Brooks - Cork Library
Shelton State
Community College

DISCARDED

SEPARATION OF CHURCH AND STATE

DISCARDED

SEPARATION OF CHURCH AND STATE

PHILIP HAMBURGER

Brooks - Cork Library
Shelton State
Community College

HARVARD UNIVERSITY PRESS
Cambridge, Massachusetts
London, England

DISCARDED

Copyright © 2002 by the President and Fellows
of Harvard College
All rights reserved
Printed in the United States of America

Third printing, 2002

Library of Congress Cataloging-in-Publication Data

Hamburger, Philip, 1957–
Separation of church and state / Philip Hamburger.
p. cm.
Includes bibliographical references and index.
ISBN 0-674-00734-4 (alk. paper)
1. Church and state—United States.   I. Title.
BR516.H19 2002
322'.1'0973—dc21   2002020111

To the memory of my father,
Joseph Hamburger

Congress shall make no law respecting an establishment of religion, or prohibiting the free exercise thereof . . .

U.S. Constitution, First Amendment (1791)

I contemplate with sovereign reverence that act of the whole American people which declared that *their* legislature should "make no law respecting an establishment of religion, or prohibiting the free exercise thereof," thus building a wall of separation between Church & State.

Thomas Jefferson, Letter to the Danbury Baptist Association (1802)

In the words of Jefferson, the clause against establishment of religion by law was intended to erect "a wall of separation between church and State."

Hugo Black, *Everson v. Board of Education* (1947)

CONTENTS

ACKNOWLEDGMENTS

My debts are numerous, and it is a pleasure to acknowledge them. Intellectually, as in so much of my life, my most profound obligations are to my late father, Joseph Hamburger. To his memory this book is dedicated as a small token of my feelings.

I am also deeply obliged to various colleagues and friends, and to none am I more indebted than to three at George Washington University, where I began the writing of this book. Ever generous with his time and knowledge, Scott B. Pagel helped me to navigate some poorly charted bibliographic oceans. No less valuable was the assistance of Robert E. Park, with whom I had the opportunity to discuss the complexities of American religion and culture. Last, but not least, Robert W. Tuttle offered learned, thoughtful suggestions about theology and church government. Most important, he long ago clarified my understanding of authority, especially within churches.

Much of the assistance I received can only be summarized here. At Boston University, the University of Chicago, George Washington University, the University of Pennsylvania, Northwestern University, and Samford University, the participants in faculty workshops patiently read portions of my manuscript and helped me to reconsider my views. Among those who kindly read more substantial sections of the manuscript were Marc M. Arkin, Richard Audet, Thomas C. Berg, Joseph Carrig, Bradford R. Clark, Adam S. Cohen, Jacob I. Corré, Daniel R. Ernst, Dennis J. Hutchinson, Robert Katz, Renée B. Lettow, Ira C. Lupu, Martha Nussbaum, David M. Rabban, Linda Safran, Steven D. Smith, and Winnefred Fallers Sullivan. Even among my family, I was able to rely upon the learning of others. My mother, Lotte Hamburger, suggested numerous changes; my brother, Jeffrey Hamburger, pointed out some medieval illuminations; my sister and brother-in-law, Annette and Stuart Levey, saved me from considerable errors and infelicities. Moreover, a series of remarkably bright and energetic research assistants, Selim Ablo, Robert Bailey, Jason Callen, Zachery Cunha, Joseph Gentile, and Christopher Skinnell, generously came to my aid—for example, by helping me to search and copy the dizzyingly small print of nineteenth-century newspapers. When I attempted to learn about the Stephenson trial, John L. Wright, Jr., of Birmingham, Alabama, shared his extensive knowledge of it, and Joyce Sims—the librarian of the John Carroll Catholic High School—undertook the arduous task of photocopying the trial transcript for me. Among the many other scholars and librarians who came to my aid, I particularly must thank Margaret Duczynski and Greg Nimmo of the University of Chicago Law School; Shane Blackman and Barbara B. Oberg of the Papers of Thomas Jefferson, at Princeton University; Susan Brosnan of the Archives of the Knights of Columbus; and Joan E. Sansbury of the House of the Temple Library and Museum, Supreme Council, 33°, Scottish Rite of Freemasonry, Southern Jurisdiction, U.S.A. I am also grateful to William Bartlett for his assistance with my research on the Masons, to the *Supreme Court Review* for publishing in 1992 an earlier version of my arguments in Chapter 4, and to Hugo L. Black, Jr., Baylor University, the Harvard University Archives, the Knights of Columbus, and Yale University Archives for permission to quote materials in their custody or over which they possess rights. Perhaps most fundamentally, I am indebted to Shauna Clarke, Jennifer Ewald, Ronna Reimer, Valerie Scott, Marlene Vellinga, and Liane Walters, who carefully typed portions of this book, and to Stephanie Boyd, whose painstaking efforts with another manuscript, which I was editing, freed up her colleagues to work on this one.

Finally, I must mention my gratitude for that great aid to scholars, serendipity. Several years ago, while browsing through some eighteenth-century pamphlets and newspapers, I stumbled across some discussions of religion that did not quite fit with the standard accounts of constitutional history. In particular, I found writings in which establishment ministers attempted to discredit religious dissenters by suggesting that the dissenters sought a separation between religion and government. It was intriguing that these establishment ministers employed separation—at least one kind of it—as an accusation. Of course, I could not long suppress my curiosity. One thing led to another, and eventually the resonance of this minor chord, sounded by some rather traditional clergymen, drew my attention to much larger developments, full of disharmonies I never expected to study.

Introduction

JEFFERSON's words seem to have shaped the nation. Beginning with his draft of the Declaration of Independence, Jefferson's taut phrases have given concentrated and elevated expression to some of the nation's most profound ideals.

Few of Jefferson's phrases appear to have had more significance for the law and life of the United States than those in which he expressed his hope for a separation of church and state. In 1802, in a letter to the Danbury Baptist Association, he quoted the First Amendment and interpreted it in rather different words: "I contemplate with sovereign reverence that act of the whole American people which declared that *their* legislature should 'make no law respecting an establishment of religion, or prohibiting the free exercise thereof,' thus building a wall of separation between Church & State."[1] Two centuries later, Jefferson's phrase, "separation between church and state," provides the label with which vast numbers of Americans refer to their religious freedom. In the minds of many, his words have even displaced those of the U.S. Constitution, which, by contrast, seem neither so apt nor so clear. Thus,

---

[1] Thomas Jefferson, Letter to Messrs. Nehemiah Dodge, Ephraim Robbins, and Stephen S. Nelson, a Committee of the Danbury Baptist Association in the State of Connecticut (Jan. 1, 1802), in Daniel L. Dreisbach, "Sowing Useful Truths and Principles: The Danbury Baptists, Thomas Jefferson, and the 'Wall of Separation,'" *Journal of Church and State*, 39: 468 (1997). Although, of course, not the first to publish this and related documents, Dreisbach provides by far most accurate transcript of them. To Dreisbach's work James H. Hutson adds an infrared photograph that reveals the deleted words in Jefferson's letter. Hutson, "Thomas Jefferson's Letter to the Danbury Baptists: A Controversy Rejoined," *William & Mary Quarterly*, 56 (no. 4): 779 (3d ser., October 1999).

refracted through Jefferson's letter, the religious liberty guaranteed by the Constitution often appears to be a separation of church and state.[2]

Notwithstanding the authority of Jefferson and those who have followed him, it may be useful to reconsider whether the First Amendment actually guaranteed a separation of church and state and, further, how Jefferson and other Americans came to assume that it did so. Certainly, there is reason to wonder why the religion clauses of the First Amendment differ from the words with which these clauses are most commonly interpreted. According to the First Amendment, "Congress shall make no law respecting an establishment of religion, or prohibiting the free exercise thereof." Yet Jefferson and numerous other Americans, including many judges and scholars, have understood this phrase, especially its establishment clause, in terms of the "separation between church and state"—indeed, a "wall" of separation.

The difference between the Constitution's phrase and Jefferson's is significant because Jefferson's has tended to mean much more. Of course, the phrase "separation between church and state" has had a range of meanings. At the very least, it alludes to a differentiation or distinction between church and state. More substantively, it is often used to denote a freedom from laws instituting, supporting, or otherwise establishing religion. Yet the phrase "separation between church and

---

[2] Daniel Dreisbach writes: "Occasionally a metaphor is thought to encapsulate so thoroughly an idea or concept that it passes into the vocabulary as the standard expression of that idea. Such is the case with the graphic phrase 'wall of separation between Church and State,' which in the twentieth century has profoundly influenced discourse and policy on church-state relations. Jefferson's 'wall' is accepted by many Americans as a pithy description of the constitutionally-prescribed church-state arrangement. More important, the federal judiciary has found the metaphor irresistible, elevating it to [an] authoritative gloss on the First Amendment religion provisions." Dreisbach, "Sowing Useful Truths and Principles," 456. Among those quoted by Dreisbach is R. Freeman Butts, who writes that Jefferson's words about separation "are not simply a metaphor of one private citizen's language, they reflect accurately the intent of those most responsible for the First Amendment; and they came to reflect the majority will of the American people. The words 'separation of church and state' are an accurate and convenient shorthand meaning of the First Amendment itself; they represent a well-defined historical principle from the pen of one who in many official statements and actions helped to frame the authentic American tradition of political and religious liberty." Butts, *The American Tradition in Religion and Education*, 93 (Boston: Beacon Press, 1950), quoted by Dreisbach, "Sowing Useful Truths and Principles," 456. Dreisbach, ibid., also quotes Edwin S. Gaustad as saying that "this powerful metaphor, once employed, became even more familiar to the American public than did the constitutional language itself." Gaustad, "Religion," in *Thomas Jefferson: A Reference Biography*, 282, ed. Merrill D. Peterson (New York: Scribner, 1986).

state" has also pointed to something more dramatic—a distance, segregation, or absence of contact between church and state. Rather than simply forbid civil laws respecting an establishment of religion, it has more ambitiously tended to prohibit contact between religious and civil institutions. Thus the phrase "separation between church and state" has lent itself to a notion very different from disestablishment. Recognizing the disparity between separation and disestablishment, this book attempts to understand how Americans came to interpret the First Amendment in terms of separation of church and state, and through this inquiry it traces how Americans eventually transformed their religious liberty.

The Standard History

The standard history of separation has some of the qualities of a myth. Certainly, it makes its hero seem larger than life, it celebrates his deeds (or, at least, his words), and it serves a valuable explanatory role. The conventional account of separation emphasizes the heroic role of Jefferson by suggesting that he employed a previously obscure phrase to illuminate the First Amendment's establishment clause. Apparently drawing upon ideas first enunciated by an earlier giant, Roger Williams, Jefferson in 1802 gave currency and constitutional significance to the phrase about separation, which was later employed in 1875 by President Grant, in 1878 by Chief Justice Waite, and in 1947 by Justice Black, whose opinion that year in *Everson v. Board of Education of Ewing* made Jefferson's separation the foundation of subsequent establishment clause jurisprudence. In this spare, bold account of the utterances of great men, Jefferson's influence exerts itself in leaps and bounds across the centuries. An ancient phrase to which Jefferson gave new life, his statement about separation seems both venerable and original, both authoritative and a creative act of genius.

According to the proponents of this conventional account, Jefferson's phrase has not only been immensely influential but also appropriately so—his views being the profoundly thoughtful conclusions of a philosopher-president who devoted himself to the cause of religious liberty. Although at least one scholar has questioned whether Jefferson gave much thought to what he wrote to the Danbury Baptist Association, others have insisted that he wrote with care, and most commentators have joined a resounding chorus of praise for the farsighted, even prophetic vision of religious liberty bequeathed to Americans by the most intellectual of their presidents.[3]

It is odd, however, that this standard history of separation is so remarkably free of detail. Little is said of the genealogy of the phrase during the generations—even centuries—between the pronouncements of the great men, and nothing is said of the contexts in which they used it. To be sure, there are numerous scholarly and popular histories of American religious freedom—histories that could be considered accounts of a generic separation of church and state. Yet these accounts hardly discuss the history of the phrase "separation of church and state" and therefore are rarely informative about the specific idea or ideas to which that phrase may have referred. As a result, the meaning of "separation of church and state" remains obscure.

Fortunately, some important work has been done on the specific phrase and idea of separation. Perry Miller, Edmund S. Morgan, and various other scholars have explored Roger Williams's notion of separation of church and state.[4] Writing on a later period, Daniel L. Dreisbach observes that the phrase about a wall of separation between church and state may have been known to Jefferson, not from Roger Williams, but from an eighteenth-century writer, James Burgh, whom Jefferson much admired.[5] In two particularly suggestive pieces, Thomas E. Buckley examines the political successes of religious dissenters, especially Baptists,

---

[3] For the most perspicacious query concerning Jefferson's letter, see Edward S. Corwin, "The Supreme Court as National School Board," in *A Constitution of Powers in a Secular State,* 106 (Charlottesville, Va.: Michie Co., 1951).

[4] Perry Miller, ed., *The Complete Writings of Roger Williams,* 7: 6 (New York: Russell & Russell, 1963); Edmund S. Morgan, *Roger Williams: The Church and the State* (New York: Norton, 1967); W. Clark Gilpin, *The Millenarian Piety of Roger Williams* (Chicago: University of Chicago, 1979); David Little, "Roger Williams and the Separation of Church and State," in *Religion and the State: Essays in Honor of Leo Pfeffer,* ed. James E. Wood, Jr. (Waco: Baylor University Press, 1985); William Lee Miller, *The First Liberty: Religion and the American Republic,* 182–183 (New York: Paragon, 1988); Glenn W. LaFantasie, ed., *The Correspondence of Roger Williams,* 2: 23 (Providence: Rhode Island Historical Society, 1988); Hugh Spurgin, *Roger Williams and Puritan Radicalism in the English Separatist Tradition* (Lewiston: E. Edwin Mellen Press, 1989); Edwin S. Gaustad, *Liberty of Conscience: Roger Williams in America* (Grand Rapids: William B. Eerdmans, 1991); Timothy L. Hall, "Roger Williams and the Foundations of Religious Liberty," *Boston Univ. Law Review,* 71: 455, 482 (1991); Dreisbach, "Sowing Useful Truths and Principles," 483; Timothy L. Hall, *Separating Church and State: Roger Williams and Religious Liberty,* 72–98 (Urbana: University of Illinois, 1998).

[5] Dreisbach, "Sowing Useful Truths and Principles," 455.

in late eighteenth-century Virginia. Buckley concludes that Virginia's 1786 Act for Establishing Religious Freedom, which was drafted by Thomas Jefferson, "did not disentangle religion from politics or sever relations between church and state. Nor did Virginians understand Jefferson's statute to require that separation." On the contrary, the act (together with the subsequent sale of establishment glebe lands) ensured Baptists and other evangelicals an equal religious liberty and thereby allowed evangelicals to cooperate in pursuit of their legislative agenda, with which they hoped "to impose their religious values and culture upon American society." Buckley also examines the early nineteenth-century debate in Virginia concerning that state's power to incorporate religious societies—a controversy in which many Virginians argued that incorporation risked the creation of a religious establishment. It was a dispute in which the term "separation" was not ordinarily employed, but it reveals, as Buckley points out, that a standard of liberty in some ways similar to separation had onerous consequences for religious minorities seeking to enjoy religious freedom.[6]

Yet none of these accounts directly examines the broad history of separation of church and state as a constitutional standard in America, let alone its relationship to the religious liberty guaranteed by the First Amendment. Indeed, the work most directly pertinent to this inquiry consists only of very brief historical observations. For example, according to Mark DeWolfe Howe, whereas the First Amendment was understood in the eighteenth century to protect religion and churches from the state, Jefferson sought to protect the state from the demands of churches.[7] This contrast is suggestive, but it overlooks a third possibility, that Jefferson desired not only to preserve government but also, more fundamentally, to protect individuals from churches so that Americans might be

---

[6] Thomas E. Buckley, "Evangelicals Triumphant: The Baptists' Assault on the Virginia Glebes, 1786–1801," *William & Mary Quarterly*, 45: 68–69 (1988); Thomas E. Buckley, "After Disestablishment: Thomas Jefferson's Wall of Separation in Antebellum Virginia," *Journal of Southern History*, 61 (no. 3): 445 (August 1995).

[7] Mark DeWolfe Howe, *The Garden and the Wilderness: Religion and Government in American Constitutional History*, 19 (Chicago: University of Chicago Press, 1965). Although roughly accurate, even this remark obscures almost as much as it illuminates. For example, in 1777, an antiestablishment pamphlet published in Virginia stated that "[t]he very establishment corrupts the Church: And such a Church will consequently corrupt the State." "A Freeman of Virginia," *The Freeman's Remonstrance against an Ecclesiastical Establishment: Being Some Remarks on a Late Pamphlet, Entitled The Necessity of an Established Church in Any State*, 8 (Williamsburg: 1777).

free and uninfluenced in thought and politics. Edward S. Corwin, in a lone remark, intimates that Jefferson's phrase about separation "was not improbably motivated by an impish desire to heave a brick at the Congregationalist-Federalist hierarchy of Connecticut, whose leading members had denounced him two years before as an 'infidel' and 'atheist.'"[8] Corwin, however, does not pursue this hint that Jefferson aimed his words about separation at politics as much as religious liberty. Most recently, in a manner similar to Corwin, James H. Hutson proposes that "Jefferson's principal motive in writing the Danbury Baptist letter was to mount a political counter-attack against his Federalist enemies." Yet Hutson undermines some of the possibilities his brief observation might seem to imply, arguing that Jefferson wrote his letter as part of a "strategy of conciliation" and that Jefferson's separation was "consistent" with the religious liberty of "his fellow founders." From Jefferson's 1802 letter, Hutson then jumps forward 150 years to conclude that "the wall of separation is still an acceptable metaphor, if it is understood as a wall of the kind that existed during the cold war."[9] Thus the scholarship—particularly this nonmythical variety—contains valuable hints about the concept of separation between church and state but provides no sustained examination of its history.

The Tenacity of Separation

The concept of religious liberty employed by Jefferson has been tenacious. So strongly has it become part of American understandings of religious liberty that even the twentieth-century commentators who question the idea of separation often have difficulty dislodging it from their own thought.

The doubts about separation have been long-standing. Only five years after the Supreme Court's adoption of Jefferson's phrase in 1947 in *Everson*, Justice William O. Douglas, in *Zorach v. Clauson*, declared his adherence to the idea of separation but expressed concern about the length to which its implications could be taken. He opined that the First Amendment reflected the "philosophy" of separation and that "the

[8] Corwin, "The Supreme Court as National School Board," 106.
[9] James H. Hutson, "Thomas Jefferson's Letter to the Danbury Baptists: A Controversy Rejoined," 776, 780, 789; James H. Hutson, *Religion and the Founding of the American Republic,* 94 (Washington, D.C.: Library of Congress, 1998).

separation must be complete and unequivocal" but added that the First Amendment did "not say that in every and all respects there shall be a separation of Church and State." If it had said this, "the state and religion would be aliens to each other": on the one hand, "[c]hurches could not be required to pay even property taxes"; on the other, "[m]unicipalities would not be permitted to render police or fire protection to religious groups."[10] Similarly, although Justice Warren Burger in 1971 enforced the principle of separation with vigor in *Lemon v. Kurtzman*, he also equivocated: "The line of separation, far from being a 'wall,' is a blurred, indistinct and variable barrier depending on all the circumstances of a particular relationship."[11] Indeed, in 1984, in *Lynch v. Donnelly*, Burger acknowledged that "[n]o significant segment of our society and no institution within it can exist in a vacuum or in total or absolute isolation from all the other parts, much less from government."[12] Most emphatically, in 1985 Justice William H. Rehnquist, in a dissent, argued that separation is a standard that lacks historical support and has "proved all but useless as a guide to sound constitutional adjudication."[13] Some academics agree. For example, Sidney E. Mead suggests that "Jefferson's words have been the source of much confusion and conflict because they have helped to perpetuate thinking about the situation in the United States with the traditional concepts of 'church' and 'state' which are really not applicable to the experienced order of Americans." He also observes that "the reference to a 'wall' conjures up the image of something quite tangible and solid, which was built once and for all in the beginning."[14] Adding to these scholarly doubts, some popular authors

[10] Zorach v. Clauson, 343 U.S. 306, 312 (1952). Nonetheless, according to Justice Douglas, "[t]here cannot be the slightest doubt that the First Amendment reflects the philosophy that church and State should be separated." Ibid.
[11] Lemon v. Kurtzman, 403 U.S. 602, 614 (1971).
[12] Lynch v. Donnolly, 465 U.S. 668, 673 (1984).
[13] Wallace v. Jaffree, 472 U.S. 38, 107 (1985). See also Brief of Appellant, George C. Wallace, in Wallace et al. v. Jaffree et al. and Smith et al. v. Jaffree et al., 36–37 (October Term, 1983, U.S. Supr. Ct.).
[14] Mead, "Neither Church nor State: Reflections on James Madison's 'Line of Separation,'" in James E. Wood, Jr., *Readings on Church and State*, 41–42 (Waco: J. M. Dawson Institute of Church-State Relations, Baylor University, 1989). See also Wilfrid Parsons, *The First Freedom: Considerations on Church and State in the United States* (New York: Declan X. McMullen Co., Ca. 1948); James M. O'Neill, *Religion and Education under the Constitution* (New York: Harper, 1949); Edward S. Corwin, "The Supreme Court as National School Board," 98; Joseph Brady, *Confusion Twice Confounded* (South Orange: Seton Hall University Press, 1954); Charles Rice, *The Supreme Court and Public Prayer: The Need for Restraint* (New York:

bluntly challenge separation as a myth.[15] Generalizing about the developments of the past few decades, Ira C. Lupu notes that "separationism is on the wane" and that there is a "strong trend away from the separationist ethos . . . that prevailed . . . after the end of the Second World War."[16]

Yet even those who have questioned whether the First Amendment really required separation of church and state have had difficulty escaping this concept. For example, as already seen, although Justices Douglas and Burger doubted there could be a thorough separation of church and state, they nonetheless analyzed the religion clauses of the First Amendment in terms of "separation"—Burger attempting to soften the conventional phrase by substituting a "line of separation," which he borrowed from one of Madison's letters.[17] More typically, the commentators who question separation do not even attempt to dislodge the phrase "separation of church and state." For example, in interpreting the First Amendment, Mark DeWolfe Howe merely contrasts two versions of separation, that of Roger Williams and that of Jefferson, arguing that Williams and Jefferson each was ahead of his time, and that Williams's "figure of speech luminously reflects the political theory of the eighteenth century"—indeed, that the First Amendment was then "generally understood to be more the expression of Roger Williams's philosophy than

---

Fordham University Press, 1964); Mark DeWolfe Howe, *The Garden and the Wilderness: Religion and Government in American Constitutional History,* 176 (Chicago: University of Chicago Press, 1965); Elwyn A. Smith, *Religious Liberty in the United States: The Development of Church-State Thought since the Revolutionary Era,* 246, 252, 322 (Philadelphia: Fortress Press, 1972); Robert L. Cord, *Separation of Church and State: Historical Fact and Current Fiction* (New York: Lambeth Press, 1982); Norman DeJong, with Jack Van Der Slik, *Separation of Church and State* (Jordan Station, Ontario: Paideia Press, 1985); Gerard V. Bradley, *Church-State Relationships in America* (New York: Greenwood Press, 1987); Steven D. Smith, "Separation and the 'Secular': Reconstructing the Disestablishment Decision," *Texas Law Review,* 67: 955 (1989); Michael W. McConnell, "Christ, Culture, and Courts: A Niebuhrian Examination of First Amendment Jurisprudence," *DePaul Law Review,* 42: 191 (1992); Thomas Berg, *The State and Religion in a Nutshell* (St. Paul: West Group, 1998).
[15] John W. Whitehead, *The Separation Illusion: A Lawyer Examines the First Amendment* (Milford, Mich.: Mott Media, 1977); David Barton, *The Myth of Separation: What Is the Constitutional Relationship between Church and State? A Revealing Look at What the Founders and Early Courts Really Said* (Aledo, Tex.: Wallbuilder Press, 1992).
[16] Lupu, "The Lingering Death of Separationism," *George Washington Law Review,* 62: 230, 256, 267 (1994).
[17] Lemon v. Kurtzman, 403 U.S. at 614. Madison's 1832 letter is also quoted approvingly by Sidney E. Mead, "Neither Church nor State: Reflections on James Madison's 'Line of Separation,'" in Wood, *Readings on Church and State,* 41.

of Jefferson's."[18] As will be seen, it is misleading to understand either eighteenth-century religious liberty or the First Amendment in terms of separation of church and state, whether the separation be that of Williams or that of Jefferson. Yet Howe prefers to describe different types of separation than to discuss the phrases and concepts actually used by eighteenth-century advocates of religious liberty. Another historian, E. R. Norman, protests that "[t]he separation of church and state in the federal constitution of the United States was not originally intended to disconnect Christianity and public life; it was a device to prevent the supremacy of one sect over another."[19] Unselfconsciously using a phrase not in the Constitution, this historian has to struggle to make clear that the Constitution's religious liberty was not that apparently implied by his own words. These commentators who attempt to wiggle free from the clear implications of Jefferson's phrase make no effort to shake off the phrase itself and thereby reveal how much it has become part of American culture and constitutional thought. Although some have rejected the phrase as ahistorical, most judges, lawyers, academics, journalists, and other Americans—even those who reject its implications— repeatedly talk about religious liberty and especially that of the First Amendment in terms of a "separation of church and state."

Separation and the Constitutional Religious Freedom

To understand the idea of separation of church and state and how it became part of American constitutional law, this book examines two questions, the first being whether separation was the religious liberty protected by the First Amendment. According to the myth, the idea of separation of church and state was widely accepted by the time of the nation's establishment and was the freedom desired by religious dissenters and protected by the Constitution. Yet the idea of separation of church and state was very different from the religious liberty desired by the religious dissenters whose demands shaped the First Amendment, and it had its own quite distinct path of development. The dissenters were the adherents of minority denominations that refused to conform

---

[18] Howe, *The Garden and the Wilderness*, 18–19.
[19] Norman, *The Conscience of the State in North America*, 4 (London: Cambridge University Press, 1968).

to the churches established by law. These established churches (Episcopal in the southern states and Congregationalist in most New England
states) were established through state laws that, most notably, gave government salaries to ministers on account of their religion. Whereas the
religious liberty demanded by most dissenters was a freedom from the
laws that created these establishments, the separation of church and
state was an old, anticlerical, and, increasingly, antiecclesiastical conception of the relationship between church and state. As might be expected, therefore, separation was not something desired by most religious dissenters or guaranteed by the First Amendment. Indeed, it was
quite distinct from the religious liberty protected in any clause of an
American constitution, whether that of the federal government or that
of any state.

   A second, no less significant question is how the U.S. Constitution's
religious liberty came to be perceived as a separation of church and state.
If separation was an idea radically different from what dissenters and
other early Americans considered their religious liberty, how did it come
to be revered as their founding conception of this freedom? To ascertain
this is to understand some of the ways in which constitutions, for better
or for worse, can evolve.

   The explanation of how separation became the U.S. Constitution's
religious liberty has much to do with majority perceptions. Jefferson suggested that the U.S. Constitution guaranteed separation, but the idea of
separation did not become popular until the mid-nineteenth century,
when opponents of Catholicism—many of them nativists—depicted it
as a principle of government evident in most American constitutions,
even if it was not guaranteed by these documents. Allied with the nativists were theological liberals, especially anti-Christian "secularists," who
worried that separation had not been fully assured by any American
constitution, and who therefore demanded a federal constitutional
amendment. These secularists organized a political movement, including
a presidential campaign, on behalf of this alteration to the U.S. Constitution. Only when their movement for an amendment failed did they
abandon their argument that the U.S. Constitution had not already guaranteed separation. With little hesitation they switched tack and argued
that American constitutions had historically guaranteed separation. Similarly, nativist Protestants, who had also hoped for amendments to the
U.S. Constitution, turned away from the disappointments of the amend-

ment process and increasingly argued that separation had been guaranteed in American constitutions and especially in the U.S. Bill of Rights. In these and other ways, Protestants, nonbelievers, and numerous other Americans came to understand the religious liberty protected by American constitutions as a separation of church and state.

Related to these two inquiries about the distinct development of separation and about its subsequent association with the First Amendment's religious liberty is an incidental inquiry concerning Jefferson's reputation for a thoughtful analysis of separation and for influencing constitutional law on the subject. Ever since the *Everson* case in 1947, innumerable judges, lawyers, and other Americans have assumed that the constitutional separation of church and state was one of Jefferson's great contributions to American liberty. Accordingly, it would be valuable to learn whether Jefferson wrote about separation in a manner that deserves constitutional weight and whether his words were as influential before 1947 as is commonly supposed. There is much reason to believe that modern suppositions about the wisdom and influence of Jefferson's words regarding separation have developed largely as part of a twentieth-century myth—an account that has become popular precisely because it has seemed to provide constitutional authority for separation.

Contrasting Implications

Americans took their religious liberty in a new direction when they reconceived their constitutional freedom from an establishment as a separation between church and state. The significance of the shift is apparent from the contrasting practical implications of these two ideals. Neither has been self-defining, but those who in the late eighteenth century sought constitutional guarantees against establishments and those who later sought a separation of church and state revealed much about what they understood to be the implications of their different conceptions of religious liberty.

In late eighteenth-century America the dissenters from the established churches sought limitations on civil government and did so in arguments that conformed to recognizable patterns.[20] The states with

---

[20] Philip A. Hamburger, "Equality and Diversity: The Eighteenth-Century Debate about Equal Protection and Equal Civil Rights," *Supreme Court Review*, 295, 336–345 (1992).

establishments had once passed laws imposing penalties on dissenters but now more typically enacted only privileges for their established denominations—notably, salaries for the established clergy. Against these establishments of religion most dissenters sought not only a freedom from penalties (whether in terms of the "freedom of worship" or the "free exercise of religion") but also guarantees against the unequal distribution of government salaries and other benefits on account of differences in religious beliefs. Some dissenters even demanded assurances that there would not be any civil law taking "cognizance" of religion. As a result, the American constitutions that were drafted to accommodate the antiestablishment demands of dissenters guaranteed religious liberty in terms of these limitations on government—specifically, limits on discrimination by civil laws and on the subject matter of civil laws.

In contrast, separation has often seemed to imply rather different conclusions. First, it has implied limits upon government far beyond, and even contrary to, what dissenters demanded. The dissenters or religious minorities whose views were reflected in the First Amendment assumed that legislation should not discriminate among religions and even that it should not take cognizance of religion. Yet separation has often been taken to imply that even if legislation does not take cognizance of religion, such legislation is suspect if it has a religious purpose or if it substantially benefits religion—particularly when the religion is that of a "church" or group. For example, on the ground of such religious purposes or benefits, legislators and judges since the mid-nineteenth century have often questioned the constitutionality of Sunday closing laws and school-aid statutes, even if the statutes do not take cognizance of religion.[21] Moreover, whereas the First Amendment, following the demands of most religious dissenters, seems to have placed limits only on civil legislation, the concept of separation of church and *state* has long appeared, in addition, to impose limits on what government can do even beyond legislation—for example, in executive acts (such as thanksgiving proclamations) and in nonlegislative acts of the legislature (such as the

---

[21] For the most prominent recent expression of such concerns, note the first two parts of the standard proposed in Lemon v. Kurtzman, 403 U.S. 602 (1971). "First, the statute must have a secular legislative purpose; second, its principal or primary effect must be one that neither advances nor inhibits religion . . . finally, the statute must not foster 'an excessive government entanglement with religion.'" Id. at 612–613 (citations omitted).

appointment of chaplains). Thus, in various ways, separation has histori-cally gone much further in implying limits on government than did the liberty sought by dissenters and protected by the First Amendment.

Second, unlike the liberty sought by dissenters, separation of *church* and state has often implied limitations not only upon government but also directly upon religions. As already observed, separation is often un-derstood to suggest that churches cannot receive government benefits, even if the benefits are distributed on the basis of entirely secular quali-fications. In addition, for almost two centuries separation has seemed to imply that clergymen and religious organizations ought not attempt to influence voters or governments, and thus separation has implied that these individuals and groups ought not fully exercise the rights of politi-cal speech and association held by other Americans. Indeed, for at least 150 years separation has frequently been understood to imply doubts about the legitimacy of otherwise secular laws enacted with vigorous or partisan support based on religious views, especially if from religious organizations. Thus separation has suggested limits on religion and reli-gious groups—constraints not sought by dissenters.

Both of these developments—limiting government and limiting churches—have been magnified by a third, more general, implication of separation that if church and state are to be separate, they should not have too much contact. For example, it is said that these institutions should avoid close relations or any substantial involvement in each oth-er's activities. In the parlance of its advocates, separation bars "entangle-ments" between church and state.[22]

On account of all three of these lines of reasoning, the First Amend-ment has often been understood to limit religious freedom in ways never imagined by the late eighteenth-century dissenters who de-manded constitutional guarantees of religious liberty. For example, the dissenters who campaigned for constitutional barriers to any govern-ment establishment of religion had no desire more generally to prevent contact between religion and government. Yet separation has seemed to forbid contact. Moreover, these dissenters and their allies sought to prohibit laws establishing religion, and in making such demands, they

---

[22] Again, compare *Lemon*, 403 U.S. 602. Of course, other standards or ideals of religious liberty can also suggest the three implications recited here, but none has done so more consistently than the separation of church and state.

did not attempt directly to limit religion. Yet the conception of the First Amendment in terms of separation directly constrains church as much as state. Not least, the dissenters sought the First Amendment and other constitutional provisions to prevent government from discriminating on account of religious differences. Yet these guarantees have increasingly been interpreted on the basis of an idea that typically has seemed more applicable to members of churches than to persons who merely have an individual religiosity. This last point—that separation discriminates among religions—is evident in the expectations that government should deny secularly defined benefits to religious groups and that clergymen should not speak about politics on behalf of their churches. As these examples illustrate, the principle of separation limits religious groups and individuals within them more severely than other types of religion, thus transforming the constitutional guarantees against discrimination on grounds of religious differences into provisions that necessitate it. To some Americans, the various implications of separation may seem reassuringly familiar and not necessarily invidious. Nonetheless, in all of the ways outlined here, separation has had a severe effect, particularly upon individuals whose religious beliefs lead them to worship and otherwise act as part of a religious group. The federal and state constitutional provisions designed to protect religious liberty have, ironically, come to be understood in terms of an idea that substantially reduces this freedom.

Separation and Society

In order to trace how American religious liberty came to be conceived as a separation between church and state, this book must examine how the idea of separation flourished among broader cultural and social developments, including ideals of individual independence, fears of Catholicism, and various types of specialization. Although often omitted from the history of religious liberty, these more general tendencies can suggest much about the growing popularity of separation.

Separation often attracted Protestants who felt individualistic fears of religious groups. Many nineteenth- and twentieth-century Americans worried about the power of government. In addition, however, numerous Protestants felt anxiety about nongovernmental groups and hierarchies, particularly churches and their clergies. From the perspective of these Protestants, the claims of authority made by churches—even if merely claims of moral rather than legal authority—could be oppressive and dangerous to the freedom of individuals. Accordingly, in the nineteenth and twentieth centuries separation often appealed to Americans who thought of themselves as mentally independent—particularly to those who conceived of themselves as independent of their churches. Of course, in America's ever more secular society, separation also attracted expanding numbers of nonreligious persons.[23] More generally and pervasively, however, it appealed to those whose liberal theology or whose sense of distance from communal, clerical religion led them to think of themselves as intellectually independent of any ecclesiastical dictates.

This distrust of church authority increasingly permeated American Protestantism and its often nativist critique of the Catholic Church. Fearful of Catholic immigrants, many native-born Protestants emphasized the Protestant character of their American identity. In particular, they adopted heightened expectations of intellectual independence. Believing that this individual independence was essential for both genuine religion and American citizenship, they demanded that Catholics adhere to hyper-individualistic ideals of mental freedom. In this spirit, nativist Protestants worried that the pope's claims of ecclesiastical authority would stultify the minds of Catholics, rendering them unfit to vote and giving the Church an influence that would allow it to threaten freedom through the institutions of republican government. Against these and related dangers, growing numbers of Protestant Americans demanded a separation of church and state. Thus nativist demands for mental independence and for a separation between church and state took aim at Catholics for their failure to adopt supposedly Protestant and American

---

[23] It is often assumed that separation of church and state became popular as a secular principle. Yet this conclusion—when stated this simply—is misleading. There was no single secularism in England or America during the period covered by this book. Indeed, "secularism" was a term popularized for polemical purposes in the mid-nineteenth century precisely in order to minimize the differences among quite divergent tendencies, many of which were candidly religious. See Chapter 11, note 20. Although some secularizing developments (such as social specialization and antiecclesiastical suspicions) drew Americans toward a separation of church and state, other secularizing developments did not so clearly have such an effect. Accordingly, it seems useful to focus on separation's relatively concrete historical circumstances rather than generalizations about secularism.

beliefs.[24] In such ways, religious liberty itself—even an unusually individualistic conception of it—was often employed to demand conformity.

The separation of church and state had particular appeal in an age of specialization. Separation often attracted individuals who—whether in fact or in their minds—divided their lives into distinct activities and sought to maintain their freedom within each such activity by restricting the demands of the others. Jefferson, his allies, and many subsequent Americans attempted, on occasion, to limit religion to a private, personal, or nonpolitical realm so that it would not intrude too much (whether by force of law or only by force of argument) on various other aspects of their lives. To such Americans, the moral claims of an entirely voluntary, disestablished church could seem threatening. Accordingly, increasing numbers of Americans attempted to escape these constraining demands of churches by welcoming various separations between organized religion and other facets of their lives, particularly a separation between church and state.

Ironically, however, religion was not so easily confined. The very parties and groups that in the nineteenth century most vigorously condemned church participation in politics simultaneously encouraged a much more direct and individualized pursuit of religious yearnings in this secular arena and, in this way, rechanneled profoundly religious passions and aspirations from Christian churches to egalitarian politics. Their efforts, however, probably were only part of a broader displacement of aspirations—a transference of religiosity to various specialized, secular activities—that may have been almost inevitable with the fragmentation of society and the decline of localized "social worship." In their increasingly fractured and secular circumstances, Americans who found their desires for purity and transcendence unsatisfied in the communal worship of traditional religion often pursued these goals in more specialized endeavors but most commonly in politics. Thus the separation of church and state may have been part of a specialization of religion, politics, and much of the rest of life that simultaneously contributed to the secularization of most activities and left many Americans to

---

[24] Of course, as John Higham and others have pointed out, anti-Catholicism can be distinguished from nativism. Higham, *Strangers in the Land: Patterns of American Nativism, 1860–1925*, 5 (1955; New York: Atheneum, 1977). Nonetheless, much anti-Catholicism was distinctly nativist.

pursue in their specialized, secular endeavors the sort of yearnings they once more typically satisfied in their religious groups.[25]

These cultural and social contexts—ranging from fears of group authority to the displacement of yearnings—suggest that the evolution of American religious liberty into a separation of church and state cannot be understood simply as the product of great men, whether Roger Williams, Thomas Jefferson, or Hugo Black. Nor can it be understood merely as an institutional development, whether in the documents of the U.S. Constitution or in the opinions of the U.S. Supreme Court. Instead, the redefinition of American religious liberty as a separation of church and state needs to be considered within the context of America's broader ideas, culture, and society. Amid these wider circumstances, including changing popular perceptions and fears, Americans gradually transformed their understanding of religious liberty. Increasingly, Americans conceived their freedom to require an independence from churches, and they feared the demands of one church in particular. To limit such threats, Americans called for a separation of church and state, and eventually the U.S. Supreme Court gave their new conception of religious liberty the force of law.

[25] R. Laurence Moore, "The End of Religious Establishments and the Beginning of Religious Politics: Church and State in the United States," in *Belief in History: Innovative Approaches to European and American Religion*, 237, ed. Thomas Kelsman (Notre Dame, Ind.: University of Notre Dame Press, 1991).

I

<hr>

LATE EIGHTEENTH-CENTURY
RELIGIOUS LIBERTY

Although today it is often assumed that eighteenth-century American religious dissenters sought a separation of church and state, they in fact struggled for a very different type of religious liberty. That the eighteenth-century Americans who dissented from their state establishments did not desire a separation of church and state may seem strange to modern Americans. Certainly, in an era in which separation of church and state is widely accepted as a fundamental American ideal, an effort is required to imagine a world in which separation was neither so familiar nor so admired—a world in which separation of church and state was, at best, only one of various types of religious liberty. Such, however, was the world in which American religious dissenters demanded religious liberty.

Indeed, separation of church and state first became widely familiar as the fear of establishment ministers rather than as the desire of religious dissenters. Beginning in the late sixteenth century, some prominent establishment ministers worried that the religious liberty sought by dissenters would have the effect of separating religion and thus also morality from civil government. Accordingly, from the late sixteenth century through the late eighteenth, establishment clergymen occasionally accused dissenters of separating church and state or even of separating religion and government. In fact, this was a caricature of the religious liberty sought by dissenters. Almost none of the dissenters who struggled for their liberty from religious establishments revealed any desire for a separation of church and state or for a separation of religion and government.

Eventually, however, some anticlerical intellectuals embraced this establishment misrepresentation. These advocates of separation tended to distrust the clergy and the worldly institutions of the church. They therefore welcomed the almost unearthly purity of the separation metaphor, which depicted the church as existing apart from the world and worldly government. Looking back to these few anticlerical writers, many historians have assumed that the religious dissenters who organized against establishments, including late eighteenth-century American dissenters, also supported separation.

Yet most dissenters did nothing to deserve either the establishment accusation of separation or the later historical attribution of it. They were neither so indifferent to the religious and moral foundations of government nor so hostile to clergymen and church institutions as to seek a segregation of church and state. Ever conscious of the broad relevance of their beliefs, their congregations, and the Christian church to their lives in this world, late eighteenth-century American dissenters advocated conceptions of religious liberty more compatible with their hopes for themselves and their Christianity.

1

⇒·◇·⇐

Separation, Purity, and Anticlericalism

LONG before separation became an American icon, it offered an image of purity. Like so many metaphors, that of the separation of the church was put to different uses. Yet, in all of its diverse contexts, this image of separation lent itself to portrayals of extreme demarcation. Repeatedly, it was adopted for its depiction of a purified church segregated from worldly things, not least the state.

The power of separation as an image of purity did not necessarily make it a popular vision of the Christian church's relation to the state and the world. In a corrupt world an image that emphasized the purity of the church could seem almost otherworldly and therefore could seem to challenge conventional Christian assumptions about church and clergy and their role in the world. Accordingly, in the centuries prior to 1800 the idea of the separation of church and state appealed to only a tiny fraction of Europeans and Americans—a small number who not only distrusted the clergy but also hoped to purify the church beyond what was ordinarily considered possible. Yet, even while the idea remained unpopular, there were already hints as to why it might one day seem more attractive.

Some Early Conceptions of the Relationship between Church and State

Since the time of Jesus, Christians discussed the relationship between church and state. They developed various conceptions of this relationship, and, in so doing, they often took for granted that church and state were distinct institutions, with different jurisdictions and powers. Yet, even when drawing a distinction between church and state, they typically did not conceive that the church should be kept separate or apart from the state.

From their beginnings Christians had differentiated church and state. Jesus had declared (in John 18.36) "My kingdom is not of this world," and, on such foundations, the Church Fathers and the Catholic Church distinguished the church from civil government. Later, Martin Luther also differentiated between the "two kingdoms, one the kingdom of God, the other the kingdom of the world" and argued that "these two kingdoms must be sharply distinguished" and even that they "must be kept apart." He meant, however, that they should be kept apart conceptually and recognized as very different institutions, and it was in this sense that "we must clearly distinguish these two kingdoms from each other."[1] Similarly, when commenting on the "two kingdoms," Calvin began by pointing out that "these two . . . must always be examined separately; and while one is being considered, we must call away and turn aside the mind from thinking about the other." He followed this approach in order to expound the "[d]ifferences between spiritual and civil government," insisting that "we must keep in mind the distinction . . . so that we do not (as so commonly happens) unwisely mingle these two, which have a completely different nature."[2] In examining these kingdoms separately and, in this way, keeping them apart and not mingling them, these Christians emphasized that church and state were distinct institutions but hardly concluded that they should be segregated and kept separate or apart from each other. On the contrary, Luther held that "the temporal government is a divine order" and urged all cities in Germany to establish Christian schools.[3] Calvin described both church

---

[1] *An Open Letter Concerning the Hard Book against the Peasants* (1525), in *Works of Martin Luther,* 4: 265 (Philadelphia: A. H. Holman Co., 1931); *Secular Authority: To What Extent It Should Be Obeyed* (1523), in ibid., 3: 237; *Sermons of Martin Luther,* 5: 319 (23rd Sunday after Trinity), ed. John Nicholas Lenker (Grand Rapids: Baker Book House, 1983); ibid., 5: 280 (22nd Sunday after Trinity).

[2] Calvin, *Institutes of the Christian Religion,* 1: 847 (IV.xix.15), 2: 1486 (IV.xx.1), trans. Ford Lewis Battles (Philadelphia: Westminister Press, 1960). He also wrote: "But whoever knows how to distinguish between body and soul, between the present fleeting life and that future eternal life, will without difficulty know that Christ's spiritual Kingdom of Christ and the civil government are things completely distinct." Ibid., 2: 1488 (IV.xx.1).

[3] *To the Councilmen of All Cities in Germany That They Establish and Maintain Christian Schools* (1524), in *Works of Martin Luther,* 4: 121. Such were his views even before he adopted more severe doctrines. For the latter, see Joseph LeCler, *Toleration and the Reformation,* 1: 154–164 (New York: Association Press, 1960).

and state as divinely ordained and hoped each would sustain the other in fulfilling their divine obligations. In particular, the "spiritual polity," although "quite distinct from the civil polity, . . . greatly helps and furthers it." By the same token, "civil government" had "the duty of rightly establishing religion" and had as its "appointed end" to "cherish and protect the outward worship of God, to defend sound doctrine of piety and the position of the church."[4] Clearly, the distinction between church and state, by itself, hardly amounted to the notion that they should be separated or walled off from one another.

Indeed, the distinction between church and state seemed fully compatible with a relatively rigorous establishment of religion. In the sixteenth and seventeenth centuries this was demonstrated by Luther in Germany, Calvin in Geneva, and the Congregationalists in New England. In the eighteenth century in England, the most prominent Enlightenment defender of establishments, William Warburton, justified an establishment as an alliance between two different institutions—the distinct existence of church and state making their alliance necessary. Gradually, the distinction between church and state (and, underlying it, the distinction between the two kingdoms) also came to be employed as the foundation for ideas about freedom from religious establishments. In the nineteenth century the distinction even seemed to legitimate a separation between church and state. Yet, as may be illustrated by Warburton and his numerous imitators, the distinction between church and state continued to be understood by many Christians to justify various modes of collaboration and even alliance between the two. Evidently, the distinction did not in itself imply either a disestablishment or a separation of church and state.

In distinguishing between the state and the church, Christians also differentiated between civil and ecclesiastical jurisdiction—between the powers of *regnum* and *sacerdotium*—but Christians did not employ these jurisdictional differences to demand a separation of church from state.

---

[4] *Institutes of the Christian Religion,* 2: 1211 (IV.xi.1); ibid., 2: 1487–1488 (IV.xx.2–3). Quoting these texts, John Witte observes that Calvin also suggested church and state were "conjoined"—further evidence, if any were needed, that "Calvin's principle of separation of church and state bore little resemblance . . . to the modern American understandings of 'a high and impregnable wall between church and state.'" John Witte, Jr., "Moderate Religious Liberty in the Theology of John Calvin," in Noel B. Reynolds and W. Cole Durham, eds., *Religious Liberty in Western Thought,* 117–118 (Atlanta: Scholars Press, 1996).

As recorded in Matthew 22.21, Jesus had admonished "Render therefore unto Caesar the things which are Caesar's; and unto God the things that are God's." Medieval Christians also repeatedly distinguished between what was owed to the state and what was owed to a higher power, and in doing so they discussed the different powers of the state and the church.[5] During the Reformation Protestants relied upon the contrast between these jurisdictions in their arguments against the Catholic Church, and eventually dissenting Protestants employed this contrast to challenge Protestant establishments. Indeed, much later, in the nineteenth century, Americans would allude to this jurisdictional difference in their arguments for a separation of church and state. Yet, until the late eighteenth century in America, and until later centuries elsewhere, most Christians understood this differentiation of jurisdictions, like the distinction between church and state, to be entirely compatible with one or another type of establishment, including Calvin's vision of mutually supportive institutions and Warburton's alliance.

Some Christians reached the conclusion that church and state must have different personnel. Most prominently, Calvin argued that officers of the church should not also be officers of civil government: "If we seek the authority of Christ in this matter, there is no doubt that he wished to bar the ministers of his Word from civil rule and earthly authority." According to Calvin, Christ held "not only that the office of pastor is distinct from that of prince but also that the things are so different that they cannot come together in one man."[6] In sixteenth-century England some dissenters demanded this division of offices, and in seventeenth-century New England the Congregational establishments put it into practice by excluding ministers from civil positions. Yet none of these Christians, from Calvin to the Congregationalists, thought that they were thereby separating church and state. On the contrary, they expected the state to protect the church and its ministers and, in turn, to enjoy the support and moral guidance of the church.

---

[5] Ewart Lewis, *Medieval Political Ideas,* 2: 506 (London: Routledge & Kegan Paul, 1954). Lewis writes: "Certainly no absolute dualism, completely separating the spheres of church and state, could logically be derived from the continuing medieval conviction of the primary importance of salvation and of the role of the priesthood as the necessary agency through which divine law was interpreted and salvation mediated. . . . [A] state with purely secular concerns was inconceivable and an absolute dualism was a *non sequitur.*" Ibid., 555.
[6] Calvin, *Institutes of the Christian Religion,* 2: 1220 (IV.xi.8).

More broadly, some Christians considered themselves a people separate or apart from other peoples. The Jews had felt obliged to maintain their identity separate from other nations or peoples, and some Christians drew upon this tradition. For example, St. Paul (in 2 Corinthians 6.17) told the Corinthians to leave behind unbelievers and idol worshipers, saying, "come out from among them, and be ye separate, saith the Lord, and touch not the unclean thing; and I will receive you." Later Christian writers, ranging from some of the Church Fathers to Calvin and many New Englanders, echoed this sense that Christians stood apart. They sometimes even used the metaphor of a wall. For instance, in his Commentary on Jeremiah, Calvin wrote that "God built, as it were, a wall to separate his people from aliens" and thereby gave "some preludes of his favor, and of the calling of the Gentiles."[7] Jesus had "pulled down" the "wall of separation" between Jew and Gentile in order to favor the Gentiles with a wall that separated them from other peoples.[8] Yet not all Gentiles would be so favored, and Calvin reminded his readers that many who considered themselves Christian might not be called—that some might be distinct from others. Of course, some of the Calvinists who considered themselves favored wanted sharper demarcations between themselves and those who were not so fortunate. On this account, they particularly welcomed the idea of a separation from other peoples—a tendency that led some of the regenerate elect to call themselves "Separatists." Yet this notion of a people separated from others—even if separated by a wall—did not constitute or even necessarily imply a separation of church and state. Indeed, as will be seen, those who wrote about themselves as separate from others did not demand a separation between church and state.

Some Christians hoped to separate or disentangle themselves from

---

[7] Calvin, *Commentary on the Prophet Jeremiah*, lecture 173 (Jer. 2.49.6), in *Calvin's Commentaries*, 11 (part 1): 63 (Grand Rapids: Baker Book House, 1984). Similarly, he wrote of the Jews in Egypt that "their mean and contemptible mode of life proves a wall of separation between them and the Egyptians; yea, Joseph seems purposely to labor to cast off, in a moment, the nobility he had acquired, that his own posterity might not be swallowed up in the population of Egypt." Calvin, *Commentary on Genesis* (Gen. 47.3), in *Calvin's Commentaries*, 18 (part 2): 437.

[8] Calvin, *Commentaries on the Acts of the Apostles* (Acts 10.28), in *Calvin's Commentaries*, 18 (part 2): 437. In the mid-sixteenth century the English reformer, Cox, wrote to the chief pastor at Worms, Weidnerus, that the English "were breaking down the popish hedge, and restoring the Lord's vineyard." Letter of Cox to Weidnerus (May 20, 1559), in John Strype, *Annals of the Reformation*, 1 (part 1): 197 (Oxford: Clarendon Press, 1824).

the world, but this too was very different from a separation of church and state. Cyprian had noted that "the Lord tells us that he becomes perfect and complete who sells all his goods, and distributes them for the use of the poor," to which Cyprian added that, according to Jesus, "that man is able to follow Him" who "is involved in no entanglements of worldly estate."[9] Somewhat differently, Augustine wondered how an incorporeal deity could speak to corporeal men and urged them, if they would hear, to "disentangle" themselves "from the world."[10] Exactly how Christians were to separate themselves from the world was a question to which medieval Christians found different answers—whether in convents and monasteries walled off from the world or in the mendicancy by which some Franciscans and others separated themselves from worldly goods. They did not, however, conceive themselves to be separating church from state.

Similarly, in the sixteenth century Anabaptists withdrew from worldly affairs. In the words of the *Schleitheim Confession* of 1527: "A separation shall be made from the evil and from the wickedness which the devil planted in the world; in this manner, simply that we shall not have fellowship with them [the wicked] and not run with them in the multitude of their abominations." In such attempts to "withdraw from Babylon and the earthly Egypt," Anabaptists not only questioned the use of civil force against dissentient beliefs but also doubted whether a Christian who served as a magistrate could long retain his Christianity. Many felt, as stated in the *Schleitheim Confession,* "that it is not appropriate for a Christian to serve as a magistrate because of these points: The government's magistracy is according to the flesh, but the Christians' is according to the Spirit; their houses and dwelling remain in this world, but the Christians' citizenship is in heaven." The Anabaptists withdrew so far from civil government as to hold that Christian individuals ought not seek justice in courts of law.[11] Thus, in separating from the world,

[9] Cyprian, Treatise 4, *On the Lord's Prayer* (para. 20), in Alexander Roberts, ed., *Ante-Nicene Fathers,* 5: 453 (New York: Charles Scribner's Sons, 1926).

[10] Augustin, *Homilies on the Gospel of St. John,* Tractate no. 23 (para. 8) (John 5.19–40), in Philip Schaff, ed., *A Select Library of the Nicene and Post-Nicene Fathers,* 7: 154 (Grand Rapids: Eerdmans Publishing, 1983).

[11] *Schleitheim Confession* (1527), in William R. Estep, Jr., *Anabaptist Beginnings (1523–33),* 102, 103 (Niewkoop: DeGraaf, 1976); Robert Kreider, "The Anabaptists and the State," in Guy F. Hershberger, ed., *The Recovery of the Anabaptist Vision: A Sixtieth Aniversary Tribute to Harold S. Bender,* 193 (Scottdale, Pa.: Herald Press, 1957). See also George Huntston

Anabaptists withdrew from civic life. They conceived themselves to be separating not simply the church, but all Christians, from civil government, and they did so as part of their broader renunciation of worldly abominations. This separation of Christian individuals from worldliness was very different from a separation of church and state.

When distancing their church from corrupt alternatives, Christians often adopted the image of an adulterous union. The Book of Revelation had described the church as the bride of Christ and had seemed to hint at the dangers of a corrupt union with others, and, already during the early history of Christianity, commentators used such ideas against those whom they considered heretics. For example, one Donatist complained: "Christ . . . committed His bride to our care: do we keep her uncorrupt and undefiled, or do we betray her purity and chastity to adulterers and corrupters? For he who makes the baptism of Christ common with heretics betrays the bride of Christ to adulterers."[12] The potential faithlessness of the Christian church became a common theme, and more than a thousand years later, when Protestants departed from Rome, they remonstrated against its adulterous "union" of church and state. Eventually Protestant dissenters employed this metaphor in their critiques of Protestant establishments. For example, in 1777 an English Baptist, Robert Robinson, condemned both Catholics and Anglicans for arguing that church and state had interlocking hierarchies, and he mocked the concept of a universal Christian church united in what he considered an adulterous union with the state. The "imaginary being called the *church* . . . has *sex*, in violation of the English language, and the laws of precise argumentation—*She* is either married or a prostitute. . . .—All this may be rhetoric; but nothing of this is reason, less still can it be called religion, and least of all is it that religion which Jesus taught."[13] Across the Atlantic, during the same year, a dissenter in Virginia wrote: "A virgin, however chaste before, when once deflowered, loses her native modesty;

William and Angel M. Mergal, eds., *Spiritual and Anabaptist Writers: Documents Illustrative of the Radical Reformation* (Philadelphia: Westminister Press, 1957); Walter Klaassen, *Anabaptism in Outline: Selected Primary Sources* (Waterloo, Ont.: Herald Press, 1981); Robert Kreider, "The Relation of the Anabaptists to the Civil Authorities in Switzerland, 1525–1555" (Ph.D. diss., University of Chicago, Dept. of History, 1953).

[12] The Seven Books of Augustin . . . on Baptism, Against the Donatists (bk. 7, ch. 13, para. 24) (quoting Venantius of Tinisia), in *A Select Library of the Nicene and Post-Nicene Fathers*, 4: 503.

[13] Robert Robinson, *The History and the Mystery of Good-Friday*, 15 (1777; London: 1823).

and ten to one but she becomes a common strumpet." Enticed and even "intoxicated" by her "fornications," many "Monarchs and Emperors . . . committed adultery with her."[14] This image of an adulterous and unnatural coupling (together with related metaphors of prostitution and rape, of virginal purity and corrupted wine) would continue to enliven antiestablishment arguments for centuries, including, eventually, arguments for the separation of church and state.

Yet, even as dissenting Protestants objected to the "adulterous union" of church and state and attempted to "sever" any "unnatural alliance," they did not thereby clearly endorse a separation of these institutions. On the contrary, their attacks on a union or alliance left open the possibility of other, nonestablishment connections. There were many potential connections, ranging from the cooperative to the merely moral and sociological, that came nowhere near a formal "alliance" or establishment, let alone a genuine union of church and state. For example, even most churches that were not established prayed for the government, taught obedience to law, expected to be protected in their legal rights, and hoped for legal recognition of their property and some of their rituals, such as that of marriage. All of these were connections between church and state, and many of these connections were essential parts of religious liberty. Therefore, the overwhelming majority of Protestants who criticized religious establishments and the union of church and state did not understand themselves to be seeking separation. Indeed, they carefully avoided making such a claim. Thus an attack on the union of church and state was not a demand for separation, and although in retrospect the notion of the separation of church and state has seemed to harmonize with the idea of opposition to an impure union, the two concepts should not be confused.

Last but not least, Christians gradually developed ideas about the inviolable authority of individuals and the limited authority of civil government with respect to religious belief. Continental Anabaptists in the sixteenth century and English Baptists in the seventeenth made arguments about the freedom of an individual's belief within his conscience, and, later, seventeenth-century dissenters and allied philosophers, such

---

[14] "Freeman of Virginia," *The Freeman's Remonstrance against an Ecclesiastical Establishment: Being Some Remarks on a Late Pamphlet, Entitled The Necessity of an Established Church in Any State,* 8, 12 (Williamsburg: 1777).

as John Locke, generalized these ideas into conceptions of religious freedom eventually employed by most American dissenters. Increasingly
joined with such ideas about belief and conscience were notions of the
limited jurisdiction of civil government, which dissenters gradually
adapted into arguments about equal rights and about government's lack
of power to grant financial privileges to churches. In these concepts of
individual freedom and limitations on government power, Englishmen
and Americans developed what would become the religious liberty guaranteed in American constitutions. Strikingly, however, as will be seen
in more detail below, they thereby conceived of their freedom in ways
very different from a separation between church and state.

Such were some of the traditional Christian ideas of religious liberty
and of the church's relationship to the state. Later, advocates of a separation between church and state would draw upon these various ideas,
viewing them retrospectively as nascent manifestations of the principle
that church should be kept separate from civil government. Earlier
Christians, however, did not go so far. They adopted many different conceptions of the relationship between church and state, but they did not
ordinarily, if ever, propose a separation, let alone a wall of separation,
between these institutions.

The Wall Separating the Garden and the Wilderness

The wall separating church and state was built upon the remains of an
earlier wall, which separated the garden from the wilderness. This metaphor of a wall separating the garden was applied in many ways but always in a manner that suggested the purity of the church. Whether the
wall represented the separation of the church from the world, the separation of the regenerate from the unregenerate, or the separation of particular "gathered" churches from a national church, it consistently depicted the church set apart from the taint of worldly things.

Early and medieval Christians found in the distinction between the
enclosed garden and the wilderness a profound image of their church
and its purity. They read in Genesis of the Garden of Eden, and, more
commonly, they read in the Song of Songs (4.12) of the enclosed garden
or *hortus conclusus:* "A garden inclosed is my sister, my spouse; a spring
shut up, a fountain sealed." Whether imagining the garden surrounded
by a hedge, fence, or wall, Christians perceived this enclosure as signifi-

cant, seeing it as a type or intimation of their walled monasteries and convents, of their faith and inner life, of Mary's virginity, and of the church itself—each of these being distinct from the world and its pollutions. Strengthening this image of purity was another, contrasting type, the wilderness of Sinai, in which the Jews had to wander before reaching the Promised Land—a wilderness with its own antitypes in the physical and spiritual wilderness of the world.

Although sixteenth-century Protestants pulled down the walls that surrounded medieval monasteries, some of them continued to rely upon the walled garden as an image of the Christian church. Luther mocked the early Christian monks who lived inside the enclosure formed by "a simple fence or hedge such as is made of bushes and plants and shoots to keep in cattle or as a pen for sheep" and who thus "led a separated life." Yet he himself could refer to "the garden of the Church."[15] With greater emphasis on the enclosed character of the garden, other Protestants—notably Calvin—still described the Christian church as a garden walled off from the threats of the world. For example, Calvin alluded to Israel and the church when, in commenting on Ezekiel, he wrote of "builders, who, if they see a breach in a wall, instantly and carefully repair it: they are like gardeners who do not allow either a field or a vineyard to be exposed to wild beasts."[16]

For many seventeenth-century Englishmen this image of the garden separated from the world illustrated the interior, mental state of individuals seeking spiritual development. As shown by Stanley Stewart, numerous Englishmen portrayed the garden as a place for contemplation, as the location in which individuals could reject vain strivings after worldly honors, and as a state of mind in which, under the protective shade of grace, the soul flourished and achieved transcendence. It was a verdant image of contemplation most sympathetically cultivated by Andrew Marvell, in whose poetry it remains memorable even though its theological foundations are usually forgotten:

> Mean while the Mind, from pleasure less,
> Withdraws into its happiness:

---

[15] Luther, *On the Councils and the Churches*, Part 2 (1539), in *Works of Martin Luther*, 5: 246–247.

[16] Calvin, *Commentary on the Prophet Ezekiel*, lecture 13 (Ezek. 13.10–11), in *Calvin's Commentaries*, 12 (part 1): 19.

> The Mind, that Ocean where each kind
> Does streight its own resemblance find;
> Yet it creates, transcending these,
> Far other Worlds, and other Seas;
> Anihilating all that's made
> To a green Thought in a green shade.[17]

In meditation the mind could reach beyond this world and even beyond the worldly metaphors of the garden and its shade.

Associating the garden with grace, Englishmen often perceived the enclosed garden as an apt depiction of the purified church. For example, in his 1623 volume, *Strange Vineyard in Palæstina*, Nehemiah Rogers merged the image of the enclosed garden with Isaiah's depiction of Israel as a vineyard to emphasize the role of the greatest of gardeners in establishing his church:

> A Vineyard we know is a place severed and hedged in from the open champaine or common. It doth not of it selfe spring up, or naturally grow; but it is planted by hand and Art, and so it is made a *Vineyard:* And thus the Church is called and separated from the rest of the world both in life and conversation, and is gathered by the word.

In this Protestant adaptation of Catholic imagery, the church, like Israel, was "called" and "gathered by the word" and thus was "separated" or "severed and hedged in" from the open, uncultivated land. "God hath taken it in out of the vast wildernesse of this wretched world, and hath imparked it with the pales of his mercy, and separated it from all other grounds whatsoever, to be a Vineyard for himself."[18] As William Prynne rhymed:

> Gardens enclosed are with walls, pales, bounds,
> Hedges, dikes, and more fenc'd than other grounds:
> So God his Church and chosen doth enclose,
> And fence with walls, pales, dikes against all foes.[19]

---

[17] Stanley Stewart, *The Enclosed Garden: The Tradition and the Image in Seventeenth-Century Poetry*, 162, 170–171 (Madison: University of Wisconsin Press, 1996), quoting Marvell.
[18] Ibid., 54, quoting Nehemiah Rogers, *Strange Vineyard in Palæstina* (1623). As Stewart explains, the "enclosure . . . represents the chosen Bride, whether she be Israel or the Church." Ibid.
[19] Ibid., 197, note 45, quoting William Prynne, "A Christian Paradise," in *Mount-Orgueil*, 152 (1641).

No longer the church as conceived by Catholics, this walled garden enclosed the elect. Clearly, the garden held different meanings for Catholics and for Protestants. For both, however, it provided an image of the church in a fallen world—an image in which the church had been set apart from the world and its impurity.

Richard Hooker

The wall separating church and state evolved from the wall separating the garden and the wilderness. Yet, unlike its predecessor, the wall between church and state seems to have become popular as an object of derision rather than as an ideal. In particular, it first became widely known in England when Richard Hooker ungenerously used it to characterize the position of Protestant dissenters who sought to purify the English Church.

In the 1590s, the learned Anglican apologist Richard Hooker wrote his voluminous *Of the Laws of Ecclesiastical Polity,* in which he defended the English middle ground between Catholicism and Puritanism. He published five books of his monumental work before his death in 1600 and left among his papers the rough manuscript notes for three additional parts. The Eighth Book was eventually published in 1648, and, near the beginning of this book, Hooker posthumously but prominently accused dissenters of seeking a separation of church and state.

Hooker's accusation echoed earlier Anglican attacks upon dissenters—most significantly, one by Hadrian Saravia. A Dutch Calvinist, Saravia would later, in 1607, become one of the translators of the King James Bible. He arrived from the Continent at a time when English dissenters were challenging the Anglican bishops on many grounds, including their wealth and civil offices. Troubled by these attacks, Saravia in 1590 published his *De Gradibus*—a defense of the Anglican hierarchy—in which, among other things, he repudiated the assault of dissenters upon the right of the clergy to hold civil office. Saravia held that church and city "both derived from one and the same author" and that the "two divers and distinct estates" were both part of one society: "the same societie is both Church & Cittie, and the authority of them is both drawen from the same head." On such assumptions, Saravia argued against those who "either exclude the Magistrate from causes Ecclesiasticke, or sequester the Minister from affaires politike." He even objected to this as a dangerous divorce of Minister and Magistrate: "But these two (the Magistrate and the Minister) so long as they shalbe distracted into partes, and as it were divorsed in state the one from the other, and shall not take sweete counsell together like friends, or not communicate in consent for their common benefite, they cannot but conceive divers and doubtfull surmises, fonde yea, and some times false opinions of each otheres governement." Of course, as Saravia explained in a paraphrase of Cyprian, the clergy *"should by no meanes bee called away from their devine function, neither shuld be intangled with troubles and worldlie affaires."* Nor was it "any part of the Ecclesiasticall function, to intermeddle in civil affaires, the which indeed is out of all controversie." Instead, Saravia simply argued that the same individual could hold both ecclesiastical and civil positions— that the *"diverse functions"* of these different persons *"are not confounded, albeit undertaken of one man."* Accordingly, "ᴛʜᴀᴛ which is commonly said of the state Ecclesiastique, *(that it is distinct from the Civil estate,)* is altogeather impertinent to this question: seeing both callings become not one, though one man be called to them both." For example, he argued, "Are not the parts of a Lawyer diverse, and the partes of a Physicion diverse? yet the same party may play both partes, and proove as good a Lawyer as a Physicion. In like manner, the same man may be both Physicion and Divine."

Not only could a man have two functions or callings but also no such specialization deprived a man of his place in society. Pointing out that "Curriers, Diers, Weavers, Beere-brewers, Smithes, Fullers, Marchauntes and Pedlers, furnish the common house, and give their voyce in things concerning the common wealth," Saravia concluded that if "the Pastors of Churches shoulde stande excommunicate out of their generall assemblies," it would be "a thing utterly against the equal right of al Cittizens." In such ways, Saravia attacked dissenters for taking a position that "as it were divorced" minister from magistrate.[20] It was a mischaracterization of dissenters to which Hooker would give much

---

[20] D. Saravia, *1. Of the Diverse Degrees of the Ministers of the Gospell. 2. Of the Honor Which Is Due unto the Priestes and Prelates of the Church. 3. Of Sacrilege, and the Punishment Thereof,* 32, A3, 143, 166, 180, 184 (1590; London: 1591). (Incidentally, the paraphrase of Cyprian was from his Epistle 65, although a printer's error alludes to Epistle 66.) Saravia, ibid., 143. Saravia also wrote that "when as Church and common wealth are imbarked in the same vessell, & saile together in the same danger: how should the devout minister be lesse solicited for the safety of the common state, then are the common Burgesses." Ibid., 185.

greater prominence when he attributed to them the position that there should be a wall of separation between church and state.

Among the dissenters, only the so-called "Separatists" demanded any sort of "separation," but even they did not seek a separation of church from state. On the contrary, they aimed to separate the regenerate from the unregenerate by disavowing any national church. Most Protestant dissenters felt that the Church of England, through its unscriptural prelacy and its accretion of "Popish" ceremonies, had deviated from early Christian practices and therefore needed to be reformed or purified. In place of the government-appointed Anglican hierarchy, some of these reformers hoped to impose Scottish-style presbyteries. Others aimed to substitute congregations "gathered" from among the regenerate. Of course, neither Presbyterians nor those who would later come to be known as "Congregationalists" offered much hope of toleration, except for themselves, for they had Calvinist expectations of a national church in which they—the regenerate elect—would set standards coercively enforced by a civil government attentive to their aspirations. The advocates of congregational organization feared that Anglican churches corruptly gave membership to the unregenerate, and therefore these dissenters believed that a true Gospel church had to be "gathered" and "covenanted" from among the regenerate. Accordingly, they sought the reconstruction of the English Church by forming their own, independent congregations, which were, in effect, regenerate substitutes for Anglican parish churches.

Some purifiers, however—the Separatists—sought a more thorough reformation by pursuing the congregational model with greater rigor. Taking congregational principles to their logical conclusion, the Separatists argued that no church defined by a parish, nation, or other geographic boundary could be gathered or covenanted among the regenerate alone, for if it included all inhabitants of a parish or nation, it would embrace the unregenerate. On this basis, the Separatists argued that the Church of England, being a national church, could never become a true church. They therefore felt obliged not only to depart physically into congregations of their own (as did the Congregationalists) but also to reject the very concept of a Church of England, and it was in this sense that they separated from it. More generally, Separatists abandoned covenant theology. Whereas Anglicans and Congregationalists elevated England or, at least, New England as a new Israel—as a chosen nation with its own church—the Separatists openly challenged expectations that a national or other territorial church was even possible, and they thereby, not suprisingly, separated their theology as well as themselves from their nation's church.[21] Yet even these, the most purifying of the purifiers, did not go so far as to advocate the separation of church and state. Anxious to separate the regenerate from the unregenerate, the Separatists sought a type of separation very different from that between church and state.

Although most dissenters never sought a disestablishment, and although even the Separatists apparently never asked for a separation of church and state, many Congregational dissenters demanded the end of the Anglican prelacy on grounds that distinguished between civil and ecclesiastical power, and it was these dissenters against whom Saravia and then Hooker most clearly aimed their allegations of divorce and separation. Without typically rejecting cooperation between church and state or the power of civil government to enforce religious conformity, these dissenters sought what they believed was a more scriptural church government, in which, following Calvin's admonitions, there would be a division of labor among civil and ecclesiastical officers, the latter belonging to presbyteries or congregations rather than an episcopal hierarchy appointed by the civil magistrate. Thus such dissenters argued that the same person could not hold both civil and spiritual office—that a single individual could not simultaneously be an officer of the Crown and an officer of the Church—but they did not ordinarily conceive of this as an attempt to "divorce" the clergy from the magistrates or as a separation of church and state.[22]

Nonetheless, drawing upon Saravia's polemical mischaracteriza-

---

[21] This account of the Separatists more or less follows the analysis of Edmund S. Morgan, *Roger Williams: The Church and the State* (New York: Norton, 1967).

[22] For example, in 1591 Henry Barrow argued that Anglican bishops were "no christian bishopps, in that they exercise som civile office or offices together with this their pretended ministrie . . . God himself hath made two distinct offices, and appointed unto them two distinct and several persons for ministers; it being no more lawfull for a bishop to execute the civile magistrate's office, than for the civile magistrate to administer the sacraments." Barrow, *A Plaine Refutation*, 111, in Leland H. Carlson, ed., *The Writings of Henry Barrow 1590–91*, 201, Elizabethan Non-Conformist Texts, vol. 5 (London: George Allen & Unwin, 1966). See also Henry Barrow, *A Petition Directed to Her Most Excellent Majestie*, 8 (1591). "Martin Marprelate" argued: "No civill magistrate can be an ordinary preacher without sinne." Martin Marprelat, *Oh read Over, D. John Bridges/for it is worthy worke: Or an epitome of the fyrste Booke/of that right Worshipfull volume/written against the Puritanes/in the defence of the noble cleargie/by as worshipfull a prieste/John Bridges/*. . . (quire E4v) (1588). See also *Theses Martinianae: That is, Certaine Demonstrative Conclusions* . . . , Nos. 67 and 68 (ca. 1589).

tions, Hooker suggested that the arguments of dissenters rested upon an unstated assumption that church and state should be kept separate.[23] According to Hooker, the arguments of the dissenters against the government-appointed Anglican prelacy did not make sense, "unless they against us should hold that the *Church* and the *Commonwealth* are two both distinct and separate societies, of which two the one comprehendeth always persons not belonging to the other." Indeed, in Hooker's view, dissenters seemed to be arguing from the position that there was a wall of separation between church and commonwealth. They appeared to believe "that *Bishops* may not meddle with the affayrs of the commonwealth, because they are governours of an other corporation, which is the *Church*, nor *Kings*, with making laws for the *Church* because they have governement not of this corporation, but of an other divided from it, the *Commonwealth*, and the walles of separation between these two must for ever be upheld." Although, as Hooker practically admitted, dissenters had not demanded "walles of separation" between church and commonwealth, he must have been pleased to believe that dissenters built their arguments upon this foundation, for he could easily demolish it.[24] All Hooker had to do was to point out that Englishmen were members simultaneously of England's church and of its commonwealth. If a person could be both an Anglican and an Englishman—both a servant of Christ and a subject of the Crown—there was no wall of separation between church and commonwealth.

In accusing dissenters of seeking walls of separation, Hooker went out of his way to admit that his own position could be considered a sort of separation, but he did so largely to avoid any "childish" tendency "to

[23] Isaac Walton records that the "learned Doctor" Saravia sought Hooker's friendship, and that in 1595 "these two excellent persons began a holy friendship, increasing daily to so high and mutual affections, that their two wills seemed to be but one and the same: and their designs both for the glory of God, and peace of the Church, still assisting and improving each other's virtues, and the desired comforts of a peaceable piety"—a passage that led an early nineteenth-century editor of Saravia to suggest the importance of "the sentiments of the less celebrated of the two." Hadrian Saravia, *A Treatise on the Different Degrees of the Christian Priesthood*, vi–vii (Oxford: 1840). See also *The Works of That Learned and Judicious Divine Mr. Richard Hooker*, 3: 330–331, ed. John Keble (Oxford: Clarendon Press, 1888).

[24] Hooker revealed his understanding that the dissenters had not sought a separation when he indulged in the supposition, "unless they against us should hold that the *Church* and the *Commonwealth* are two both distinct and separate societies." *Of the Laws of Ecclesiastical Polity*, in *Works of Richard Hooker*, 3: 319 (VIII.i.2), ed. W. Speed Hill (Cambridge, Mass.: Belknap, 1981).

lurk under shifting ambiguities and equivocations of wordes." Both he and his opponents sought types of what could be called "separation," but he distinguished between two types, the personal and the natural. Dissenters held "the necessitie of personall separation, which," according to Hooker, "cleane excludeth the power of one mans dealing in both [church and commonwealth]." In contrast, Hooker supported only a "natural" separation—a mere distinction between the church and the commonwealth—"which doth not hinder but that one and the same person may in both bear a principal sway."[25] Of course, dissenters did not exclude all members of the church from the commonwealth. They simply wanted different civil and ecclesiastical officers. Hooker, however, suggested that a more sweeping separation underlay dissenting positions.

The "separation" sought by Hooker was simply the age-old distinction between church and state, which, for Hooker, as for so many earlier Christians, seemed perfectly compatible with an established religion, including the combination of civil and church authority in any one person. Hooker readily would "graunt" this "difference," which posed no obstacle to his traditional view that both church and commonwealth "may and should always lovingly dwell together in one subject." Like Saravia, he therefore brushed off arguments based on the distinction between church and state as irrelevant:

> I shall not need to spend any great store of wordes in answearing that which is brought out of holy *Scripture* to shewe that secular and Ecclesiasticall affayres and offices are distinguished, neither that which has been borrowed from antiquitie using by phrase of speech to oppose the *Commonwealth* to the *Church* of *Christ;* neither yet the reasons, which are wont to be brought forth as witnesses that the *Church* and *Commonwealth* are alwayes distinct. For whither *a Church* and *a Commonwealth* doe differ is not the question we strive for, but our controversyie is concerning the kinde of distinction, whereby they are severed the one from the other.

According to Hooker, the words "church" and "commonwealth" referred to different or "several functions of one and the same *Communities*," and he noted that even a Catholic apologist, Cardinal William Allen, admitted that, *"in Christian Commonwealths,"* political power and spiritual power were *"joyned though not confounded."* Thus "[t]he difference . . .

---

[25] Ibid., 3: 318, 319–320 (VIII.i.2).

either of affayres or offices Ecclesiasticall from secular is no argument that the *Church* and the *Commonwealth* are always separate and independent the one from the other."[26] Anything more than the "natural" separation between these institutions went beyond the traditional Christian concept of a distinction between church and state, and therefore a more substantial separation seemed vulnerable to Hooker, who all too readily assumed that it underlay the claims of dissenters.

Roger Williams

A half century later, drawing upon some of the same Christian sources familiar to Hooker, Roger Williams adopted the wall of separation as an image of the purity he sought in religion. Yet what Hooker depicted as an unrealistic assumption of the dissenters and what other Protestants employed as a poetic image of the regenerate church, Williams took almost literally. So far did Williams pursue spiritual purity and a separation from the corruptions of this world that he separated himself from all of his contemporaries.[27]

[26] Ibid., 3: 322–325 (VIII.i.4–5).

[27] My interpretation of Williams's separatism and his desire for purity follows some of the rich modern scholarship, especially that of Morgan, Gilpin, and Hall. Edmund S. Morgan, *Roger Williams: The Church and the State* (New York: Norton, 1967); W. Clark Gilpin, *The Millenarian Piety of Roger Williams* (Chicago: University of Chicago, 1979); Timothy L. Hall, "Roger Williams and the Foundations of Religious Liberty," *Boston Univ. Law Review,* 71: 455, 482 (1991); Timothy L. Hall, *Separating Church and State: Roger Williams and Religious Liberty,* 30, 72–98 (Urbana: University of Illinois, 1998). See also Richard Martin Reinitz, "Symbolism and Freedom: The Use of Biblical Typology as an Argument for Religious Toleration in Seventeenth Century England and America," 143–144 (Ph.D. diss., University of Rochester, 1967); David Little, "Roger Williams and the Separation of Church and State," in *Religion and the State: Essays in Honor of Leo Pfeffer,* ed. James E. Wood, Jr. (Waco: Baylor University Press, 1985); William Lee Miller, *The First Liberty: Religion and the American Republic,* 182–183 (New York: Paragon, 1988); Glenn W. LaFantasie, ed., *The Correspondence of Roger Williams,* 2: 23 (Providence: Rhode Island Historical Society, 1988); Hugh Spurgin, *Roger Williams and Puritan Radicalism in the English Separatist Tradition* (Lewiston: E. Edwin Mellen Press, 1989); Edwin S. Gaustad, *Liberty of Conscience: Roger Williams in America* (Grand Rapids: William B. Eerdmans, 1991).

There is a possibility that Roger Williams had read the Eighth Book of Hooker's *Of the Laws of Ecclesiastical Polity.* Probably about 1630, various Hooker manuscripts, including the surviving drafts for the Eighth Book, had been acquired for Lambeth Palace. On June 27, 1644, however, during the tumult of the Civil War, the House of Commons gave the Lambeth Palace Library to Hugh Peters "as a reward for his remarkable service in those sad times of the Church's confusion." *Of the Laws of Ecclesiastical Polity,* in *Works of Richard Hooker,* 3: xviii (VIII). This prompted Bishop King to say that Hooker's manuscripts "could hardly fall into a fouler hand." Ibid., xxviii, note 21. Roger Williams may well have had

Williams was a Separatist. Whereas Anglicans and those who would eventually be known as Congregationalists looked back to the example of Israel to suggest that their entire nation had a divine covenant and were a chosen people, Separatists feared that, under the New Dispensation, nations necessarily included the unregenerate. Therefore, as has been seen, Separatists not only gathered in their own congregations, in the manner of Congregationalists, but also declared themselves and their "particular" churches separate from any national church. Williams joined his fellow Separatists in breaking away from Anglicans and their conception of a national church, and, beginning at least in 1631 when he arrived in Boston, he further separated from the Puritans of Massachusetts and their Congregational version of a national English church. In adhering to his Separatist principles, Williams on more than one occasion sacrificed valued friendships, and when quarreling with the Congregationalists, he increasingly found himself opposed to an old friend, John Cotton, who had become the most persistent advocate of the Massachusetts colony's national Congregational vision.

Williams took his Separatism so far as to insist on separating even from most Separatists. Like other Separatists, he argued that particular churches or congregations were obliged to separate from territorial, national churches, whether the Church of England or the Congregational churches of Massachusetts. Yet, for Williams, not only a particular congregation but each individual member of it had to be fully separated from the impurity of the unregenerate. Most Separatists had no complaint about fellow congregants who, when visiting England, occasionally attended Anglican services. Williams, however, could not tolerate such impurity, and accordingly he lasted only briefly in any congrega-

---

a different view, for, already in 1637, he referred to Peters as "my worthy friend." Roger Williams, Letter to John Winthrop (July 21, 1637), in LaFantasie, *The Correspondence of Roger Williams,* 1: 106. Even before June 1644 Hooker's manuscripts probably attracted interest, for Bishop King, after disparaging Hugh Peters, added, "yet there wanted not other endeavours to corrupt and make them speak that language, for which the faction then fought." *Works of Richard Hooker,* 3: xxviii, note 21. Both before the summer of 1644 and after, Hooker's manuscripts would have been the focus of some attention, and by 1648 the printer's notice to the first publication of the Eighth Book could observe that "Copies are abroad." Indeed, the 1648 edition was based on six manuscripts, and today at least ten are extant, none of which can certainly be identified as one of the six relied upon by the editors of the 1648 edition. Ibid., xxix. Accordingly, by the time Williams published his *Mr. Cotton's Letter, Lately Printed, Examined and Answered* in February 1644, he may have seen either Hooker's drafts or copies of them.

tion. Williams "refused to join with the congregation at Boston, because they would not make a public declaration of their repentance for having communion with the churches of England, while they lived there."[28] From Boston he went to the Separatist church at Salem and finally retreated to the Separatist church at Plymouth, the most separate of the Massachusetts Separatist congregations. Yet Williams felt obliged to leave even this congregation "something abruptly" in 1633 when he could not persuade its members to adopt his "rigid separation." Although he went back to the church at Salem, he later refused to take communion there on account of its impurity.[29] With an abhorrence of any taint upon the regenerate, he insisted that women "cover themselves with veils when they went abroad, especially when they appeared in publick assemblies," and that church members not pray with the unregenerate. He apparently even held that a man should not pray with his wife if she were unregenerate. He also argued that "a magistrate ought not to tender an oath to an unregenerate man," and he rejected the Boston churches "as full of antichristian pollution."[30] All of this seemed scandalous to Cotton and other Congregationalists, who understood their churches to be fully regenerate and who sought to purify the Church of England.

In questioning the purity of the churches of Massachusetts, Roger Williams also challenged the colony's use of its civil power to force the regenerate to mix in churches with the unregenerate. Such coercion seemed, to Williams, to threaten the freedom of individuals and the purity of the regenerate. Accordingly, Williams argued that "the magistrate ought not to punishe the breache of the first table [of the Ten Commandments], otherwise then in suche Cases as did disturbe the Civill peace."[31] Only civil offenses—breaches of the peace—were subject to civil sanctions.

For years, the General Court of Massachusetts attempted to persuade Williams to abandon his errors. Finally, however, in October 1635

---

[28] LaFantasie, *The Correspondence of Roger Williams*, 2: 12 (quoting Winthrop's *History*, 1: 63).
[29] Ibid., 13–14 (quoting Morton's *Memorial*, 102–103), and 21.
[30] Ibid., 16, 19–21; Morgan, *Roger Williams*, 27; James D. Knowles, *Memoir of Roger Williams*, 68 (Boston: 1834).
[31] *The Journal of John Winthrop 1630–1649*, 150 (July 8, 1635), ed. Richard S. Dunn, James Savage, and Laetitia Yeandle (Cambridge, Mass.: Belknap Press, 1996). Although these words came from the accusation against Williams in the General Court, there is no reason to doubt the accuracy of this charge.

Massachusetts made tangible its claim that, like ancient Israel, it could use civil power to enforce conformity to its national church. Williams had reiterated his views that the Boston magistrates had acted oppressively and that the church in Salem should fully separate from other Massachusetts churches and renounce communion with them.[32] In so doing, he simultaneously repudiated religious beliefs he considered false and rejected the impure use of civil power in a realm governed by a higher power. It was a stance that left the General Court little choice. With a punishment that aptly expressed its national understanding of religion, the General Court banished him, and early the next year he departed to seek freedom in Rhode Island, in a place he and his fellow settlers called "Providence."

Williams argued against infringements on religious liberty by adopting the arguments of the early seventeenth-century Baptists who attributed different objects and weapons to Christ's kingdom and to civil government.[33] For example, in explaining the limits of civil jurisdiction, Williams drew upon Jesus' parable of the tares and the wheat. According to Jesus (as recounted in Matthew 13.24–44), a man planted wheat, and, when the "enemy" sowed tares among the wheat, the man's servants asked whether they should weed out the tares, but the man said: "Nay, lest while ye gather up the tares, ye root up also the wheat with them. Let both grow together until the harvest." From this, Williams concluded that, "as the *civill State* keepes itselfe with a *civill guard*, in case these *Tares* shall attempt ought against the *peace* and *welfare* of it, let such *civill offences* be punished, and yet, as *Tares* opposite to *Christs Kingdome*, let their *Worship* and *Consciences* be tolerated." The civil state could apply its civil penalties to civil offenses, as these were opposed to the state, but it could not apply such punishments to consciences or worship, as these related to Christ's kingdom. Concomitantly, Christ's kingdom had complete jurisdiction over conscience and worship but none over civil offenses. "But as the *Civill Magistrate* hath his charge of the *bodies* and *goods*

---

[32] LaFantasie, *The Correspondence of Roger Williams*, 1: 20–21.

[33] For Williams's views on these different jurisdictions, see Little, "Roger Williams and the Separation of Church and State"; Miller, *The First Liberty*, 182–183; Hall, "Roger Williams and the Foundations of Religious Liberty," 482; Hall, *Separating Church and State*, 72–98; Gilpin, *The Millenarian Piety of Roger Williams*; Morgan, *Roger Williams*; Spurgin, *Roger Williams and Puritan Radicalism*; Daniel L. Dreisbach, "Sowing Useful Truths and Principles," *Journal of Church and State*, 39: 483 (1997).

of the *subject:* So have the *spirituall Officers, Governours* and *overseers* of *Christs City* or *Kingdome,* the charge of their *souls,* and *soule safety."*[34] Thus, in contrast to Cotton and the others in Massachusetts who held that there, as in Israel, the magistrate possessed both civil and spiritual power, Williams believed that civil governments had not been given authority over spiritual matters.

Yet Williams took the division between the worldly and the spiritual far beyond this conventional Baptist argument about religious liberty. For example, he argued that an exclusively worldly foundation was adequate for specialized worldly activities, including government, family life, and commerce. "And hence it is true, that a *Christian Captaine, Christian, Merchant, Physitian, Lawyer, Pilot, Father, Master,* and (so consequently) *Magistrate, &c.* is no more a *Captaine, Merchant, Physitian, Lawyer, Pilot, Father, Master, Magistrate, &c.* then a *Captaine, Marchant, &c.* of any other Conscience or Religion," and "A *Pagan* or *Antichristian Pilot* may be as skillfull to carry the Ship to its desired Port, as any *Christian Mariner* or *Pilot."*[35] So severe was Williams's division between the spiritual and the worldly that they seemed almost irrelevant to each other, leaving worldly activities—or at least those so specialized as to seem secular— unburdened by spiritual concerns. This transcended the religious liberty Baptists had demanded and hinted how social specialization was secularizing human life, stripping religion of much of its worldly significance. By no coincidence, such observations came from the man who, more than any other, rejected the hopes of his contemporaries for churches that included entire communities, local or national.

In 1644 Williams wrote his famous *Bloudy Tenent of Persecution.* In 1643, when England was in the middle of its civil war, Williams hoped to obtain a charter for his new home, Rhode Island, and he therefore sailed to London. He arrived in the autumn at a dramatic moment. In an attempt to solicit the support of Scotland against the king, the House of Commons adopted the Solemn League and Covenant, by which the Commons agreed to reform the Church of England on the Scottish Presbyterian model. Of course, those who were not Presbyterians feared that

---

[34] *The Bloudy Tenent, of Persecution, for Cause of Conscience, discussed, in a Conference between Truth and Peace* (1644), in *The Complete Writings of Roger Williams,* 3: 111, 127 (New York: Russell & Russell, 1963).

[35] Ibid., 3: 398–399. For this interpretation of this passage, see Morgan, *Roger Williams,* 118.

the Solemn League and Covenant would threaten their freedom. In these circumstances, beginning in the winter of 1644, Roger Williams wrote his *Bloudy Tenent of Persecution,* which he cautiously published, however, only in July 1644, after he had obtained his charter and was ready to return to Rhode Island. Although he took aim most directly at "Mr. Cotton, and the New England ministers," he wrote his *Bloudy Tenent* as a methodical compendium of all the arguments for freedom of conscience. He designed it to contain the "whole *Body*" of the "Controversies of *Persecution* for cause of *Conscience,*" which was something "beyond what's extant." Intending to present for the first time the whole of the debate over persecution, Williams methodically included "*Arguments from Religion, Reason,* [and] *Experience.*" Strikingly, however, in a book designed to compile all known arguments against persecution, Williams did not present his most purifying image, the wall of separation.[36]

Instead, Williams discussed the wall of separation in another pamphlet published almost six months earlier. In 1636, shortly after Massachusetts banished Williams, John Cotton had written to Williams to justify the colony's refusal to reject the Church of England and its civil enforcement of its Congregational establishment. Toward the end of his letter, Cotton condemned Williams for separating from English parish churches and from the churches of New England that allowed their members to attend such parish churches:

> It is not to helpe Jehovah, but Satan against him, to withdraw the people of God from hearing the voyce of Christ which is preached in the evidence, and simplicity, and power of his Spirit in sundry Congregations (though they be Parishes) in our native Country. In which respect,

---

[36] *The Complete Writings of Roger Williams,* 3: 5–6 (dedication). Williams's contemporary, William Chillingworth, alluded to walls of separation in his arguments for religious liberty but only as a metaphor for the sectarian opinions that divided Christians: "[T]his deifying our own interpretations, and tyrannous forcing them upon others; this restraining the word of God from that latitude and generality, and the understandings of men from that liberty wherein Christ and the apostles left them, is and hath been the only fountain of all the schisms of the church, and that which makes them immortal. Take away these walls of separation, and all will quickly be one. Take away this persecuting, burning, cursing, damning of men for not subscribing to the words of men as the words of God; . . . I say, take away tyranny, and restore Christians to their just and full liberty of captivating their understanding to Scripture only; and as rivers, when they have a free passage, run all to the ocean, so it may well be hoped, by God's blessing, that universal liberty, thus moderated, may quickly restore Christendom to truth and unity." Chillingworth, *The Religion of Protestants: A Safe Way to Salvation,* 250 (1638; London: H. G. Bohn, 1846).

though our people that goe over into England, choose rather to heare in some of the Parishes where the voyce of Christ is lifted up like a trumpet, then in the separated Churches (where some of us may speak by experience we have not found the like presence of Christ, or evidence of his Spirit).

Against the separated churches, Cotton added: "It is not Chirurgery, but Butchery, to heale every sore in a member with no other medicine but abscission from the body."[37] Accordingly, to prevent this separation, civil government had to enforce conformity by law. Williams had replied with a letter of his own, and there the matter rested until the fall of 1643, when someone (perhaps Williams himself) arranged to have Cotton's letter published in London. Finally, having reason to respond publicly, Williams in February 1644 published his own letter under the title *Mr. Cotton's Letter, Lately Printed, Examined and Answered.*[38]

According to Williams, Cotton and the other Massachusetts Congregationalists failed to separate their churches from worldly impurities. The Congregationalists combined the regenerate with the unregenerate, and their dependence upon state coercion amounted to an admission of this impurity. "[B]y compelling all within their *Jurisdiction* to an outward *conformity* of the *Church worship,* of the *Word* and *Prayer,* and *maintenance* of the *Ministry* thereof, they evidently declare that they still lodge and dwell in the confused mixtures of the *uncleane* and *cleane,* of the *flock* of *Christ* and the *Herds* of the *World* together, I mean in *spirituall* and *religious* worship."[39] The Congregationalists coercively mixed in their congregations both the regenerate and the unregenerate, the clean and the unclean, and thus seemed to hold that "the *Garden* and the *Wildernesse,* the *Church* and the *World* are all one."[40]

In contrast, Williams hoped to wall off the garden from the wilderness. The book of Isaiah (5.5–6) had warned that the wall protecting the vineyard or garden would be broken down as a divine punishment: "I will tell you what I will do to my vineyard: I will take away the hedge thereof . . . and break down the wall thereof. . . . And I will lay it waste."

---

[37] *A Letter of Mr. John Cottons Teacher of the Church in Boston in New-England to Mr. Williams a Preacher There* (London: 1643), in LaFantasie, *The Correspondence of Roger Williams,* 1: 42–43.

[38] LaFantasie, *The Correspondence of Roger Williams,* 1: 31–32.

[39] *The Bloudy Tenent, of Persecution,* in *The Complete Writings of Roger Williams,* 3: 234.

[40] Ibid., 3: 233.

In requiring the regenerate to mix with the unregenerate, the Congregationalists and other established churches breached the wall or hedge separating the church from the world, and they thereby brought about the reduction of the garden to a wilderness—a wasteland in which the regenerate were deprived of divine light:

> [T]he faithful labours of many Witnesses of *Jesus Christ,* extant to the world, abundantly proving, that the Church of the Jews under the Old Testament in the type, and the *Church* of the Christians under the New Testament in the Antitype, were both separate from the world; and that when they have opened a gap in the hedge or wall of Separation between the Garden of the Church and the Wilderness of the world, God hath ever broke down the wall it selfe, removed the Candlestick, &c. and made his Garden a Wilderness, as at this day.

Therefore, if he were "ever please[d] to restore his Garden and Paradise again, it must of necessitie be walled in peculiarly unto himselfe from the world."[41] Williams desired religious liberty of a sort enunciated by the Baptists, but, clearly, he also hoped to build a wall separating the regenerate from the unregenerate and the church from the world.

New Light on an Old Metaphor

Although Williams has become famous for his wall of separation, he in fact combined two images: the wall and the candlestick. He placed the candlestick in the enclosed garden of the church, and he thereby shed much light on his radically individualistic and anticlerical understanding of the church he would keep separate from the world.

Although not necessarily individualistic or anticlerical, the image of a candlestick could have such implications, and to discern these, it is necessary to look back briefly to the late Middle Ages and the illuminated books of hours and prayer books frequently used for private devotions. In the northern Netherlands, as shown by James Marrow, the prayers contained in such books sometimes described John the Baptist as the "lantern of the Lord" or the "lantern of the world," and the accompanying illustrations sometimes depicted him holding a lantern. Later, in

---

[41] *Mr. Cotton's Letter, Lately Printed, Examined and Answered* (London: 1644), in ibid., 1: 392 (ch. 28). Williams added that "all that shall be saved out of the world are to be transplanted out of the Wilderness of the world, and added unto his Church or Garden." Ibid.

at least one mid-sixteenth-century panel painting, he holds a burning candle. In the words of the Gospel of John (5.35), the Baptist was a "bright and shining light."[42] Eventually, however, as also shown by Marrow, some books of hours made for the English market displayed the lantern on the ground or hanging from a tree in an expanse of unimproved land of the sort that was known as a "desert" or "wilderness." In these illustrations the Baptist stood nearby—in one instance, pointing to the lantern—suggesting an appreciation of another passage in John (1.8): "He was not that light, but was sent to bear witness of that light."[43] Now Jesus himself, rather than the Baptist, appeared as the light of the world. It was a portentous change—suggesting profound possibilities for individual enlightenment and, concomitantly, dark suspicions of the clergy.

These evolving images may reveal an interest in the claims of John Wycliffe and other reformers who urged individuals to find illumination by reading the Bible for themselves. In early fifteenth-century England those sympathetic to Wycliffite views—the so-called "Lollards"—had recited Proverbs (6.23) that "Goddis comaundementis ben a lanterne & that lawe is light," and, even more radically, they had argued that "the wit of Crist is so clere light that in hise wordis ther may no man erre; he takith the persoone of pore nedi & spekith in poore men as in him silf."[44] Each person, even the poor and needy, could read the Bible and find Christ's light himself, without clerical assistance. Accordingly, the "Lantern of Light" was adopted as the name of a Wycliffite tract popularizing such ideas and, more broadly, became a Wycliffite symbol of the illumination each person might find for himself in the Scriptures.[45] In

---

[42] James Marrow, "John the Baptist, Lantern for the Lord: New Attributes for the Baptist from the Northern Netherlands," *Oud Holland,* 83: 13 (1968), quoting John 5.35.

[43] James Marrow, "John the Baptist, Lantern for the Lord: A Supplement," *Oud Holland,* 85: 188 (1970).

[44] Lilian M. Swinburn, ed., *The Lantern of Li[gh]t,* 123, 30 (London: Early English Text Society, 1917). The second quotation cited "Mat. xxv." (Quotations from the *Lantern* are made more readable here by modernizing punctuation and orthography and dropping the editor's italicization of letters inserted to fill in contractions.)

[45] Ibid., viii. This individual enlightenment could cast a strong shadow. On the one hand, "Light & sunne is up spronngen & meke loweli ben uphaunsid [i.e., enhanced]." On the other, "What euere that ony man doith that failith this light it ledith blyndingis to the dungun of helle." Ibid., 28–29.

Incidentally, the key texts recited in the *Lantern* were not from John, but Wycliffites seem to have understood the importance of what John had to say about the light. Revealing what may have been anxiety that Jesus would not be understood as having given the

these circumstances some Englishmen and women, even if not Lollards, seem to have preferred images in which the Baptist was not the light but merely the witness of it. Eventually, especially in the aftermath of the Reformation, the Baptist dropped out of the picture altogether, and the lantern or a candlestick stood on its own in the wilderness—a representation of scripture lighting the way for individuals living in the world.[46]

---

light to individuals, some versions of the Wycliffe Bible provided alternative readings to John 5.35: "Sothli he was a lanterne brennyinge and schynynge," to which some copies added "or [g]yvynge light." Josiah Forshall and Frederic Madden, eds., *The Holy Bible Containing the Old and New Testaments . . . in the Earliest English Versions Made from the Latin Vulgate by John Wycliffe and His Followers*, 3: 249 (Oxford: 1850).

[46] Such an image, with the words "Praelucendo Pereo," was used as a printer's device in London in the 1620s and 1630s—as was the more common variant that emphasized the role of scripture, the candle on a Bible. Ronald B. McKerrow, *Printers and Publishers' Devices in England and Scotland 1485–1640*, 155 and illustration nos. 413 and 412 (London: Bibliographical Society, 1913). For other variants, see, e.g., [Jacques Callot?], The Maidservant (woman sitting on hillock holding a candlestick); Daniel Cramer, *Emblemata Sacra*, 37 (Frankfurt: 1624) (seeing heart in unimproved land, with shining lantern above held by arm from cloud, illustrating Psalm 36, v.10, "In deinem liecht sehen wir das liecht"); Francis Quarles, *Emblemes*, 128 (London: 1635) (angel holding a shining lantern at night in unimproved land, approached by a woman with outstretched arms, illustrating Psalm 29, v.6, "My soule hath desired thee in the night"). According to John (1.9), Jesus had said "let your light shine," and, in this spirit, Augustine had written that "all men are lamps," which could be "both lighted and extinguished"—a common Christian metaphor adapted by many seventeenth-century artists to depict the light, life, grace, inspiration, or talents within individuals. Augustin, *Homilies on the Gospel of John*, Tractate 23 (John 5.19–40), in *A Select Library of the Nicene and Post-Nicene Fathers*, 7: 151. See also "Liceat Sperare Timenti," in *Emblemata Moralia et Æconomica*, 40 (emblem 20), in Jacob Catz, *Proteus ofte Minne-Beelden Verandert in Sinne-Beelden Door* (Rotterdam: 1627); Francis Quarles, *Hieroglyuphikes of the Life of Man* (London: 1638). Incidentally, in employing the image of the light in the lantern, the great Quaker apologist, Robert Barclay, seems to have alluded to an oral tradition on the subject among Quakers. Barclay, *An Apology for the True Christian Divinity: Being an Explanation and Vindication of the Principles and Doctrines of the People Called Quakers*, 147 (Propositions V & VI, sec. 16) (1676; Providence: 1840). For further variants, see Arthur Henkel and Albrecht Schöne, *Emblemata Handbuch zur Sinnbildkunst des XVI. und XVII. Jahrhunderts*, 1362–1373 (Stuttgart: J. B. Metzlersche, 1967).

The basic motif could, of course, be deployed for very different purposes. In the 1640s it was used to illustrate "The Royal Flame" on the frontispiece to a volume of cases of conscience by the man who would soon become chaplain to the unfortunate King Charles I, Henry Hammond—an image that simultaneously depicted the light of conscience and the obligation in conscience to the Lord's anointed, a message made clear by the quotation inscribed on the base of the candlestick from 2 Samuel 21.17, "Quench not the Light of Israel." Hammond, *A Practical Catechisme* (1644; 2d ed., 1646). See also *Allegory of Charles I of England and Henrietta of France in a Vanitas Still Life* (after 1669), in Birmingham Museum of Art, Atlanta.

This bright image of individual illumination had a somber alternative, as became apparent in some early seventeenth-century pictures, in which the light was removed or snuffed out by the clergy. According to the Book of Revelation (1.12–13, 20, and 2.4–5), John turned to "see the voice that spake with me. And being turned, I saw seven golden candlesticks; And in the midst of the seven candlesticks one like unto the Son of man," who told John that the "seven candlesticks which thou sawest are the seven churches." John was instructed to write to "the angel of the church" of Ephesus: "Nevertheless I have somewhat against thee, because thou hast left thy first love. Remember therefore from whence thou art fallen, and repent, and do the first works; or else I come unto thee quickly, and will remove thy candlestick out of his place, except thou repent." Some seventeenth-century printmakers applied this Biblical vision to the Church of England by portraying the attempts of the clerical hierarchy to extinguish or remove a candlestick that stood in the wilderness. In one print, a lighted candlestick rested on a Bible, which lay in unimproved ground within a landscape. The candle was held by three hands—two apparently trying to dislodge it, and a third, coming out of a cloud, keeping it steady. Below, a caption complained to an authority higher than the episcopy:

> Prevailing Prelat[e]s strive to quench our Light,
> Except your sacred power quash their might.[47]

Similarly, a woodcut emblem showed a burning candlestick standing in a wilderness—the candle being grasped by three truncated hands. Two of these hands belonged to the bishops:

---

[47] John Leighton, *An Appeal to the Parliament; or Sions Plea against the Prelacie* (1629) (STC 15428.5). See Frederick George Stephens, *Catalogue of Political and Personal Satires Preserved in . . . British Museum*, 1: 64 (no. 104) (British Museum, 1978). These motifs may have played off earlier Catholic images. Already in Robert Campin's Annunciation Triptych of ca. 1425–1430—the Merode Altarpiece in the Cloisters—the descent of the Holy Ghost rushing through the air toward Mary seems to extinguish the solitary candle by which she was reading. A trail of smoke rises from the dying ember of the wick. Although the painting may allude to the extinguishing of the man-made light of reformers, this is purely speculative, and there are many other possible interpretations. For a description, see Maryan W. Ainworth and Keith Christianen, eds., *From Van Eyck to Bruegel: Early Netherlandish Painting in The Metropolitan Museum of Art*, 89 (New York: Metropolitan Museum of Art, 1998). For one of many accounts of the painting's iconography, see William S. Heckscher, "The Annunciation of the Merode Altarpiece: An Iconographic Study," in *Miscellanea Jozef Duverger: Bijdragen tot de kunstgeschiedenis der Nederlanden* (Gent: Vereniging voor de Geschiedenis der Textielkunsten, 1968).

> Two hands together heere with griping hold,
> And all their force, doe striue to take away
> This burning Lampe, and Candlestick of Gold,
>> Whose light shall burne in spite of Hell . . .
>> For tis the Truth so holy and divine.
> Which soule Ambition hath so often vext,
> And swelling pride of Praelates put in doubt,
> With covetuousnes that greedie Monster next,
> That long I feare me since it had bene out,
>> Did not thy hand (deare Saviour) from above
>> Defend it so, that it might never moue.[48]

Only a hand "from above" could protect this "burning Lampe, and Candlestick of Gold" from the grasping hands of the prelates, who strove to take it away. It was this candlestick—the light of divine truth illuminating individual conscience in the wilderness of this world, a light the prelates and now also the Congregationalists threatened to extinguish or remove—that Williams described as threatened by a breach in the wall separating the garden from the wilderness.

Unlike the pictures, Williams envisioned the candlestick in the garden of the church rather than in the wilderness, and he thereby separated it from the world. Williams explained: "The Nationall Church of the Jewes . . . were as a silver candlestick, on which the light of the Knowledge of God and the Lord Jesus in the type and shadow was set up [and] shined. That Silver Candlestick it pleased the most holy and only wise to take away, and in stead thereof to set up the Golden Candlesticks of particular Churches (*Revel.* I.) by the hand of the Son of God himselfe."[49] Williams associated these golden candlesticks with particular separated churches rather than the wilderness of the world. Accordingly, the light was in peril, for as already seen, when Christians "opened a gap in the hedge, or wall of separation, between the garden of the church and the wilderness of the world, God hath ever broke down the wall

---

[48] Henry Peacham, *Minerva Britanna*, 3 (1612). For variants, see, e.g., Daniel Cramer, *Emblemata Sacra*, 137 (Frankfurt: 1624) (man with bleeding nose in unimproved land with candle extinguished by arm from cloud); see also variants in Henkel and Schöne, *Emblemata Handbuch zur Sinnbildkunst*, 1364, 1375, 1376. According to Calvin, the "Papists . . . abuse the *lamps* for extinguishing the light of God." *Calvin's Commentaries*, 17 (part 2): 214 (John 5.35).

[49] Roger Williams, *Mr. Cotton's Letter, Lately Printed, Examined and Answered* (London: 1644), in *The Complete Writings of Roger Williams*, 1: 356.

itself, removed the candlestick, &c. And made his garden a wilderness, as at this day."

Both in adhering to convention and in departing from it, Williams revealed the radicalism of his ideas. In using the metaphor of the removed or extinguished candle, Williams participated in the traditions of radical antiepiscopal imagery. Yet, by transposing the light from the wilderness into the garden, he suggested his high expectations for the purity of the church and his very different expectations for the wilderness of the state. At the same time, when he put the light in the garden, he brought together images of individual conscience and of the church, clarifying that there was little room for the clergy in Williams's purified Christianity. Thus the candlestick hints at the significance of Williams's more famous image, the wall of separation, and suggests the ways in which this separation was not simply a matter of religious liberty.

Williams's Anticlericalism

In his desire for purity and his suspicion of the clergy, Williams stood well beyond the Christianity of most other Christians. He sought a faith untainted by clerical corruption, and to this end he separated himself from all institutionalized religion, including even that of his fellow Separatists.

The length to which Williams carried his anticlericalism is most clearly evident in his opposition to any "hireling" clergy, even in their own, voluntary churches. In 1652 Williams, like the Quakers, questioned the legitimacy of any formal and, particularly, any paid clergy, whose spiritual qualifications were tainted by worldly things. Believing that Constantine, through his supposed donation of the western empire to the pope, had introduced the reign of the anti-Christ, Williams doubted whether "the *Feeding* and *Nourishing Ministry* of *Pastors* and *Teachers,* according to the first *Institution* of the *Lord Jesus,* are yet restored and extant," and he opposed any ministry other than "the true *Ministry* appointed by *Christ Jesus.*"[50] Cotton interpreted Williams to mean "that the Apostacie of Antichrist hath so farre corrupted all, that there can be no

---

[50] Roger Williams, *A Hireling Ministry None of Christs* (London: 1652), in *The Complete Writings of Roger Williams,* 7: 160; also quoted by Edward Bean Underhill, ed., *The Bloudy Tenent of Persecution for Cause of Conscience Discuss'd,* xxvii (London: Hanserd Knollys Society, 1848).

recovery out of that Apostacie, till Christ shall send forth new Apostles to plant Churches anew."[51] What Williams advocated, however, was the ministry of those who were converted and called by Jesus. Complaining of *"how greatly some mistake, which say I* declame *against all* Ministries, *all* Churches, *all* Ordinances," he explained that, *"since the* Apostasie, *and the* interrupting *of the first ministry and* order, God *hath graciously and immediately stirred up and sent forth the* ministrie *of his* Prophets, *who during all the* raigne *of* Antichrist, *have prophesied in* sackcloth, *and the* saints *and* people of God *have more or less gathered to and assembled with them."*[52] He did not deny the possibility of "an Externall *Test* and *Call,* which was at first and shall be againe in force at the *Resurrection* of the *Churches.*" Yet, "in the present *State* of things, I cannot but be humbly bold to say, that I know no other *true Sender,* but the most *Holy Spirit.* And when he sends, his *Messengers* will goe, his *Prophets* will *prophecy,* though All the *World* should forbid them." Unlike these prophets, the clergy of existing churches were "hirelings," for "[i]n their *Wages,* whether by *Tithes* or otherwise, they have alwayes run in the way of an *Hire,* and rendred such *Workemen* absolute *Hirelings* between whom and the true *Sheapheard* (Joh[n]. 10.) the *Lord Jesus* puts so expresse and sharp a *Difference:* so that in all humble submission, I am bold to maintaine, that it is one of [the] grand *Designes* of the most *High,* to breake downe the *Hireling Ministry,* that *Trade, Faculty, Calling,* and *Living,* by *Preaching."*[53]

Although today Roger Williams has come to be celebrated as a prophet in the wilderness—a prophet of modern separation of church and state—his understanding of religious liberty needs to be understood as part of his relentless quest for religious purity.[54] It was a quest that led him to separate from the Church of England, from the Congregationalists, and even from other Separatists. He so urgently desired purity that he forbade the clergy from earning their living within their own, purely voluntary churches, lest they defile themselves with power, money, or other impure things of this world. For Williams, therefore, any separa-

---

[51] John Cotton, *A Reply to Mr. Williams His Examination* (1647), in *The Complete Writings of Roger Williams,* 2: 19; also quoted by Underhill, ed., *The Bloudy Tenent,* xxvii.

[52] Roger Williams, *A Hireling Ministry,* in *The Complete Writings of Roger Williams,* 7: 155–156.

[53] Ibid., 160, 163. For a discussion of these issues, see Hugh Spurgin, *Roger Williams and Puritan Radicalism,* 45–47.

[54] Morgan, *Roger Williams,* 27; Hall, *Separating Church and State,* 24–25, 30; Reinitz, "Symbolism and Freedom."

tion of church and state he may have imagined was but part of a broader separation of the garden from the wilderness of the world—a separation that tore through the logic of establishments but also through the human distinctions and institutions of which churches in this world were made. So great was his discomfort with any impure clerical authority that he abandoned his own tiny Baptist congregation in Rhode Island only months after joining it, apparently with the intention of becoming a seeker. Not merely opposed to religious establishments, their penalties, and privileges, Williams questioned the very possibility of Christian ministers or churches in any of their external, institutional manifestations until the *"Resurrection* of the *Churches."*

Williams's anticlerical stance was not lost on at least one eighteenth-century commentator. Baptist dissenters, such as John Callender in 1739 and Isaac Backus at the end of the century, had nothing but praise for Williams as an opponent of establishments, but, whether from ignorance or convenience, they said nothing about his ideas concerning either a hireling ministry or the separation of the church from the world.[55] More willing to focus on Williams's anticlericalism was a defender of Connecticut's establishment, the great lexicographer, Noah Webster, who recognized (in his Americanized spelling) that "Roger Williams and hiz adherents imbibed an inveterate hatred against the colony of Massachusetts, and in particular against the clergy, whoze rigid zeel occasioned their expulsion from the colony." With his own "zeel," Webster added that in Rhode Island this "prejudice" of Williams and his followers "continued among their desendants, and to this day the inhabitants boast of their liberality of sentiment and their freedom from the bigotry of clergymen, which, they say, enslaves the peeple of Massachusetts and Connecti-

---

[55] John Callender, *An Historical Discourse on . . . Rhode-Island,* ed. Romeo Elton, Collections of Rhode Island Historical Society, vol. 4 (Providence: 1838); Isaac Backus, *History of New England* (1871; New York: Arno, 1969). See also Thomas Crosby, *The History of the English Baptists,* 1: 117 (London: 1738). Although many Baptists did not formally distinguish their pastors as ministers, this was changing rapidly toward the end of the eighteenth century. Moreover, although some eighteenth-century Baptists doubted whether preachers should enter subscriptions or other contracts with their flock, or whether preachers should enforce such contracts at law, Baptists ordinarily had no qualms about a preacher's receipt of voluntary contributions, and increasingly they did enter contracts. Indeed, many New England congregations eventually incorporated so that they could collect funds with assistance of the tax collector.

cut."[56] Webster recognized that Williams's reputation would suffer if his "aversion to the clerical order" became known to the many eighteenth-century Americans whose Protestantism did not go to such extremes of anticlericalism. In this respect, Webster understood the character of Williams's unusual opinions far better than have many subsequent observers.[57]

Later Seventeenth- and Eighteenth-Century Advocates of Separation

The separation of church and state found little support during the seventeenth and eighteenth centuries, except among some English and French critics of the clergy. Like Roger Williams, these enlightenment writers opposed establishments from a distinctively anticlerical perspective, and therefore they felt no qualms about the separation Hooker condemned.[58] Of course, they probably did not know Williams's writings and certainly had more secular beliefs, but they, like Williams, distrusted institutional churches and clergy and therefore did not worry that separation might limit such institutions more than a mere disestablishment.

Already in the late seventeenth century John Locke alluded to a sort of separation, but only a very limited sort, which he employed to defend toleration. In his 1689 *Letter Concerning Toleration*, Locke argued for toleration, but he made no direct objection to government support for religion, and he insisted that civil government could deny toleration for opinions that tended to undermine the safety of government

---

[56] Noah Webster, "Miscellaneous Remarks on Divizions of Property, Guvernment, Education, Religion, Agriculture, Slavery, Commerce, Climate and Diseezes in the United States" (Philadelphia: 1787), in *A Collection of Essays and Fugitiv Writings*, 336 (Boston: 1790). Such attitudes about Rhode Island were common among Federalists. See Cynthia Louise Kersten, ed., "Isaac Backus's Remarks on Morse's Geography," 10 (master's thesis, Brown University, 1963).

[57] The radical character of Williams's views in his *Hireling Ministry* may perhaps explain the reluctance of the editors of the Narragansett edition of his works to publish this pamphlet. Perry Miller observed that "[t]he Editors were certainly aware of its existence, since the title appears in their bibliography of his writings. The reasons behind this omission remain obscure, and no plausible explanation comes readily to mind." Roger Williams, *A Hireling Ministry*, in *The Complete Writings of Roger Williams*, 1: 145.

[58] Hooker's account of separation was widely known, as may be illustrated by Warburton's discussion of it, which, in turn, was quoted by Priestley. *The Theological and Miscellaneous Works of Joseph Priestley*, 16: 4, ed. John T. Rutt (London: 1817–1832).

and civil society, including "opinions contrary to human society, or to those moral rules which are necessary to the preservation of civil society." Although these arguments would eventually become important in America, only one aspect of Locke's *Letter*—a brief allusion to separation—needs to be considered here. In examining "what the duty of toleration requires from . . . the clergy," Locke wrote: "This only I say, that whencesoever their authority be sprung, since it is ecclesiastical, it ought to be confined within the bounds of the church, nor can it in any manner be extended to civil affairs, because the church itself is a thing absolutely separate and distinct from the commonwealth. The boundaries on both sides are fixed and immoveable."[59] Although Locke wrote of the church as "absolutely separate and distinct from the commonwealth," and although he used this separation to limit the power of the clergy, it was not clear that he was arguing more than that the church and the commonwealth were distinct institutions with different origins, purposes, and powers. As he explained in the following sentence: "He jumbles heaven and earth together, the things most remote and opposite, who mixes these two societies, which are in their original, end, business, and in everything perfectly distinct and infinitely different from each other." Locke's emphasis upon the distinction and difference between church and state reinforces the impression that his description of the church as "absolutely separate and distinct from the commonwealth" was merely an expression of his pervasive and hardly original argument about the difference between religious and civil jurisdiction. As he concluded in his next sentence: "No man, therefore, with whatsoever ecclesiastical office he be dignified, can deprive another man that is not of his church and faith either of liberty or of any part of his worldly goods upon the account of that difference between them in religion."[60] Thus, although

---

[59] John Locke, *A Letter Concerning Toleration*, 50, 27, ed. Patrick Romanell (New York: Macmillan, 1950). In the printed Latin version the sentence about separation ended "quandoquidem ipsa ecclesia a re publica rebusque civilibus prorsus sejuncta est et separata." John Locke, *A Letter Concerning Toleration: Latin and English Tests Revised and Edited with Variants and an Introduction,* 38, ed. Mario Montuori (The Hague: Martinus Nijhoff, 1963). Locke seems to have carefully chosen his language here to condemn claims of ecclesiastical authority over civil matters, without criticizing clerics who held civil office or advised the civil magistrate on civil matters.

[60] Locke, *A Letter Concerning Toleration,* 27, ed. Romanell. Locke's account drew upon similar arguments in earlier writings, both ancient and quite recent. For example, according to Sir Charles Wolseley, the "Magistratical power" was quite "mixed" with the *"Jewish Church."* In contrast: "The *Church* of the Gospel is totally of another nature, perfectly dis-

Locke used the word "separate," he focused on the distinction between religious and civil jurisdictions.

In a very different, more theological tradition, some Europeans and Americans condemned the union of church and state in allusive sexual language developed from the Book of Revelation. Yet they did not quite advocate separation. In 1777, for example, a dissenter in Virginia employed sexual rhetoric against an advocate of the Anglican establishment. The latter had relied upon the, by then, rather antiquated notion that the "interest of Church and State should be so blended together as that of man and wife." The dissenter responded:

> The Church has been long since betrothed to another. She is espoused as a chaste virgin unto Christ. He is her husband; and she is the bride, the lamb's wife. And if so, was she to be joined to the State, it would be committing spiritual adultery, the most detestable of all enormities!
> . . . This union we know, has often been productive of the most pernicious consequences. They have always corrupted, and often ruined one another; as wine and water mingled, turns to vinegar. The State, I say, has always corrupted the Church. . . . The very establishment corrupts the Church. And such a Church will consequently corrupt the State.[61]

Like this dissenter, American opponents of establishments vigorously condemned any adulterous union of church and state, but almost never embraced the other extreme of a separation between these institutions.

The separation of church and state that Hooker condemned and Williams almost espoused seems not to have been revived and directly advocated until the last half of the eighteenth century, when fears of an establishment merged with a sharply Protestant and Enlightenment animus against the clergy. For example, as shown by Daniel Dreisbach, the British Whig, James Burgh, denounced the Anglican establishment in terms of separation in 1767.[62] Yet Burgh took this position in his *Crito*, a two-volume set of essays in which he attacked not only the English establishment but also all clerical authority and human inventions in religion. Notwithstanding that he was the son of a Scottish Presbyterian

---

tinct from the Civil State, can well subsist without a relation to it, and is no way intermixed in its Concerns with it." Wolseley, *Liberty of Conscience upon Its True and Proper Grounds Asserted and Vindicated*, 30 (2d ed., 1668).

[61] "Freeman of Virginia," *Freeman's Remonstrance against an Ecclesiastical Establishment*, 6, 7–8.

[62] Dreisbach, "Sowing Useful Truths and Principles," 486–490.

minister, Burgh joined Joseph Priestley in becoming a Unitarian, and, although Burgh later acquired popular fame, he achieved this for his critique of politics rather than for his religious views. Like other radical Protestants, he had come to conceive of religion in terms drawn from arguments about religious liberty—an approach that allowed him to depict religion as utterly unsocial: "I cannot, for my part, help looking upon religion as a matter, which lies wholly between God and a man's *conscience*, exclusive of all interposition; and as what, from its specific nature, necessarily *individuates* mankind; while civil power necessarily regards them as collected into *societies*." Accordingly, when he attacked the "*alliance* between *church* and *state*," Burgh had little reason to worry about the broader implications of his suggestion "that the less the church and the state had to do with one another, it would be the better for both."[63] Throughout his book Burgh condemned English Protestants for persecuting Catholics, but he did so largely to suggest that England's "pretended Protestants" were equivalent to Catholics—for example, in honoring a corrupt clergy and fostering a "*persecuting* spirit."[64]

In his second volume Burgh became, as he acknowledged, "rather more severe." Whereas he humorously dedicated his first volume to a three-year-old prince who had been made a bishop, he addressed his second volume "To the Good People of BRITAIN OF THE TWENTIETH CENTURY" and urged "[m]y dear little Non-entities" to avoid Britain's errors in politics and religion. In the eighteenth century, "we have been doing our best to prove Christianity a mere *human* invention," and "[w]e have bestowed much honest pains in endeavoring to shew, that a sett of sordid *Jews* might naturally be expected to give the world a system of ethics and theology, whose *purity* and *sublimity* should make those of the *polite*

---

[63] James Burgh, *Crito, or, Essays on Various Subjects*, 1: x–xi (London: 1766–1767).

[64] Ibid., 2: 192 and 1: xiv. Burgh rarely used the English language as richly as when abusing both Catholics and "pretended Protestants"—the Catholics for being superstitious and the Protestants for being intolerant. He wrote that "we pretend, we do not molest the papists on account of their worshiping a god made of dough, or for speaking nonsense to the Almighty in *Latin* (it is well enough if we ourselves do not sometimes address him in *English* nonsense)." Foolishly, English Protestants sought security from the Catholic threat by "driving a set of nonsensical *Ave-Maria*-mummers from jabbering their holy spells in a mass-house." Ibid., 1: xii–xiii. Later, in a postscript to his second volume, Burgh explained that "I intended nothing less than the *destruction* of that diabolical superstition" and argued that "the *tolerating* protestant" was "in fact a more dangerous enemy to the *religion* of the papists" than "the protestant persecutor." Ibid., 2: 191.

and *learned Greeks* contemptible."[65] In contrast, he had higher hopes for his twentieth-century readers: "Set up none of your blundering human-invented jargon, solemnly drawn out into articles, creeds, or confessions; nor pretend, I charge you, to call your absurdities sacred mysteries, or to palm them off upon the ignorant people for divine truth, threatening them with *damnation* for rejecting your clumsy inventions. . . . The heavenly authors knew better than *you*, how to *express* themselves. Do not therefore presume to establish any summaries, or compends, of their sublime sense. . . . do not attempt what is beyond the *reach of human capacity*." Rather than "subscribing to an inconsistent *farrago* of human inventions," the "public dispensers of religion" were "to be *masters* of *reason*, that they may convince the opposers of truth." In such ways, Burgh desired "that there may not be among you so much as a shadow of *authority* in *religious* matters," and he condemned the doctrines that distinguished "every puny subdivision of religionists."[66]

With this rarified conception of religion as something that *"individuates"* mankind, it should be no surprise that Burgh advocated a sort of separation. He assumed that *"ecclesiastical* corruption" was "the most odious of all corruption," and therefore, when he blasted England's "mixed-mungrel-spiritual-temporal-secular-ecclesiastical establishment," he was content to envision an English Church that "stands wholly unconnected with *secular* concerns." At one point, when Burgh urged the future inhabitants of Britain to abandon the practice of imposing religious tests on military officers, he even adopted an image similar to that which Hooker had attributed to dissenters:

> Build an impenetrable wall of *separation* between things *sacred* and *civil.* Do not send a *graceless* officer, reeking from the arms of his *trull*, to the performance of a *holy* rite of *religion*, as a test for his holding the command of a regiment. To *profane*, in such a manner, a religion, which you pretend to *reverence*; is an impiety sufficient to bring down upon your heads, the roof of the sacred building you thus defile.

This was not quite a wall of separation between church and state. Nonetheless, it came close. From a perspective Burgh understood to be un-

---

[65] Ibid., 2: 188, Dedication, 105, 106.
[66] Ibid., 2: 109–111. In rejecting legal penalties upon Catholics, he bluntly wrote that *"human* authority is *tyranny*, when exerted in matters of *religion*." Ibid., 2: 193.

usual in his own century, he urged the British of the twentieth century to build a "wall of *separation*."[67]

The closest American dissenters came to demanding separation of church and state may have been in a Virginia memorial of 1783 from the General Association of Separate Baptists. Assembling at Dupuy's Meeting House in Powhatan County, the Association petitioned the House of Delegates for greater equality under the laws regulating vestries and marriages. These Baptists sought revisions to "the vestry law" because, under the existing statute, Episcopalian vestries set parish poor rates, and therefore Baptists were "liable to be taxed, without representation." The Baptists also wanted amendments to "some parts of the marriage act," which, in 1780, had given legal recognition to marriages conducted by dissenting ministers but had not gone so far as to put these clergymen "on an equal footing" with their Episcopalian counterparts. Although these Baptists sought laws recognizing Baptist religious ceremonies and altering Episcopal vestries, they concluded by praying "for redress of our grievances, & that no law may pass, to connect the

---

[67] Ibid., 2: 116–117, 119. In his closing paragraphs Burgh acknowledged the unconventional character of his views, observing that "[m]ost minds . . . are too *weak* to disengage themselves from the prejudices of *education* and *fashion*" and that "[m]ost people hate the *trouble* of groping to the bottom of the well." Ibid., 2: 245–246. Certainly, it is difficult to find other antiestablishment writers who advocated separation. One who came close was the Rev. John Hildrop—a dissentient Anglican—who compared church and state to parallel lines. Hildrop argued that sacred and civil power should be "independent," and in the course of making this relatively conventional argument, he responded to the objection that an independent church would amount to an "Imperium in Imperio." He wrote: "A Church absolutely independent of the State, in Things civil as well as sacred, would indeed be setting up one Power and Government within another, perpetually clashing and interfering; which, without doubt, would produce nothing but confusion. But whilst the sacred and civil Powers run each in their proper Channels, they will be like two parallel Lines, that never can meet or interfere, but are perfectly consistent and assistant to each other." Hildrop suggested that church and state should never "meet," but even he thought they should be "parallel," "consistent," and "assistant." *The Contempt of the Clergy Considered in a Letter to a Friend*, 165–166 (London: 1739). Similarly, a Scottish minister, William Graham, used language suggestive of separation. In 1792 this minister in the United Secession Church attacked the incorporation of religious societies on the assumption that incorporation would necessarily convey special privileges. In making this argument, he wrote: "The ADVANTAGES, which would result from a total disengagement of Church and State, are *great, universal and lasting*." Yet he seems to have been referring to "a total subtraction of ecclesiastical affairs from the constitutions of civil societies" rather than a separation between church and state. Graham, *A Review of Ecclesiastical Establishments in Europe*, 198, 209 (Windham, Conn.: 1808).

church, & State in the future."[68] In light of their specific requests it may be doubted whether they considered the potential implications of a disconnection. They probably were merely responding to conventional fears of an illicit connection or union—the sort of connection that amounted to an establishment. Nonetheless, this Baptist petition reveals how already in the eighteenth century Americans could begin to conceive of disestablishment as a rejection of all connection between church and state.

Although few Englishmen or Americans appear to have demanded separation of church and state during the late eighteenth century, an eminent French intellectual, the Marquis de Condorcet, briefly adopted a version of the idea. In 1785, in his editorial notes on Voltaire, Condorcet wrote a little essay on religious liberty, in which he observed: "The interest of the princes was not to seek to regulate religion, but to

---

[68] Memorial of Ministers of the Ministers, & Messengers of the Several Baptist Churches in Virginia (Nov. 6, 1783), Virginia State Library, Richmond, microfilm, Misc. Ms. 425. These Baptists met at a time when they assumed they had obtained their freedom from the most severe injustices of an establishment and had only a few minor issues to address. On such assumptions in 1782, they had voted to disband their General Association after their next annual meeting and thereafter to entrust their work for religious liberty to a committee or "standing sentinel for political purposes." Robert B. Semple, *A History of the Rise and Progress of the Baptist in Virginia,* 67 (Richmond: 1810). Although these and other Virginia Baptists continued to work for religious freedom, none of them apparently in the eighteenth century again demanded that church and state be disconnected.

Incidentally, there is reason to believe that the former members of the General Association soon realized that their fall 1783 memorial needed some correction. In the 1783 document they had generalized that laws should not connect church and state. At the same time, they had indicated a desire to share the same privileges—the same representation in vestries and the same legal authorization to conduct marriages—as enjoyed by Episcopalians. This openness to sharing legislated privileges with Episcopalians was likely to seem quite incompatible with any conception of disconnecting church and state. It even was at odds with the Baptists' usual requests for a full equality of rights, let alone their more severe demands for no laws taking cognizance of religion. Therefore, these Baptists had reason to worry that both the generalities and the details of their fall 1783 memorial contradicted their usual antiestablishment demands. Such a reevaluation became evident in May 1784, when members of the former General Baptist Association reassembled and petitioned once again against the vestry and marriage laws. In their new document they dropped both their condemnation of laws connecting church and state and their demand for shared privileges. In particular, after referring to the earlier petitions of Baptists, they told the legislature that on account of the inequality of the vestry law they wanted it repealed, and that as marriage "is in our esteem, but a civil contract" they desired to have it entrusted to local justices. Memorial of Baptist Association Met at Noel's Meeting-House, May 8, 1784 (May 26th, 1784), Virginia State Library, microfilm, Misc. Ms. 425.

separate religion from the State, to leave to the priests the freedom of sacraments, censures, ecclesiastical functions; but not to give any civil effect to any of their decisions, not to give them any influence over marriages or over birth or death certificates; not to allow them to intervene in any civil or political act; and to judge the lawsuits which would arise, between them and the citizens, for the temporal rights relating to their functions, as one would decide the similar lawsuits that would arise between the members of a free association, or between this association and private individuals."[69] Condorcet's theory of separation seems to have made little impression upon his countrymen during the remaining years of the eighteenth century, when France was convulsed by its Revolution, but he introduced to French intellectuals a concept with which they would eventually provoke a papal response—a reaction that would be felt as far away as America.[70]

More immediately, an American in Paris, Thomas Paine, came close to advocating separation of church and state when he condemned "[t]he adulterous connection of church and state." Paine borrowed the concept from Christian theology, but he gave it a more radical context and a more radical meaning. In 1794 in his *Age of Reason*, Paine took aim at establishments and, more broadly, the clergy, their power, and the impurity of their creeds, which he blasted in radical Protestant and enlight-

---

[69] In French, he wrote: "L'intérêt des princes a donc été, non de chercher à régler la religion, mais de séparer la religion de l'Etat, de laisser aux prêtres la libre disposition des sacremens, des censures, des fonctions ecclésiastiques; mais de ne donner aucun effect civil à aucune de leurs décisions, de ne leur donner aucune influence sur les mariages, sur les actes qui constatent la mort ou la naissance; de ne point souffrir qu'ils interviennent dans aucun acte civil ou politique, & de juger les procès qui s'élèveraient, entre eux & les citoyens, pour des droits temporels relatifs à leurs fonctions, comme on déciderait les procès semblables qui s'élèveraient entre les membres d'une association libre, ou entre cette association & des particuliers." *Oeuvres Completes de Voltaire*, 18: 476 (Paris: 1784). In the nineteenth century this note was republished under the title "Sur l'intérêt des princes à séparer la religion de l'État," in *Oeuvres de Condorcet*, 538–539 (Paris: 1847). For a discussion of Condorcet's views, see Karl Rothenbücher, *Die Trennung von Staat und Kirche*, 72 (Munich: 1908).

[70] In diluted form, a version of some such rhetoric reached America already in the 1790s. Writing about subjects with respect to which opinions could not be based on the senses— that is, religious matters—Volney argued that "in order to live in peace and harmony, we must consent not to pronounce upon such subjects, or to annex to them importance; we must draw a line of demarcation between such as can be verified and such as cannot, and separate by an inviolable barrier the world of fantastic beings from the world of realities: that is to say, all civil effect must be taken away from theological and religious opinions." C. F. Volney, *The Ruins: or a Survey of the Revolutions of Empires*, 169–170 (1791; Albany: 1822).

enment fashion as human inventions. He rejected all distinct religions, including Christianity, on behalf of a universal deistical faith in human reason, which, he believed, would lead to a secular millennium—the so-called "age of reason." For Paine, the connection of church and state was the means by which churches (whether the "Jewish church," the "Roman church," or the "Greek church") had enlisted the power of government to suppress doubts about the truth of their doctrines. Therefore, a revolution in government was necessary to end the "adulterous connection" of church and state and bring about a revolution in religion:

> Soon after I had published the pamphlet, *Common Sense*, in America, I saw the exceeding probability that a revolution in the system of government would be followed by a revolution in the system of religion. The adulterous connection of church and state, wherever it had taken place, whether Jewish, Christian, or Turkish, had so effectually prohibited, by pains and penalties, every discussion upon established creeds and upon first principles of religion, that until the system of government should be changed those subjects could not be brought fairly and openly before the world; but whenever this should be done, a revolution in the system of religion would follow. Human inventions and priestcraft would be detected, and man would return to the pure, unmixed, and unadulterated belief of one God, and no more.

Like religious dissenters, Paine assumed that the American Revolution would destroy "[t]he adulterous connection of church and state." Yet, unlike the dissenters, he also hoped that Americans would then challenge all clergies and creeds and would thereby so completely alter the character of religion as to bring conventional Christianity to an end.

In condemning "[t]he adulterous connection," Paine clearly demanded disestablishment, but he is unlikely to have felt qualms about the possibility that his language would be interpreted more broadly. Certainly, his individualism and his deism left him indifferent to all sorts of connections between church and state and even hostile to what ordinarily were considered churches. Paine declared: "My own mind is my own church," for "it is necessary to the happiness of man, that he be mentally faithful to himself. Infidelity does not consist in believing, or in disbelieving; it consists in professing to believe what he does not believe."[71] Earlier, in their struggle for religious liberty, dissenters had al-

---

[71] Thomas Paine, *The Age of Reason*, 2–3 (1794; Exton, Pa.: Wet Water Publications, 1992).

ready argued that each individual had a right and even a duty to conform to his own belief—the duty being to the Almighty and, by extension, to the individual and his future happiness. On this basis dissenters claimed that if an individual deferred to the coercion or emoluments of any civil government, he failed to adhere to his own beliefs. Some radically anticlerical Protestants took this argument further, holding that, even if an individual merely deferred to the human creed of a church, he gave up his individual liberty of belief and reduced his faith to a hypocritical conformity. Drawing upon this heritage (and revealing how conceptions of religious liberty were shaping notions of religion), Paine and growing numbers of Protestants concluded that religion not only required but largely consisted of being "mentally faithful" to oneself. With such views, Paine felt that not only civil government but also churches, clergy, and their human creeds threatened religion and individual freedom, and he therefore welcomed, in addition to disestablishment, the diminution of clerical opinion and influence. Yet whether he went so far when he condemned "[t]he adulterous connection of church and state," or whether he merely rejected establishments, remains unclear. Undoubtedly, his phrase alluded to establishments, but it did not necessarily refer to all types of church-state connections. Through its context and tone, however, Paine's French encomium of reason could easily be read with some breadth, and, at least in this way, it came much nearer to a demand for separation than most other American critiques of religious establishments.

After the publication of Paine's *Age of Reason*, some petitioners in Virginia echoed the bold tone of Paine's anticlerical rhetoric and even his condemnation of the "adulterous connection." In the mid-1790s the Episcopal Church in Virginia was no longer established, but it owned various glebe lands, which had been given to it by the colonial government and, to a lesser extent, by individual donors. Baptists and Presbyterians resented that the Episcopalians continued to enjoy this benefit of their earlier establishment, and therefore these former dissenters petitioned the House of Delegates to authorize the sale of the glebe lands and the use of the proceeds for public purposes, such as the reduction of parish poor rates.[72] Their petitions tended to adopt Paine's audacious

---

[72] Thomas E. Buckley, "Evangelicals Triumphant: The Baptists' Assault on the Virginia Glebes, 1786–1801," *William & Mary Quarterly*, 45: 33 (1988).

style of writing, and one 1795 petition—from the parishioners of King William Parish in the counties of Powhatan and Chesterfield—deplored the adulterous connection. Complaining about the Episcopal Church's acquisition of its glebes, this petition regretted that in colonial times, "through the adulterous connection between Church and State, the impositions of king craft and priest craft . . . cherish'd and supported each other."[73] Like Paine, these petitioners did not clearly condemn all connections between church and state. Yet, in light of the 1783 Baptist petition, which more certainly condemned all connections, this 1795 petition from King William Parish may perhaps suggest some continuity in seeking a freedom at least close to a separation between church and state.

Thus James Burgh, the Marquis de Condorcet, and (on at least one occasion) the General Association of Separate Baptists in Virginia advocated versions of separation, but they apparently failed to persuade many of their contemporaries to adopt any such idea. American religious dissenters were not shy about demanding their freedom. Vigorous, insistent, and well organized, they wrote incessantly about their religious liberty and created a highly successful popular movement to achieve this end. Accordingly, if the separation of church and state had been one of their demands, one would expect to find this principle discussed repeatedly in their writings. Yet amid hundreds upon hundreds of dissenting petitions, sermons, pamphlets, newspaper essays, letters, and memoranda, the idea of separation remains quite elusive. Even in Virginia, where Baptists in 1783 urged the legislature not to connect church and state, they did not again make such a demand in their petitions, even during the great antiestablishment struggle of 1784 and 1785. Accordingly, what is striking is not that some Europeans and Americans occasionally supported a separation between church and state or something like it, but rather that dissenters, including American dissenters, clearly did not make separation one of their demands.

From a twenty-first-century perspective, the difficulty of locating advocates of separation may seem puzzling. It may seem particularly odd that one cannot identify American religious dissenters who made such

[73] Petition of a number of the parishioners of King William Parish in the Counties of Powhatan and Chesterfield (Nov. 24, 1795), Virginia State Library, microfilm, Misc. Ms. 425.

demands. Yet this should hardly be a surprise. American religious dissenters distrusted civil establishments of religion, but they were unlikely to embrace a position that also seemed to evince hostility toward churches and their clergy. Accordingly, notwithstanding the enthusiasm of a few intellectuals in Europe and the brief support of one group of Baptists in Virginia in 1783, it is difficult to find dissenting denominations or even many individuals in America prior to 1800 who clearly advocated the separation of church and state.

2

Accusations of Separation

SEPARATION first appeared in popular American debates about religious liberty not as a demand but as an accusation. As already seen, a few somewhat anticlerical intellectuals had sought versions of separation of church and state. Accordingly, it may be thought that in the late eighteenth century, when evangelical dissenters were engaged in their dramatic struggle against the establishment of religion in some American states, they may have demanded a separation of church and state. Yet they typically did not do so. On the contrary, in the late eighteenth-century controversies over religious liberty, it was the advocates of establishments who alluded to a sort of separation—the separation of religion and government—and following the example of Richard Hooker, they treated separation as an accusation.

In the contest over religious establishments, disputants on both sides gave in to their worst fears and attributed extreme positions to their opponents—separation being only one of these slurs. From the dissenting side came the accusation that the establishment churches "united" or "blended" church and state—an allegation powerfully suggestive of papal oppression. It was an accusation deeply resented by establishment ministers, who pointed out that their tolerant establishments were merely alliances between distinct civil and religious bodies—church and state being closely affiliated but different institutions.[1] In

---

[1] In late eighteenth-century England and America, establishments were ever less frequently defended as a combination or blend of church and state, for, by the early eighteenth century, William Warburton and others had developed the alternative theory of an alliance. Warburton's counterintuitive defense of establishment privileges rejected the

contrast to the dissenters' accusation of union, establishment clergymen occasionally reciprocated by hinting that dissenters sought to separate religion and government. This too was a mischaracterization, for dissenters rarely, if ever, demanded such a separation. These charges, therefore, are less revealing about the beliefs of the accused than about the anxieties of the accusers.

The Establishment Accusation

In a society in which it was widely accepted that civil government depended upon religion and upon the morality it inculcated, any hint that dissenters aimed to separate religion from government was a potent accusation. It insinuated that dissenters desired to undermine the moral foundations of government, and it thereby appealed to those who worried that religious dissent threatened moral and political order.

Government and especially republican government seemed inescapably dependent upon religion. Establishment clergymen once had justified their civil privileges—most important, salaries raised by special taxes or assessments—by emphasizing that religion needed the support of civil government. Following the example of John Locke, however,

---

tradition that the English government and the English church were so intertwined as to be, in some respects, almost indistinguishable and instead accepted the arguments of dissenters that church and state should be considered distinct institutions. Indeed, Warburton insisted upon the distinction between church and state, and, on this ground, argued for the dependence of each upon the other and for the necessity, on secular grounds of self-preservation, of an alliance between these institutions. William Warburton, *The Alliance between Church and State* (London: 1736). It was a rhetorically brilliant reply to the critics of establishments. On the assumption that church and state were distinct, all defenders of establishments in America, Anglican or Congregational, could defend themselves by insisting that church and state were allied or connected rather than blended together. Accordingly, it was a rare instance when, in 1776 or 1777, a Virginian wrote that it was "necessary, for domestic peace, that the interest of Church and State should be so blended together as that of man and wife." *The Necessity of an Established Church in any State,* as quoted in *The Free Man's Remonstrance against an Ecclesiastical Establishment: Being Some Remarks on a Late Pamphlet, Entitled The Necessity of an Established Church in Any State; by a Free Man of Virginia,* 5–6, and 15 (Williamsburg: 1777). More typical was Timothy Dwight. He argued that "THE first duty of a ruler, and the first concern of a virtuous ruler, is the support of religion," but immediately cautioned that, in urging government support for religion, he did not support any union or blend: "Let not my audience from this remark imagine, that I wish a revival of that motley system of domination which in Europe has so long, so awkwardly, and so unhappily blended civil and spiritual objects." Dwight, *Virtuous Rulers a National Blessing,* 18 (Hartford: 1791).

dissenters had increasingly argued that religion did not depend upon human institutions and that civil government was established for exclusively civil purposes. In response, late eighteenth-century establishment writers revised their position and stressed that civil government financed religion for civil ends—that religion had civil benefits, which civil government supported for its purely civil purposes.[2] In support of this secular argument, establishment clergymen repeatedly reminded Americans that republican government depended upon the morality of its citizens and that morality depended upon religion.

Establishment ministers often alluded to these commonplace assumptions about the civil benefits of religion by speaking of the necessary connection between religion and government. Establishment ministers emphasized that government depended upon religion in all societies, and, in this way, they made the connection of government to religion seem almost sociological. Yet the connection was not merely sociological, for the dependence of government upon religion seemed to suggest that government should support religion—in particular, that government should encourage religion and its secular benefits by paying ministers' salaries from tax revenues. Government had to reinforce the sociological connection with a financial one.[3] Thus, by insisting that religion and civil government were necessarily connected, these establishment clergymen conveniently elided their explicit and utterly conventional assumption that religion was a necessary basis of the morality required for government and their more controversial and understated assumption that the preservation of religion required government financing.

In contrast to the established ministers who frequently asserted the sociological connection of religion to government, dissenters sometimes sounded as if they considered religion an entirely private matter, without

[2] For the most prominent exposition of this argument, which many American clergymen had read, see Warburton, *The Alliance between Church and State.*

[3] For example, some Episcopalians in Virginia argued: "We are fully convinced of the importance of religion and its happy influence upon the temporal interests of society, as well as the future happiness of individuals." "To Richard Bibb and John Clarke, Esquires, Representatives in the General Assembly, for Prince Edward County," in *Virginia Gazette,* No. 152 (Nov. 20, 1784). In the 1770s a dissenter noted: "I cannot but observe how people of this . . . cast have lately changed their note. Formerly, when any of the nations made the least attempt to recover, or to maintain their liberty, the prevailing outcry was the CHURCH, the CHURCH is in danger! But now it is the STATE, the STATE is in danger!" *The Free Man's Remonstrance against an Ecclesiastical Establishment,* 11.

public, social consequences, and they thereby left themselves open to the establishment accusations that they sought a separation of religion and government. To be sure, almost all of the dissenters who participated in the campaign against establishments assumed that religion was the foundation of morality and that government therefore depended upon religion.[4] Such beliefs constituted a significant part of their piety. Yet in their arguments for religious liberty, dissenters frequently proposed that their different religious opinions should not have legal consequences, and, on behalf of this position, dissenters sometimes came close to suggesting that variations in religious opinions had no material consequences. Earlier, dissenters had emphasized that material, worldly matters—civil matters—were the things over which civil government had jurisdiction. But what if, as establishment ministers claimed, religious beliefs had worldly ramifications? Did this not justify civil legislation to support some such beliefs, even if not to penalize others? Against such an argument, it was not sufficient simply to insist that civil government had jurisdiction only over civil, material matters; it was also necessary to assert a stronger proposition, that civil government lacked jurisdiction over religion. It was to persuade themselves and others that civil government should not have jurisdiction over religion that dissenters felt tempted to deny the material or worldly significance of religious differences. Whether or not dissenters actually went so far, establishment writers were pleased to point out that dissenters seemed to question the significance of religion for morality and government. By implication, dissenters and their demands for religious liberty were a threat to morality, including the moral obligations necessary for the successful functioning of government.

As early as the 1740s at least one establishment minister, in Massachusetts, adumbrated the accusation that dissenters were threatening to separate religion and civil government. Having departed or separated from the established churches, some religious dissenters in New England came to be known as "Separates" (not unlike earlier "Separatists"), and because these Separates departed from what often was the sole church in a town, they were accused of causing "separations" or divisions in

---

[4] A dissenting leader with views that departed, in some respects, from these assumptions about government's dependence upon religion was John Leland, about whom more will be said later. See Chapter 7 at notes 21–25 and 40–46.

civil society. In 1749 the Rev. William Balch built upon such usage to suggest that dissenters desired something even worse: "Religion is a Sacred Thing, and Worthy of the Regards of the Highest & Wisest of Mankind: Nor is Civil Order and Government or the Establishment & Practice of Justice and Righteousness Among a People ever to be separated therefrom."[5] Government and the practice of justice and righteousness were not to be separated from religion, by which, of course, Balch meant the established religion, his implication being that dissenters sought such a separation.

In the late eighteenth century it became commonplace for establishment ministers and their allies to defend establishments by emphasizing the value of a connection between religion and civil government and, in so doing, they sometimes aimed an understated but pointed accusation at dissenters. In Virginia in 1785 an Anglican or Presbyterian advocate of establishment wrote an entire essay against the position he attributed to dissenters, that there should be no connection between religion and civil government. "IT is an opinion confirmed by the united suffrage of the thinking part of mankind in all former ages; 'that the *general belief* and *public acknowledgment* of the great principles of religion are necessary to secure the order and happiness of civil societies.'" At the very least, even according to the "enemies" of religion, "the *belief* of its truth was necessary to deceive mankind into a regard to order." Yet dissenters and their allies appeared to hold otherwise:

> But this opinion . . . it now seems, is founded only on mistake and prejudice; and it has been reserved, as a most important discovery for the present enlightened age, that civil society, so far from receiving any aid, from religion, cannot even form the most distant connexion with her, but on terms dangerous and fatal to both.

Responding to this supposedly enlightened view that "civil society" could not safely form even "the most distant connexion" with religion, the essayist proposed "to re-consider the subject" by inquiring "whether

---

[5] William Balch, *A Sermon* (Boston: 1749). He added: "For, the Religion we plead for, is, not that of a *Party*, but the Religion of the *Bible:* a Religion of which it may be truly said, 'that it is the Life of a People'; including in it every social Virtue; requiring Submission and Obedience to lawful Authority in the People, as well as Integrity and a public Spirit in Rulers; and enjoining Industry, Frugality, Temperance, and every Virtue that tends to a People's outward Prosperity." Ibid.

the general acknowledgment and influence of religious principles be re-ally of importance to *secure* the morals and good order, and . . . the happi-ness of societies."[6]

His response—that society needed religion or, at least, a general ac-knowledgment of it—accentuated the remarkably sociological character of the establishment argument about a necessary connection. Other than religion, there were three possible ways of constraining human beings, but each of these was itself dependent upon religion. "Exclusive of the influences of religion," the only means of restraining individuals were "the powers of *reason*[;] the active principles of *benevolence* and *public spirit;* or the *power* of the *civil magistrate.*" Yet, without religion, even these failed, for little could "ordinarily be expected from *any* or *all* of these, should we . . . part with . . . the *fear of God.*" Without the "supposition of a Deity," individuals acting in accord with reason would pursue imme-diate, selfish interests rather than the more distant and social interests that only religion could reconcile with "self-love." Without the supposi-tion of a Deity, even persons influenced by benevolence and public spirit might not be able to resist the influence of more "selfish and overbearing passions," and the "few" who nonetheless retained a disposition "in fa-vour of the public" would thereby only be rendered "a more easy prey to the force or fraud of an infinitely greater number." Without the sup-position of a Deity, civil government could not rely upon oaths, and, even if individuals respected their oaths, civil government would not be able to restrain secret crimes or offences by the overwhelmingly numer-ous or the powerful, for such crimes typically were beyond the "censure of human laws." For these reasons, "civil government *always has* called in the influences of religion to its assistance and support; and in the nature of things *always must* do so."

More broadly, religion was the source of the social confidence upon which government depended.

> [W]ithout *religion* 'tis hard to say what foundation there could be for any such mutual *trust* and *confidence* among men as is necessary to the support of government, the very being of society. Without supposing each other under the influence of this principle, every man might too justly be in perpetual fear of every other, who should be either stronger or more subtle than himself.

[6] "On the Importance and Necessity of Religion to Civil Society," in *Virginia Gazette* (Rich-mond: Nicolson) (Aug. 6 and 13, 1785).

In contrast, with the assistance of religion, men were sociable and their government salutary: "BUT when we take into our account the general acknowledgment of a God, a Providence, a future state; the face of the moral world is changed: Society becomes practicable, and government a blessing. Where religious principles prevail, rulers may govern with security to themselves, and benefit to the people." For example, "[s]ubordinate magistrates will know themselves to be under the strongest obligation, the most powerful engagement, to *decree justice*."[7]

Similarly, in the North, in the wake of the French Revolution, an establishment minister from Connecticut, the Rev. Timothy Stone, preached that "the connection, between religion and good government is evident—and all attempts to separate them are unfriendly to society, and inimical to good government."[8] Interpreting dissenters to argue that

---

[7] Ibid. The essayist concluded: "And now having, I think, sufficiently proved the premises, *the importance and necessity of religion to civil society;* I think it must undeniably follow that the *civil magistrate* and all who are intrusted with the care of public order and happiness, are, for that very end, highly concerned to encourage and support religion." Ibid.

Incidentally, without using the words "connection" or "separation," numerous proponents of an establishment suggested that dissenters and their allies were blind to what seemed the obvious significance of religion and the morality it inculcated for government, liberty, and other civil blessings. In response to Jefferson's 1786 Act for the Establishment of Religious Liberty, John Stanwick protested in almost sociological terms: "'That our civil rights have no dependence on our religious opinions, any more than our opinions in physic or geometry,' is an assertion contradicted by the experience of mankind. Since nothing is more evident, than that in proportion as the minds of men have become enlightened by the influences of a pure and free system of religion, their civil rights have become more perfectly enlarged and ascertained. So that the genius of government in all nations has ever borne great affinity to the state of religion therein; being either arbitrary, liberal, or free, in proportion as their spiritual systems were so." "Citizen of Philadelphia" [John Stanwick], *Considerations on an Act of the Legislature of Virginia, Entitled, An Act for the Establishment of Religious Freedom,* 12 (Philadelphia: 1786). According to a Virginia Episcopalian: "[T]he most approved and wisest legislators in all ages, in order to give efficacy to their civil institutions, have found it necessary to call in the aid of religion," but, "in no form of government whatever has the influence of religious principles been found so requisite as on that of a republic," for "mankind require the awe of some power to confine them within the line of their duty," and without religion, the citizens of a republic might appreciate the "dread of a rapacious tyrant" to "preserve quiet and order." Of course, he believed that the Christian religion comprehended "the most complete system of ethics, calculated to harmonize society by laying a restraint on the passions and regulating the affections of its votaries," and on this account, even "motives of policy alone" would persuade persons to support it. "A.B.," Letter to Mr. Davis, in *Virginia Independent Chronicle,* No. 67 (Oct. 31, 1787).

[8] Timothy Stone, *A Sermon,* 24 (Hartford: 1792). He also wrote: "The ignorance and folly of that principle, that there is no connection between religion and civil policy, is most happily refuted, when the followers of JESUS act in character, and demonstrate to the world, that real Christians are the best members of society in every station." Ibid., 32. The Rev.

religious opinions had no worldly consequences and thus were of no concern to civil government, Stone thought they denied a connection between religion and government. Attempting to understand so strange an opinion, he speculated:

> The idea that there is, and ought to be no connection between religion and civil policy, appears to rest upon this absurd supposition; that men by entering into society for mutual advantage, become quite a different class of beings from what they were before, that they cease to be moral beings; and consequently, loose their relation and obligations to GOD, as his creatures and subjects: and also their relations to each other as rational social creatures.

Those who apparently denied a connection between religion and government seemed to rely upon the assumption that citizens had relations with each other only through government. Stone responded that the attempts "to distinguish between moral and political wisdom" would not "destroy the connection between religion and good government."[9]

Stone defended the connection between religion and government as compatible with religious liberty. He fended off dissenters' accusations about the blending of church and state by acknowledging that "RELIGION and civil government, are not one and the same thing." He also conceded that the former "hath rights and prerogatives, with which the latter may not intermeddle." Yet this was not to say that religion and civil government were or should be unconnected. Against this position—"that there is, and ought to be no connection between religion and civil policy"—

Nathan Strong presented a variation of such arguments: "THO a distinction is made in the state, between the civil and Ecclesiastical departments, neither of them is independent of the other. Civility and good order of political regulations are a great advantage to religion; religion and its institutions are the best aid of government, by strengthening the ruler's hand, and making the subject faithful in his place, and obedient to the general laws." Nathan Strong, *A Sermon*, 15 (Hartford: 1790).

[9] Stone, *A Sermon*, 23–25. In this passage, and in his comment about the attempts "to distinguish between moral and political wisdom," Stone probably took aim not only at American dissenters but also at the English and Continental defenders of the French Revolution who, after establishing or assuming the moral foundation of rights, argued from rights without further reference to their moral basis, lest the strength and absolute character of rights be questioned and qualified. For the best-known contemporary defense of such argumentation, albeit in a slightly different vocabulary, see James Mackintosh, *Vindiciae Gallicae* (1790), in *The Miscellaneous Works of the Right Hon. James Mackintosh,* 3: 101 (London: 1846).

Stone held that "there are many ways, in which civil government may give countenance, encouragement, and even support to religion, without invading the prerogatives of the Most High: or, touching the inferior, tho sacred rights of conscience: and in doing of which, it may not only shew its friendly regard to christianity, but derive important advantages to itself."[10] The connection of religion to government, which dissenters seemed to threaten, could benefit government without endangering religious liberty.

The Dissenters' Defense

The accusation that dissenters sought to separate religion and civil government left dissenters in a quandary. They surely resented this charge. Yet they could not easily respond with the demotic simplicity they needed if they were to prevail in popular debate.

On the one hand, dissenters could not deny that there was a connection between religion and government. Prudentially, they could ill afford to invite further accusations that they were undermining one of government's moral foundations. More substantively, they agreed with establishment writers that religion and especially the religion of their country provided an essential moral basis for government, and they assumed that government ought to govern in sympathy with Christianity to the extent compatible with religious freedom. In this sense, dissenters did not question the necessary connection between religion and government. On the other hand, if dissenters had prominently admitted this connection (or denied that they sought a separation), they would have had to explain why the connection did not justify government subsidies for religion.

Of course, dissenters might have attempted to explain their middle ground. They might have asserted that there was a limited connection compatible with their understanding of religious liberty. In acknowledging even a partial connection, however, they would have risked being misunderstood or misrepresented as justifying an establishment. To show that religion and government were sufficiently connected as to justify government accommodation and even solicitude but not so connected as to justify an establishment was a complicated, difficult task,

[10] Stone, *A Sermon*, 25.

and therefore dissenters largely avoided the rhetoric of connection and separation.

The difficulty of acknowledging the connection while condemning establishments had been prominently illustrated by the English scientist and notorious Unitarian, Joseph Priestley. William Warburton and his intellectual followers had justified the English establishment as an "alliance" between church and state, each of which necessarily depended upon the other. In response, Priestley argued in 1771 against the necessity of such a connection. Yet even Priestley understood that he could not afford to reject the sociological connection. "I am aware that the connexion between *civil* and *religious* affairs will be urged for the necessity of some interference of the legislature with religion; and, as I observed before, I do not deny the connexion." Instead, Priestley repeatedly affirmed it, while explaining that it was less necessary than in earlier, more primitive eras: "But as this connexion has always been found to be the greatest in barbarous nations and imperfect governments, to which it lends an useful aid; it may be presumed, that it is gradually growing less necessary; and that, in the present advanced state of human society, there is very little occasion for it. For my own part, I have no apprehension but that, at this day, the laws might be obeyed very well without any ecclesiastical sanctions, enforced by the civil magistrate." Thus, "religious motives may still operate in favor of the civil laws, without such a connexion as has been formed between them in ecclesiastical establishments; and I think this end would be answered even better without that connexion." Religion could encourage morals and obedience to law without the sort of connection that amounted to an establishment. In defense of this position, however, Priestley had to argue that all religions more or less reinforced the morals necessary for civil order:

> In all the modes of religion which subsist among mankind, however subversive of virtue they may be in theory, there is some *salvo* for good morals; so that, in fact, they enforce the more essential parts, at least, of that conduct which the good order of society requires. Besides, it might be expected, that if all the modes of religion were equally protected by the civil magistrate, they would all vie with one another, which should best deserve that protection. This, however, is, in fact, all the alliance that can take place between religion and civil policy, each enforcing the same conduct by different motives. Any other "alliance between church and

state" is only the alliance of different sorts of worldly minded men, for their temporal emolument.[11]

This argument—in which Priestley ostentatiously acknowledged the sociological connection between church and state but denied that it any longer justified an establishment—required all of the dexterity and doctrinal laxity for which he was infamous, and it remains suggestive as to why American dissenters apparently felt discretion was the better part of valor. Unpersuasive in London, Priestley's overly sophisticated position could not have recommended itself to dissenters who needed to prevail in Boston, Hartford, or Richmond.

Although American dissenters did not often respond directly to the slur about disconnecting religion and government, they emphatically rejected related accusations that, in seeking religious liberty, they denied the civil utility of religion. For example, in 1777, after an establishment minister, Phillips Payson, preached on the "utility" of religion to civil society, not least "in a free government," the great Baptist leader, Isaac Backus, responded: "I am as sensible of the importance of religion and of the utility of it to human society as Mr. Payson is. . . . But I am . . . far from thinking with him that these restraints would be broken down if equal religious liberty was established."[12] Another eminent Baptist,

[11] Joseph Priestley, *An Essay on the First Principles of Government and on the Nature of Political, Civil, and Religious Liberty* (London: 1771), in *The Theological and Miscellaneous Works*, 22: 56–57 (1817–1832). Later, in 1787, he came close to what, on its face, seemed a more direct rejection of a connection: "I have even no doubt, but that, as Christianity was promulgated, and prevailed in the world, without any aid from civic power, it will, when it shall have recovered its pristine purity, and its pristine vigour, entirely disengage itself from such an unnatural *alliance* as it is at present fettered with, and that our posterity will even look back with astonishment at the infatuation of their ancestors, in imagining that things so wholly different from each other as *Christianity* and *civil power* had any natural connexion." Indeed, he said, "I look with satisfaction to a future and a better state of things, in which the *religion of Christ* will be as much detached from all connexion with *civil power* as it was in its best days, before the time of Constantine; since which time it has always been kept in chains, and made subservient to the most unworthy purposes. It will then be supported, not by the compulsory payment of tithes, or any compulsion at all, but by the voluntary attachment of its friends, who will understand and value it." Priestley, *A Letter to the Right Hon. William Pitt . . . on the Subjects of Toleration and Church Establishments; Occasioned by His Speech against the Repeal of the Test and Corporation Acts* (London: 1787), in ibid., 19: 119, 131. Even in this 1787 pamphlet, however, Priestley did not deny that a connection might be valuable in some circumstances.

[12] Phillips Payson, *A Sermon*, 19 (Boston: 1777); Isaac Backus, *Government and Liberty Described* (1778), in William G. McLoughlin, ed., *Isaac Backus on Church, State, and Calvinism, Pamphlets, 1754–1789*, 353, 358 (Cambridge, Mass.: Belknap, 1968).

Samuel Stillman, noted in 1779: "ɪᴛ may be said, That religion is of importance to the good of civil society," and that "therefore, the magistrate ought to encourage it under this idea." Rather than directly dispute this, Stillman emphasized that all persons, as individuals, including persons in government, had the obligation to encourage religion: "ɪᴛ is readily acknowledged that the intrinsic excellence and beneficial effects of true religion are such, that *every man* who is favored with the christian revelation, ought to befriend it. . . . And there are many ways in which the civil magistrate may encourage religion, in a perfect agreement with the nature of the kingdom of Christ, and the rights of conscience."[13] Further south, in Virginia in 1785, Presbyterians who questioned the necessity of government support for Christianity more forcefully argued: "We are fully persuaded of the happy influence of Christianity upon the morals of men; but we have never known it, in the history of its progress, so effectual for this purpose, as when left to its native excellence and evidence to recommend it . . . free from the intrusive hand of the civil magistrate."[14] Rather than the dissenters, it was their political allies, such as James Madison or Thomas Jefferson, who tended to doubt the secular benefits of religion. Yet in disputes about religious liberty, even Madison preferred to change the focus of the debate than to challenge the widely held assumption that a connection was necessary. As Madison told the Virginia House of Delegates, the "[t]rue question [was] not—Is Rel[igion] nec[essar]y?" Instead, it was "are Relig[ou]s Estab[lishmen]ts necess[ar]y for Religion?"[15]

Baptists repeatedly had to fend off arguments that they sought a religious liberty incompatible with moral legislation. For example, in Vermont in 1792, when Caleb Blood argued against the state establishment on behalf of an "equal religious liberty," he felt obliged to add that

---

[13] Samuel Stillman, *A Sermon,* 28–29 (Boston: 1779).

[14] Memorial of the Presbyterians of Virginia to the General Assembly (Aug. 13, 1785), in William Addison Blakely, ed., *American State Papers Bearing on Sunday Legislation,* 114 (Washington, D.C.: Religious Liberty Association, 1911). For similar sentiments about the civil value of religion from what may have been a Baptist petition, see The Petition of Sundry Inhabitants of the County of Powhatan (June 4, 1784), in the Virginia State Library, Richmond, microfilm, Misc. Ms. 425.

[15] Notes on General Assessment Bill, Outline B (Dec. 23–24, 1784), in R. A. Rutland et al., eds., *Papers of James Madison,* 8: 198 (Chicago: University of Chicago Press, 1973). Of course, his answer was "no."

such a freedom would not prevent the enactment of moral legislation: "This however, by no means prohibits the civil magistrate from enacting those laws that shall enforce the observance of those precepts in the Christian religion, the violation of which is a breach of the civil peace; viz. such as forbid murder, theft, adultery, false witness, and injuring our neighbor, either in person, name, or estate." In addition, the precept "of observing the Sabbath, should be enforced by the civil power." In defending this last point, concerning Sabbath legislation, he not only mentioned religious reasons but also, more prominently, secular ones, such as that "tyrannical and cruel masters would be allowed to subject their servants to a constant series of labour without proper time to rest, or attend to the important concerns of a future world. One reason given by Moses for keeping the Sabbath, was, that thy manservant and thy maiden servant may rest as well as thou."[16] A religious liberty against an establishment would still permit the civil enforcement of moral duties, for such duties were founded on both religious and civil obligation.

Baptists responded with special vigor to the malicious suggestions that they sought a religious liberty at odds with government. Some establishment ministers persistently hinted that Baptists were Anabaptists like those of Münster—antinomian enthusiasts who denied the obligation of all civil laws to which they had religious objections. In defense against these crude and utterly groundless attacks, Isaac Backus again and again felt obliged to declare that he and his coreligionists were not Anabaptists. Baptists, he explained, distinguished themselves in various ways, not least by obeying civil laws.[17] In Virginia, in 1790, John Leland similarly felt obliged to respond to insinuations of an immoral antinomian disregard for law: "[T]he Baptists hold it their duty to obey magistrates, to be subject to the law of the land, to pay their taxes, and pray for all in authority. They are not scrupulous of taking an oath of God upon them to testify the truth before a magistrate or court. . . . Their religion also allows them to bear arms in defense of their life, liberty and

---

[16] Caleb Blood, *A Sermon*, 35 (Vermont election sermon, 1792). Blood adroitly cast the standard dissenting aspersion on the members of the establishment in his audience, declaring that he (presumably unlike them) was "far from wishing to have America involved in the great error of blending the government of church and state together." Ibid., 27.

[17] *Isaac Backus on Church, State, and Calvinism*, 131, 168, 173, 179, 276n, 325, 294, 395, 420, and 486.

property. . . . From this account of the Virginia Baptists, they appear to be a very different sect from the German Anabaptists."[18]

Like most other Americans, Baptists gave support to civil government through many aspects of their religious life. In their religious conformity to legal duties, in their pious adherence to the moral obligations not enforced by law (including charity and forgiveness), in their oaths taken in court, and in their prayers for the nation and its leaders, Baptists and many other Americans eased the burdens of government, helping it in ways it could not help itself. Thus, even while dissenters avoided convoluted distinctions about the permissible degree or type of connection between religion and government, they vigorously protested that their religious liberty was no threat to government, to Christian morality, or to the laws enforcing such morality—indeed, that their religion supported government and law. Committed to a vision of society in which their religion permeated their lives, and struggling to overcome the prejudice of their fellow citizens who feared religious dissent as a threat to morality and law, these dissenters had every reason to seek religious liberty and no reason to demand the disconnection of religion and government.

Separation of church and state is often assumed to have been the demand of eighteenth-century American dissenters, but these dissenters seem to have said little, if anything, about it. Ironically, to the extent anything like separation was widely discussed in America, it was a topic addressed by establishment ministers, who accused dissenters of seeking to disconnect religion and civil government. In making this allegation, establishment ministers attributed to dissenters a desire to separate religion and therefore also morality from government. A scurrilous misrepresentation, it revealed much about the fears of establishment ministers but little about the hopes of dissenters.

[18] *The Virginia Chronicle* (1790), in *The Writings of the Late Elder John Leland,* 120, ed. L. F. Greene (New York: 1845).

3

The Exclusion of the Clergy

THE ROLE of separation in the controversy over establishment found quiet echoes in the occasional disagreements as to whether clergymen should be excluded from civil office. In retrospect, it may be thought that advocates of exclusion would have argued on the basis of separation, but it is difficult to locate any American who demanded clerical exclusion as a separation of religion and government, let alone a separation of church and state. Once again, separation was not a demand but an accusation.

Arguments for Exclusion

The arguments for the exclusion of the clergy from civil office were quite varied. None of them, however, came even close to separation. In seventeenth-century Massachusetts, for example, Congregationalists excluded ministers on religious grounds. In particular, they followed the approach of Calvin and some of his English dissenting followers in holding that no man should hold both temporal and ecclesiastical office. Calvin had argued that Christ wanted to "bar the ministers of his Word from civil rule and earthly authority," and when Congregationalists came to America and established a government in Massachusetts, they also assumed that civil and ecclesiastical offices "cannot come together in one man."[1] Although some later historians have characterized the division of offices in Massachusetts as a nascent separation of church and state,

---

[1] Calvin, *Institutes of the Christian Religion*, 2: 1220 (IV.xi.8), trans. Ford Lewis Battles (Philadelphia: Westminister Press, 1960).

the Congregationalists of this colony surely did not share the latter perspective any more than did Roger Williams.[2] On the contrary, they excluded ministers from civil office while encouraging substantial cooperation between church and state. Indeed, their exclusion of ministers was part of their religious establishment, in which, as stated in their 1641 Body of Liberties, "Civill Authoritie hath power and libertie to see the peace, ordinances and Rules of Christ observed in every church according to his word[,] so it be done in a Civill and not in a Ecclesiastical way."[3] This was hardly a conception of separation between church and state.

Later, at the time of the American Revolution, some inhabitants of Massachusetts argued for exclusion on secular rather than Calvinist grounds, as may be illustrated by a petition from the Town of Pittsfield in 1776. After electing a Baptist elder to the state's House of Representatives, the town asked the House to disqualify him. Although the town may have been simply trying to change its representative, it petitioned on the ground that he ought not levy taxes if he was exempt from paying them:

> [W]e Conceive it has been the Constant Sence and Opinion of your Honours that no Minister of the Gospel ought, to be admitted to a Seat in the House of Representatives in the General Court of this colony; on the General Principle that no Persons, not Contributing to the Support of Publick Burthens, and payment of Publick Taxes, ought to have a Voice in giveing or granting, the Property of others, not so Exempted, or in Meking, and Passing any acts, or Laws, not Equally Binding on themselves, and their Constituants unless for mere Political Purposes Excused.[4]

---

[2] Edmund S. Morgan, *Puritan Political Ideas*, xxix–xxx, xxxii (Indianapolis: Bobbs-Merrill, 1965). Morgan calls this a type of "separation of church and state," although, of course, he does not suggest that Congregationalists described their civil and ecclesiastical arrangements as such. Ibid., xxxii.

[3] "A Coppie of the Liberties of the Massachusets Collonie in New England" (1641), in *Collections of Massachusetts Historical Society*, 226 (3d ser.; Boston: 1843).

[4] Pittsfield Petition (May 29, 1776), in Oscar and Mary Handlin, eds., *The Popular Sources of Political Authority: Documents on the Massachusetts Constitution of 1780*, 93–94 (Cambridge, Mass.: Belknap, 1966). The petition continued: "We further would inform your Honours that notwithstanding the Same has also been the Sence of this Town, as appears by the Instructions they gave their Representatives the year Past, injoining them to Do their utmost to prevent any Minister of the Gospel from having a Seat in the House of Representative[s]. The Inhabitants of said Town have by some Extraordinary Means Chosen one Mr. Valentine Rathbone to Represent them in this Honorable Court—Which Said Rathbone

An argument from American principles of taxation and representation, this was no more a separation of church and state than Calvin's division of offices.

In justifying constitutional prohibitions on the admission of ministers to state legislatures, Americans typically questioned whether it was proper for men of the cloth to hold office of a sort that could only distract them from higher obligations. For example, the 1778 South Carolina Constitution declared: "And whereas the ministers of the gospel are by their profession dedicated to the service of God and the cure of souls, and ought not to be diverted from the great duties of their function, therefore no minister of the gospel or public preacher of any religious persuasion, while he continues in the exercise of his pastoral function, and for two years after, shall be eligible either as governor, lieutenant-governor, a member of the senate, house of representatives, or privy council in this State."[5]

Notwithstanding that this constitutional exclusion purported to be sympathetic toward the clergy, some exclusion clauses clearly attempted to elicit anti-Catholic support. For example, in 1777 the earlier, New York version of the provision quoted above specified that "no priest of any denomination whatsoever" should be eligible for office. This anti-Catholic wording came from the document's primary drafter, John Jay, whose preamble to the Constitution's religious freedom clause pointedly declared that "we are required, by the benevolent principles of rational liberty, not only to expel civil tyranny, but also to guard against that spiritual oppression and intolerance wherewith the bigotry and ambition of weak and wicked priests and princes have scourged mankind."[6] Yet

---

we aver to your Honours, is and has been ever Since he lived in this Town the Minister or Elder of a Baptist Church and Congregation in this Town, and that he had never paid any Taxes either Public or private in the Town, or been assessed to the payment thereof but has from year to year for four or five years past given Certificates to the members of his Church and Congregation In the Capacity of an Elder thereof, in order to obtain their Exemption from the payment of Ministerial Charges etc.—We Therefore pray your Honours would Take the premises into your wise Consideration, and that the Said Mr. Rathbone may be Dismissed from giveing his attendance as a Member of this Honorable Court, and this we are the more imboldened to ask as the Town have also made Choice of another Person to Represent them whom We Conceive to be not thus incapacitated and who upon Notice will Doubtless attend—And as in Duty Bound Shall pray." Ibid.

[5] S.C. Const., Art. XXI (1778).

[6] N.Y. Const., Arts. XXXVIII and XXXIX (1777); Tenn. Const., Art. VIII (1796). Shorter exclusion clauses appeared in the constitutions of Va. (1776); Del., Art. 29 (1776); Del., Art. VIII, §9 (1792); Md., Art. XXXVII (1776); N.C., Art. XXXI (1776); and Ky., Art. I, §24

most Americans hesitated to endorse this intemperate anti-Catholicism, and even when in 1796 the drafters of the Tennessee Constitution copied the anti-Catholic allusions in New York's exclusion provision, they did not adopt New York's diatribe about the "bigotry and ambition of weak and wicked priests."[7]

With or without any overt anti-Catholicism, many Americans, especially in frontier areas, probably also welcomed the exclusion of the clergy from civil office on the basis of a general suspicion of clergymen, but the evidence of this anticlerical support for exclusion remains elusive. In 1783, in Virginia and what would become Kentucky, Thomas Jefferson hoped that a new constitution would exclude "Ministers of the Gospel" from the General Assembly. His discriminatory proposal, however, elicited skepticism from James Madison:

> Does not the exclusion of Ministers of the Gospel as such violate a fundamental principle of liberty by punishing a religious profession with the privation of a civil right? Does it not violate another article of the plan itself which exempts religion from the cognizance of Civil power? Does it not violate justice by at once taking away a right and prohibiting a compensation for it? And does it not in fine violate impartiality by shutting the door against the Minister of one religion and leaving it open for those of every other?[8]

This inequality had no justification in the antiestablishment principles shared by Jefferson and Madison, and Jefferson is not known to have defended it. Nonetheless, it should not be assumed that Jefferson was easily reconciled to the prospect of clergymen in the legislature, and if Jefferson did not spell out his reasons for wanting to exclude the clergy, this may have been, in part, because it was not entirely respectable to voice doubts about the clergy as a whole. Even anonymous anticlerical writers had reason to soften their sentiments with a vague solicitude for

---

(1792). For New York, see John W. Pratt, *Religion, Politics and Diversity*, 88 (Ithaca: Cornell University Press, 1967).

[7] For the decline of anti-Catholicism in the post-Revolutionary period, see Charles P. Hanson, *Necessary Virtue: The Pragmatic Origins of Religious Liberty in New England* (Charlottesville: University Press of Virginia, 1998).

[8] Jefferson's Draft of a Constitution for Virginia, in *Papers of Thomas Jefferson*, 6: 297, ed. Julian P. Boyd (Princeton: Princeton University Press, 1952); Madison's Observations on Jefferson's Draft, in ibid., 311. More generally, see Philip Mazzei, *Researches on the United States*, 162, trans. Constance D. Sherman (Charlottesville: University Press of Virginia, 1976).

the higher occupations of ministers. In Kentucky, for example, a "Corn Planter" argued in 1788 that "[t]he necessary pastoral exercises of a faithful Gospel minister is fully sufficient to imploy his whole time and attention." He was "to give himself wholy to the work," for "[t]he faithful preacher will neither have leisure nor inclination to concern [himself] in politicks, and he who is of opposite character is not to be trusted."[9]

Thus Americans barred clergymen from civil office for many reasons, including an odd combination of Calvinism, anti-Catholicism, theories of taxation and representation, solicitude for the clergy, and suspicion of the clergy. Strikingly, however, Americans did not exclude the clergy on grounds of separation.

The Silence of Dissenters

While advocates of clerical exclusions apparently did not demand a separation of church and state, dissenters were even more reticent. They usually did not even discuss clerical exclusions.

In remaining silent about the exclusion of ministers from civil office, dissenters apparently found it politic to remain quiet about one of the few legal arrangements that, at least in some states, treated dissenting and established clergymen equally. Many evangelical dissenting leaders in the North shared the roughly Calvinist or Reformed expectations of established Congregational clergymen that ministers should not hold civil office. More generally, dissenters probably hesitated to protest an exclusion that resonated with their own doubts about excessive involvement in worldly matters, especially politics, which might distract a preacher or anyone else from his or her higher concerns. Indeed, to the extent exclusion applied not only to the legislature but also saved the clergy the trouble of serving as town and county officers, some clergymen considered it desirable.[10] Moreover, few dissenters wished to give

---

[9] "Corn Planter," Letter to Mr. Printer, in *Kentucky Gazette*, No. 46 (July 12, 1788). He was responding to the questions of a "Farmer": "Ought preachers to be allowed a seat in the Legislature? and ought they to bear arms?" "A Farmer" (Jan. 16, 1788), in ibid., No. 23 (Feb. 2, 1788).

[10] For example, in 1774 in Virginia, where dissenters were not excluded from civil office, the Presbytery of Hanover requested that "the dissenting clergy, as well as the clergy of the Established church, be excused from all burdensome offices." Petition of Presbytery

established ministers the opportunity to sit in state legislatures, where these clergymen of the majority denomination (Congregationalist in the North or Episcopalian in the South) would become more influential than ever. Not least, clerical exclusions from civil office were often paired with exemptions from civil obligations, such as the obligation to pay taxes or serve in the military. Accordingly, if ministers—established or dissenting—hoped to retain their exemptions, they had reason not to protest their exclusions.[11] Being especially vulnerable, dissenting ministers remained notably quiet.

By failing to protest these deviations from a strict equality under law, dissenters revealed that they felt no obligation to take their most radical political principles to their logical extremes. Dissenters suffered under various unequal penalties. Most dramatically, in Connecticut and Massachusetts they paid taxes for the salaries of establishment ministers and could avoid paying these taxes only by filing a certificate as to their dissenting status. In response, dissenters demanded equality under law, without respect to religious differences, and even demanded that the laws not take cognizance of religion. If dissenters took these demands to their logical conclusions, they would have had reason to doubt whether any group of persons, even the entirety of the clergy, should be privileged or penalized on account of their being clergymen.

One of the few dissenting leaders who did take his principles to their logical conclusions was one of the most prominent—the brilliant, delightfully eccentric Baptist leader, John Leland. In 1790, while still in Virginia, he admitted that "there is not a constitutional evil in the states, that has a more plausible pretext, than the proscription of gospel ministers."[12] Certainly, "to have one branch of the legislature composed of

---

of Hanover to the House of Burgesses (Nov. 11, 1774), in Charles F. James, *Documentary History of the Struggle for Religious Liberty in Virginia,* 45 (Lynchburg: 1900).

[11] Writing about militia and tax exemptions in New England, William G. McLoughlin observes: "No evidence exists that the Baptists opposed this ministerial prerogative." McLoughlin, *New England Dissent, 1630–1833,* 2: 1019 (Cambridge: Harvard University Press, 1971).

[12] *The Virginia Chronicle* (1790), in *The Writings of the Late Elder John Leland* 122, ed. L. F. Greene (New York: 1845). He added: "I say in the *states,* for most of them have proscribed them from seats of legislation, &c. The federal government is free in this point." Ibid.

McLoughlin interprets Leland as "eccentric" on account of his departure from Calvinism and on the basis of the comments of his contemporaries in New England, who recognized that Leland was unusually engaged in politics. McLoughlin, *New England Dissent,* 2: 928–

clergymen, as is the case in some European powers, is not seemly—to have them entitled to seats of legislation, on account of their ecclesiastical dignity, like the bishops in England, is absurd." Yet Americans had gone to the other extreme. "[T]o declare them [clergymen] ineligible, when their neighbors prefer them to any others, is depriving them of the liberty of free citizens, and those who prefer them, the freedom of choice." The best that could be said of the proscription was that it "den[ied] them the liberty of citizens, lest they should degrade their sacred office." Not only opposed to these exclusions, Leland also rejected exemptions, arguing that the clergy should be subject to neither "degrading checks" nor "alluring baits." More than most dissenters, Leland put his principles ahead of his personal interest and admitted of exemptions that "[t]hough this is an indulgence that I feel, yet it is not consistent with my theory of politics."[13] Strikingly, however, Leland's theory on this matter was not one of separation. Instead, it was a version of the usual dissenting demands for equality and for laws that did not take cognizance of religion. As Leland put it in 1791: "Ministers should share the

---

932. To this it might be added that the titles of his pamphlets, let alone his giant cheese, reveal a somewhat unconventional approach. (For the cheese, see the text of Chapter 7 at notes 23–25.) McLoughlin's characterization, however, has been challenged by a regional interpretation that attributes Leland's seeming eccentricity to his being a Baptist with a southern perspective who did not adapt to the prevailing views of the North when he moved there. Andrew M. Manis, "Regionalism and a Baptist Perspective on Separation of Church and State," *American Baptist Quarterly*, 2: 213, 219 (1983). Certainly, Leland's itinerancy, his revivalism, and his Arminian tendencies were traits strongly reinforced by his long sojourn in Virginia from the 1770s through the 1780s. Yet Manis's account inadequately recognizes variations within the South. Arminianism prevailed among Virginia Baptists more than among their coreligionists in other states. Even in Virginia, however, Arminians never became a majority within their denomination, and already by the 1790s their numbers had sharply declined. See Chapter 7, note 62, and Gregory A. Wills, *Democratic Religion: Freedom, Authority, and Church Discipline in the Baptist South, 1785–1900*, 171, note 18 (New York: Oxford University Press, 1997). Still more significant, Leland's very personal, quirky style of writing was neither peculiarly northern or southern, and his degree of political involvement with the Republicans was as notable in the South as further North. To understand the remarkably political tone of many of Leland's pamphlets, one need only observe the very different character of most other Baptist publications.
[13] *The Writings of the Late Elder John Leland*, 122. Leland made clear, however, that he was more concerned about the exclusions than these exemptions, for "an exemption from bearing arms, is, but a *legal indulgence*, but the ineligibility is *constitutional proscription*, and no legal reward is sufficient for a constitutional prohibition. The first may be altered by the caprice of the legislature, the last cannot be exchanged, without an appeal to the whole mass of constituent power." Ibid.

same protection of the law that other men do, and no more. . . . The law should be silent about them; protect them as citizens, not as sacred officers, for the civil law knows no sacred religious officers."[14]

An Accusation of Separation

By now it should hardly come as a surprise that clerical exclusion was discussed in terms of separation neither by advocates of exclusion nor by dissenters, but by a defender of the New England establishments—as it happens, Noah Webster. Like Leland, Webster opposed clerical exclusions on grounds of equality. Yet the lexicographer did so for very different reasons and in a manner that played upon anxieties about separation. Webster was accustomed to defending New England's religious establishments on the ground that the clergy exerted a highly beneficial influence in society, and he therefore thought it incongruous that the clergy were excluded from some state legislatures. Accordingly, he demanded equal rights and hinted that exclusions manifested anticlerical animus and a desire for separation.

According to Webster, Americans irrationally discriminated against clergymen on account of the clergy's specialized duties. The exclusion of the clergy "iz founded on just az good reezons, az the old laws against witchcraft; a clergyman being no more dangerous in a civil office, than a witch in civil society."[15] Nonetheless, too many American constitutions took for granted that clergymen "should hav no concern with politics." This was an "enormous error" that "seems to be rivetted in popular opinion, *that the functions of clergymen are of a spiritual and divine nature, and that this order of men should hav no concern with secular affairs.*"[16] Yet, if the objection stood against the clergy, it "iz equally good against merchants, mechanics and farmers, who hav no immediate concern with legisla-

---

[14] *The Rights of Conscience Inalienable, and therefore, Religious Opinions not Cognizable by Law; or, the High-Flying Churchman, Stripped of his Legal Robe, Appears a Yaho* (1791), in *The Writings of the Late Elder John Leland,* 188. He also wrote: "To proscribe them from seats of legislation, etc., is cruel. To indulge them with an exemption from taxes and bearing arms is a tempting emolument." Ibid. The unusual character of Leland's position is born out by McLoughlin, *New England Dissent,* 2: 1019.
[15] "Miscellaneous Remarks *on* Divizions *of* Property, Guvernment, Education, Religion, Agriculture, Slavery, Commerce, Climate *and* Diseezes *in the* United States" (Philadelphia: 1787), in Noah Webster, *A Collection of Essays and Fugitiv Writings,* 346 (Boston: 1790).
[16] Ibid., 346, 364.

tion." Although almost all men pursued specialized activities, "every citizen haz a concern in the laws which guvern him; and a clergyman haz the same concern with civil laws, az other men."

The real danger lay not in the specialized vocation of the clergy but in the legal exclusion of the clergy from political office, which created a separation of interests. "There hav been bad clergymen and tyrannical hierarkies in the world; but the error lies in separating the civil from the ecclesiastical government. When separated they become rivals; when united, they hav the same interest to pursu."[17] By encouraging a separation of religious and civil government, the irrational fear of clergymen "haz laid the foundation of a separation of interest and influence between the civil and ecclesiastical orders; haz produced a rivalship az fatal to the peece of society az war and pestilence, and a prejudice against *all orders* of preechers, which bids fair to banish the 'gospel of peece' from some parts of our empire."[18] This prejudice against clergymen—a prejudice that encouraged a dangerous separation of interests within society—arose in response to extraordinary claims of power by the popes: "The separation of religion and policy, of church and state, waz owing at first to the errors of a gloomy superstition, which exalted the ministers of Christ into Deities; who, like other men, under similar advantages, became tyrants." Such had been the "papal hierarky."[19] Fortunately,

---

[17] Ibid., 346. He continued: "A clergyman's business iz to *inform* hiz peeple, and to make them *good men.* This iz the way to make them *good citizens.*" Ibid. To this end, Webster suggested that the clergy should mingle in society: "The clergymen in Boston take the right method to accomplish this business; they throw aside all *divine airs* and imperious grave superiority; they mingle in the most familiar manner, with other peeple; they are social and facetious, and their parishoners delight to hav them at all entertainments and concerts. This conduct remoovs the awful distance between them and other descriptions of men; they are not only esteemed and respected, but luved; their decent department iz imitated; their churches are crowded, and their instructions listened to with plezure. Such men are blessings to society." Ibid.

[18] Ibid., 364.

[19] Ibid., 347, 363. Probably following Webster, Zephaniah Swift also hinted that a separation of the clergy from the rest of society had papal and clerical origins: "The clergy usurped an uncontroverted authority in all matters, which they pretended, were of an ecclesiastical nature. They separated themselves from the civil state, they became a distinct order of men, devoted to the sole employment of religion, and forever ready to interrupt the tranquility, or impede the administration of government, when they thought it necessary to guard, or extend the rights of the church. Hence originated a government within a government, and a separation of interest between the clergy and the laity, which produced perpetual discord and contention." Zephaniah Swift, *A System of the Laws of the State of Connecticut,* 1: 134 (Windham: 1795).

there was a better solution to the political aspirations of clergymen than a mischievous separation: "The way to check their ambition, and to giv full efficacy to their administrations, iz to consider them az *men* and *citizens,* entitled to all the benefits of guvernment, subject to law, and designed for *civil* az wel az *spiritual* instructors."[20] To avoid clerical tyranny, it was only necessary to give the clergy the rights and interests enjoyed by other citizens.

Far from threatening free government, a learned clergy supported it. "That clergymen ought not to meddle with politics, iz so far from truth, that they ought to be *well* acquainted with the subject, and *better* than most classes of men, in proportion to their literary attainments." With such qualifications, they could sustain good citizenship by inculcating morality. Accordingly, "Religion and policy ought ever to go hand in hand; not to raize a system of despotism over the consciences, but to enlighten the minds, soften the harts, correct the manners and restrain the vices of men."[21] Webster hoped for a clergy fully integrated and even prominent in the life of their communities, and, from this perspective, he saw clerical exclusions as an irrational attempt to separate politics from the religion that was the basis of political and moral edification.

Thus, yet again, separation was an accusation. Richard Hooker and, much more recently, some American ministers had defended their different religious establishments by intimating that dissenters desired a separation of one sort or another. Drawing upon such accusations, Webster opposed clerical exclusions by hinting that they had been adopted in order to separate clergymen from politics and church from state. As in the establishment controversy, this was a mischaracterization, which reflected fears rather than facts. Neither the advocates of religious liberty nor the proponents of clerical exclusions appear to have sought a separation, and, if they ever did, they seem to have done so only rarely or in a most understated and elusive manner.

[20] "Miscellaneous Remarks *on* Divizions *of* Property," in Webster, *A Collection of Essays and Fugitiv Writings,* 347.
[21] Ibid., 346.

4

Freedom from Religious Establishments

IF IN their struggle against the state establishments American religious dissenters did not demand a separation of church and state, what sort of liberty did they seek? Centuries have passed since Roger Williams dreamed of a separation between church and world, and since some later anticlerical writers, such as the Marquis de Condorcet, called for a sort of separation of church and state. So too, centuries have passed since establishment ministers attributed to dissenters a desire to separate religion from government, and since Noah Webster similarly discredited the supporters of clerical exclusions. After the passage of so much time, it should be possible to step back from all of these contentious assertions and to examine dispassionately the religious liberty sought by the late eighteenth-century Americans who struggled against establishments. If not separation, what did they request? An examination of their demands, as expressed in their own terms, will be seen to vindicate these dissenters not only from the aspersions of their opponents but also, ironically, from the accolades of their later admirers, who, with very different motives, have likewise attributed to them a desire for separation.

The Character of American Establishments

During the Revolution, American establishments lost their severity. Some colonies had once penalized religious dissenters with laws constraining unauthorized worship and preaching, but, in their struggle against Britain, the states abandoned what remained of their direct penalties on religion. As a result, such establishments of religion as still survived in America consisted mostly of legal privileges for the established religion in a state—most prominently, the privilege of the established clergy to receive salaries paid from state taxes.

The War of Independence left Americans largely free of direct penalties on religion. Prior to the Revolution various state governments not only gave financial and other privileges to their established denominations but also imposed penalties on the free exercise of religion by dissenters. In Connecticut in the 1740s, the Separates had been fined and imprisoned for preaching and meeting, and in Virginia, as recently as the early 1770s, Baptists had been incarcerated for such offences. Yet at the onset of the Revolution numerous evangelical dissenters (and even a few Quakers) found common cause with their fellow patriots and joined the Revolutionary armies. These dissenters fought for a regime in which they could attain equality within their own states as well as from Britain and, in the new atmosphere created by their participation in the Revolution, the states could no longer punish them merely on account of their religious differences. After 1776, therefore, all that plausibly remained of any American establishment were various forms of government support. In some states religious tests admitted only Christians or even only Protestants to public office. More troubling to most dissenters, the constitutions of some states allowed establishment ministers to collect salaries raised by state taxes and permitted laws that gave the established clergy the exclusive right to conduct marriages. Accordingly, privilege more than penalty now seemed to be at stake. Even the advocates of religious establishments often joined dissenters in praising religious liberty, seeking to defend establishment privileges by disclaiming any desire for penalties.

To be sure, establishment privileges might also be considered penalties on the free exercise of religion. For example, in Virginia in the 1780s, when Anglicans—now Episcopalians—proposed taxes in support of ministers' salaries, dissenters complained that the taxes not only would give privileges to establishment clergymen but would also penalize dissenters. Similarly, in Connecticut and Massachusetts, Congregationalists taxed individuals, including dissenters, for the salaries of ministers selected by Congregational majorities, unless the dissenters signed certificates attesting to their dissenting status. Dissenters often refused to sign such certificates and had difficulty recovering such taxes as were collected.[1] All of these arrangements imposed burdens on dissenters, who frequently complained about them as penalties.[2]

Nonetheless, the remaining infringements on the religious liberty of evangelical dissenters consisted mostly of establishment privileges, and these seemed far less threatening than earlier persecutions. Establishment benefits and associated assessments or taxes paled in comparison with the fines and imprisonment that had once been imposed upon dissenters simply for meeting and preaching.[3] During the Revolution, moreover, some southern states, such as Virginia, abandoned tax support for Episcopalian ministers, leaving dissenters to worry not so much about establishment privileges as about the revival of these benefits. Accordingly, by the end of the War of Independence, many dissenters felt they had largely achieved religious liberty. For example, in 1782 the General Association of Separate Baptists in Virginia concluded that they had "already secured their most important civil rights" and therefore decided that their next meeting should be their last.[4] Only the 1784 Episcopalian proposal to restore tax support for ministers again concentrated the minds of Virginia Baptists and led them to resume their campaign for a constitutional or equivalent prohibition on an establishment.[5] Thus, having already obtained constitutional guarantees against direct penalt-

[1] William G. McLoughlin, *New England Dissent, 1630–1833*, 1: 644–647 (Cambridge: Harvard University Press, 1971).

[2] Dissenters were particularly apt to complain about establishment privileges as "penalties" in states in which dissenters had obtained a constitutional guarantee of free exercise but not a prohibition on establishments. For this dynamic in Virginia, see Philip Hamburger, "Equality and Diversity: The Eighteenth Century Debate about Equal Rights and Equal Protection," *Supreme Court Review*, 347–355 (1992).

[3] Moreover, even the penalties on religion in Virginia had not amounted to anything like what had been common in Europe. As Leland observed in 1790: "The dragon roared with hideous peals, but was not *red*—the Beast appeared formidable, but was not *scarlet colored*. Virginia soil has never been stained with vital blood for conscience sake." *The Virginia Chronicle* (1790), in *The Writings of the Late Elder John Leland*, 107, ed. L. F. Greene (New York: 1845).

[4] Robert B. Semple, *A History of the Rise and Progress of the Baptist in Virginia*, 67 (Richmond: 1810). It was at their final 1783 meeting that, before disbanding, they petitioned on the relatively minor issues of vestries and marriages, requesting "that no law may pass, to connect the church, & State in the future." See Chapter 1, note 68.

[5] In December 1784 Jefferson wrote, "I am glad the *Episcopalians* have again shown their teeth & fangs. The *dissenters* had almost forgotten them." Letter of Thomas Jefferson to James Madison (Dec. 8, 1784), in *Papers of James Madison*, 8: 178, ed. Robert A. Rutland et al. (Chicago: University of Chicago Press, 1973).

ies, evangelical dissenters increasingly struggled, more narrowly, for constitutional guarantees against establishment privileges.

The Demands of the Dissenters

In their attack upon the remaining establishments, dissenters and their political allies created an intellectually cohesive movement, which made relatively uniform requests for limitations upon government. The various evangelical dissenters who opposed establishments often cooperated across state and denominational lines and acted with an awareness that they were participating in a broader struggle for religious freedom. In so doing, they shared many assumptions about religious liberty, and, although they disagreed about numerous details, they made remarkably similar demands.[6]

Evangelical dissenters dominated the antiestablishment struggle that shaped the First Amendment. In New England, Baptists led the assault on the Congregational establishments with little help from Presbyterians, who shared deep theological sympathies with the Congregationalists. In the South, Baptists opposed the Episcopalian establishments with greater but not entirely uniform assistance from Presbyterians, Methodists, and some liberal-minded Episcopalians. Yet Quakers, Mennonites, and other nonevangelical sects increasingly took only a peripheral role in these struggles. In part, these nonevangelicals withdrew from the organized antiestablishment movement because they had already achieved a substantial freedom from the burdens of state establishments. By far the largest and most politically active of the nonevangelical sects, the Quakers, had concentrated their settlements in Pennsylvania and Rhode Island, where they and others had long ago determined that there would be no establishment. Moreover, in the states that levied taxes in support of establishment clergymen, Quakers often secured statutory exemptions. The events of 1775 and 1776, however, finally prompted these nonevangelicals to depart from the struggle against establishments.

In these years, as Americans began to quarrel with Britain, the

---

[6] Extensive cooperation across denominations and far-flung colonies is documented by John Wesley Brinsfield, *Religion and Politics in Colonial South Carolina*, 84, 105, 107–108, 121 (Easley, S.C.: Southern Historical Press, 1983). For Baptists in Virginia and New England, see Thomas E. Buckley, "Evangelicals Triumphant: The Baptists' Assault on the Virginia Glebes, 1786–1801," *William & Mary Quarterly*, 45: 42 (1988).

Quakers and other nonevangelicals came to realize with new clarity that they needed a different sort of religious liberty than that demanded by evangelical dissenters. Prior to the Revolution, Quakers and most other dissenters could share a common cause against the state establishments. Yet beginning in 1775 evangelical dissenters took a route Quakers could not follow. The evangelical dissenters, having joined American demands for equal liberty against the British, similarly opposed American establishments with arguments that emphasized the need for equal rights. The evangelicals thereby began to insist upon the principle of equality in all rights and obligations, including the duty to fight and pay taxes. In this manner, the Quakers, who had conscientious objections to fighting and to paying taxes for war, were reminded that they needed a different, less egalitarian type of religious freedom. Unlike the evangelical dissenters who campaigned against establishments on the principle of equal rights under law, without respect to different religious beliefs, Quakers increasingly saw that they needed a religious liberty from law precisely on account of their distinct religious views. In particular, if the establishments were defeated on the egalitarian principles asserted by evangelical dissenters, the Quakers might lose any possibility of even legislative exemptions from law. Accordingly, the Quakers (and the other peace churches) largely dropped out of the organized agitation against establishments. For example, in New England many Quakers refused to sign an antiestablishment petition circulated by Baptists.[7] In Virginia, although Quakers petitioned against an establishment on at least one occasion (in November 1785), the Quaker leadership more typically petitioned for conscientious exemptions from militia duty and from other legal requirements incompatible with Quaker beliefs.[8] Thus, in the catalyst of the Revolution, Quakers and evangelical dissenters came to perceive that they needed distinctly different types of religious liberty, and as a result Quakers withdrew from the campaign against establishments, leaving evangelical dissenters to carry this struggle forward.[9]

[7] McLoughlin, *New England Dissent*, 1: 277, 595, 607, note 33.
[8] On November 14, 1785, some Quakers submitted two versions of a memorial against an assessment. The Memorial of the People Called Quakers (Nov. 14, 1785), Virginia State Library, Richmond, microfilm, Misc. Ms. 425. For the more typical Quaker petitioning, see Robert Pleasants, Letterbook and Bundle of Letters, Valentine Museum, Richmond, Valentine Shelf No. 289.6y F912, vols. 3 and 4 (typescript copy of originals in possession of Haverford College Library, on loan from Baltimore Orthodox Friends).
[9] Philip Hamburger, "Religious Liberty and Constitutional Language" (manuscript).

The evangelical dissenters who worked against establishments in the late eighteenth century were united by some assumptions about the need to limit government. Most immediately, these evangelical dissenters hoped to secure constitutional provisions preventing civil government from legislating clerical salaries or other special privileges on account of religious differences. More broadly, underlying this goal were a host of beliefs drawn from earlier antiestablishment literature, such as that civil government could not give authority to a higher realm and that civil government lacked the jurisdiction to legislate over Christ's kingdom. Having these views, the late eighteenth-century dissenters who campaigned against religious establishments did not attempt to limit churches or to deprive government of the moral influence of Christianity. Instead, they hoped to constrain governmental and especially legislative power.

Specifically, the numerous demands of these dissenters can be understood as variations on two basic requests. Of course, in agitating for a freedom from establishments, dissenters relied upon far more than two arguments or principles. For example, dissenters reasoned from Biblical texts, natural rights, the limited purpose and power of government, economics, and prudence. Yet these were not the practical, legal ends demanded by the dissenters who struggled against establishments. Ultimately, notwithstanding their multitudinous arguments, these dissenters sought constitutional provisions securing their conceptions of religious liberty, and their demands for these provisions tended to fall into two categories, both of which limited government but in conceptually different ways. One type of demand, for equal rights, was a request for a freedom from laws that discriminated on the basis of religious differences. The other type of demand, for a freedom from legislation that took cognizance of religion, was a request that law take no notice of religion.[10] In contrast to a separation of church and state, which con-

---

[10] Of course, some constitutional clauses against establishments did not fit into either of the two general categories discussed here. Most notably, clauses in some state constitutions specified that government could not compel individuals to pay, without their consent, for the support of ministers and churches. Such clauses departed from the standard pattern of antiestablishment demands. Yet they did so for a reason. They were antiestablishment clauses that mimicked the logic of free exercise provisions. In effect, they portrayed establishment privileges as constraints on belief—an approach with obvious rhetorical advantages. This type of attempt to treat support for an establishment as part of the more basic religious freedom from compulsion is most clearly evident in the New Jersey Constitution

strained both institutions, these antiestablishment demands for religious liberty constrained only government.

Variations

Different evangelical dissenters opposed establishments in slightly different ways, and it is amid the variety of their demands that common patterns are discernible. Although some evangelical dissenters occasionally departed from their shared standards and few fully lived up to any professed standard, the vast majority made clear that the legal guarantees they sought embodied some version of either equal rights under law or a freedom from legislation taking cognizance of religion.[11]

Dissenters often asserted their freedom against establishments in generic terms—such as "rights of conscience" or "freedom of religion"— even though they ultimately sought more precisely defined constitutional limitations.[12] For example, in the South Carolina Assembly, a Pres-

---

of 1776. In its article protecting the right of worship, this constitution also stated that no person shall ever "be compelled to attend any place of worship, contrary to his own faith and judgment; nor shall any person . . . ever be obliged to pay tithes, taxes, or any other rates . . . for the maintenance of any minister or ministry, contrary to what he believes to be right." N.J. Const., Art. 18 (1776). Only in the next article did the constitution declare "That there shall be no establishment of any one religious sect . . . in preference to another." Ibid., Art. 19.

[11] For more details, see Hamburger, "Equality and Diversity," 346–353. Incidentally, Steven D. Smith points out that the late eighteenth-century politicians who drafted the U.S. Constitution may have shared only very limited assumptions about religious liberty and therefore may have drafted it with words that were conveniently imprecise. Smith, *Foreordained Failure: The Quest for a Constitutional Principle of Religious Freedom*, 19–22, 26–27 (New York: Oxford University Press, 1995); Smith, "The Religion Clauses in Constitutional Scholarship," *Notre Dame Law Review*, 74: 1040–1041 (1999). This is a valuable caution, which has some relevance for the eighteenth-century phrases that were used to refer to a generic religious liberty, the most common such phrase being "the rights of conscience." As illustrated in the text, however, various other phrases were frequently used to allude to specific types of religious liberty and even to quite refined variants of these.

[12] According to a minority of the Pennsylvania ratification convention, "[t]he right of conscience shall be held inviolable." "The Address and Reasons of Dissent of the Minority." Merrill Jensen, ed., *Documentary History of the Ratification of the Constitution*, 2: 623 (Madison: State Historical Society of Wisconsin, 1976). Similarly, in 1780 Backus wrote: "Our Convention at Cambridge passed an act last Wednesday to establish an article in our bill of rights which evidently infringes upon the rights of conscience." McLoughlin, *New England Dissent*, 1: 604. Also in Massachusetts, Joseph Hawley wrote: "Pray give over the impossible (task) of endeavoring to make a religious establishment, (consistent) with the unalienable Rights of Conscience." Hawley, "Protest to the Constitutional Convention of 1780," in Mary C. Clune, ed., "Joseph Hawley's Criticism of the Constitution of Massachusetts," *Smith College Studies in History*, 3: 50 (1917). According to Leland, "[t]he question

byterian who advocated equal rights on behalf of a coalition of dissenting groups, the Rev. William Tennent, argued that "[m]y first, and most capital reason, against all religious establishments is, that *they are an infringement of Religious Liberty.*"[13] Members of establishments and even many dissenters had often used this sort of phrase more narrowly to refer to a freedom from penalties. Yet then, as now, "liberty" had layers of meaning, and many dissenters such as Tennent also described themselves as seeking religious liberty when they condemned the unequal privileges enjoyed by establishments.

Although dissenters often argued in terms of the appealing rhetoric of liberty, they also enunciated their demands in more precise terms— most commonly in terms of some degree of equality. For example, many claimed equal liberty or an equality of religious liberty. Thus Samuel Stillman—a prominent Baptist with a fashionable Boston congregation—preached in a Massachusetts election sermon that the governor should secure to all peaceable Christians "the uninterrupted enjoyment of equal religious liberty." Even this language, however, could be ambiguous, for it could refer either to the equal natural right of free exercise (a freedom from government penalty) or to a broader, antiestablishment liberty involving equal legal rights (a freedom from both penalty and unequal privileges). Stillman, however, clarified that, for him, "equal religious liberty" was the latter—an equality of all rights held under civil law without regard to religious differences: "The authority by which he [i.e., the 'magistrate'] acts he derives alike from *all the people*, [and] consequently he should exercise that authority *equally* for the benefit of

---

is, 'Are the rights of conscience alienable, or inalienable?'" *The Rights of Conscience Inalienable* (1791), in *The Writings of the Late Elder John Leland*, 180. Although Leland discussed rights of conscience as inalienable and natural, he had a broad view of them, apparently considering them a freedom from all legislation concerning religion, including taxes in support of religion. In many writings the significance attached to the phrase "the rights of conscience" is less clear.

[13] William Tennent, *Mr. Tennent's Speech on the Dissenting Petition, Delivered in the House of Assembly, Charles-Town, South-Carolina, Jan. 11, 1777*, 5 (1777). Tennent made it clear that he understood religious liberty in terms of equality. See Brinsfield, *Religion and Politics in Colonial South Carolina*, 107–108, 116, 120–122. Incidentally, when recalling how he had collected signatures for the petition supported by Tennent, Colonel William Hill later wrote of himself that "in order to get as many names as possible—(and not believing in the doctrine of the turks that women have no souls) he got the women to sign their names with the men." Ibid., 111.

all, without any respect to their different religious principles." Indeed, Stillman wanted *"equal treatment of all the citizens."*[14] As his fellow Baptist, Isaac Backus, boldly wrote: "I challenge all our opponents to prove, if they can, that we have ever desired any other religious liberty, than to have this partiality entirely removed."[15]

One version of the equality standard required an equality of "civil rights." For example, the Pennsylvania Constitution of 1776 declared: "Nor can any man, who acknowledges the being of a God, be justly deprived or abridged of any civil right as a citizen, on account of his religious sentiments or peculiar mode of religious worship."[16] Similarly, at least with respect to a narrower class of individuals, the New Jersey Constitution stated "[t]hat there shall be no establishment of any one religious sect in this Province, in preference to another; and that no Protestant inhabitant of this Colony shall be denied the enjoyment of any civil right, merely on account of his religious principles; but that all persons, professing a belief in the faith of any Protestant sect . . . shall fully and

---

[14] Samuel Stillman, *A Sermon*, 29 (Boston: 1779). Stillman also said that "as all men are equal by nature, so when they enter into a state of civil government, they are entitled *precisely* to the same rights and privileges; or to an *equal degree* of political happiness." Ibid., 11. Other uses of the phrase "equal liberty" or "equal religious liberty" to refer to equal rights under law are quite common. In Virginia, Baptists petitioned that "the full equal and impartial Liberty of all Denominations, may be indubitably secured." Petition of the Ministers and Messengers of the Baptist Denomination, Assembled at Noel's Meeting House in Essex County on May 3, 1783 (May 30, 1783), Virginia State Library, microfilm, Misc. Ms. 425. Baptists also told the legislature: "Your Memorialists have hoped for a removal of their Complaints, and the enjoyment of equal liberty; . . . And that in every Act, the bright beams of equal Liberty, and Impartial Justice may shine." Memorial of the Committee of Several Baptist Associations, Assembled at Dover Meeting House, Oct. 9, 1784 (Nov. 11, 1784), Virginia State Library, microfilm, Misc. Ms. 425. Similarly, the Presbytery of Hanover, Virginia, optimistically interpreted the 1776 Declaration of Rights as "declaring that equal liberty, as well religious as civil, shall be universally extended to the good people of this country." Memorial of the Presbytery of Hanover to the General Assembly of Virginia (April 25, 1777), in William Addison Blakely, ed., *American State Papers Bearing on Sunday Legislation*, 96 (Washington, D.C.: Religious Liberty Association, 1911). In contrast, the July 1789 House Committee Report on the Bill of Rights may have equated equal rights of conscience merely with the natural right of free exercise: "No religion shall be established by law, nor shall the equal rights of conscience be infringed." House Committee Report of July 28, 1789, in Helen E. Veit, Kenneth R. Bowling, and Charlene Bangs Bickford, eds., *Creating the Bill of Rights: The Documentary Record from the First Federal Congress*, 30 (Baltimore: Johns Hopkins University Press, 1991).

[15] Isaac Backus, *An Appeal to the People* (Boston: 1780), in William G. McLoughlin, ed., *Isaac Backus on Church, State, and Calvinism*, 396 (Cambridge, Mass.: Belknap Press, 1968).

[16] Pa. Const. of 1776, Art. 2.

freely enjoy every privilege and immunity, enjoyed by others their fellow subjects."[17] These pronouncements against discriminatory denials of any "civil right" were attractively simple. Yet they did not become popular because the term "civil rights" increasingly was understood to refer only to the natural rights held under the laws of civil government rather than to all rights held under such laws. In other words, it increasingly seemed to refer only to such freedom from government penalty as was permitted by law.[18] Accordingly, the provisions that referred to equal civil rights did not prohibit unequal establishment privileges as clearly as they were designed to do.

Therefore, a more common variant of the equality standard deliberately employed the vocabulary of natural law to distinguish between natural rights and the privileges or benefits of civil government. Natural law theory posited a largely hypothetical condition, the state of nature, which was the condition in which individuals had no common superior—in which there was no civil government. Natural rights were portions of the liberty enjoyed in the state of nature—portions of the freedom from civil government and its constraints or penalties—and, as already observed, civil rights (at least as increasingly understood) were such natural rights as continued to be enjoyed after the imposition of the laws of civil government. In contrast to natural rights were the privileges, benefits, emoluments, or favors of government—rights that could exist only under government and that, presupposing government, could not exist in the state of nature. It was such privileges—notably, government-supported salaries for ministers—that distinguished American establishments. Therefore, to prohibit establishments in utterly unequivocal language, dissenters often sought constitutional provisions that required equality (or nondiscrimination) for both the natural right of religious liberty and any privileges.

---

[17] N.J. Const. of 1776, Art. 19. The 1778 South Carolina Constitution provided that Protestants "shall enjoy equal religious and civil privileges." S.C. Const. of 1778, Art. 38. In this context the word "privileges" appears to have been interchangeable with "rights." The Presbytery of Hanover, Virginia, asked the legislature "to restrain the vicious and to encourage the virtuous, by wholesome laws equally extending to every individual." Memorial of the Presbytery of Hanover to the General Assembly of Virginia (Oct. 24, 1776), in *American State Papers*, 94; see also the same language in the Memorial of April 25, 1777, in ibid., 97.

[18] For the changing understanding of "civil rights," see Hamburger, "Equality and Diversity," 386.

This bifurcated approach, which specified that both the natural right and any privileges had to be equal, was very common. In particular, although many Americans used the words "liberty" and "privilege" interchangeably to denote either a natural right or a right existing only under civil government, they often employed these words to distinguish between the two types of rights and demanded not only the natural right of religious liberty but also equal privileges. For example, some dissenters in Virginia petitioned that, being "[f]ully Persuaded . . . That the Religion of JESUS CHRIST may and ought to be Committed to the Protection Guidance and Blessing of its Divine Author, & needs not the Interposition of any Human Power for its Establishment & Support[,] We most earnestly desire and Pray that not only an Universal Toleration may take Place, but that all the Subjects of this Free State may be put upon the same footing and enjoy equal Liberties and Privileges."[19] For purposes of this bifurcated analysis, Americans also used the words "discrimination" and "preference." Thus in New York, where antiestablishment sentiment found strength in the state's religious diversity, the 1777 Constitution prohibited an establishment by requiring that "the free exercise and enjoyment of religious profession and worship, without discrimination or preference, shall forever hereafter be allowed."[20] Not only would the natural right be shielded from discriminatory restraints but also preferences based on religious differences would be prohibited.[21]

In contrast to these versions of the demand for equal rights was a

[19] Petition of Divers of the Freeholders and Other Free Inhabitants of Amherst County (Nov. 1, 1779), Virginia State Library, microfilm, Misc. Ms. 425.

[20] N.Y. Const. of 1777, Art. XXXVIII. In 1790 South Carolina employed the same language as New York to prohibit an establishment. S.C. Const. of 1790, Art. 8, §1.

[21] The bifurcated analysis had many variants. In 1788 New York's ratification convention proposed as an amendment to the U.S. Constitution: "That the People have an equal, natural and unalienable right, freely and peaceably to Exercise their Religion according to the dictates of Conscience, and that no Religious Sect or Society ought to be favoured or established by Law in preference of others." Helen E. Veit et al., eds., *Creating the Bill of Rights: The Documentary Record from the First Federal Congress*, 22 (Baltimore: Johns Hopkins University Press, 1991). Virginia's proposal concluded with a similar guarantee: "[A]ll men have an equal, natural and unalienable right to the free exercise of religion according to the dictates of conscience, and that no particular religious sect of society ought to be favored or established, by Law, in preference to others." Ibid., 19. In Delaware, section 3 of the Declaration of Rights stated that Christians "ought . . . to enjoy equal Rights and Privileges in this State, unless, under Colour of Religion, any man disturb the Peace, Happiness or Safety of Society." Del. Const. of 1776, Bill of Rights, §3. See also N.J. Const. of 1776, Art. 19, and proposal of 1788 North Carolina ratification convention. Jonathan Elliot, *Debates in the Several State Conventions*, 4: 244 (Washington, D.C.: 1854).

position that went further in limiting the legislative power of civil government—an approach that denied civil government any jurisdiction over religion. As put by a leading ally of dissenters in Virginia, James Madison, "in matters of Religion no mans right is abridged by the institution of Civil Society, and . . . Religion is wholly exempt from its cognizance."[22] Often the dissenters who took this approach emphasized not government in general, but civil law. Thus in 1791 the peripatetic Baptist, John Leland, entitled one of his most famous pamphlets *The Rights of Conscience Inalienable, and Therefore, Religious Opinions Not Cognizable by Law.*[23] In his struggle against the New England establishments, Leland continued to assert this standard, as when in 1794 he wrote: "The rights of conscience should always be considered inalienable—religious opinions are not the objects of civil government, nor any way under its jurisdiction. Laws should only respect civil society; then if men are disturbers they ought to be punished."[24]

[22] James Madison, *Memorial and Remonstrance* (1785), in *Papers of James Madison,* 8: 78.
[23] Leland also wrote: "The principle, that civil rulers have nothing to do with religion in their official capacities, is as much interwoven in the Baptist plan, as Phydias's name was in the shield. The legitimate powers of government extend only to punish men for working ill to their neighbors, and no way affect the rights of conscience." *The Virginia Chronicle* (1790), in *The Writings of the Late Elder John Leland,* 117–118. According to Isaac Backus, in a case arising in Attleboro, Massachusetts, "[t]he chief pleas for the appellant were that RELIGION was prior to all states and kingdoms in the world and therefore could not in its nature be subject to human laws." Backus, *A Door Opened for Christian Liberty* (Boston: 1783), in McLoughlin, ed., *Isaac Backus on Church, State, and Calvinism,* 432. In Virginia an antiestablishment petition urged: "Civil Government & Religion are, and ought to be, Independent of Each other. The one has for its object a proper Regulation of the External conduct of men . . . ; [the other] our internal or spiritual welfare & is beyond the reach of human Laws." Petition from Botetourt County (Nov. 29, 1785), as quoted by Rhys Isaac, *The Transformation of Virginia 1740–1790,* 291 (Williamsburg: Institute for Early American History and Culture, 1982). Isaac interprets the word "independent" as suggesting "separateness," but it seems to have referred to the traditional distinction between the jurisdictions of the two kingdoms.
[24] "Jack Nips," *The Yankee Spy: Calculated for the Religious Meridian of Massachusetts, but Will Answer for New Hampshire, Connecticut, and Vermont, without any Material Alterations* (1794), in *The Writings of the Late Elder John Leland,* 228. Establishment ministers deliberately adopted rhetoric similar to that of dissenters but in ways that clearly had different implications. For example, in Vermont an establishment minister, the Rev. Peter Powers, preached in his election sermon: "Once more here, ecclesiastical power is wholly of a spiritual nature, and no ways connected with either civil or military power. Christ's *kingdom* is *not of this world,* not of a worldly nature. The constitution is spiritual, *the covenant of grace.* The laws are spiritual, and the ordinances of a spiritual nature, given us in the word of truth, the great statutes of heaven; and the punishments are spiritual, being the sentences of Christ's mouth, who is the only king, Lord and law-giver of his church, and pronounced against offenders in his name, by his ministers. Therefore the civil magistrate has nothing

The First Amendment

Among the many versions of the no-cognizance standard, the one adopted in the First Amendment to the U.S. Constitution was the most prominent. It also probably was the most carefully drafted.

Like some earlier constitutional provisions concerning religion, the First Amendment drew upon the bifurcated approach that distinguished between natural rights and government privileges. As indicated above, the bifurcated analysis took various forms. Some state constitutions, for example, protected the natural right in one clause and proscribed unequal privileges in a second. Other constitutional documents, including New Hampshire's 1787 proposal to amend the U.S. Constitution and, later, the First Amendment, took a similar bifurcated approach but, in place of the clause prohibiting unequal privileges, more generally forbade legislation "touching" or "respecting" religion.[25]

A prohibition, however, of all legislation with respect to religion may have been considered too broad by some dissenters. In particular, it might have precluded legislation protecting the free exercise of religion or otherwise concerning religion without establishing it. Americans of many persuasions, both dissenters and members of establishments, had argued that not only constitutions but also, more generally, governments should protect individuals in the free exercise of their religion.[26]

---

to do with this government. Only the civil rights, privileges and properties of the church are to be secured and defended by the civil powers." Powers, *Jesus Christ the True King and Head of Government: A Sermon,* 15 (Newburyport: 1778). Of course, these privileges and properties were neither equal nor negligible. They were the essence of the establishment. Thus, while conceding much to dissenting ideas, Powers justified the establishment in Vermont. Although he disclaimed any connection between civil and ecclesiastical power and held that "the civil magistrate has nothing to do" with Christ's kingdom, he refrained from saying that the civil magistrate had nothing to do with the church, the civil benefits of religion, or the civil privileges and property of the Congregational churches.

[25] The New Hampshire ratification convention proposed that "Congress shall make no Laws touching Religion, or to infringe the rights of Conscience." Veit, Bowling, and Bickford, eds., *Creating the Bill of Rights,* 17. Typically, as has been seen, it was dissenters who sought a prohibition of legislation with respect to religion, but, for purposes of the federal government, this position of dissenters may have also appealed to state establishments. See note 40 below.

[26] For example, the president of Princeton, John Witherspoon (who thought that "[t]he magistrates . . . have a right to instruct, but not to constrain") argued: "At present, as things are situated, one of the most important duties of the magistracy is to protect the rights of conscience." Jack Scott, ed., *An Annotated Edition of Lectures on Moral Philosophy by John Witherspoon,* 160–161 (lecture XIV) (Newark: University of Delaware Press, 1982).

They thereby in effect added a caveat to the commonplace that government was created only to protect civil or temporal interests. In the words of some of Virginia's Presbyterians in 1785, "The end of civil government is security to the temporal liberty and property of mankind, and to protect them in the free exercise of religion."[27] Therefore, when, in opposition to establishments, various dissenters asserted that government should not make laws taking cognizance of religion, some of these dissenters—including many Presbyterians in Virginia—hastened to add in qualification that government should, of course, be able to provide protection for the free exercise of religion.

Presbyterians particularly emphasized this perspective, for it allowed them, even as they opposed an establishment, to persist in their belief that civil government should protect the church—albeit now by protecting the free exercise of religion rather than by granting special privileges.[28] For example, as early as 1777 a petition from the Presbytery of Hanover asked that "the civil magistrates no otherwise interfere [in

---

[27] Memorial of the Presbyterians of Virginia (Aug. 13, 1785), in *American State Papers*, 113.

[28] This was not exclusively a Presbyterian position. Thomas Paine wrote: "As to religion, I hold it to be the indispensable duty of all government, to protect all conscientious professors thereof, and I know of no other business which government hath to do therewith." *Common Sense* (1776), in Paine, *Collected Writings*, 43 (New York: Library of America, 1995). A 1785 petition from Rockbridge, Virginia, requested: "Let the Ministers of the Gospel of all denominations enjoy the Privileges common to every good Citizen protect them in their religious exercises in the Person and Property and Contracts and that we humbly conceive is all they are entitled to and all a Legislature has power to grant." Petition from Rockbridge County, Virginia, in H. Eckenrode, *Separation of Church and State in Virginia*, 97 (Richmond: Superintendent of Public Printing, 1910). See also petition of October 16, 1776, in Charles F. James, *Documentary History of the Struggle for Religious Liberty in Virginia*, 69 (Lynchberg: J. P. Bell Co., 1900).

In related language Americans could request that government equally protect individuals in their religious liberty. For example, the Presbytery of Hanover, Virginia, wrote that the legislature should be "[t]he common guardian and equal protector of every class of citizens in their religious as well as civil rights." Memorial of the Presbytery of Hanover to the General Assembly of Virginia (May 1784), in *American State Papers*, 103. An Antifederalist minority in the Maryland ratification convention proposed as an amendment to the Constitution: "That there be no national religion established by law; but that all persons be equally entitled to protection in their religious liberty" (April 21, 1788), Elliot, *Debates*, 2: 553. Of course, Federalists argued that, even without a bill of rights, the Constitution provided equal protection: "Partiality to any sect, or ill treatment of any, is neither in the least warranted by the constitution, nor compatible with the general spirit of toleration; an equal security of civil and religious rights, is therefore given to all denominations, without any formal stipulations; which, indeed, might suggest an idea, that such an equality was doubtful." Nicholas Collin, "Remarks on the Amendments to the Federal Constitution" (No. 9), in *Federal Gazette*, No. 42 (Philadelphia: Nov. 18, 1788).

religion], than to protect them all [i.e., 'every individual'] in the full and free exercise of their several modes of worship."[29] Similarly, in 1785 the Presbyterians of Virginia petitioned that "it would be an unwarrantable stretch of prerogative in the legislature to make laws concerning it [i.e., religion], except for protection."[30] Further north, where the proximity of the Congregational establishments kept alive more traditional Calvinist hopes for state support, some Presbyterians revealed a hope that government would protect not only the free exercise of religion but also religion itself—in particular, Christianity.[31] In Virginia, however, many Presbyterians—at least many of the laity—felt their minority status and either specified that government should do no more than protect the free exercise of religion or else conveniently left unmentioned what sort of protection they had in mind.

This Presbyterian version of the no-cognizance standard or some-

[29] Memorial of the Presbytery of Hanover to the General Assembly of Virginia (April 25, 1777), in *American State Papers*, 97.

[30] Memorial of the Presbyterians of Virginia to the General Assembly (Aug. 13, 1785), in *American State Papers*, 114.

[31] In particular, many Presbyterians in the New York and Pennsylvania regions wanted government to promote and, in this sense, protect religion rather than just the free exercise of religion—provided the government did not discriminate among Christian or at least Protestant sects. For example, the New York and Philadelphia Synod of the Presbyterian Church stated in 1792 that "Civil Magistrates may not assume to themselves the administration of the word and sacraments . . . or, in the least, interfere in matters of faith. Yet, as nursing fathers, it is the duty of civil magistrates to protect the church of our common Lord, without giving the preference to any denomination of Christians above the rest." *The Constitution of the Presbyterian Church in the United States of America*, 35 (1792). In the introduction to their 1787 draft, the Synod had revealed some sympathy for the more liberal position: "They do not even wish to see any religious constitution aided by the civil power, further than may be necessary for protection and security, and, at the same time, may be equal and common to all others." *A Drought of the Form of the Government and Discipline of the Presbyterian Church in the United States of America*, iii (1787). Indeed, earlier, in 1783, the Synod of New York and Philadelphia declared: "It having been represented to Synod, that the Presbyterian Church suffers greatly in the opinion of other denominations, from an apprehension that they hold intolerant principles, the Synod do . . . declare, that they ever have, and still do renounce and abhor the principles of intolerance; and . we do believe that every peaceable member of society ought to be protected in the full and free exercise of their religion." *Records of the Presbyterian Church in the United States of America*, 499 (1904), quoted in James H. Smylie, "Protestant Clergy, the First Amendment and Beginnings of a Constitutional Debate, 1781–91" in Elwyn A. Smith, ed., *Religious Liberty in the United States: The Development of Church-State Thought since the Revolutionary Era*, 116, 141–142 (Philadelphia: Fortress Press, 1972). Concerning Presbyterians in Virginia, see Thomas E. Buckley, *Church and State in Revolutionary Virginia, 1776–1787*, 177 (Charlottesville: University Press of Virginia, 1977). See also David Parsons, *A Sermon*, 13 (Boston: 1788). In general, see McLoughlin, *New England Dissent*, 1: 610.

thing similar to it seems to have caught the attention of James Madison. During the mid-1780s some Episcopalians in Madison's home state attempted to resurrect the Virginia establishment—no longer in a narrowly Anglican form but as an incorporation of the Episcopalian clergy and an ecumenical assessment in support of Christians in general. Some Presbyterians, especially the Presbyterian clergy, were willing to join Episcopalians in supporting a version of this nondenominational assessment, as the Hanover Presbytery revealed in its petitions of 1784. Significantly, these petitions refrained from taking the Presbyterian antiestablishment position that the legislature ought to make no laws regarding religion, except to protect its free exercise.[32] Many other Presbyterians, however—mostly, members of the laity—and even substantial numbers of Episcopalians declined to support the coalition on behalf of a Christian assessment. Accordingly, in the struggle against the revival of an establishment on an ecumenical basis, Madison apparently found allies among most Baptists and many lay Presbyterians and Episcopalians.[33] In this context, in November 1784, when the House of Delegates considered an assessment bill that "comprehends Christians alone and obliges other sects to contribute to its maintenance," Madison reported to Richard Henry Lee that there was opposition both on the ground that the bill violated the Virginia Declaration of Rights and "on the general principle that no Religious Estab[lishmen]ts was within the purview of Civil authority."[34] Like the Presbyterian antiestablishment position, this

---

[32] Memorials of the Presbytery of Hanover to the General Assembly of Virginia (May and October 1784), in *American State Papers*, 100–111.

[33] Buckley, *Church and State in Revolutionary Virginia*, 138–139. In 1810 Robert Baylor Semple—the Baptists' historian of their churches in Virginia—wrote: "The Baptists, we believe, were the only sect who plainly remonstrated. Of some others, it is said, that the laity and ministry were at variance upon the subject, so as to paralyze their exertions either for or against the bill. These remarks, by the by, apply only to religious societies, acting as such. Individuals of all sects and parties joined in the opposition." Semple, *History of the Rise and Progress of the Baptist in Virginia*, 72–73.

[34] Letter of James Madison to Richard Henry Lee (Nov. 14, 1784), in *Papers of James Madison*, 9: 430. He continued by pointing out that the majority in favor of the assessment "was produced by a Coalition between the Episcopal & Presbyterian Sects. A Memorial presented since the vote by the Clergy of the latter shews that a Schism will take place. They do not deny but rather betray a desire that an Assessment may be estabt. but protest ag[ain]st any which does not embrace all Religions, and will not coincide with the Decl[aration] of Rights." Ibid., 430–431. Later, Madison's letters recorded how the Presbyterian clergy came around to the position of the laity. Letter of James Madison to James Monroe (April 12, 1785), in *Papers of James Madison*, 8: 261; Letter of James Madison to James Monroe

general principle permitted some legislation concerning religion, and on this principle, at least according to Madison, his allies opposed the assessment.[35]

Although Madison joined forces with dissenters who held that religious establishments were beyond the purview of civil authority, he apparently considered his own position to be slightly different. In his notes for the debates on the 1784 assessment bill, he more broadly wrote, "*Rel[igion]:* not within purview of Civil Authority."[36] Similarly, when, a year later, Madison wrote his *Memorial and Remonstrance* in opposition to an ameliorated general assessment bill "establishing a Provision for Teachers of the Christian Religion," he emphasized the unqualified character of his claim, maintaining "that in matters of Religion, no mans right is abridged by the institution of Civil Society and that Religion is wholly exempt from its cognizance."[37]

Significantly, this unqualified prohibition was not what Madison proposed or what Congress included in the U.S. Bill of Rights. In June 1789, when Madison introduced the constitutional amendments that became the Bill of Rights, he proposed: "The civil rights of none shall be abridged on account of religious belief or worship, nor shall any national religion be established, nor shall the full and equal rights of conscience be in any manner, or any pretext infringed."[38] This was a far cry from Madison's position in 1785 that religion was "wholly exempt" from the cognizance of civil society. In the months that followed, as the House of Representatives considered various phrases, only one, put forward by Congressman Samuel Livermore on August 15, came close to Madison's perspective in 1785. Livermore suggested: "Congress shall make no laws touching religion or the rights of conscience."[39] Although a committee of the whole House approved Livermore's language, the House did not.

(May 29, 1785), in ibid., 286; Letter of James Madison to Thomas Jefferson (Aug. 20, 1785), ibid., 345.

[35] Of course, the position described by Madison and that taken by antiestablishment Presbyterians could have slightly different practical implications because one excluded religious establishments from the cognizance of government and the other defined the power of government in relation to religion more narrowly to include only the protection of the free exercise of religion.

[36] Papers of James Madison, 8: 198.

[37] *Memorial and Remonstrance* (ca. June 20, 1785), in *Papers of James Madison* 8: 299.

[38] James Madison's Resolutions (June 8, 1789), from *N.Y. Daily Advertizer* (June 12, 1789), in Veit, Bowling, and Bickford, eds., *Creating the Bill of Rights,* 12.

[39] *N.Y. Daily Advertizer* (Aug. 17, 1789), in *Creating the Bill of Rights,* 150.

After considering other proposals, both the House and the Senate eventually adopted the words currently in the Constitution: "Congress shall make no law respecting an establishment of religion."[40] These words were similar to those Madison had used to characterize his allies in Virginia, and they identified a position from which he had once sought to distinguish his own.

Whatever Madison thought about the words finally adopted in the First Amendment, he clearly did not mind language less severe than that which he had used in 1785. Perhaps he did not think the precise wording mattered much. More certainly, he assumed that a federal bill of rights would be more valuable for political than legal reasons.[41] Yet it is also possible that, in the years since 1785, Madison had slightly modified his views about the appropriate prohibition on establishments. In particular, he may have learned some moderation from religious minorities— whether his fellow opponents of establishments or the Quakers—who, in differing ways, had reason to fear a constitutional proscription so broad that it would stand in the way of all legislation taking cognizance

---

[40] First Amendment (1791) to U.S. Constitution. Prior to the adoption of this language, Congressman Fisher Ames proposed the words: "Congress shall make no law establishing religion." Marc M. Arkin, "Regionalism and the Religion Clauses: The Contribution of Fisher Ames," *Buffalo Law Review*, 47: 764, 789 (1999).

Incidentally, some scholars go so far as to argue that the words of the First Amendment about an establishment of religion merely precluded federal interference with state establishments. See, e.g., Joseph M. Snee, "Religious Disestablishment and the Fourteenth Amendment," *Washington Univ. Law Quarterly*, 371 (1954); Smith, *Foreordained Failure*, 22–26; Steven D. Smith, *The Constitution and the Pride of Reason*, 31–47 (New York: Oxford University Press, 1998); Kurt T. Lash, "The Second Adoption of the Establishment Clause: The Rise of the Nonestablishment Principle," in 27 Arizona L. J. 1085 (1995). Yet the establishment clause also clearly stood in the way of a federal establishment. The relations between civil government and religion had been discussed in jurisdictional terms since early Christian times, and therefore the jurisdictional wording of a provision prohibiting an establishment can hardly be taken to suggest that the provision was not substantive. As seen above in the text, the notion that civil government had no cognizance of religion— or at least no cognizance of establishments of religion—was understood as a substantive claim against establishments. Versions of the no-cognizance standard had been much discussed as barriers to state establishments, and it therefore is difficult to believe that when Americans employed such a standard in the federal constitution, they did not understand it to prohibit state establishments. As one might expect, there is no evidence that advocates of an enumerated right against a federal establishment felt that the First Amendment failed to accomplish this goal. On the contrary, Americans (including religious dissenters) were confident that the amendment prohibited a federal establishment of religion.

[41] Paul Finkelman, "Madison's Reluctant Paternity of the Bill of Rights," *Supreme Court Review*, 301 (1990).

of religion. Even the evangelical opponents of establishments had no desire for an antiestablishment clause so strong as to forbid laws protecting their property or recognizing their marriages, and Quakers hardly wanted a guarantee that would have nullified legislative exemptions. Whatever the basis of his decision, Madison reconciled himself to language less sweeping than that he had used in 1785, and Congress adopted a moderated version of the no-cognizance standard, which did not forbid all legislation respecting religion.

Thus it is possible to ascertain the constitutional demands of dissenters and their allies with enough precision to observe that their demands typically had little to do with a separation of church and state. The religious dissenters who participated in the campaign against establishments and whose claims seem to have affected the wording of the constitutional guarantees against establishments made demands for a religious liberty that limited civil government, especially civil legislation, rather than for a religious liberty conceived as a separation of church and state. Moreover, in attempting to prohibit the civil legislation that would establish religion, they sought to preserve the power of government to legislate on religion in other ways. Accordingly, American constitutions, whether those of the states or that of the United States, said nothing about separation. Nor should any of this be a surprise. All of the dissenting denominations that struggled against establishments had clergy, structures of authority, and other conventional characteristics of institutional churches. Even highly decentralized denominations, such as the Baptists, typically deferred to their preachers and elders, consulted with their associations, and vigorously adhered to their congregational authority and discipline.[42] Thus, while a few exceptional, anticlerical thinkers in Europe urged versions of a separation of church and state, and while some establishment ministers in America abused their opponents by attributing to them a desire for a sort of separation, the dissenters who campaigned against American establishments, including Baptists, usually revealed little desire for separation of church and state or any other concept that constrained clergy and churches. Instead, these dissenters typically sought constitutional limitations on the power of government, particularly on government's power to legislate an establishment.

[42] Gregory A. Wills, *Democratic Religion—Freedom, Authority, and Church Discipline in the Baptist South, 1785–1900,* chapter 1 (New York: Oxford University Press, 1997).

II

EARLY NINETEENTH-CENTURY
REPUBLICANISM

I N THE opening years of the nineteenth century some Republicans, including eventually Thomas Jefferson, began to advocate versions of
separation. In so doing, they intimated for the first time that the religious
liberty protected by American constitutions should be understood as
a separation between religion and government or, at least, between
church and state. Yet the religious dissenters in New England, who still
lived under establishments, did not adopt the Republican ideal of separation or otherwise deviate from their traditional demands for religious
liberty. Accordingly, while Part II of this inquiry must begin to examine
how the constitutional religious liberty of Americans came to be viewed
as a separation, it also must continue to explore the wide gulf between
these concepts.

It is usually assumed that in the period following the adoption of
the Bill of Rights in 1791, Jefferson was the first to give expression to
the hopes of dissenters by expounding the First Amendment as a wall
of separation between church and state. In his letter to the Danbury
Baptist Association, America's most philosophical president is thought
to have penned one of his succinct declarations of American freedom.
Apparently, a brilliant, even profound contribution to American liberty—simultaneously an embodiment of constitutional principles and
an eloquent expression of an original mind—this letter has lent Jefferson's authority as a founder of the nation to separation's status as a constitutional principle.

Yet Jefferson's letter was not entirely a declaration of liberty. Separation was an idea first introduced into American politics by Jefferson's

allies, the Republicans, who used it to elicit popular distaste against Federalist clergymen in their exercise of their religious freedom. The religious dissenters, including the Baptists, sympathized with the Republicans and distrusted Federalists, particularly the Federalist clergy. Yet, when invited by Jefferson to join the Republican demand for separation, the Baptists quietly declined. Much misunderstood, this episode reveals less about the Constitution than about its evolution. In particular, it suggests how separation first became popular among relatively secular, political, and anticlerical Americans, even as it remained disreputable among religious dissenters, who continued patiently to seek the rather different religious liberty they had been demanding for so very long.

5

Demands for Separation: Separating Federalist Clergy from Republican Politics

THE IDEA so frequently portrayed as one of Jefferson's profound contributions to American liberty was introduced into the presidential campaign of 1800 by leading Republican intellectuals as a means with which they hoped simultaneously to attract antiestablishment votes and to browbeat Federalist clergy for preaching about politics. Often assumed to have been a demand for religious liberty, it was also a rather less elevated attempt to deter Federalist clergymen from exercising their freedom of religion and speech. It was, in this respect, a demand that the clergy constrain themselves in the exercise of rights enjoyed by other Americans.

During the election of 1800, Republicans had reason to try to separate Federalist clergymen from politics. Beginning in the 1790s, and now with renewed effort, Federalist ministers inveighed against Jefferson, often from their pulpits, excoriating his infidelity and deism. For some politicians, such as Alexander Hamilton, this onslaught was part of a deliberate plan of "opposing the honest enthusiasm of Religious Opinion to the phrenzy of Political fanaticism."[1] Most clergymen, however, were hardly so calculating. Understanding their religion as a fully integrated part of the life of the nation, and oblivious to the risks to themselves

---

[1] Believing this a measure "of the most precious importance," he also wrote, "We must oppose to political fanaticism religious zeal." Alexander Hamilton, Letter to James McHenry (January–February 1798), and Letter to Timothy Sedgwick (March 1798), as quoted by Charles Ellis Dickson, "Jeremiads in the New American Republic: The Case of National Fasts in the John Adams Administration," in *New England Quarterly*, 60: 192 (1987).

and the country of employing their pulpits for partisan ends, Federalist ministers felt obliged to bring their faith to bear upon party politics, especially against the man who, more than any other American, seemed to regard religion with indifference—who was notorious for apparently suggesting that religion and morality and thus also religion and politics were specialized, less than fully integrated, features of human life.

In defense of Jefferson, Republicans argued that clergymen ought not preach about politics, and eventually, beginning in 1800, some made such arguments in terms of separation—in particular, a separation of religion and politics.[2] Seizing upon the idea of separation—a concept that until 1800 had been unusual and anything but popular—these Republicans elevated it to a political principle. Although establishment ministers had caricatured dissenters as seeking a separation of religion from civil government, and although dissenters had declined to seek separation, Republicans now endorsed it as a means of discouraging Federalist clergy, especially in Congregational New England, from preaching against Jefferson.

Federalist Clergy on the Civil Importance of Religion

Many Federalist clergymen claimed that Jefferson was not a Christian, and they thereby introduced into a national political campaign the old

---

[2] Prior to 1800 Republican objections to the political activities of Federalist clergymen seem to have focused on arguments other than separation. Some of the Jeffersonian criticisms of the late eighteenth century are discussed by Dickson, "Jeremiads in the New American Republic," 187; Donald H. Stewart, *The Opposition Press*, 403–404 (Albany: State University of New York, 1969), notably a series of critiques in the Boston *Independent Chronicle*. For example, in 1796 one writer told the clergy that he had no desire "to deprive you of the rights of Citizens in judging and determining for yourselves on men and measures," but he hoped "your prudence will naturally lead you to distinguish between the patriot and partisan." "A Serious, Candid, and Plain Address, to the Clergy," in ibid., vol. 28, no. 1585 (May 26, 1796). In 1797 a "Friend to the Clergy" advised Federalist ministers: "you were not settled in the Ministry to preach Politics, nor to profane the sacred desk by party rage, therefore, a less attention to politics, and a greater to the religion you profess, would be more congenial to the principles of the gospel, and consequently more useful to the people." "A Friend to the Clergy," "To the Association of Ministers in and about Cambridge," in ibid., vol. 29, no. 1728 (Oct. 12–16, 1797). In Philadelphia the Tammany Society assembled at the "Fish-house" on the Schuylkill, where "having spent the day with innocent mirth and brotherly harmony," and "after partaking of a frugal repast," the members less frugally drank numerous toasts—the predictable culmination of so many American activities—one of which was: "The rights of Conscience—May political tenets never be fulminated from the pulpit, nor religious opinions be enforced by the sword of the law." "Domestic Intelligence," in ibid., vol. 28, no. 1581 (May 12, 1796).

issue of religion's civil importance. Establishment ministers had long asserted that religion was essential to government, but they had done so in English and local American debates about establishments. In the 1790s, however, Federalist clergymen, including many establishment ministers, employed this idea against Republicans, eventually giving it great prominence in the presidential election of 1800. It was this Federalist emphasis on the political importance of religion that would provoke a Republican demand for the separation of religion and politics.

The onslaught against Jefferson began in earnest when Federalist pamphlets charged that Jefferson was a deist and an infidel. William Linn and John Mitchell Mason—the one a Dutch Reformed pastor in New York City, the other a Presbyterian minister of the city's Associate Reformed Church—initiated the assault, and numerous other Federalists quickly joined the fray. Soon Republicans and Federalists were trading insults with abandon, including lurid allegations of an infidelity that extended beyond religion. By the end of the election Republicans (or "Democrats," these being more or less interchangeable party labels) could fairly complain that "President Jefferson has been called an infidel philosopher" and that "the democrats have been called atheists."[3] Indeed, to Republicans it seemed that "[f]or many weeks federalism and Christianity were used synonymously and all advocates for a change of political men and measures were regarded as heretics." In contrast, Federalist clergy could legitimately protest that Republicans had attacked their right to engage in politics. As a result "[a]ll New England" was "agitated with church and state alarms."[4]

---

[3] Abraham Bishop, *Oration Delivered in Wallingford on the 11th of March 1801, before the Republicans of the State of Connecticut, at Their General Thanksgiving, for the Election of Thomas Jefferson,* 87 (New Haven: 1801).

[4] Ibid., 40. In these ways, the attacks upon Jefferson's character, for which the election of 1800 is legendary, were part of a more general controversy about the role of religion in America. Charles F. O'Brien, "The Religious Issue in the Presidential Campaign of 1800," *Essex Institute Historical Collections,* 107: 82 (1971); Norman de Jong, with Jack Van Der Silk, *Separation of Church and State: The Myth Revisited,* 154–163 (Jordan Station, Ontario: Paideia Press, 1985); Mark Noll, *One Nation under God? Christian Faith and Political Action in America,* 75 (San Francisco: Harper & Row, 1988). For a greater emphasis on the election's abusive rhetoric, see, e.g., Charles O. Lerche, Jr., "Jefferson and the Election of 1800: A Case Study in the Political Smear," *William & Mary Quarterly,* 5: 467 (3d ser., 1948); Constance B. Schulz, "'Of Bigotry in Politics and Religion': Jefferson's Religion, the Federalist Press, and the Syllabus," *Virginia Magazine of History and Biography,* 91: 73 (1983); James H. Hutson, "Thomas Jefferson's Letter to the Danbury Baptists: A Controversy Rejoined," in *William & Mary Quarterly,* 56 (no. 4): 781 (3d ser., October 1999).

Although the nation's chief officer possessed little constitutional power over the people's faith, Federalists worried that he could exert a dangerous influence upon religious and moral opinion. One who made this point was an anonymous Federalist who published his pamphlet in Philadelphia and called himself a "Layman"—no doubt to distinguish himself from the establishment ministers of New England. Preparing a foundation for his arguments, he asked the reader to imagine a "familiar." This Republican spirit supposedly whispered in the reader's ear that an infidel president would pose no danger, for, even if inclined to threaten religion, such a president would lack the constitutional power to "meddle" with "our consciences." Thus: "All his power to shake our religious principles, must rest in him, as a man. It is by his converse and writings only, that he is a formidable enemy. By raising him to office, we in no respect enlarge his power." Of course, the "Layman" employed the whisperings of the Republican familiar to set up his real argument—that even without the power to establish "unbelief," the religion of the president had consequences for morality and thus also the nation. In a president, private beliefs became influential. True, "he will not be a Chinese or Russian despot!" Yet, as the "Layman" sarcastically recited:

> He will *only* be looked upon as a sample of his countrymen. His example will *only* be rendered an hundred times more extensive in its influence. Instead of being overlooked as heretofore by the eyes of the multitude, he [will] *only* become incessantly and unboundedly conspicuous. Fashions will take their birth from his elevation; his opinion will be quoted to countenance the audacity of numbers, and an argument will be put into the mouth of those with whom you shall venture to remonstrate on the folly, and to descant on the evils of *unbelief;* an argument which you will find it impossible to elude.[5]

As the Rev. William Linn observed, "the election of any man avowing the principles of Mr. Jefferson" would "destroy religion, introduce immorality, and loosen all the bonds of society."[6]

At one point the "Layman" supposed the familiar to argue that self-interest was an adequate substitute for religion in providing moral direction—"that, though religion be of use, to give the due direction and force

---

[5] A Layman, *The Claims of Thomas Jefferson to the Presidency*, 29, 46, 45 (Philadelphia: 1800).
[6] William Linn, *Serious Considerations on the Election of a President: Addressed to the Citizens of the United States*, 24 (New York: 1800).

to our principles, yet, self-interest, when it chances to impel to the same course of action, with virtue and religion, will, of itself, be strong enough to keep us in the safe and honest path." In response, like so many establishment writers, the "Layman" argued that religion was not only "sacred, and true" but also "necessary": "And why? Does it not impart force and harmony to morals? Does it not inspire . . . a just zeal in the cause of human happiness? Does it not make the hands strong and the heart strenuous, and while it furnishes the only adequate motive, supplies the only certain clue to the great end of individual and national good?" Not only did religion teach "that virtue has a sure and liberal reward, in another state" and "that vice will hereafter meet with condign and inevitable punishment," but also "does it not teach us what virtue is, and what is vice?" Religion provided both a motive for virtue and a clear definition of it that could not be derived from worldly interest. Accordingly, if Americans elected Jefferson, they would endorse the view that religion was unimportant for morality and government. To elect a man of Jefferson's views would be to create a conspicuous and long-lasting "monument of the *nothingness* of piety" and "of its remoteness from the judgments" and "its disconnection with the affairs of mankind."[7] Similarly, the Rev. John Mitchell Mason urged, "By giving your support to Mr. Jefferson, you are about to strip infidelity of its ignominy. . . . By this act, you will proclaim to the whole world . . . that you do not believe it subversive of moral obligation and social purity."[8]

Public indifference to Jefferson's religious views seemed all the more dangerous on account of the common theological assumption that, whereas the sins of individuals were punished in the next world, the

---

[7] A Layman, *The Claims of Thomas Jefferson,* 35–36, 46.

[8] John Mitchell Mason, *The Voice of Warning, to Christians, on the Ensuing Election of a President of the United States,* 35 (New York: 1800). Federalists assumed that religion might seem particularly important in an election as a guarantee of "political rectitude." Of course, Republicans ridiculed Federalist ministers for sanctimoniously assuming that they had, by virtue of their religious calling, any special claim to good political judgment. For example, in Connecticut one of the most gifted of Republican writers, Abraham Bishop, distinguished between his opponents' professions of piety and their politics, arguing that "their holiness may recommend them to heaven, but is no GUARANTEE FOR THEIR POLITICAL RECTITUDE." In response, David Daggett, a Connecticut lawyer, asked: "What security then have we for 'political rectitude'?" *Three Letters to Abraham Bishop,* 26–27 (Hartford: 1800). Mockingly, the "Layman" had his "familiar" whisper: "Thomas Jefferson, to be sure, would be less exceptionable, if he had religion; but let us overlook his errors in that respect, for the sake of his political rectitude." A Layman, *The Claims of Thomas Jefferson,* 28.

sins of nations were punished in this one. The Rev. Linn warned about "the dishonor which would be done to God" and about the danger of God's displeasure "if an opposer of Christianity should be preferred." Linn elaborated: "Though there is nothing in the constitution to restrict our choice, yet the open and warm preference of a manifest enemy to the religion of Christ, in a Christian nation, would be an awful symptom of the degeneracy of that nation, and . . . a rebellion against God."[9] Indeed, Mason put the Constitution's silence about Christianity to advantage. Noting that the federal Constitution *"makes no acknowledgement of that God* who gave us our national existence, and saved us from anarchy and internal war," he argued that "[t]he only way to wipe off the reproach of irreligion, and to avert the descending vengeance, is to prove, by our national acts, that the Constitution has not, in this instance, done justice to the public sentiment."[10] As the people had not, through their Constitution, acknowledged the source of the nation's blessings, they now had to do so in their votes.

Federalists agreed with Jefferson that religious opinion should not be subject to civil penalties, but they worried that this philosophizing Virginian, discontent with so mundane an observation, had argued for religious liberty on the ground that religion was without civil importance. In 1782, in his *Notes on the State of Virginia,* Jefferson had held: "The legitimate powers of government extend to such acts only as are injurious to others. But it does me no injury for my neighbor to say there are twenty gods, or no God. It neither picks my pocket nor breaks my leg."[11] Looking back, the Connecticut lawyer, David Daggett, approved of Jefferson's attempt "to show the impropriety of legislative interference in matters of religion" but feared that Jefferson's arguments for this position had gone further: "If he had said that faith was not a subject of legislation I would subscribe to the opinion; but he unquestionably means that it is not injurious to individuals or society for a man to declare that there are twenty Gods, or that there is no God."[12] The Rev. Linn shared these doubts: "It is true that a mere opinion of my neighbor will do me no injury. Government cannot regulate or punish

[9] Linn, *Serious Considerations,* 27–28.

[10] Mason, *Voice of Warning,* 33–34.

[11] Thomas Jefferson, *Notes on the State of Virginia,* 152 (Query XVII) (1782; New York: Harper & Row, 1964).

[12] Daggett, *Three Letters to Abraham Bishop,* 30.

it. The right of private opinion is inalienable. But let my neighbor once persuade himself that there is no God, and he will pick my pocket, and break not only my *leg* but my *neck*."[13]

In these attacks on Jefferson for his indifference to religion, Federalist clergymen argued that religion had civil importance, and they thereby gave religion not only civil but also, more narrowly, partisan significance. Little did they realize that, in bringing religion to bear upon a political campaign, they would provoke their opponents to question not so much the importance of religion for civil government as the right of clergymen to make politics the subject of religion.

Republicans Defend Jefferson

Republicans responded to the Federalist charges. Republicans wanted to gain establishment votes in New England and to avoid losing dissenting votes, and therefore they could not ignore the Federalist allegations that Jefferson had questioned the moral and civil value of Christianity. No less than establishment ministers, the numerous evangelical dissenters in New England (including Baptists, Episcopalians, and Methodists) tended to believe that religion, particularly Christianity, was an essential foundation of morals and therefore also of civil government. Accordingly, when Federalists suggested that Jefferson had abandoned Christianity and had challenged the civil value of religion, Republicans felt obliged to refute these charges as best they could.

Some Republicans argued that Jefferson had not rejected Christianity, even if his views were unusual. For example, a leading New York politician, DeWitt Clinton, hinted that Jefferson was yet another religious dissenter, who adhered to one of the many varieties of Christian belief:

> The Christian world is divided into a great variety of sects, differing in their doctrines and discipline, but all agreeing in the divinity of the religion of Christ, and all admitting each other to be entitled to the denomination of Christians. . . . Any peculiar opinions which do not go directly to a disbelief of the divinity of the religion, but which are in themselves erroneous, may be named heretical, but can by no means come under the description of deistical.[14]

[13] Linn, *Serious Considerations*, 19.
[14] "Grotius" [DeWitt Clinton], *A Vindication of Thomas Jefferson*, 6–7 (New York: 1800).

Similarly, after the election the boldest of Jefferson's Connecticut allies, Abraham Bishop, lectured the Federalists: "It will cost you many years to learn the variety of opinions, which Christians . . . have entertained on the leading subjects of Christianity."[15]

Republicans also attempted to show that Jefferson had not denied the civil utility of religion. When opposing establishments in his *Notes on the State of Virginia*, Jefferson had not revealed much concern for the worldly consequences of religion. Nonetheless, in defense of Jefferson, a New York Republican, Tunis Wortman, pointed out that Jefferson's "only object" in discussing religion was "to discountenance political establishments in theology." If Jefferson's argument seemed to go too far, it did so merely because his vigorous language revealed his strong attachment to religious liberty:

> [I]mpressed with its importance, his language glows with animation; it is upon a single expression used in the warmth of sensibility, and in the ardor of argument, that peculiar reliance has been placed[:] "it does me no injury for my neighbor to say, there are twenty Gods, or no God, it neither picks my pocket nor breaks my leg." The expression is a strong one, but it is strictly true in the sense in which it was applied.

According to Wortman, Jefferson merely distinguished between civil jurisdiction over acts and the absence of such jurisdiction over opinions:

> Belief indeed may, nay will influence our conduct; the errors of my neighbor may be dangerous, I would distrust the man who would palliate adultery, or endeavor to excuse a theft; but the manner in which Mr. Jefferson applies the sentiment renders it perfectly correct, he distinguishes between our *actions* and our *opinions*, for the former we are amenable to the civil magistrate, for the latter he expressly tells us we *"are answerable to our GOD."*

Thus, rather than deny that atheistical belief could cause injury, Jefferson had only claimed that it caused no injury of the tangible sort cognizable by law:

> Speaking of the rights of conscience, he says, that—"we never submitted them to our civil rulers, we could not submit them, the legitimate powers of government extend to such *acts*, only as are injurious to others"; it is therefore demonstrable that Mr. Jefferson exclusively contemplates civil

---

[15] Bishop, *Oration Delivered in Wallingford*, 94.

injuries: that is to say, injuries visible and palpable, and for which human laws afford redress; in this legal sense, the sentiments of my neighbor are no injury to me.[16]

Jefferson questioned whether individuals were responsible to government for their religious opinions, but he said nothing against the civil utility of belief.

Unfortunately for his defenders, Jefferson had suggested that the Bible ought not be used as a school book, and he thereby had seemed to disconnect religion from morality. Schoolchildren, he claimed, were too immature to read the Bible, which could be replaced with volumes teaching historical facts and "the first elements of morality."[17] In response, Linn asked: "Why not the first elements of religion, which are the foundation of all sound morality? Are the minds of children *matured* for the one, and not for the other? He has not told us when it is proper to teach them a little religion; and how we may prevent, in the mean time, irreligious principles."[18] Coming to Jefferson's defense, DeWitt Clinton argued that "the primary design of sending children to school, is to *learn to read, and write, not to learn religion.* That to teach the latter is a more appropriate duty and concern of parents and clergymen." Education and even, perhaps, religion were specialized activities and therefore belonged in different places. "That if the Bible ought not to be employed as a book from which to be taught spelling and reading, it does not follow that it ought not to be adopted as an infallible source of religious education and instruction; and that if it be inexpedient to resort to it in the school, it may be still obligatory to use it in the family, and to teach it from the pulpit."[19]

Although Wortman, Clinton, and other Republican writers vigorously denied suggestions that Jefferson had rejected Christianity or had repudiated the civil value of religion, they typically declined to make the more positive argument that their candidate warmly adhered to conventional Christianity or cared much about its beneficial civil conse-

---

[16] Tunis Wortman, *A Solemn Address to Christians and Patriots* (New York: 1800), in *American Political Sermons of the Founding Era, 1730–1805*, 1516–1517, ed. Ellis Sandoz (Indianapolis: Liberty Press, 1991). See also "Grotius" [DeWitt Clinton], *A Vindication of Thomas Jefferson*, 18.

[17] Jefferson, *Notes on the State of Virginia*, 141 (Query XIV).

[18] Linn, *Serious Considerations*, 15.

[19] "Grotius" [DeWitt Clinton], *A Vindication of Thomas Jefferson*, 25–26.

quences. Republicans would have found such arguments difficult to sustain. Indeed, a few Republicans may have been saving their vehemence for another very different argument: that religion and politics should be kept separate.

Republicans Demand the Separation of Religion and Politics

In response to the critiques of Federalist clergymen, some leading Republicans demanded that religion be separated from politics. Adopting a hyper-rigorous understanding of the purity required in religion and in government, these Republicans argued that any failure to disconnect religion and politics would leave both contaminated.

For Republicans, the demand for separation had the virtue of blending their opposition to the New England establishments with their denunciation of the political preaching against Jefferson. Implicitly and often explicitly, separation was an accusation that the Federalist clergy supported a union of church and state. Using separation in this way, Republicans could garner antiestablishment votes against Federalists— even against Federalists who had no establishment affiliation and in states that had not possessed an establishment for decades. Yet separation was not merely an antiestablishment ideal. In addition, it was an attack on all connection between religion and politics, including political preaching. Accordingly, Republicans could use separation to impugn Federalist ministers—again, even nonestablishment ministers—who preached against Jefferson. As Republicans intended, the position that there should be a separation of religion and politics obscured the distinction between state support for a religious establishment and clerical participation in the full life of the nation. In particular, it lent the legitimacy of the dissenters' complaints against establishments to the Republicans' complaints against the clergy—thus justifying Republican attacks on the political participation of individuals with religious authority, whether in established or purely voluntary churches.

In using the notion of separation to associate Federalists with a union of church and state, the Republicans played upon earlier establishment arguments about the necessary connection between religion and government. Establishment clergymen had long defended their special privileges on the ground that religion was necessarily connected to government, and in New England many of these established clergymen sympathized with the Federalists. During the election of 1800, however, Federalists needed to attract nonestablishment votes, and therefore the Federalist clergy avoided making arguments specifically associated with establishments and cautiously adopted the more generic claim that religion had civil importance. Notwithstanding that these Federalists tended to shy away from explicit references to a "connection," Republicans responded by demanding the separation of religion and politics and thereby suggested that Federalists (including Linn, Mason, and others unassociated with any establishment) were making the establishment argument about a necessary connection. Thus Republicans attributed the establishment position to Federalists and even flipped it around by seeking a separation. Much earlier, Roger Williams had adopted a position close to that with which Richard Hooker had caricatured early English dissenters, and, now, probably more self-consciously, the Republicans adopted the position with which recent establishment writers had caricatured American dissenters. It was a rhetorically playful response that radically reversed establishment arguments in a way eighteenth-century American dissenters had almost never done. Accordingly, in a period in which dissenters in New England still struggled against their establishments, this sly Republican demand for a separation of religion and politics all the more effectively associated religious commentary upon politics with religious oppression.[20]

The most prominent argument for separation of religion and politics appeared in 1800 in *A Solemn Address to Christians and Patriots,* published anonymously by the New York Republican, Tunis Wortman. Against the Federalists, Wortman wrote that "it is your duty, as Christians, to maintain the purity and independence of the church, to keep religion separate from politics, to prevent an union between the church and the state, and to preserve your clergy from temptation, corruption and reproach."[21] Apparently solicitous of religious purity, Wortman hoped for a separation of religion and especially the clergy from politics.

---

[20] Of course, none of this is to say that Republicans actively opposed the New England establishments or sought to aid the dissenters. As William G. McLoughlin observes about Connecticut: "Although the 1800 election campaign was filled with anticlerical speeches by the Republicans, none of them touched upon the issues so important to the Baptists. Disestablishment simply was not an issue in Connecticut in the 1800 election." McLoughlin, *New England Dissent, 1630–1833,* 2: 1004 (Cambridge: Harvard University Press, 1971).
[21] Wortman, *A Solemn Address,* in *American Political Sermons,* 1482.

The connection of religion and government threatened both church and state. "Religion and government are equally necessary, but their interests should be kept separate and distinct. No legitimate connection can ever subsist between them. Upon no plan, no system, can they become united, without endangering the purity and usefulness of both— the church will corrupt the state, and the state pollute the church." Working upon anti-Catholic fears, Wortman alluded to "the inquisition, . . . the sufferings of the wretched Huguenots. . . . the fires of Smithfield, and . . . the massacre of St. Bartholomews" to suggest that any connection between religion and government would destroy liberty. Such a connection also undermined religion: "Christianity becomes no longer the religion of God—it becomes the religion of temporal craft and expediency and policy." Indeed, "[w]hen a church becomes directly or indirectly connected with a state, it may still retain its external form and appearance, but Christianity no longer remains, the heavenly virtues become extinct, and the pure spirit of piety disgusted by its avarice, ambition and impiety takes wings and flies to heaven." Thus "[n]othing is left but a state without liberty and a church without religion." Attributing these horrors to Federalists, Wortman exclaimed: "God of heaven, . . . preserve thy church from the pollution and abomination which accompanies a connection with the state."[22]

In particular, Wortman urged a separation of preachers from politics. "It is essential to the interests of religion, that its teachers should be set apart, to the performance of their sacred duties. . . . The charge of their flocks requires all their pastoral care; their attention should always be directed heavenward; if they mingle too deeply in the affairs of this world, they are apt to become unmindful of the prospects of the next." In religious tones, he declared: "Let me conjure you then, to purify the altar, to keep things sacred from intermingling with things profane, to maintain religion separate and apart from the powers of this world."[23]

Wortman directed his principle of separation not merely at establishments and establishment clergy, but at all preachers who mixed politics with the Gospel to attack Republicans. He was a New Yorker, and he made clear that his targets were Linn and Mason—two New York

[22] Ibid., 1488, 1495.
[23] Ibid., 1485, 1489.

clerics opposed to Jefferson—neither of whom received privileges from an establishment, there being none in New York. Thus, even while Wortman appealed to religious minorities and others distrustful of establishments, he also propounded the higher goal of censuring and discouraging all ministers who inveighed against Republicans from their pulpits.

To induce Federalist ministers to perceive the wisdom of his ideas, Wortman knowingly urged a congregational remedy. "If it is the duty of the clergy to watch over the conduct of their congregations, it is equally incumbent upon congregations, to be mindful of the conduct of their pastors—they should confine their ministers to the duties of their sacred calling, and above all things, beware how they permit them to acquire a political ascendancy." Wortman invited congregations to hold their ministers to account and, in this way, had hopes of "confining them, with the utmost rigor, to the duties of their profession."

Wortman recognized that he might seem to be discouraging clergymen from exercising their rights to declare their opinions and to participate in politics as did other citizens. Yet he remained unmoved. Both "as men and as citizens, they have an equal right to express their opinions and give their suffrages; but they should never be permitted to carry their politics into the sacred desk, and more especially, they should not be suffered to make religion an engine of politics."[24] Such were Wortman's views in 1800 in his anonymous electioneering pamphlet, *A Solemn Address*. Ironically, in the same year he published his *Treatise Concerning Political Enquiry, and the Liberty of the Press*—a book still celebrated for its abstract, even "philosophic," defense of freedom of political discussion.[25]

After Jefferson finally triumphed in the election, some Republicans continued to demand separation, especially in New England. Yet Republicans who needed to get elected within this Congregationalist stronghold were cautious enough to talk about separation less directly than had Wortman in New York. In Congregationalist New England, where local Republicans still faced formidable Federalist and establishment opponents, the idea of separation remained valuable both against the Congregationalist establishments and against Federalist preachers. None-

---

[24] Ibid., 1486.
[25] Leonard W. Levy, *The Emergence of a Free Press*, 328 (New York: Oxford University Press, 1985).

theless, a direct advocacy of separation carried risks, as many New Englanders, even dissenters, still assumed that there was a necessary and valuable connection between religion and government. Particularly in Connecticut, a sophistication about such sensibilities was required, and it was there that the brilliant Republican polemicist, Abraham Bishop, railed against the union of church and state—always suggesting the need for separation but rarely being so explicit as to use the words that could only alienate his more traditional readers.

Bishop sought to "[d]etach politics, offices, applause and honors from New-England religion!"[26] Like Wortman, Bishop held that "Church and State always contaminate each other, so far as their union extends," and he used this argument not only to attack establishments but also to demand that preachers keep out of politics—to insist that "[t]he clerical *politician* is an useless preacher; the *political* christian is a dangerous statesman."[27]

In his 1802 pamphlet, *Church and State, A Political Union, Formed by the Enemies of Both,* Bishop wrote that ministers had forfeited some of the rights enjoyed by other citizens: "These men claim a *right* to be *active partisans,* in our choice of public officers. They would have had such right, had they not undertaken a business inconsistent with this right."

> Many things were lawful for the Apostle Paul, but they were not *expedient.* It is criminal in a preacher to do those things, which are manifestly inexpedient and inconsistent with his profession, though they may be strictly legal, and in any other character, proper. Man has rights in a state of nature, which he cannot exercise in society. Men have rights in their private capacities, which as Presidents or Ambassadors they cannot exercise. Certainly those men must be eminent among delinquents, who, spurning at expediency, neglecting a profession which requires all their faculties, neglecting the families of the sick and dying, neglecting alarmed consciences and enquiring souls, devote their time and talents to the interests of a political party, which has set itself up in opposition to the general government.[28]

---

[26] Abraham Bishop, *Proofs of a Conspiracy, against Christianity, and the Government of the United States, Exhibited in Several Views of the Union of Church and State in New England,* 109 (Hartford: 1802).

[27] Bishop, *Oration Delivered in Wallingford,* 41.

[28] Abraham Bishop, *Church and State, A Political Union, Formed by the Enemies of Both,* iv (n.p.: 1802).

Although the partisanship of ministers was "strictly legal," it was not a right they could appropriately exercise.

Without going so far as to say that Federalist ministers had violated the law, Bishop suggested as much. "Adverse combinations, oppugnations, disrespect, reproach and systematic revilings, are (in the essence and nature of the crimes) sedition, treason, and rebellion." These "obnoxious acts, are evils in themselves, and if they were not forbidden by positive statutes, they would be a violation of the spirit of all law, and the great and salvable principles of social preservation." Bishop gave force to his somewhat equivocal words by suggesting that Jefferson and other Republican officials had been elevated above Federalist criticism: "These servants of the public, are the creatures of the people's sovereignty. Contumeliously and falsely to reproach them, is slandering and insulting the majesty of the people; and to thwart and oppose, is to resist their will; is insurrection, is, virtually, treason." Lest this be considered an idle threat, Bishop reminded his readers that Federalists had recently prosecuted Republicans: "For less, infinitely less, was Lyon convicted; Callender and Cooper punished." Indeed, "[t]he charges of the courts, on those trials, would be excellent lessons, for the perusal of Clergymen on the doctrines of Sedition and government."[29] Federalist clergy seemed to have conspired against the choice of the people, and so, for the "clerical Federalists" and others who had "combined together," Bishop posed the questions: "What is their object? Is it a legal, a laudable one?"

Notwithstanding his threat of treason prosecutions, Bishop, like Wortman, had a more practical remedy. "Republicans have no delay in thinking, and want no apology for saying, that clergymen, who will allow themselves aspersing the first officers of the General government, who will wilfully excite . . . opposition to its constitutional and deliberate measures; and spread . . . falsehood, misrepresentation, and calumnies concerning them, ought not to be supported by their parishioners."

Yet Bishop hoped for more than a merely congregational response. Hinting at changes in the legal status of the clergy, he first took aim at the establishment clergy, arguing that they had abandoned their religious duties. "It is absurd to suppose a legal or a constitutional obligation to support the clergy, when the very object, for which the duty devolved,

[29] Ibid., 54–55, 57.

is defeated, by its performance." More broadly, he threatened all clergy with a loss of their exemptions:

> It is truly marvelous that of an order of men, exempted from civil office, exempted from military duties, separated from secular, on account of their spiritual concerns; professing to be the disciples of him, whose kingdom is not of this world, any should be found to engage, or be made subservient to, the setting of one part of his common charge against the others; of supporting confusion against order, faction against Government, the dogmas of a party, against the injunctions of religion.[30]

This privileged order engaged in politics against the very government that exempted them from secular duties so that they could attend to higher matters. The implications were clear enough.

Not merely opposed to an establishment—a union of church and state—Wortman, Bishop, and the Republicans who followed them sought a separation of religion and politics. These Republicans assumed that religion did not extend to politics, and that the clergy should confine their clerical conduct to religion. Accordingly, clergymen were to stay out of politics, especially partisan politics, in which they seemed particularly out of place.

Federalists Defend the Rights of the Clergy

In response to Republican demands for a separation of religion and politics, Federalists protested that the clergy, like any other class of citizens, had a right to participate in debates about government. Clergymen, according to Federalists, even had a duty to preach on politics.

Mason replied to Wortman's attack upon Linn and himself by observing the novelty of Wortman's claim that religion had no right to concern itself with politics: "That religion has, in *fact*, nothing to do with the politics of many who profess it, is a melancholy truth. But that it has, of *right*, no concern with political transactions, is quite a new discovery. If such opinions, however, prevail, there is no longer any mystery in the character of those whose conduct, in political matters, violates every precept, and slanders every principle, of the religion of Christ."

In explaining the right of "religion" to concern itself with politics, Mason argued that religion concerned all life, including politics:

---

[30] Ibid., 55, 56.

And what is religion? Is it not an obligation to the service of God, founded on his authority, and extending to all our relations personal and social? Yet religion has nothing to do with politics! Where did you learn this maxim? The Bible is full of directions for your behavior as citizens. It is plain, pointed, awful in its injunctions on rulers and ruled as such: yet religion has nothing to do with politics. You are commanded "in ALL your ways to acknowledge him." In EVERY THING, by prayer and supplication, with thanksgiving, to let your requests be made known unto "God," "And WHATSOEVER YE DO, IN WORD OR DEED, to do ALL IN THE NAME of the Lord Jesus." Yet religion has nothing to do with politics! Most astonishing! And is there any part of your conduct in which you are, or wish to be, without law to God, and not under the law of Christ?

Accordingly, religion was relevant to politics:

Can you persuade yourselves that political men and measures are to undergo no review in the judgment to come? That all the passion and violence, the fraud and falsehood, and corruption which pervade the systems of party, and burst out like a flood at the public elections, are to be blotted from the catalogue of unchristian deeds, because they are politics? Or that a minister of the gospel may see his people, in their political career, bid defiance to their God in breaking through every moral restraint, and keep a guiltless silence because religion has nothing to do with politics?

On the contrary, American politics needed more religion. "Yes, if our religion had more to do with our politics; if, in the pride of our citizenship, we had not forgotten our Christianity: if we had prayed more and wrangled less about the affairs of our country, it would have been infinitely better for us at this day."[31] It was an irenic thought—but utterly sanctimonious, even hypocritical, in an election pamphlet so critical of Jefferson.

A more systematic defense of political preaching as a right and even a duty came from the Congregationalist minister, Simon Backus. In 1802 Abraham Bishop had pointedly condemned Backus for preaching a Connecticut election sermon *"the object of which was to expose to ridicule and contempts the republicans of this State."*[32] Backus responded in 1804 with a *Dissertation on the Right and Obligation of the Civil Magistrate*—the right and obligation being, of course, to support religion. From this obligation, he

---

[31] Mason, *Voice of Warning*, 25, 26–27.
[32] Bishop, *Oration Delivered in Wallingford*, 45 (note) and 94.

drew a series of corollaries about the role of religion in the election of
rulers and, ultimately, about the right and duty of ministers to preach
politics:

> 1st. That one important qualification of magistrates or civil rulers, is that
> they should be men of religion. . . . [J]ustice and the fear of God, or a
> devout reverence of the divine majesty, are . . . inseparably connected;
> . . . we can have no security for the justice of a ruler's administration,
> who is destitute of the fear of God.
>
> Corol. 2d. . . . it is the duty of those who are entrusted with the ap-
> pointment of rulers, to have a respect to the religious character of those
> for whom they give their suffrage. . . . To commit the most important
> interests of the community, as well as our own, both civil and religious,
> into the hands of men, whom we have no reason to apprehend, have
> the fear of God before their eyes, is a most irrational and preposterous
> as well as criminal piece of conduct; a betraying the public trust. . . .
> What security can we have, that infidels, or persons who have no regard
> to religion, or reverence for the Deity, when advanced to places of public
> trust, will not at every opportunity sacrifice the interest of their constit-
> uents, to their own private passions, or emolument?
>
> 3d. Corol. That it belongs to the duty and office of the ministers, or
> public teachers of religion, to inculcate these duties, and make them the
> occasional subjects of their public preaching.
>
> 4th Corol. That the censures passed upon ministers by many at the
> present day, for occasionally making some of these duties the subjects
> of their preaching; stigmatizing them as political preachers, &c. is very
> unreasonable and injurious. . . . Nay, it is an essential part of the duty
> of his function to preach politics.[33]

---

[33] Simon Backus, *A Dissertation on the Right and Duty of the Civil Magistrate,* 26, 27, 29 (Middletown, Conn.: 1804). He also observed: "Perhaps the real ground of the grievous accusations
against the clergy, which are exhibited by many at the present day, for preaching what
they call politics, may not be their simply explaining and inculcating the duties and qualifications of civil rulers, and those of electors, but rather the particular sentiments relative to
those subjects which they endeavor to impress upon the minds of their hearers.—Should
ministers adopt the other side of the question, and boldly assert and maintain from the
desk, that civil government has nothing to do in matters of religion; and that electors are
under no obligations to respect the religious characters and qualifications of those whom
they elect to places of power and trust in the government; that it is a matter of perfect
indifference to society whether their rulers believe in one God, in twenty Gods, or no God;
it may be queried, whether they might not probably escape those severe censures, and
that volley of calumnies which are so liberally bestowed upon them by a certain class of
men for preaching politics?" Ibid., 32.

It was desirable for ministers "to preach politics" not only because religion could help preserve civil justice but also because ministers had an obligation "to declare the whole counsel of God," which encompassed all human relations:

> All moral, relative and social duties are to be explained, and inculcated by the public teachers of religion: such are the duties of husbands and wives, parents and children, rulers and subjects, &c. And one class of these duties are no less properly the subjects of a minister's preaching than an other, for they all equally constitute a part of the counsel of God; being particularly, and explicitly enjoined and inculcated in the sacred scriptures.[34]

Like other human relationships, politics was a matter of religion.

Indifferent to these protests, Republicans demanded a separation of religion and politics and thereby altered the way many Americans perceived the rights of their clergy. Nothing Mason or Backus said about "the whole counsel of God" could prevent Republicans from using their "cant phrases designed to fix a stigma upon the clergy, or to possess the minds of the more illiterate and undiscerning, with an idea that ministers have abandoned the appropriate duties of their function."[35] Nor could Mason or Backus provide much comfort to Federalist clergymen in Republican towns. These lonely ministers understood the power of their congregations and apparently abandoned political sermons.[36] Although introduced for the transient purposes of an election conflict, the Republican demand for a separation of religion and government shook many New England ministers and resonated among the people, who would not entirely forget this concept or its anticlerical implications.

[34] Ibid., 29–31.
[35] Ibid., 31.
[36] Richard J. Purcell, *Connecticut in Transition 1775–1818*, 202 (Middletown, Conn.: Wesleyan University Press, 1963).

⇒•◦•⇐

6

Keeping Religion Out of Politics and Making Politics Religious

IN DEMANDING the separation of religion and politics, Republicans hoped, more broadly, for an America in which individuals would engage equally in politics, free from the interference of antiquated religious and social hierarchies. Yet at the same time that Republicans sought to exclude clerical religion and other interfering influences from politics, they themselves made politics the object of almost religious aspirations.

The Republican Vision of the Role of Religion in American Politics

Republicans demanded separation not only to gain votes but also as part of their vision of American society. Particularly in Connecticut and other areas of New England where the traditional character of society seemed to linger, Republicans argued that the relation of individuals to the government should be unimpeded by other ties—that inegalitarian connections and hierarchies, whether religious or social, should not interfere with the equal participation of individual citizens in politics.

In the Republican conception of America's changing society, clergymen could not expect deference to their political views. According to Republicans, each American (at least, each adult, white, male American) had an equal right to participate in politics and was as capable in political matters as a clergyman. Abraham Bishop, for example, argued that clergymen had no legitimate claim upon political loyalties and complained that Federalist clergymen exerted political influence only by threatening damnation:

Do our clergy understand politics? Certainly no other class of men is so indifferently informed on that subject.—Whence then arises their right to dictate political opinions?—Is it because they occupy the pulpit? *Aye, there's the rub.*—Are they to be witnesses for or against you on a future day? They tell you so.—Are they envoys of heaven? They say so.

Addressing himself to "Ye clerical 'friends of order,'" Bishop told them in his "plain republican English":

You are not in the habit of hearing from men, who attach to you no more respect than your knowledge and piety demand. You have talked and preached very freely about republicans: You have abused them. On this occasion, I am their organ for speaking to you, and they take high ground, when they claim of you to PREACH THE GOSPEL.[1]

Clergymen could claim respect for preaching the gospel, not politics.

Most preachers with settled ministries could ill afford to split their congregations by taking sides in politics. Whether establishment ministers (dependent upon public funds) or dissenting clergymen (dependent upon voluntary contributions), they often had reason to avoid divisive political issues. As Abraham Bishop noted:

Political wranglings, and party strife . . . will inflict . . . deep and dangerous wounds. . . . A clergyman is the pastor of an entire church, the minister of an undivided parish, the shepherd of the whole flock. His usefulness, and his living, depend on harmony, brotherly love, and the confiding affection of an united people. The siding with a party in a cause of contention, involves engendered strife, and is a root of bitterness, which will poison religious intercourse at its source, and turn the consolations of social worship, into an embittered task, or at least a joyless exercise. The shepherd and the sheep will become estranged, or if penned together, will, like the wolf and dog, tear and devour each other.

Regretting that the clergy "engaged as partisans," Bishop declared: "What a wound has the Christian Religion received in this house of its friends, which many Sermons on its truth and excellency cannot heal."[2]

---

[1] Abraham Bishop, *Oration Delivered in Wallingford on the 11th of March 1801, before the Republicans of the State of Connecticut, at their General Thanksgiving, for the Election of Thomas Jefferson,* 88, 91 (New Haven: 1801).

[2] Abraham Bishop, *Church and State, A Political Union, Formed by the Enemies of Both,* 53–54, 52, 61 (n.p.: 1802). Of course, this was not an exclusively Republican position. Against Richard Price's pulpit exposition of the principles of the French Revolution, Edmund Burke wrote: "[P]oliticks and the pulpit are terms that have little agreement. No sound ought to be heard in the church but the healing voice of Christian charity. The cause of civil liberty

Bishop never aspired to the tone of dispassionate balance that would later be brought to the topic by Alexis de Tocqueville, but he recognized that in America's relatively free, diverse, egalitarian circumstances, the clergy would voluntarily have to submit to constraints more confining than any imposed by law.

Bishop and other Republicans who opposed clerical intervention in politics had an idealized image of American society that they often framed in opposition to the no less idealized vision held by Connecticut Federalists and their clerical allies. According to Federalists, the people of Connecticut distinguished themselves by their "steady habits"—by their habitual attachment to custom, self-restraint, and virtue. Unusually capable of this sort of self-government, the inhabitants of Connecticut reputedly required little law and so possessed greater freedom, with more security, than the people of any other state. Federalists understood that the steady habits and freedom of Connecticut thrived amid the state's intertwined familial ties, social connections, and religious establishment, and that, of these, the religious establishment, known as the "standing order," had a particularly important role in inculcating the people's steady habits. Thus steady habits and the standing order—tradition and established clerical authority—formed a social landscape in which, according to Federalists, the people enjoyed exceptional virtue and freedom.

In contrast, Republicans envisioned a nation of equal citizenship. Resentful of the standing order and its inegalitarian privileges and expectations of deference, Republicans hoped for a society in which individuals engaged in politics independently, unburdened by the customs of their forefathers or the authority of their ministers. Accordingly, Republicans urged that, especially in Connecticut, each man should free him-

---

and civil government gains as little as that of religion by this confusion of duties. Those who quit their proper character, to assume what does not belong to them, are, for the greater part, ignorant both of the character they leave, and of the character they assume. Wholly unacquainted with the world in which they are so fond of meddling, and inexperienced in all its affairs, on which they pronounce with so much confidence, they have nothing of politics but the passions they excite. Surely the church is a place where one day's truce ought to be allowed to the dissensions and animosities of mankind." Edmund Burke, *Reflections on the Revolution in France*, in *The Works of the Right Hon. Edmund Burke*, 5: 42–43 (London: 1803). Yet, for Burke, as for members of Connecticut's standing order, church and state were to be mutually supportive. Although persons of all persuasions had occasion to condemn the political preaching of their opponents, the Republicans found this position peculiarly compatible with their other views.

self of clerical influence and interference. Of course, this is not to say that all Republicans were, in fact, more independent than Federalists of their society's customs and religion. At the very least, however, Republicans perceived themselves as opposing habitual and clerical authority and seeking instead equal individual freedom, and their perception was not without consequence. In Connecticut, Republicans pursued this vision until 1818, when they adopted a new constitution, abolished the standing order, and even altered the people's steady habits, thereby changing the state forever.[3]

Thus, especially in Connecticut, Republicans took an anticlerical view of politics and argued that political preaching threatened the independence of the people. At least, this was the perspective Republicans attempted to impose upon Federalists. It coexisted and blended, however, with another Republican vision of politics—a more religious vision—which Republicans claimed for themselves.

Republicans and the Millennial Republic

Ironically, while Republicans demanded that Federalist clergymen separate religion from politics, Republicans themselves imbued their secular politics with profoundly religious sentiments. They sought to transform the politics of this world, and in so doing they often described secular politics as the means of achieving religious and even millennial ends.

Millennialism could take various forms. As shown by Nathan Hatch, the New England clergy, especially Federalist establishment ministers, espoused a type of national millennialism. According to these clergymen, Christianity and free government each flourished in the context of the other. Inextricably connected, Christian liberty and civil liberty would therefore progress in America as they had not elsewhere, giving Federalist clergymen hopes that theirs was the blessed land that would usher in the millennium.[4] In contrast, a rather different millennial vision prevailed among some leading Republican politicians. Adopting an almost

---

[3] At least to contemporaries, the changes in manners seemed connected to the political transition. For example, S. G. Goodrich later observed that "[t]he change in manners had no doubt been silently going on for some time; but it was not distinctly visible to common eyes till the establishment of the new constitution." Goodrich, *Recollections of a Lifetime*, 1: 129 (New York: 1858).

[4] Nathan O. Hatch, *The Sacred Cause of Liberty*, 137–179 (New Haven: Yale University Press, 1977).

otherworldly perfectionism, these Republicans described their political
aspirations in religious terms and spoke of themselves as the secular instruments of a millennial era.[5]

In this civic appropriation of religious expectations, Republicans
learned much from writings associated with the French Revolution,
most notably the voluble eloquence of Volney and Paine. Thomas
Paine—a critic of the "adulterous connection between church and
state"—perceived in the recent history of France not merely a revolution, but a "REGENERATION OF MAN."[6] It was, however, the Comte de Volney who, both in print and in person, gave Americans their most popular
glimpse of a Republican millennium. In 1791, in a surreal fantasy of
rational, anticlerical, and antimonarchical legislators (whom he imagined himself to be viewing from the gondola of a hot-air balloon), Volney
predicted an end to prejudice and passion, warfare and intolerance.
Among the rational people of his reconstructed world, the *"religions of
errour and delusion"* would be replaced by *"the religion of evidence and
truth,"* leading to unanimity in the perception of the laws of nature,
which, in turn, would permit the attainment of harmony on earth.[7] Describing a secular millennium, in which priests and monarchs would give
way to a perfection of self-government, Volney attacked religions and
their clergies while imbuing the people of the new age with a religious
sense of their own reason.

At about the same time, some Americans began to attribute a millennial character to their republican government. Most attractively, Joel
Barlow—the Connecticut poet and friend of Jefferson who would later
translate Volney's work—suggested the "progressive paths" by which
"full perfection" would eventually encompass the globe:

> See, thro' the whole, the same progressive plan,
> That draws, for mutual succour, man to man,
> From friends to tribes, from tribes to realms ascend,
> Their powers, their interests and their passions blend; . . .

---

[5] For a discussion of such tendencies in the context of nationalism, see Michael Lienesch,
"The Role of Political Millennialism in Early Modern Nationalism," *Western Political Quarterly,* 36: 458 (1983).

[6] Thomas Paine, *The Age of Reason,* in Paine, *The Collected Writings,* 667 (1794; New York:
Library of America, 1995); Thomas Paine, *Rights of Man,* 99 (part 1) (1791; London: Ev-
eryman, 1969).

[7] C. F. Volney, *The Ruins: Or a Survey of the Revolutions of Empire,* 270 (Albany: 1822).

> Till each remotest realm, by friendship join'd,
> Links in the chain that binds all human kind.

As Barlow explained in the more prosaic language of a footnote, "such a state of peace and happiness as is foretold in scripture and commonly called the millennial period, may be rationally expected to be introduced without a miracle."[8]

At New Haven's celebration of Independence Day in 1799, the leading defender of Connecticut's standing order, David Daggett, questioned the Republicans' secular millennialism. Daggett compared the perfectionist fantasies he saw among Republicans to the utopian projects that Jonathan Swift, in *Gulliver's Travels*, had attributed to the Academy of Projectors—a pseudo-scientific body that Gulliver encounters in Lagado. Referring to one of these projects, Daggett, with a rare flash of wit, entitled his oration *Sun-Beams May Be Extracted from Cucumbers, But the Process Is Tedious*. According to Daggett, "the modern Literati are attempting to extract sun-beams from Cucumbers—to travel without exertion—to reap without sowing—to educate children to perfection—to introduce a new order of things as it respects *morals* and *politics, social* and *civil duties,* and to establish this strange species of credulity."[9] In France these fantasies of the philosophes had left millions dead. Their pursuit of a secular millennium had "driven men from one species of error and superstition to another," and "what consolation is it to the wretched worshippers of stones to forget these Gods, and adore reason, fortitude and virtue?"[10] Of course, Republicans rejected such accusations. Two years later, Abraham Bishop would ask, "has any class of men avowed their preference for immorality and anarchy? Has any class assumed upon themselves, and faithfully promised to maintain, and circulate, the

---

[8] Joel Barlow, *The Vision of Columbus,* 240–241, 216, 242 (Hartford: 1787), in William K. Bottorf and Arthur L. Ford, eds., *The Works of Joel Barlow,* 340–341, 316, 342 (Gainesville: Scholars' Press, 1970), quoted and discussed by William C. Dowling, *Poetry and Ideology in Revolutionary Connecticut,* 3, 98–101 (Athens: University of Georgia Press, 1990).

[9] David Daggett, *Sun-Beams May Be Extracted from Cucumbers, But the Process Is Tedious,* 17 (New Haven: 1799).

[10] Ibid., 18, 22. In the wake of the election of 1800 some observers, such as Ezra Witter, reminded Republicans that they were likely to "find . . . their extravagant expectations frustrated—that the millennium is not immediately ushered in, and much the same natural and moral evils continue to scourge our country and the world, which existed before." Witter, *Two Sermons on the Party Spirit,* 14 (1801), as quoted by Daniel Sisson, *The American Revolution of 1800,* 440 (New York: Knopf, 1974).

dreams of Condorcet, or the absurdities of Godwin? If so, let evidence of the fact be produced."[11]

Although Bishop and his fellow Republicans never rose to the sophistication of Condorcet or Godwin, they were not without their own, sometimes distinctively American, dreams. In 1796 in New York, in an *Oration on the Influence of Social Institutions*, Tunis Wortman had argued that human character was so completely malleable as to permit hopes for secular perfection. Through the progress of the human mind, the increase of science, and the advancement of the arts, human knowledge had "already arrived to a degree of perfection that has exceeded the hopes of the most sanguine and enthusiastic visionary." Accordingly, "[m]oral light" had "diffused its invigorating influence throughout every department of social life, and exalted the human character to a state of splendid greatness and perfectibility, that no former age has ever yet realised or experienced." Citing "the acute and penetrating Godwin" on the malleability of the mind—on its "plastic nature," which was "fitted for the reception of every impression" and was "capable of becoming moulded in almost any shape"—Wortman concluded that individuals needed relatively little government and could be perfected by means of education.[12] Thus a "happy modification of social life" would bring about "that ultimate state of perfection of which the human character is susceptible," and mankind would satisfy its "final hopes and expectations" for a time when "[p]ersecution and superstition, vice, prejudice and cruelty will take their eternal departure from the earth," when "[n]ational animosities and distinctions will be buried in eternal oblivion" and "the sounds of war [will] no more be heard." In contrast to this pleasing fantasy was "that monkish and dishonorable doctrine which teaches the original depravity of mankind"—a "false and pernicious libel upon our species, issuing from the former spurious connexion between the spiritual and temporal hierarchies." Wortman, however, "particularly leveled" this criticism "at the former union between the church and the

---

[11] Abraham Bishop, *Proofs of a Conspiracy, against Christianity, and the Government of the United States, Exhibited in Several Views of the Union of Church and State in New England,* 17 (Hartford: 1802).

[12] Tunis Wortman, *An Oration on the Influence of Social Institutions upon Human Morals and Happiness, Delivered before the Tammany Society, at Their Anniversary, on the Twelfth of May, 1796,* 3, 8 (New York: 1796). Accordingly, "[s]ystems of jurisprudence and forms of government, and not physical causes, have produced that astonishing dissimilarity with which the human character abounds." Ibid., 10.

state." Fortunately—"Heaven be praised!"—a "more liberal and benevolent philosophy" had "compleatly vindicated the human character" and man would "continue to make accelerated advances in wisdom and in virtue until he hath rendered himself the vanquisher of misery and vice, and until *'Mind hath become omnipotent over matter.'* "[13]

If Wortman's secular perfectionism reached dizzying heights, it was nothing compared to the less obviously secular fantasies of many other Republicans, such as Abraham Bishop and his ally, the Rev. David Austin. Even as Republicans sought to keep Federalist clergymen from bringing their religion to bear upon politics, Republicans—as illustrated by these two residents of New Haven—could give their worldly opinions some of the peculiar intensity of their otherworldly faith. After growing up in New Haven and graduating from Yale, David Austin eventually became a Presbyterian minister in Elizabeth, New Jersey. He prospered there until the mid-1790s, when a combination of "natural eccentricity" and a "violent attack of scarlet fever" left him persuaded that, in the manner of Joshua and John the Baptist, he was "appointed of God"— his task being to bring in the millennial reign on earth. Although crowds congregated to hear him preach, his parishioners feared for his mind and requested his departure. Undeterred, Austin believed that the millennium could not occur until the Jews returned to the Promised Land, and, expecting that they would assemble in New Haven so as to await the Messiah in the new Jerusalem, he returned to his hometown to build them houses and a wharf.[14] Perhaps because the Jews did not share Austin's enthusiasm for New Haven, or perhaps because Republicans seemed more interested than the Jews in Austin's millennial prophesies, Austin soon concluded that the Israelites would go directly to Washington, D.C., where they would await the second coming following the election of Thomas Jefferson.

On such assumptions Austin published his millennial dreams. Addressing himself to "THE SEED OF ABRAHAM," he told them in October 1800: "The moment of your restoration fast approaches. From the regions of your dispersion, look *to the west*," for in "this western world, the God of

[13] Ibid., 24–25, 26–27. He also urged his countrymen to teach their sons "to reverence TRUTH, LIBERTY and JUSTICE more than they regard *Constitutions*." Ibid., 30.
[14] Nicholas Murray, "David Austin," in William B. Sprague, *Annals of the American Pulpit*, 2: 195–199 (New York: 1866); Harris Elwood Storr, "David Austin," in *Dictionary of American Biography* (New York: C. Scribner's Sons, 1943).

your fathers is preparing for you an habitation." Indeed, "[t]he advancing glory of the New Jerusalem, waits your presence. Behold these tribes, in Esau's dominion, inviting you into their bosom." Anxious, as ever, about accommodations for the Jews, Austin reassured them that "[a]ny persons disposed, without delay, to purchase lots in the Federal City, and to set buildings thereon, answerable to the design, will not fail to see their accompt in the enterprize." The restoration of the Jews would usher in the millennium: "From the top of this American mountain the arm of the Lord will be extended.—The throne of your national edifice is the place, where the introductory power of the mediatorial reign will take its seat. From thence will go forth the law of peace, in behalf of him who comes, *the desire of all nations.*" Thus "[t]he New Jerusalem-day is at the door": "Foundation is laid for the unloosing of the bonds of nature and of grace. The *New Heavens and the New Earth* shall open a dispensation of righteousness, as yet unrevealed to the sons of men. . . . The book of the revelations will soon be opened. Its seals are now in breaking." Not being so completely distant from reality as to think such utterances required no explanation, Austin added in less Biblical tones that "the preceding papers are calculated to invite your attention and suffrage towards the object *designated by heaven,* shortly to wield the sceptre of the *mediatorial administration* from the summit of that mountain, which, through your instrumentality, Almighty God had reared and protected."[15]

With such predictions this preacher who had so recently been dismissed for mental eccentricity found a following among Republicans, including Thomas Jefferson himself. After the inauguration Austin was invited to preach on July 4, 1801, before Congress, and he set himself up in the District of Columbia at what he called "Lady Washington's Chapel," presenting himself as "struck in prophesy under the style of

---

[15] David Austin, *The Dawn of Day, Introductory to the Rising Sun, Whose Rays Shall Gild the Clouds; and Open to a Benighted World the Glowing Effulgence of That Dominion, That Is to Be Given to the People of the Saints of the Most High. In Nine Letters,* 15, 18, 19, 21, 24, 25 (New Haven: 1800). He also explained: "Almighty God hath set before you the work. You that wish well to the American revolution: to the labors of Washington: and design stability to the work of his hands have but to put your hand to the present work, and send the Ark of God to its place. It is the Empire of the Redeemer, *in a covered Chariot,* that awaits your suffrage. The highest condescension imaginable is expressed in this act towards the sons of men. The Redeemer awaited the approving voice of his own: but his own received him not.—Again he appears in the vehicle of prudence and waits your assent, that his visible operations may commence." Ibid., 17.

'Joshua' of the American Temple." Jefferson had admired the millennial perspective adopted by Volney and Barlow, and, within fourteenth months of taking office, he encouraged Austin with three substantial gifts, totaling seventy-five dollars.[16]

Even Abraham Bishop declared that "this redeemed continent was to be the grand theater of the millennial reign." In a blasphemy that would be recalled with repugnance even half a century later, he suggested that Jesus and Jefferson had some striking similarities. Addressing a crowd of Republicans who met in Wallingford, Connecticut, to celebrate the president's inauguration, this most calculating of politicians slyly began by protesting that he would not "compare the illustrious chief, who, once insulted, now presides over the union, with him who, once insulted, now presides over the universe." Instead, he explained, he would merely show that Federalists and other "friends of order" who opposed Jefferson perpetuated the errors of the Jews, who refused to accept Christ.[17] This was not a casual or momentary exaggeration. Elaborating his theme at great length, Bishop claimed that Federalist clergymen "would, if they had power, and really believed themselves, actually crucify the republicans." Certainly, they made such an attempt against Jefferson. Seeking vengeance, as had the opponents of Christ, they cried out "crucify him, crucify him." Thus the Federalists continued in the tradition of the Jews and "all the friends of order" who "have been unchangeable: The obstinate jew will wander forever in error—The Catholic will be always infallible and cruel. . . . The character is fixed on them as indelible as colour is on the Ethiopian—they will hate equal rights and economy and republicanism throughout, as long as the Ethiopians shall be black."

It was an appeal to prejudice in religion, as in race, with which Republicans—the popular party—had already distinguished themselves,

---

[16] James H. Hutson, *Religion and the Founding of the American Republic,* 84–85, 119, note 45 (Washington, D.C.: Library of Congress, 1998), citing A. P. C. Griffin, "Issues of the Press in 1800–1802," *Records of the Columbia Historical Society,* 4: 58 (1901); *Alexandria Advertizer* (July 14, 1801); *National Intelligencer* (June 29 and July 1, 1801). See also Lienesch, "The Role of Political Millennialism in Early Modern Nationalism."

[17] Bishop, *Oration Delivered in Wallingford,* 7. See Richard Hildreth, *The History of the United States,* 5: 429 (1851; revised, 1879). Bishop also declared that Federalists were "political levites" who "teach a religion extremely like that of the Jews, consisting of an ostentatious display of tenets. They persecute, and bless not. They pray for the downfall of their enemies, and assume the reverse of what the Saviour recommended on the mount." Bishop, *Proofs of a Conspiracy,* 16–17. See also ibid., 69.

but it now took on millennial proportions.[18] Lest Bishop's implications were unclear, he added with rhetorical flourish: "Look at the Jewish 'friends of order:' he healed their sick and wrought miracles before them; and though he opened the eyes of a blind man, in a manner too open and convincing to admit the doubt, yet they evaded the force of the miracle by saying to the multitude, 'Give glory to God, we know that this man is a sinner.' . . . [T]hese 'friends of order' never relented."[19] Like Christ, Jefferson brought the truth to the friends of order, who were obstinate and would not relent.

The millennial Republican visions of Austin and Bishop coalesced most spectacularly during an event Bishop organized in the town that Condorcet had misspelled "New-Heaven."[20] The occasion was a Republican festival held on March 9, 1803, to celebrate the second anniversary of Jefferson's inauguration. Following artillery salutes from high atop East Rock, the approximately 1,000 celebrants paraded around the Green to one of the churches, where they listened to prayers, speeches, instrumental music, and the "Republican Festival Proclamation, and New Jerusalem"—a presentation scripted by the Rev. David Austin and read by the sonorous Roswell Judson.[21] Combining religious and political

---

[18] Bishop, *Oration Delivered in Wallingford*, 41, 70, 7. Racial prejudice was widespread in 1800, but during the election it was more prominently employed by the defenders of the candidate from Virginia. For example, on the basis of passages in Jefferson's writings, including his *Notes on the State of Virginia* (1782), Federalists observed that Jefferson was willing to question the humanity of slaves and, from this, argued that he would deny them the opportunity of Christian salvation. Jefferson's supporters responded in terms that provided little comfort to northern Federalists. One Republican wrote: "If the blacks do not appertain to the human race, then it is no more anti-Christian to say so, than it is to affect it of the Orang Outang, or the monkey. If they do belong to it, we may suppose them a distinct race, made so by time and circumstances, and inferior in the endowments both of body and mind to the whites, without impeaching the doctrine of a first pair." "Grotius" [DeWitt Clinton], *A Vindication of Thomas Jefferson: Against the Charges Contained in a Pamphlet Entitled, "Serious Considerations," &c.*, 16 (1800).

[19] Bishop, *Oration Delivered in Wallingford*, 71.

[20] See Simeon E. Baldwin, "The Authorship of the Quatre Lettres d'un Bourgeois de New-Heaven sur l'Unité de la Législation," in *Papers of the New Haven Colony Historical Society*, 6: 263 (New Haven: 1900).

[21] For relatively clear accounts of the order of proceedings, see *American Mercury* (March 3, 1803, and March 17, 1803). The second of these issues estimated that over 1,000 were present in the procession by the time it reached the meeting house. For a less friendly estimate of about 850 in the procession, see *Connecticut Gazette* (March 23, 1803). The attempts of Republicans to draw women to the festival provoked much commentary. Although the managers sought to have the occasion "numerously attended by both sexes," few of "the respectable ladies of New-Haven" agreed to attend. Moreover, some not quite

metaphor, it presented strange verbal descriptions of mental stage sets or "scenes," such as that of the "REPUBLICAN DIOCESE," which was described as "A COUNTERPART TO THE REPUBLICAN ADMINISTRATION OF THOMAS JEFFERSON." In one scene "[t]he Republican administration . . . rises on the base, and relies on the strength of popular suffrage, and the unfailing support of Almighty God." While "Federal religion fades with federal glory" and "the federal priesthood" is left "upon a lee shore," "Republicans now advance," and "[t]hey bear upon their surface the testimony of 'the Ark of the Testament' as it relates to things which are 'to be hereafter.'" Echoing Federalist millenarianism but with new import, Austin's Republicans confidently proclaimed: "We are at this moment on the evening of the gospel day, and approach the rising of 'the morning after.' A new day opens upon the gospel field and upon the American nation, and through them *to all nations*." Indeed, Jefferson's election "was of God." With this blend of civil and religious dreams, the participants who congregated in New Haven were asked "What can the restoration of the gospel Jerusalem be, but 'the New Jerusalem?' Who can describe the 'new Heaven and the new earth'—'the holy city, New Jerusalem, coming down from God out of Heaven?'"[22] Those present on the ninth of March had met for a sanctified purpose, and they would

---

respectable young men sought to obtain tickets to the ball that was planned to close the event. In part on this account, the ball was canceled, and Federalists made the most of this. "Circular" (New Haven, Feb. 1, 1803), in *Connecticut Journal*, 26 (no. 1843): 3 (Feb. 14, 1803); Correspondence (Hartford, March 16), in *Connecticut Gazette*, 2 (March 23, 1803). One of the most scurrilous Federalist critiques matched its ill humor with poor rhymes:

> Behold a motley crew
>   Comes crowding o'er the Green,
> Of every shape and hue,
>   Complexion, form and mien.
>   With deafening noise,
>   Drunkards and Whores
>   And Rogues in scores,
>   They all rejoice.

"Moll Carey," in Jared Potter Kirtland, ed., *Song of Jefferson and Liberty*, 9 (East Rockport, Ohio: 1874). Incidentally, "Moll Carey" was the proprietor of a notorious house of ill repute. This song first appeared in the *Connecticut Courant* (March 3, 1803). For Republican festivals, including some allusions to this one, see David Waldstreicher, *In the Midst of Perpetual Fetes: The Making of American Nationalism, 1776–1820* (Chapel Hill: University of North Carolina Press, 1997).

[22] *Republican Festival Proclamation, and New Jerusalem: New Haven, March 9th*, A.D. *1803*, 3, 4, 6–7, 8, 14 (New Haven: 1803).

meet again. "On the *fourth of July* next, (for there is no impiety in recording the wonders which God hath wrought) *let the same people who were
at New Haven on the ninth of March,* and as many more as may be disposed
to join, *appear there again!* The fourth of July will then be kept as unto
the Lord."

Those who met in New Haven even celebrated Jefferson's piety. In
a scene called "The State of Connecticut Revolutionized," Jefferson was
described as one who "says nothing against the Christian religion: but
pays well for its support"—that is, he opposed taxes for establishments
but paid money voluntarily in support of Christianity. Indeed, "[h]e
practices gospel principles on a national scale" and was "the first parish-
ioner, in the 'Republican Diocese.'"

In the secular New Jerusalem, Republican politics was religious, but
religion would not interfere with politics. One scene depicted the Constitution as a bastion that posed no threat to religious liberty. Through its
silence this fort left government without power over religion and left
religion powerless against Republicans:

> Fort CONSTITUTION mounts no guns against the liberty of Zion. It says noth-
> ing about religion; and the voice of the nation in its constitutional utter-
> ance at the lips of *three millions* of people hath said that *it shall say nothing
> about it!* Of consequence, the legs of national power, in this matter, are
> *set in the stocks.* There is no "Pharaoh and his host"—no "Gog nor Magog"
> in the American land. . . . Instead of being swallowed up in the Gulph
> of national turmoil and of broil; instead of thundering against T. Jefferson
> on religious subjects, a matter foreign to his jurisdiction; let the *spiritual
> eye* pass from the national to the spiritual line.[23]

The Constitution did not take aim at "the liberty of Zion," and the people
had confirmed in the recent election that it would continue to say "noth-

---

[23] Ibid., 9, 12, 13, 15–16. Having read the advertisements for this "sublime" event, Noah
Webster prepared an anonymous pamphlet to be published in New Haven on the day of
the festival. In his pamphlet he also used Biblical analogies but in a very different way.
"Chatham" [Noah Webster], *An Address to the Citizens of Connecticut* (New Haven: 1803).
See also Emily Ellsworth Ford Skeel and Edwin H. Carpenter, Jr., eds., *A Bibliography of
the Writings of Noah Webster,* 321 (New York: New York Public Library, 1958). Republicans
complained about the sanctimonious Federalist use of religion. For example, one Republican wrote: "We use scripture phrases without any affectation of parading religion in our
news-papers, but in mere reference to our subject, and we hope that the time is approaching, when religion and civil government, shall cease to corrupt and contaminate
each other." *American Mercury,* 3 (March 24, 1803).

ing about religion." In addition, however, the *"spiritual eye"* was to stop "thundering against Jefferson on religious subjects" and was to keep to spiritual matters.

It was a strangely circular phenomenon. Republicans demanded the separation of religion and politics but simultaneously introduced religious aspirations into their own politics. Of course, Republicans had practical reasons for drawing upon religious sentiments. By this means they could mobilize the passions of multitudes and could emphasize their radical, uncompromising political stance. Yet the Republicans' religious approach was by no means merely instrumental, and therefore if, while segregating clerical religion from politics, Republicans made American politics more directly religious, their experience may provide an initial hint as to what it might mean to separate church and state.

7

Jefferson and the Baptists: Separation Proposed and Ignored as a Constitutional Principle

AFTER Republicans in 1800 blasted their candidate's clerical opponents with the concept of separation between religion and politics, Jefferson himself in 1802 advocated the related idea of separation between church and state, which he asserted as an interpretation of the First Amendment's religion clauses. No doubt, Jefferson was pleased to support his Baptist allies. More broadly, he hoped to reprimand his clerical and Federalist opponents and to propagate his own, profoundly anticlerical, vision of the relationship of religion to politics.

Yet the Baptist dissenters for whom Jefferson wrote about separation did not, in response, adopt this concept as one of their demands for religious liberty. Separation had not been and would not soon become their goal. Indeed, they had ample reason to fear the separation of church and state as a concept that would bring Baptists into disrepute, that departed from their beliefs about the worldly role of Christianity, and that might deprive their leaders of valuable civil liberties enjoyed by other Americans. Not surprisingly, therefore, Baptists, like other dissenters, stuck to their traditional claims of religious liberty.

Revolutionizing Rhetoric, Mental Freedom, and Social Specialization

Although bolder with a pen than a sword, Jefferson, when writing to the Danbury Baptist Association, conceived of himself and his fellow Republicans as engaged in a revolutionary struggle. Federalism was their immediate target, but they reserved their greatest animus for New England's clergy, which nowhere was more entrenched than in Connecticut. Republicans perceived Connecticut's steady habits and standing order—its customs and religious establishment—as bulwarks of prejudice and inequality that rested upon the foundation of clerical authority. Therefore, by undermining the clergy Jefferson and his allies hoped to bring down not only Connecticut's religious establishment but also its antiquated mores. In particular, Jefferson and his fellow Republicans aspired to remove the clerical and other impediments to emancipated social relations and thus to leave individual citizens standing equal and independent, if also alone, in relation to government. On such principles Jefferson and his allies hoped to reform Connecticut and, more broadly, planned to make his election a second, more thoroughgoing revolution—the Revolution of 1800.

In completing what was begun in 1776, Jefferson understood the power of well-chosen words to awaken the power of the people. Looking back in 1819, Jefferson claimed that "the revolution of 1800 . . . was as real a revolution in the principles of our government as that of 1776 was in its form; not effected indeed by the sword, as that, but by the rational and peaceable instrument of reform, the suffrage of the people." Flattered by public perceptions, which he did not discourage, that his words had ushered in the first American Revolution, Jefferson seems to have come to believe that he could liberate a people through his writings. He recognized his ability to write in prose that resonated with Americans, and he hoped that his words, together with those of his allies, could overturn prejudices and open the minds of the people to new ways of seeing their world—leading eventually to radical changes.[1]

Other Republican leaders assumed that with mere words they could defeat Federalism even in the place where it found its greatest strength in tradition and deference. Congressman Matthew Lyon of Vermont boasted "that if he should go into Connecticut, and manage a press there six months, although the people of that State were not fond of revolutionary principles, he could effect a revolution, and turn out their present representatives." Indeed, he claimed that "nothing would be more easy than for him to change the Sentiments of the Connecticut people . . . he would want but one hour in Each Town, in the hearing of all

---

[1] Daniel Sisson, *The American Revolution of 1800*, 437 (New York: Knopf, 1974); Letter of Thomas Jefferson to Spencer Roane (Sept. 6, 1819), in *Writings of Thomas Jefferson*, 15: 212, ed. Andrew A. Lipscomb, quoted in Sisson, *American Revolution of 1800*, 437.

the people."[2] This was what Abraham Bishop attempted through his speeches and pamphlets, becoming "a flaming street orator" and "a blazing meteor of republicanism."[3] If necessary, he could also be surreptitious—as in the town of Hamden. He "went there several times in the dead of night—distributed nominations for assistants, . . . directed the men to be voted for in the delegation to Congress," and, according to one Federalist, "propagated the most palpable falsehoods." Returning to New Haven, Bishop boasted that he had "revolutionized Hamden."[4] On a larger scale, Jefferson sought to revolutionize Connecticut, New England, and the nation.

One of the ways Jefferson had long been revolutionizing or at least liberating the minds of Americans was by using familiar words in unfamiliar contexts, in which their meaning was altered and expanded so as to give readers new ways of seeing themselves and their liberty. Jefferson excelled at this means of making an idea, word, or phrase seem novel or paradoxical. Taking delight in his own creativity, even while he wrote with a most serious sense of his purposes, Jefferson, in these verbal changes of context, revealed himself at both his most playful and his most earnest, as may be illustrated by two of his pronouncements on religious liberty.[5] In 1779, when drafting his statute to prohibit any reli-

---

[2] Aleine Austin, *Matthew Lyon: "New Man" of the Democratic Revolution, 1749–1822,* 96, 126 (University Park: Pennsylvania State University Press, 1991), quoting Isaac Tichenor, Letter to Mr. Jacobs (Feb. 14, 1799), in Wilbur Library, University of Vermont, Burlington. From the first of these statements arose the incident in which Lyon spat in Roger Griswold's face.

[3] Contance B. Schulz, "'Of Bigotry in Politics and Religion': Jefferson's Religion, the Federalist Press, and the Syllabus," in *Virginia Magazine of History and Biography,* 91: 77 (1983), quoting the rather unfriendly *Washington Federalist* (Aug. 5 and Oct. 21, 1801).

[4] David Daggett, *Three Letters to Abraham Bishop,* 32 (1800). Like Jefferson, Bishop could be quite self-conscious about his rhetoric. In 1805, when advising his brother on how to give a political speech, he explained, "Avoid adjectives and participles as much as possible: they are the dead branches of our language. Obscurity in an oration is preferable to prolixity." Letter of Abraham Bishop to Jonathan Law (New Haven, Aug. 8, 1805), in "Letter Book of Abraham Bishop 1804–16," Misc. Ms. 137, in Yale University Archives, Group 352, Series XV, Box 77, Folder 1602. See David Waldstreicher, *In the Midst of Perpetual Fetes: The Making of American Nationalism, 1776–1820* (Chapel Hill: University of North Carolina Press, 1997). See also Kenneth Cmiel, *Democratic Eloquence: The Fight over Democratic Speech in Nineteenth Century America* (New York: W. Morrow, 1990).

[5] Jefferson also changed the context of ideas in matters not involving religious liberty. For example, he asserted that individuals do not give up any natural right when entering into society. See Philip A. Hamburger, "Natural Rights, Natural Law, and American Constitutions," *Yale Law Journal,* 102: 907, 958 (1993). Although other writers adopted similar ideas, Jefferson's formulation was unusually dramatic.

gious establishment in Virginia, Jefferson entitled it "A bill for establishing religious freedom."[6] Against the establishment of religion, Jefferson sought to establish religious liberty, and, by changing the context of "establishment," he flipped the word back at his opponents. Later, in his 1802 letter to the Danbury Baptist Association, Jefferson would tweak establishment ministers who doubted his reverence for Christianity by writing that he contemplated the First Amendment's protection for religious liberty "with sovereign reverence." Jefferson's irreverent style— his tendency to give words and phrases new contexts in which they acquired fresh, often polemical significance—endowed his writing with a resonance and a boldness that thrilled many of his contemporaries.

Of all the prejudices, customs, and other mental burdens from which Americans suffered, none seemed to Jefferson more pernicious and more in need of his liberating prose than the continued deference of many Americans to the clergy. Although most historians have "glossed over" Jefferson's anticlericalism, Fred C. Luebke shows that, in response to Federalist clerical attacks in the election of 1800, Jefferson came to feel and express his anticlerical attitudes with new intensity and even hatred. Having "never permitted myself to meditate a specified creed," Jefferson was already unsympathetic to organized religion, but he sharpened and hardened his antagonisms during the election.[7] From

---

[6] Julian P. Boyd et al., *Papers of Thomas Jefferson*, 2: 545 (Princeton: Princeton University Press, 1950).

[7] Letter from Thomas Jefferson to Rev. Thomas Whittemore (June 5, 1822), in Lipscomb, ed., *Writings of Thomas Jefferson*, 15: 373. More generally, Republicans "made anticlericalism a political plank before 1800"—indeed, had done so by the mid-1790s. James R. Beasley, "Emerging Republicanism and the Standing Order: The Appropriation Act Controversy in Connecticut, 1793 to 1795," *William & Mary Quarterly*, 29: 604 (3d ser., 1972). For the limited character of Jefferson's purified Christianity and the ways in which Jefferson found the views of Joseph Priestley gratifying, see Paul K. Conkin, "Priestley and Jefferson: Unitarianism as a Religion for a New Revolutionary Age," in Ronald Hoffman and Peter J. Albert, eds., *Religion in a Revolutionary Age*, 290 (Charlottesville: U.S. Capitol Historical Society, 1994). In 1810 Jefferson wrote that the clergy "themselves are the greatest obstacles to the advancement of the real doctrine of Jesus, and do, in fact, constitute the real Anti-Christ." Letter from Thomas Jefferson to Samuel Kercheval (Jan. 19, 1810), in Lipscomb, *Writings of Thomas Jefferson*, 12: 345–346, as quoted by Fred C. Luebke, "The Origins of Thomas Jefferson's Anti-Clericalism," in *Church History*, 32: 353 (1963). In 1819 Jefferson described himself as "of a sect by myself." He praised Jesus, who "told us only that God is good and perfect, but has not defined Him. I am, therefore, of His theology, believing that we have neither words nor ideas adequate to that definition. And if we could all, after this example, leave the subject as undefinable, we should all be one sect, doers of good, and eschewers of evil. No doctrines of His lead to schism. It is the speculations of crazy theologists which have made a Babel of a religion. . . . These religious animos-

the enactment of his bill establishing religious freedom in 1786 through the end of the eighteenth century, Jefferson wrote little on religion. From January 1800 to August 1801, however, he "wrote more letters with religious content than during his entire life prior to that time, and . . . every one of those letters, without exception, contains criticisms of the clergy, either directly or by innuendo."[8] In his "strongly emotional reaction to the fulminations of Federalist clerics, most of whom were honestly but mistakenly concerned about the status religion would have under a Republican administration," Jefferson lashed out against the established clergy of New England and, more generally, against all clergymen since the foundation of Christianity. The strength of his animosity against those who did not accept his Republican gospel became most astonishingly evident when he suggested that the clergy were crucifying him: "[F]rom the clergy, I expect no mercy. They crucified their Savior, who preached that their kingdom was not of this world; and all who practice on that precept must expect the extreme of their wrath. The laws of the present day withhold their hands from blood; but lies and slander still remain to them."[9]

The clergy threatened freedom, he felt, not merely through their power and privileges under a legal establishment but also, far more invidiously, through their mental tyranny. In New England, he wrote, the established clergy "believe that any portion of power confided to me, will be exerted in opposition to their schemes. And they believe right: for I have sworn upon the altar of God, eternal hostility against every form of tyranny over the mind of man." More generally, he blamed the clergy for inculcating the steady habits or deference to custom of which Federalists were so enamored, declaring that "the Gothic idea that we are . . . to recur to the annals of our ancestors for what is most perfect in government, in religion, and in learning, is worthy of those bigots in religion and government, by whom it has been recommended, and whose purposes it would answer." Shortly after the election, he ex-

---

ities I impute to those who call themselves His ministers, and who engraft their casuistries on the stock of His simple precepts. I am sometimes more angry with them than is authorized by the blessed charities which He preaches." Letter from Thomas Jefferson to Rev. Ezra Styles (June 25, 1819), in Lipscomb, 15: 203–204.

[8] Luebke, "The Origins of Thomas Jefferson's Anti-Clericalism," 344, 352.

[9] Letter from Thomas Jefferson to Levi Lincoln (Aug. 26, 1801), in Paul L. Ford, ed., *Works of Thomas Jefferson*, 9: 290 (New York: G. P. Putnam's Sons, 1905), as quoted by Luebke, "The Origins of Thomas Jefferson's Anti-Clericalism," 352.

claimed to Joseph Priestley: "What an effort . . . of bigotry in politics and religion have we gone through! The barbarians really flattered themselves they should be able to bring back the times of Vandalism, when ignorance put everything into the hands of power and priestcraft." Yet while Republicanism had brought Jefferson into office, it still struggled to prevail in New England, and this was no surprise: the New England states would "be the last to come over, on account of the dominion of the clergy, who had got a smell of union between Church and State." Extolling a purified Christianity—the religion "most friendly to liberty, science, and the freest expansion of the human mind"—Jefferson condemned the Christianity of the priests, from whom he expected only obfuscation and tyranny.[10]

Jefferson particularly hoped to undermine clerical influence in Connecticut, where the standing order had done so much to preserve the steady habits of the people and thus keep them in subjugation to prejudice and inequality. Unfortunately, as Jefferson explained to one of his Connecticut allies, Pierrepoint Edwards, "[t]he nature of your government being a subordination of the civil to the ecclesiastical power, I consider it as desperate for long years to come." Inculcated by the clergy, Connecticut's "steady habits exclude the advances of information," leaving the people of that state "exactly where they were" when their ancestors first came to America, "[a]nd there your clergy will always keep them if they can." Accordingly, Connecticut would "follow the bark of liberty only by the help of a tow-rope." Nonetheless, Jefferson still aspired to revolutionize Connecticut. In 1803 he complained to Postmaster General Gideon Granger that "clerical bondage is the root of the evil," but Jefferson could "rejoice that in some forms, though not in all, republicanism shows progress in Connecticut." In 1805, although Jefferson regretted that "Connecticut is still federal by a small majority," he confidently told the Comte de Volney that "[s]he will be with us in a short time."[11]

---

[10] Letter from Thomas Jefferson to Benjamin Rush (Sept 23, 1800), in Lipscomb, ed., *Writings of Thomas Jefferson*, 10: 175; Letter from Thomas Jefferson to Joseph Priestley (Jan. 27, 1800), in ibid., 10: 148; Letter from Thomas Jefferson to Joseph Priestley (March 21, 1801), in ibid., 10: 228; Letter from Thomas Jefferson to Moses Robinson (March 23, 1801), in ibid., 10: 336–337, all as quoted by Luebke, "The Origins of Thomas Jefferson's Anti-Clericalism," 350, 351.

[11] Letter from Thomas Jefferson to Pierrepoint Edwards (July 1801), in Ford, ed., *Works of Thomas Jefferson*, 8: 74; Letter from Thomas Jefferson to Gideon Granger (May 1801), in ibid., 8: 232; Letter from Thomas Jefferson to C. F. Volney (July 1801), in ibid., 4: 573.

Federalists recognized that not only their power but also the very nature of their society was under assault. Preeminent among these Federalists was David Daggett, who wondered why Jefferson and other officers of the federal government were "engaged, with a furious zeal, to subvert the institutions of this state?"[12] Daggett urged the people of Connecticut in his 1805 pamphlet, *Steady Habits Vindicated*, to adhere to the government "you . . . received as a legacy from your ancestors." Thus far, the people of Connecticut had "steadily cleaved to the civil, religious, moral and literary institutions which have been handed down from one generation to another"—institutions that "have formed the opinions, manners and habits of the people." By the same token, "the opinions, manners and habits of the people have supported the institutions out of which they grew." It was an ancient system, in which "[t]he institutions for religious and moral instruction and of common and grammar schools, were planned and established with the government itself, having been interwoven in its very nature," and these interconnected institutions had "grown with the people's growth and have strengthened with their strength."[13]

This interconnected, evolutionary character of Connecticut life depended upon the influence of the clergy, and therefore when in 1817 Republicans finally captured the state, Jefferson rejoiced that the clergy had been vanquished. Looking ahead to the opportunities for Republicanism, liberty, and, most profoundly, for enlightenment, he wrote to John Adams:

> [W]hat need we despair of after the resurrection of Connecticut to light and liberality? I had believed that the last retreat of monkish darkness, bigotry, and abhorrence of those advances of the mind which had carried the other States a century ahead of them. They seemed still to be exactly where their forefathers were when they schismatized from the covenant of works, and to consider as dangerous heresies all innovations, good or bad. I join you, therefore, in sincere congratulations that this den of the priesthood is at length broken up, and that a Protestant Popedom is no longer to disgrace the American history and character.[14]

---

[12] David Daggett, *Steady Habits Vindicated: Or a Serious Remonstrance to the People of Connecticut, against Changing Their Government*, 7 (Hartford: 1805).
[13] Ibid., 4–5.
[14] Letter from Thomas Jefferson to John Adams (1817), in Lipscomb, ed., *Writings of Thomas Jefferson*, 15: 1108–1109.

Connecticut's "Popedom" and "monkish darkness" had been resurrected to "light and liberality."

Two years earlier, in 1815, Jefferson wrote a letter arguing that the exclusion of the clergy from politics was one of various intellectual and social specializations, and he thereby revealed much about his understanding of the separation between church and state. In his letter he had occasion to explain why the clergy should not have "the right of discussing public affairs in the pulpit," and his extraordinary explanation suggests how his advocacy of separation may have been a response not merely to the New England establishments, but to the bondage of clerical influence in a society in which steady habits, Federalist politics, and clerical authority were closely intertwined.

Jefferson wrote his letter to a newly elected Republican congressman, Peter Hercules Wendover of New York. A stranger to Jefferson, Wendover had sent the great man a volume of political sermons or "discourses" by the Rev. Alexander M'Leod, who was one of Wendover's constituents. M'Leod was a Presbyterian minister whose eloquence regularly attracted throngs of worshipers to his church in New York City, and he was no stranger to political preaching. When at the start of his career he was called to take charge of another congregation, among whom there were slaveowners, M'Leod had maintained that they could not retain their church membership while holding slaves—a position he elaborated in a sermon, *Negro Slavery Unjustifiable*.[15] Now in his more recent discourses, published as *A Scriptural View of the Character, Causes, and Ends of the Present War*, M'Leod preached in favor of the war against Britain, arguing that the conflict was "in the Providence of God for extending the principles of *representative democracy*."[16] He introduced this polemical point, however, with a more fundamental argument: "IN a free country, it is the privilege of the subject to examine, and to judge the measures of the government."

On this basis, M'Leod rejected a separation of religion and politics.

[15] Alexander M'Leod, *Negro Slavery Unjustifiable* (Advertizement) (New York: 1802). In this sermon he recommended the example of Christians—including, presumably, the members of his congregation—who had "sacrificed, on the altar of Religion, the property which the civil law gave them in their fellow men." Ibid. See Paul Patton Harris, "Alexander McLeod," in *Dictionary of American Biography* (New York: C. Scribner's Sons, 1943).

[16] Alexander M'Leod, *A Scriptural View of the Character, Causes, and Ends of the Present War*, 10, 15 (New York: 1815).

He devoted his first discourse to showing that *"Ministers have the right of discussing from the pulpit those political questions which affect Christian morals."* Yet his argument went further than a simple assertion of equal rights for clergymen. Like his eighteenth-century predecessors, he held that "[t]he spirit of true religion is friendly to civil liberty." Moreover, in response to increasingly popular nineteenth-century fears, he carefully disclaimed any "right of enslaving the minds of my hearers into passive obedience to sacerdotal claims." Most fundamentally, he argued that religion "is useful for man, in every relation of life," including politics, and that the exclusion of politics from the pulpit would "produce a separation between the two subjects." Worst of all would be a complete separation, for "the separation cannot be complete, unless all christians are secluded from every concern in national politics; and the entire management devolved upon those, who will not be tempted to think of the bible, as the rule, or of piety, as the principle, according to which civilians should act: and where would this end; but in the transfer of the undivided management of national affairs into the hands of infidels."[17]

In thanking Wendover for M'Leod's volume, Jefferson responded that the clergy were specialists who were obliged to confine their preaching to their area of expertise. The breadth of human knowledge necessitated specialization:

[17] Ibid., 15, 10, 16, 223. M'Leod acknowledged that it might be imprudent for preachers to exercise their right to preach politics. "There are many, who admit that the public teachers of the Christian churches have a right, both as citizens of the commonwealth, and as interpreters of the oracles of God, to express their sentiments on political subjects," but "who, nevertheless, deem it inexpedient to exercise the right." Ministers could have such doubts from prudence but also from less admirable motives: "Prudence, lest by giving offence, they frustrate the more important objects of their ministry; personal timidity, lest they provoke disrespect and opposition; christian tenderness, lest they should wound the feelings of a pious hearer; and in some, perhaps, a sense of their own incompetency, or an ignoble pusillanimity, prevent the ministers of religion generally from introducing political remarks in their discourses." Although suspicious of preachers who disdained politics, M'Leod conceded that "[i]n abstaining from the exercise of this right, let christian pastors use their own discretion: I am willing to admit, that we ought rarely touch on such points; but an absolute prohibition cannot be supported by any solid reasonings." Ibid., 29.

M'Leod bluntly rejected the objection that "[p]olitical remarks are unfavorable to devotion; and therefore unsuitable to the pulpit." He responded: "The principle of this objection, while it appears to proceed from spiritual-mindedness, is near of kin to the unenlightened devotion of the recluse or the hermit, who retires from the world into a life of solitude. It approaches monastic holiness more than the piety of Abraham, of Elijah, of Daniel, of Paul, and of John the Divine." These pious men "taught, and they practised the duties of political life, both in peace and in war, without thinking that it injured devotion." Ibid., 38–39.

The mass of human concerns, moral and physical, is so vast, the field of knowledge requisite for man to conduct them to the best advantage is so extensive, that no human being can acquire the whole himself, and much less in that degree necessary for the instruction of others. It has of necessity, then, been distributed into different departments, each of which singly, may give occupation enough to the whole time and attention of a single individual. Thus we have teachers of Languages, teachers of Mathematics, of Natural Philosophy, of Chemistry, of Medicine, of Law, of History, of Government, &c.

A curious argument from America's greatest polymath, it permitted him to conclude: "Religion, too, is a separate department." This happened to be the only area of knowledge "deemed requisite for all men," and it therefore led them to "associate together, under the name of congregations, and employ a religious teacher," but preachers were not hired to preach beyond their specialty. "I suppose there is not a single instance of a single congregation which has employed their preacher for the mixed purposes of lecturing them *from the pulpit,* in Chemistry, in Medicine, in Law, in the science and principles of Government, or in anything but Religion exclusively." As a result, preachers who opined on other matters violated their contracts:

> Whenever, therefore, preachers, instead of a lesson in religion, put them off with a discourse on the Copernican system, on chemical affinities, on the construction of government, or the characters or conduct of those administering it, it is a breach of contract, depriving their audience of the kind of service for which they are salaried, and giving them, instead of it, what they did not want, or, if wanted, would rather seek from better sources in that particular art or science. In choosing our pastor we look to his religious qualification, without enquiring into his physical or political dogmas, with which we mean to have nothing to do.

Ministers were specialists in religion, hired for their expertise, and had no business instructing their congregants on other matters. Significantly, this limitation applied to all preachers, even if not members of religious establishments.

Of course, Jefferson well understood that most clergymen would have insisted that religion concerned all aspects of human life, including politics. As he put it, "I am aware that arguments may be found, which may twist a thread of politics into the cord of religious duties." Indeed, "every other branch of human art or science" could be said to involve religious duties. Yet the clergy could not provide instruction in these other areas. Otherwise, the clergy might presume to teach all specialties:

> Thus, for example, it is a religious duty to obey the laws of our country; the teacher of religion, therefore, must instruct us in those laws, that we may know how to obey them. It is a religious duty to assist our sick neighbors; the preacher must, therefore, teach us medicine, that we may do it understandingly. It is a religious duty to preserve our own health; our religious teacher, then, must tell us what dishes are wholesome, and give us recipes in cookery, that we may learn how to prepare them.

In this way, one might "amalgamate all the branches of science into any one of them, and the physician who is paid to visit the sick, may give a sermon instead of medicine; and the merchant to whom money is sent for a hat, may send a handkerchief instead of it." In opposition to "this possible confusion of all sciences into one," Jefferson argued that "common sense draws the lines between them sufficiently distinct for the general purposes of life, and no one is at a loss to understand that a recipe in medicine or cookery, or a demonstration in geometry, is not a lesson in religion."[18]

Jefferson closed by asking for confidentiality from his correspondent. In particular, he worried about his clerical enemies in New England who, although about to succumb in Connecticut, remained powerful in Massachusetts:

> Unaccustomed to reserve or mystery in the expression of my opinions, I have opened myself frankly on a question suggested by your letter and present. And although I have not the honor of your acquaintance, this mark of attention, and still more the sentiments of esteem so kindly expressed in your letter, are entitled to a confidence that observations not intended for the public will not be ushered to their notice, as has happened

---

[18] Letter from Thomas Jefferson to P. H. Wendover (March 13, 1815), in Lipscomb, ed., *The Writings of Thomas Jefferson,* 14: 279–283. With apparent graciousness Jefferson admitted that "I do not deny that a congregation may, if they please, agree with their preacher that he shall instruct them in Medicine also, or Law, or Politics. Then, lectures in these, from the pulpit, become not only a matter of right, but of duty also." Yet this nonreligious instruction "must be with the consent of every individual; because the association being voluntary, the mere majority has no right to apply the contributions of the minority to purposes unspecified in the agreement of the congregation." Similarly, Jefferson added, "I agree, too, that on all other occasions, the preacher has the right, equally with every other citizen, to express his sentiments, in speaking or writing, on the subjects of Medicine, Law, Politics, &c., his leisure time being his own, and his congregation not obliged to listen to his conversation or to read his writings." Ibid.

to me sometimes. Tranquility, at my age, is the balm of life. While I know I am safe in the honor and charity of a Macleod, I do not wish to be cast forth to the Marats, the Dantons, and the Robespierres of the priesthood; I mean the *Parishes*, the *Ogdens*, and the *Gardiners* of Massachusetts.

As he elaborated his fears of exposure, Jefferson apparently doubted the wisdom of sending such a letter. How would his clerical enemies respond to his view of clergymen as religious specialists, who lacked "the right of discussing public affairs in the pulpit"? What, for that matter, would their congregants say? Accordingly, after signing the letter, Jefferson docketed it: "On further consideration, this letter was not sent, Mr. Wendover's character & calling being entirely unknown." So bold on paper, and yet so timid in life, Jefferson filed it for the benefit of a more appreciative posterity.[19]

In such ways, Jefferson struggled for mental freedom and the social specialization that permitted it. He despised what he considered the mental and political bondage of New England, and he rejected the Federalist suggestions that Connecticut was a society all the more free on account of its steady habits and its deference to an intertwined social, political, and religious elite. Not least, in opposition to the clergy whose authority sustained such a society, Jefferson and his fellow Republicans attempted to separate religion from politics and church from state.

Jefferson's Letter to the Danbury Baptists

In 1802, with the election of 1800 behind him, and with the continuing struggle against Connecticut's standing order still ahead, Jefferson responded to a petition from some Connecticut Baptists in a way that gave new, constitutional significance to the election rhetoric about separation. Variants of separation had thus far been employed in anticlerical and political contexts, and now Jefferson advocated the separation of church and state as an interpretation of the U.S. Constitution's First Amendment.

---

[19] Ibid.; Jefferson Papers, Series I, General Correspondence, fol. 36, 189, microfilm, in Library of Congress. Jefferson similarly hesitated to discuss his religious views, treating them as utterly private. He told Charles Clay: "I not only write nothing on religion, but rarely permit myself to speak on it, and never but in a reasonable society. I have probably said more to you than to any other person, because we have had more hours of conversation in *duetto* in our meetings at the Forest." Letter from Thomas Jefferson to Charles Clay (Jan. 29, 1815), in Lipscomb, ed., *The Writings of Thomas Jefferson*, 14: 233.

The New England Baptists were struggling for their religious liberty, and, if only on this account, had sympathy for Jefferson.[20] Baptists had to sign certificates as to their minority status in order to avoid paying taxes for support of the Congregationalist religious majority in each town, and therefore Baptists resented the establishments and looked to Jefferson for support. The Baptists of New England found an especially strong connection to Jefferson in John Leland. Originally from Massachusetts, he spent fourteen years preaching in Virginia, where he also campaigned for religious liberty and, in early 1789, encouraged Baptists to vote for James Madison so that he might propose what became the First Amendment.[21] Shortly afterward, however, Leland returned to Massachusetts, eventually settling in the Berkshire town of Cheshire.[22] In 1801 he simultaneously advertised a local agricultural product and reminded Jefferson of his friends in New England by organizing the farmers of Cheshire to make an enormous cheese for the president. After Leland proposed the plan from his pulpit, the townspeople approved it— although in the spirit of voluntariness, no contribution was taken from the cows of Federalists. On July 20, 1801, Leland's supporters pressed the gigantic mass of curds into a cheese ultimately weighing (after shrinkage) 1,235 pounds.[23] In December a chosen few carried the cheese down through New York to Washington on a wagon, accompanied by Leland, who "preached all the way there."[24] Finally, on January 1, 1802, Leland presented it to the president in Washington, taking the opportunity to praise the Constitution and to "humbly claim" for the inhabitants of Cheshire "the right of judging for ourselves." Leland also expressed his belief that "the supreme Ruler of the Universe . . . has raised up a Jefferson at this critical day to defend *Republicanism* and to baffle the arts of *Aristocracy.*" Jefferson reciprocated by lauding the cheese, the people of Berkshire, and his "reverend and most respected friend." Jefferson

[20] It should not be assumed, however, that Baptists were without disagreement or that in Connecticut they were yet very directly involved in partisan Republican activities. William G. McLoughlin, *New England Dissent, 1630–1833,* 988 (Cambridge: Harvard University Press, 1971).

[21] Both Leland and another Baptist preacher, George Eve, were active on Madison's behalf. See Robert A. Rutland, ed., *Papers of James Madison,* 11: 304, 442 (Charlottesville: University Press of Virginia, 1977).

[22] Samuel Chiles Mitchell, "James Madison and His Co-worker, John Leland," *Religious Herald,* 107: 4–5 (Oct. 18, 1934).

[23] C. A. Browne, "Elder John Leland and the Mammoth Cheshire Cheese," *Agricultural History,* 18: 145, 147 (1944).

[24] *The Writings of the Late Elder John Leland,* 32, ed. L. F. Greene (New York: 1845).

then, of course, proceeded "to have this monster cut"—which, notwithstanding some decay, was in excellent state "for its age."[25] Although the presentation of Leland's cheese was prompted by regional more than Baptist interests, it suggests how Jefferson's supporters, particularly Baptists, made use of public communications to the president.

The Danbury Baptist Association, which elicited Jefferson's famous letter concerning separation between church and state, consisted of some twenty-six churches in the Connecticut Valley. In 1800 it initiated a campaign to petition the General Assembly of Connecticut for religious liberty—in particular, for a freedom from the state's religious establishment.[26] Although the Danbury Association directed its complaints to the local legislature that propped up the standing order, and although it hesitated to petition in ways that might be thought partisan, the Association in October 1801 wrote to President Jefferson in the hope that his response might influence public opinion on their behalf.[27]

The Association drafted its letter to Jefferson in traditional antiestablishment terms:

> That Religion is at all times and places a Matter between God and Individuals—That no man ought to suffer in Name, person or effects on account of his religious Opinions—That the legitimate Power of civil Government extends no further than to punish the man who *works ill to his neighbor.* But Sir, . . . such had been our Laws & usages, & such still are; that

---

[25] Browne, "Elder John Leland and the Mammoth Cheshire Cheese," 150, 151. The cheese came to be identified with Jefferson, and Federalists attributed to the president words of bitter self-recognition:

> In this great cheese I see myself portray'd
>   My life and fortunes in this useless mass,
> I curse the hands, by which the thing was made,
>   To them a cheese, to me a looking-glass.
> Once I was pure—Alas, that happy hour,
>   E'en as the milk, from which this monster came,
> Till turn'd by philosophic rennet sour
>   I barter'd virtue for an empty name. . . .
>
> Like to this cheese, my outside, smooth and sound,
>   Presents an aspect kind and lasting too;
> When nought but rottenness within is found,
>   And all my seeming rests on nothing true.

Schulz, "'Of Bigotry in Politics and Religion,'" 81, quoting "Reflections of Mr. Jefferson, over the Mammouth Cheese."

[26] McLoughlin, *New England Dissent,* 2: 986.

[27] For the Association's caution, see ibid. 987–988.

religion is consider'd as the first object of Legislation: & therefore what religious privileges we enjoy (as a minor part of the state) we enjoy as favors granted, and not as inalienable rights.[28]

[28] "The Address of the Danbury Baptist Association, in the State of Connecticut; Assembled October the 7th, 1801, to Thomas Jefferson, Esq. President of the United States of America," as quoted by Daniel L. Dreisbach, "Sowing Useful Truths and Principles: The Danbury Baptists, Thomas Jefferson, and the 'Wall of Separation,'" *Journal of Church and State*, 39: 460–461 (1997). It was "signed in behalf of the Association" by Nehemiah Dodge, Ephraim Robbins, and Stephen S. Nelson. The letter in its entirety read as follows:

Sir,

Among the many millions in America and Europe who rejoice in your Election to office; we embrace the first opportunity which we have enjoy'd, in our collective capacity, since your Inauguration, to express our great satisfaction, in your appointment to the Chief Magistracy in the United States: And though our mode of expression may be less courtly and pompious than what many others clothe their addresses with, we beg you, Sir to believe, that none are more sincere.

Our sentiments are uniformly on the side of Religious Liberty—That Religion is at all times and places a Matter between God and Individuals—That no man ought to suffer in Name, person or effects on account of his religious Opinions—That the legitimate Power of civil Government extends no further than to punish the man who *works ill to his neighbor*. But Sir, our constitution of government is not specific. Our ancient charter, together with the Laws made coincident therewith, were adopted, as the Basis of our government, at the time of our revolution; and such had been our Laws & usages, & such still are; that religion is consider'd as the first object of Legislation: & therefore what religious privileges we enjoy (as minor part of the state) we enjoy as favors granted, and not as inalienable rights: and these favors we receive at the expence of such degrading acknowledgements, as are inconsistent with the rights of freem[e]n. It is not to be wondered at therefore; if those, who seek after *power & gain* under the pretense of *government & Religion* should reproach their fellow men—should reproach their chief Magistrate, as an enemy of religion Law & good order, because he will not; dares not assume the prerogative of Jehovah and make Laws to govern the Kingdom of Christ.

Sir, we are sensible that the President of the united States, is not the national Legislator, & also sensible that the national government cannot destroy the Laws of each State; but our hopes are strong that the sentiments of our beloved President, which have had such genial Effect already, like the radiant beams of the Sun, will shine & prevail through all these States and all the world till Hierarchy and tyranny be destroyed from the Earth. Sir, when we reflect on your past services, and see a glow of philanthropy and good will shining forth in a course of more than thirty years we have reason to believe that America's God has raised you up to fill the chair of State out of that good will which he bears to the Millions which you preside over. May God strengthen you for the arduous task, which providence & the voice of the people have cal'd you to sustain you and support you in your administration against all the predetermin'd opposition of those who wish to rise to wealth & importance on the poverty and subjection of the people–

And may the Lord preserve you safe from every evil and bring you at last to his Heavenly Kingdom, through Jesus Christ our Glorious Mediator.

Ibid.

These Baptists, like so many of their predecessors, argued that the power of government did not extend to religion, and that government should not deprive individuals of their rights on account of their religious opinions.

As has been observed by Daniel Dreisbach, Jefferson saw the Danbury petition as an unexpected but welcome opportunity to disseminate his views. To his attorney general, Levi Lincoln, Jefferson wrote: "Averse to receive addresses, yet unable to prevent them, I have generally endeavored to turn them to some account, by making them the occasion, by way of answer, of sowing useful truths and principles among the people, which might germinate and become rooted among their political tenets." In particular, "[t]he Baptist address now inclosed admits of a condemnation of the alliance between church and state, under the authority of the Constitution."

Eager to make the best of this opportunity, Jefferson also hoped finally to explain his opposition to the proclamation of fast days and thanksgiving days. "It furnishes an occasion too, which I have long wished to find, of saying why I do not proclaim fastings and thanksgivings, as my predecessors did." Jefferson conceded that, "to be sure," the address "does not point at this," and therefore he worried that "it's introduction is awkward." Yet he could "foresee no opportunity of doing it more pertinently." After spelling out these desires and concerns to his attorney general, Jefferson more generally requested advice about his draft letter:

> I know it will give great offence to the New England clergy: but the advocate for religious freedom is to expect neither peace nor forgiveness from them. [W]ill you be so good as to examine the answer and suggest any alterations, which might prevent an ill effect, or promote a good one, among *the people?* [Y]ou understand the temper of those in the North, and can weaken it therefore to their stomachs: it is at present seasoned to the Southern taste only.[29]

Clearly, Jefferson hoped his response would influence the public.

Lincoln urged Jefferson to moderate his criticism of fast and thanksgiving proclamations. The people of New England, other than Rhode Island, had "always been in the habit" of observing the days proclaimed

---

[29] Letter from Thomas Jefferson to Levi Lincoln (Jan. 1, 1802), in Dreisbach, "Sowing Useful Truths and Principles," 465.

by their executives, and "this custom is venerable[,] being handed down from our ancestors." Indeed, "[t]he Republicans of those States generally have a respect for it," and they "regretted very much the late conduct of the legislature of Rhode Island," which in 1801 had declined to ask the governor to proclaim a day of thanksgiving. Accordingly, while acknowledging that "the religious sentiment expressed in your proposed answer" was "of importance to be communicated," Lincoln suggested "that it would be best to have it so guarded, as to be incapable of having it construed into an implied censure of the usages of any of the States." Lincoln then proposed language that would temper Jefferson's criticism of proclamations—that would express deference not only (as Jefferson had) to "the voluntary regulations & discipline of each respective sect, as mere religious exercises" but also (as Lincoln thought advisable) "to the particular situations, usages & recommendations of the several States, in point of time and local circumstances."[30] This cumbersome language of the attorney general could hardly have appealed to a philosophizing president hoping to sow "useful truths and principles among the people."

Another New Englander whom Jefferson consulted took a different tack and unctuously congratulated the president. After presenting "his compliments," Postmaster General Gideon Granger wrote that Jefferson's answer "will undoubtedly give great Offence to the established Clergy of New England while it will delight the Dissenters as they are called." Yet "[i]t is but a declaration of Truths which are in fact felt by a great Majority of New England, and publicly acknowledged by near half of the People of Connecticut." Although he acknowledged that "[i]t may . . . occasion a temporary Spasm among the Established Religionists," Granger wrote that "his mind approve[d] of it, because it will 'germinate among the People' and in time fix 'their political Tenets.'" Granger concluded that he therefore "cannot . . . wish a Sentence changed, or a Sentiment expressed equivocally—A more fortunate time can never be expected."[31] Notwithstanding Granger's enthusiasm, Jefferson heeded Lincoln's advice. Indeed, avoiding the equivocation required by Lincoln's phrasing, Jefferson simply dropped the entire sentence condemning the proclamations, lest it "give uneasiness to some of our re-

---

[30] Letter from Levi Lincoln to Thomas Jefferson (Jan. 1, 1802), in ibid., 466, 462.
[31] Letter from Gideon Granger to Thomas Jefferson (December 1801), in ibid., 466.

publican friends in the eastern states."[32] With this modification, Jefferson sent his letter to the Danbury Baptist Association on January 1, 1802—the very day he received John Leland and his mammoth cheese at the White House.[33]

Jefferson's letter elevated anticlerical rhetoric to constitutional law. Two hundred years earlier, Richard Hooker had accused dissenters of seeking walls of separation between church and state, and, similarly, in the late eighteenth century establishment ministers in America had suggested that dissenters aimed to separate religion and government. In 1800, however, Tunis Wortman and others flipped this accusation around, turning it into a demand. Now, echoing the words he surely had read in Hooker's *Ecclesiastical Polity*, Jefferson adopted the demand of his partisans, arguing that the First Amendment built "a wall of separation between church and state":

> Believing with you that religion is a matter which lies solely between Man & his God, that he owes account to none other for his faith or his worship, that the legitimate powers of government reach actions only & not opinions, I contemplate with sovereign reverence that act of the whole American people which declared that *their* legislature should "make no law respecting an establishment of religion, or prohibiting the free exercise thereof," thus building a wall of separation between Church & State. [A]dhering to this expression of the supreme will of the nation in behalf of the rights of conscience, I shall see with sincere satisfaction the progress of those sentiments which tend to restore to man all his natural rights, convinced he has no natural right in opposition to his social duties.[34]

[32] Ibid., 462, note 14. The final version of the deleted sentence (which followed Jefferson's language concerning separation of church and state) had read: "Congress thus inhibited from acts respecting religion, and the Executive authorized only to execute their acts, I have refrained from prescribing even occasional performances of devotion, prescribed indeed legally where an Executive is the legal head of a national church, but subject here, as religious exercises only to the voluntary regulations and discipline of each respective sect." Ibid., 462. For the earlier version of this sentence and other deletions, see James H. Hutson, "Thomas Jefferson's Letter to the Danbury Baptists: A Controversy Rejoined," *William & Mary Quarterly*, 56 (no. 4): 779 (3d ser., October 1999).

[33] Ibid., 785.

[34] Letter of Thomas Jefferson to Messrs. Nehemiah Dodge, Ephraim Robbins, and Steven S. Nelson, a Committee of the Danbury Baptist Association in the State of Connecticut (Jan. 1, 1802), in Library of Congress, microfilm, Jefferson ms., fol. 20,594. See also Hutson, "Thomas Jefferson's Letter to the Danbury Baptists: A Controversy Rejoined," 778. Incidentally, Jefferson opened his letter: "The affectionate sentiments of esteem and approbation which you are so good as to express towards me, on behalf of the Danbury Baptist

Jefferson interpreted the U.S. Constitution to require a version of what his supporters had sought in the heat of the campaign.

Jefferson recognized the radical character of his letter, for he took measures to protect himself from what he assumed would be a clerical onslaught. On January 3, 1802, John Leland took advantage of his visit to Washington to preach in the House of Representatives, and on that day Jefferson, apparently for the first time during his presidency, attended services in the House. As James H. Hutson has pointed out, "It is no accident that Jefferson issued the Danbury letter on Friday, January 1, 1802, and two days later, on Sunday, January 3, 'contrary to all former practice,' went to his first church service in the House, which he attended 'constantly' for the next seven years." In short, "[b]y attending church services in Congress, Jefferson intended to send to the nation the strongest symbol possible that he was a friend of religion." Being "a master of symbolic politics," and being as cautious in person as he was bold in his imagination, Jefferson balanced his anticlerical words with acts of personal religiosity.[35]

If Jefferson had high hopes that his letter would promptly sow useful truths and principles, he must have been disappointed, for his epistle was not widely published or even noticed. In one respect this is not altogether surprising, for his phrase about the separation of church and state probably seemed to reiterate the Republicans' anticlerical rhetoric. Yet there was another reason the letter eluded the public's attention. Jefferson miscalculated dissenting and especially Baptist opinion.

---

association, give me the highest satisfaction. [M]y duties dictate a faithful & zealous pursuit of the interests of my constituents, and in proportion as they are persuaded of my fidelity to those duties, the discharge of them become more and more pleasing." After the paragraph in the text above, he closed: "I reciprocate your kind prayers for the protection and blessing of the common father and creator of man, and tender you for yourselves & your religious association, assurances of my high respect & esteem." Library of Congress, microfilm, Jefferson ms., fol. 20,594.

[35] James H. Hutson, *Religion and the Founding of the American Republic,* 93 (Washington: Library of Congress, 1998). Hutson, however, does not interpret Jefferson's attendance at sermons in the House as evidence that Jefferson understood the radical character of his Danbury letter. On the contrary, Hutson assimilates Jefferson's religion and his separation of church and state to the views of most of his contemporaries: "The Danbury Initiative— the letter plus the attendance at worship—demonstrates that the mature Jefferson's views on religion and public policy were consistent with those of his fellow Founders, the only difference being the mode of expression, his being symbolic, theirs rhetorical." Ibid., 94. See also Hutson, "Thomas Jefferson's Letter to the Danbury Baptists: A Controversy Rejoined," 785, 789.

The Baptists

Upon receipt of Jefferson's letter, the Baptists might have turned it to their advantage by publishing it and adopting its phrase about separation. Certainly, other Baptist associations that corresponded with the president went out of their way to advertise their support from the great man. Yet the Baptists of the Danbury Association did not publish their letter from the president, and, far from employing Jefferson's words about separation, they continued to demand their freedom with the vocabulary and concepts they had used in the past. Apparently, separation was not what the Baptists wanted. Indeed, it was incompatible with their understanding of the pervasive value of Christianity.

The Danbury Baptist Association had solicited the support of Jefferson at the beginning of its petition campaign for religious liberty. In October 1800, at its annual meeting, the Danbury Association formed a joint committee with the nearby Stonington Baptist Association to petition the Connecticut General Assembly. Unable to collect enough signatures in time to submit their petition to the Assembly at its May 1801 session, these groups decided to wait until the following May. Accordingly, at its October 1801 meeting the Danbury Association urged the persons circulating copies of the petition to "get as many of the Freemen of the State to sign them as they can."[36] At this meeting—when the Danbury Association still needed signatures—it wrote to Jefferson, requesting his support, and it would have received his reply the following January, four or five months prior to the submission of its petition to the Assembly in May 1802.

Strikingly, however, the Danbury Baptists did not publish or otherwise take notice of the letter they received from Jefferson. When writing to him, the Danbury Baptists were "sensible that the President of the united States, is not the national Legislator, & also sensible that the national government cannot destroy the Laws of each State; but our hopes are strong that the sentiments of our beloved President, which have had such genial Effect already, like the radiant beams of the Sun, will shine & prevail through all these States and all the world till Hierarchy and tyranny be destroyed from the Earth." After seeking the president's radiant influence, however, the Danbury Baptists did not make use of his letter.

---

[36] McLoughlin, *New England Dissent*, 2: 986–988.

Some Republican papers in the Northeast, mostly in Massachusetts, published the correspondence, but the Danbury Baptists made no attempt to draw attention to it and seem to have been content for it to go largely unnoticed.[37] In a state well known for the strength of its Congregational establishment and its Federalism, these Baptists may have cautiously delayed publicizing a letter that Jefferson and his advisers understood might give "great Offence." Yet even after the Connecticut General Assembly rejected the Baptist petition in the spring of 1802, the Danbury Baptists did not publish or quote the letter either in their printed minutes or elsewhere. Indeed, as William G. McLoughlin points out, whereas the 1801 minutes of the Danbury Association recorded its decision to write to Jefferson, the 1802 minutes remained silent about his response.[38] This was in sharp contrast to the practice of other Baptist associations. Later in Jefferson's presidency, when several Baptist associations that regularly published their minutes wrote to the great man, they consistently recorded the resulting correspondence and published it with their proceedings.[39]

---

[37] Daniel Dreisbach points out: "This suggests that Jefferson was writing for an audience beyond the Danbury Baptists—namely, the New England Federalists and Congregationalists." Dreisbach, "Thomas Jefferson and the Danbury Baptists Revisited," *William & Mary Quarterly*, 56 (no. 4): 809 (3d ser., October 1999). For the publication of the correspondence in America, see ibid., 809, note 15. For its publication in England, see *Baptist Annual Register, for 1801 and 1802*, 854–855 (London: 1802). In his diary the Unitarian minister of the East Church in Salem, Massachusetts, William Bentley, noted the publication of Jefferson's response to the Baptists. Although Bentley sympathized with Jefferson, he did not have such warm feelings for the Baptists, and he viewed Jefferson's letter in entirely political terms. "The Baptists by attaching themselves to the present administration have gained great success in the United States & greater in New England than any sect since the settlement, even beyond comparison. This seems to be a warning to the Churches of the other denominations. The late address of the Danbury Association of Baptist Churches to President Jefferson with his answer of the present month are before the public. The president is in full consent with them upon the use of civil power in the Church. The Baptists are in their constituencies more republican then the Methodists." *The Diary of William Bentley, D.D.*, 2: 409 (Jan. 24, 1802) (Gloucester: Peter Smith, 1962).

[38] McLoughlin, *New England Dissent*, 2: 1005, note 23. For a hint that Leland may have hoped to publish Jefferson's letter but changed his mind, see note 43 below.

[39] All of the Baptist associations that regularly published their minutes (other than the Danbury Association) included their presidential correspondence in their printed minutes. *Minutes of the North-Carolina Chowan Baptist Association, Holden at Cashie Meeting House, Bertie County, the 2, 3 and 4 of May, 1807*, 4 (Halifax, N.C.: 1807); *Minutes of the Baltimore Baptist Association, Held in the City of Washington, District of Columbia, on the 14th, 15th, 16th and 17th days of October, 1808*, 14–15 (Baltimore: 1808); *Minutes of the Ketocton Baptist Association, Holden at New Valley, Louden County, Virginia, August 17, and Continued by Adjournment till 20* [1809], 13–16 (Baltimore: 1810). At least four other Baptist groups wrote to Jefferson, but none of them were in the habit of publishing minutes, and unfortunately their manu-

The Danbury Association, however, acted as if its correspondence had never taken place.

To understand why Baptists who sought the support of the president were so silent about his letter, it may be useful to begin by considering their awkward situation. As already observed, establishment ministers had long accused dissenters of advocating separation, whether of church from state or religion from government. Most recently, establishment clergymen had suggested that Baptists and other opponents of the financial connection denied that there was a necessary sociological or moral connection. Of course, Baptists merely sought disestablishment and did not challenge the widespread assumption that republican government depended upon the people's morals and thus upon religion. Yet such was the implication of the establishment charge. In these circumstances, in which the Baptists' opponents could bring them into disrepute by hinting that they wanted a separation of religion and government, the Baptists may have been hesitant to publish a letter that would have seemed to confirm this allegation.

A couple of New England Baptists came close to adopting Jefferson's words about separation, one of these being Jefferson's friend and ally, the irrepressible John Leland. This itinerant, who traveled tirelessly even when settled with a congregation, vaguely associated himself with a version of Calvinism more Arminian than was typical among New England Baptists. Having as little formal learning as many of those to whom he preached, he expressed indifference to the finer points of doctrine and even espoused a liberal disregard for these stumbling blocks to evangelization.[40] He ardently supported Jefferson and Madison, with whom he

---

script minutes have not yet been located. Incidentally, Baptist associations could be quite assiduous in obtaining the desired response. When the Chowan Baptist Association realized that the president's response had probably been misaddressed to Salem, the Association wrote to solicit another copy. It then published all of these communications in its minutes and in a local newspaper. *Minutes of the North-Carolina Chowan Baptist Association, May, 1807*, 4.

[40] Leland's restless, itinerant preaching carried him far, even in an age of itinerant preachers. Looking back in 1825, he wrote: "I have preached in four hundred and thirty-six meeting-houses, thirty-seven court-houses, several capitols, many academies and school-houses; barns, tobacco-houses and dwelling-houses: and many hundreds of times on stages in the open air." No place was too informal, and no congregation was too small or too large: "My congregations have consisted of from five hearers to ten thousand." Measuring his travels, he calculated that, "[s]ince I began to preach in 1774, I have traveled distances, which, together, would form a girdle nearly sufficient to go round the terraqueous globe three times." *The Writings of the Late Elder John Leland*, 35. Like Jefferson, he hoped his

had worked for religious liberty in Virginia, and, not averse to preaching politics, he celebrated Jefferson's 1801 inauguration with a sermon on religious liberty. On such occasions Leland adopted a stance that was as much Republican as Baptist. "What may we not expect, under the auspices of heaven, while JEFFERSON presides, with *Madison* in state by his side. Now the greatest orbit in America is occupied by the brightest orb."[41] Similarly, in 1802, following Independence Day, he preached that "the late change has been as radical in its tendency, as that which took place in 1776." Sharing the president's distaste for the establishments of New England, he urged: "May the combination of rulers and priests, church and state, be dissolved, and never re-unite."[42]

------

tomb would record his contributions to religious liberty. "When I die, I neither deserve nor desire any funeral pomp. If my friends think best to rear a little monument over my body, 'Here lies the body of JOHN LELAND, who labored . . . to promote piety, and vindicate the civil and religious rights of all men,' is the sentence which I wish to be engraved upon it." Ibid., 38. For his relatively liberal version of "Calvinism" and the contrasting version that prevailed among New England Baptists, see McLoughlin, *New England Dissent*, 1: 928–931.

[41] John Leland, *A Blow at the Root: Being a Fashionable Fast-Day Sermon, Delivered at Cheshire, April 9, 1801*, in *Writings of the Late Elder John Leland*, 255. In 1801, after the election, he wrote: "I may be enthusiastical; but I feel a strong persuasion, that America's God presided, and seemed to be addressing Americans thus: 'My children . . . I raised up a JEFFERSON to state your abuses and tell the world, in *the Declaration of Independence*, your burden, your wishes, and your rights. . . . Being now in a land of peace, . . . as you are not all instructed in your inalienable rights and the nature of a republican government, I have preserved Jefferson to be a guide and father unto you. I have raised him up in righteousness, and will strengthen his hands. . . . I have taught him . . . that the religious opinions of men, are not objects of civil government, nor anyways under its controul." John Leland, *A Storke at the Branch: Containing Remarks on Times and Things*, 12–13 (1801). He even wrote: "How confidently it is circulated thro' all these northern and eastern states, that JEFFERSON is a *deist*, for which, no proof is brought; but if it could be supported that he was a *deist*; there is this for our consolation, that he cannot possibly be a religious persecutor while he remains such. Whenever men adopt the religion of Pagans, Jews, Turks or Christians; or the religion of reason, and exert legal authority to force others to embrace *this* and reject *that*, they are persecutors; but no man can do this, until he [a]postatizes from deism and turns *religious biggot*." Ibid., 19. See also John Leland, *An Oration, Delivered at Cheshire, July 5, 1802, on the Celebration of Independence*, in *Writings of the Late Elder John Leland*, 264.

[42] Ibid., 263, 270. Incidentally, Leland, like many Baptists and Republicans, harbored deep suspicions of clerical hierarchies and believed that "[t]he groundwork of these establishments of religion is, *clerical influence*." *The Rights of Conscience Inalienable, and Therefore, Religious Opinions Not Cognizable by Law; or, the High-Flying Churchman, Stripped of His Legal Robe, Appears a Yaho* (1791), in *Writings of the Late Elder John Leland*, 185. Yet this is hardly to say that he opposed spiritual leadership. He was himself an elder. More generally, not all Baptists were anticlerical, and, against the anticlericalism of rationalist attacks on Christianity, some Baptists reacted with vigor. For example, at the 1797 commencement of Rhode Island College, Benjamin Allen preached: "While men have been pleading an uni-

Yet even this Jeffersonian, who condemned the combination of church and state, did not unequivocally seek their separation. Like other Republicans, Leland rejected any illicit or unnatural connection. For example, in 1802, when condemning the union of church and state, he wrote, "Let us . . . endcavor to divorce them, to dissolve their unnatural connection." Similarly, Leland denounced the existing connection between church and state, as when he complained in 1806 about "the present connection that exists between religion and property—religion and honor—religion and education, &c."[43] Of course, he may have opposed any connection. In his numerous writings on religious liberty, however, it is difficult to find even one passage in which he clearly attacked all connection between church and state or otherwise advocated their separation. Instead, although Leland enlivened his prose with Republican rhetoric, he sought religious liberty in traditional Baptist arguments, with which he repeatedly condemned laws that took notice of what was "no part of human legislation."[44] As late as the 1830s, he wrote

---

versal toleration of religious opinions, we rejoiced at their success," but "[t]hey have with great exaltation vilified the character of the clergy. We are sensible of ecclesiastical abuses; they cannot be too much exposed: but while we depreciate the ambition of the clergy, so destructive to the peace of civil society, when strengthened by the arm of the magistrate, let us not abuse indiscriminately an order of men so important and useful to mankind. Society, in an improved state, cannot exist without them. . . . [T]hey form the mind and mend the heart." Benjamin Allen, *An Oration, in Defence of Divine Revelation; Together with the Valedictory Addresses; Delivered in the Baptist Meeting-House, in Providence at the Commencement of Rhode Island College, September 6, A.D. 1797*, 5 (Providence: 1797).

[43] John Leland, *The Connecticut Dissenters' Strong Box, No. I*, 39 (New London: 1802); John Leland, *Van Tromp Lowering His Peak with a Broadside. Containing a Plea for the Baptists of Connecticut*, 35–36 (Danbury: 1806). Although in the *Strong Box No. I*, Leland came close to advocating the ideal Jefferson had mentioned in his letter to the Danbury Baptists, it is notable that Leland never published part II of this publication, which was to have contained "The Beauties of Washington and Jefferson; OR, THEIR choicest Observations on Religion and Religious Toleration." Leland, *Connecticut Dissenters' Strong Box, No. I*, 40.

[44] *Virginia Chronicle* (1790), in *Writings of the Late Elder John Leland*, 119. In 1790 Leland opposed religious proclamations and Sabbath laws that established days for worship—not because such laws violated separation but rather because these were beyond the power of civil government: "As the appointment of such days is no part of human legislation, so the breach of the Sabbath (so called) is no part of civil jurisdiction. . . . [T]hese times should be fixed by the mutual agreement of religious societies, according to the word of God, and not by civil authority. I see no clause in the federal constitution, or the constitution of Virginia, to empower either the federal or Virginia legislature to make any Sabbathical laws." Ibid. Even later, when Leland opposed Sabbath laws, as in 1815, he did not do so in terms of separation. John Leland, *Remarks on Holy Time*, 18–19 (Pittsfield: 1815).

Although Leland opposed the payment of government chaplains, he did not complain of their appointment: "I shall also take notice of one thing, which appears to me unconsti-

that "the only way to prevent religion from being an engine of cruelty, is to exclude religious opinions from the civil code." He declared: "Let every man be known and equally protected as a citizen, and leave his religious opinions to be settled between the individual and his God."[45] Looking back on his relentless efforts for religious liberty, Leland observed in conventional Baptist terms that "[t]he plea for *religious liberty* has been long and powerful; but it has been left for the United States to acknowledge it a right inherent, and not a favor granted: to exclude

---

tutional, inconsistent with religious liberty, and unnecessary in itself; I mean the paying of the chaplains of the civil and military departments out of the public treasury. . . . If legislatures choose to have a chaplain, for Heaven's sake, let them pay him by contributions, and not out of the public chest." *Virginia Chronicle,* 119. See also, incidentally, *Journal of the Senate . . . of Kentucky,* 6 (Nov. 7, 1793) (Lexington: 1793). Indeed, on January 3, 1802—two days after Jefferson sent his letter to the Danbury Baptist Association—Leland preached to the House of Representatives. Hutson, "Thomas Jefferson's Letter to the Danbury Baptists: A Controversy Rejoined," 785.

Leland summarized his views in his proposals for constitutional guarantees of religious liberty. In 1794, in Massachusetts, he wrote: "If the constitution should be revised, and anything about religion should be said in it, the following paragraph is proposed:—'To prevent the evils that have heretofore been occasioned in the world by religious establishments, and to keep up the proper distinction between religion and politics, no religious test shall ever be requested as a qualification of any officer, in any department of this government; neither shall the legislature, under this constitution, ever establish any religion by law, give any one sect a preference to another, or force any man in the commonwealth to part with his property for the support of religious worship, or the maintenance of ministers of the gospel.'" Jack Nips [John Leland], *The Yankee Spy: Calculated for the Religious Meridian of Massachusetts, but Will Answer for New Hampshire, Connecticut, and Vermont, without any Material Alterations* (1794), in *Writings of the Late Elder John Leland,* 229. In 1806 he proposed for Connecticut that:

> [I]n some prominent part of a constitution, an article should be fixed, tantamount to the following. As divine worship is a matter that lies between men and their God, and as religious opinions are not subjects of civil government not any ways under its controul; therefore the legislature of Connecticut shall have no authority under this constitution to establish any kind of religion, force any man to attend or support any order of worship contrary to his own will: but all men shall be left at liberty to worship their God, in that mode which their consciences dictate; free from the disturbances of others. Nor shall any man be proscribed, disgraced, or any ways rendered ineligible to office, on account of his religious opinions. But when any church or religious society shall voluntarily coalesce, and of their own free will, without the force of law, purchase lands or build houses for worship for their social use; they shall be entitled to such lands and houses without molestation.

He added that "anything short" of such an article "would not place *religion* on its proper footing, in its relation to government. In this opinion I am supported by the voice of thirteen states out of seventeen, either by their constitutions or laws." Leland, *Van Tromp Lowering His Peak with a Broadside,* 35–36.

[45] John Leland, *Transportation of the Mail* (1830), in *Writings of the Late Elder John Leland,* 565.

religious opinions from the list of objects of legislation."[46] In politics and religious liberty Leland approached the views of Jefferson as much as any leading evangelical dissenter, and, as has been seen, he visited the White House on the day that Jefferson sent his letter mentioning separation. Even Leland, however, did not clearly wish to separate church and state. Although, in attacking the existing connection between church and state, he used language that may, in retrospect, seem to come close to a demand for separation, he did not unequivocally go so far, and, indeed, he typically demanded a religious liberty that remained unmistakably within Baptist and other evangelical dissenting traditions.

Another of Connecticut's unusually liberal Baptists with Jeffersonian sympathies was Nehemiah Dodge (who later went so far as to become a Universalist), and he, more than Leland, focused on "the connection of Church and State." Yet, as with Leland, it is unclear whether he opposed all connections, though he castigated "our Connecticut Church and State blenders." Assuming that in Connecticut there was not "any distinction between the church and nation"—that "all are blended in one Covenant; all governed by one code of laws"—Dodge had no difficulty denouncing "your Church and State connection," without going so far as to condemn all such connections. At one point he warned Congregationalists against "the corrupt fruit, which has been always springing from a connection of Church and State." Yet even in this statement he was merely condemning "all religion in any and every country" that was "established and defended by civil law."[47] Although

---

[46] *Writings of the Late Elder John Leland,* 39.

[47] Nehemiah Dodge, *A Discourse Delivered at Lebanon, in Connecticut, on the Fourth of March, 1805: Before a Large Concourse of Respectable Citizens, Met in Honor of the Late Presidential Election of Thomas Jefferson,* 21, 42, 23, 31–32, 40, 24 (Norwich: 1805). McLoughlin describes him as one of Connecticut's "eccentric liberal Baptists." McLoughlin, *New England Dissent,* 2: 1024. See Chapter 3, note 12. For his Universalism, see ibid., 1008, note 2.

Incidentally, Dodge repeatedly used conventional Old Testament rhetoric to make unmistakably anti-Semitic allusions. He associated the established Congregationalism with the "the same old Judaizing creed" that had been rejected by Christ and accused Congregationalist ministers of meeting secretively to advance "their Jewish plan." *A Discourse Delivered at Lebanon,* 24, 28. Moreover, in urging lay Congregationalists not to remain in what he considered "Jewish churches," he told them that, as matters stood, they were paying "to support those Judaizing teachers, who are constantly trying to gull you out of your inalienable rights." Ibid., 33. Dodge also associated Congregationalists with "the Church of Rome, the mother of harlots, the whore of mystical Babylon." Reaching deep into the violent sexual imagery of anti-Catholicism, he asserted that the advocates of the established religion "denied to the Redeemer a rightful sovereignty in his own house, by bursting into the chambers of the heavenly bride, and ro[b]bing her of her innocence, by forcing her into the chambers of mystical prostitution, by kingly, national or legislative power."

Dodge had been one of the three members of the Danbury Baptist Association who had signed the letter to Jefferson, and although he therefore may have read the president's response, he did not unequivocally go beyond a critique of the existing connection between church and state. Even so, in their occasional ambiguity about this, he and Leland went further than most of their denomination. Unconventional among Baptists in the extent of their departure from Calvinism, and in their active political participation, Leland and Dodge probably moved nearer to Jefferson's separation of church and state than any other Baptist leaders.[48]

In contrast, most Baptists clearly refrained from demanding the separation of church and state or denouncing all connection between them. Notwithstanding the efforts of Wortman, Bishop, and Jefferson to propagate Republican principles and the somewhat different arguments by Leland and Dodge, the Baptists of Connecticut continued to demand religious liberty in their traditional terms. After their first petition was dismissed in 1802, the Danbury, Stonington, and Shaftesbury Associations held a meeting in Bristol in February 1803 to renew their campaign. At this meeting they prepared a new, more detailed petition, which they submitted to the legislature in May 1803. Not succeeding with this petition, they submitted a "slightly reworked" version of it again in 1804 and 1806.[49]

In this reiterated 1803 petition the Baptists objected to the union of church and state:

> [T]he doctrines of the gospel . . . retained much of their primitive purity, until the clergy became corrupted by a legal establishment under the Emperor Constantine; then, when church and world became united, and

---

Nehemiah Dodge, *A Sermon Delivered, at West-Springfield, Massachusetts, on the 5th of July,* 19 (Hartford: 1802).

[48] McLoughlin, *New England Dissent,* 2: 1024. Jonathan Maxcy—the president of the College of Rhode Island, who had flirted with Unitarianism—used language that could easily be interpreted as favoring a separation of religion and civil government but that probably was simply an expression of his relatively conventional antiestablishment views. "Religious liberty exists in these States, but not without some restraints. These restraints have originated in an unjustifiable interference of civil authority. To the everlasting honour of Rhode-Island be it said, that her legislature has never assumed the authority of regulating ecclesiastical concerns. Religion here, stands, as it ought to, on its own basis, disconnected with all political considerations." Jonathan Maxcy, *An Oration, Delivered in the Baptist Meeting-House in Providence, July 4, A.D. 1795 at the Celebration of the Nineteenth Anniversary of American Independence,* 17 (Providence: 1796).

[49] McLoughlin, *New England Dissent,* 2: 1000.

the clergy furnished with rich livings, and large salaries, the constant and main object of every such establishment, civil and religious oppression united their strength to the great injury of mankind.

Yet rather than seek a separation of church and state or denounce a connection, the Baptists stuck to their old antiestablishment claims. Human laws should not regulate worship, compel the payment of taxes in support of religion, or discriminate among religions:

> THAT your petitioners believe that all mankind are entitled to equal rights and privileges, especially the rights of conscience, or worshiping their *great creator* when, where, and in what manner they believe to be right, so far as not to interfere with the rights of others; and that all human laws, which oblige a man to worship in any law-prescribed mode, time or place, or which compel him to pay taxes, or any way assist in the support of a religious teacher, unless on his voluntary contract, are unjust and oppressive. That all law-made subordination of one or more denominations of professing christians to *another*, is productive of evil, both to the sect exalted, and to those who are depressed.

The Connecticut Baptists summed up:

> In short, your petitioners humbly conceive, that the christian religion is not an object of civil government, not any ways under its controul; that the interference of Magistrates to befriend it, has never done it any good, but much harm; and that it is best situated, when left on the same footing where the LORD JESUS himself placed it, and where the constitution of the United States, and most of the States in the union consider it, *distinct from the laws of state.*
>
> . . . We wish to be in subjection to all equitable laws, . . . but Gentlemen, in the case of the laws establishing religion in this State, it appears to us that we are deprived of those *rights of conscience,* which the *Almighty* GOD hath given us, by that, which we humbly conceive, to be the usurpation of men.[50]

This assertion of "rights of conscience" against laws that made Christianity "an object of civil government" hardly adopted the language of separation between church and state.

While this public petition for religious liberty remained distant from Republican demands for separation, the internal communications of

---

[50] To the Honorable General Assembly of the State of Connecticut, to Be Holden at Hartford, on the Second Thursday of May, 1803, the Remonstrance and Petition of a Convention of Elders and Brethren of the Baptist Denomination, Assembled at Bristol, on the First Wednesday of February, 1803 (Feb. 2, 1803).

Connecticut Baptists often ventured even further from the Republican ideal. For example, in 1805 the Danbury Baptist Association complained to other Baptist associations about its failure to obtain relief from the oppression of Connecticut's establishment, but it desired to proceed with appropriate humility:

> We still feel the burden of ecclesiastical oppression in this State, and do not enjoy that liberty which is the happy lot of many of our sister Associations with whom we correspond.
>
> But while we see our brethren who are in covenant-relation with us, distrest by having their property taken by force of law, and sold at the post to pay preachers whom they do not hear, and whose profession and practice they cannot fellowship; we would desire to be humble under the dispensation of divine Providence, and use every laudable and christian exertion to be freed from the tryannical yoke.
>
> May God grant that we may continually trust in him, who hath said, "I have chosen thee in the furnace of affliction;—And in the world ye shall have tribulation."[51]

Although only months earlier, in his attack on the "Church and State connection," Dodge had echoed something like Jefferson's separation of church and state, the Association of which he was a leader revealed no trace of such ideas.

In the same year, in a circular letter to its member churches, the Stonington Association urged Baptists to avoid excessive involvement in politics—not because Baptists should be unconcerned about the world but rather because an otherworldly approach was more efficacious:

> And be not *too much* engaged (as we fear, too many are) in Political disputes, and State politics: but let us earnestly commit the affairs of all things both Spiritual and Temporal to him with whom we have to do, who sees and knows all things in Heaven and Earth; and doth his pleasure and none can hinder: who hath the hearts of all men in his hand, and can turn them, as the Rivers of water are turned; and while others are perplexing themselves in those disputes, let us retire to our closets and with earnest and unfeigned desires wrestle with God for his Divine interposition for our good, and his Glory; that he would gratiously turn the hearts of the children of men to himself, and purify a peculiar People, zealous of good works; and dispose the hearts of Kings, Rulers and all men to peace, and that he would purge our land from the many growing

[51] Corresponding Letter, in *Minutes of the Danbury Baptist Association, Together with Their Circular and Corresponding Letters*, 7 (Oct. 2 and 3, 1805) (1805).

and gross Evils and Abominations, which call aloud for Judgements on the sinful inhabitants of the Earth. O Brethren can we not do more in a few moments with God through Jesus Christ than all the vain disputes:—all the laborious Assemblies of States and Empires without him, in bringing about those great and desirable objects; that our land may become Emanuel's; and the wilderness blossom like a Rose.[52]

Far from adopting a Republican, rationalist confidence in mankind, the Stonington Association Baptists, like so many others, saw little hope in this world or the next, except by committing all things, spiritual and temporal, to the ruler of heaven and earth. By this means—by "wrestl[ing] with God for his Divine interposition"—Baptists could do more than worldly leaders to make America's wilderness "blossom like a Rose."

As in Connecticut, so too elsewhere in the United States, Baptists held religion to be of pervasive significance—not least for those in government. The Cayuga Baptist Association observed in 1808 that "[w]hatever may be the object of moral reflections, whether it respects the present or the coming world; of matters civil or religious; of industry or economy; of things ancient and modern; the fountain of information is opened to view in Divine Revelation."[53] Further south, the Charleston Baptist Association, meeting in Euhaw, South Carolina, reminded its member churches that religion was to be the concern of every person in every office, religious or civil:

> Each Christian has his sphere of action, in the Church, in civil society, and in relative connection; in which it must be his care to move with regularity and faithfulness. Some are called to offices in the Church, others in the State; the rest occupy private stations; but all are concerned in the duties of relative life. To arrive at the highest usefulness in either character or station, the love of God and man must be our leading motive, and religion our governing principle.

[52] Circular Letter, in *Minutes of the Stonington Baptist Association*, 6 (Oct. 15 and 16, 1805) (Norwich: 1805). Less severe than the Stonington Association, the New York Baptist Association merely sought to limit political discussion during periods of religious fellowship: "To the practice of discussing politics on seasons of religious fellowship, we are utterly opposed; knowing it to be injurious to spiritual prosperity, and contrary to the declaration of Christ, 'My kingdom is not of this world.'" Circular Letter, in *Minutes of the New-York Baptist Association Holden in the City of New-York*, 15 (May 20 and 21, 1807) (New York: 1807).
[53] Circular Letter, in *Minutes of the Cayuga Baptist Association*, 9 (Sept. 28 and 29, 1808) (Canandaigua, N.Y.: 1808).

This principle had consequences for those who held power, including public officers, parents, and teachers, whom the Charleston Association admonished: "In the exercise of authority, whether in public or domestic life, unite with it mercy and kindness; that, if possible, you may rule by consent of the governed, and promote their happiness; but support your authority with purity, dignity, and firmness; for rulers are the ministers of God, and accountable to him"—a conclusion unpropitious for a separation of church and state.[54]

Some Baptists emphasized assumptions even less compatible with separation. If not only individuals but also nations depended upon the Almighty—nations being rewarded and punished in this world rather than the next—it was incumbent upon nations, as upon individuals, to express gratitude to the Almighty for their blessings. In particular, Jefferson had declined to proclaim days of thanksgiving, prompting the Savannah Baptist Association of South Carolina, in its 1804 circular letter, to demand a national acknowledgment of a power greater than civil government:

> It is an obvious dictate of reason that as nations are indebted to God for their security and prosperity that they ought to acknowledge him as nations. Their neglecting to do this or attempting to dishonor him will be resented by him. Of these truths we have clear declarations and striking examples in sacred scriptures; "righteousness exalteth a nation but sin is the reproach of any people." This neglect or contempt of God is punished by dreadful judgments and especially by that most awful of all, of being left to themselves to harden their hearts and to proceed in a rapid declension of holiness, the most awful as being the fore-runner & the cause of most of their calamities. What an impressive example has France exhibited of this truth.

These national sins and calamities were encouraged by the rulers of nations who neglected to acknowledge their Ruler:

> The rulers then cause a declension of holiness when they neglect to acknowledge the hand of God in prosperity and in adversity by rendering public thanks for their benefits and by humbling themselves before him under his chastisements. By this neglect they act as tho' they thought these events were fortuitous, instead of directing the eyes of the commu-

---

[54] Circular Letter, in *Minutes of the Charleston Baptist Association Convened at the Euhaw,* 7–8 (Nov. 3, 1804) (n.p.: 1804).

nity to that Being from whom they proceed, who reigneth in the heavens and in the earth.

In particular, political leaders exacerbated the problem "by violating the sabbath, by acts of legislation either in their legislative capacity, or in their various committees, by neglecting public worship and other instituted means of grace, by intemperance in their conduct or indecorum in their language."

In addition, the people had to take responsibility. "The ruled in general participate directly in some of these violations and neglects where they prevail, and are further reprehensible in being too indifferent about the religious qualifications of those whom they elect to serve them. We have been astonished at being informed that professors of Christianity have expressed an indifference about the religious sentiments of their rulers. Such indifference is inconsistent with a regard for the word of God." Lest Republicans protest that presidents needed to meet other qualifications, the Savannah Baptist Association added: "Being religious will not alone qualify men for office, . . . but candidates should be sought for among the most pious or least impious and their freedom from gross vices, and especially their possessing piety, ought to be a ground of decided preference before those of different characters."[55] These Baptists would rest content with the "least impious," but they expected at least some personal piety and, if possible, a freedom from "gross vices."

More broadly, Baptists understood the civil significance of religion and could discuss it in conventional eighteenth-century terms. For example, on Washington's death, a Savannah Baptist, Henry Holcombe, like so many other clergymen, praised America's first president for recognizing the "essential advantages of religion, in a political light." Holcombe, who, as a young officer in the Revolutionary War, is said to have preached to his troops from his saddle, had no doubt about the secular importance of religion:

> And may that firm persuasion of the importance of Religion, which eminently distinguished the invaluable deceased, so pervade and penetrate our own, and the minds of our fellow-citizens, that the blessed Gospel may diffuse its divine influence, and exert its transforming efficacy throughout this favored land! that all vice may be suppressed, virtue and

[55] Circular Letter, in *Minutes of the Savannah Baptist Association, Held at Black Swamp, in the State of South Carolina,* 5–7 (Nov. 24–27, 1804) (1804).

piety promoted, our excellent government perpetuated, and our civil and religious liberties and privileges, transmitted unimpaired to the latest posterity![56]

Similarly, on July 4, 1802, in Charleston, the pastor of the Baptist Church, Richard Furman, preached to the Society of the Cincinnati and the Revolution Society on the role of religion in securing American liberty during the Revolution—a theme that led him to discuss, in addition, "[t]he proper means for securing our liberties, and for improving the blessings conferred on us."

> On this subject, I humbly conceive, the first article, in order and importance, which presents itself to an enlightened mind, is a strict attention to religion. This is, at once, the most suitable expression of our gratitude to God; and the best means of securing happiness to ourselves. I do not mean the establishment of a national religion, by civil authority; this does not correspond either with our principles or feelings; but a personal attention and regard to the important subject; such as becomes a rational, immortal creature, accountable for his actions, and under infinite obligations to his Creator.
>
> It is the chief concern of man as an individual; and cannot be overlooked in a just estimation of the duties and interests of society: without virtue there can be no real happiness, either to individuals or the body politic; and without religion there can be no genuine, stable virtue.[57]

[56] Henry Holcombe, *A Sermon, Occasioned by the Death of Lieutenant-General George Washington, Late President of the United States of America; . . . First Delivered in the Baptist Church, Savannah, Georgia, January 19th, 1800, and Now Published, at the Request of the Honorable City Council,* 13 (Savannah: 1800). See also John Donald Wade, "Henry Holcombe," in *Dictionary of American Biography.*

[57] Richard Furman, *America's Deliverance and Duty, A Sermon, Preached at the Baptist Church in Charleston, South Carolina, on the Fourth Day of July, 1802, before the State Society of the Cincinnati, The American Revolution Society, and the Congregation Which Usually Attends Divine Service in the Said Church,* 16–17 (Charleston: 1802). Two years earlier, on Washington's death, Furman observed: "That the General possessed a high sense of the importance and excellency of religion, his public declarations on almost every occasion abundantly manifested. God's superintending Providence; his special interposition in favor of the just and innocent; his attention to the prayers of his supplicating people; and the necessity of religion, for the support of morality, virtue, and the true interests of civil society; are articles which he has fully stated in them, and zealously supported." Richard Furman, *Humble Submission to Divine Sovereignty, the Duty of a Bereaved Nation: A Sermon, Occasioned by the Death of His Excellency General George Washington, Late Commander in Chief of the Armies, and Formerly President, of the United States of America. Preached in the Baptist Church, in Charleston, South-Carolina, on the 22d of February, 1800, before the American Revolution Society, The State Society of the Cincinnati, and a Numerous Assemblage of Citizens,* 13 (Charleston: 1800). Similarly, the New York Baptist Association wrote to its member churches that not only in the next world but also in this one, religion—that is, true religion—was essential: "Force,

The Baptists adhered to their faith with profound anticipations of the next world but not without consciousness of the value of their religion in this world.

An American Baptist—somewhere at some time during the early nineteenth century—may have demanded a separation of church and state, but no Baptist organization or even any individual Baptist has thus far been identified who unmistakably took such a position. As William G. McLoughlin points out with respect to New England, "No . . . Baptists . . . ever utilized Jefferson's phrase about the wall of separation, though he had obviously coined this term with the Connecticut Baptists specifically in mind."[58] Some leading Baptists surely knew of the idea of separation—whether from Richard Hooker's *Ecclesiastical Polity,* from the election of 1800, or from Jefferson's 1802 letter. Yet Baptist churches and associations seem to have gone no further than to denounce the union between church and state—that is, an establishment—and only a few individual Baptists during the early decades of the nineteenth century, such as Leland and Dodge, seem to have come even close to advocating separation of church and state. In all probability, therefore, only a handful of Baptists, if any, and no Baptist organizations made separation their demand. Instead, Baptists focused on other, more traditional, claims of religious liberty.

What Baptists sought not only differed from separation of church and state but also conflicted with it. Tactically, dissenters could not afford to demand separation, for a potent argument against them had been

---

fraud and interested combinations in politics, in false religion, and in the *externals* of true religion, have all been used, in vain, to promote and secure the happiness of mankind. Still, some contend, that by prudently adding delegated power to general information on moral and political subjects, we may effectually guard against the dangers, and enjoy all the attainable advantages of society. This, it must be allowed, is plausible in theory: But it is an awfully attested fact, that wherever these means have been, *exclusively,* depended upon for the regulation of human affairs, anarchy and despotism have borne alternate sway, and our nature has bled at every pore." Circular Letter, in *Minutes of the New-York Baptist Association, Holden in the City of New-York,* 5 (May 22 and 23, 1805) (n.p.: 1805).

[58] McLoughlin, *New England Dissent,* 2: 1013. Indeed, according to McLoughlin, the "only incident which indicates that Jefferson's and Madison's radical views" on separation "influenced any Connecticut Baptists (with the notable exception of Leland)" was an 1810 tract against thanksgiving and fast proclamations by Elder Henry Grew. Yet even Grew adopted a "pietistic" argument and agreed with Jefferson only in concluding that such proclamations were inappropriate. Ibid., 1013–1015. More generally, McLoughlin writes of the Connecticut Baptists that in 1818 "they had still not reached the point of complete separation." Ibid., 1048.

that they denied the connection between religion and government—a serious charge in a society in which religion was widely understood to be the necessary foundation of morality and government. Nor could Baptists or other evangelical dissenters, whose preachers had long campaigned for religious liberty, accept separation's implication that the clergy had no right to preach politics. Certainly, Baptists had no interest in silencing their own preachers who spoke and wrote for religious liberty in polemics that were, as Leland entitled one of his efforts, *Politics Sermonized*.[59] Baptists also had no desire to deny themselves the advantages of civil laws that recognized their marriages, protected their church property, and otherwise accommodated their needs.[60]

---

[59] John Leland, *Politics Sermonized* (Springfield: 1806).

[60] Traditionally, Baptists had emphasized that they were grateful for such laws. In 1773 Isaac Backus wrote: "We would be far from forgetting or undervaluing of our privileges but are willing thankfully to acknowledge that our honored rulers do protect our societies so as not to allow them to be interrupted in their worship. And as the taking cognizance of marriage belongs to them, we take it as a favor that they grant our ministers power to administer it so that we may have marriage solemnized among ourselves. Many other liberties we also enjoy under the government that is set over us for which we desire to be thankful both to the Author and to the instruments of them." Backus, *An Appeal to the Public* (1773), in *Isaac Backus on Church, State, and Calvinism*, 325, ed. William G. McLoughlin (Cambridge, Mass.: Belknap Press, 1968).

Although Baptists needed laws protecting their church property, many Baptists opposed the incorporation of churches. For example, in 1804 the Goshen Association, in Virginia, refused to approve the incorporation of congregations "from a conviction that such incorporating acts may tend to lay the foundation of religious tyranny, contrary to our bill of rights." *Minutes of the Baptist Association in the District of Goshen, Held at Bethel Meeting-house, Caroline County, Virginia*, 5 (October 1804) (Fredericksburg: 1804). In taking such positions, Baptists seem to have assumed that they could continue to hold their church property without risk in other ways. Eventually, however, they came to understand that they may have been mistaken about this. Thomas E. Buckley, "After Disestablishment: Thomas Jefferson's Wall of Separation in Antebellum Virginia," *Journal of Southern History*, 61 (no. 3): 445 (August 1995). Outside of Virginia, Baptists recognized what was at stake both earlier and with much greater clarity. For example, the Leyden Baptist Association responded to a query on incorporation: "Though Christ's kingdom is not of this world, yet parishes or religious societies have many things in common with all other societies, and christian men have a right to the protection of the laws of the land; and as such incorporations are designed exclusively to protect men in the enjoyment of their religious rights; they are not inconsistent with the gospel, but should be left solely to the discretion of those concerned." *Minutes of the Leyden Baptist Association, Holden at Wendell, Mass.*, 6 (Oct. 13 and 14, 1819) (Greenfield: 1819).

Baptists also desired legal prohibitions on Sunday activities. As McLoughlin has observed, Baptists were "undoubtedly divided" about compulsory church attendance, but "they clearly believed the state had the right to prohibit all work, amusement, travel and other nonessential labor on that day." McLoughlin, *New England Dissent*, 2: 758.

More substantively, separation undermined much that Baptists and most other dissenters took for granted about the role of religion in this world. Many Baptists celebrated the president who had done so much to ensure religious liberty. Yet they assumed that all human endeavors, including government, rested ultimately in the hands of a higher power: "altho' the helm may be in the hands of those that administer the government, still the Almighty is on board the ship, and her safe coming into port depends on his attendant providence."[61] Like other evangelicals, Baptists took a broad view of religious obligation and its appropriate sphere. Many Baptists seem to have held that all human beings and all legitimate human institutions, including civil government, had Christian obligations, and some Baptists felt obliged to remind Americans and their governments of their Christian duties. Throughout the North, and probably in much of the South, there were Baptists who hoped that American individuals and institutions, informed by a shared sense of scriptural duties, would voluntarily live together and even cooperate in sympathetic Christian harmony.[62] Although some, such as John Leland, hesitated to

---

[61] Circular Letter, in *Minutes of the Ketocton Baptist Association, Holden at Ebenezer Meeting House in Loudoun County,* 8 (Aug. 18–21, 1808) (Alexandria: 1808).

[62] Writing about New England, William G. McLoughlin explains: "As pietists the Baptists were never greatly interested in political activity as such," but "a steady devotion to good order and a Christian nation pervaded their political outlook." McLoughlin, *New England Dissent,* 2: 752. Indeed, "[t]he Baptists, like most New Englanders, thought of the good society as a Christian Commonwealth in which a 'sweet harmony' existed between church and state." Ibid. McLoughlin adds: "Despite the intrinsically individualistic aspect of experimental religion, the Baptists had not yet adopted an atomistic view of society. . . . Although the logic of their theological doctrines regarding experimental religion, believers' baptism, lay ordination, and the priesthood of all believers led them into the Jeffersonian anti-Federalist camp (and later into laissez-faire Jacksonianism), at the same time their beliefs in the sovereignty of God, original sin, and the depravity of man kept them wedded to many aspects of the Puritan (and later the Whig) conceptions of an organic Bible Commonwealth." Ibid., 2: 752–753.

Incidentally, by 1800 most American Baptists were in some rough sense "Calvinist." For the Calvinism of Baptists in the North, see ibid. In the 1770s and 1780s, in the West and South, Baptists had been divided, and although, by 1775, Baptists of a more Calvinist persuasion prevailed in numbers, they did not have a very large predominance. Robert Baylor Semple, *The History of the Baptists of Virginia,* 60 (Richmond: 1810); David Thomas, *The Virginian Baptist or A View and Defense of the Christian Religion As It Is Practiced by the Baptists of Virginia,* 10 (Baltimore: 1774). Gradually, however, this changed. Writing of the aftermath of the 1791 Mercer-Walker debate over the merits of Arminianism and Calvinism, Semple wrote that the "ultimate consequence of this investigation of principles, was, a decrease of Arminianism among the Baptists of Virginia, and a much greater uniformity in the doctrines of grace." Semple, *History of the Baptists,* 83. According to Gregory A. Wills, "As early as 1800, most Arminian Baptists in the South had either died or been converted

embrace this perspective, even he emphasized the social character of religious duty when he defended Baptists from allegations that they aimed to escape the obligations of law. He argued not only that "their religion allows them" to take oaths and to bear arms but also that "the Baptists hold it their duty to obey magistrates, to be subject to the law of the land, to pay their taxes, and pray for all in authority."[63] At the very least, in their social attitudes Baptists seem to have had no quarrel with the commonplace that religion was essential for morality, republican government, and freedom. More personally, they cultivated an intense consciousness of "God's presence" and hoped to conform to their Christian obligations in all aspects of their lives.[64]

Thus Jefferson sowed a truth or principle that was not likely to flourish among the Baptists—let alone other dissenters. As in the past Jefferson took a phrase developed in one context and brought it to bear in another, and he surely hoped, as did Gideon Granger, that his words would "delight the Dissenters." Undoubtedly, he said something original about the religious liberty protected by the U.S. Constitution, but he did not assist the dissenters. Nor did he "delight" them. Instead, he asserted an idea that, at best, proved awkward for the Baptists and, more seriously, conflicted with much of what they sought.

---

to Calvinistic ideas." Wills, *Democratic Religion: Freedom, Authority, and Church Discipline in the Baptist South, 1785–1900,* 103 (New York: Oxford University Press, 1997). See also Sidney Ahlstrom, *A Religious History of the American People,* 441–442 (1972; New Haven: Yale University Press, 1979).

[63] *Virginia Chronicle* (1790), in *Writings of the Late Elder John Leland,* 120. Earlier, in 1774, when summarizing the duties required of believers, David Thomas had written that they "should obey earthly kings, and all in lawful authority, as far as they rule in righteousness. They should be just and honest in all their dealings with men. As well sober, temperate, and industrious toward themselves in their several stations." Thomas, *The Virginian Baptist,* 16. He explained of "civil Privileges, and Immunities" that "[w]e believe, that it is lawful for Christians to marry. To take an oath for confirmation of the truth, before a magistrate: To bear arms in defense of their country, when unjustly invaded: to clothe their bodies decently, and becoming their station in the world: To eat and drink temperately." Ibid., 20.

[64] Circular Letter, in *Minutes of the Charleston Baptist Association Convened at the Euhaw,* 7–8 (Nov. 3, 1804) (n.p.: 1804). According to the Letter, these Baptists hoped to live "under a habitual sense of God's presence." Ibid. See, e.g., Circular Letter, in *Minutes of the Baltimore Baptist Association, Held in the City of Washington, District of Columbia, on the 14th, 15th, 16th and 17th days of October, 1808,* 12 (Baltimore: 1808). More generally, see John G. West, Jr., *The Politics of Revelation and Reason: Religion and Civil Life in the New Nation,* 115, 117 (Lawrence: University of Kansas Press, 1996); Richard Carwardine, *Evangelicals and Politics in Antebellum America* (New Haven: Yale University Press, 1993).

The Republican Tradition

In the early nineteenth century the concept of separation continued to find support not among Baptists, but among some Republicans and their intellectual successors. Yet even this Republican advocacy of separation was sporadic and was not of a character likely to win wide approval.

After writing to the Danbury Baptist Association in 1802, Jefferson himself apparently did not again directly advocate separation. He continued to denounce the union of church and state, but he seems not to have expressly urged separation. For example, when, as already seen, he denounced political preaching in 1815, he did not do so in terms of the separation of church and state.

Following 1802 the most prominent Republican to advocate something like the separation of church and state was Jefferson's old ally in the struggle for religious freedom, James Madison. In a memorandum written between 1817 and 1832, Madison discussed a sort of separation and, perhaps not coincidentally, also revealed, to an extent not apparent in his eighteenth-century writings, a fear of the influence of religious groups.[65] Abandoning the studied moderation characteristic of so many of his published writings, Madison worried that America's churches would overpower the civil government. The initial problem was religious prejudice: "[B]igotry may introduce persecution; a monster, that feeding and thriving on its own venom, gradually swells to a size and strength overwhelming all laws divine & human." According to Madison, "the

---

[65] In 1774, in one of the most anticlerical comments to be found in his eighteenth-century writings, Madison complained about "Pride ignorance and Knavery among the Priesthood and Vice and Wickedness among the Laity" in Virginia. Letter of James Madison to William Bradford (Jan. 24, 1774), in William T. Hutchinson, ed., *Papers of James Madison,* 1: 106 (Chicago: University of Chicago, 1962). In 1784, against a pro-establishment petition in Virginia, Madison wrote: "But that part of the petition, which concerns me most, as well as every Non-Episcopalian in the state, is, where these Clergymen pray for an act of the Assembly to *Enable,* them to regulate all the spiritual concerns of that Church &c. This is an express attempt to draw the State into an illicit connexion & commerce with them, which is already the ground of that uneasiness which at present prevails thro' a great part of the State." Letter from James Madison to John Blair Smith (June 21, 1784), in Robert A. Rutland, ed., *Papers of James Madison,* 8: 81 (Chicago: University of Chicago, 1973). Although critical of "an illicit connection," this passage does not clearly indicate a distaste for all connections. Indeed, in the mid-1780s, although Madison opposed the incorporations bills desired by some Episcopalians, he acknowledged that "the necessity of some sort of incorporation for the purpose of holding & managing the property of the Church could not well be denied." Letter from James Madison to Thomas Jefferson (Jan. 9, 1785), in ibid., 8: 228–229.

separation between Religion & Gov[ernmen]t in the constitution of the United States" was "[s]trongly guarded," but he still worried about the "danger of encroachment by Ecclesiastical Bodies." Madison illustrated this ecclesiastical threat by mentioning not only a congressional bill reserving land in the Mississippi territory for a Baptist church but also matters that went beyond what were ordinarily considered problems of religious establishments: an "attempt in Kentucky . . . to exempt houses of Worship from taxes" and a congressional bill for incorporating the Episcopal Church in Alexandria that specified rules for electing and removing the Church's minister.[66] Eventually, in this memorandum, Madison acknowledged that he feared more than "the danger of a direct mixture of Religion & civil Government"—that he also worried about the "evil" of "the indefinite accumulation of property from the capacity of holding it in perpetuity by ecclesiastical corporations." This "accumulation of ecclesiastical wealth . . . beyond its object" could be subject to "abuses," including "corruption," and thereby could render even voluntary religious societies unsafe. Thus he applied, even against disestablished churches, the rhetoric ordinarily used against monopolies and business corporations—an approach he disclosed in the title to his memorandum: "Monopolies. Perpetuities. Corporations. Ecclesiastical Endowments." In Madison's view "all corporations," ecclesiastical or other,

---

[66] Elizabeth Fleet, ed., "Madison's Detached Memoranda," *William & Mary Quarterly,* 3: 554–555 (3d ser., October 1946); David P. Currie, "God & Caesar & President Madison," *Green Bag,* 3: 17 (2d ser., Autumn 1999); David P. Currie, *The Constitution in Congress: The Jeffersonians 1801–1829,* 352 (Chicago: University of Chicago Press, 2000). Currie points out that, although Madison acknowledged the necessity of some type of incorporation of churches, he vetoed the incorporation of the Alexandria Episcopalian Church in 1811 largely because the act specified matters of internal governance. Madison argued: "The bill enacts into and establishes by law sundry rules and proceedings relative purely to the organization and polity of the church incorporated, and comprehending even the election and removal of the minister of the same, so that no change could be made therein by the particular society or by the general church of which it is a member, and whose authority it recognizes. This particular church, therefore, would so far be a religious establishment by law, a legal force and sanction being given to certain articles in its constitution and administration." *Annals of Congress,* 22: 351, 982–983, as quoted by Currie, *The Constitution in Congress,* 354. Yet without civil recognition of such "rules and proceedings," a congregation could have difficulty preserving its doctrines or preventing internal advocates of other beliefs from seizing control of its property. In this sense, Madison's position had some similarities to that increasingly taken by Unitarians and rejected by more traditional denominations, except, of course, in their dealings with Catholics. For still broader differences over incorporation in nineteenth-century Virginia, see Buckley, "After Disestablishment," 445.

"ought to be limited" in their power to accumulate property in perpetuity. Not so much a problem of establishment, this was an issue of mortmain and monopolies, and it suggests that Madison's growing fear of church influence affected his views on religious liberty, including his willingness to conceive of the constitutional religious freedom as a "separation of Religion & Gov[ernmen]t."[67]

Separation was a conception of disestablishment that allowed Madison to express his hopes that Christianity would be so pure as to focus only on the next world, and it thereby permitted him to hint at broader prohibitions than those implied by more conventional antiestablishment ideas. In 1819 Madison described Virginia's disestablishment and concluded that "the number, the industry, and the morality of the Priesthood, & the devotion of the people have been manifestly increased by the total separation of church and state."[68] In 1822 he complained about congressional chaplains and about executive proclamations of fasts and festivals and then denounced any corrupting alliance between religion and government—a passage he concluded by declaring: "Every new and successful example . . . of a perfect separation between ecclesiastical and civil matters, is of importance; and I have no doubt that every new example will succeed, as every past one has done, in shewing that religion and government will both exist in greater purity the less they are mixed together."[69] Repeatedly, Madison expanded his more traditional anties-

---

[67] Fleet, "Madison's 'Detached Memoranda,'" 554–555. Madison also wrote: "The growing wealth acquired by them [i.e., all corporations] never fails to be a source of abuses. . . . The excessive wealth of ecclesiastical Corporations and the misuse of it in many Countries of Europe has long been a topic of complaint. In some of them the Church has amassed half perhaps the property of the nation." He then asked: "Are the U.S. duly awake to the tendency of the precedents they are establishing, in the multiplied incorporations of Religious Congregations with the faculty of acquiring & holding property real as well as personal? Do not many of these acts give this faculty, without limit either as to time or as to amount? And must not bodies perpetual in their existence, and which may be always gaining without ever losing, speedily gain more than is useful, and in time more than is safe?" Ibid., 556–557.

[68] Letter from James Madison to Robert Walsh (March 2, 1819), in *Writings of James Madison,* 8: 432, ed. Gaillard Hunt (New York: Putnam's Sons, 1908).

[69] Letter from James Madison to Edward Livingston (July 10, 1822), in *Letters and Other Writings of James Madison,* 3: 275 (Philadelphia: 1865). In contrast, in the late eighteenth century, criticisms of chaplains and of fast proclamations did not rest upon the principle of separation of church and state. For example, in 1790 a Virginian argued that the state legislature lacked express authorization in the state constitution to appoint a chaplain: "[I]t is not constitutional: No part of the Virginia constitution authorizes such acts, nor does the federal constitution honor them." Drawing on typical antiestablishment language,

tablishment ideas into a notion of separation, as when in 1823 he wrote that: "The settled opinion here [in Virginia] is, that religion is essentially distinct from civil Government, and exempt from its cognizance; that a connexion between them is injurious to both."[70] Although Madison occasionally acknowledged that some connections (such as some types of incorporation) might be lawful, he increasingly used varying phrases that indicated his desire not merely for a conventional disestablishment, but for some broader sort of disconnection between religion and government or between church and state.

Such views found their way into the Virginia House of Delegates. In 1826 a Methodist preacher, Humphrey Billups, got himself elected as a delegate, but the House refused to admit him because the state constitution excluded "all Ministers of the Gospel" from political office. As a deacon in the Methodist Church, Billups lacked the power to administer the sacraments, and, in this sense, he was not a minister. Yet the House Committee on Privileges and Elections interpreted the Constitution's disqualification to reach "all those, whose business it is to preach or minister the Gospel," and it justified its exclusion of preachers as well as ministers by relying upon the idea of separation between church and state:

> It is certain that our civil rights have no dependence on our religious opinions, and it is also certain, that our ancestors knowing this, intended

---

he added: "The moment that a Minister is so fixed by law, as to obtain a legal claim on the treasury, for religious services, that moment he becomes a Minister of state, and ceases to be a Gospel-Ambassador. This is the very principle of religious establishment, and should be exploded forever. If government has a right to make a law to support one religious teacher, it has the same claim to support all." A.B., Letter (from *Virginia Independent Chronicle*), in *Kentucky Gazette*, vol. 3 (no. 28) (March 6, 1790). See also "On Public Fasts," *The Bee*, vol. 2 (no. 87) (New London, Conn.: April 10, 1799), cited by Donald H. Stewart, *The Opposition Press of the Federalist Period*, 790 (Albany: State University of New York Press, 1969).

[70] Letter from James Madison to Edward Everett (March 19, 1823), in *Letters and Other Writings of James Madison*, 3: 307. In 1833, in a letter to Jasper Adams, Madison wrote favorably of circumstances in which the "connexion" between government and religion "has been entirely dissolved," adding that "[i]n the Papal system, Government & Religion are in a manner consolidated; & that is found to be the worst of Governments." Letter from James Madison to Jasper Adams (September 1833), in Daniel Dreisbach, *Religion and Politics in the Early Republic: Jasper Adams and the Church-State Debate*, 117–118 (Lexington: University Press of Kentucky, 1996). Incidentally, this was the letter in which Madison also wrote about a "line of separation," which suggests that Madison was not using this phrase to describe a different, more moderate, principle.

to keep separate Church and State. No mode was calculated more certainly to effect this object, than by denying a participation in the civil
government, to all those, whose high and influential stations gave them
an opportunity by preaching, of working upon and inflaming the minds
of their sect, and bringing with them into the councils of the nation, all
the prejudices which might be engendered under circumstances of high
sectarian feeling in Church matters.

This separation seemed all the more necessary on account of the "demagogues . . . who address themselves to the fears, prejudices and passions
of their congregations" rather than "applying reason and sound gospel
doctrine." The House agreed and, by an overwhelming majority of 179
to 2, refused to seat the minister.[71]

In the 1830s Andrew Jackson and his supporters adopted the idea
of separation, and, like Republicans earlier in the century, Jacksonians
employed it to condemn religious connections not clearly prohibited by
constitutional provisions against establishments. Of course, some Americans spoke almost casually of their support for separation and revealed
little understanding of its potential breadth.[72] Jacksonians, however,
seem to have recognized the potential of the idea to go beyond the antiestablishment religious liberty more specifically guaranteed in many
American constitutions. For example, Andrew Jackson himself refused
to proclaim a fast day. In 1832, when cholera threatened the United
States, the General Synod of the Dutch Reformed Church responded to
this "awful pestilence" by establishing a committee to "correspond with
other denominations, and with the civil authorities of our land, . . . in
order to obtain the general observance of a day of fasting, humiliation
and prayer, that if it please God that our country may be preserved from
the attacks of the pestilence." Yet when asked to proclaim the fast day,

---

[71] *Journal of the House of Delegates of the Commonwealth of Virginia*, 132 (Feb. 1, 1827) (Richmond: 1826 and later), cited and discussed by Buckley, "After Disestablishment," 475. For
a repeat performance, see *Journal of the House of Delegates of the Commonwealth of Virginia*,
70 (Jan. 8, 1830) (Richmond: 1829 and later), also cited by Buckley.

[72] For example, in 1818 Henry Clay rejected suggestions that the Catholicism of South
America would prevent that continent from achieving freedom. On the contrary, separation would permit South America to become free: "All religions united with government,
are more or less inimical to liberty. All, separated from government, are compatible with
liberty." This separation remained a possibility in South America and, therefore, the people of that continent, as they liberated themselves from Spain, might progressively follow
the example of the United States. "On the Emancipation of South America" (H.R., March
24, 1818), in *The Life and Speeches of the Hon. Henry Clay*, 1: 331 (New York: 1843).

President Jackson declined, explaining that he could not comply "without transcending the limits prescribed by the constitution for the President; and without feeling that I might in some degree disturb the security which religion now enjoys in this country, in its complete separation from the political concerns of government."[73]

Similarly, the radical Jacksonian essayist, William Leggett, condemned fast and thanksgiving proclamations on the principle of separation.[74] The constitutions of the United States and of New York did not specifically forbid executive acts concerning religion, such as proclaiming thanksgiving days, but Leggett discerned in American constitutions the principle that civil and ecclesiastical matters should not be mingled:

> In framing our political institutions, the great men to whom that important trust was confided, taught, by the example of other countries, the evils which result from mingling civil and ecclesiastical affairs, were particularly careful to keep them entirely distinct. Thus, the Constitution of the United States mentions the subject of religion at all, only to declare that "no religious test shall ever be required as a qualification to any office or public trust in the United States." The Constitution of our own state specifies that "the free exercise and enjoinment of religious professions and worship, without discrimination or preference, shall forever be allowed in this state to all mankind."[75]

Indeed, the framers of the New York Constitution were "so fearful of the dangers to be apprehended from a union of political and religious concerns, that they inserted a clause of positive interdiction against min-

---

[73] Correspondence, in *Daily Albany Argus* (June 26, 1832). The governor of New York also declined, explaining that "although a proclamation does not issue as a command, yet the design of proclaiming it in an official character, is to give the influence of a mandate to an unauthorized act." In addition, he made clear he had other reasons and drew attention to the dangerous "influence of the clergy, in ages of ignorance and superstition." Ibid. For the various ironies of this episode, not least those involving Clay, see Charles Warren, *Odd Byways in American History*, 228 (Cambridge: Harvard University Press, 1942); Dreisbach, *Religion and Politics in the Early Republic*, 24, note 12.

[74] Leggett once declared: "Convince me that a principle is right in the abstract, and I will reduce it to practice if I can"—an approach with which, during the brief remainder of his life, he alienated relatively staid Jacksonians and delighted New York's radical Loco-Focos. Fitzwilliam Byrdsall, *The History of the Loco-Foco or Equal Rights Party* (title page) (New York: 1842).

[75] William Leggett, "Thanksgiving Day" (from the *Plain Dealer*, Dec. 3, 1836), in Theodore Sedgwick, Jr., ed., *A Collection of the Political Writing of William Leggett*, 2: 113–114 (New York: 1840).

isters of the gospel, declaring them forever ineligible to any civil or military office or place within the state."[76] In these constitutional clauses Leggett observed a separation that was violated by thanksgiving and fast-

[76] Ibid., 114. As it happened, Leggett felt that "[i]n this last step"—the exclusion of ministers—"the jealousy of religious interference proceeded too far." He saw "no good reason why preachers of the gospel should be partially disfranchised, any more than preachers against it, or any more than men devoted to any other profession or pursuit." Instead, according to Leggett, "neither of them should be proscribed. They should both be left to stand on the broad basis of equal political rights, and the intelligence and virtue of the people should be trusted to make a selection from an unbounded field." This was "the true democratic theory; but this is a subject apart from that which it is our present purpose to consider." Ibid.

Some ministers more forcefully challenged the inequality of clerical exclusions. For example, the pastor of the Congregational Church in Chester, Vermont, preached:

> The ministers of the gospel, so far from being a privileged order in our country, are in some instances deprived of the privileges of common citizens; and there seems to be an effort to deprive them still more. In the state of New-York (I will not say positively in any other state) ministers are not permitted to hold civil offices. They cannot be represented in the Legislature.
>
> Now, I would not say, that it is expedient for ministers to hold civil offices to much extent. More important duties demand their energies. But this does not render it consistent with the principles of our government, that they should be legally *disabled*. Like other men, they are required to pay taxes; they have families; they are interested in the political condition of our country, and are justly entitled to all the privileges of American citizens. It may seldom, if ever, be expedient for ministers to engage in mercantile concerns; but would it be proper to forbid them, by law, to engage in such business? According to the principles of our national constitution, what propriety is there in depriving them of the privileges of common citizens? Are not all classes of men entitled justly to a share in the government, until some criminal act shall disqualify them? We would have no legislation to favour ministers, nor would we have any against them. Let them stand on a level with other citizens, so far as legal rights and privileges are concerned.

Accordingly, this minister suggested a constitutional amendment:

> I will close this essay by suggesting the propriety of altering our National constitution. If it is dangerous to the interests of our country that the ministers of the gospel should have the liberty of speech, and the privileges of common citizens, would it not be best to begin efforts against them, by a proposal to alter the constitution, so that they should be deprived of all the ordinary legal privileges of the country, and not be permitted *to speak any more in the name of Jesus?* In this way, a fair experiment might be made of the reign of licentiousness, and the glory, which would follow. Let the Sabbath be annihilated; let every sanctuary be burned down; let every moral and religious institution be swept away; let the last ray of *moral influence* depart from our land; let the line of distinction between good and evil be blotted out; and let the pillars of our liberty be founded upon moral anarchy.

U. C. Burnap, *Priestcraft Exposed. A Lecture Delivered in Chester, April 9, 1830. Being the Annual Fast; Together with An Essay on the Clergy of the United States*, 26–28 (Windsor, Vt.: 1830).

day proclamations. These proclamations amounted to a "mingling of civil and ecclesiastical affairs," and Leggett "regret[ted] that even this single exception should exist to that rule of entire separation of the affairs of state from those of the church, the observance of which in all other respects has been followed by the happiest results." According to Leggett, "[w]e cannot be too careful to keep entirely separate the things which belong to government from those which belong to religion."[77]

Far more controversially, and with hints of things to come, Abner Kneeland came close to questioning any connection between church and state when defending himself from charges of blasphemy. Federalist officials in Boston prosecuted this Jacksonian and notorious skeptic for articles he had written in his periodical, the *Investigator*. To the dismay of his prosecutors, however, Kneeland took his case to the public, arguing for the severance of any union or alliance of church and state and even almost arguing for the disconnection of church and state. It was on this ground rather than on the basis of ordinary antiestablishment principles that Kneeland could most clearly denounce his accusers and the law of blasphemy upon which they relied.

> If the kingdom of Christ is not of this world (as most assuredly it was not, and never ought to be) what have the governments of this world to do with it, or that to do with the government? This holy (or rather unholy) alliance should be completely dissolved and nothing heard of religion or anything that appertains to it on the floor of Congress, in our Halls of Legislation, in our colleges or schools, (excepting theological) on board any of our naval ships, or in any of our armies. These all relate to the government and concerns of this world, which should have no connection with religious dogmas, religious rites, or religious ceremonies. But confine these all to the sanctuary, to the church, and to religious associations.[78]

---

[77] *Collection of the Political Writing of William Leggett,* 2: 115, 118.

[78] Having urged a disconnection, however, Kneeland continued by blending this position with a much more conventional denunciation of establishments: "And let the laws take cognizance of their acts so far as to keep them [religious associations] as much as possible from quarreling among themselves, and as relates to their civil matters only. Tolerate no religion exclusively; for this supposes that some one of them all is right; and that the others may be tolerated; but give equal protection to all sects, opinions and denominations, and exclusive privileges to none. And let the world see that both government and morals may get along just as well without as with; and then you will let every body have his own religion at his own expense." Abner Kneeland, *An Introduction to the Defence of Abner Kneeland, Charged with Blasphemy . . . January Term, in 1834,* 42 (Boston: 1834).

As one of Kneeland's supporters argued, "The entire severance of church and state is the great boast of American liberty."[79]

Clearly, in the 1820s and 1830s the Republican tradition of separation found a following, but it enjoyed this occasional support among the political successors to the Republicans rather than among Baptist or other evangelical dissenters who campaigned against establishments. Separation conflicted with the religious and moral assumptions of such Christians, and it was unlikely to become a religiously respectable position through arguments to limit the rights of the clergy, to end fast and thanksgiving proclamations, or to reject blasphemy laws. Nor was it likely to become respectable through the advocacy of writers such as William Leggett, let alone Abner Kneeland. As a result separation became a popular American principle only later, in subsequent decades, when Protestant fears transformed American conceptions of identity, religion, and religious liberty in ways that would make separation more attractive.

---

[79] *An Appeal to Common Sense and the Constitution in Behalf of the Unlimited Freedom of Public Discussion Occasioned by the Late Trial of Abner Kneeland for Blasphemy*, 3 (Boston: 1834), in Leonard W. Levy, ed., *Blasphemy in Massachusetts: Freedom of Conscience and the Abner Kneeland Case, A Documentary Record*, 295 (New York: Da Capo Press, 1973).

III

MID-NINETEENTH-CENTURY AMERICANISM

P ARTS I and II have traced the development of separation as a perspective distinct from the antiestablishment religious liberty protected by the First Amendment. Now Parts III and IV must shift the focus of this inquiry to consider the ways in which Americans came to conflate these rather different conceptions of their freedom. Some hints as to how Americans began to assume that separation was a constitutional right have already been observed, but the more complete evolution of separation as a constitutional freedom remains to be considered.

According to the modern myth, separation of church and state has been an American ideal and even a constitutional right since the eighteenth century. Yet if separation has seemed one of the nation's fundamental constitutional and cultural principles, this was because it became popular not in the eighteenth-century struggle to obtain constitutional guarantees of religious freedom, but rather in the nineteenth-century movement to impose an aggressively Protestant "Americanism" on an "un-American" Catholic minority. Separation of church and state had severe implications for religious groups and their clergies—especially for any group so bold as to claim to be *the* Church—and therefore separation seemed to give positive, idealistic expression to the fears so many Americans cultivated in their animosity toward their most despised and insufficiently submissive white population.

This anti-Catholicism and the separation of church and state became popular in America as part of an individualistic transformation of religious liberty, Protestant religion, and American identity. As Americans escaped their more confining political and social circumstances, and as they idealized their individual independence, many of them came to worry that their liberty was threatened not only by governmental power but also by assertions of religious authority. They came to fear even the claims made by their own, disestablished, Protestant churches, but particularly those asserted by the Catholic Church. With this understanding of what they conceived to be the ecclesiastical and, above all, the Catholic threats to their individual independence, they adopted the separation of church and state as a Protestant and American ideal.

Of course, not all of those who thought of their religious liberty as a separation of church and state harbored anti-Catholic or other suspicions of ecclesiastical authority. Yet fears of church authority and especially of the Catholic Church made separation respectable as an "American" principle. Accordingly, amid anti-Catholic, nativist demands for conformity to American principles, Americans increasingly assumed that separation was their nation's religious liberty. In this way, as a result of anti-Catholicism even Americans without animosity toward any church or its authority frequently adopted nativist conceptions of national ideals.

Incidentally, even more than the rest of this book, Part III examines the attitudes of Americans rather than any particular events. The organized popular agitation for separation first developed in response to an educational controversy in 1840, and afterward, in each decade, the principle of separation became ever more widely accepted. Yet separation became popular not so much because of any one dispute in 1840, as because of a long-term shift in theological and social perspectives. Accordingly, it is necessary to examine the broad direction of these attitudes—about religion, churches, and the Catholic Church—across much of the nineteenth century.

8

A Theologically Liberal, Anti-Catholic, and American Principle

IN THE middle of the nineteenth century some Americans employed the idea of separation of church and state against Catholicism and thereby made it a popular "American" principle. During the beginning of the century, as has been seen, some secular political writers had occasionally advocated separation as a constitutional principle in a spirit that was recognizably Republican—that was anticlerical but not specifically anti-Catholic. By the middle of the century, however, Protestants began to employ separation in a manner more likely to have widespread appeal. Eager to prevent the Catholic Church from exercising political or religious authority in America, many Protestants were all too willing to perceive their religious liberty as a separation of church and state, and increasing numbers of Protestant leaders therefore opposed the Catholic "union" of church and state by urging a separation of these institutions. Of course, American Protestants had long differentiated between church and state and had justified their religious liberty with related distinctions concerning the limited jurisdiction of civil government. Therefore, many of the Protestants who began to assert a separation of church and state probably assumed that they were not making any significant change. Nonetheless, in demanding the separation of church and state and claiming that it was a constitutional principle, they took a momentous step, for they thereby initiated a redefinition of American religious liberty.

When advocating separation against Catholics, Protestant Americans voiced not only a fear of the Church's temporal power but also, more fundamentally, an individualistic suspicion of its theological authority. Even more than the Church's secular power, its assertions of theological authority seemed incompatible with freedom—especially with the individual independence and personal authority that were increasingly felt to be at the core of Protestant and American identity— and, in this respect, anti-Catholic demands for separation echoed and drew upon liberal Protestant rejections of creeds. Reacting to the hierarchical, group claims of Catholicism, Protestants ever more emphatically defined themselves, their citizenship, their religion, and their liberty in terms of their individualism and independence, and, in separation's limits on churches as well as government, these Americans found the most positive articulation of what their increasingly individualistic religious and civil identity implied for the Catholic Church and eventually other religious groups.[1]

Liberal Protestantism and Its Challenge to Authority

In America anti-Catholicism adopted some of the assumptions of liberal theology. American anti-Catholicism developed in response to many circumstances and came in many varieties, but much of what distinguished it from European anti-Catholicism was the degree to which it flourished with the growth of liberal Protestant ideas and became an avenue for liberal rejections of ecclesiastical authority. Rather than follow the path of European liberals in going to extremes of anti-Christian skepticism, American liberals explored the further reaches of individualistic Protestantism and questioned the authority of churches, clergymen, and creeds. They thereby developed an antiecclesiastical perspective, from which growing numbers of Protestants, whether or not theologically liberal, perceived the Catholic Church as a threat to individual mental freedom. In particular, Protestants could put aside their own differences over liberal theology and could unite by adopting a theologically liberal stance against Catholicism. As Rabbi Isaac Wise remarked about the anti-

---

[1] Aspects of these themes appear in Sidney E. Mead, *The Lively Experiment: The Shaping of Christianity in America,* 134 (New York: Harper & Row, 1963); Mark DeWolfe Howe, *The Garden and the Wilderness: Religion and Government in American Constitutional History* (Chicago: University of Chicago Press, 1965); Elwyn A. Smith, *Religious Liberty in the United States: The Development of Church-State Thought since the Revolutionary Era,* 97 (Philadelphia: Fortress Press, 1972); Elizabeth B. Clark, "Anticlericalism and Antistatism" (unpublished manuscript).

Catholic prejudice of his Protestant contemporaries: "The liberality of the Protestant churches is something unknown and strange."[2]

American Protestants had departed from established churches, including those of Rome and Canterbury, but now increasing numbers of American Protestants questioned the authority of entirely disestablished Protestant churches. Most evangelicals belonged to churches that retained creeds, clergies, and structures of church discipline.[3] Nonetheless, ever more Protestants felt their individual liberty to require a freedom not only from government but also from their own purely voluntary religious societies.

In effect, these Protestants declined to distinguish between what one minister, Samuel Lothrop, called "internal" and "external" religious liberty. The external was the liberty "which the individual claims of the government as a civil right, and relates to the extent of his exemption from penalties, privations or disabilities, on account either of his articles of faith, or modes of worship." In contrast, the internal was "the liberty which the individual claims of the church or ecclesiastical body, and relates to his freedom to form and express his own opinions of religious truth, without loss of religious privileges and fellowship, on account of those opinions."[4] The New England establishments had most clearly threatened the external liberty, but, with the decline of these establishments in the early nineteenth century, Unitarians in particular demanded internal as well as external liberty and, indeed, hardly differentiated them. In the words of William Ellery Channing—the most prominent advocate of internal liberty:

> There are countless ways by which men in a free country may encroach on their neighbors' rights. In religion the instrument is ready made and always at hand. I refer to Opinion, combined and organized in sects, and

[2] Isaac Wise, "Politics," in *The Israelite*, 2 (no. 2): 12 (Cincinnati: July 20, 1855). He also spoke about Protestants who "conjure up the spectre of fanaticism." Ibid. More generally, see Philip Gleason, "American Catholics and Liberalism, 1789–1960," in *Catholicism and Liberalism: Contributions to American Public Philosophy*, 51, ed. R. Bruce Douglass and David Hollenbach (Cambridge: Cambridge University Press, 1994).

[3] Even Baptists had a system of elders, discipline, churches, and associations, and nonevangelical sects, such as the Quakers, retained versions of their old systems of discipline.

[4] S. K. Lothrop, *The Nature and Extent of Religious Liberty. A Sermon Preached at the Church in Brattle Square . . . June 17, 1838*, 3 (Boston: 1838). Lothrop, however, was preaching about the first sort of freedom. More generally, see Smith, *Religious Liberty in the United States*, 96.

swayed by the clergy. We say we have no Inquisition. But a sect, skillfully organized, trained to utter one cry, combined to cover with reproach whoever may differ from themselves, to drown the free expression of opinion by denunciations of heresy, and strike terror into the multitude by joint and perpetual menace,—such a sect is as perilous and palsying to the intellect as the Inquisition.

Fearing that individuals would "lose themselves in masses," "identify themselves with parties and sects," and "sacrifice individuality," Channing urged an "Inward" or mental freedom from "the bondage of habit," from the slavery of "precise rules," and from anything by which the "mind" might be "merged in others."[5] Channing was seconded by many others, such as Bernard Whitman, who more concretely argued that "the use made of human creeds by the leaders of the orthodox denomination is subversive of free inquiry, religious liberty, and the principles of Congregationalism."[6] What often was at stake in practical terms was whether Unitarian congregants could be prevented from obtaining control of church buildings and other property—whether they could be stopped from taking over a congregation and changing its doctrine. Yet more than property was in dispute. As the New England establishments passed into oblivion, at issue was whether the creeds of even voluntary religious societies should be feared as threats to liberty.

This Unitarian demand for liberty from not only civil government but also Congregational churches was part of a broader liberal challenge to ecclesiastical authority, which no denomination could escape. For example, the assault on church authority found its way into that bastion of Presbyterian orthodoxy, the Princeton Theological Seminary. In May 1824, when the Seminary invited the Rev. John M. Duncan of Baltimore to preach the annual discourse to students, he disparaged "subjugation"

---

[5] William E. Channing, *A Sermon*, 27–28, 10 (Boston: 1830). As the Rev. Huntington put it, there could be a "persecuting spirit" even "where the civil arm is wanting." "There is a persecuting heart, and a persecuting tongue, as well as a persecuting sword. Hard names, uncharitable censures, rash dealings, are the very essence of it." D. Huntington, *An Intolerant Spirit, Hostile to the Interests of Society. A Sermon*, 10–11 (Boston: 1822). Of course, this liberal theology was hardly original. For example, almost a century earlier, William Dudgeon had written that "Persecution" included "the least uneasiness given to our neighbor upon account of different belief." "A Catechism Founded upon Experience and Reason" (1739), in William Dudgeon, *The Philosophical Works*, 190 (1765).

[6] Bernard Whitman, *Two Letters to the Reverend Moses Stuart; on the Subject of Religious Liberty*, 2 (2d ed., Boston: 1831).

to "sectarian principles" as an impediment to "ministerial liberty."[7] This was quite unexpected, and, in response, Professor Samuel Miller felt obliged to introduce the Seminary's summer session with a lecture in defense of creeds and confessions of faith. "If every christian were a mere insulated individual, who inquired, felt and acted for himself alone, no Creed of human formation would be necessary for his advancement in knowledge, comfort or holiness." Yet "the case is far otherwise," for Christians were not so insulated and did not act for themselves alone. "The church is a *society;* a society which, however extended, is 'one body in Christ,' and all who compose it, 'members one of another.'" Moreover, the members of a religious society surely had a "privilege to judge *for themselves;* to agree upon the plan of *their own association;* to determine upon what principles they will receive other members into their brotherhood."[8] Miller's vigorous defense of creeds suggests the degree to which even traditional Presbyterians felt they had to fight off manifestations of liberal theology.

Much later, in 1877, the Scottish-born Baptist preacher, George Lorimer, who preached at the Tremont Temple in Boston, would look back and complain about the ways in which religious liberty had been taken beyond a freedom from the state:

> [F]or half a century or longer, and especially in our day, efforts have been made to give it a wider, and, in some cases, a misleading application. . . . There is a tendency, more wide-spread than is generally supposed, to complain that articles of faith cramp intellectual liberty, and that the laws and rules of religious communities restrict unduly inclination and action. In the name of liberty, . . . fixity is unfixed, and the solidities of Christian societies reduced to a state of flux.

This rejection of creeds and discipline in "the name of liberty" was an "evil . . . not confined to any particular denomination." On the contrary: "It shows itself among the Presbyterians and Episcopalians, as distinctly as among the Congregationalists and Baptists."[9] Pervading American de-

---

[7] John M. Duncan, *A Plea for Ministerial Liberty. A Discourse, Addressed, by Appointment, to the Directors and Students of the Theological Seminary of the Presbyterian Church at Princeton, on the 17th of May, 1824,* 41, 56 (Baltimore: 1824). For a brief account of the ensuing dispute, see Whitman, *Two Letters to the Reverend Moses Stuart,* 11.

[8] Samuel Miller, *The Utility and Importance of Creeds and Confessions: An Introductory Lecture, Delivered . . . July 2, 1824,* 9, 44 (Princeton: 1824).

[9] George C. Lorimer, *The Great Conflict: A Discourse, Concerning Baptists, and Religious Liberty,* 127–129 (New York: 1877). Focusing on more recent manifestations of such tendencies,

nominations, it was a suspicion of clerical authority that Protestant clergymen (even those who were not theologically liberal) would soon redirect against Catholicism, especially after they felt its sting themselves.

Evangelical Protestant clergymen learned about the necessity of deflecting sharply liberal and anticlerical suspicions when these ministers attempted to influence American politics in naively imprudent ways. In the 1820s and 1830s, as the New England establishments collapsed, and as Protestants increasingly cooperated without fear of legal inequalities, evangelicals sought, through the power of Christian opinion, to establish a Christian society or nation—to substitute a voluntary and harmonizing moral establishment in place of the coercive and divisive legal establishments. In so doing, they hoped to persuade legislatures to adopt secular laws on matters of moral and social importance, and they assumed that their advocacy of such laws would pose no threat to freedom. Indeed, they hoped to reinforce freedom's moral foundations. Other Americans, however, objected to these clerical forays into politics, fearing that clerical influence, even on behalf of laws that did not establish religion, might encourage dangerous clerical ambitions.

In the late 1820s these opponents of clerical influence found a tangible object for their fears in the Rev. Ezra Stiles Ely—a Presbyterian and the organizer of the Sunday School Union, who lacked the gentle character of his namesake. On July 4, 1827, in Philadelphia, this imprudent clergyman boldly preached that Christians should form a "union of church and state." Far from being a legal union, it was to be "a new sort of Union; or, if you please, *a Christian party in politics, . . .* not by *subscribing a constitution* and the formation of a new society, . . . but by adopting,

---

the Rev. A. H. Granger—pastor of the Fourth Baptist Church in Providence—preached against John Stuart Mill and in defense of "creed-statements": "A church adopting certain articles as expressing its convictions on essential doctrines, and separating itself from those who do not subscribe to the same confession of faith, does thereby trench on no one's private rights, touch no one's inner life. Membership in a church, is voluntary, never compulsory. The constitution of a church must not be confounded with that of a state. This remark would be superfluous, if men of intelligence even did not persist in likening the action of a church in withdrawing from doctrinal dissentients, to that of the Puritans in banishing Roger Williams from their jurisdiction. In the very act of contending for the broadest liberty of thought and of worship, our fathers claimed for themselves the right to separate from those whose opinions they deemed inimical to the truth, or subversive of scripture teaching. They strongly insisted on their right thus to withdraw. This was their liberty." Rev. A. H. Granger, *History of the Rhode Island Baptist State Convention, 1825–1875*, 43, 45 (Providence: 1875).

avowing and determining to act upon, truly religious principles in all civil matters." By sheer numbers rather than by law, "[w]e are a Christian nation: we have the right to demand that all our rulers in their conduct shall conform to Christian morality; and if they do not, it is the duty and privilege of Christian freemen to make a new and a better election." Ely emphasized that "I do not wish any religious test to be prescribed by constitution and proposed to a man on his acceptance of any public trust." Instead, "[l]et it only be granted, that Christians have the same rights and privileges in exercising the elective franchise which are accorded to Jews and Infidels." Ely believed that, "[w]hile every religious opinion is tolerated and no one is established by law, it is still possible for me to think, that the friend of Christianity, will make a much better governor of the United States, than the advocate of Theism or Polytheism." He asked, "Are Christians the only men in the community who may not be guided by their judgment, conscience, and choice, in electing their rulers?"[10]

Ely's emphasis upon a "union of church and state" and "a Christian party in politics" was singularly ill-chosen. He sought no legal establishment, and, at a time when all denominations had abandoned their pretensions to a legal superiority, he merely described an evangelical alliance of a sort that was already occurring without much objection. Yet he adopted phrases that revived among other denominations all of their old suspicions about the intolerance of the Presbyterians. Accordingly, the following year, when Ely sought an act incorporating his Sunday School Union, Jacksonians in the state legislature defeated his proposal on the ground that he sought a religious tyranny. Typical of the Jacksonian protests was a placard denouncing Ely's "union of church and state." In the view of one contemporary "all that was wanting to make it perfect was to have a likeness of poor Dr. Ely placed at the top in the shape of a Pope."[11]

---

[10] Ezra Stiles Ely, *The Duty of Christian Freeman to Elect Christian Rulers*, 8, 5, 6, 11, 10 (Philadelphia: 1828). See John R. Bodo, *The Protestant Clergy and Public Issues 1812–1848*, 46–48 (Princeton: Princeton University Press, 1954); Morton Bordon, *Jews, Turks, and Infidels*, 60, 144 (Chapel Hill: University of North Carolina Press, 1984); Daniel Dreisbach, *Religion and Politics in the Early Republic: Jasper Adams and the Church-State Debate*, 7–11 (Lexington: University Press of Kentucky, 1996). The Ely dispute was not soon forgotten, and, strikingly, it engaged the interest of nativists. Lewis C. Levin, *A Lecture on Irish Repeal*, 34 (Philadelphia: 1844); Justus E. Moore, *The Warning of Thomas Jefferson as a Brief Exposition of the Dangers to Be Apprehended to our Civil & Religious Liberties, from Presbyterianism* (Philadelphia: 1844).
[11] Ely, *The Duty of Christian Freeman to Elect Christian Rulers*, 19.

The Jacksonians and theological liberals who joined in the condemnations of the Rev. Ely soon protested even more vocally against the clerical opponents of Sunday mails. In 1829 and 1830 evangelical clergymen petitioned the U.S. Congress to end the delivery of mail on Sundays by the United States Post Office. To their astonishment, these ministers elicited as much fear as sympathy. Numerous Americans sent counterpetitions, and when Congress rejected the clergy's attempt to prevent Sunday mails, Senator Richard M. Johnson of Kentucky—an ally and friend of President Jackson—wrote committee reports that echoed and amplified popular fears of clerical influence. "All religious despotism commences by combination and influence; and when that influence begins to operate upon the political institutions of a country, the civil power soon bends under it; and the catastrophe of other nations furnishes an awful warning of the consequence."[12] The history of Christianity revealed that "many of its professors, as soon as clothed with political power, lost the meek spirit which their creed inculcated, and began to inflict on other religions, and on dissenting sects of their own religion, persecutions more aggravated than those which their own apostles had endured"—a point Johnson illustrated with "massacres and murders perpetrated by Christian hands," the *"holy inquisition,"* and the danger of "[t]he bigot, in the pride of his authority."[13] Accordingly, in 1832, when Johnson ran for vice president, the New York labor leader Ely Moore could claim that Johnson "has done more for liberal principles . . . than any man in our country—by arresting the schemes of an ambitious, irreligious priesthood. Charge him not with hostility to the principles of religion, because he opposed the wishes and thwarted the designs of the clergy."[14] Observing such responses to the Rev. Ely and the opponents

[12] Sunday Mails, Communicated to the Senate, Janurary 19, 1829, *American State Papers,* Class VII, 211 (Washington, D.C.: 1834). For the politics of the controversy, see Dreisbach, *Religion and Politics in the Early Republic,* 4–7; John G. West, Jr., *The Politics of Revelation and Reason: Religion and Civil Life in the New Nation,* 137–170 (Lawrence: University of Kansas Press, 1996).

[13] Sunday Mails, Communicated to the House of Representatives, March 4 and 5, 1830, in *American State Papers,* Class VII, 230. Incidentally, Johnson wrote that "the line cannot be too strongly drawn between church and state." Ibid. Although most memorials in defense of Sunday mails assailed the influence of the clergy without mentioning separation, the memorial of the General Assembly of Indiana went further, arguing that "we consider every connexion between church and state at all times dangerous to civil and religious liberty." Memorial of the General Assembly of the State of Indiana, in ibid., 240.

[14] William Emmons, *Authentic Biography of Col. Richard M. Johnson,* as quoted by William Addison Blakely, ed., *American State Papers Bearing on Sunday Legislation,* 269 (Washington, D.C.: Religious Liberty Association, 1911).

of Sunday mails, evangelical Protestants had ample opportunity to contemplate the risks of asserting clerical and church authority.[15]

The assaults on the Protestant authority portended ill for Catholics. Protestants had long despised the Catholic Church. Yet the theologically liberal attacks by Protestants upon their own churches gave the animus against the Catholic Church an altered character and force. As evangelical clergymen in the 1820s and 1830s came under criticism for their attempts to assert moral leadership beyond their churches, these ministers increasingly took gratification in pointing to the dangerous authority claimed by the Catholic Church. Being themselves the object of liberal and anticlerical suspicions, these ministers welcomed the opportunity to deflect such sentiments toward Rome, and their conduct suggests how Protestants divided over theological liberalism could join together in adopting a theologically liberal attitude against the Catholic Church. Most dramatically, Presbyterians could hope to lead their fellow Protestants in the new voluntary or moral establishment of Christianity in America not by asserting church authority, but rather by opposing the authority claimed for Catholicism.[16] In such ways liberal suspicions of authority simultaneously divided Protestants among themselves and united them against Rome.

Anti-Catholicism

Although American Protestants had long felt a profound animus against the Catholic Church, they gave this antagonism new intensity in the

---

[15] After the Sunday mails debacle and "after all the noise which the cry of *'Church and State'* has made through the country, and all the prejudices which it has excited," most evangelicals simply retreated from the Sabbath campaign and refocused their efforts on causes more likely to elicit popular support. Harmon Kingsbury, *The Sabbath: A Brief History of Law, Petitions, Remonstrances and Reports*, 263–264 (New York: 1840). Harmon Kingsbury—a stalwart advocate of the Sabbath—complained that "Some friends of the Sabbath say, that . . . it must not be generally known that any systematic efforts to this end are being made." According to these cautious evangelicals, "[w]e must use such means only as will not awaken suspicion, or excite opposition." Even Kingsbury "conceded that we ought to be wise in projecting plans, and inoffensive, as far as may be, in executing them." Ibid., 147. Indeed, after the third anniversary in 1831 of the General Union for Promoting the Observance of the Sabbath, "[n]o public meeting was held," and the "Society and its auxiliaries were soon considered defunct." In their fear of causing offense, the "friends of the Sabbath" recognized a growing indifference to the Sabbath among almost all groups of Americans. Even the officers of the Society "did not refrain from traveling on the Lord's day" and did not "evince that devotedness to the cause that was requisite." Ibid., 145–146.

[16] See text below at note 52.

nineteenth century. They had inherited some very traditional fears about the anti-Christian character of Catholicism and its union of church and state. In addition, they now combined these with more modern, theologically liberal anxieties about Catholic ecclesiastical authority and its threat to individual mental freedom. Viewing themselves as intellectually independent individuals, who followed their consciences rather than the authority of any church or priest, many Protestants assumed that the Catholic Church, because of its apparent threat to intellectual independence, was all the more likely to obtain political power and revive a medieval intolerance. In response to this combination of liberal and more traditional fears, Protestants would eventually elevate separation of church and state as an American ideal.

Much anti-Catholicism had little to do with religion. In the 1830s and especially the 1840s and 1850s, Catholic immigrants from Germany and especially Ireland arrived in the United States by the thousands and eventually the hundreds of thousands each year. Crowding into America's cities, most were destitute and had little familiarity with American ways. Those from Ireland, moreover, belonged to an ethnic group not traditionally beloved by Americans of English and Scottish descent, and numerous Protestants complained of both the indolence of the Irish and their economic competition. Fearful of the foreigners, many native-born Protestants self-consciously identified themselves with America and its native population and, on this basis, these "nativists" opposed foreign immigration, especially by Irish Catholics. Yet even this sort of secular ethnic and class animosity often blended into the religious prejudice that would do so much to popularize the separation of church and state. For example, in displaying his solicitude for Irish Catholics, one Protestant hoped that "when drunkenness shall have been done away, and, with it, that just, relative proportion of all indolence, ignorance, crime, misery, and superstition, of which it is the putative parent; then truly a much smaller portion of mankind may be expected to follow the dark lanthern of the Romish religion."[17]

---

[17] Lucius Sargent, *An Irish Heart, Founded on Fact*, 120 (1836; Boston: 1843). To this, Hughes sarcastically said, "And, unless we send our children to imbibe these lessons, we are going to overturn the system!" Catholics eventually threw the "dark lantern" caricature back at nativists, calling, for example, the American Republicans the "Dark Lantern Party." "Second Day's Speech before the Board of Aldermen and Councilmen" (Oct. 30, 1840), in *Complete Works of the Most Rev. John Hughes*, 1: 145 (New York 1865).

American Protestants often expressed their revulsion against Catholicism in remarkably traditional theological ways. Like numerous other Protestants since the Reformation, Americans of various denominations complained about the pope and the Church of Rome in terms drawn from the Book of Revelation. For example, a mid-nineteenth-century Presbyterian speaker on church history declared "the Pope of Rome to be Anti-Christ" and, on this ground, concluded that "his ministers must be excluded from the Christian ministry." Far from being *the* Christian Church, Rome was not even one such church. It was, instead, an eschatological machine of intolerance—"the scarlet harlot, riding on the beast with seven heads and ten horns . . . drunk with the blood of saints." Commenting on these utterly commonplace remarks, a Southern Baptist reviewer confidently added: "This is most unquestionably so and all Protestant sects so affirm." As even this reviewer understood, he may have been too optimistic about his fellow Protestants, for many, regrettably, might "shrink from" these conclusions.[18] Nonetheless, vast numbers of Protestants shared the suspicions of the reviewer, and a newspaper published in Philadelphia and New York from 1834 through 1837 could flourish under the title, *The Downfall of Babylon; or, the Triumph of Truth over Popery.*[19] Thus Catholics had ample reason to worry that "the American people have inherited, even in their political freedom, the prejudices of their ancestors."[20]

Yet this very old-fashioned Protestant revulsion against Catholicism could find more modern expression in an evolving Protestant, Enlightenment, and, eventually, liberal redefinition of religion. In distinguishing themselves from Catholics, Protestants had long emphasized justi-

---

[18] J. R. Graves, Review of G. H. Orchard, "History of Foreign Baptists," in *Southern Baptist Review and Eclectic*, 1: 23 (January 1855).

[19] Ray Allen Billington, *The Protestant Crusade 1800–1860: A Study of the Origins of American Nativism*, 92, 94 (Chicago: Quadrangle Books, 1964).

[20] "Reflections and Suggestions, in Regard to What Is Called the Catholic Press in the United States" (November 1856), in *Complete Works of the Most Rev. John Hughes*, 2: 695. For anti-Catholicism in eighteenth-century America, see Sister Mary Augustine (Ray), *American Opinion of Roman Catholicism in the Eighteenth Century* (New York: Columbia University Press, 1936). In the late eighteenth century at the time of the American alliance with France, anti-Catholicism declined. Charles P. Hanson, *Necessary Virtue: The Pragmatic Origins of Religious Liberty in New England* (Charlottesville: University of Virginia Press, 1998). In the nineteenth century, however, one of America's more dispassionate historians observed "the diligent stirring up of old prejudices against the Catholics, on the part of spiritual rivals." *Richard Hildreth: An American Utilitarian*, 195 (New York: Columbia University Press, 1948).

fication by faith alone, and they gave even greater emphasis to belief when, in the seventeenth and eighteenth centuries, they increasingly contrasted their conscientious gospel beliefs to the hypocrisy and human interpositions of the Catholic Church. In England and America, where Protestant dissenters struggled against established Protestant churches, the dissenters asserted religious liberty by focusing on the importance of freedom of conscience, and they thereby appeared, in some of their petitions for freedom, much closer than they really were to the position that unimpeded belief was the only essential in religion. By the nineteenth century some Protestants—not only Unitarians but also others—came close to reducing their religion to freedom, as when the expansive Congregationalist, Leonard Bacon, declared in 1845 that *"Protestantism is the love of Spiritual Liberty."*[21] Implicitly, such a claim called into question the religious character of a church that did not give theological prominence to faith and freedom of individual conscience. In addition, some Enlightenment Protestants attempted to reconcile religion and reason by accentuating what could be inferred from reason and by reducing religion to what was reasonable. Associating reason with the purity of their own faith, Protestants condemned Catholicism as not only unfree but also irrational and superstitious—thereby joining earlier Protestants who classed it with the mummery and horrors of paganism. A worship of things human, in response to terrors knowingly inculcated by priests, Catholicism seemed a cynical invention imposed by force and mental stultification rather than a free, rational, and pure faith. In these ways (usually for limited, polemical purposes) many Protestants came to view their own religion and, indeed, religion itself as essentially a matter of

---

[21] *The Christian Alliance, Addresses of Rev. L. Bacon, D.D., and Rev. E. N. Kirk, at the Annual Meeting of the Christian Alliance Held in New York, May 8, 1845,* 19 (New York: 1845). Bacon assumed the evangelical Protestant character of Christianity and, like so many of his contemporaries, took for granted a mutually supportive relationship between Christianity and civil liberty, especially in the institutions of local government. "But if we reverse this view, and instead of Protestant Evangelical Christianity establishing itself in these institutions of local self-government which are so congruous to its nature, suppose the ascendancy of a different system, establishing itself, according to its nature, in the form of a consolidated spiritual despotism, how different the result!" This despotism would "teach the American citizen everywhere to bow in awe before the divine authority of the priesthood," and, in accord with its "despotic genius," it would "extinguish the characteristic spirit of our existing American civilization." Leonard Bacon, *The American Church. A Discourse in Behalf of the American Home Missionary Society, Preached in the Cities of New York and Brooklyn, May 1852,* 20–22 (New York: American Home Missionary Society, 1852).

conscientious faith and the freedom necessary for this—a perspective with which they could attractively identify Protestantism as the foundation for rational inquiry, truth, morality, and progress. It was an astonishingly broad view of Protestantism and a remarkably narrow conception of religion, and, in accord with more venerable condemnations of the Whore of Babylon, it suggested that Catholicism—"this system of so-called religion"—was not a religion at all.[22]

American fears were not limited to either eschatological terror about the Whore and the Beast or enlightenment revulsion against unfree and irrational superstition, for the Church, through its temporal power and union of church and state, had long seemed to threaten, in a very worldly way, both religious and political liberty. In parts of both the Old World and the New, the Church had the direct power or at least the influence to stifle and punish religious dissent, and, although it did so with only a shadow of its former vigor, it thereby seemed to confirm that it still lusted after temporal power.[23] Nursed for centuries on stories of martyrs burning at Smithfield, English Protestants had long viewed Catholic political ambition with trepidation. They carefully preserved memories of the Gunpowder Plot and numerous other treacheries, real and imagined, and feared even their tiny Catholic minority on the ground that it seemed to pay allegiance to a foreign temporal prince. English governments tended to recognize that most Catholics posed no threat, but the Protestant populace was by no means so confident. Blending distant history with present reality, and fantasy with fact, their fears of Catholic power and treachery became the inheritance of American Protestants—a legacy somewhat neglected during the late eighteenth century but increasingly regarded with appreciation.[24] Particularly as Catholic immigrants populated the western states, and as

---

[22] "The New York Tribune and the Church Property Question," *Daily American Organ*, 4 (March 2, 1855) (quoting the *Boston Bee*).

[23] In fact, the Catholic tradition of exercising temporal power was tempered, particularly in America, by prudential and canon law prohibitions on the capacity of the clergy to hold political office—prohibitions that were not, however, bars to political activity. For some of the nuances of canon law, see James H. Provost, "Priests and Religious in Political Office in the U.S.: A Canonical Perspective," in Madonna Kolbenschlag, ed., *Between God and Caesar: Priests, Sisters and Political Office in the United States*, 74 (Mahwah, N.J.: Paulist Press, 1985). An account of the various ways in which Catholics participated in American politics may be found in Gerald P. Fogarty, "Priests in Public Office: An Historical Overview," in ibid., 21.

[24] Hanson, *Necessary Virtue*.

Catholic missionaries boldly tried to convert other Americans, Protestants feared that Catholics would attempt to subvert representative government or would even gain enough adherents to impose religious tyranny by democratic means. On this reasoning innumerable American Protestants, like their English predecessors, argued that, to prevent Catholics from capturing free, Protestant government and imposing a union of church and state, Catholics had to be denied equal civil and political rights unless they first renounced their allegiance to the pope.[25]

This denial of rights was harsh, but it seemed fully justified by the threat of Catholic beliefs. In the prior century Jefferson had argued that civil government should not penalize opinion because there was "time enough for the rightful purposes of civil government for its officers to interfere when principles break out into overt acts against peace and good order."[26] Vast numbers of Americans, however, held that civil government had to interfere before Catholic principles broke out into overt acts.

Of course, Catholicism was not, in reality, so monolithic, powerful, or dangerous. For example, Irish immigrants had various traditions about temporal power, including at least one that denounced the adulterous connection between church and state. Such was the perspective espoused on behalf of Catholics in Ireland by an Irish barrister, Charles Phillips, whose speeches—running through at least nine American editions between 1817 and 1823—seem to have been widely read by Irish Catholic immigrants. Phillips confessed that "there was a day, when I was bigoted as the blackest." No longer. In particular, he now declaimed against a parliamentary bill that offered Catholics toleration on odious terms. Like earlier proposals for toleration, the bill granted Catholics the civil privileges they had long been denied (such as the right to vote or hold office), provided they took oaths disclaiming allegiance to the pope. In response, Phillips urged Irish Catholics that "the time is come to give that calumny the lie, which represents you as subservient to a foreign influence."[27] Irish Catholics, Phillips said, deferred to the spiritual au-

---

[25] In general, see David Brion Davis, "Some Themes of Counter-Subversion: An Analysis of Anti-Masonic, Anti-Catholic, and Anti-Mormon Literature," *Mississippi Valley Historical Review*, 47: 205 (September 1960).

[26] An Act for Establishing Religious Freedom (1786), in Henning's Virginia Statutes, 12: 84.

[27] *The Speeches of Charles Phillips, Esq. Delivered at the Bar, and on Various Public Occasions, in Ireland and England*, 3, 5 (New York: 1817).

thority of the pope but not to any claims for his temporal authority and thus were both good Catholics and loyal subjects of the crown.[28] Were the pontiff to interfere with the civil allegiance of Irish Catholics— which, according to Phillips, he surely would not do—they would distinguish between their religious and civil duties: "Separating, as we do, our civil rights from our spiritual duties, we humbly desire that they may not be confounded."[29] Phillips emphasized this separation, arguing that the ungenerous Emancipation Bill "was suited to increase" the "anti-Christian connexion between church and state," which had "done more mischief to the Gospel interests, than all the ravings of infidelity since the crucifixion." Echoing Paine, he explained: "It is at best but a foul and adulterous connexion, polluting the purity of heaven with the abomination of earth, and hanging the tatters of a *political piety* upon the cross of an insulted Saviour."[30]

With or without the benefit of reading Phillips's speeches, American Catholics, including even bishops, often adopted a liberalized, American understanding of their Church. For example, in the 1830s John England, bishop of Charleston, argued in his pastoral letters that in America "the duty of a Roman Catholic legislator is to be regulated by the power which is conferred upon him. His duty is to legislate only for the temporal welfare of the State, not upon the religious concerns of the people. . . . It would on his part be an usurpation, which would be criminal, to use his power openly or covertly for the checking of heresy, or the elevation of his own Church." Indeed, he explained that the pope's temporal power in Europe was distinct from his spiritual power within the Church and that "the Pope's authority" as head of the Church "is merely of a spiritual nature and can never interfere with the temporal authority of our government."[31] In a similar spirit American Catholics frequently

---

[28] "The Irish Catholic, firm in his faith, bows to the pontiff's spiritual supremacy, but he would spurn the pontiff's temporal interference. If, with the spirit of an earthly denomination, he were to issue to-morrow his despotic mandate, Catholic Ireland with one voice would answer him: 'Sire, we bow with reverence to your spiritual mission: the descendant of Saint Peter, we freely acknowledge you the head of our church, and the organ of our creed: but, Sire, if we have a church, we cannot forget that we also have a country; and when you attempt to convert your mitre into a crown, and your crozier into a septre, you degrade the majesty of your high delegation, and grossly miscalculate upon our acquiescence. No foreign power shall regulate the allegiance which we owe to our sovereign. . . .'" *Speeches of Charles Phillips*, 55–56.
[29] Ibid., 72.
[30] Ibid., 7. See also ibid., 79.
[31] Smith, *Religious Liberty in the United States*, 178–180.

went out of their way to demonstrate their love of freedom. For example, in 1848 they organized a meeting to declare their happiness that the
pope himself had adopted a "Liberal Policy" toward the independence of
Italy—a celebration for which they carefully solicited support from notable Protestants.[32]

More fundamentally, as a Baptist writer, Thomas Curtis, acknowledged, Catholics in America increasingly felt individualistic expectations,
albeit within a system that remained hierarchical: "In the United States,
. . . we find a variety of the Roman Catholic religion springing up vastly
different from that even of Ireland. We find lay trustees of Catholic
Churches capable, sometimes by themselves, of resisting the priesthood.
We find the Douay Bible more generally permitted, sermons more fre-
quent and confessions more rare." In particular, Catholics were beginning to partake of the "public sentiment, and the unwritten Christianity
of the country" that seemed "to suggest instinctively that none ought to
be received as full members of any church, or regarded as true Christians,

---

[32] *Proceedings of a Public Meeting of the Citizens of the City and County of Philadelphia, Held January 6, 1848 to Express Their Cordial Approval of the Liberal Policy of Pope Pius IX. In His Administration of the Temporal Government of Italy* (Philadelphia: 1848). Many Protestants vigorously challenged the hopes for a liberalized Catholicism. One anti-Catholic writer, John
Dowling—an English-born Baptist who had been pastor of the Berean Church in New
York and in 1853 was pastor of the Sansom Street Church in Philadelphia—observed that
"some have fondly hoped that Pius was about to extend these liberal movements into the
domain of religion, and that, perchance, Popery itself might change its character, and instead of being, as heretofore, a system of spiritual despotism, falsehood, and tyranny, that
it was about to become a religion of truth, of gentleness, and of love." Dowling, however,
pointed to Catholic sources to contradict these ecumenical assumptions. "No mistake could
be greater than this. . . . None are more strenuous than Roman Catholics themselves in
denying that the liberality of the Pope as a Prince is to be regarded as any indication of
his feelings as a Priest." Quoting Catholic denials in the *Freeman's Journal,* Dowling explained that the "boasted reforms of Pope Pius are nothing more than 'concessions to the
spirit of the time.'" Dowling, *The History of Romanism from the Earliest Corruptions of Christianity to the Present Time,* 666, 667 (New York: 1853). More broadly, anti-Catholic writers
repeatedly insisted that Catholicism could not change and that a Catholic who deviated
from Catholic doctrine was not really a good Catholic. For example, the Rev. Boardman
argued that "Romanism is avowedly an *'unchangeable'* system." H. A. Boardman, *A Lecture
Delivered in the Walnut Street Presbyterian Church,* iv–v (Philadelphia: 1841). In 1844 it was
said that the Church "declares itself 'unchangeable' and *'infallible.'* It cannot, it never has,
it never will be otherwise; though the Roman priests may make fools of some in this
country by saying that popery 'is changed' here, &c." *The Crisis! An Appeal to Our Countrymen, on the Subject of Foreign Influence in the United States!* 74 (New York: 1844). On later
Catholic attempts to reconcile Catholicism with American institutions, see Charles Louis
Sewrey, "The Alleged 'Un-Americanism' of the Church as a Factor in Anti-Catholicism in
the United States, 1860–1914," 32 (Ph.D. thesis, University of Minnesota, 1955).

with whom sound morality and steady piety is not a matter of established personal influence and supremacy." As a result, "the priest is no longer the mere tool of the bishop, nor the layman of the priest." It was "not simply that both are more free, but also that both have a stronger sense of direct personal responsibility to God; not simply that the layman will not perform what he considers an arbitrary penance, but that he will claim his right to read the Word of God."[33]

Yet even amid this gradual Americanization of Catholics, many Catholic leaders did anything but allay the fears of Protestants. Indeed, Catholic leaders vigorously asserted extreme positions, which spurred Protestants to their own excesses. In Europe, as the popes lost their temporal power, they asserted it all the more vigorously, and, echoing papal views, many American Catholic leaders repeatedly spoke of dominating the nation in religion and even politics.[34] Bishop Hughes of New York declared: "Everybody should know that we have for our mission to convert the world—including the inhabitants of the United States—the people of the cities, and the people of the country, the officers of the navy and the marines, commanders of the army, the Legislatures, the Senate, the Cabinet, the President, and all!"[35] Such ambitions

---

[33] Thomas F. Curtis, *The Progress of Baptist Principles in the Last Hundred Years,* 61–62 (Boston: 1855). He continued: "And probably more Bibles are circulated and read by the Roman Catholics in this country than in any, perhaps, of all the countries of Europe. Large numbers of copies of the Douay version are freely to be obtained with the approbation of the priests themselves." Ibid. Similarly, he wrote: "When M. de Tocqueville visited the institutions of the country, a few years ago, he went, among other places, of a Sabbath morning to one of the largest Sabbath Schools in the city of New York. Brought up in roman Catholic or infidel France, he had never beheld such a sight before. Some hundreds of happy children all had *Bibles* in their hands. He had only seen them taught religion by Catechisms and forms of prayer. 'What,' he exclaimed, 'do you let each of these young people read the Bible?' 'Yes.' 'And do you found your whole system of instruction directly on the Bible?' 'Yes.' 'And is this done in your Sabbath Schools generally throughout the country?' 'Yes.' 'And do all the children attend?' 'Very generally.' 'It must produce a profound impression upon the national character,' was the reply of that sagacious philosopher." Ibid., 314–315. This "silent change, giving to every man's religion a closer personal character," which had affected Catholics and other religious groups in America, he understood to be the product of "the entire separation of the church from the State." Ibid., 63. In some respects, Curtis was observing features of a devotional revival that had already begun among European Catholics. For this revival and its relationship to American Catholicism, see James Turner, *Without God, Without Creed: The Origins of Unbelief in America,* 209 (Baltimore: Johns Hopkins, 1985). In America especially, however, this emphasis on individual piety was linked, at least by Protestants, to a relaxation of hierarchical authority.
[34] Billington, *The Protestant Crusade,* 289–321.
[35] Ibid., 291.

for conversion were frightening enough, but they were accompanied by direct challenges to religious liberty. For example, Orestes Brownson wrote that "we assert the most rigid theological intolerance, and the wisdom and justice of the political intolerance which nobody denies was during many centuries asserted, and sometimes practiced, by Catholic states." Brownson hastened to qualify this intolerance by explaining that a different policy was appropriate in a modern era—that "we are bound by Catholic principles to assert for our times the toleration of all religions."[36] This hardly reassured Protestants, however, who worried about future times, when Catholics might attain a majority. Confirming Protestant fears, the St. Louis *Shepherd of the Valley* bluntly declared: "The Church, we admit, is, of necessity, intolerant. . . . Her intolerance follows necessarily from her claim of infallibility; she alone has the right to be intolerant. . . . Heresy . . . she endures . . . when and where she must, but she hates it and directs all her energies to effect its destruction. . . . If the Catholics ever gain . . . an immense numerical superiority, religious freedom in this country is at an end. So say our enemies. So we believe."[37] Although the premise of a numerical superiority was improbable, Catholics and Protestants readily contemplated its consequences.

While Catholics indulged in these astonishing claims, Protestants could rationalize their terror about a Catholic plot to overturn republican government. A nativist paper observed that "the Church itself avows its political character and intentions, and boldly asserts that it will succeed in accomplishing its nefarious purpose."[38] It was only prudent to worry

---

[36] "Civil and Religious Toleration," *Brownson's Quarterly Review,* 298 (July 1849). In early 1855 Brownson conceded that at least other Catholic writers had shown a lack of judgment: "Undoubtedly, there have been journals circulating chiefly amongst Catholics, and regarded as Catholic by outsiders, and demagogues enough, nominally Catholic perhaps, that have talked in a boastful way of a Catholic party and the great things it would do, and have endeavored to make use of the influence they exerted to commit the Catholic body as such, and to turn over the so-called 'Catholic vote' to one party or another. There has been, no doubt, too much of this, and Catholics and Catholic interests are suffering not a little from it. But the Church is not responsible for it, for she never inspired it, and they who have done it have acted without her authority and against her wishes. Her wish is to pursue her spiritual mission in peace, and keep aloof from politics, so long as they leave her the opportunity." "The Know-Nothings," *Brownson's Quarterly Review,* 117 (January 1855).

[37] "Religious Toleration," *Shepherd of the Valley,* 2 (no. 7) (St. Louis: Nov. 22, 1851). This passage was quoted, for example, by the Nashville *Banner of Peace* (June 28, 1855) and by Brownlow, *Americanism Contrasted with Foreignism,* 28 (Nashville: 1856). See W. Darrell Overdyke, *The Know-Nothing Party in the South,* 216 (Gloucester, Mass.: Peter Smith, 1968).

[38] "An Astounding Confession," *Republic,* 4 (no. 2): 100 (August 1852).

that "the Pope and his adherents have formed the deliberate design of obtaining the ascendency in the United States," if "Popish priests and editors make no secret of this design, and expect its realization at no distant day."[39] Thus the Church's untempered ambitions seemed to justify a new version of an old fear—the Protestant nightmare of treason and torture, disloyalty and despotism, now coming to life, incongruously, in the daylight of modern American democracy, a Roman *imperium* in the democratic *imperio*.[40] Catholic mobs, which violently disrupted nativist meetings, and Catholic gangs, which mixed crime with politics, seemed to confirm the threat. Although some American Catholics, not least some bishops, tried to calm Protestant anxieties, they could not suppress the unrealistic hopes of many Catholics and the morbid apprehensions of Protestants.[41]

Not only the Church's claims of temporal power but also its claims of authority in purely religious matters seemed oppressive, and, in this sense, the objection to Catholicism was as much theological as political. The Church claimed authority to interpret the Bible and to demand faith in Catholic dogma and thereby seemed, to many Protestants, to violate the consciences of individuals, who had a right to think for themselves. Echoing earlier liberal attacks upon their own creeds and clergy, Presbyterians and Congregationalists led the assault on the Catholic hierarchy as "the foe of mental liberty," arguing, in the words of a Presbyterian, John Breckinridge, that the "Roman Catholic Church in America is anti-American, anti-liberal." It was so fixed in its dogma that it "*cannot become liberal,* and they [Catholics] will not renounce it; and here we join issue—here we fix our final opposition to it, as anti-American, as well as anti-Christian."[42] In particular, Protestants argued that the Church

---

[39] Dowling, *The History of Romanism,* 643.

[40] More generally, see Davis, "Some Themes of Counter-Subversion," 205.

[41] Overdyke, *The Know-Nothing Party in the South,* 217, 223; Smith, *Religious Liberty in the United States,* 100.

[42] "Kirwan," *Letters to the Rt. Rev. John Hughes,* 90 (1st series; Philadelphia: Presbyterian Board of Publication, 1851); John Hughes and John Breckinridge, *Discussion of the Question Is the Roman Catholic Religion, in Any or in All Its Principles or Doctrines Inimical to Civil or Religious Liberty? And of the Question, Is the Presbyterian Religion, in Any or in All Its Principles or Doctrines, Inimical to Civil or Religious Liberty?* 301, 337 (Baltimore: John Murphy & Co., 1869). See also ibid., 236. Similarly, Thomas Smyth rejected charges of Presbyterian "illiberality, bigotry, and exclusiveness" by writing a volume that contrasted the "liberality" of Presbyterianism to the "illiberality" of the papacy. Thomas Smyth, *Ecclesiastical Republicanism; or The Republicanism, Liberality, and Catholicism of Presbytery, in Contrast with Prelacy and*

required a "substitution of authority for conscience."[43] As the Rev. Samuel Barnum later summarized, "[t]he denial of the right of private judgment . . . and the alleged supremacy and infallibility of the pope . . . logically involve (so Protestants think) the substitution of a corporate or foreign or artificial 'conscience' (so-called) in the place of that conscience which God has put into every man to bear witness for Him."[44] This denial of private judgment appeared all the more stultifying among recent immigrants, whose social cohesion often reinforced their deference to clerical authority. Against these foreign-born Americans, Samuel F. B. Morse—the frustrated painter who found greater success as an inventor and bigot—declared that Catholics were "human priest-controlled machines."[45] In more conventional terms, "Junius Americus" held that Protestantism and Catholicism were "essentially opposite. . . . The former admits diversity of opinions, and freedom in the enjoyment of those opinions: the latter demands that there shall be but one faith."[46] As a result, in the words of John Breckinridge, the Catholic Church was "the only church in America in which perfect *uniformity prevails;* and whose members all speak one language and breathe one spirit. The agitated and heterogenous mass of protestantism can never feel, *think,* or act together; though each of the thousand and one sects were ever so well disposed to govern the nation." Whereas Protestants were free and resisted mental conformity, "[a] real *'Catholic'* is another name for a *slave for life.*"[47] From

---

Popery, 202 (Boston: 1843). Indeed, he argued that "there can be no greater liberality, nor any protest against . . . intolerance, more powerful than that delivered in the standards of our church." Ibid., 234. Of course, he had to add that *"[t]he presbyterian church is at once liberal and orthodox."* Ibid., 239. For more on "the illiberal creed and practices of the Roman Catholic Church," see *The Crisis! An Appeal to Our Countrymen,* 73.

[43] Samuel Seabury, *The Supremacy and Obligation of Conscience: Considered with Reference to the Opposite Errors of Romanism and Protestantism,* 21 (New York: 1860).

[44] Samuel W. Barnum, *Romanism As It Is, An Exposition of the Roman Catholic System,* 788 (1871; Hartford: 1882). He held that "Romanism or orthodox Roman Catholicism steps in between man and his God who has ordained that 'everyone of us shall give account of himself to God' (Rom. xiv, 12), and claims perfect submission and obedience to the Pope as occupying the place of God, clothed with the authority of God." Ibid., 788–789.

[45] Dale T. Knobel, *"America for the Americans": The Nativist Movement in the United States,* 121 (New York: Twayne, 1996).

[46] "Junius Americus," in William H. Ryder, *Our Country: The American Parlor Keepsake,* 96 (Boston: 1854).

[47] Hughes and Breckinridge, *Discussion of the Question,* 470, 472, 537. Breckinridge continued: "The system is so constructed in its doctrines, institutions, and discipline, as to receive a man into *bondage* when he *comes in to the world; to lead him through life in bondage;* and send him out of the world bound hand and foot, dependent on priestly *acts* and *intentions*

such a perspective, a Yale-educated Presbyterian, Henry A. Boardman, preached, with no irony, in 1855: "The servitude of the laity to the priest-hood, is in some respects the most complete slavery of which the world furnishes any example—for it is the slavery of the conscience."[48]

In questioning Catholic claims of authority, Protestants found a means of transcending the differences within and among their own churches. The last remaining establishments—those of Connecticut and Massachusetts—had been abolished in 1818 and 1833, and, no longer divided by the special privileges once accorded establishments, the Prot-estant majority could finally sense its unity as the dominant religious and moral voice of the nation. Accordingly, the old vision of a society unified in its Christianity—a perspective once much beloved by estab-lishments—seemed to find new possibilities in America's freedom, per-mitting evangelicals to assert, without any sense of contradiction, their devotion to individual religious freedom and their satisfaction in belong-ing to a nation harmonized by its Protestantism.[49]

Yet dissensions over liberal theology and innumerable other issues flourished at the same time as the evangelical dream of unity, and as different denominations increasingly indulged in internal quarrels, they found anti-Catholicism all the more important for its capacity to bind them together. John Forney—the prominent Democratic newspaper

---

whether he be saved or lost, and whether if he get into purgatory and not into hell, he shall stay there a long or a short time, before he *rises* to Heaven!" Ibid., 537. Moreover: "In the Papal Church, baptism, which is a *brand of slavery for life,* is at the same time made *absolutely necessary to salvation;* so that none can be saved *without* it; no, not even the *dying infant;* and those babes who die without it are forever lost." Ibid., 470. Similarly, "AURICULAR CONFESSION, which is *required* in the roman Church, *in order to salvation,* is in the highest sense an INVASION of personal liberty." Ibid.

[48] Boardman, *A Lecture Delivered in the Walnut Street Presbyterian Church,* iv–v. Giving this common religious sentiment a political emphasis, the nativist politician Thomas R. Whit-ney declared: "In a word, American Republicanism is FREEDOM; Romanism is *slavery.*" Whit-ney, *A Defence of the American Policy, as Opposed to the Encroachments of Foreign Influence, and Especially to the Interference of the Papacy in the Political Interests and Affairs of the United States,* 96 (New York: 1856). Incidentally, Boardman was also the author of *The Christian Ministry Not a Priesthood* (1855).

[49] Thomas E. Buckley, "Evangelicals Triumphant: The Baptists' Assault on the Virginia Glebes, 1786–1801," *William & Mary Quarterly,* 45: 68–69 (1988). As early as 1803, for example, a Baptist Circular letter observed: "And the dear people of God in different parts and among different denominations are pursuing the same precious cause with increasing zeal. Prejudice and party spirit are on the margin of oblivion, and christianity has now more generally become a common cause." Circular Letter, in *Minutes of the New-York Baptist Association, Holden in the City of New-York, May 18th and 19th, 1803,* 7 (n.p.: 1803).

editor—observed that "while an attempt is made to combine all other religious denominations against the Catholic Church, . . . the very denominations thus sought to be combined, are torn with all manner of dissensions," and, against these divisions, anti-Catholicism was a cohesive force.[50] Anti-Catholic writers encouraged Protestants to join forces across denominational lines in their hopes of "extending light throughout our yet happy America, and of thus arresting the efforts of Rome to spread over the western continent, the darkness, the superstition and the mental and spiritual thraldom of the middle ages." On such a basis, "all Protestants should unite in the conflict with Rome."[51] Having long been accused of oppressing fellow Protestants, Congregationalists and Presbyterians could now vindicate themselves by rushing to the forefront of the crusade against Catholicism and turning the accusation of oppression against Catholics. It was an approach that allowed them the gratification and advantage of inveighing against tyranny while, in fact, reclaiming a role of leadership and authority among Protestants.[52] Presbyterians and Congregationalists, however, were hardly on their own. Clergymen from almost all denominations joined the assault on Catholicism in one way

---

[50] John W. Forney, *Address on Religious Intolerance and Political Proscription, Delivered at Lancaster, Pa., on the Evening of the 24th of September*, 30 (Washington: 1855).

[51] Dowling, *The History of Romanism*, v.

[52] Speaking of the anti-Catholic "crusade" in Philadelphia, James Roosevelt Bayley, bishop of Newark, later observed that "Presbyterians, in particular (the 'Presby-tyrants,' . . .), were always ready for this sort of work." Bayley, "The Substance of a Discourse on the Life and Character of the Most Rev. Archbishop Hughes" (Feb. 28, 1864), in *Complete Works of the Most Rev. John Hughes*, 2: vii (Introduction). In 1835 Hughes said: "The man must be blind to clear evidence, who does not see the existence of a dark conspiracy, having for its ultimate object, to make the Presbyterian Church the dominant religion of this country. . . . Under the pretense of solicitude for the preservation of CIVIL AND RELIGIOUS LIBERTY, the Catholics are to be robbed of both. They are to be denounced as 'foreigners;'—and foreigners are at the bottom of the plot for their destruction. These intriguing adventurers, who come inflated with the spirit of John Knox, care not what dissensions may ensue, what charities may be broken up, what blood may flow, provided that, under the plea of guarding against 'foreigners,' they may be allowed to sting the Republic, and distil into its veins the poison of bigotry and intolerance, which will soon reach its heart. But they would have the work of their own creation to appear as the spontaneous manifestation of *American* feeling." Hughes and Breckinridge, *Discussion of the Question*, 281–282. To Hughes it seemed that Presbyterians were, ironically, accusing Catholics of what at least some of the Presbyterians had hoped for: "We all remember the boast of Dr. Ely, that Presbyterians alone could bring half a million voters to the poll, and his effort to establish 'a Christian party in politics.' All these efforts failed. But the untiring, indomitable spirit of Presbyterian ambition returns to the onset, and out of pure, disinterested zeal 'for civil and religious liberty' undertaken to deprive Catholics of both. It will be again defeated;—as soon as it will be discovered that there is an ulterior object towards which the putting down of the Catholics is but the first stepping-stone." Ibid., 289.

or another, making anti-Catholicism the shared religious expression of an otherwise increasingly fragmented Protestant majority.

As if this were not enough, many Protestants took prurient pleasure in lurid tales of sexual excess by Catholic priests—stories that excited Protestant fears for both political and mental liberty. Unnaturally deprived of conjugal satisfactions, priests were said to have their way in convents and to employ the rite of confession to seduce young virgins. "NUNNERIES" had "*uniformly* been *prisons* to the *inmates,* and *generally brothels* for the priests,*" who pursued their insatiable sexual desires and then covered up their crimes by murdering unwanted babies and the nuns who sought freedom.[53] What priests enjoyed by physical force in convents, they also obtained by spiritual seduction in confessionals. A woman "was wax in her spiritual director's hands; she has ceased to be a *person,* and is become a *thing."* Indeed, "*Romish priests now in this country,* hearing confessions perhaps at the moment I write," were "debauching their penitents, aye, even in New England, the land of the pilgrims." Worrying about the absolute power of the hierarchy, many Protestants saw dangers to both freedom and purity—threats in which sexual anxieties about "our hitherto virtuous mothers and chaste daughters" seemed intimately intertwined with religious and political fears for the nation.[54] Thus the Church's requirement of celibacy had consequences far beyond convent walls, "convert[ing] monasteries, nunneries and nations into one vast brothel."[55] Through auricular confession, priests would "rivet the chains of slavery" on the "souls as well as the bodies of men." In the confessional "the priesthood" not only took advantage of innocent virgins but also could, "at their discretion, exercise a more thorough despotism than that of any Asiatic sovereign."[56] A fantasy of relentless sexual subjugation, this pornographic vision of despotism depicted the fate of the republic in the hands of the priests.

Amid this hysteria, nativists urged the "inspection of nunneries and

---

[53] Hughes and Breckinridge, *Discussion of the Question,* 537. An opponent of nativists complained that "[t]he country is flooded with a spurious literature, in which the imagination of its authors has been stimulated into activity to portray the fancied horrors of cloister and cell, and describe the Catholic priesthood as clothed in the garments of every crime." Philip Phillips, *Letter . . . on the Religious Proscription of Catholics,* 5 (Washington: 1855).

[54] William Hogan, *Popery As It Was and As It Is. Also Auricular Confession and Popish Nunneries,* 259, 257, 457 (Hartford: 1854).

[55] *Protestant Vindicator* (Dec. 1, 1842), as quoted by Billington, *The Protestant Crusade,* 67.

[56] Hogan, *Popery As It Was and As It Is,* 271 (quoting unspecified writer); Boardman, *A Lecture Delivered in the Walnut Street Presbyterian Church,* iv–v.

convents." Eager for such inspection, a Massachusetts House committee intruded itself so vigorously into female Catholic institutions as to prompt even a Protestant protest about unconstitutional searches (not to mention less elevated discussion about the female company kept by one committee member when not inspecting the nuns).[57] It was an occasion on which Orestes Brownson's heightened rhetoric was thoroughly justified, for the committee members seemed "to have been wholly under the influence of their lecherous tastes and prurient fancies, and to have imagined they were sent to visit a brothel, and not the residence of reputable and highly respectable ladies."[58]

Aroused by religious prejudice, fears about political and mental liberty, and fantasies about sexual violation, American mobs violently attacked Catholics.[59] In the 1830s Protestants initiated the practice of burning down Catholic churches, their most notorious achievement being the destruction in 1834 of the Ursuline convent in Charlestown, Massachusetts. For decades afterward, Protestant mobs sporadically indulged in open conflict, often stimulated by both settled ministers and less respectable but gifted street preachers, such as the self-proclaimed Angel

---

[57] Charles Hale, *"Our Houses Are Our Castles": A Review of the Proceedings of the Nunnery Committee* (Boston: 1855).

[58] "A Know-Nothing Legislature," *Brownson's Quarterly Review*, 406 (July 1855). Brownson also wrote: "One of the most subtle devices of modern tyranny has been to seize upon education, and to subject it to the absolute control of the public authority. In denying the freedom of education, in subjecting private schools to public inspection, and forbidding any one to teach even in his own house without a license or certificate from public authority, the order or party strike at the rights of parents, and make war on family, the basis of the whole social fabric." Ibid., 405. Incidentally, much modern regulation of private schools was built upon the foundation of this and subsequent episodes of the inspection movement.

Anti-Catholic prurience was such that, on both sides of the Atlantic, there were prosecutions for publications about confessionals. The leading English case, which was much followed in America, was R. v. Hicklin, 3 L.R. 360 (Q.B. 1868), in which Henry Scott—the publisher of *The Confessional Unmasked*—unsuccessfully appealed an order for the destruction of all copies of his book. The judges rejected Scott's argument that his goal was to expose the errors of the Roman Church rather than to encourage depravity among the English, a ruling that probably dismayed not only pornographers and their customers but some Protestant clergy.

[59] Mob violence against Catholics in America differed from that in England, as did the response to it. For example, whereas most propertied Englishmen viewed mob power of any sort with deep apprehension and therefore repeatedly—especially from 1780 onward—restrained anti-Catholic mobs with vigor, American authorities often were elected by anti-Catholic majorities and did not always view anti-Catholic violence with so clear a sense of its threat to the underpinnings of their society.

Gabriel, who—dressed in a white robe and announcing his presence with a brass horn—incited Protestants to attack Catholics and torch their houses and churches.[60] In 1844, after an orchestrated campaign of anti-Catholic preaching, Protestants in the city of brotherly love ignited churches and battled against Catholics and local military companies, sometimes using cannons, and causing the streets to be "baptized in blood."[61] A decade later, in the mid-1850s, Protestants burned a dozen churches in different towns. In Sidney, Ohio, and Dorchester, Massachusetts, enterprising Protestants blew up churches with gunpowder.[62] Riots between nativists and Catholic immigrants—often on the occasion of elections—left numerous injured and dead in the streets and engulfed portions of American cities, from Lawrence to New Orleans and from Louisville to St. Louis. Observing the mayhem in 1855, John Forney complained that Protestant leaders sought a sort of political proscription, "hunting down the Catholics as if they were so many wild beasts."[63] Bishop Hughes did not bother with a metaphor: "Convents have been burned down. . . . Catholic churches have been burned down, while whole neighborhoods have been, under the eye of public officers, reduced to ashes. People have been burned to death in their own dwellings, or, if they attempted to escape, have been shot down."[64] In the midst of this arson, Hughes—who saved Catholic churches in New York City by arming congregants—asked "whether there be not some more Christian mode of *illuminating* the minds of the 'Papists' than that of burning their churches?"[65]

---

[60] Billington, *The Protestant Crusade*, 309; Gustavus Myers, *History of Bigotry in the United States*, 305–306 (New York: Random House, 1943).

[61] *Richard Hildreth: An American Utilitarian*, 194.

[62] Billington, *The Protestant Crusade*, 309; Myers, *History of Bigotry*, 196–199.

[63] Forney, *Address on Religious Intolerance and Political Proscription*, 31–32.

[64] "Reflections and Suggestions, in Regard to What Is Called the Catholic Press in the United States" (November 1856), in *Complete Works of the Most Rev. John Hughes*, 2: 695.

[65] "Letter to Col. William L. Stone" (1844), in *Complete Works of the Most Rev. John Hughes*, 1: 499. Spontaneous as much of the combustion must have been, it was stimulated—even if not planned—by popular Protestant preachers and newspapers during controversies over public schools and other issues. In New York, Hughes looked back on the origins of the public school controversy and complained that "as the occupants of many of the pulpits of the city had entertained their congregations with political sermons on the School Question, for months before—so also, for months after, what ever might be their text from the Bible, the abuse of the Catholic religion under the nickname of papacy, together with all the slang, and all the calumnies furnished by the *New York Herald*, the *Commercial Advertiser*, and the *Journal of Commerce*, and other papers of that stamp, was sure to make the body

Among fiery Protestant sermons, inflamed prejudices, and their very worldly consequences, Protestant Americans increasingly defined themselves and their freedom in opposition to Catholicism. A nativist gift book held that "the American idea is *liberty, civil* and *religious:* whilst the Catholic idea is submission to the church, and implicit obedience to all its behests."[66] Contrasting the papal and the republican systems, a leading nativist policitian elaborated: "In the one, the individual is held to be a free agent, social and religious; in the other, the individual possesses not freedom either of conscience or allegiance."[67] As the editor of a Protestant journal put it already in 1835: "The abhorrence of papacy has become an instinct almost—a part of our personal identity."[68]

It was a personal identity that increasing numbers of Americans asserted by doing what Tocqueville said they did so effectively—by forming numerous associations, albeit not of the sort that this political scientist hoped would mitigate "the tyranny of the majority." In particular, they joined various "nativist" orders and political parties that were organized on behalf of native-born Protestants. Most notorious were the secretive Know Nothings. Evolving out of the Order of the Star-Spangled Banner, the Know Nothings acquired their peculiar name because of their first-degree ritual, in which they swore they would not disclose anything about the organization, even binding themselves to deny any knowledge of its existence. In this ceremony they vowed that they were native-born Protestants and that they would "vote only for native born American citizens . . . to the exclusion of all . . . Roman Catholics." Of course, they also learned the secret hand signal and secret handshake, which would reveal their membership to fellow initiates.[69] With such

---

of the sermon. By this process the minds of the people were excited, their passions inflamed, their credulity imposed upon, and their confidence perverted." "Letter to Mayor Harper" (May 17, 1844), in ibid., 1: 455. Later, the bishop of Newark observed a similar pattern in Philadelphia: "According to their usual tactics on such occasions, a number of their ablest preachers were instructed to administer to their congregations for a number of successive Sundays, good large doses of anti-Popery, prepared according to the most approved receipts." James Roosevelt Bayley, "The Substance of a Discourse on the Life and Character of the Most Rev. Archbishop Hughes," in ibid., 2: vii (Introduction).

[66] "Junius Americus," in Ryder, *Our Country*, 100.

[67] Whitney, *A Defence of the American Policy*, 99.

[68] B. B. Edwards, Review of Isaac Taylor, *Spiritual Despotism*, in *Biblical Repository and Quarterly Observer*, 6: 216 (1835).

[69] James P. Hambleton, *A Biographical Sketch of Henry A. Wise, with a History of the Political Campaign in Virginia in 1855*, 51–52 (Richmond: 1856); Mark C. Carnes, *Secret Ritual and Manhood in Victorian America*, 7 (New Haven: Yale University Press, 1989).

vows and rituals, nativists could enjoy the satisfactions of an intense fraternalism and a sense of independence from Catholic conformity and submission.[70]

In the intensity of these fears, images of religion and nation merged. On July 4, 1844, when 70,000 Protestants were said to have paraded through the streets of Philadelphia to protest against Catholics, the Protestants celebrated their ideals with banners depicting the Bible and the Constitution, including one displaying "[a] bust of the mother of Washington resting on a pedestal. . . . An eagle hovering over it, holding the American flag in its beak, which fell in graceful folds over the bust and the pedestal." Supporting this icon wrapped in a flag, the pedestal displayed the inscription, "To Mary the mother of Washington."[71] In New York the American Republican Party urged Americans "to congregate themselves around the GREAT ALTAR of their common country."[72] Typically, however, nativist Protestants felt more fearful than triumphant. Dreading Catholic domination, Protestants—even as they terrorized Catholics—identified with Reformation martyrs and imagined that they, their freedom, and thus their nation would be sacrificed to Roman tyranny. Gazing upon a cross surmounting a church spire, a Know Nothing was supposed to have imagined:

> Upon that lofty cross methought I saw
> The image of my country crucified.[73]

Publicly Funded Schools

The idea of separation of church and state first attracted widespread support and even national attention in 1840, when Protestants and Catho-

---

[70] Knobel, *"America for the Americans,"* 121. In condemning Catholicism, a nativist gift book observed that the *"spiritual worth of every man"* was "THE AMERICAN IDEA." E. H. Chapin, "The American Idea," in Ryder, *Our Country*, 214, 208. Chapin's excerpt was part of an oration he delivered in the New York Crystal Palace on July 4, 1854. Significantly, Chapin alluded to theologically liberal conceptions of religious liberty. One result of the "American Idea," according to Chapin, was freedom of conscience—"a freedom . . . that is violated by ignorant denunciation as much as by the wheels of the Inquisition; violated by calumny as cruelly as by the stake." Ibid., 216.

[71] John Hancock Lee, *The Origin and Progress of the American Party in Politics: Embracing a Complete History of the Philadelphia Riots*, 149 (New York: 1855); Billington, *The Protestant Crusade*, 227.

[72] *Address of the General Executive Committee of the American Republican Party of the City of New-York, to the People of the United States*, 14 (New York: 1845).

[73] Samuel R. Phillips, *Know Nothing: A Poem, for Natives and Aliens*, 13 (Cleveland: 1854).

lics in New York City quarreled over public school funds. Upon arriving in America from Ireland and elsewhere, many Catholics settled in New York, and eventually they grew numerous and confident enough to claim equal rights in receiving public school funds. This presumptuous demand shocked Protestants, many of whom responded by asserting separation of church and state as a constitutional principle.[74]

The existing publicly funded schools in New York City were, in fact, Protestant in character. In contrast to the rest of New York State, which left public school funds in the hands of local school districts that could adapt to the needs of their populations, the city disbursed its funds centrally. Since the early 1820s, when it first acquired authority to distribute public school funds, New York's City Council had denied such funds to all sectarian institutions, including Baptist, Methodist, and Catholic schools. Instead, it gave most of its funds to the schools run by the Public School Society—a privately operated nondenominational organization. Yet the ostensibly nonsectarian schools of the Public School Society had some broadly Protestant, even if not narrowly sectarian, characteristics. One goal of the Society was "to inculcate the sublime truths of religion and morality contained in the Holy Scriptures," and its schools required children to read the King James Bible and to use textbooks in which Catholics were condemned as deceitful, bigoted, and intolerant.[75] Catholics objected to what seemed to them little more than publicly funded Protestant schools and insisted that their own schools also receive public

[74] Elwyn Smith writes: "In the wake of the great school controversy, the concept of separation of church and state was persistently fouled by the association with nativism." Smith, *Religious Liberty in the United States,* 134. To this he might have added that this association was what popularized separation. The New York school controversies have been recounted in considerable detail by William Oland Bourne, *History of the Public School Society of the City of New York* (New York: 1870); Vincent P. Lannie, *Public School Money and Parochial Education: Bishop Hughes, Governor Seward, and the New York School Controversy* (Cleveland: Case Western University Press, 1968); Diane Ravitch, *The Great School Wars* (New York: Basic Books, 1974).

[75] Billington, *The Protestant Crusade,* 143, 144; Lannie, *Public Money and Parochial Education,* 103–113. On the background to these developments, see John Webb Pratt, *Religion, Politics, and Diversity: The Church-State Theme in New York History,* 158 (Ithaca: Cornell University Press, 1967). When Tocqueville wrote that the clergy "filled no public appointments" in America, his American editor, the New York politician John C. Spencer, noted in 1838 after the word "appointments": "Unless this term be applied to the functions which many of them fill in the schools. Almost all education is intrusted to the clergy"—by which, of course, he meant Protestant clergy. Alexis de Tocqueville, *Democracy in America,* 1: 313 (1835; London: 1875).

support. In the circumstances, their demand that the city fund Catholic schools was not clearly a request for a privilege that Protestants did not already enjoy. Indeed, far from attempting to establish their own religion, Catholics, in their own view, merely wanted equality in response to the majority's establishment of Protestantism. Among Protestants, the education provided by the Public School Society seemed neutral and nonsectarian, but for Catholics it was quite prejudicial.

As early as 1825, when the Common Council of New York City first considered whether to distribute some of its school fund to Catholic and other church schools, advocates of the Public School Society argued that such a disbursement would create a forbidden connection between church and state. "The churches," they said, "ought not to participate in this fund, because it would be in violation of that rule of civil policy admitted to be prevalent, which forbids all connection between matters of Church and those of State. Upon this same policy, the State's constitution had long forbidden 'any minister of the gospel from holding any civil or military office.'"[76] Although no one claimed that the New York constitution, let alone its religious liberty clauses, actually required this "policy" against a connection, the Common Council's Law Committee perceived such a policy underlying the state's constitution and, on this ground, recommended that the Council deny funds to Catholic schools.

In 1840 the Protestant argument for separation became more prominent. The year before, some upstate Whig leaders, including Governor William Henry Seward and Thurlow Weed, had attempted to counter the popularity of their Jacksonian opponents by wooing Irish Catholic voters with hints of educational equality—Seward speaking of schools "in which their children shall enjoy advantages of education equal to our own, with free toleration of their peculiar creeds and instructions."[77] When Governor Seward presented such a proposal to the legislature in January 1840, Catholics in New York City petitioned the Common Council and then the Board of Assistants to provide public funding for Catholic schools.[78] Other religious minorities soon joined the fray. Some

---

[76] *Report of the Law Committee of the Common Council* (April 28, 1825), in Bourne, *History of the Public School Society,* 718.

[77] Pratt, *Religion, Politics, and Diversity,* 174, quoting G. E. Baker, ed., *Works of William H. Seward,* 2: 199 (New York: 1853–1854).

[78] Pratt, *Religion, Politics, and Diversity,* 176. Pratt provides the best account of the politics of this dispute, which divided the Whigs and failed to separate the Irish from the Democrats.

Jews and Scottish Presbyterians argued that they too should receive funding. The Reformed Protestant Dutch Church, however, protested that the Catholic proposal could only be regarded as "in effect creating an odious union between Church and State: an union, not less repugnant to the sentiments and wishes of the Protestant portion of this community, than it is forbidden by the genius of our republican institutions."[79] Similarly, the Public School Society protested, "The political compact by which these United States are governed, divorced the unholy alliance between Church and State."[80]

The Board of Assistants' committee on schools rejected the Catholic petition and, in its widely disseminated report, argued not merely against the alliance of church and state, but for their separation. Using code words that played upon popular fears of Catholicism, the Committee hinted at the danger of religious bloodshed:

> Religious zeal, degenerating into fanaticism and bigotry, has covered many battle-fields with its victims; the stake, the gibbet, and the prison have fallen to the lot of countless martyrs; exile from the land of their nativity, expulsion from the seats of civilization to the wilderness of the savage, have been experienced by hundreds, of almost every sect, who could not honestly subscribe to the religious opinions of the majority.

It was "[t]o prevent, in our day and country, the recurrence of scenes so abhorrent to every principle of justice, humanity and right" that the constitutions of the United States and of the states had "declared in some form or other":

> [T]hat there should be no establishment of religion by law; that the affairs of the State should be kept entirely distinct from, and unconnected with those of the Church; that every human being should worship God, according to the dictates of his own conscience; that all Churches and religions should be supported by voluntary contributions; and that no tax should ever be imposed for the benefit of any denomination of religion, for any cause, or under any pretense, whatever.

---

[79] "Remonstrance of the Ministers, Elders and Deacons of the Reformed Protestant Dutch Church, in the City of New-York" (March 15, 1840), in *Report of the Committee on Arts and Sciences and Schools of the Board of Assistants, on the Subject of Appropriating a Portion of the School Money to Religious Societies, for the Support of Schools*, 385 (Document No. 80) (New York: 1840).

[80] "Remonstrance of the Public School Society, by their Executive Committee, to the Honorable, the Common Counsel of the City of New-York" (March 2, 1840), in ibid., 375.

"These principles" (including the one that affairs of the state were to be kept entirely "distinct" from, and "unconnected" with, those of the church) were "either expressly declared in the several Constitutions, or arise by necessary implication from the nature of our governments, and the character of our republican institutions."[81] This was practically an admission that one of these principles, separation, arose merely by "implication." Yet separation also had its utility to recommend it: "The purity of the Church and the safety of the State, are more surely obtained, by a distinct and separate existence of the two, than by their union."[82]

Notwithstanding these emphatic resolutions in favor of separation of church and state, the allies of the Public School Society seem briefly to have dropped their rhetoric about separation when they were forced to admit that they wanted students to continue to read the Bible and other religious materials. The Public School Society defended its position that its publicly supported schools were nonsectarian by offering to black out the most bigoted anti-Catholic references in its textbooks. It refused, however, to withdraw the King James Bible, which, although Protestant, no longer seemed to belong to any one church.[83] When the advo-

---

[81] Ibid., 346–347.

[82] Ibid., 352. Later, in May 1841, when Catholics, in seeking for public funds for secular education, proposed that they would give no religious instruction "during the usual school hours," the Public School Society asked whether, "even if literally complied with, could it be considered such a separation of the two objects as the public might of right demand if taxed to support the schools." "Memorial and Remonstrance of the Trustees of the Public School Society of the City of New York to the Senate of the State of New York" (May 21, 1841), in Bourne, *History of the Public School Society*, 410.

[83] In January 1841 a special committee reported that it "discovered to be not wholly unfounded" the allegations that "the books used in the public schools contain passages that are calculated to prejudice the minds of children against the Catholic faith." *Report of the Special Committee to Whom Was Referred the Petition of the Catholics Relative to the Distribution of the School Fund: Together with a Remonstrance against the Same*, 560 (Document No. 40, Board of Aldermen, Jan. 11, 1841). More generally, the committee defended the nonsectarian Protestant character of the schools: "Though religion constitutes no specific part of the system of instruction, yet the discipline of the schools, and the well arranged and selected essays and maxims which abound in their reading books, are well calculated to impress upon the minds of children, a distinct idea of the value of religion; the importance of the domestic and social duties; the existence of God, the creator of all things; the immortality of the soul; man's future accountability; present dependence upon a superintending providence; and other moral sentiments, which do not conflict with sectarian views and peculiarities." Ibid., 561. Having said this, it could reject funding of Catholic schools: "So long as government refuses to recognize religious sectarian differences, no danger need be apprehended from this source; but when it begins to legislate with particular reference to any particular denomination of Christians, in any manner which recognizes their reli-

cates of the Public School Society initially had difficulty explaining why they sought to keep the Bible, they apparently found it easier to denounce Catholics than to argue from the principle of separation. As John Hughes—soon to be appointed bishop—observed in the summer of 1841: "The charge of Church and State is now no longer heard, and they appear only to labor to prove that we are CATHOLICS, and, as such, unworthy to be heard."[84]

Although, in their desire to retain the Bible, Protestants seem momentarily to have backed down from insisting on a separation of church and state, they continued to accuse Catholics of uniting church and state:

> And shall our Common Schools, the republic's strongest hope
> Be wielded by deceitful Priests, a Bishop or the Pope?
> No! answers free-born millions; give them a traitor's grave,
> Advance, advance, Americans—your boasted bulwarks save.
>   Loud sounds the sacred bugle, the American youth dash on,
> Base foreigners shall bite the ground—our war-cry, Washington.[85]

Accused of "aiming at the subversion of the Constitution, and effecting a union between the State Government and the Catholic Church," Catholics responded by throwing these "absurd accusations" back at the Protestants.[86] "We have been charged with advocating the doctrine of the *'Union of Church and State!'* And this, too when a *union of Church and State*

---

gious peculiarities, it oversteps a boundary which public opinion has established; violates a principle which breathes in all our Constitutions; and opens a door to that unholy connection of politics with religions, which has so often cursed and desolated Europe." Ibid., 563. Catholics were appalled at the Protestants' position that no religious instruction "but what is 'exclusively general and scriptural in its character should be introduced into the schools under their charge.' Here, then, is their own testimony that they did introduce and authorize 'religious instruction' in their schools. And that they solved, with the utmost composure, the difficult question on which the sects disagree, by determining *what kind* of *'religious instruction'* is *'exclusively general and scriptural in its character.'*" Ibid., 572. Accordingly, Catholics believed that "[t]he contest is between the *guarantied* rights, civil and religious, of the citizen on the one hand, and the pretensions of the Public School Society on the other." Ibid., 575.

[84] "Important Meeting of the Friends of Freedom of Education, in Washington Hall" (June 1, 1841), in *Complete Works of the Most Rev. John Hughes*, 1: 267.

[85] Ibid., 1: 490–491 (Hughes's italics not reproduced).

[86] "James W. White, et al., Letter to Bishop Hughes, at Great Meeting at Washington Hall of Catholics and Others Favorable to an Alteration in the Present Public School System" (Nov. 16, 1841), in *Lectures, Letters, Speeches and Sermons of Archbishop Hughes*, 3: 117 (New York: American New Co., 1864).

was one of the identical political heresies against which we had so resolutely arrayed ourselves!" The real threat of a union of church and state, Catholics argued, came from the publicly funded schools, which, under the guise of neutrality, imposed a nondenominational Protestantism on New York's children: "The present Public School System of New York, we esteem as but the old system of a LAW-ESTABLISHED CHURCH IN DISGUISE— a scheme that seeks, by the sickly substitute of a *State system of education* to achieve the same end that was formerly accomplished by the establishment of a *State system of Religion,* namely, *to promote certain religious doctrines, and t[o] discountenance others."*[87] To the nativist editor of the *Commercial Advertizer,* Bishop Hughes complained: "[Y]ou maintain 'the existence and necessity of a NATIONAL PREDOMINANT RELIGION which is neither established nor unestablished.' You maintain the necessity of a scheme of public education, to which 'discontented fragments MUST CONFORM, and towards which *they can exercise no veto power?'* This, sir, is strong language to use toward a people who suppose themselves free."[88]

Among the Protestants who understood the danger of forcing a minority to submit to choices made by a majority—even a heterogeneous majority—was John C. Spencer. The secretary of state of New York and one of Governor Seward's political allies, Spencer had recently become a friend of Alexis de Tocqueville. Spencer and Tocqueville had met in July 1831, when Tocqueville and Gustave de Beaumont were visiting the United States to interview Americans and learn about their society. Responding to questions from the Frenchmen, Spencer explained that in America "it's a generally accepted opinion, in which I concur, that some sort of religion is necessary to man in society, the more so the freer he is." In this way, Spencer became the first to share with Tocqueville this commonplace of eighteenth- and nineteenth-century American thought, which would make such a profound impression upon the Frenchman and his understanding of democracy. Spencer further told Tocqueville that the Catholic religion was "less apt than the reformed to accord with ideas of liberty," although the New Yorker added that "if the [Catholic] clergy were entirely separated from all temporal power,

[87] Ibid., 3: 120.
[88] "Letter to Col. William L. Stone" (1844), in *Complete Works of the Most Rev. John Hughes,* 1: 499.

I cannot but believe that with time it would regain the intellectual influence which naturally belongs to it."[89]

Seven years later, in 1838, Spencer edited the American edition of
Democracy in America, and in 1841, in his position as secretary of state
(and thus ex-officio state superintendent of schools), Spencer proposed
a decentralized solution to the educational controversy—a solution that
would have allowed Catholics considerable local control over their education. Spencer worried that, although religious instruction was indispensable, it would inevitably be somewhat sectarian and thus, under the
existing system, would unavoidably give offence to religious minorities.
Indifferent to neither the danger of a tyrannous majority nor the votes of
the oppressed minority, he therefore suggested a plan of neighborhood
control that would shift power from the larger "masses" to the smaller.
The defect of the existing system was "necessarily inherent in every form
of organization, which places under one control large masses of discordant materials, which, from the nature of things, can not submit to any
control." Spencer therefore hoped to remedy the situation "by depriving
the present system in New York, of its character of universality and exclusiveness, and by opening it to the action of smaller masses, whose

---

[89] George Wilson Pierson, *Tocqueville and Beaumont in America,* 220 (New York: Oxford University Press, 1938). Spencer continued: "I have heard it said that in France the temptation
was strong to abandon all positive religion. If that is true you are not, even with your spirit
of liberty, near to seeing free institutions establish themselves among you, and you cannot
hope before the next generation." Ibid. According to Pierson, "it would be almost impossible
to overstate" the influence of Spencer's remarks. Ibid., 221. Nonetheless, the thoughts enunciated by Spencer had long been commonplace in America, and such views probably came
to Tocqueville's attention on various occasions as the Frenchman continued his travels.
  Incidentally, Tocqueville's depiction of Catholicism could elicit suspicion from Protestant
readers. The Frenchman wrote: "I think that the catholic religion has erroneously been looked
upon as the natural enemy of democracy. Among the various sects of Christians, catholicism
seems to me, on the contrary, to be one of those which are most favorable to the equality of
conditions. . . . If catholicism predisposes the faithful to obedience, it certainly does not prepare
them for inequality; but the contrary may be said of protestantism, which generally tends to
make men independent, more than to render them equal." To the last sentence, a Protestant
reader reacted sympathetically in the margin, "This is true *(sadly)*." Yet when Tocqueville went
so far as to argue that "the catholics of the United States are at the same time the most faithful
believers and the most zealous citizens," the reader replied, *"not so!"* Alexis de Tocqueville,
American Institutions and Their Influence, 305–306 (1835; New York: 1854) (a school text reprint
of volume I of *Democracy in America*) (copy in author's possession). Tocqueville believed he
had shown "what the direct influence of religion upon politics is in the United States," but
his reader altered it to say that he had shown the influence of "[the catholic] religion." Ibid.,
307. When, six pages later, Tocqueville revealed that he was "a member of the Roman catholic
church," the reader triumphantly declared: "I said so!" Ibid., 313.

interests and opinions may be consulted in their schools, so that every denomination may freely enjoy its 'religious profession' in the education of its youth."[90] His decentralized neighborhood approach had the advantage of breaking up the "universality and exclusiveness" of the Protestant system without distributing public funds to specifically Catholic schools. Of course, Catholics were grateful. In New York City, however, nativist Whigs resented the Catholic alliance sought by Seward and Spencer and blocked the proposal's enactment.

As it became clear that Seward and Spencer could not deliver the support of their party, Catholics realized they had to show their political power at the polls, and it was in these circumstances, in October 1841, that Hughes ventured to form his "Carroll Hall" ticket. In effect, he raised the specter of an independent Catholic party. A fateful step, which Hughes's enemies would never let him forget, it provoked horror among many Protestants, both Whigs and Democrats. Most immediately, in 1842 it stimulated the Democrats, frightened that they might lose Irish votes,

---

[90] John C. Spencer, *Report of the Secretary of State upon Memorials from the City of New York, Respecting the Distribution of the Common School Moneys in That City, Referred to Him by the Senate,* 11–12 (State of New York Senate Document No. 86, April 26, 1841). See also the contemporary argument of Hurlbut that the laws should leave to each school district the decision as to whether religion should be taught, which was republished in E. P. Hurlbut, *Essays on Human Rights and Their Political Guarantees,* 82 (New York: 1848). For Spencer's relationship to Seward and his status as state superintendant, see Pratt, *Religion, Politics, and Diversity,* 182.

Versions of the localized approach urged by Spencer remained commonplace throughout the nineteenth century. For example, in Madison in 1879 the superintendent of schools, Samuel Shaw, noted: "Whether religious instruction should be blended with moral depends much upon the district, very much upon the teacher; hence our law as it now stands is eminently wise, in allowing each board of education to decide the question for themselves; they are supposed to know somewhat of the views of their teachers; a great deal of the religious complexion of the district. They are within easy reach of their constituents and can be rotated out of office if they misrepresent them. Thus the majority rules, which is consistent with American doctrine in other directions. Yet the minority is protected from oppression by the constitutional provisions, and by their power to have their children excused from any exercise on the programme. Unless the voters in a district are unanimous, or nearly so, in wishing religious instruction in school as a means for moral culture, I believe it is better to confine attention to the latter, and try to have *every* pupil receive the benefit of such teaching." *Annual Report of the Board of Education, of the City of Madison, for the Year 1879,* 20 (Madison: 1880). Incidentally, in commenting on the state's requirement that "[n]o sectarian instruction shall be allowed," Shaw observed that he could not "presume to predic[t] what our court would decide sectarian instruction to consist of. Sect in a specific sense, means a denomination which descends from an established church; in a more general sense, it means a religious denomination. There are those in our country who hold that Christianity is the Sectarianism of more than one sect. I confess I do not believe this, particularly when I consider the historic relations of this government to Christianity." Ibid., 13.

to support a school bill that put New York City schools under the control of local districts, where they remained for the rest of the century.[91]

Yet even this modest Catholic victory had a price: the organization of nativists and the popularization of the idea of separation between church and state. The threat of overtly Catholic participation in politics appalled Protestants, many of whom responded by forming and joining anti-Catholic, nativist organizations. Most of these groups denounced Catholicism in traditional antiestablishment terms, not least as a union of church and state. Some leading nativist organizations, however, went further and demanded the separation of church and state—a principle they understood to advance the liberty of individuals by constraining churches, especially the Catholic Church.

With the concept of separation of church and state, nativists could most clearly exclude Catholicism from the public schools without removing Protestantism. Protestants tended to assume that, whereas Catholics acted as part of a church, Protestants acted in diverse sects as individuals. Therefore, as the school-funding controversy progressed, Protestants increasingly took for granted that the separation of church and state forbade public funding for Catholic education of any sort, even as it permitted such funding for nonsectarian Protestant teaching. In particular, from this perspective, separation allowed the Bible to remain in public schools. The presence of the Bible was desired by many sects and, indeed, by individuals rather than by any one sect. It therefore seemed that Protestants did not act as a church and did not violate the separation of church and state when they formed a majority and placed the Bible in their publicly funded schools. In 1845, in New York, the American Republicans announced:

> Our sole object is to form a barrier high and eternal as the Andes, which shall forever separate the Church from the State. While we regard the religion of the Bible as the only legitimate element of civilized society, and the single basis of all good government, we are greatly opposed to the introduction of sectarian dogmas into the science of our civil institutions, or the incorporation of Church creeds into the political compact of our government.
>
> We believe the Holy Bible, without sectarian note or comment, to be a most proper and necessary book, as well for our children as ourselves,

---

[91] Pratt, *Religion, Politics, and Diversity*, 183–190; Billington, *The Protestant Crusade*, 150–152.

and we are determined that they shall not be deprived of it, either *in*, or *out* of school.[92]

Even more astonishingly, the Native Americans who assembled in Philadelphia in 1844 declared: "We . . . recommend to the native Americans of the several states, in their systems of education, a full recognition of the Bible, as Divine authority for the rights of man, as well as for the separation of church and state, on which depends so essentially the pursuit of happiness and freedom of conscience. To the Bible we are indebted for the wand that broke the scepter of tyrants, and crumbled to atoms the church and state despotisms of those potentates, who associate religion with their political systems."[93] Far from being a violation of separation of church and state, the Bible, which had atomized church and state despotisms, would reveal to students the divine authority for separation. In such ways the school-funding controversy led nativists to identify with the separation of church and state.

Responses to the Pope

In the aftermath of the New York school dispute, many Protestant ministers added their voices to the nativist claims demanding separation of church and state and thereby lent clerical respectability to an idea from

---

[92] *Address of the General Executive Committee of the American Republican Party of the City of New-York*, 9–10. Earlier, at a mass meeting in 1843 in New York, the American Republicans observed, among other things, that "papal power is directly opposed in its end and aim to a republican form of government," that papal power "has been exercized in this city to such an extent that our common school system . . . has been bartered away as a price for the votes of the organized followers of Bishop Hughes," and that "there has been a pre-conceived determination . . . to put out of our schools the Protestant Bible, and to put down the whole Protestant religion as being sectarian." The American Republicans then resolved to seek a repeal of the school law, which was the produce of "papal influence"— in fact, it made few concessions to Catholics—and, more generally, "That in every particular, and throughout all time, we are in favor of an entire separation of religion and politics, and that we will put down the attempt to unite them." Louis Dow Sisco, *Political Nativism in New York State*, 41–42 (1901; New York: AMS Press, 1968), quoting *Journal of Commerce* (Nov. 4, 1843). Thomas Thorpe wrote: "We must maintain the peculiarities of our social and civil life. We must maintain our Christian character as a nation. We must still enforce the observation of the Christian Sabbath. We must continue scrupulously to preserve the Church and the State separate from each other. We must again avow and maintain the Christianity of our public education. Shall children be taught here in heathen schools? Shame on the defenders of such a measure!" Thomas Bangs Thorpe, *A Voice to America, or, The Model Republic, Its Glory, or Its Fall*, 313 (New York: 1855).
[93] Lee, *The Origin and Progress of the American Party in Politics*, 247.

which they had earlier remained distant. A profoundly significant shift in attitude, this change can be documented in the evolving responses of the Protestant clergy to Pope Gregory XVI's encyclical denunciation of separation.

Of course, vast numbers of clergymen continued to value a connection between religion and government. Even with the growth of Unitarianism, Universalism, transcendentalism, and other deviations from orthodoxy, many clergymen persisted in their adherence to a version of Calvinism and, on this account, envisioned the church as the religious and moral guide for the state. More generally, numerous clergymen, whether or not they were orthodox, continued to assume that morality, freedom, and government depended on a mutually cooperative and even supportive relationship between government and religion. Accordingly, many ministers still spoke about the "connection" between religion and government that they hoped would flourish all the more profoundly in the absence of an establishment. Even the many others who hesitated to speak of a connection, lest they seem orthodox or seem to justify an establishment, at least refrained from endorsing separation, for fear that they would thereby subvert the moral basis of free government. Nonetheless, in opposition to the pope, some of these various clergymen would embrace the concept of separation of church and state.

The pope had condemned the separation of church and state when rejecting the stance taken by a small group of European Catholic clerics and intellectuals. Perhaps following Condorcet, these liberal French Catholics opposed the union of church and state by advocating separation. Most prominently, the French cleric, Abbé Lamennais, together with his associates, supported separation in his periodical, *Avinir*. Eventually, the pope reprimanded Lamennais, but this dissentient priest declared his intent to continue publishing the journal. For the pope, this blatant declaration of disobedience by one of his own clergy, in support of a position that, in his view, encouraged the state's indifference to religion, was intolerable. In this context, in his 1832 encyclical, *Mirari Vos*, Gregory XVI condemned the separation of church and state.[94] "Nor can we augur more consoling consequences to religion and to govern-

---

[94] C. S. Phillips, *The Church in France 1789–1848: A Study in Revival*, 252–253 (1929; New York: Russell & Russell, 1966). For some later French developments, see Evelyn Martha Acomb, *The French Laic Laws (1879–1898): The First Anti-Clerical Campaign of the Third French Republic* (New York: Columbia University Press, 1941).

ment, from the zeal of some to separate the church from the state, and to burst the bond which unites the priesthood to the Empire. For it is clear that this union is dreaded by the profane lovers of liberty, only because it has never failed to confer prosperity on both."[95] It was a reaction that gave all the more prominence to the idea of separation. From this time, separation would increasingly become an indispensable ideal of secularizing European liberals. Of greater interest here, the pope's denunciation of separation allows a measurement of how American clerical opinion about separation changed in response to the New York school debates.

Many American clergymen criticized the pope's pronouncement against separation, and, among their responses, a change can be detected. The pope's encyclical seemed to confirm the worst suspicions of American Protestants—that Catholicism threatened American liberty, not least by uniting church and state. Yet, in their initial replies to the pope, American Protestant clergymen typically hesitated to endorse a separation of these institutions, preferring, instead, merely to condemn the pope's advocacy of a union.[96] After the New York school controver-

---

[95] *Mirari Vos* (1832), as quoted by Henry A. Boardman, *Is There Any Ground to Apprehend the Extension and Dangerous Prevalence of Romanism in the United States. A Lecture,* 28–29 (Philadelphia: 1841).

[96] For example, in 1835 the Rev. John Breckinridge—a Presbyterian—focused on the pope's words about union. "Here it is plain that the Pope declares it *profane* to sunder this tie." Hughes and Breckinridge, *Discussion of the Question,* 301. Of course, in believing that it was desirable to "sunder" the "union" of church and state, Breckinridge was not clearly seeking to sunder church and state or otherwise to sever all connections. Some Protestants even more obviously went out of their way to avoid endorsing separation. For example, after quoting Gregory's Encyclical, William C. Brownlee of the Collegiate Protestant Reformed Dutch Church in New York wrote: "We have here established *two* things: First, that the union of church and state is an essential dogma of the popish church . . . 2nd, the popish union of church and state is of *the most mischievous kind.*" Brownlee, *Popery an Enemy to Civil and Religious Liberty; and Dangerous to Our Republic,* 126 (New York: 1836). Similarly, the Rev. Henry A. Boardman—pastor of the Walnut Street Presbyterian Church in Philadelphia—wrote of Gregory:

> In the first passage, he advocates a union of Church and State. "Nor can we augur more consoling consequences, (says the letter,) to religion and to government, from the zeal of some to *separate the Church from the State,* and to burst the bond which unites the Priesthood to the Empire; for it is clear that this union is dreaded by the profane lovers of liberty only because it has never failed to confer prosperity on both."
>
> . . . Here, then, is the Popery of the nineteenth century. Do the American people know that in the judgment of the *present Pope,* the CHURCH (that is, the Roman Catholic Church,) ought to be "UNITED WITH THE STATE;" and that "LIBERTY OF CONSCIENCE,

sies, however, Protestants responded to Gregory's words by demanding separation, which they declared to be an American principle. For example, in 1843 clergymen of various denominations organized the American Protestant Association to "awaken" Americans to the "assaults of Romanism," and, in this spirit, they embraced the separation that the pope rejected:

> [W]e have it officially promulgated by the *present Pope*, that LIBERTY OF CONSCIENCE, LIBERTY OF OPINION, the LIBERTY OF THE PRESS, and the SEPARATION OF CHURCH AND STATE, are four of the sorest evils with which a nation can be cursed! Both as Protestants and as American citizens, we count the rights which are here assailed as among our dearest franchises: and we cannot look on in silence and see the craft and power of Rome systematically and insidiously employed to subvert them.[97]

Similarly, in his 1845 *History of Romanism*, the English-born Baptist, John Dowling, observed that in "its hostility to the separation of church and state . . . Popery is even now the same that we have seen it throughout the career of ages. . . . It might be expected that a power which is thus bitterly hostile to liberty of opinion, should be equally *opposed to the separation of church and state*, which has always been regarded by every enlightened friend of freedom, as one of the surest safeguards of the liberty of nations."[98] Protestant clergy were beginning to define their liberty not only against the papal union of church and state but also in favor of

---

LIBERTY OF OPINION, AND THE LIBERTY OF THE PRESS," are three of the SOREST EVILS WITH WHICH A NATION CAN BE CURSED?

Boardman, *A Lecture Delivered in the Walnut Street Presbyterian Church*, 28–30. Gregory had condemned separation and three other freedoms, and these last three, which were traditional in America, Boardman defended; the first, however, separation, he transmuted into its opposite, which he condemned as characteristic of the Catholic Church. Incidentally, although these American clergymen distanced themselves from separation when defending American religious liberty, some American clerical writers in the 1830s quoted or described European discussions of separation. See, e.g.: "The Religious Prospects of France," *Princeton Review*, 3: 386 (July 1831); "The Church Establishment of England," in ibid., 6: 523 (October 1834).

[97] *Address of the Board of Managers of the American Protestant Association; with the Constitution and Organization of the Association*, 7, 23 (Philadelphia: 1843). Of course, these clergymen believed that "Popery was the great ANTI CHRIST." Ibid., 14. See also Smyth, *Ecclesiastical Republicanism*, 267.

[98] Dowling, *The History of Romanism*, 618, 619.

separation. Rejecting one extreme, they were beginning to embrace another.

Among those who noticed some of the early steps in this direction was an advocate of Sabbath legislation, Harmon Kingsbury. He was one of the clergymen who sought to preserve a middle ground, in which religion legitimately exercised influence without being legally established. Increasingly, however, he felt himself on the defensive, not least because he had to answer critics who condemned his proposed Sabbath legislation as a union of church and state. Some of these critics apparently even desired a separation of these institutions. In response, in 1840 Kingsbury rejected both extremes. On the one hand, to those who told him that he "would 'unite Church and State,'" he responded that "only fools, the devil, and his emissaries, would have them united, . . . for, thus *united, the Church* falls." On the other hand, if "separated, the *State* falls." Accordingly, Kingsbury took an intermediate stance that both separated and united church and state: "[P]roperly united and separated, they stand and flourish together. Separate the Church from the State, in all her influence, and by going to pagan lands, you may see in what condition the State would be. Unite Church and State, and Europe can tell how many tales of sorrow, scenes of discord and bloodshed, which have occurred in consequence of it."[99]

Notwithstanding such protests, American Protestant clergymen increasingly responded to Catholicism and its union of church and state by endorsing a separation. The pope's response to Lamennais and other liberal European Catholic clerics was understood by these American Protestant clergymen to be an assault upon themselves, and what the pope feared, they made an American ideal. Ironically, these Americans thereby adopted the pope's view that separation was the only alternative to the union of church and state. This was but one indication that, following the first demands by American Catholics for equal rights in American schools, many Protestant clergymen abandoned their distaste for separation. In this way separation became a respectable position not only among nativist political organizations but also among Protestant

---

[99] Kingsbury, *The Sabbath,* 305. He also wrote: "Civil liberty, ardent piety, and Christian privilege, are too closely allied ever to be separated." Ibid., 305–306. See also Hubbard Winslow, *Christianity Applied to Our Civil and Social Relations,* 114, 124 (Boston: 1835).

clergy. It was a change in posture with portentous consequences for Catholics and, eventually, for vast numbers of other Americans.

Politics and Religion

Many Protestants used the principle of separation to argue against Catholic participation in politics. Catholics had failed to remove Protestantism from most publicly funded schools. Nonetheless, their demonstration of political strength in limiting the attempts to impose Protestantism upon their children made a profound impression on many Protestants. In response, many Protestants demanded that Catholics separate themselves from American politics.

The most outspoken of the Protestants who made these demands desired to "Americanize America." For example, one nativist political organization, the American Party, sought to develop even among native-born citizens the "national characteristics of which they have heretofore been unmindful."[100] Similarly, in its "higher and holier" aspirations, the American Republican Party hoped to displace other religious or ethnic affiliations: "TO NATIONALIZE THE INSTITUTIONS OF OUR LAND, AND TO IDENTIFY OURSELVES ALONE WITH OUR COUNTRY."[101]

In their zealous defense of this Americanism, these nativists argued that foreign-born Catholics who voted in a bloc endangered the republic. In part, the threat was that Catholics would use their political power to unite church and state. "*The American Ballot Box*, then, is to be the battleground of European Monarchy and Papal Superstition"—a battleground on which Catholics planned "to vanquish our Republican Institutions, and organize a Party in Political Power, in favor of the intentions of the Pope!"[102] It was "dangerous to commit the ballot-box, *the Ark of*

---

[100] Lee, *The Origin and Progress of the American Party in Politics,* 205, 198. See Dale T. Knobel, *"America for the Americans."*

[101] *Address of the General Executive Committee of the American Republican Party of the City of New-York,* 14.

[102] Levin, *A Lecture on Irish Repeal,* 15. In response to the presentment of the grand jury that condemned Catholics after anti-Catholic riots in Philadelphia, Catholics protested: "As Catholics, we are free in our political sentiments, uninfluenced by our religious tenets or by our spiritual guides. We belong to different political parties, according to our judgement and choice." *Address of Catholic Laity of Philadelphia* (June 20, 1844), as quoted by A Catholic Layman, *Religious Liberty in Danger. A Vindication of the Whig Party from the Charge of Hostility to Catholics and Foreigners,* 2 (Philadelphia: 1844).

our Freedom's Covenant, to foreign hands"—to persons who "may be foreigners in *heart,* and American in *form* only."[103] More fundamentally, many Protestants feared Catholicism in American politics because of the authority claimed by the Church—an authority that in its breadth, its apparent inflexibility, and its hierarchical character appeared to deprive Catholics of the independence that increasingly seemed essential in citizens and voters. According to the nativist editor and politician, Thomas Whitney: "The individual who places his conscience in the keeping of another, divests himself of all individuality, and becomes the creature, the very slave of his conscience-keeper. In every sense, moral, social, and religious, he becomes a mere instrument, and as a natural consequence his whole being, his happiness or misery, his successes and defeats, his condition and circumstances, all are made dependent on the will or caprice of another." Divested of individuality, Catholics lacked the essential qualification for voting: "The exercise of the right of suffrage is, in its legitimate sense, an *intellectual* act; and the conferring of that right upon minds like these—minds incapable of understanding the purport or power of the ballot—seems little less than an act of madness or imbecility."[104] Of course, in complaining that Catholics failed to exercise their individual judgment, nativists said as much about themselves as about Catholicism, for what irked nativists was that Catholics exercised their judgment in deference to the wrong authorities. As one nativist candidly

---

[103] Lee, *The Origin and Progress of the American Party in Politics,* 248.

[104] Thomas R. Whitney, *An Address Delivered . . . at Hope Chapel . . . on the Occasion of the Seventh Anniversary of Alpha Chapter, Order of United Americans,* 10 (New York: 1852). He also wrote: "These qualifications are rarely found in one trained to submission, and imbued with a sense of his own inferiority. Such a man, coming from the twilight of bondage into the broad meridian of freedom, is dazzled with the unaccustomed glory that surrounds him. His confused senses cannot endure the light. He is lost, bewildered. He can neither comprehend nor realize his new position. Accustomed to cringe in the presence of his 'betters,' he looks in vain for a living shrine that will accept the homage of his bended knee." Thomas R. Whitney, *A Defence of the American Policy,* 129. He asked: "Is such a man in a condition to exercise the right of suffrage side by side with the free-born, and free-cultured intelligence? Should the vote of such a man be permitted to neutralize and render nugatory the vote of the most enlightened mind in the nation? Such is its effect." Ibid., 130. James Putnam—state senator from Buffalo—argued: "If he surrender a portion of his franchise to his spiritual teacher, he will soon be prepared to surrender all his judgment, all his political individuality, to the same ambition." *Ecclesiastical Tenures. Speech of James O. Putnam, of Buffalo, on the Bill, Providing for the Vesting of the Title of Church Property in Lay Trustees, Delivered in the Senate of New York, January 30, 1855,* 21 (Albany: 1855).

explained, the Catholic laity "needs to have a proper direction and example set, from which to mold their opinions and principles."[105]

Many nativists opposed Catholic suffrage and other Catholic threats
to American politics by demanding a separation of church and state. To
be sure, numerous advocates of Americanism said nothing at all about
separation and merely accused Catholics of wanting to unite church and
state—a formulation attractive to the Protestants who regretted any establishment but still perceived the necessity of a moral connection between government and the Christian church. Other nativists similarly
hesitated to reject a connection but wanted to seem bold and therefore
went out of their way to sound as if they desired a separation. For example, in 1845 in Philadelphia the American Party demanded "the universal toleration of every religious faith and sect, and the total separation
of all sectarianism and politics."[106] According to the *American's Text-Book,*
"We would preserve separate and inviolable our political and religious
liberty." Desirous of preserving "immaculate that other light, which is
'light from Heaven,'" the author of the *Text-Book,* quoting Paine, "would
sever forever the *adulterous connection* between the Church and the
State—between the Throne and the Altar."[107] These nativists used language suggestive of separation but did not go so far as to demand separation of church and state. Some advocates of Americanism, however,
were not so hesitant. As one nativist explained: "The Republicans profess
to take a stand against Church and State connection in any form. They
wish to keep the Church from interfering to control State action. This
principle of non-interference is a sound and constitutional one. It is the
Republican principle, and should be boldly and openly maintained by

---

[105] *Republic,* 3 (no. 2): 105 (February 1852). See also Whitney, *A Defence of the American
Policy,* 69. In Tennessee an "American" quoted Jefferson against immigrants: "In proportion
to their numbers, they will share with us in the legislation. They will infuse into it their
spirit, warp and bias its direction, and render it a heterogeneous, incoherent, distracted
mass. . . . May not our government be more *homogeneous, more peaceable, more durable?*"
An American, *The American's Text-Book: Being a Series of Letters . . . to the Citizens of Tennessee,*
38 (Nashville: 1855).

[106] Lee, *The Origin and Progress of the American Party in Politics,* 250.

[107] An American, *The American's Text-Book,* 23. Somewhat similarly, a nativist gift book
admonished: "The danger we apprehend . . . arises from the fact that Catholicism is . . .
essentially *an unit.* Its religious and political creed are one and the same. Church and State,
under its dominion, are indissolubly united. Now, it has ever been our aim, as Protestants,
to divorce Church and State, politically, and to leave each to its appropriate sphere"—this
divorce being the source of "the freedom of the people." Ryder, *Our Country,* 101. Of course,
to divorce church and state "politically" might be to leave them connected in other ways.

every Republican, no matter what his creed and politics. Church interference in the affairs of the State never has resulted in good."[108]

Notwithstanding the apparently positive sound of the principle of
separation of church and state, it was, as nativists occasionally conceded,
part of a campaign to limit the freedom of Catholics. One nativist stated:
"The profession of any particular creed or rule of religious faith, unconnected with civil matters or the rights and interests of those differing in
opinion therefrom, has justly been regarded as a right which no one in
this country is justified in disturbing or destroying."[109] By implication, it
was justifiable to "disturb" even the mere "profession" of a creed or faith
that was connected with civil matters. Similarly, American Republicans
"as a Political Party, entertain no unfriendly feelings whatever toward
any *Religious Institution, disconnected with the politics of our country,* and
which does not SEEK an alliance with matters of State." They were "disposed to extend a free and impartial toleration to All. But while we do
this, it should be—MUST be—upon the condition that they or any of
them, shall not interfere with the civil and political departments of
City, State, or Union."[110] Merely by believing in the authority of their
church—a church that defended a union of church and state—and

---

[108] Orvilla S. Belisle, *The Arch Bishop: or, Romanism in the United States,* 181, 389, note 53
(to page 182) (Philadelphia: 1855). (This passage was quoted from *The Independent.*)

[109] *The Crisis! An Appeal to Our Countrymen,* 73. To bolster this, the author suggested that
Catholics advocated the violation of law and that "[o]ur fathers never contemplated, when
they framed the Constitution of the United States, that there would be those establishing
themselves among us whose rule of religious faith and practice would prove inimical or
opposed to the laws of the land." Ibid.

[110] *Address of the General Executive Committee of the American Republican Party of the City of New-
York,* 9. Already in 1835 Samuel F. B. Morse argued that Catholics deserved toleration
only for their religious principles, not their political beliefs, and that, if they could not
separate the two, they had only themselves to blame for the consequences. "[A]lthough
Popery is a religious sect, and on this ground claims toleration side by side with other
religious sects, yet Popery is also a political, a despotic system, which we must repel as
altogether incompatible with the existence of freedom. . . . Is it asked, how can we separate
the characters thus combined in one individual? How can we repel the politics of a Papist
without infringing upon his religious right? I answer, that this is a difficulty for Papists
have made their religion and despotism identical, that is not our fault. Our religion, the
Protestant religion, and Liberty are identical. . . . Let Papists separate their religious faith
from their political faith, if they can, and the former shall suffer no political attack from
us." Their tyrannical principles were "separable from religious belief," and "if Papists will
separate them, and repudiate these noxious principles, . . . the political duty of exposing
and opposing Papists, on the ground of the enmity of their political tenets to our republican
government will cease." Morse, *Foreign Conspiracy against the Liberties of the United States,*
118, 119, 138 (New York: 1835).

merely by speaking, meeting, voting, and otherwise participating in American politics with a sense of their Catholic identity, Catholics seemed to connect their church to civil government, and, for this, they deserved to lose their religious liberty.

Among those who condemned nativist "proscription" and "intolerance" were many southerners, who regularly adopted the concept of separation in order to turn it against its more bigoted proponents. In Louisville, at a mass meeting at the "Whig Pavilion," the local Whigs castigated a nativist newspaper article that reflected upon "the Catholic persuasion, and especially the Catholic priesthood, charging them [the Catholics] with hostility to American liberty." In response to the article, those present at the meeting resolved: "That the Whigs of this city regard the continued separation of Church and State as essential to the perpetuity of our free institutions; and we hereby denounce the efforts of the Locofoco party to array against each other the different religious persuasions, and to create a line of political demarcation between the Protestants and the Catholics, as subversive of the best interests of religion and inimical to the perpetuity of civil and religious liberty."[111] Similarly, the Jewish Democratic congressman from Alabama, Philip Phillips, "treated the movement of the 'Know Nothings' as a direct attack upon the constitution itself."

> There is nothing clearer than that in the formation of the constitution it was intended emphatically to exclude all connection with any religious faith whatever. Separation of Church and State, eternal divorce between civil and ecclesiastical jurisdiction, were cardinal principles with the sages and patriots to whom not only we, but all mankind, are indebted for this model of a republican government.

Adopting the nativist principle of separation, he asked: "When before has it been found proper to introduce religion into our political organizations? When before was the fitness for political office tested not by the honesty or capability of the candidate, but by the religious faith he professed?"[112]

---

[111] "Whigs of Louisville on the Same Subject," reprinted in Michael W. Cluskey, *The Political Text-Book, or Encyclopedia*, 682 (Philadelphia: 1860). The exact date of this resolution is unclear. Southern opposition to nativism obviously went beyond a concern for Catholics. For some but, perhaps, only some of the complexities of nativism in the South prior to the Civil War, see Overdyke, *The Know-Nothing Party in the South.*
[112] Philip Phillips, *Letter . . . on the Religious Proscription of Catholics,* 8, 5, 6.

Southern nativists who were Catholic or who had Catholic constituents joined the resistance to nativist intolerance. For example, Representative George Eustis of Louisiana rejected the prejudice of his fellow advocates of separation: "I am in favor of maintaining and keeping up the divorce between Church and State which has been established by our great fathers. But, sir, that very same reason which makes me a deadly enemy of Catholic interference with our institutions, makes me blush for my countrymen when I see the Protestant Church soiling its robes by dragging them in the mire of politics. Your legislatures are filled with gentlemen who wear white cravats and black coats. Your Congress has a large proportion of these clerical gentlemen. And I ask you, with all due respect and all due courtesy to gentlemen of the cloth, to show me a Catholic priest or an accredited agent of the Church of Rome in this hall. Gentlemen who talk about the Pope of Rome ought to recollect that poor old man, who is an object of such terror to them, is now in the custody of a guard of French Soldiers."[113]

It is striking that many of those who condemned anti-Catholic prejudice felt obliged to declare their support for separation. Nativists claimed to speak for "true" Americans and impressed upon their contemporaries the necessity of conforming to "American" ideals. Accordingly, even those who denounced nativist intolerance—perhaps especially these Americans—were quick to declare their own support for American principles, particularly separation. In this way, opponents of anti-Catholicism ended up adopting an anti-Catholic ideal.

Of course, the accusations of intolerance irked most nativists, who thought of themselves as idealistic advocates of liberty. Nativists felt they were simply protecting American politics and freedom from the influence of churches. One nativist protested: "The truth is, no party more earnestly opposes connecting the affairs of church and State, in any manner, than the American party; and it is because we will tolerate no influence which any religious body is disposed to bring to bear upon the politics of the day—because we promptly and frequently rebuke such intolerant and impertinent interference—that this charge is frequently iterated and re-iterated against us."[114] Condemning the "intolerant and

---

[113] Cluskey, *The Political Text-Book, or Encyclopedia*, 282, quoting speech by George Eustis of Louisiana in House of Representatives (Jan. 7, 1856).

[114] "Politics and Religion," in *Republic*, 4 (no. 5): 266 (November 1852). Another nativist wrote: "The American Party opposes no man's franchises, interferes with no man's reli-

impertinent interference" of "any religious body," nativists assumed they were opposing intolerance and preserving liberty.

Hughes's Defense

Catholics defended their right to engage in politics on behalf of their religious liberty, and none did so more prominently than Bishop John Hughes of New York. In 1840 this determined Irish American priest had led the fight over publicly funded schools, and, after his appointment in 1842 as bishop of New York, he continued vigorously to defend the rights of his coreligionists. On the basis of this personal experience, he understood that, if Catholics were to preserve their freedom, they had to be bold, but they could never appear to be engaged in partisan politics.

Hughes resented accusations in the press that Catholics confused religion and politics more than did Protestants, especially as Catholics merely spoke and voted to defend themselves from an aggressive majority:

> When several strong denominations attack one that is weaker, in a manner which turns religion into politics, and politics into religion, the sentinels of our liberties at the press are asleep. But when that one assailed denomination meets the assault and repels the assailants with the same weapons which the latter had selected, then the danger of mixing religion with politics, is for the first time trumpeted in the public ear! If Protestants mingle religion with politics to abridge the Catholics of a common right, it is all well enough; but if Catholics do the same for the purpose of protecting common rights, then it is all wrong.[115]

The real threat of a union of church and state came from the tyranny of the Protestant majority. "If ever the spirit or the letter of the Constitution of the country shall be violated in this particular, it will happen, not from any one sect rising above and lording it over all others, but from the coalition of all the others to depress, first the weakest or most unpopular, and then the next, and so on, until finally a few of the most

---

gion, proscribes no man politically because of his religious faith, and means to suppress that interference with our constitutional freedom which forbids and excludes all connection whatever between Church and State!" Anna Ella Carroll, *The Great American Battle; or the Contest between Christianity and Political Romanism,* 125 (New York: 1859).

[115] "Reply to Address" (Nov. 29, 1841), in *Lectures, Letters, Speeches and Sermons of Archbishop Hughes,* 3: 122.

powerful will arise and remain in the ascendent." Therefore, as Hughes told a sympathetic crowd, all Americans had to demand equal protection, particularly for the weak:

> It behooves you all, therefore, and every citizen, to see that all are protected alike—the weakest as well as the strongest, but the weakest especially. No matter what sect is assailed, extend to it, in common with all your fellow citizens, a protecting hand. If the Jew is opposed, then stand by the Jew. [Loud and long-continued cheering.] Thus will all be secured alike in the common enjoyment of the blessings of civil and religious liberty, and the justly obnoxious union of Church and State be most effectually prevented.[116]

Against a Protestant union of church and state, minorities—especially non-Protestant minorities—had to unite.

Hughes emphasized that Catholics were engaged not in a political contest, but in a struggle for their liberty. "Our meetings are not then political; we meet for the purpose of . . . extracting light that we may see, and understand, and be enabled to vindicate our rights. Neither should it be wondered at by political men that we should assemble here to discuss the question of our rights, and that we should complain of our grievances. . . . If they tickle us we must laugh—if they bruise us we must complain."[117] To the extent Catholics engaged in politics, he claimed, they only acted in self-defense: "Now I agree with the public press in the *principle*, that one of the greatest evils which could happen to society is the mixture of religion with politics. But in the application of that principle, I hold that it is those who *first* introduce the evil, who employ it in *assailing* the common rights of others, and not those who employ it in their own defense, who are entitled to blame." Protestants had first introduced the evil by insisting that Catholic political activity "was 'union of Church and State,'—'bringing religion into politics,' a 'Roman Catholic Bishop in the political arena,' etc., etc." Yet, "[n]ot a word or syllable of truth in all this! It was simply a pastor warning his flock against a politico-religious intrigue already sprung upon them, having for its object to brand the word 'Ignorance' on the foreheads of their

---

[116] "Speech at Meeting of the Friends of Freedom of Education, in Washington Hall" (June 1, 1841), in ibid., 3: 101.
[117] "Speech at Meeting in Basement of Saint James' Church" (Sept. 7, 1840), in ibid., 3: 37.

children, as the penalty of *not conforming* to the sectarianism of the public schools."[118]

Yet Hughes had to go further in disclaiming political participation. In the early 1850s nativists in New York and elsewhere adopted church property laws that attempted to deprive Catholic bishops of control over Catholic churches—a measure designed to shift authority to the laity and to Protestantize the Catholic Church. Proponents of this assault on the Catholic Church sometimes defended it as a sort of separation, as when one nativist leader sanctimoniously explained: "The purity of the clergy, depends upon their separation from the secularizing tendencies of politics and power. There can be no just respect for that office, when associated with secular affairs." Of course, the secular affairs from which the Catholic clergy were to be separated most prominently included their property, which many nativists eagerly hoped would escheat to the state.[119] Amid these threatening demands, Hughes felt obliged to declare his complete rejection of politics. He admitted one instance of "meddling with politics"—his formation of the Carroll Hall ticket in 1841—but "in no other case have I ever aided or abetted, or been in connection with any political party, or any individual of any party since the world began. On the contrary, when I was appointed to take charge of this diocese, I prescribed for its numerous clergy, as a rule of conduct, to abstain from all interference in politics. I did not deny them the right to vote as other citizens merely in consequence of their being clergymen. That right I

---

[118] "Reply to Address," in ibid., 3: 122.

[119] *Ecclesiastical Tenures. Speech of James O. Putnam*, 22. Introducing a new bill, requiring the Catholic Church to adopt lay trustees in conformity with New York's 1784 incorporation act, Senator James O. Putnam of Buffalo—a Whig who became a member of the nativist National American Party—described himself as restoring the separation of church and state. The 1784 act, according to Putnam, manifested a "jealousy of the power of the priesthood" and "secured the rights of conscience and the freedom of worship." Indeed, "It realized a central idea of the revolution—a separation of Church and State. It was a practical embodiment of the American sentiment. 'A PRIEST FOR THE PEOPLE, AND NOT, THE PEOPLE FOR A PRIEST.'" Ibid., 6. The more tangible hopes of many nativists may be illustrated by the view of the *New York Herald*, which looked forward to the possibility that Hughes and his fellow Catholics would defiantly refuse to name lay trustees and that therefore "the Attorney General will be bound forthwith to proceed against the tenants of the property with a view to its escheat to the State. If, therefore, they obey the Archbishop and not the law, it is not impossible but the State may find itself two or three millions richer one of these fine days—a consummation by no means to be despised at a time when canal mismanagement has reduced us to a state of quasi-bankruptcy." "Archbishop Hughes and the Roman Catholic Church Property," *New York Herald* (April 14, 1855).

believe they have seldom if at all exercised. I myself have not exercised it."[120] A Catholic cleric, he could not admit that he engaged in politics, and he even felt a need to refrain from voting.

The Protestant Clergy

In contrast to Hughes, who felt obliged to proclaim his abstention from politics, Protestant ministers had no need to be so delicate. Protestant ministers tended to view themselves as the moral light of the nation, and vast numbers of them did not hesitate to participate in politics in ways Catholics could not afford.

Much of the Protestant clergy had never substantially involved themselves in partisan politics or had withdrawn from it. In early nineteenth-century New England, for example, most Baptist preachers ignored party politics, and many Congregationalist ministers, chastened by their experiences surrounding the 1800 election, withdrew from party conflicts. Yet these and increasingly many other Protestant clergymen turned their energies to the social crusades that would shape nineteenth-century America, and, in this way, they reentered politics. Attentive to the risks of direct support for partisan politics, and less engaged than they once had been in disputes about the next world, the evangelical clergy, especially in the North, found new ways to participate in the struggles of this world, learning to preach not against Jefferson, but against the removal of the Cherokees, against the delivery of mail on Sundays, and, with more success, against alcohol and slavery.[121]

---

[120] *Brooksiana; or the Controversy between Senator Brooks and Archbishop Hughes, Growing Out of the Recently Enacted Church Property Bill, with an Introduction by the Most Rev. Archbishop of New York,* 93–94 (New York: 1855). Hughes emphasized that he abstained to avoid disputes with his flock: "There are few congregations in which the members are not divided in their political opinions and the Catholic clergymen who would take sides on such occasions would be sure to impair the usefulness of his own ministry." Ibid.

[121] Dreisbach, *Religion and Politics in the Early Republic,* 4–7, 24–27; West, *The Politics of Revelation and Reason,* 137–206. For continuities in leaders, ideas, and rhetoric between the Federalists and the abolitionists, see Marc M. Arkin, "The Federalist Trope: Power and Passion in Abolitionist Rhetoric," *Journal of American History* 88 (no. 1): 75 (June 2001). Of course, the temperance campaign was a model for much of what followed. See, e.g., Lyman Beecher, *Six Sermons on the Nature, Occasions, Signs, Evils, and Remedy of Intemperance,* 90–92 (4th ed., Boston: 1828). Writing in 1826, shortly before the formation of the American Society for the Promotion of Temperance, Beecher hoped that "[a]ll denominations of Christians in the nation may . . . be united in the effort to exclude the use and the commerce in ardent spirits . . . through the medium of a national society." By this means Christians could influence public opinion and politics so that "[s]omething may be done

Unashamedly and even militantly engaged in the cultural and social politics of the nation, the vast body of Protestant clergymen felt free to preach on almost any issue. From the pulpit of New York's Bleeker Street Church, Thomas Skinner—a Presbyterian clergyman—explained in 1850:

> [T]hough the Church in this land be separate from the State, there is no power which can be brought into action in favor of the nation's happiness, equal to that of the Pulpit. . . . [T]here is no place near or remote, no person high or low, no subject whether of politics, legislation, morals, religion, science or art, to which it may not boldly apply its appropriate influence, under protection of the government, so long as it violates no one's civil rights. This privilege has the American Pulpit. Its field is boundless, . . . the Gospel ministry is the best friend to all human interests, national and individual; the State will reverence and cherish, though it cannot espouse, the Church; and the peace of our rising and spreading Republic, will flow as a river, and its righteousness as the waves of the sea.

He acknowledged: "The Pulpit is often charged with occupying a sphere not its own, and there teaching *against* the Gospel, in its strictures on civil and political matters." This, however, would not stop him: "Ministers of the Gospel are not to hold themselves aloof from observing or criticizing the doings of magistrates and politicians. The kingdom of Christ, though not of this world, is over all kings and kingdoms, and governments of whatsoever kind; and of this kingdom the earthly administrators are Ministers of the Gospel; and if they do not appropriately assert the universal supremacy of its Lord and its laws, there is no unfaithfulness so great as that of which they are guilty."[122] Skinner was a Protestant and could afford to be audacious.

In the mid-1850s, when Hughes had to go so far as to proclaim that he did not vote, the Protestant clergy felt no need to demonstrate such restraint. Against the Nebraska bill, which left open the possibility of slavery in the Kansas and Nebraska territories, Protestant ministers in New England and New York preached over 3,200 sermons in the space

---

by legislation." In particular, "the suffrage of the community may be expected to put in requisition men of talents and integrity, who, sustained by their constituents, will not hesitate to frame the requisite laws, and to give them their salutary power." Ibid., 94.

[122] Thomas H. Skinner, *Love of Country: A Discourse Delivered on Thanksgiving Day, December 12th, 1850, in the Bleeker Street Church*, 15–16 (New York: 1851).

of only six weeks, and more than 3,000 New England clergymen signed a memorial to Congress.[123] Of course, these Protestants had no concern about violating the separation of church and state:

> The undersigned, clergymen of different religious denominations in New England, hereby, in the name of Almighty God, and in his presence, do solemnly protest against the passage of what is known as the Nebraska Bill, or any repeal or modification of the existing legal prohibitions of slavery in that part of our national domain which it is proposed to organize into the territories of Nebraska and Kansas. We protest against it as a great moral wrong, as a breach of faith eminently unjust to the moral principles of the community, and subversive of all confidence in national engagements; as a measure full of danger to the peace and even the existence of our beloved Union, and exposing us to the righteous judgments of the Almighty: and your protestants, as in duty bound, will ever pray.[124]

When these New Englanders presented themselves to Congress as clergymen rather than as citizens and even presumed to speak "in the name of Almighty God," southerners expostulated about political preaching, the union of church and state, and the subordination of the state to the church. Yet these southern critics carefully limited their attacks. Even from the assiduous author of a 600-page tract against the offending northern clergy came the conclusion: "The question is not, whether clergymen have the same rights, politically, as other citizens; this no one denies; but their indulgence in political preaching . . . presents a subject for prudential consideration alone, as it affects their usefulness among those amidst whom they labor."[125]

---

[123] Victor B. Howard, *Conscience and Slavery: The Evangelistic Calvinist Domestic Missions, 1837–1861,* 133 (Kent, Ohio: Kent State University Press, 1990).

[124] Protest of 3,050 New England Clergymen (March 1, 1854), in David Christy, *Pulpit Politics; or Ecclesiastical Legislation on Slavery,* 598–599 (1862; New York: Negro University Press, 1969). In Chicago more than 500 signed such a memorial. Others were active in New York. Observing the prominent political role of Protestant ministers, and that "Protestant ministers may, in fact, be said to be at the head of the Abolition party in the North," many Catholics felt that "[i]t is they, and not the Catholics, who have thus attempted to mingle religion with politics." *Civil and Religious Liberty Defended. Speech of John Kelly in Reply to the Charges of Hon. Thomas R. Whitney against Catholicism. Delivered in the House of Representatives, August 9, 1855,* 14–15 (Washington, D.C.: 1856). One historian observes that in their responses to the Kansas-Nebraska Act and the 1856 election, Calvinist clergy in New England went far in "convincing their followers that there was a direct connection between piety and public duty." Howard, *Conscience and Slavery,* 154.

[125] Christy, *Pulpit Politics,* 598.

In contrast, the Catholic clergy had to show more caution. Far more than the Federalist ministers in 1800 or the Protestant clergy of New England in 1854, the Catholic clergy found it difficult simultaneously to fulfill the duties of a clergyman and to exercise the rights of citizenship.

An American Principle and the Coming Conflict

Fearful of the threat from Catholics and their clergy, Protestants viewed the separation of church and state as an embattled principle of American government that they would soon have to defend in a final conflict with the Catholic Church. At stake, these Protestants assumed, was nothing less than American constitutional freedom and the possibility that it would be replaced with Roman ecclesiastical servitude.[126]

For nativists, separation seemed a principle of American constitutions, even if not precisely guaranteed in any of these documents. The various religion clauses of the federal and state constitutions had all distinguished religion from government in one way or another, and, on this basis, nativists casually assumed that separation was the nation's underlying constitutional principle of religious liberty. According to Daniel Ullmann—the Yale-educated lawyer and Know Nothing candidate for governor of New York in 1854—"All these constitutions aim to provide against spiritual domination and to establish full personal religious freedom. In this, the nation agrees in all its utterances—written Constitutions and unwritten law. The general sentiment, and the settled determination—the profound convictions of the American people are, that there shall be, forever, under this government, an entire and absolute separation between church and state; and that perfect, full religious liberty shall always exist." Taking these sentiments to the height of religion itself, he envisioned "the Temple of American Liberty": "Let the mighty fabric rise, its majestic dome swelling in all its magnificent proportions, until it reaches the heavens." Shortly afterward, in 1856, in his *Outlook of Freedom or The Roman Catholic Element in American History*, Justin D. Fulton echoed Ullmann's thoughts. One of the most popular of nativist writers, this Baptist—who would go on to write such classics as *Why Priests Should Wed* (1884) and *Washington in the Lap of Rome*

---

[126] For the tradition of Christian fantasies about a final conflict, see Norman Cohn, *The Pursuit of the Millennium* (London: Secker & Warburg, 1957).

(1888)—argued that the religious liberty clauses of the federal and state constitutions, although "uttered in different forms," concurred in "these two fundamental principles: first, that there shall be no connection between church and state; and secondly, that religious liberty, the rights of conscience, and freedom to worship . . . are guaranteed to the citizens of the United States." Just as the Declaration of Independence "made every man feel his individuality—his sovereignty"—so too American constitutions evinced the principle of separation.[127]

Following the Civil War, when the crisis over slavery no longer eclipsed anti-Catholicism, many theological liberals and nativist Protestants feared that the nation stood on the brink of another great constitutional struggle—this time with the Catholic Church over the principle of separation. For example, in 1870 a former judge of the New York Supreme Court, Elisha P. Hurlbut, argued that there was an irreconcilable conflict between "Democracy and Theocracy"—a conflict "stronger and fiercer" than that between "freedom and slavery." This was not mere hyperbole, for Hurlbut thought that "[t]here are bondmen still on our soil, subjects of a foreign tyranny, in comparison with whose bondage, African slavery, with intellectual freedom, was as nought." Fearing that democracy and theology "cannot coexist in the same nation, without deadly strife until a triumph is secured to one or the other," he argued that "the theocracy of Rome and the democracy of America, being utterly antagonistic, have no other way to peace, but by an entire separation." Indeed, "There can exist an American Catholic church, as well as an American Protestant church; and all can freely worship the Divine Power of the Universe, without interfering with each other, or endangering the peace of the state; provided they all concur in sinking the theocratic element in civil government, and carry not one iota of it to the polls."[128] To this end, Hurlbut published a proposal for a constitutional amendment that would alter the First Amendment to give the federal

---

[127] Justin D. Fulton, *The Outlook of Freedom or The Roman Catholic Element in American History*, 230–231 (Cincinnati: 1856). In chapters on the public schools and church property, Fulton clarified the consequences of such constitutional views, asking his Protestant readers about the property of the Catholic Church: "will you now lay the legislative axe to the root of this upas, or will you leave it to be uptorn at a future day, by the storm of REVOLUTION?" Ibid., 289. Incidentally, in 1863 Daniel Ullmann would receive the first order to raise colored troops.

[128] E. P. Hurlbut, *A Secular View of Religion in the State and the Bible in the Public Schools*, 18, 21–22 (Albany: 1870).

government power to enact *"such laws as it shall deem necessary to control or prevent the establishment or continuance of any foreign hierarchical power in this country, founded on principles or dogmas antagonistic to republican institutions."*[129] In a less lawyerly fashion, he proposed: "Suppose then, we indulge in a familiar piece of surgery, and cut the umbilical cord which binds the spiritual fœtus of America to the great mother of superstition, and thus stunt a growth, whose completed proportions would be likely, upon a successful delivery, to ruin the nurse into whose arms it should fall. It is not murder for the midwife humanely to stifle the birth of a monster." Such was Hurlbut's remedy for the pope's "spiritual *imperium* within our democratic *imperio.*"[130] Commenting on Hurlbut's constitutional proposal, Orestes Brownson pointed out that it would give the government "the power to suppress any church or religious institution that is based on a theory or principle different from its own." It would thus rewrite and nullify "the very amendment" that denied Congress "the power to prohibit to any one the free exercise of his religion!"[131]

A year later, in 1871, the Rev. Henry W. Bellows spoke in even more dire terms about the battle over separation. A radical Unitarian who "craved popularity," Bellows had already, two decades earlier, entered the fray against Bishop Hughes, arguing that "a new struggle has begun between the Catholic Church and the Protestant." This was a struggle "between the elements of religious authority and religious liberty"—between "a conscience in charge of a church and a conscience

---

[129] Ibid., 5. Hurlbut explained: "Under this amendment congress would be authorized to forbid, under effective penalties, the exercise of any priestly office under a foreign appointment, by any order of religionists, whose organization, discipline and teachings among us, were antagonistical and dangerous to our political institutions. Candor compels the admission, that this provision points to the Roman pontiff, his high dignitaries, and his doctrines." Ibid., 16.

[130] Ibid., 20, 27.

[131] "The Secular Not Supreme," *Catholic World,* 13: 690–692 (August 1871). In "prohibiting the free exercise" of religion, Hurlbut's amendment "gives to Congress full power to control or prevent the establishment or the continuance—that is, to prohibit—the free exercise by Catholics of their religion, under the flimsy pretence that it is a foreign hierarchy founded on anti-republican principles." Yet, as Brownson explained, the "hierarchy is an essential part of our religion, and any denial of its freedom is the denial of the free exercise of his religion to every Catholic, and of the very principle of religious liberty itself, which the constitution guarantees." Admittedly, the hierarchy was "not founded on democratic principles, . . . but there is nothing in its principles or dogmas antagonistical to republican government, if government at all." Ibid.

in charge of its owner."[132] Now, in 1871, shortly after the Civil War, Bellows felt obliged to warn Catholics of their fate if they continued to threaten American liberty by failing to keep church and state separate:

> Will the American people—a Christian, Protestant nation—see any form of sacramental, hierarchical, theological priestcraft, getting possession of their politics and government, cheating them before their very eyes out of their rights and liberties, and not, sooner or later, treat it just as they treated slavery?—nay, override the Constitution to save the nation threatened with a government of priests?
>
> It is the certainty of this result, so much more fearful for them than for us, that makes it the duty of Protestants to warn the Catholic hierarchy and the politicians that support them, whither they are tending; while they carefully cleanse their own skirts from every stain of political commerce, or want of fidelity to the fundamental law that keeps Church and State apart in our country.[133]

---

[132] Henry W. Bellows, *Religious Liberty. The Alleged Failure of Protestantism. A Sermon Preached in the Unitarian Church at Washington, on Washington's Birth-Day, February 22, 1852*, 6–7 (Washington: 1852). It "was written, and first preached in New York . . . and was called forth by Bishop Hughes's sermon on the 'Decline of Protestantism.'" At Bellows's death, a fellow liberal theologian, Frederic Henry Hedge, observed: "He craved popularity. . . . And he *was* popular. Innocent of duplicity, by virtue of a never-failing suavity, he could be all things to all men, conciliating the self-willed, humoring the weak, noticing the obscure, acknowledging the claims of the eminent, paying tribute where it was due, and collecting it from all." Frederic H. Hedge, *Memorial Address, Spoken on the 30th of May, 1882 (Decoration Day) at the Annual Meeting of the American Unitarian Association*, in Joseph Henry Allen, *Our Liberal Movement in Theology, Chiefly as Shown in Recollections of the History of Unitarianism in New England, A Closing Course of Lectures Given in the Harvard Divinity School*, 205–206 (Boston: American Unitarian Association, n.d.).

[133] Henry W. Bellows, *Church and State in America. A Discourse Given at Washington, D.C., at the Installation of Rev. Frederic Hinckley, as Pastor of the Unitarian Church, January 25, 1871*, 20 (Washington, D.C.: 1871). He also said: "Now, as an American Citizen, I say nothing against the equality of the rights of the Roman Catholics and the Protestants—both may lawfully strive, in their unpolitical spheres, for the mastery, and the law may not favor or disfavor either; nor can anything be done to prevent Roman Catholics from using their votes as Roman Catholics, if they please. It is against the spirit, but not against the letter of the Constitution. At any rate it cannot be helped; only, it may compel Protestants to form parties and vote as Protestants against Roman Catholic Interests, which would . . . lead, sooner or later, through religious parties in politics, to religious wars. The way to avoid such a horrible possibility—alas, such a threatening probability for the next generation— is at once to look with the utmost carefulness and the utmost disfavor upon every effort on the part of either Protestants or Catholics to mix up sectarian or theological or religious questions, with national and State and city politics." Ibid., 18. Incidentally, Bellows knew what he was talking about when he warned Catholics of another war, for he had led the U.S. Sanitary Commission. Similarly, a Universalist sympathetic to separation, J. C. Adams,

Protestants would resort to a civil war, even an unconstitutional conflict, against Catholics who entered politics in violation of the principle
of separation. Therefore, it was incumbent upon responsible Protestant
preachers to warn Catholics of the danger they risked at the hands of
freedom-loving Americans.

Again, Orestes Brownson recognized the violence of the prejudice.
Catholics had merely voted to protect their religious liberty, and, "as
long as any religion, even the reading of the Bible, is insisted on in the
public schools, . . . what is to prevent Catholic citizens from making it
a political question and withholding their votes from the party that refuses to respect their rights of conscience and to do them justice?" The
retort from Bellows, as understood by Brownson, was grim: "we [Catho-
lics] cannot legally be prevented from doing so, but, if we do so, it will
be the worse for us; for if we carry our religion to the polls the Protestant
people will, as they should, rise up against us and overwhelm us by their
immense majority, perhaps even exterminate us."

Of course, not all Protestants went to these extremes, but many
feared or could be induced to fear an impending conflict between Roman
slavery and Republican freedom—often depicted as a contest between
Catholic union and American separation. Without carefully examining
the history of the notion of separation, numerous Protestants concluded
that the Catholic Church had long been at war against this principle. In
particular, they looked back at the history of Christianity and of America and observed Catholic opposition to ideas of religious liberty that,
in retrospect, they easily and conveniently confused with separation.
Accordingly, these Protestants believed they were approaching the culmination of an historic struggle with the Catholic Church. For example,
Joseph Smith Van Dyke wrote that "Romanism" had long been hostile
to "the separation of Church and State," which was a "principle of our
national life" and "which Protestants have ever viewed as one of the
defences of civil liberty." This principle "has been and now is the object of
incessant attack"—as evidenced by the popes who "for the last thousand

---

observed: "Our next war—if one must come—will be between Romanist and Protestant."
"Church and State" (from *The Universalist*), in *Boston Investigator*, 4 (Sept. 15, 1875). Writing
of the state and religion, Adams concluded: "The existing relations of the two, evidently
cannot last long unmodified. And what changes will be made, depends very much upon
the thoroughness and scope of the agitation now begun." Rev. J. C. Adams, "The Church
and the State," *Universalist Quarterly and General Review*, 14: 308 (new ser., 1877).

years" had "pronounced it a 'damnable heresy.'"[134] So popular was this fantasy that national politicians sought votes by writing about it. For example, in 1876, in his *The Papacy and the Civil Power*, a leading Republican, Richard W. Thompson, contributed to his party's victory in the presidential election by reminding voters of the struggle for separation and individual freedom:

> The two systems stand in direct antagonism with each other. The Protestant has separated the State from the Church; the papal proposes to unite them again. The Protestant has founded its civil institutions upon the *will of the people;* the papal proposes to reconstruct and found them upon the *will of the pope.* The Protestant secures religious freedom; the papal requires that every man shall give up his conscience to the keeping of ecclesiastical superiors.

Incidentally, in observing these tensions, Thompson, like so many other Protestants, linked the Church's claims of political authority to its claims of theological authority—the fundamental problem being that, for Catholics, "the personality of the believer is merged in the superior personality of the pope." It was a view one Catholic reviewer called "sheer, unmitigated twaddle."[135]

With these dire visions of the Catholic Church and its threat to the political and mental freedom of individuals, many Protestants found satisfaction in conceiving of their religious liberty, especially their freedom from establishments, as a separation of church and state. In so doing, they took for granted that separation was a principle of government with historical foundations vaguely evident in American constitutions. Yet they repeatedly revealed that it had a more substantial basis in their fears of the Catholic Church and in their contrasting sense of their own individual independence as Protestants and Americans.

---

[134] Joseph Smith Van Dyke, *Popery the Foe of the Church, and of the Republic,* 263 (Philadelphia: Peoples Publishing Co., 1872).

[135] R. W. Thompson, *The Papacy and the Civil Power,* 53, 76 (New York: 1876); see also ibid., 218–219; B. A. Harper, Review of R. W. Thompson, *The Papacy and the Civil Power,* in *American Catholic Quarterly Review,* 2: 516 (Philadelphia: January to October 1877). The reviewer argued that it was "the State" that "even yet more violently endeavors to submerge in itself the personality of the citizen." Ibid., 518–519. Incidentally, it is suggestive of the continuity maintained by nativists that the passage in the block quotation was adopted later without attribution and with only minor changes by the Central Committee for Protecting and Perpetuating the Separation of Church and State, *To the People of the State of New York. Appeal No. 4,* 16 (1886).

9

Separations in Society

THE SEPARATION of church and state seems to have been part of a wider array of separations in society. These separations included not only suspicions of ecclesiastical authority but also the whole range of specializations through which individuals segregated religion or otherwise escaped the religious expectations of their society—a series of separations that had obvious secularizing effects. In this context some Americans welcomed the separation of church and state as part of the broader segregation of church and of religion from their specialized activities. As has been seen, the separation of church and state became popular mostly as an anti-Catholic and more broadly antiecclesiastical conception of religious liberty. At the same time, it probably also appealed to Americans as yet another form of specialization that limited the role of religion, especially the communal religion of churches.

At least some Americans had already perceived that the separation of the church was a type of specialization. In 1644, Roger Williams, who sought to separate the church from the world, also separated religion from worldly endeavors that required professional or other specialized knowledge. A Christian, according to Williams, could not, on account of his religion, perform professional activities better than, for example, a pagan, and this seemed to suggest that such activities were unconnected to religion. More directly, in 1815 Jefferson recognized that the separation of clergymen from politics was part of the broader specialization of professional knowledge that has subsequently come to be associated with modernity. The exact relationship of the separation of church and state to these more general social specializations is difficult to document, but in the writings of some nineteenth-century Americans it is possible to obtain at least glimpses of how the one sort of separation developed among others.

Specialization

Some educators and theological liberals self-consciously recognized the attractions of specialization, including a separation of church and state. For example, the first president of the University of Michigan, Henry P. Tappan, welcomed the separation of church and state in education as the first stage in the broader progress of the separation of religion from education. Since his appointment in 1852, Tappan had struggled to make Michigan a center of learning in accord with the Prussian model and therefore had appointed professors on the basis of their academic qualifications. He thus directly repudiated Michigan's tradition of dividing such appointments among each of the leading Protestant sects in the state. So completely did he embrace his professional role that, although a Dutch Reformed minister, he went out of his way to worship at the churches of other denominations and discouraged student prayer meetings.[1] Such was the man who in 1858 took pleasure in observing "separation" not only in common schools, which were publicly funded, but also in all higher institutions of learning, without distinction between public and private:

> Men who immigrated to this country from religious principles, naturally connected all their institutions both educational and political, with their peculiar church organization.
>
> But it did not follow, because, this connection was originally demanded, or could not be avoided, on account of the peculiar exigencies of the times, that it was to continue when these exigencies had passed away. Hence, in time, the Church and State came to be separated; and education in the common schools, at least, came to be separated from the Church also. This movement has proceeded further and further; and we now have not only common schools, but also, High Schools, and Academies, Normal Schools, and even many Colleges and Universities, removed from particular ecclesiastical connections.

[1] Wilfred B. Shaw, ed., *The University of Michigan: An Encyclopedic Survey*, 45–46 (Ann Arbor: University of Michigan Press, 1942).

Indeed, it is hard to perceive any necessity for such a connection in any instance, save where a sect desires to create a Theological Faculty.[2]

Having separated their states and state schools from particular churches and sects, Americans would now, in Tappan's vision of professional specialization, separate almost all education, both public and private, from sectarian influence.

This separation of education from particular religious denominations resonated with the aspirations and self-image of theological liberals. Not so clearly because of any fragmentation of their lives as because of their Protestant image of their individuality, Unitarians and other theological liberals gave unusual emphasis to the importance of an individual's freedom of belief, uninhibited by the constraints of a creed. These opponents of Calvinist orthodoxy did not deny religion's moral role in the world, but, with visions of religion so focused on the individual, they saw no harm in segregating their communal religious life—their churches and denominations—from their secular activities, such as education, and even saw this separation as a valuable means of restraining other, more traditional, denominations.

This theologically liberal desire to separate conventional denominations from education can be illustrated by the views of Octavius Brooks Frothingham—the Unitarian and Transcendentalist minister who would soon establish his Independent Liberal Church and who would support separation of church and state as a vice president of the National Liberal League. Taking what initially seemed a remarkably tolerant position, he asked his fellow Protestants in 1866 why they singled out Catholics

---

[2] Henry P. Tappan, *The University: Its Constitution, and Its Relations, Political and Religious: A Discourse Delivered June 22d, 1858, at the Request of the Christian Library Association*, 22 (Ann Arbor: 1858). After Tappan was forced out of his position, largely because of his refusal to make appointments on religious grounds, his successor as president of the university, Erastus Otis Haven, attempted to reverse Tappan's policies. In so doing, Haven recognized the difficulty of explaining how a public institution could support religion without infringing on religious liberty. For example, in 1867 he told the graduating class that the university, like the nation of which it was a part, had to reconcile its religiosity and its religious freedom: "You are about to graduate from a University conducted by the State, and which received its existence from the nation—a nation whose destiny it is to solve practically the difficult problem how to favor religion and to be religious, and at the same time guarantee to all perfect freedom of religious opinion and practice. Its institutions must partake of its own character, sharing in its difficulties and its advantages, and in no particular is this characteristic more conspicuous than in their relations to religion." E. O. Haven, *Public Education and Religion. A Baccalaureate Sermon Delivered June 23, 1867*, 4 (Ann Arbor: 1867).

when complaining about the influence of clergymen teaching in public schools. "But why confine our jealousy to the Romanist? Why not suspect every *religionist* as such—the Episcopalian, the Baptist, the Methodist, the Presbyterian, the Unitarian, the Universalist? Why not suspect everything that threatens to color common-school teaching with sectarian hues?" On this apparently equal basis, he questioned whether most clergymen should teach in public schools: "'Is a teacher less prepared to instruct the people in letters, because to the learning of the schools and the wisdom of men he adds divine teaching and the Word of God?' We answer frankly, 'Yes'; if the two classes of learning are mingled together, or if the teaching of divinity and the Word of God crowds out, takes precedence of, limits, defines, or colors the instruction in letters and the wisdom of men." The religious and the secular classes of learning were to be compartmentalized. Accordingly,

> Rationalists and Unitarians—who reject the scheme of salvation, whose religion is chiefly ethical, who preach up the interests of this life, intellectual culture, domestic virtue, social kindness, the priceless worth of the simply human relations—may mingle such religion as they have with education, because education is their religion. But evangelical men, who are supremely interested in the salvation of souls, cannot confound them with secular interests, without encountering the dangers of compromising both.[3]

Unlike those who advocated the religion of this world, those who believed in the religion of the next world could not safely be allowed to teach in public schools.

In liberal theological circles a segmentation of life increasingly seemed respectable, allowing liberal ministers to justify a separation of church and state as one of various beneficial specializations.[4] For exam-

---

[3] O. B. Frothingham, "Education and Religion," *New York Independent*, 17 (no. 919) (July 12, 1866). According to one critic, Frothingham "avowed that, not only the Bible, and all religious instruction, but all evangelical men, also, are to be excommunicated from our public schools." R. Patterson, *The Free Thinkers and the Free Schools*, 12–13 (Chicago: 1870).

[4] A liberal supporter of separation of church and state, Frederic Henry Hedge—who was also a leading Transcendentalist and who presided over the American Unitarian Association—exhorted Harvard to abandon its attempt to control both the intellectual and the moral lives of students: "Professors should not be responsible for the manners of students beyond the legitimate operation of their personal influence. There should be no penalty beyond that of expulsion, and that only in the way of self-defence against positively noxious and dangerous members. Let the civil law take care of civil offences." He apparently also argued: "Abolish . . . your whole system of marks, college rank, and compulsory tasks."

ple, in the 1870s, when some Presbyterians and Episcopalians proposed a Christian amendment to the U.S. Constitution, a Universalist minister, the Rev. John Coleman Adams, opposed such an amendment on the basis of "the secular theory of the State," which aimed "at the complete separation of the church and the State" and thereby offered all of the advantages of a "division of labor." This division benefited not only the state but also the church: "[I]t is not a wise plan to have one institution undertake too many things. For while it may do some things very well, if it attempted certain others, it might fail in them very signally." Thus "[i]f a religious society, in addition to its legitimate work, were to try and run a savings-bank or carry on a horse railroad, it would miss its vocation."[5] Treating the separation of church and state as part of this specialization, Adams pointed out that organizations specializing in government, like those focused on railroads, did not profess their religious faith in their articles of incorporation. In Adams's vision of society "the Church by no means loses her influence" over the state, but this influence was fragmented: "She still brings her power to bear upon it, through the consciences of her members." Indeed, this absence of communal religious influence was a strength, for "the influence is real, and not fictitious, because it will always be exactly equal to the thorough convictions of men's minds. The State will not be controlled by what men's creeds say, but by what their hearts say."[6]

Politicians, Lawyers, Merchants, and Consumers

Like the educators and theological liberals who self-consciously advocated separation of church and state as one of the valuable separations in society, many others, with more practical concerns—politicians, lawyers, and merchants—also supported separation. Although these practical-minded men tended not to justify separation with the eloquence of their more theologically inclined countrymen, they seem to have recognized the connection of this ideal to their own divided lives.

As quoted by Patterson, *The Free Thinkers and the Free Schools,* 13. Incidentally, Hedge was the author of the "oft-quoted" saying, "Reason or Rome—there is no middle ground." Francis Ellingwood Abbot, "Christianity and Free Religion Contrasted as to Corner-Stones," *Index,* 1 (no. 4): 2 (Jan. 22, 1870).
[5] Rev. J. C. Adams, "The Church and the State," *Universalist Quarterly and General Review* 14: 313 (new ser., 1877).
[6] Ibid., 321.

Many nineteenth-century politicians lived in a manner unlikely to give them second thoughts about the separation of church and state. Not only could they gratify their more prejudiced Protestant constituents by attacking Catholics on grounds of separation, but they could do so at little cost, for many politicians participated in religious life in a rather detached way, without strong ties to any one denomination. Although only a small proportion of mid-nineteenth-century Americans were full members or communicants in their churches, a majority seem to have been at least associated with one or another denomination.[7] Politicians, however, had a reputation for religious affiliations of a weaker sort. As Bela Bates Edwards—an Andover-trained clergyman and editor—complained in 1835: "A great majority of the members of our successive legislatures are not connected with the churches of any denomination."[8] Over the century, the association of politicians with churches may have increased, but, if politicians typically did not adhere to much more than an unspecific Protestantism, they were unlikely personally to feel the limiting implications of a separation of church and state for religious groups. Even if firmly affiliated with a specific denomination, a politician usually represented constituents of diverse denominations and therefore had reason to emphasize a generalized, nondenominational Protestantism (or, if he also needed Catholic support, a broad Christianity). Accordingly, even more than other Americans, politicians tended not to appreciate the constraints on group religion that might arise from a separation of church and state.

[7] Robert Baird counted more than 2.8 million "members in full communion" and more than 15.3 million individuals "more or less under the influence" of the "evangelical denominations," out of a U.S. population he estimated to be about 18.5 million. Baird, *Religion in America* (1844), in William G. McLoughlin, *The American Evangelicals, 1800–1900: An Anthology,* 33, 35 (Gloucester: Peter Smith, 1976). Of course, as Baird himself cautioned, the accuracy of such numbers cannot be taken for granted.

[8] B. B. Edwards, Review of Isaac Taylor, *Spiritual Despotism* (1835), in *Biblical Repository and Quarterly Observer,* 6: 207, 209, 214 (1835). Two years later, Edwards joined the Andover faculty. Forty years afterward, another clergyman made a more optimistic estimate about legislators but ended up observing the weakness of their connections to Christianity: "[A]fter all, quite likely we need apprehend no danger. . . . More than two thirds of our legislators, probably, are in some sort of connection with the Churches. If not personally allied as communicants, they are held by domestic ties or by their own preference as members of the congregation." Rev. E. M'Chesney, "Taxation of Church Property: Review of Charles Eliot, *The Exemption from Taxation of Church Property* . . . & Alvah Hovey, *Religion and the State,*" in *Methodist Quarterly Review,* 68: 256 (vol. 28 of 4th ser., 1876). Obviously, domestic ties and preferences about congregations were not exactly attachments to a particular denomination.

An 1849 rumor about President Taylor and the newspaper dispute that ensued can illustrate how a segregation of religion and politics could appeal to politicians, or at least some of their supporters, who sought to insulate themselves from the less welcome demands of their fellow Christians. The *Baltimore Sun* reported: "The story is, that a committee of one of the Methodist Societies of Georgetown waited upon the President to ask a donation towards enabling them to build a church. It is said that the General replied, 'No: I will not give you a cent; the People did not put me here to build churches.'" The Baltimore *Sun*, which was "quite Taylorwise," defended the president by pointing out that, although his "language may have acquired a twang of rudeness in its transference to a political use, . . . it is the language of sound discernment and good common sense." According to the *Sun*, "[t]he office of the President is exclusively secular, and for his religious sentiments he is responsible to no earthly being. He had, therefore, a perfect right to refuse the donation upon any ground, and without explanation; and the attempt to make him amenable for it, is an outrage upon his individual rights as a citizen of the United States." To this, the District of Columbia's *National Era* replied that secular office did not separate individuals from their religious and moral obligations:

> The Sun . . . justifies him, on the ground that his office is "exclusively secular!" Ridiculous! Do Virtue, Knowledge, and Religion, cease to have claims upon a man because he happens to hold a civil office? We believe in the separation of Church and State, but not in the divorce of Religion and Rulers. According to the new light of the Sun, no office-holder ought to contribute to the building of churches, to the payment of expenses of religious worship, to the support of ministers, to the circulation of the Bible, to the prosecution of Missions, or to any other religious object: his office is "exclusively secular!"

Far from being relieved of his individual religious obligations because of his secular office, the president was subject to higher expectations:

> The act of refusing to aid in the building of a place of religious worship, where neither want of means nor a disbelief in religion exists, is discreditable to any man, specially to one holding high office from the people. True, they may not have put him there to build churches; neither did they put him there to stifle the generous instincts of his nature, and set an example of penuriousness. The people of the United States are distinguished for their liberal contributions to all good works; and their public

servants cannot do better than to rival them in their charities, and gracefully reflect the national spirit.[9]

In this way the *National Era* repudiated the *Sun*'s suggestion that secular office divorced men from their obligation to support religion. To the Baltimore *Sun*, however, and, no doubt, to various politicians, such a claim seemed plausible.

Lawyers and judges similarly had reasons to put aside some of the implications of religion. Even if these professionals were worried about the secularizing consequences of specialization, they typically had to ignore their religious concerns and follow the law.[10] Indeed, lawyers were inclined to look for evidence of the constitutional status of separation, and therefore they, more than other Americans, turned to Jefferson's words about a *wall* of separation—a formulation singularly incompatible with the common assumption that religion had implications for all features of human life. As Daniel Dreisbach has pointed out, Jefferson's letter to the Danbury Baptist Association was first widely disseminated in the 1853 edition of his works.[11] Three years later, in an 1856 commencement address on religious liberty, Justice Jeremiah S. Black of the Pennsylvania Supreme Court—who would soon become Attorney General of the United States—adopted the wall metaphor, without apparent concern:

> The manifest object of the men who framed the institutions of this country, was to have a *State without religion*, and a *Church without politics*—that is to say, they meant that one should never be used as an engine for any purpose of the other, and that no man's rights in one should be tested by his opinions about the other. As the Church takes no note of men's political differences, so the State looks with equal eye on all the modes of religious faith. The Church may give her preferment to a Tory, and the State may be served by a heretic. Our fathers seem to have been perfectly sincere in their belief that the members of the Church would

[9] "General Taylor and the Church," *National Era*, 3 (no. 134): 118 (July 26, 1849).
[10] In some cases they had occasion to observe that America was a Christian nation, but, as Stuart Banner shows, they usually did so merely to confirm their secular legal arguments. Banner, "When Christianity Was Part of the Common Law," *Law & History Review*, 16: 27 (1998).
[11] Henry A. Washington, ed., *The Writings of Thomas Jefferson* (Washington, D.C.: 1853–1854), discussed by Daniel L. Dreisbach, "'Sowing Useful Truths and Principles': The Danbury Baptists, Thomas Jefferson, and the 'Wall of Separation,'" *Journal of Church and State*, 39: 491 (1997).

be more patriotic, and the citizens of the State more religious, by keeping their respective functions entirely separate. For that reason they built up a wall of complete and perfect partition between the two.[12]

Similarly, in 1878, in *Reynolds v. United States,* Justice Waite of the U.S. Supreme Court even treated Jefferson's letter to the Danbury Association as an authoritative interpretation of the First Amendment. A Mormon polygamist, George Reynolds, who had been convicted under a federal bigamy statute, argued that he had married again in accord with his religious obligations and that therefore his criminal conviction violated the First Amendment. In rejecting his claim, the Court quoted Jefferson's letter about separation and concluded that, "[c]oming as this does from an acknowledged leader of the advocates of the measure, it may be accepted almost as an authoritative declaration of the scope and effect of the amendment thus secured." For decades, nativists had complained that Catholic doctrine elevating church law over secular law violated the separation of church and state, and now, although the Court did not clearly rely upon separation and thus did not yet elevate it to constitutional law, it assumed that the principle of separation prevented Reynolds from relying upon a claim of obedience to his church. Of course, in employing the idea of separation against polygamy, Waite and the other justices were unlikely to worry whether separation had some costs, but, further, as professionals, they were accustomed to isolating peripheral concerns. Indeed, being judges of law rather than of American life as a whole, they had little reason and, perhaps, even only a limited right to consider separation's broader implications for the role of religion in America.[13]

---

[12] "Religious Liberty" (1856), in *Essays and Speeches of Jeremiah S. Black,* 53 (New York: 1885).
[13] Reynolds v. United States, 98 U.S. 145, 164 (1878). In contrast to this case, in which the Supreme Court perceived a claim of religious obligation to a church, the Court later looked more favorably upon assertions of individual conscientious objection—typically made by members of Protestant sects. For more on the exemption issue, see Chapter 14, note 112.

Justice William Strong's acquiescence in the *Reynolds* opinion is particularly suggestive of the narrow professional focus of lawyers and judges. An active member of the Presbyterian Church and president of the American Tract Society and of the American Sunday-School Union, Strong became president of the movement for a Christian amendment to the Constitution in the 1870s. This movement opposed the separation of church and state. Yet in *Reynolds,* Strong did not distance himself from the language in Waite's opinion about separation of church and state. In all probability, Strong allowed the phrase to pass into the reports because of his satisfaction with the judgment against the Mormons and polygamy and because of his reluctance to dissent from an inessential portion of the Court's opinion. Therefore, little can be inferred from his failure to object. Nonetheless, it is clear that, as a judge, he did not object to what he surely would not have written as a Christian.

In addition to politicians and lawyers, many merchants and businessmen wished to keep communal religious expectations from limiting their professional activities, and they therefore embraced the separation of church and state. The most entertaining of the businessmen who saw the separation of church and state as part of a larger separation of religion from secular activity was Phineas Taylor Barnum. After pursuing various less than reputable moneymaking schemes, he anointed himself Proprietor of The Greatest Show on Earth and had the satisfaction of writing books such as *How I Made Millions.* Yet Barnum faced religious opposition to his career of "duplicity" and "persistent deception." For example, according to the *Ladies Repository*—a popular outlet for the Methodist Church—Barnum was "an unscrupulous and successful manipulator of public gullibillity."[14] Accused of humbuggery, he responded with a volume on *The Humbugs of the World,* in which he lashed out at "the doctrine of 'special providence'"—a concept he compared to the medieval ordeal, in which defendants were subjected to burning hot iron or submersion in water as means of discerning divine judgment. The irrationality of the ordeal suggested to Barnum the value of separating the religious from the secular, including the church from the state: "Looked at as a superstition . . .—considered as a humbug—the history of ordeals show how corrupt becomes the nuisance of religious ways of deciding secular business, and how proper is our great American principle of the separation of state and church."[15] Barnum had suffered the nuisance of religious complaints about his business, and, not surprisingly, he appreciated a broad range of separations between the religious and the secular.

Thus numerous legislators, judges, merchants, and others seemed to keep their religion—especially the religion of their churches—out of their professional tasks. As early as 1835, the popular pastor of Boston's Bowdoin Street Church, the Rev. Hubbard Winslow, summed up the issue in a complaint about legislators and judges:

> The notion that religion and politics must have nothing to do with each other, has too often induced Christians, whenever they approached politics, to leave their religion behind. Of our legislators and judges, how few bring their religion with them to the hall and the bench. They even make a *duty* of leaving it at home, or in the sanctuary, because they are profes-

[14] Rev. T. M. Eddy, "Barnum," *Ladies Repository,* 15: 175 (March 1855).
[15] P. T. Barnum, *The Humbugs of the World,* 415 (New York: 1866).

sionally to serve their *office*, and not Christ! And of all subjects, how few bring religion practically to bear upon their relations and duties to our government. They seem to have, as is said of some merchants, *two* consciences; one for religion, and one for other purposes. Now if even Christians do thus, what will others do?[16]

Eager to participate in their professional and other secular activities without the constraint of religious obligations, these specialized Americans elevated the sequestration of religion to an ideal.

Even consumers had reason to support this separation, as may be illustrated by a story about a cigar. Evangelicals had long feared "that an irresistible flood of business and pleasure" would "roll over the sacred institutions of religion," and by the end of the century, this flood of desires—even merely the need for a smoke—carried increasing numbers of Americans toward the separation of religion, especially a separation of church and state.[17] One of the late nineteenth-century organizations

---

[16] Hubbard Winslow, *Christianity Applied to Our Civil and Social Relations*, 130 (Boston: 1835). This was not merely a Congregationalist position. William Ellery Channing's associate, Ezra S. Gannett, preached: "It is said, that men need not be as scrupulous in their public as in their private relations. There is a morality for the public man, and another for the private citizen. There are two standards of conduct even for the same person, in his private and in his public capacity. I have heard it said by those who knew him well that an individual of great influence, who had been placed in the most elevated offices within the people's gift, was a man of strict integrity and the mildest character in his private connexions, though as a politician he was distinguished for his disregard of truth, his violence, and his use of any means to carry the ends which his party espoused." Gannett, *The Religion of Politics. A Sermon*, 27–28 (Boston: 1842). In Philadelphia Stephen Colwell wrote: "THERE is no small confusion of ideas . . . on the subject of the bearing of Christianity on social and political questions. 'Do you suppose I mingle my religion with my politics?' replied, not long since, a man of standing in his church, to a gentleman who had taken him to task for political conduct inconsistent with his religious profession. There are not a few who seem to be of the same opinion; that, in the way of politics and business, they can be perverse, rabid, undermining, overreaching, overbearing, if not dishonest and indecent, provided they keep their every-day conduct quite distinct from their religious observance and Sunday demeanor. Christianity permits no such distinction. . . . It is true that the great Author of Christianity . . . enjoins no interference with political institutions. His instructions in reference to our conduct in this life are elementary; they reach to the soul and inward character, and thence mould the outward man." Colwell, *Politics for American Christians: A Word upon Our Example as a Nation, Our Labour, Our Trade, Elections, Education, and Congressional Legislation*, i (Philadelphia: 1852). See also Sidney E. Mead, *The Lively Experiment: The Shaping of Christianity in America*, 137 (New York: Harper & Row, 1963).

[17] *An Account of Memorial Presented to Congress during Its Last Session, by Numerous Friends of Their Country and Its Institutions; Praying That the Mails May Not Be Transported, Nor Post-Offices Kept Open, on the Sabbath*, 4 (New York: May 1829). Similarly, in his *Address to the People of the United States*, Lyman Beecher wrote that "the respect of former generations for the Sabbath was in many places gone, and in all places fast failing before the innundation of

that advocated separation of church and state, the American Secular Union, held its 1888 annual congress in Pittsburgh, where on Sundays "[n]othing can be legally sold—not even grocery, candy, or cigar stores can be kept open." Accordingly, "[e]verybody must lay in on Saturday night the solid and liquid refreshments for the following day," and "[t]he improvident man who neglects to provide his spiritual food from the saloon on Saturday must take it on Sunday from the churches, or not at all." In these circumstances a reporter for the *Truth Seeker* came across an improvident delegate:

> One of the delegates who likes a good cigar . . . was the most disgusted person in the city. The Editorial Reporter met him on Sunday morning walking up and down in front of the hotel and swearing earnestly. He had had his breakfast but not his cigar. He approached the Editorial Reporter and unbosomed himself. His language would not do to print. All at once a thought hit him, and he went plunging upstairs to his room, and punched the button of the electric bell till it went out of sight. When the hallboy made his appearance he shouted: "Bring me a cigar!" It came at once. And thus did ingenuity on the part of the guest and hypocrisy on the part of the hotelkeeper triumph over Pittsburgh puritanism. When [a leader of the American Secular Union, Samuel] Putnam was asking the audience for a campaign fund, that man's name went down for $50, and he wants it all applied to repealing Sunday laws.

A cigar could go a long way.[18]

---

business and pleasure; that commerce . . . is putting in motion a secular enterprise, which is fast and fearfully annihilating the national conscience in respect to the Sabbath." As quoted by Harmon Kingsbury, *The Sabbath: A Brief History of Law, Petitions, Remonstrances and Reports,* 143 (New York: 1840). See also ibid., 316–317, 346, 356.

[18] "Scraps from the Congress. From E. M. McDonald's Report in the *Truth Seeker,*" in *Free-thought, A Liberal Journal,* 1 (no. 43): 521 (San Francisco: Oct. 27, 1888). On the other hand, as will be seen, cigars and other Sunday conveniences, such as Sunday trains and newspapers, hardly sufficed to hold together the American Secular Union or any of the other late nineteenth-century "Liberal" groups that worked on behalf of separation. At the very least, the individualism and the resentment of communal demands that stimulated support for separation may also have left many proponents of this principle unwilling to make sacrifices for their own organizations. A late nineteenth-century advocate of separation from Pittsville, Wisconsin, complained: "But as a class Liberals are content with theoretical advantages, and consequently the orthodox reap all practical benefits. There are too many professed Liberals who giv[e] no support to Liberal propaganda. They buy no books, read no papers, contribute to no lectures; their whole energy is bent to the acquisition of wealth, disregarding those noble principles which, if carried into effect, would contribute to the welfare and happiness of themselves and their fellow men." G. H. Dawes, "Principles of American Liberty," *Truth Seeker,* 355 (June 8, 1889).

The various economic and cultural divisions in American society were hardly new, but they increasingly contributed to suspicions of the demands made by organized Christianity. The religion that once had seemed to "bridge" divisions among classes and interests was itself becoming a source of division, especially between the populace and "the more cultivated classes." To some observers this widening "gulf between the average and the higher mind of the day" seemed "far more dangerous than the 'old sectarian divisions,'" for "when the visible differences among men, as to their religious sympathies and views, coincide with the grades of intellectual and social rank, the distrust and dread run deeper." On this basis, a Unitarian clergyman, Joseph Henry Allen, feared that Americans would soon find that "intellect is utterly divorced from the popular faith, and such a thing as a common Christian civilization becomes impossible." More than most of his contemporaries, Allen understood that the failure of the "popular faith" was "more real and more formidable, because the separation which threatens it is going on in other things as well as in religion." The whole of "[r]epublican society among us is going through a process of 'differentiation' and 'individuation,' which, as the science of the day informs us, is the needful preliminary to higher forms of life." Accordingly, this development seemed attractively progressive, but it placed American "political institutions" under "a strain which their founders never anticipated," for "civilization means division of interest and division of labor. Education means a gradual widening and separating of mental sympathies. Trade means speculation, and the increasing differences and contrasts of wealth."[19] On these secular grounds as well as religious ones, Americans were becoming fragmented, and many of them therefore increasingly had reason to call for various separations from the demands of their churches—not least for a separation of church and state.

---

[19] J. H. Allen, "Liberalism in Church and State" (reviewing Samuel Osgood, *Faith and Freedom in America. Sermon at the Consecration of the Church of the Messiah,* April 2, 1868), in *Christian Examiner,* 85: 85–87 (July 1868). Revealingly, at the same time that Allen worried about the dangers of "differentiation" and "individuation," he attacked Catholics for their cohesion. "Where Protestantism deals with individuals as individuals, unorganized and dispersed, Romanism deals with them as a mass, to be trained as willing recruits, and drilled into an effective army." Ibid., 96. Of course, Unitarians had particular reason to worry about the religious alignment of different classes. As Henry W. Bellows had said a decade earlier, "our faith is very thin air to the majority of lungs accustomed to the damp atmosphere of the prevailing Christianity." Henry W. Bellows, *The Christian Liberal. A Sermon, Delivered before the Western Unitarian Conference, at Buffalo,* 19 (Buffalo: 1855).

Moral Costs

Especially when allied with other separations in American society, the separation of church and state could have a moral cost. This became particularly clear when the principle of separation was raised as a barrier to the moral claims sometimes made against property owners. Although Americans only occasionally employed separation in this manner, their efforts suggest much about the role of this idea in allowing Americans to fend off moral demands with which they did not wish to comply. For example, on the ground of separation, some Americans opposed taxes for the support of the poor. In the words of an 1859 New York manual on local government:

> If our legislatures ordain that the counties shall have power to establish poorhouses, and tax the people to raise the funds for their support, they assume that the supporting of poor men is a political business, while I call it a mere charitable private personal act of brotherly love. The Christian church, from its beginning, took hold of this business, tried to introduce communism on this account, and later, when united with the states, transferred it to them. We have separated the church from the state, and the church has to take back this charity business, if it may not be entirely left with the benevolent, as a mere personal private affair; instead of doing so we have, by bad centralization, made it a county business.[20]

Charity belonged to the church and needed to be separated from the state.

Although separation rarely became an issue in the debates over slavery, the possible implications of the principle were not entirely ignored. It has already been seen that many Americans, especially in the South, rejected clerical intervention in the politics of slavery but did not typically go so far as to demand a separation of church and state. Similarly, when abolitionists demanded that churches take a strong stand against slavery, some clergymen, fearful that their denominations would be sundered over this issue, argued that the Christian church lacked the authority or competency to condemn slavery. According to these Christians, slavery (unlike, apparently, temperance and education) was a matter belonging exclusively to civil government. It was an argument

[20] Maurice A. Richter, *Internal Relations of the Cities, Towns, Villages, Counties, and States of the Union; or, The Municipalist: A Highly Useful Book for Voters, Tax-Payers, Statesmen, Politicians and Families,* 218 (New York: 1859).

often cast in Biblical terms (about what was due unto Caesar and how the church ought to confine itself to Christ's kingdom). Yet it also could be stated in other ways. For example, in 1851, when the Methodist Church was splitting apart, one of its members, Thomas J. Taylor, protested that, because of the separation of church and state, although individuals could oppose slavery, "the Church, in her organized capacity," was "not competent" to take a stand:

> We find, in the teaching and example of Christ and the apostles, a recognition of the separation of the Church and State, Luke xii, 14; and also of the supremacy of the civil power in all the duties of civil or organized society. . . . Therefore we conclude, that whatever we, as individual members of the Church, and as subjects of the civil power, may regard as our duty toward the government under which we live, it is not competent for the Church, in her organized capacity, to array herself against the powers that be, or any of the civil duties legitimately growing out of the constitution under which we live, when they do not conflict with the law of God.[21]

[21] Thomas J. Taylor, *Essay on Slavery*, 23 (New York: 1851). For more typical examples, not in terms of separation, see Anson Phelps Stokes, *Church and State in the United States*, 2: 210, 212, 240 (New York: Harper, 1950); An American [James Birney], *The American Churches: The Bulwarks of American Slavery* (Newburyport: 1842). Even those critics of political preaching who evidently were reluctant to rely upon the principle of separation between church and state sometimes clearly were conscious of it. For example, in 1859 the Rev. William C. Richards of Rhode Island preached to the Rhode Island Baptist State Convention that the use of the pulpit for political purposes was a divorce of pulpit and cross:

> The pulpit and the Cross of Christ are bound together by the two bonds of Divine commission and Apostolic practice. To undo those bonds, to divorce the pulpit from the Cross for any purpose, however noble in the estimation of human wisdom, however dear to the heart of human philanthropy, however sacred to the beating bosom of humanity, however imperative by the will of the world—is to put asunder what God hath joined together; is to deny the wisdom which ordained the Gospel, as the remedy for human woes . . . ; is to put human wisdom above Divine; man's philanthropy above God's mercy; humanity above immortality; the will of the world above the authority of God. Where is the man that dares to do this? Let him stand forth and confront the Apostle of the Gentiles; and when he has vaunted, in all the eloquence of speech, the freedom of the pulpit to thunder forth its anathemas against political men and political measures; . . . to lend its sacred influence to sanctify the clamours of the multitude shouting for partisan issues; to suspend its diviner messages for a season, that it may proclaim the doctrines of humanity; to put the Cross aside, that it may display the pole of Liberty; to forget the Divine martyr of Calvary, that it may canonize some bleeding advocate of political reform; when he has boasted of the license of the pulpit to do all this, the Apostle shall lift his earnest eyes into the face of the time-server, and exclaim, "God forbid that *I* should *glory* save in the cross of our Lord Jesus Christ."

Like so many others in America who, in more mundane matters, hoped to avoid the religious and moral expectations of their fellow countrymen, this apologist for a church unwilling to condemn slavery found comfort in separation. Of course, more typically, Americans relied upon separation in order to escape the demands of their churches rather than to allow their churches to elude the demands of their members. Nonetheless, Taylor's views on slavery suggest how far Americans could take their ideal of separation as they sought to segregate portions of their lives from the religious expectations of their contemporaries.

In adopting this separation of the pulpit from politics, Richards fully understood that he was leaving slaves to find freedom in their faith. On his title page he quoted Cowper:

> He is a freeman whom truth makes free;
> and all are slaves beside.

Richards, *The Pulpit and True Freedom: A Sermon, Preached before the Rhode Island Baptist State Convention, at Pawtucket, R.I., April 26, 1859,* 34–35 (New York: 1859). (Actually, Cowper wrote, "He is the freeman.")

10

Clerical Doubts and Popular Protestant Support

THROUGHOUT the last half of the nineteenth century, some Protestant clergymen continued to voice theological and moral doubts about the separation of church and state. They feared that this principle amounted to a separation of religion and government—in particular, that it deprived government of religion's moral guidance and support and that it thereby challenged religion's relevance to society as a whole. Yet even as these clergymen cautiously weighed the risks of a separation between church and state, many others casually accepted the more popular Protestant assumption that such a separation would not undermine the ties between religion and government. On this basis clergymen increasingly joined lay Protestants in adopting the separation of church and state as their conception of religious liberty.

Theological and Moral Doubts

Protestant clergymen from various theological perspectives, especially those derived from Calvinism, often had layers of reasons for worrying that a separation of church and state might lead to a separation of religion and government. Assuming that Christianity was a necessary moral guide for human life, most Protestant ministers hesitated to believe that their faith had no relevance to government. They ordinarily took for granted that religion was the foundation of morality and therefore also of civil government and the liberty enjoyed under it. Many further assumed that, even though they did not have a Christian government, they lived in a Christian nation, in which the predominant faith of the people had a moral influence on almost all individuals and institutions, including government. Some additionally held that not only individuals but also the people as a whole had moral responsibilities and that, beyond individual ministers, the Christian church had a duty to instruct the public in their obligations. Indeed, if Americans lived in a nation of special providence—a new Israel—then nation and church had inescapable responsibilities. In such ways Protestant clergymen tended to envision an informal, disestablished but profoundly sympathetic cooperation between religion and government.[1]

Relatively traditional Presbyterians were particularly apt to distrust a separation of church and state, lest it become a separation of religion and the state. For example, in 1856, in response to those who assumed that the separation of church and state was an American principle, the Rev. Erasmus Darwin MacMaster—a former president of Miami University—argued that there was not really a separation of religion and government in America. Unlike most of his fellow Presbyterians, he advocated a Christian amendment to the U.S. Constitution. More conventionally, like other Reformed Protestants, he understood government, even popular government, to have been divinely instituted and therefore to have moral obligations, which necessarily meant religious obligations. "The State, founded in Divine institution, appointed for the attainment of moral ends, and conversant about moral objects, is itself a *moral person*, possessed of *moral character*, and as such is bound to act in conformity to the principles of the moral law of God, as the supreme standard by which it shall conduct its affairs." Not only did the state have moral obligations, but also it regulated many matters of religious significance. It was obvious "how many civil and political questions, about which the administration of justice is conversant, . . . run directly and immediately into the domain of religion." Such were "the questions concerning the conjugal, parental, and filial relations; and the rights and obligations pertaining to these relations; to education; to the Sabbath; to blasphemy and obscenity; to systems of religion which are directly

---

[1] John R. Bodo, *The Protestant Clergy and Public Issues 1812–1848* (Princeton: Princeton University Press, 1954); Sidney E. Mead, *The Lively Experiment: The Shaping of Christianity in America*, 67 (New York: Harper & Row, 1963); Thomas G. Sanders, *Protestant Concepts of Church and State: Historical Backgrounds and Approaches for the Future* (New York: Holt, Rinehart & Winston, 1964); Elwyn Smith, *Religious Liberty in the United States: The Development of Church-State Thought since the Revolutionary Era*, 68–90 (Philadelphia: Fortress, 1972).

subversive of morals; and, in short, to the whole rationale of crime and its punishment." Thus there were various "direct and indirect" ways in which "the institutions of the Christian religion are recognized in the Constitutions and laws of the United States and of the particular States, and in their daily practice." Accordingly, it was "not true, then, that there is made by our nation the entire separation of religion from the State and all political affairs which is often alleged."[2]

At the other end of the theological spectrum, some Unitarians similarly feared that separation had the potential to disconnect religion and government. In 1842, shortly after nativists began to popularize the idea of separation, William Ellery Channing's younger associate, the Rev. Ezra S. Gannett, observed that "[t]he bare mention of religion and politics in connexion alarms some minds, who fear lest the liberties of the people be invaded by zealous religionists, or the public affairs of the time be handled by honest or ambitious preachers—in either case wandering beyond their appropriate limits." Yet he was not put off by such alarms, and, distinguishing between the effect of law and of religious opinion, he explained: "It is not a national Christianity, but a Christian nation, which I desire to see." With this goal he hoped that politicians, like others "in the midst of life's cares, temptations and labours," would "be religious, heartily, truly, constantly religious."[3] Even more directly, the Rev. Edward E. Hale observed in 1859 that "careless political speakers, and speakers from the pulpit as careless, are, indeed, apt to say, that under our system, the Church and the State are entirely divorced from each other." Hale condemned this "careless proposition" as "radically false," for, although church and state had distinct "functions," this was not "to say that there is no intimate relation between the Church and State."[4]

In the 1870s, when the separation of church and state had become

---

[2] E. D. MacMaster, *The True Life of a Nation: An Address Delivered at the Invitation of the Erodelphian and Eccritean Societies of Miami University, the Evening Preceding the Annual Commencement, July 2d, 1856,* 11, 10, 21 (New Albany: 1856). Like later advocates of a Christian amendment, MacMaster argued that the amendment could be consistent with religious liberty. Ibid., 21–25.

[3] Ezra S. Gannett, *The Religion of Politics. A Sermon,* 6, 8, 42–43 (Boston: 1842). Later, Gannett exclaimed: "Church and State! words of wonderful power over our fears and our imaginations. But who can for a moment seriously believe that such a purpose is entertained by one who loves, or by one who understands, American institutions? A State religion does any one dread? I should think there was just now more danger of almost any thing else." Ibid., 46.

[4] Edward E. Hale, *A Sermon,* 9 (Boston: 1859).

an almost irresistible dogma of Americanism, an Andover-trained Congregationalist, the Rev. Richard Gleason Greene, gave a Massachusetts election sermon in which he defensively asked: "Is Christianity to be recognized as standing in any organic and legal connection, whatever, with our civil government?" He observed: "You must have noticed that the answers to this question from the high places of both the State and the Church, are different to-day from the answers given by our fathers, or even from those of less than a score of years since." In particular: "The public drift, already strong toward utter separateness in the administration of these two great elements, is setting in with increasing power in each successive year. The question now wakes negative answers on all sides, like echoes,—fervent negatives from the Pulpit, learned negatives from the Bench, crisp negatives from the Press, thunderous negatives from the Political Rostrum." In contrast, Greene took the "liberty of noting that not always do these swift, popular, easy answers of the day fit the great question which we are impelled to ask."

> Thus, when it is asked by earnest men, "Is Christianity to have any recognized administration in our civil government?" it will not suffice to cast up coruscating negatives to the questions whether there shall be a persecution for opinion's sake; whether there shall be a usurpation of the liberty of conscience; whether there shall be a union of Church (meaning a sect) and State; whether it be fit or safe for the State to teach a theology; whether the nation shall be compelled to enact the dumb show of a formal compliment in recognition of God by crowding his great name edgewise into its Constitution.

Greene understood that "[a]ll these questions may be magnificently answered on any Fourth of July, before applauding crowds," but he reminded his more sedate audience—the assembled officialdom of Massachusetts—that there was a more traditional, measured answer. In his vision America was "a place which rustles with open Bibles." Christianity therefore could have connections to American government that did not amount to persecution, a union of church and state, or any usurpation of conscience.

Ultimately, Greene insisted upon an almost sociological explanation of the necessity of religion:

> Every civil government must unavoidably have a religion of some kind, and must stand in some recognized administration of it. The question

here is not what governments *ought* to do, but what they cannot avoid doing; and the fact, as stated, is involved in the very nature and idea of government among men. It is impossible to conceive of a civil State as existing altogether aside from some embodiment of ethical relations; and it is impossible to think of ethical relations, except as rooted in some ground of moral principles; and moral principles which we may well say cannot exist without a spiritual basis, we may surely assert cannot be enforced without a reference to some facts and forces which stand above man, yet which testify of themselves within man; and the recognition and application of these facts and forces to human conduct is one of the main workings of religion. The ethical conceptions may be rude, the moral principles dimly seen, the spiritual facts greatly obscured or greatly misapprehended; but these, such as they are, give a religion, and they give it, and they must give it, to every national organism among men.

"If, then, it be impossible for man to divest himself of his moral and spiritual attributes in any realm of his activity, how evident is that impossibility in the department of *government*, which expressly involves his morality in its relations to society." Accordingly, the displacement of Christianity would simply invite the introduction of other religions. "If you thrust forth Christianity from its recognized administration in your government, then what religion will you put in its place? for we have seen that government cannot exist in organic perpetuity without some civil administration of some religion. Shall it be Mohammedanism, Buddhism, Spiritism, Pantheism, Materialism, Atheism,—all equally religions or phenomena of certain transition from one religion to another? The question is its own reply."[5]

Anxious to avoid a disconnection of government and religion, many Protestant clergymen propagated their own, moderated versions of the separation of church and state. For example, Philip Schaff—the Lutheran theologian—refused to endorse separation of church and state as an ideal in all circumstances, but he declared a version of it appropriate in America, where, by not completely carrying out the principle, Americans had created a type of separation appropriate for their country. Writing in 1854, near the height of the mid-century anti-Catholic fervor, Schaff worried not about the implications of separation for Catholicism, but about its consequences for Christianity in general and for American

---

[5] Richard Gleason Greene, *Christianity a National Law. An Election Sermon,* 8–10, 11–12, 14, 28, 50 (Boston: 1874). Of course, Congregationalists had long taken such positions.

Protestantism in particular. He could not regard the "abstract separation of Church and State . . . as the perfect and ultimate condition of things; for Christianity aims to leaven and sanctify all spheres of human life, as well as all the powers of the soul."[6] Yet he much preferred separation to "a police guardianship of the church," and he considered separation peculiarly appropriate in America, for this principle was "connected with the Protestant origin and character of the country" and was "favorable to her religious interests."[7] In America, unlike Europe, separation hardly implied a rejection of Christianity:

> [I]t is by no means to be thought, that the separation of church and state there is a renunciation of Christianity by the nation. . . . It is not an annihilation of one factor, but only an amicable separation of the two in their spheres of outward operation; and thus equally the church's declaration of independence towards the state, and an emancipation of the state from bondage to a particular confession. The nation, therefore, is still Christian, though it refuses to be governed in this deepest concern of the mind and heart by the temporal power.

Though not by law, nonetheless by conviction America remained a Christian nation, and, far from treating separation as a matter of hostility to the church, "the state, as such, to some extent officially recognizes Christianity."

> Congress appoints chaplains (mostly from the Episcopal, sometimes from the Presbyterian and the Methodist clergy) for itself, the army, and the navy. It opens every day's session with prayer, and holds public worship on the Sabbath in the Senate Chamber at Washington. The laws of the several States also contain strict prohibitions of blasphemy, atheism, Sabbath-breaking, polygamy, and other gross violations of general Christian morality.

Pleased that, in these ways, "the separation is not fully carried out in practice, on account of the influence of Christianity on the popular mind," Schaff endorsed this incomplete American separation.[8]

---

[6] Philip Schaff, *America: A Sketch of Its Political, Social, and Religious Character*, 11, ed. Perry Miller (Cambridge, Mass.: Belknap Press, 1961; reprint of 1855 ed.). Similarly, Schaff was not inclined to "vindicate this separation of church and state as the perfect and final relation between the two," for he believed that "[t]he kingdom of Christ is to penetrate and transform like leaven, all the relations of individual and national life." Ibid., 75.
[7] Ibid., 73, 75–76.
[8] Ibid., 76–77.

Likewise, in 1876 Jeremiah Lewis Diman—a Congregationalist academic, who had been educated not only at Brown but also at Heidelberg and Berlin—accepted separation with the caveat that it should not be understood to deny the moral and thus also religious character of the nation:

> [I]n the deeper life of the nation, the spiritual and the temporal can never be divided. The mere government may be secular, but the state is built on everlasting moral foundations. We may do away with an established church, but we can never emancipate ourselves from the restraints and obligations of Christian civilization; they are part of our history, they are inwrought into our being, we cannot deny them without destroying our identity as a people! For in its deepest analysis, the state is a moral person. . . . However, in common and limited transactions, we may discriminate between the spiritual and the temporal, we cannot do so when dealing with those supreme interests and relations, from which the ultimate ends of human action, and the sanctions of civil society, derive their meaning. The life of a nation, like the life of an individual, forms an indivisible whole. . . . We cannot at one moment be spiritual beings, and at the next be released from spiritual restraints . . .

Accordingly, "[t]he principle of the separation of church and state receives an unwarranted and most pernicious interpretation, when it is understood to mean, as it so often is, that religion and politics occupy two wholly distinct provinces."[9] Together with most other clergymen, Diman accepted disestablishment and a division between the spiritual and the temporal in "common and limited transactions." Yet he feared that the popular understanding of separation disconnected religion and politics at a "deeper," moral level, and therefore he joined those who interpreted this principle narrowly.

[9] J. Lewis Diman, *The Alienation of the Educated Class from Politics*, 31–32 (Providence: 1876). In the same year Theodore Dwight Woolsey—former president of Yale—reported to the General Conference of the Congregational Churches of Connecticut: "I must declare myself unable on any ground of theory, to accept the total separation of church and state. If a state may foster education, or the fine arts, or the industrial, or even may furnish help to the poor, it may for aught I see give aid to religion provided only that perfect freedom of opinion and worship is not invaded. Religion . . . is in fact the principal auxiliary in all common interests." Yet any plan other than separation was impracticable: "But, while religion is a prime interest of the state, and may be allied with it on some plan or other, without injustice, in practice it must be separated, because men of equal rights cannot agree what is the truth." Woolsey, "Address before General Conference of the Congregational Churches of Connecticut" (Nov. 16, 1876), as quoted in Samuel W. Barnum, *Romanism As It Is*, 782 (Hartford: 1882).

Popular Support

Unlike these clerical rejecters and reinterpreters of separation, numerous American Protestants, including many clergymen, welcomed a separation of church and state. Confident that the religion of the nation—at least, the religion of its Protestant majority—stood independent of any church, these Americans optimistically assumed that they could separate church from state without segregating religion from government.

Some Protestant clergymen, believing that separation conformed to their various theological traditions, assumed that separation posed no threat to the religious foundation of American government. For example, unlike MacMaster, who emphasized the theological risks of separation, many other Presbyterians simply wrote that, according to the New Testament, "Christ did institute a church separate from the state, giving it separate laws and officers."[10] Unlike Schaff, many other Lutherans blandly said that "in the United States, where Church and State are happily separate, . . . the rights of both are legally secured."[11] Unlike Diman, many other Congregationalists assumed that "the principle of the separation of Church and State, and the principle of Congregationalism" amounted to "the independence of each individual church and society."[12] These Protestant clergymen so successfully reconciled the American ideal of separation with their denominational traditions that they

[10] "Relation of Church and State," *Princeton Review*, 35: 692 (October 1863). Similarly, an 1849 Presbyterian report had stated, "In this land where church and state have their separate organizations, the church may extend her bounds and fulfill her destiny by her own resources and in her own way," and that "[t]he church in this country has her own organization. She stands separate and complete in herself. Her government is in no way interwoven with the government of the state." "Annual Report of the Board of Missions of the General Assembly, of the Presbyterian Church of the United States of America," *Princeton Review*, 21: 222–223 (July 1849).

[11] Samuel Simon Schmucker, *The Church of the Redeemer as Developed within the General Synod of the Lutheran Church in America*, 77 (Baltimore: 1868). Elsewhere Schmucker had written that "in our land of constitutional divorce between church and state," it was "one grand part of the vocation of the American churches . . . to throw off the shackles of traditionary, patriarchic, and symbolic servitude; and availing themselves of the liberty secured by the divorce of church and state, to review the ground of Protestant organization, and to resume the Scripture lineaments of Christianity." S. S. Schmucker, *The American Lutheran Church, Historically, Doctrinally and Practically Delineated, in Several Occasional Discourses*, 91, 260 (Philadelphia: 1852).

[12] G. W. Warren, in *Debates and Proceedings of the National Council of Congregational Churches Held at Boston, Mass., June 14–24, 1865*, 194 (Boston: American Congregational Association, 1866).

did not feel obliged to mention and, perhaps, did not even notice that separation might endanger the connection between religion and government.

To be sure, these ministers may have felt some pressure to avoid expressing doubts about separation. The pressure felt by ministers to join the popular acclaim for this conception of religious liberty is suggested by the experiences of those clergymen who publicly questioned separation on the ground that it might amount to a separation of religion and government. Clearly, they felt they had to struggle against popular opinion. Diman himself described disestablishment in America as "the entire separation that obtains, both in our Federal and State systems, between the ecclesiastical and the civil province," and he observed, "So heartily is this accepted, and so unhesitatingly is it maintained, that it ought, perhaps, to be regarded less as an external feature than as a fundamental maxim of our body politic. He who should deny it would find it hard to gain a hearing, and would be fortunate if he escaped the reproach of holding an unfriendly attitude towards popular liberty itself."[13] In these circumstances few doubted whether American religious liberty was a separation of church and state and still fewer questioned it.

Yet growing numbers of Protestants seem to have embraced separation without feeling pressed by popular opinion, for they assumed that this idea permitted and even stimulated an intense relationship between the state and religion—between, that is, the state and a generic Protestantism.[14] Of course, many probably adopted the phrase "separation of church and state" as a label for religious liberty, without giving any thought to what such a separation might imply for the role of religion. Many, however, clearly did consider this issue and felt confident that a separation between church and state would not jeopardize the connection between religion and government. For example, an essayist writing in 1849, in the *American Whig Review,* endorsed separation as a constraint on religious groups but not religious individuals. He took for granted that separation usefully constrained religious groups, particularly their "pride of sect" and "desire of propagandism"—a point he elaborated with unmistakable references to Catholics and their "superstition," "dogma,"

---

[13] Jeremiah Lewis Diman, "Religion in America, 1776–1876," *North American Review,* 122: 4 (January 1876).
[14] Mead, *The Lively Experiment,* 67.

and "cruelty." Yet, if an individual's religious belief concerned all of his conduct, an individual could not easily separate his religion from politics: "As the religious belief of each man is the height and sum, the last fruit, of all his knowledge, and consequently the light and guide of his moral conduct, it is indeed difficult to conceive of a separation between Church and State in the individual. If obedience to the laws is a consequence of the virtue of the man, and that virtue itself a consequence of Christian education, then, indeed, the republic does rest primarily upon Christianity as its foundation."[15]

Even more vigorously, the Rev. Horace Bushnell—a leading Congregationalist—responded to those who wondered whether separation would disconnect religion from the state. They had asked, "Is it not one of the excellent modern discoveries . . . that church and state should be separate?" and "What then has religion to do with the state?" In 1856 Bushnell responded that government depended upon religion and would not be disconnected from it:

> Is there no connection of dependence between the family, or family virtue, and the state, because there is no legal and constitutional union? And as one state, the Spartan, undertaking to have no families and training the children at the public tables, was able to create no art or ornament, to furnish no great philosopher, statesman, or speaker, becoming, even amid the splendor of Greece, nothing better than a nest of hornets, or a den of lions, so too, it may finally be found that a state separated from religion, as well as from the church, had, in fact, some dependence on it. When the social inventory of its history comes to be made up of patent ballot-boxes, pistols, bowie-knives, cork-screws, and coffins interspersed here and there with a treatment of halter practice, it will be strange if some few do not begin to suspect that a state, separated from the church, even the more stringently needs religion.[16]

The separation of church and state did nothing to disturb the role of religion—that is, individual and familial belief—which now might seem all the more important to government.

During the last half of the nineteenth century many nativist Protestants used cruder versions of this Protestant perspective to defend the

---

[15] "Freedom of Opinion," *American Whig Review* 18: 54 (June 1849).
[16] Horace Bushnell, *Society and Religion, a Sermon for California, Delivered on Sabbath Evening, July 6, 1856. At the Installation of Rev. E. S. Lacy*, 9 (San Francisco: 1856). More generally, see Smith, *Religious Liberty in the United States*, 127.

political ascendency of their faith. As Rufus Clark explained in 1870: "We propose to show that while we do not and cannot tolerate the union of church and state, we, at the same time, cannot divorce from the state the idea of religion,—*of some religion*,—and that it is the duty of the state to provide for the religious or moral education of its youth." This religious education "permeates all other interests, shapes all other institutions" and "makes the political, social, and domestic condition of the people."[17] Similarly, in 1890 Isaac J. Lansing argued that "[t]he moral trend and purpose of this nation is so distinctively religious that it may be said we cannot think of the nation as divorced from religion," but this did not prevent his pamphlet from being sold in the cause of *"the American Idea of Separation of Church and State, and no appropriations for Sectarian Institutions."* Lest his meaning was unclear, Lansing elaborated: "There is a linking and blending together of religion, not the church as an organization, but religion and the nation, such that their enemies are identical."[18] It was this sort of thinking that in 1869 provoked Rabbi Max Lilienthal to complain about Protestants: "Afraid of standing up for a union of church and state, they invented the new theory of uniting religion and state, as if both sentences were not equivalent."[19] Yet, at least in the popular Protestant perspective, these were far from equivalent. Indeed, the relation of Protestantism to government was precisely what gave Protestants confidence in the separation of church and state. As these Americans realized that the separation of church and state would not jeopardize the connection between religion and government, they increasingly joined the ranks of those who welcomed separation.

Baptists on Separation

Protestant denominations were divided over separation but increasingly endorsed it, and for no denomination would these developments be more significant than for the Baptists. Many Baptists and Baptist organizations refrained from adopting the notion of separation, which seemed

---

[17] Rufus W. Clark, *The Question of the Hour: The Bible and the School Fund*, 9, 12 (Boston: 1870).
[18] Isaac J. Lansing, *National Danger in Romanism or Religion and the Nation*, "To the Reader" and page 9 (Boston: Arnold Publishing Assn., 1894).
[19] Letter to the *Jewish Times* (Dec. 10 and 17, 1869), in David Philipson, *Max Lilienthal, American Rabbi: Life and Writings*, 486 (New York: Bloch Publishing Co., 1915).

incompatible with some of their assumptions about government and about the religious obligations of the Christian church. Other Baptists, however, identified with this popular idea, finding in it an apt expression of their anti-Catholicism and, more generally, their individualistic conception of their faith.[20]

Separation had not been a Baptist position earlier in the century. Instead, as already discussed, Baptist associations had typically opposed establishments by requesting that the laws not take cognizance of religion or at least not discriminate on the basis of religious differences. Shortly after the election of 1800, John Leland and Nehemiah Dodge may have adopted the idea of separation of church and state but not with great clarity, and it is difficult to identify other individual Baptists who advocated separation. Certainly, early nineteenth-century Baptist associations did not make separation one of their demands.

In the middle of the century Baptist associations typically continued to advocate religious liberty without mentioning separation. For example, in 1855 the Southern Baptist Convention made no reference to separation when it adopted a somewhat anti-Catholic resolution on behalf of the "religious liberty" of "American citizens residing in foreign lands under the flag of our country, which is guaranteed to all foreigners residing on American soil."[21] Similarly, in 1866 the Convention did not depart from older Baptist conceptions of religious liberty when, after the Civil War, it protested the laws passed by southern states, under federal pressure, that required ministers to take loyalty oaths. The Convention's resolutions on behalf of "religious liberty" proclaimed "the principles of 'Soul Liberty,' which our fathers were the first to publish, for the maintenance of which they suffered persecution, in which they have for ages gloried, and which we should be the last to abandon." Specifically, these principles included "[t]hat Christ is the Supreme Ruler of the Church—that it is his prerogative to put men into the gospel ministry, and that they are amenable only to him for the discharge of its functions—that all interference with these functions on the part of civil rulers transcends their legitimate authority, and is a usurpation of the rights of con-

---

[20] More than most commentators, Thomas G. Sanders points to the divisions over separation in each of the larger Protestant denominations in America, although he often fails to distinguish between separation and a more generic disestablishment. Sanders, *Protestant Concepts of Church and State* (New York: Holt, Rinehart & Winston, 1964).
[21] *Proceedings of the Southern Baptist Convention*, 10 (1855).

science." This was bold language, but it described an utterly traditional division of jurisdictions. In this 1866 declaration of principles, the closest the Convention came to anything remotely like separation of church and state was in the last clause, in which the Convention reassured civil authorities "[t]hat in adopting these resolutions, the Convention expressly disavow any disposition to interfere with political affairs, and have regard solely to the question of religious liberty."[22]

The black Baptist conventions stayed even further from separation. Unlike the Southern Baptist Convention, they could hardly afford to disavow interference with political affairs, for their conventions had to struggle to sustain the political strength of their people. As the American National Baptist Convention explained in 1889, "Our political leaders are few, and even those we have cannot reach the people; therefore it becomes our duty to speak out upon all questions that affect our people socially and economically, as well as religiously."[23] In addition, like many of their white brethren, the black Baptist conventions probably had theological objections to separation. Certainly, although they adopted resolutions on both religious and political issues, they adopted none on behalf of the separation of church and state.

Notwithstanding the reticence about separation among most Baptist organizations and individuals, some individual Baptists began in the 1840s to follow the example of the nativists in urging a separation of church and state. Northerners writing for a popular, anti-Catholic audience seem to have led the way. In 1845 John Dowling wrote a widely

---

[22] *Proceedings of the Southern Baptist Convention,* 22 (1866), quoted by Edward Earl Joiner, "Southern Baptists and Church-State Relations 1845–1954," 339–340, App. II (Doctor of Theology thesis, Southern Baptist Theological Seminary, 1959). Similarly, see *Proceedings of the Southern Baptist Convention,* 25 (1871). In 1878 a report on Indian mission schools simply described "no union of Church and State" as among "Baptist principles." *Proceedings of the Southern Baptist Convention,* 28 (1878).

[23] *Journal of the American National Baptist Convention. Three Sessions,* 19 (Sept. 17, 1889) (Journal for 1889, 1890, and 1892) (Louisville: 1892). No less than many white Baptists, black Baptists took a broad view of Christianity's role in the world. For example, the opening words of a report on the "State of the Country," adopted by the 1898 National Baptist Convention, declared: "Christianity should have an opinion about all that pertains to the interest of man morally, intellectually and materially. It should give shape as far as may be consistent to the sentiment of a community, a State or a nation." Just how seriously the Convention took its duty to shape public sentiment is suggested by the topics covered by the report: the freedom of Cuba, the injustice of lynching, and the evils of Sabbath railroad excursions. *Journal of the Eighteenth Annual Session of the National Baptist Convention Held in the Second Baptist Church, Kansas City, Mo, . . . 1898,* 54–55 (Nashville: 1899).

circulated *History of Romanism* that treated *"the separation of church and state"* as "one of the surest safeguards of the liberty of nations."[24] Similarly, in 1856, in his *Outlook of Freedom or The Roman Catholic Element in American History*, Justin D. Fulton perceived in American constitutions the "fundamental" principle "that there shall be no connection between church and state."[25] Like other nativists, these Baptists adopted separation against Catholicism.

Yet Baptists could find much in separation that resonated with their unusually antihierarchical, antiecclesiastical, and individualistic sentiments, and therefore some, more broadly, asserted separation as a Baptist idea in opposition to other Protestants as well as Catholics. For example, after a Congregationalist preached the Massachusetts election sermon in 1851 on the "Indebtedness of the State to the Clergy," the pastor of the First Baptist Church of Boston, Rollin H. Neale, responded with an 1852 election sermon in favor of religious liberty, including separation. Without denying the civil benefits of religion, he argued: "Religious liberty . . . secures most fully and most effectively to our nation, the influence of the pulpit. The 'Indebtedness of the State to the Clergy,' was ably shown by the gentleman who preceded me in this public service. But it is to the entire separation of the church from the state, and the perfect freedom we enjoy in our religion, that the pulpit is indebted

---

[24] John Dowling, *The History of Romanism*, 619 (New York: 1845).

[25] Justin D. Fulton, *The Outlook of Freedom or The Roman Catholic Element in American History*, 230–231 (Cincinnati: 1856). For a review of various Baptist attitudes to Catholicism, see James Leo Garrett, Jr., *Baptists and Roman Catholicism*, 10 (Nashville: Broadman, 1965).

The anti-Catholicism of numerous Baptists had much in common with that of other Protestants, as may be illustrated by some mid-century Southern Baptists. For example, in 1853, adopting a common theme familiar from Edward Beecher and others, a committee of the Southern Baptist Convention reported that "[a] mighty conflict is now going on between the friends of a pure Christianity and Romanists . . . for ascendency in the west." It quoted Dr. Inkyn that in the rapidly approaching "collision of conflicting principles" in the Mississippi Valley, "the lines are now drawing for a deadly conflict." *Proceedings of the Southern Baptist Convention*, 22 (1853). When reviewing anti-Catholic literature, the *Southern Baptist Review and Eclectic* gave encouragement. Of *The Secret Instructions of the Jesuits*, it observed that, at a time "when an apprehension of the encroachments of Romanism on the Republican liberties of this country have called into being the mysterious order of 'Know-Nothings,' the re-publication of this little work is decidedly opportune." It concluded: "Let . . . [it] be widely circulated." "P," Review of *The Secret Instructions of the Jesuits*, in Notices of New Publications, in *Southern Baptist Review and Eclectic*, 1: 58 (January 1855). It similarly stated that publication of *The Battle Cry of Freedom* was "opportune," and it "cordially" recommended the volume, expressing a wish that it have "an extensive circulation." "P," Review of *The Battle Cry of Freedom*, in ibid., 751 (October–December 1855).

for much of the powerful good with which it is here invested." Although disestablishment was no longer in dispute, Neale had theological reasons to adopt the idea of separation in opposition to Congregationalist notions of a connection, for he associated this connection with claims of clerical authority. Observing that "free, republican institutions tend to strip off the pomp and glare of official dignity, and accord respect and honor to men for what they are in themselves," Neale believed that this tendency extended to clergymen: "The potent charm which formerly attached to the clerical name and guard, it must be allowed, does not now exist. Nor is this a matter of regret. It only tends to separate and preserve Christianity from the corrupt and corrupting influence of the world, and to keep unsoiled those pure and heavenly robes." Confident that a devolved authority was the only form of church government with a scriptural foundation, Neale condemned claims of authority by the clergy of other Protestant denominations—an authority with which, according to Baptists, ambitious ministers, like the corrupt clergy of Rome, would inevitably seek secular power and tyranny. It was a perspective with which Neale could appeal to the Unitarians among his listeners by implying that the internal authority of a church over its members was a popish threat to both internal and external liberty—a constraint that would eventually prompt a reaction in the minds of a freedom-loving people. "When the 'bull of the pope' has fallen on such a mind, or the 'edict of a bishop' oppressed it, when the congregational 'formulas' have been imposed, or the 'presbyterian book of discipline' held it down too closely, when the baptist 'articles of faith,' or the scruples of the 'dear brethren' have abridged it out of its liberty, it will stir under its burden; it will break down or leap over its safeguards, and scatter all human restraints as quickly as did the Judge of Israel the green withs that bound him."[26] In religion as in republican government, moral judgment and authority resided with individuals, and, from this perspective, Neale adopted the idea of a separation between church and state as a means of denying what he understood to be Congregationalist suggestions about the authority of their church and its clergy.

Thomas Curtis—professor of theology at Lewisburg, Pennsylvania—had similar assumptions about *the power of the priesthood residing*

---

[26] Rollin H. Neale, *Religious Liberty. A Sermon*, 24–25, 30–31 (Boston: 1852).

in every member of the whole Church," and he therefore wrote in 1855 that Baptists had long sought to "awaken a spirit in favor of perfect liberty of conscience and the separation of Church and State." Expanding upon the sort of ideas evident in Neale's sermon, Curtis emphasized that the individual and congregational authority typical of Baptists was highly consistent with American principles—that "Baptist institutions" were "powerfully friendly to free civil government by the form of their own ecclesiastical organizations."[27] Advocates of each Protestant sect tended to take such views of their own contribution to American liberty and, in so doing, often recast the old language about a connection between religion and government in terms of the sympathetic development of religion and civil liberty. Adopting the standard Protestant perspective, Curtis believed that "while the union of Church and State is a sad error, the adherence of a nation to great religious principles is the principal source of its strength." Yet he gave this argument a Baptist character by suggesting a connection between the individual religious authority espoused by Baptists and the individual political authority advocated by Americans. Although, "superficially," the "religious and civil governments of a people" seemed to have "no necessary connection with each other . . . nothing is more certain and demonstrable than that there is a constant tendency in the two to approach each other."[28] Thus, for Curtis, separation of church and state was a Baptist principle, but there was, nonetheless, a "natural and necessary connection between true religion and civil liberty"—especially between Baptist religion and American liberty.[29]

It should come as no surprise that these Baptists who spoke of separation understood it to permit connections between government and religion. Like so many other Protestants, Baptists desired to exclude any particular church from public institutions but welcomed Bible reading and other elements of Protestant religion, which seemed to be the faith of free individuals. In the 1870s, for example, although some Baptists protested the introduction of the Bible into public schools and argued that "the State had no right to teach religion," most Baptists saw no

[27] Thomas F. Curtis, *The Progress of Baptist Principles in the Last Hundred Years*, 345, 53, 363 (Boston: 1855).
[28] Ibid., 350, 363.
[29] Ibid., 347–348.

reason to go so far.[30] As one Baptist, George C. Lorimer, explained in 1877: "The position of the Bible in the schools is not the result of any union between Protestants and the State; nor was it secured by the political action of one denomination, or of all combined. The Church, as such, did not put it there, and the Church, as such, cannot take it away." Instead, the "people" put the Bible in the schools.[31]

The distinction between a church and the religion of Protestant individuals allowed growing numbers of Baptists and other Protestants to embrace the separation of church and state. Although many denominational organizations still refrained from adopting separation, an expanding range of Protestants identified with it. This conception of their antiestablishment sentiments simultaneously imposed severe constraints on Catholicism and offered Protestants a gratifying sense of their individual independence. Accordingly, separation appealed to an ever wider array of Baptists and other Protestants and became a significant element of their beliefs.

---

[30] "The Bible in the Schools," *Boston Investigator*, 5 (March 29, 1876), quoting Professor Gould of the Newton Theological Seminary speaking at a meeting of Baptists in Boston. The secularizing version of separation propounded by theological liberals and, especially, the National Liberal League probably led many Baptists in the 1870s to refrain from endorsing any version of the idea.

[31] George C. Lorimer, *The Great Conflict: A Discourse, Concerning Baptists, and Religious Liberty*, 116 (Boston: 1877).

IV

LATE NINETEENTH- AND TWENTIETH-CENTURY CONSTITUTIONAL LAW

I N THE twentieth century the popular conception of religious liberty as a separation of church and state acquired the status of constitutional law. Part III has already examined how separation of church and state became an "American" principle. It has traced how numerous Protestants responded to Catholicism and, more broadly, ecclesiastical authority by perceiving religious liberty as a separation of church and state. Looking back on their old distinctions between church and state and on their constitutional barriers to any government establishment of religion, Protestants had little difficulty in viewing these as manifestations of a broader principle of separation. Yet this popular reconceptualization of religious liberty did not by itself alter the U.S. Constitution. Therefore, although Part IV continues to trace the redefinition of religious liberty in terms of separation, it focuses on the means by which this altered perspective became part of American constitutional law. Contrary to what may be expected, the nineteenth-century advocates who desired the separation of church and state as a constitutional right did not rely upon constitutional interpretation to secure this goal. Instead, recognizing separation's inadequate constitutional foundations, they sought constitutional amendments. Only in the twentieth century, after the amendment process had been abandoned, did an interpretive approach prevail, and, by this means, separation became part of American constitutional law.

11

---·◆·---

Amendment

IN THE 1870s and 1880s anti-Christian secularists organized a national campaign to obtain a constitutional amendment guaranteeing a separation of church and state. Already during the anti-Catholic agitation of the 1840s and 1850s, nativists had popularized separation as an American principle. Now, during another surge of anti-Catholic sentiment, not only nativist anti-Catholic Protestants but also theologically liberal, anti-Christian secularists—known as "secularists" or "Liberals"—prominently advocated separation. In their constitutional objectives the Liberals failed spectacularly, but they contributed to the development of the separation of church and state in ways still evident in American culture and law.

More than any earlier group, the Liberals systematically demanded and popularized some of the broadest implications of separation. The Liberals resented all clerical hierarchies, all churches, and even all distinct religions, especially Christianity. Accordingly, they insisted upon a purely secular version of separation that would segregate government not only from any one church but also, more broadly, from all distinct religions. The Liberals thereby took separation's implications unusually far and initiated the transformation of separation from a nativist Protestant idea that tended to limit the rights of Catholics to a more radically liberal and, indeed, secular idea that had sobering consequences for any Americans participating in organized religion.

In addition, more than prior advocates of separation, Liberals self-consciously thought about this ideal as a constitutionally protected right. Nativists had tended to assume that separation was a principle of American government evident in American constitutions but not actually guaranteed in any of them. In contrast, Liberals candidly acknowledged that the U.S. Constitution had not fully provided for separation and, on this assumption, struggled to establish separation by constitutional amendment. Soon Republicans and some Protestants borrowed this approach to add demands for their own, more nativist, amendments, which, of course, were designed to protect the narrower, anti-Catholic version of separation. Although neither Liberal nor Protestant advocates of separation managed to amend the U.S. Constitution, they greatly expanded public awareness of separation as a constitutional ideal.

Free Religion, the Index, and the National Liberal League

The organized pursuit of separation of church and state by secularists or "Liberals" arose from the efforts of the newspaper of the Free Religious Association, the *Index*, to unify its heterodox readers. The *Index* sought to establish common cause among an astonishing array of theists and atheists, spiritualists and materialists, transcendentalists and positivists, and advocates of "every other phase of earnest thought" that found sympathetic expression in its pages.[1] To this end, it increasingly urged them to join a campaign for one of the few tangible goals they could share, the secularization of government or the separation of church and state.

Free Religion was a form of secular theism that placed faith in nothing so much as humanity and free inquiry. As an organized body it developed in the autumn of 1866, when, at a national meeting of Unitarians at Syracuse, New York, a group of non-Christian theists splintered off to form the Free Religious Association. The members of this group saw themselves as growing out of "the various progressive and converging religious tendencies of the time, away from the conflicting authorities of specific religious systems and from the bonds of creeds and churches, to a union as broad as humanity itself." Disappointed that the Unitarians would not "strike out . . . every implication of a creed"—disappointed, in particular, that the Unitarians would not clearly abandon Christianity—the organizers sought an association "which should be inclusive of the freest religious thought of the time, and do a work in behalf of spiri-

---

[1] "Prospectus," *Index*, 1 (no. 1) (Jan. 1, 1870).

tual unity and human brotherhood, which could not be done by any of the religious denominations."[2]

It was on behalf of this theistic humanism that a leader of the Free Religious Association, Francis Ellingwood Abbot, founded the *Index* in Toledo in 1870—his hope being to provide a forum for the various unorthodox views that might contribute to free religious investigation. Abbot sought a religion based on what was common to all human beings and free from the distinct creeds that had characterized all prior religions. Thus his paper aimed "to destroy every species of spiritual slavery, to expose every form of superstition, to encourage independence of thought and action in all matters that concern belief, character or conduct."[3] In a manner that recalled nativist critiques of Catholicism and earlier Unitarian complaints about orthodox Congregationalists, Abbot wrote that his goal in the *Index* was to "replace . . . a system of dogmas by a system of elastic principles—and thus to create intellectual and spiritual unity in the mind of the age."[4] More than most mid-nineteenth-century papers that explored theism or atheistic free thought, the *Index* appealed to authors and readers that shared little other than their earnestness in pursuing free discussion and their confidence that they were "[s]tanding squarely outside of Christianity."[5]

As the *Index* quickly became the most distinguished heterodox paper in America—supported by Wendell Phillips, William Lloyd Garrison, Rabbi Isaac M. Wise, and even Charles Darwin—it found a unifying theme in its advocacy of the separation of church and state.[6] In its early issues the *Index* devoted itself to free theistic inquiry rather than the

---

[2] "Department of the Free Religious Association," in ibid., 7. Francis Ellingwood Abbot presented Free Religion as the religious manifestation of the republican spirit: "Free Religion reduced to its lowest terms is simply the soul's Declaration of Independence in all spiritual matters. It is simply the logical result of the ideas which, less than a hundred years ago, humbled the British Empire and less then five years ago crushed into the Southern Confederacy." Abbot, "Christianity and Free Religion Contrasted as to Corner-Stones," *Index,* 1 (no. 4): 3 (Jan. 22, 1870).

[3] "Prospectus," *Index.*

[4] Letter of Francis E. Abbot to William J. Potter (Dec. 11, 1870), as quoted by Sydney E. Ahlstrom, "Francis Ellingwood Abbot: His Education and Active Career," 2: 139 (Ph.D. diss., Harvard University, 1951).

[5] "Prospectus," *Index,* 5.

[6] Later, when recording a visit from Darwin's son, Abbot noted: "He and his father have been readers and friends of the *Index* almost from the beginning, and in 1874 or 75 joined in making it a present of over $100.00." Harvard University Archives, HUG 1101.3 (Box 1), Diaries of F. E. Abbot (Nov. 1, 1878).

separation of church and state. Although Abbot interspersed his editorials about the scientific study of religion and about spiritual improvement with occasional articles against government support for religion, he focused the paper on religious inquiry rather than constitutional rights.[7] Increasingly, however, Abbot discovered that what struck a common chord among his diverse readers were shared fears and resentments of the influence of Christianity upon government—sentiments that could find expression in demands for the "secularization" of government and the "separation of church and state." Accordingly, as Abbot recalled in 1876, it was in the pages of the *Index* that "[t]he Liberal League movement, as a definite, organized endeavor to accomplish the total separation of Church and State in this country, had its beginning."[8]

Since 1863 a small proportion of American Protestants, especially

[7] At first, the *Index* did not emphasize the issue of separation. As early as 1871, however, Abbot's Toledo Liberal Alliance was demanding the "absolute separation of Church and State," and it was from this local experience that Abbot developed in the *Index* what became his national organization's main goal. *To the Liberals of America* (broadside) (Toledo: Toledo Liberal Alliance, July 1871), copy in Harvard University Archives, HUG 1101.74. Abbot recognized that "[t]he Liberal Alliance of Toledo furnishes a model for just the kind of organizations that should be multiplied from Maine to Oregon." Francis E. Abbot, "The Proposed Christian Amendment to the United States Constitution" (Dec. 21, 1871), *Index*, 3: 106 (Jan. 6, 1872).

[8] *Equal Rights in Religion. Report of the Centennial Congress of Liberals,* 8 (Boston: National Liberal League, 1876). In the first half of the 1870s, the *Index* came to advertise itself in terms of separation: "THE INDEX aims to give free utterance to the boldest and best matured thought of the age on all questions connected with religion; to secure the more complete separation of Church and State; and to promote by all fair and honorable means the great cause of RELIGIOUS LIBERTY!" *Subscribe for the Index! The Flag of American Radicalism!* (broadside, n.p., n.d. but probably ca. 1873–1875), in Harvard University Archives, HUG 1101.74, Index Association Newspapers and Clippings.

Although the *Index* was the chief publishing outlet for the local Liberal Leagues, there were other Liberal papers, such as the *Pacific Liberal,* published in San Francisco, which advertised itself as "the only Liberal journal on this coast" and as a periodical deserving "the patronage of every man and woman who feels an interest in the maintenance of religious freedom in America, the perpetuation of our glorious Free School system—in a word, the complete divorce of the Church from the State." Other publications included pamphlets, broadsides, posters, and even specialty envelopes, such as that used by E. C. Walker, a Florence, Iowa, bookseller "for all Liberal and Scientific Papers and Periodicals," whose envelopes contained various Liberal demands and the following blurb: "Have you a Liberal League in your neighborhood? Are there ten LIVE Liberals—men and women— in your town? If so go to work AT ONCE. The complete Secularization of the State, the utter separation of Government and Church, should claim the earnest thought, and secure the efficient aid of every patriotic man and woman in our land. Now is the time for action. Freethinkers! Secularists! Liberals of every shade of belief! Be up and doing." E. C. Walker, Envelope, Copy in Harvard University Archive, HUG 1101.66 (Box 6), National Liberal League Papers.

some Presbyterians, had campaigned for a Christian amendment to the U.S. Constitution. Believing that nations as well as individuals were morally accountable for their sins, including a failure to acknowledge the Almighty, they sought a national recognition of America's Christianity in the preamble to the U.S. Constitution.[9] To this end, they formed an organization, the National Reform Association, through which they proposed a Christian amendment to America's founding document. Yet such an amendment, even if only to the preamble, was more likely to provoke fear than to be adopted. When Christians had been confident in their strength, most of them, whether dissenters or members of establishments, had not wanted such an amendment. Now, when much weakened, a small number of them wanted it but lacked the necessary power.

Although the demand for a Christian amendment remained a somewhat quaint theological and social protest, the *Index* depicted the advocates of the proposal as dangerous fanatics. The *Christian Register* described the Christian amendment as the "palpably Quixotic" project of persons important only "in their villages or counties" and wondered how anyone could "keep a straight face while firing his big shot into the poor little corpse of the still-born theological amendment."[10] The *Evangelist* described the National Reform Association as "a forlorn hope."[11] Even the *Index* admitted that "the Protestant public . . . to-day" was "[u]nprepared . . . to carry out the plans" of the Association.[12] Yet the *Index* insisted that "[t]he men who are at the bottom of this movement must be grimly and dangerously in earnest—devotees of their idea—fanatics of

---

[9] As a "liberal Christian" opponent mocked, the amendment's supporters were "advocates of the union of Church and State . . . in that mild and inconsequential way, which proposes to effect the result by altering the preamble to the Constitution,—(about as effectual a plan, by the way, as it might be to alter the preface of Webster's Dictionary, in order to change its peculiarities of spelling)." Rev. J. C. Adams, "The Church and the State," *Universalist Quarterly and General Review,* 14: 318 (new ser., 1877).

[10] *Christian Register* (Feb. 10, 1872), as quoted by Ahlstrom, "Francis Ellingwood Abbot," 2: 139.

[11] Daniel G. Strong, "Supreme Court Justice William Strong, 1808–1895: Jurisprudence, Christianity and Reform," 311 (Ph.D. diss., Kent State University, 1985).

[12] "The Proposed Christian Amendment," *Index,* 3 (no. 106): (Jan. 6, 1872). On the weakness of the National Reform Association's political position, see Stow Persons, *Free Religion: An American Faith,* 116 (New Haven: Yale University Press, 1947). A lecture printed in the *Boston Investigator* complained that "even many leading minds among the Liberals declare there is no danger to be apprehended from the disjointed efforts of a few half-crazy fanatics." L. F. Hodge, "Religious Interference with Political Government. A Lecture Delivered at Investigator Hall, March 1, 1876," *Boston Investigator,* 1 (April 19, 1876).

the old, Inquisitorial stamp who, if they had the power would relentlessly put you to the rack for rejecting their gospel, not because they are harder hearted than other men but because they would think themselves doing God's service by destroying heretics."[13]

Notwithstanding that the proposals for a Christian amendment seemed more pathetic than dangerous, they proved a valuable spur to Abbot and other secularists, who began to organize around the principle of separation of church and state.[14] As early as 1871, Abbot's Toledo Liberal Alliance complained in a broadside: "The final separation of Church and State is not yet fully effected in this country. . . . [D]angerous attempts are even making to unite Church and State by a formal Christian Amendment to the United States Constitution; and in various other ways it is clear that the absolute separation of Church and State is a principle neither fully understood nor faithfully obeyed by the people of the United States."[15] Six months later, portraying itself and its readers as potential martyrs at the hands of Christians, Abbot's *Index* suggested of the Christian amendment that "[i]t will be the overthrow of the Free Republic and the creation of a Christian Theocracy instead. It will be the formal abolition of the great principle of the separation of Church and State, to which we owe the unparalleled civil liberty we enjoy. It will be the restoration to power and influence of the Christian clergy as the recognized priesthood of a Christian State."[16]

In opposition to some Christian petitions to Congress for a Christian amendment, Abbot began in January 1872 to organize in support of a

[13] "The Proposed Christian Amendment," *Index.*
[14] The Christian amendment movement probably pushed some non-Trinitarian Christians and non-Christians into the arms of the secularists. Already in 1871 one observer asked: "What must the Unitarians, the Universalists, the Christians, the Hicksite Friends, the Free Religionists, the Jews say to the proposition that the Lord Jesus Christ is the ruler among the nations?" The Christian amendment—"this keg of theological gunpowder . . . set down upon the very corner-stone of their civic temple"—would be "an attack upon the sacred divorce between Church and State." Henry W. Bellows, *Church and State in America. A Discourse Given at Washington, D.C., at the Installation of Rev. Frederic Hinckley, as Pastor of the Unitarian Church, January 25, 1871*, 13 (Washington, D.C.: 1871). See also Gary Scott Smith, *The Seeds of Secularization: Calvinism, Culture, and Pluralism in America, 1870–1915*, 65, 67 (Grand Rapids: Christian University Press, 1985).
[15] *To the Liberals of America* (broadside).
[16] "The Proposed Christian Amendment," *Index.* Taking Catholicism to be the epitome of Christianity, many Liberals adopted traditional Protestant prejudices in support of their opposition to Christianity. For example, according to Abbot, "the most consistent 'Christian'" must submit to Rome, and it "follows, therefore, that no one thoroughly imbued with the modern spirit of liberty is really a Christian: and ought not to claim the Christian name." "What Is Free Religion?" in ibid., 1 (no. 3) (Jan. 15, 1870).

counterpetition: "We protest against such proposed amendments as an attempt to revolutionize the government of the United States, and to overthrow the great principles of complete religious liberty and the complete separation of Church and State on which it was established by its original founders."[17] After Abbot and his allies collected more than 35,000 signatures, mostly in New England and the Midwest, Charles Sumner in 1874 introduced this counterpetition (all 953 feet of it) on the floor of the Senate. Almost inevitably, the Judiciary Committee rejected the Christian amendment.[18] Nonetheless, one extreme provoked another. Not content merely to resist the Christian amendment, Abbot also proposed, beginning in January 1874, an alternative amendment that would ensure and expand the secularity of American government—a goal Abbot and his allies often described as the separation of church and state. It was to pursue this objective that Abbot eventually formed the National Liberal League.[19]

[17] "To the Freemen of America," *Index Extra,* 3 (no. 108) (Jan. 20, 1872).
[18] *Congressional Record,* 2(1): 432 (Sen., Jan. 7, 1874); Sidney Warren, *American Freethought,* 177 (New York: Columbia University Press, 1943); Persons, *Free Religion,* 117; Steven Keith Green, "The National Reform Association and the Religious Amendments to the Constitution, 1864–1876," 54 (master's thesis, University of North Carolina at Chapel Hill, 1987). The Judiciary Committee reported:

> That, upon examination even of the meager debates by the fathers of the Republic in the convention which framed the Constitution, they find that the subject of this memorial was most fully and carefully considered, and then, in that convention, decided, after grave deliberation, to which the subject was entitled, that as this country, the foundation of whose government they were then laying, was to be the home of the oppressed of all nations of the earth, whether Christian or Pagan, and in full realization of the dangers which the union between church and state had imposed upon so many nations of the Old World, with great unanimity that it was inexpedient to put anything into the Constitution or frame of government which might be construed to be a reference to any religious creed or doctrine.
>
> And they further find that this decision was accepted by our Christian fathers with such great unanimity that in the amendments which were afterward proposed, in order to make the Constitution more acceptable to the nation, none has ever been proposed to the States by which this wise determination of the fathers has been attempted to be changed. Wherefore, your committee report that it is inexpedient to legislate upon the subject of the above memorial, and ask that they be discharged from the further consideration thereof, and that this report, together with the petition, be laid upon the table.

Benjamin F. Butler, *Report No. 143, 43d Congress, 1st Session. Report from the Committee on the Judiciary: Acknowledgment of God and the Christian Religion in the Constitution Feb. 18, 1874.*
[19] The only substantial study of the League is by Sydney Ahlstrom, who examines it in his dissertation on Francis Ellingwood Abbot. He concludes that "[i]n view of its short and tumultuous life, the Liberal League is difficult to assess either as to its impact or its meaning." Ahlstrom, "Francis Ellingwood Abbot," 2: 247.

Abbot and his allies called themselves "Liberals" to suggest their affinity with those who departed from orthodoxy. Since the middle of the nineteenth century, an English radical, George Jacob Holyoake, had sought to unite diverse atheists and agnostics under the appealing rubric of "secularism," which he hoped would give them a respectable common cause.[20] Similarly, Abbot hoped with the word "liberalism" to join his unorthodox allies into a politically effective alliance—an approach he publicized in 1872 in his "Demands of Liberalism," which declared "that our entire political system shall be founded and administered on a purely secular basis."[21] It was in pursuit of this secularism, especially the separa-

---

[20] Holyoake issued the first "Secular" number of his periodical, *The Reasoner,* on March 21, 1849; he said he first used the word "Secularist" in *The Reasoner* on December 3, 1851; a week later he wrote of "secularism"; beginning in 1851, moreover, he organized the Secular Society, which was the new name for the Society of Reasoners. Joseph McCabe, *Life and Letters of George Jacob Holyoake,* 1: 202, 208, 210 (London: Watts, 1908); Lee E. Grugel, *George Jacob Holyoake: A Study in the Evolution of a Victorian Radical,* 62 (Philadelphia: Porcupine Press, 1976); Owen Chadwick, *The Secularization of the European Mind,* 91, 271 note 4 (Cambridge: Cambridge University Press, 1979). A few years later, somewhat defensively, Holyoake wrote: "The term Secularism has not been chosen as a concealment, or a disguise, or as an apology for free inquiry, but as expressing a certain positive and ethical element, which the terms 'Infidel,' 'Sceptic,' 'Atheist,' do not express. *When* the term 'Infidel' is used to express fair dissent from Christianity, or 'Sceptic,' to express honest doubt of its principles, or 'Atheist,' to signify pure intellectual inability to account for the Origin of the Universe, or to accept the Christian theory of its government, none of the Secularists object to the application of such terms respectively to themselves. But as these terms usually connote guilt and dissent, they preferred the term *Secularism,* as expressive of opinions which they hold to be affirmative, virtuous, and reasonable." "Outlines of Secularism," *Reasoner: Gazette of Secularism,* 16: 17 (Jan. 8, 1854).

[21] The "Demands of Liberalism" specified:

1. We demand that churches and other ecclesiastical property shall no longer be exempted from just taxation.

2. We demand that the employment of chaplains in Congress, in State Legislatures, in the navy and militia, and in prisons, asylums, and all other institutions supported by public money, shall be discontinued.

3. We demand that all public appropriations for sectarian educational and charitable institutions shall cease.

4. We demand that all religious services now sustained by the government shall be abolished; and especially that the use of the bible in the public schools, whether ostensibly as a text-book or avowedly as book of religious worship, shall be prohibited.

5. We demand that the appointment, by the President of the United States or by the governors of the various States, of all religious festivals and fasts shall wholly cease.

6. We demand that the judicial oath in the courts and in all other departments of the government shall be abolished, and that simple affirmation under the pains and penalties of perjury shall be established in its stead.

tion of church and state, that Abbot and his allies called themselves "Liberals"—a name with which they appealed to, but also distinguished themselves from, the numerous Unitarians and other Protestants who, in varying degrees, identified themselves, in a more generic way, as theologically "liberal."

At the start of 1873 Abbot urged Liberals to organize into Liberal Leagues and then asked these groups "to lay the foundations of a great national party of freedom, which shall demand the entire secularization of our municipal, state, and national government."[22] Thus "[r]eligious radicalism" would take the momentous step of engaging in public life. It had been "long enough confined to parlors; it must now emerge into the great world of human affairs."[23] Eager to participate in a national movement that would affirm and focus their various nonconforming opinions, men and some women across the country, but especially in the Northeast and Midwest, quickly formed local leagues, and, beginning in 1875, under Abbot's direction they initiated the organization of a National Liberal League devoted to the "the ABSOLUTE SEPARATION OF CHURCH AND STATE." In particular, they wanted an association that would "secure the extension and more thorough popular comprehension of the already verbally recognized national principle of purely secular government, or absolute separation of Church and state." This association would "give definite and organized expression to the growing public sentiment in

---

7. We demand that all laws directly or indirectly enforcing the observance of Sunday as the Sabbath shall be repealed.

8. We demand that all laws looking to the enforcement of "Christian" morality shall be abrogated, and that all laws shall be conformed to the requirements of natural morality, equal rights, and impartial liberty.

9. We demand that not only in the Constitutions of the United States and of the several States, but also in the practical administration of the same, no privilege or advantage shall be conceded to Christianity or any other special religion; that our entire political system shall be founded and administered on a purely secular basis; and that whatever changes shall prove necessary to this end shall be consistently, unflinchingly, and promptly made.

"The Demands of Liberalism" (April 6, 1872), republished in *Report of the Centennial Congress of Liberals,* 8.

[22] Ibid., 8.

[23] Ibid. Ahlstrom points out that it was because of the changed tone of the *Index* during the period when the National Liberal League was being organized that "A. W. Stevens, the trusted Associate Editor, left . . . with the reminder that he was 'naturally disinclined to organized aggression.'" Ahlstrom, "Francis Ellingwood Abbot," 2: 205, quoting the *Index* (Sept. 30, 1875).

favor of the reform of the existing violations of this principle in the practical administration of the government." To these ends, they met the following year, at the 1876 Centennial Exhibition in Philadelphia, in a Congress of Liberal Leagues.[24] In this 1876 Centennial Congress, they formally created the National Liberal League—an organization designed to concentrate on this "single fixed and easily comprehensible purpose on which we all agree . . . a definite *practical object*—namely, to accomplish the total separation of Church and State."[25]

The Amendment Proposals

Believing that American constitutions did not fully guarantee the separation of church and state, the Liberals argued that the U.S. Constitution needed amendment. Liberals initially proposed a new version of the First Amendment, which would require both the federal government and the states to extend equal religious liberty to atheists and unconventional theists. Beginning on January 1, 1874, and every week for the next two years, the *Index* printed the proposed amendment:

> SECTION 1.—Congress shall make no law respecting an establishment of religion, or favoring any particular form of religion, or prohibiting the free exercise thereof; or abridging the freedom of speech or of the press, or the right of the people peaceably to assemble and to petition the Government for a redress of grievances.
>
> SECTION 2.—No State shall make any law respecting an establishment of religion, or favoring any particular form of religion, or prohibiting the free exercise thereof; or abridging the freedom of speech or of the press, or the right of the people peaceably to assemble and to petition the Government for a redress of grievances. No religious test shall ever be required as a condition of suffrage, or as a qualification to any office or public trust, in any State; and no person shall ever in any State be de-

---

[24] *Report of the Centennial Congress of Liberals,* 21. Among the vice presidents of the League were Elisha P. Hurlbut of Albany, New York, Robert Dale Owen of New Harmony, Indiana, and Rabbi Isaac M. Wise, editor of the *Israelite* in Cincinnati. Among the representatives present was Lucretia Mott.

[25] *Report of the Centennial Congress of Liberals,* 42. Abbot determinedly kept the Liberals focused on separation. "We must make that single thought, TOTAL SEPARATION OF CHURCH AND STATE, the one pithy and weighty message of the Centennial Congress of Liberals to the American people." Ibid., 38. A movement of "vast inclusiveness," it would succeed "if the Liberals should now for a while resolutely ignore all side-issues and work persistently for the ABSOLUTE SEPARATION OF CHURCH AND STATE." Ibid., 21.

prived of any of his or her rights, privileges, or capacities, or disqualified for the performance of any public or private duty, or rendered incompetent to give evidence in any court of law or equity, in consequence of any opinions he or she may hold on the subject of religion.

SECTION 3.—Congress shall have power to enforce the provisions of the second section of this Article by appropriate legislation.

The *Index* explained that "this enlargement of the First Amendment, in order to secure to the people the full and unrestricted enjoyment of religious liberty," was necessary for two reasons. First, the U.S. Constitution contained no provision prohibiting the states from restricting religious liberty.[26] Second, the ratification of the proposed amendment "would be the death-warrant of all attempts to pervert the Constitution to the service of Roman Catholicism or any other form of Christianity"—a reminder of the assumptions Liberals shared with many nativists.[27] By 1876, however, Abbot and other Liberals came to see the need for a more radical amendment, which would constrain government even further.

In seeking a more thoroughgoing separation amendment, some Liberals raised fears about the possible revival of the movement for a Christian amendment, but they worried far more about a temporizing amendment proposed by the Republican congressman, James G. Blaine. As will be seen in more detail below, President Grant in December 1875 had appealed to Liberal and nativist sentiment by proposing constitutional amendments in favor of separation. It was Blaine's amendment, however, proposed on the floor of the House a week later, that seemed likely to succeed and that most Liberals feared. Hoping for the Republican presidential nomination, Blaine rewrote the First Amendment to apply it to the states and to specify a single logical consequence of separation—the one most popular with anti-Catholic voters: "No state shall make any

---

[26] Ibid., 12. In particular, the Constitution "contains no provision prohibiting the *several States* from establishing a State religion, or requiring a religious test for office, or disqualifying witnesses in the courts on account of their religious opinions, or otherwise restricting their religious liberty." As a result "of this defect in the United States Constitution, some of the States are, as a matter of fact, actually guilty of grave infringements on the religious liberty of their citizens." Ibid.

[27] Ibid., 13. The *Index* added: "But the proposition of this new Amendment is not made at all in the spirit of a bellicose partisanship: on the contrary it is made with the strongest conviction that consistency with democratic ideas is the absolute condition of a permanent republic; that this consistency must be found both in our national and State Constitutions; and that the only way to ensure it in our State Constitutions is to assimilate them to our national Constitution by virtue of some such provision as we now propose." Ibid.

law respecting an establishment of religion or prohibiting the free exercise thereof; and no money raised by taxation in any State for the support of public schools, or derived from any public fund therefor, nor any public lands devoted thereto, shall ever be under the control of any religious sect, nor shall any money so raised or lands so devoted be divided between religious sects or denominations."[28]

The Liberals regretted this "non-committal" Blaine amendment because it conformed to the Protestant or nativist conception of separation. Although it provided that no public lands or public funds devoted to school purposes shall "ever be under the control of any religious sect" or "be divided between religious sects or denominations," it thereby would "still leave the Protestant sects undisturbed in their present collective mastery over the public school system."[29] In other words, it was an anti-Catholic measure that still permitted a generalized Protestantism in public schools as long as this was not the Protestantism of any one sect. Liberals, therefore, felt that it "ought not to be adopted, unless so amended as to prevent any sect *or number of sects* from exercising control over the public schools."[30] Fearful that the Blaine amendment was "a compromise between the ecclesiastical and the secular theories of government," and that it would "not have the effect of secularizing the pub-

---

[28] *Congressional Record,* 4(1): 205 (H.R., Dec. 14, 1875). See also ibid., 4(6): 5189 (H.R., Aug. 4, 1876). Upon being reported out of the Committee on the Judiciary on August 4, the Blaine amendment passed in the House, with modifications, by a vote of 180 to 7. In the Senate the Judiciary Committee reported an amended version, which failed to receive a two-thirds majority, the vote being 28 for and 16 against. Herman Ames, *The Proposed Amendments to the Constitution of the United States during the First Century of Its History,* 277–278 (1896; New York: Burt Franklin, 1970). Similar measures had been introduced already in April 1870 by Representative Samuel S. Burdett of Missouri and in December 1871 by Senator William M. Stewart of Nevada. For a history and analysis of such amendments, see J. B. Dunn, *Constitutional Safeguards against the Appropriation of Public Funds for Sectarian Purposes,* 5–6 (Boston: Congregational House, Committee of One Hundred Series Nos. 10, 12, July and August 1889). See also Green, "The National Reform Association," 40–41.

[29] *Report of the Centennial Congress of Liberals,* 116.

[30] Ibid. Similarly, in support of the amendment, Senator Frederick T. Frelinghuysen said: "There is nothing in it that prohibits religion as distinguished from the particular creed or tenets of religious and anti-religious sects and denominations being taught anywhere." Of course, Frelinghuysen believed that the Bible "is a religious and not a sectarian book." *Congressional Record,* 4(6): 5562 (Sen., Aug. 14, 1876). The advocates of a Christian amendment attempted to have such assumptions stated in the text of Blaine's proposal in the hope that this nativist measure would thereby secure an acknowledgment of Christianity in the Constitution. For the support by the National Reform Association, see Ahlstrom, "Francis Ellingwood Abbot," 2: 214.

lic schools, but [would] leave undisturbed the chief evil to be reformed," the Liberals proposed their new, 1876 amendment as "an eminently timely measure to bring forward now."[31]

Like the Liberals' old, 1874 proposal, their 1876 amendment did not use the words "separation of church and state," but it was understood to ensure separation by specifying the requirements of this principle. Far more than the 1874 amendment, the 1876 version moved "in the direction of greater verbal precision and comprehensiveness." The amendment read:

SECTION 1.—Neither Congress nor any State shall make any law respecting an establishment of religion, or favoring any particular form of religion, or prohibiting the free exercise thereof; or permitting in any degree a union of church and State, or granting any special privilege, immunity, or advantage to any sect or religious body or to any number of sects or religious bodies; or taxing the people of any State, either directly or indirectly, for the support of any sect or religious body or of any number of sects or religious bodies; or abridging the freedom of speech or of the press, or the right of the people peaceably to assemble and to petition the government for a redress of grievances.

SECTION 2.—No religious test shall ever be required as a condition of suffrage, or as a qualification to any office or public trust, in any State. No person shall ever in any State be deprived of any of his or her rights, privileges, or capacities, or disqualified for the performance of any public or private duty, or rendered incompetent to give evidence in any court of law or equity, in consequence of any opinions he or she may hold on the subject of religion. No person shall ever in any State be required by law to contribute directly or indirectly to the support of any religious society or body of which he or she is not a voluntary member.

SECTION 3.—Neither the United States, nor any State, Territory, municipality, or any civil division of any State or Territory, shall levy any tax, or make any gift, grant or appropriation, for the support, or in aid of any church, religious sect, or denomination, or any school, seminary, or institution of learning, in which the faith or doctrines of any religious

---

[31] "Patriotic Address," in *Report of the Centennial Congress of Liberals,* 168. The Liberals also resolved that "[t]he welfare of the country demands that no studied ambiguity should be permitted in a Constitutional amendment on this subject; and no amendment which, like Mr. Blaine's will keep the Bible in the schools, and thereby fail to separate Church and State in the public school system, ought to be adopted." Ibid. See also ibid., 168–169. For an account of the development of Liberal attitudes toward the Blaine amendment, see Green, "The National Reform Association," 89, 96–97.

order or sect shall be taught or inculcated, or in which religious practices shall be observed; or for the support, or in aid, of any religious charity or purpose of any sect, order, or denomination whatsoever.

SECTION 4.—Congress shall have power to enforce the various provisions of this Article by appropriate legislation.

According to the Liberals, "[t]his amendment is as comprehensive and as thorough as we can make it." The first section "provide[d] for the total separation of Church and State, covering the exemption of church-property from taxation."[32] More generally, the amendment would "effect the total separation of Church and State," thus limiting the power not merely of Congress but of "all branches and departments of the government, National, State, and municipal."[33]

Such an amendment was necessary because, according to Liberals, the U.S. Constitution had not guaranteed a separation of church and state. Abbot first published the 1876 amendment proposal with an editorial that adopted as its opening metaphor a story called "The Unfinished Window," about Aladdin's attempt to have built for him a window, which was completed except for one pane of glass.[34] In Abbot's view,

---

[32] *Report of the Centennial Congress of Liberals*, 13, 16. The other sections were explained as follows: "[T]he second section provides for the personal religious rights of each and every citizen; the third section (being Judge Hurlbut's admirable proposition) prohibits sectarian appropriations, and provides for a genuinely unsectarian public school system; and the fourth section provides for the efficient execution of the foregoing provisions. No measure less thorough ought to be adopted, for no measure less thorough can accomplish the entire secularization of the State." Ibid. In 1870, when Hurlbut had proposed the language on which section three was based, he explained that it was drafted "with a view to prevent the support of sectarian schools and institutions by a state tax, and to guard against gifts and grants to favorite and powerful religious sects." He thought his proposed amendment "to be as important as any which has been recently adopted." E. P. Hurlbut, *A Secular View of Religion in the State and the Bible in the Public Schools*, 54–55 (Albany: 1870).

[33] *Report of the Centennial Congress of Liberals*, 114–115.

[34] "When, at the command of Aladdin, the genie of the lamp had erected over-night the wonderful palace for the reception of the sultan's daughter, twenty-three of the windows in the great domed hall were lavishly decorated with jewels of the costliest kind; but the twenty-fourth was purposely left plain and incomplete, that the Sultan himself might have the glory of putting the finishing touch to such an incomparable structure. For a whole month all the Sultan's welders and goldsmiths labored assiduously to decorate this unfinished window in a style not unworthy of its superb companions; but, after utterly exhausting the resources of the imperial treasury, they found themselves unable to finish even one side of it. In this perplexity, Aladdin ordered them to undo their work and restore to their master his jewels. He then rubbed his lamp, and bade the genie to complete the hall; which was immediately done, to the astonishment and delight of the Sultan." *Report of the Centennial Congress by Liberals*, 13–14.

"the inadequate propositions of ex-Speaker Blaine, President Grant, the Union League, and others, to supply the omitted guarantees of religious freedom in the United States Constitution remind us irresistibly of the unfinished window in Aladdin's palace."[35] Therefore, "[t]he 'unfinished window' of the Constitution needs now to be completed." The Constitution, Abbot claimed, was a manifestly secular document, but "the imperfect guarantees of this political secularism, of this utter divorce of Church and State, need now to be perfected."[36] To correct this imperfect secularism, "[l]et such a Constitutional amendment be now adopted as shall make the separation of church and State no longer a matter merely of national tradition or disputed inference, but a great principle fully and explicitly declared in the great charter of all our civil and religious liberties."[37]

While Liberals argued for their amendment on the ground that the Constitution did not fully ensure a separation of church and state, they simultaneously insisted that their proposal merely extended and made explicit a principle already evident in the document. Thus far, separation lacked a specific guarantee. Yet it was "the general theory taken for granted in every line of our national Constitution." On this basis, Liberals could "recur to the fundamental principle of the Constitution" and make a "plea for a higher fidelity to it."[38] Abbot explained: "The principle of the total separation of Church and State is the very corner-stone of the American Republic," and it "is because this republic was founded on the idea of total separation of Church and State, and because that idea is the innermost soul of the United States Constitution, that we . . . demand

---

[35] Ibid., 15.

[36] Ibid., 71. "[I]t needs to be made no more secular than it is. All that it needs is that there should be additional guarantees and precautions . . . to preserve its own secular character." Ibid.

[37] Ibid., 15–16. Another version of the constitutional status of separation came from Hugh Byron Brown, who said, "I know that this [i.e., separation] has been supposed to be an accomplished fact, and such, no doubt, was the intention of the framers of the Federal Constitution. But such is not the result in its practical operation; as witness the exemption of church property from taxation." *Address on Thomas Paine's 139th Birthday, by D. M. Bennett, And Other Short Speeches, in New York, Jan. 29, 1876,* 28 (Truth Seeker Tract No. 80) (New York: 1876).

[38] "Patriotic Address," in *Report of the Centennial Congress of Liberals,* 164. The Address also declared: "The proposed amendment, being designed solely to preserve and perfect the existing secular character of the Constitution, is a thoroughly and wisely *conservative* measure, in the very best sense of the word. It aims not to undermine, but to confirm and strengthen and enlarge what already exists." Ibid., 168.

. . . a new and necessary extension of that principle, its larger and wider application, and its better embodiment in our general political system." In the existing Constitution the principle of separation was "manifestly insecure," and therefore Liberals felt the necessity of "defending and extending it"—"carrying out the sublime American idea to a higher, nobler, and still more beneficent fulfilment." Protesting that they were "not . . . fanatics at all," the Liberals claimed "simply to be patriots" who "grasped the fundamental idea of our country strongly and completely and earnestly, and strive to carry out to a more consistent and successful result the original and central purpose of its institutors."[39]

Practical Implications

The Liberals took the implications of separation further than any prior advocates of the idea. They understood separation of church and state to constrain not merely the Catholic Church but all Christians and even all distinct religions, and they thereby came to explore the concept's extensive implications for both government and religion—implications that were particularly severe for any organized religion.

In contrast to earlier nativists and other Protestants, who adopted separation in opposition to Catholics, Liberals ecumenically applied it to all Christians. Protestants had assumed that they acted as individuals within groups of denominations rather than as members of any one church, and they therefore had seen no need to apply the separation of church and state to themselves. Liberals, however, viewed all Christians with the same fear and horror Protestants reserved for Catholics.[40] Assuming that every distinct religion, including all Christianity, posed an ecclesiastical threat to freedom (both to the freedom of those within the religious group and to the freedom of those outside of it), Liberals applied

---

[39] *Report of the Centennial Congress of Liberals,* 37, 71. Like most other advocates of separation, the Liberals placed no special weight upon Jefferson's letter to the Danbury Baptists. Instead, they counted Jefferson as one of their intellectual forebears in a more general way as a rejecter of traditional Christianity—although they more often celebrated Ethan Allen, John Adams, Washington, and especially Thomas Paine, whose bust was a noted presence at their 1876 Congress.

[40] Liberals shared with nativist Protestants a fear of a Catholic "usurpation of power" in which Catholics would "destroy liberty of speech and of the press, stamp out all heresy, and establish ecclesiastical dungeons to be the homes of freemen." Yet Liberals held that "Catholic usurpation is no more treasonable than Protestant usurpation." B. F. Underwood, "The Practical Separation of Church and State," in *Report of the Centennial Congress of Liberals,* 98–99.

separation to all religious groups. They thereby expanded the popular Protestant version of separation into a Liberal or secular version that limited all religions with equal vigor.

The Liberals understood that, in advocating this secular separation, they had to struggle against the tendency of Americans to treat the phrase "separation of church and state" as a generic label for religious liberty. The Liberals explained: "As an abstraction, it has become a stereotyped phrase of American politics, a mere truism which nobody disputes, a mere tradition which it is the fashion to pass from mouth to mouth and not examine too closely in its bearings on existing usages or institutions."[41] Accordingly, the first object of their 1876 Congress was "to secure the extension and more thorough public comprehension of the already verbally recognized national principle of purely secular government, or absolute separation of Church and State."[42] In this, they went far beyond the religious liberty once sought by American religious dissenters and guaranteed in American constitutions—as is evident both with respect to government and religion.

First, the Liberal version of separation limited government in ways that the First Amendment, for example, had not. If church and state were to be separated, not only could Congress make no law respecting the establishment of religion, but government in general—the whole state—was to be kept apart from religion. In his "Demands of Liberalism," Abbot wrote:

> We demand that the employment of chaplains in Congress, in State Legislatures, in the navy and militia, and in prisons, asylums, and all other institutions supported by public money, shall be discontinued. . . .
>
> We demand that all religious services now sustained by the government shall be abolished; and especially that the use of the bible in the public schools, whether ostensibly as a text-book or avowedly as a book of religious worship, shall be prohibited. . . .
>
> We demand that the appointment, by the President of the United States or by the governors of the various States, of all religious festivals and fasts shall wholly cease. . . .
>
> We demand that the judicial oath in the courts and in all other departments of the government shall be abolished, and that simple affirmation under the pains and penalties of perjury shall be established in its stead. . . .

---

[41] "Patriotic Address," in ibid., 164.
[42] F. E. Abbot, "Proceedings of 1875 Convention," in ibid., 21.

We demand that not only in the Constitutions of the United States and of the several States, but also in the practical administration of the same, no privilege or advantage shall be conceded to Christianity or any other special religion; that our entire political system shall be founded and administered on a purely secular basis; and that whatever changes shall prove necessary to this end shall be consistently, unflinchingly, and promptly made.[43]

All of government had to avoid any connection with religion.

Moreover, any benefits from government, including clerical and church exemptions, seemed incompatible with separation. Accordingly,

[43] "Demands of Liberalism," in ibid., 7–8. In 1871 Abbot's Toledo Liberal Alliance declared: "The final separation of Church and State is not yet fully effected in this country. Presidents and Governors proclaim religious fasts and festivals; chaplains are supported from the public treasury in Congress and in the State Legislatures, in the army, navy, and militia, and in various public institutions; Bible-reading as a part of religious worship is maintained in the public schools; grants of money and land are made to various sectarian bodies; churches and parsonages are exempted from taxation; the Sabbath observance of Sunday is legally enforced in many places; religious Associations are actively and even openly engaged in political affairs for the furtherance of sectarian objects; religious riots, like the late outbreak in New York city, are liable to occur through the criminal connivance of public officials; dangerous attempts are even making to unite Church and State by a formal Christian Amendment to the United States Constitution; and in various other ways it is clear that the absolute separation of Church and State is a principle neither fully understood nor faithfully obeyed by the people of the United States." *To the Liberals of America* (broadside). Similarly, at the 1875 Liberal League Convention, held in Philadelphia to plan the Centennial Congress for the following year, the following resolutions were passed:

> *Resolved,* That the exemption of church property from taxation; the support of chaplains by public funds; the direct or indirect appropriation of public money for sectarian purposes of any sort; the maintenance of religious services in public institutions, and especially the use of the Bible in the public schools; the appointment of fasts or thanksgivings by public authority; the use of the judicial oath of laws for the public observance of Sunday as the Sabbath; the requirement of religious tests for office, suffrage, or naturalization,—all these and similar practices are in self-evident violation of the great national principle of the absolute separation of Church and State, and ought, therefore, to be totally discontinued.
>
> *Resolved,* That the evils here enumerated . . . constitute collectively a great public grievance to all who believe in the separation of Church and State. . . .
>
> *Resolved,* That in particular the non-taxation of church-property promotes the rapid accumulation of wealth and power in the hands of the Roman Catholic Church, and therefore directly fosters the development of an alien and formidable political power which openly claims to be supreme over all civil authorities throughout the world, and which only waits time and opportunity to press this claim vigorously in the United States; and that the enforced or permitted use of the Bible in the public schools gives to the organized power of this church a fatal weapon in its already avowed and dangerous assaults on the whole public school system.

Report of the Centennial Congress of Liberals, 22.

Liberalism demanded "that churches and other ecclesiastical property shall no longer be exempted from just taxation."[44] As Abbot put it in 1874: "If the separation of Church and State is indeed a just and righteous principle, and if it is fundamental in the theory of our political institutions, then it is fundamental in that this practical establishment of the church should cease, as a glaring violation of the religious rights of the people; and the abolition of church-exemption would be simply a due recognition of these rights."[45] Even government benefits distributed on purely secular grounds could not be given to religious organizations. Thus Liberalism demanded "that all public appropriations for sectarian educational and charitable institutions shall cease"—such institutions being precluded, on account of their religion, from receiving the benefits for which they otherwise were eligible. Of course, benefits would not be denied to qualifying individuals who were religious, but they would be denied to a qualifying group if the group was religious.

In addition, according to the Liberals, government could not enact any laws or otherwise impose any obligations that coincided with the morality of a distinct religion, such as Christianity. According to Abbot, "We demand that all laws looking to the enforcement of 'Christian' morality shall be abrogated, and that all laws shall be conformed to the re-

---

[44] "Demands of Liberalism," in ibid., 7. See also ibid., 9.

[45] Francis E. Abbot, *Just and Equal Taxation: or, No Exemption—Direct Appropriation*, 9 (Boston: 1874), copy in Harvard University Archives, HUG 1101.4. Liberals also feared that an untaxed church would acquire sufficient property and power to endanger the state. "Being relieved from the burden of taxation, it is enabled to hold it [the wealth of the people] until it becomes a power inimical to the welfare of society and the State." Speech of Hugh Byron Brown, *Address on Thomas Paine's 139th Birthday*, 28.

Of course, some Americans protested that separation required that churches be exempt from taxation. For example, after Liberals, among others, persuaded President Grant to urge the taxation of church property, an official of the New York City tax office, G. H. Andrews, skeptically remarked: "[I]t is proposed to substitute for this [present] condition of things, so as to insure mark you, the complete separation of Church and State, an entirely new relation of one to the other, that hereafter the Church shall, in specific form, contribute directly by taxation to the support of the State. That is the divorce, that the separation, with which Church and State are now for the first time to be severed. Truly this is a rare remedy for a non-existent disease." Letter No. 5, *New York Times*, 4 (Jan. 6, 1876). See also George C. Lorimer, *The Great Conflict: A Discourse, Concerning Baptists, and Religious Liberty*, 120–122 (Boston: 1877). More typically, the opponents of the Liberal position did not argue from separation at all. See, e.g., Rev. E. M'Chesney, "Taxation of Church Property: Review of Charles Eliot, *The Exemption from Taxation of Church Property* . . . & Alvah Hovey, *Religion and the State*," in *Methodist Quarterly Review*, 68: 249 (vol. 28 of 4th ser., 1876).

quirements of natural morality, equal rights, and impartial liberty."[46] For example, among the many statutes "based upon 'Christian' conceptions of morals, as distinguished from 'natural' morality," were usury laws, which were "in fact based upon the Bible conception that it is a crime to take interest for money loaned; although the common sense of mankind rejects the notion."[47] Similarly, although courts typically justified Sunday laws on at least civil grounds, the Liberals' Centennial Congress resolved that American citizens "all possess an equal right to enjoy for seven days of the week all public libraries, art-galleries, museums, parks, gardens, or other institutions or facilities for the support of which they are taxed, and not to be debarred from such enjoyment on Sunday because a part of the people do not choose to avail themselves of these things on that day; in fine, that they all possess an equal right to live under a government which shall respect all men's private religion, but favor no man's."[48]

---

[46] "Demands of Liberalism," in *Report of the Centennial Congress of Liberals*, 8. Later, in an address "elucidating the eighth Demand of Secularism," Mattie P. Krekel insisted, "[w]e demand that all laws looking to the enforcement of 'Christian' morality, as such, shall be abrogated, and that all laws shall be conformed to the requirements of natural morality, equal rights, and impartial liberty." Laws that enforced a morality that was not in conformity to secular moral reasoning were to be abrogated. She objected "to being bound by a special and technical form of asserted morality, which is less than universal in its sympathies" and argued that "[o]ur Secular constitution is the flat and uncompromising denial of the morality of organized Christianity in the affairs of men." *Freethought: A Liberal Journal* 2 (no. 47): 746–747 (Nov. 23, 1889).

[47] "Burn Your Ships," in *Report of the Centennial Congress of Liberals*, 10.

[48] *Report of the Centennial Congress of Liberals*, 115. In 1873 Abbot wrote: "Laws everywhere are in force discriminating between Sunday and the rest of the week, sometimes avowedly and sometimes covertly on Christian grounds." "Burn Your Ships," in ibid., 10. On the prevalence of the civil justification of Sunday laws, see Stuart Banner, "When Christianity Was Part of the Common Law," *Law and History Review*, 16: 27 (1998). See also R. C. Wylie, *Sabbath Laws in the United States* (Pittsburgh: National Reform Association, 1905). In 1890 William Addison Blakely complained about the advocates of Sunday laws:

> [S]ometimes they even go so far as to oppose the so-called "civil Sabbath" theory, and demand a law to enforce Sunday rest, and to "promote its observance as a day of religious worship." But they generally appear before our law-making bodies in a very different way, as is strikingly illustrated by the following extract from an open letter of the leading apostle of religious legislation on the Pacific Coast, dated at Oakland, California, February 19, 1890: . . .
>
> "You may notice how cautious we have to be in the wording of this petition, for as we have no State law recognizing the Sabbath day, we have no hope of closing the saloon on that day except as a municipal and police arrangement in the interest of sobriety, morality, law, and order. If we would undertake to close the saloons because the Sabbath is a day sacred by divine authority, we would be met at once, both by the council and by the courts, with the declaration: The State of California knows no religious Sabbath—no Sunday except a holiday. Thus we would be defeated at the very beginning. . . . As yet we hardly dare to be hopeful of success,

The Liberals did not go so far as to argue that, because charity was a responsibility of the church, government could not help the poor. Yet some of the contemporaries of the Liberals believed that the Liberal understanding of separation seemed to "lead" to such conclusions—that, from the Liberal perspective, "all care for the sick, the helplessly poor and dependent, is to be laid aside by the State" and that "Charitable institutions ought not to look for government aid in any form . . . because charity is a Christian duty."[49] By the late 1850s at least one Protestant had put forward such a position. In the 1880s, in the aftermath of the Liberal advocacy of separation, the Central Committee for Protecting and Perpetuating the Separation of Church and State—an anti-Catholic organization with support from Astor, Rockefeller, and Vanderbilt—more prominently declared:

> The appropriate spheres of the State and the Church have, perhaps, generally not been clearly apprehended.
> The duty of the State is to protect its Citizens, to preserve Order, and to *dispense Justice.*
> The duty of the Church is to teach Religion and to *dispense Charity.*
> Charity, divorced from religion, provided for by public taxation, and dispensed by the State, loses its essential quality. It then becomes a certain and secure provision which society makes for its unfortunate and pauper classes.
> The certainty of the provision thus made by the State, fosters improvidence and pauperism. Religious life also suffers by being robbed, through State provision for these classes, of one of the most important fields for the cultivation of unselfishness.[50]

Being anti-Catholic rather than anti-Christian, the Committee proceeded merely to criticize the distribution of government funds to institutions under sectarian control—that is, the distribution of funds to Catholic rather than nonsectarian Protestant bodies—but it came close

---

but the Lord of the Sabbath is supreme in California as elsewhere. By his blessing we shall succeed. May we not hope for the prayers of the friends of temperance and of the Sabbath?" "Christian Statesman," March 13.

Blakely, ed., *American State Papers Bearing on Sunday Legislation,* 87 (New York: National Religious Liberty Association, 1891).

[49] M'Chesney, "Taxation of Church Property," 251.

[50] The Central Committee for Protecting and Perpetuating the Separation of Church and State, *To the People of the State of New York: Appeal No. 4,* 11 (New York: January 1886). Somewhat similar reasoning is apparent in the comment of a later Seventh-Day Adventist magazine: "The complete separation between the proper spheres of religion and the civil government is made evident from the fact that while civil government aims at justice alone, Christianity aims at both justice and mercy." *Liberty,* 1 (no. 1): 3 (April 1906).

to suggesting that, to remain separate from the church, government had to refrain from acts of charity.

A second effect of separation was to limit religion, particularly any organized religion. For example, separation seemed to require that the clergy stay out of politics and not attempt to influence the conduct of legislators. Protestants had long complained that the creed and hierarchy of the Catholic Church threatened separation in this way, and now Liberals extended the argument to Protestant sects. Thus, when Methodists encouraged their adherents to nominate and vote for civil office only such candidates as had "true Christian character and principles," the Liberals believed that this purely internal recommendation of a voluntary religious society illustrated why America "must have a complete separation of Church and State, with such Constitutional guarantees as shall, both in the States and in the general government, make their union henceforth impossible."[51] More amusingly, a Liberal rabbi applied the idea of separation to prevent himself from advocating separation. Asked to speak on the "Separation of Church and State" at an 1889 secular convention, Rabbi J. Bloch of Portland at "first hesitated to consent," for he feared that, under the principle of separation, he was disqualified from talking about it: "Politically, I hold that no preacher should meddle with politics." There was "enough work" for preachers "within the precincts of their churches and the pulpit, and as good citizens they ought to know the first duty, viz: the separation of church and state."[52] Like most clerical advocates of separation, however, he got over this problem. Separation seemed to imply not only that clergymen should stay out of politics but also that, if they did manage to influence it, they thereby vitiated the legitimacy of otherwise secular statutes. For example, in an 1888 article called "Holy Hypocrisy," the journal of the American Secular Union, *Freethought,* complained of attempts by the clergy to obtain statutes prohibiting work on Sundays—statutes that, although ostensibly

[51] Report of the Centennial Congress of Liberals, 97, 99.

[52] "Separation of Church and State," *Freethought: A Liberal Journal,* 2 (no. 44): 697 (Nov. 2, 1889). Already in 1853, at a meeting of the General Assembly of the Presbyterian Church of the United States, Chancellor Johns argued against the adoption of a memorial from the Church to Congress on behalf of religious liberty, on the ground that by acting "in our ecclesiastical capacity"—as an ecclesiastical organization rather than as individuals—"we encroach at once upon that sacred principle of our Constitution—the perfect separation between Church and State." His perspective, however, was not warmly received. "General Assembly," *Princeton Review,* 25 (no. 3): 524 (July 1853).

not concerning religion, were, in fact, desired by the clergy to protect a religious institution, the Christian Sabbath. "These clerical mountebanks want a religious law passed by the legislature; but they conceal their design under the phraseology of asking for a civil law. . . . They ask the legislature to pass a civil Sunday law, and under cover of this they will enforce the religious observance of the day."[53] The clergy were to stay out of politics, and the religious motives underlying their political involvement rendered otherwise secular statutes illegitimate.

A third implication of separation was a prohibition on any "entanglement" of church and state, which gave emphasis to the limits on both government and religious organizations. In response to the bogeyman of a Christian amendment, the "Patriotic Address" of the National Liberal League to the people of the United States declared: "Two Constitutional amendments are offered to you for your choice, embodying two opposing principles between which human ingenuity will search in vain to find a mean. One fatally entangles the State with the Church, and plunges this young republic into all the bitterest embarrassments of the Old World."[54] Similarly, in protest "against the recent proclamation of President Grant, inviting the people to celebrate the Fourth of July by religious observances," the National Liberal League resolved: "We deny emphatically the right of the President to issue a civil proclamation of any religious fast or festival, to assume as President a strictly ecclesiastical function, to entangle the State with the Church by interfering with the people's free control of their own religious observances, and to cast the stigma of governmental disapproval on those citizens who do not choose to comply with this unwarranted, officious, and impertinent invitation." Denying the right of the president to "entangle the State with the Church," the Liberals reminded Grant of "his own advice to the people last September at Des Moines, now so glaringly disregarded by himself— 'KEEP THE CHURCH AND THE STATE FOREVER SEPARATE.' "[55]

---

[53] *Freethought: A Liberal Journal,* 2 (no. 4): 33, 38 (Jan. 28, 1888).

[54] "Patriotic Address," in *Report of the Centennial Congress of Liberals,* 168–169.

[55] *Report of the Centennial Congress of Liberals,* 117. This resolution was eventually adopted with the insertion of the phrase: "substantially reiterated in December in his Annual Message to Congress," which was added after the words, "at Des Moines." Ibid., 138.

Incidentally, entanglement and related ideas had attractions in church property and church membership disputes for the parties seeking to fend off the state's "interference," making it necessary for courts occasionally to acknowledge the principle of separation but to limit its apparent implications, as when in 1906 the Supreme Court of Washington

The metaphor of separation drew Americans to these radical conclusions with considerable logical force, as the Rev. Henry W. Bellows candidly acknowledged. Although not one of the Liberals, Bellows was a theological liberal—indeed, he was the Unitarian who had hinted at the necessity of annihilating Catholics—and his response, in 1871, to a relatively secular conception of separation reveals much about the idea's appeal.[56] Viewing separation as a constraint on both Catholics and evangelicals, he considered "an essential and permanent divorce of Church and State" as the only principle upon which "a political union" could be maintained in America.[57] Even so, he equivocated as he considered its implications for American life—that is, Protestant American life. "Doubtless political *science* would always divorce the Church and the State; but living history has not in the past forbidden the banns, nor will statesmanship yet justify the separation in all cases." Nonetheless, reluctantly, Bellows gave way to the force of separation's logic. For example, he at first resisted the conclusion that the Bible had to be excluded from public schools: "To exclude it from the public schools is to the religious affections of Protestants like Abraham's sacrifice of his only son. When it was first proposed, I felt horror-stricken, and instinctively opposed it; but I have thought long and anxiously upon the subject, and have, from pure logical necessity and consistency, been obliged to change—nay, reverse my opinion."[58] Grudgingly, Bellows applied the principle not only to Catholics but also to the Protestant Bible, and, in this sense, he moved toward a secular separation of a sort that would be systematically developed by the Liberals. To be sure, he applied separation more severely against Catholics, whom he threatened with destruction for voting as a group, but he at least felt the logical necessity of excluding the Protestant Bible from public schools.

It was in response to this disturbing logic that the Catholic essayist,

---

cautioned: "It is true that in this country there is what is termed a separation of church and state. . . . But it does not follow from this that church property is placed beyond the pale of protection by the law; or that the law will not compel the trustees of such property to honestly and faithfully carry out the duties of their trust in relation to this kind of property, as well as any other kind." W. Hendryx et al. v. People's United Church of Spokane, 42 Wash. 336, 345 (1906). See also Ex rel. H. W. Soares v. Hebrew Congregation, 31 La. Ann. 205, 206 (1879); Smith et al. v. Pedigo et al., 145 Ind. 361, 364 (1893).

[56] Notwithstanding his liberal theology, Bellows said he would "go with Orthodoxy in any form rather than with the Radicals." Abbot, "The Proposed Christian Amendment," *Index*.

[57] Bellows, *Church and State in America*, 4.

[58] Ibid., 19.

Orestes Brownson, saw that he had to distinguish between the absence of an establishment and the separation that would deprive all organized religion of its legal rights. Government "affords religion the protection and assistance of the law in the possession and management of her temporalities, her churches and temples, lands and tenements, funds and revenues for the support of public worship, and various charitable or eleemosynary institutions." Yet "[a]ll the protection and assistance the benefit of which every Protestant denomination fully enjoys, and even the Catholic Church in principle, though not always in fact, would be denied, if the divorce Dr. Bellows demands were granted, and religion, having no rights politicians are bound to respect, would become the prey of lawless and godless power, and religious liberty would be utterly annihilated."[59]

Of course, not all Americans felt separation's logic with as much clarity as Bellows or the Liberals. For example, when, as will be seen, President Grant proposed a constitutional amendment that would directly declare "Church and State forever separate and distinct," some commentators questioned whether the phrase had any clear implications of a practical character. Samuel Spear—the Presbyterian clergyman who became an editor of the *Independent*—objected that "[t]his language is altogether too general, too ambiguous, and too susceptible of diverse constructions to be of any practical service. . . . A mere general dogma on any subject will not do for a constitutional law. Making constitutions which are to be the basis of powers to be exercised, or restraints to be imposed and enforced, is a work that demands the utmost accuracy in the use of words."[60] Yet Liberal advocates of separation had no need for such fears. They sought what they considered the broadest implications of separation, and in any case they demanded a "practical" enumeration of these rather than an abstract declaration of the principle.

The Liberals felt confident that their understanding of the logic of separation would gradually prevail. In contemplating how Americans would eventually come to accept the full implications of their secular

[59] "The Secular Not Supreme," *Catholic World*, 13: 689 (August 1871). According to Brownson, Bellows "proposes to defeat the Evangelicals on the one hand, and the Catholics on the other, by separating totally religion and politics." Ibid., 686.

[60] Samuel T. Spear, *Religion and the State*, 22 (New York: Dodd, Mead & Co, 1876). See also his series of articles in the *Independent*, cited by Green, "The National Reform Association," 101 and note 100.

version of separation, Liberals thought of their ideal as an historically inevitable, even progressive, principle that had been the foundation of American government and that would, increasingly, be applied with consistency. Two decades earlier, Philip Schaff had taken comfort in the failure of Americans to live up to their ideal of separation. Now, however, it was the Liberals who acknowledged this gap between the theory and the practice, and they regretted that most other Americans did not perceive how far they still had to go. Liberals expected that the "time will come, when it will be seen . . . that the popular notion that there is an utter disconnection between Church and State in America, and that all our laws are in harmony therewith, is a notion which is *at variance with the real facts.*"[61] Indeed, by drawing attention to this variance, the Liberals brought many Americans to see the logical reach of separation—at least, that is, the logical extent of the Liberal version of the idea. Already in 1880, for example, the superintendent of public schools in Madison, Wisconsin, wrote that one of the "objections" to "the combination of religious and moral instruction" was that the "idea of separating church from state, has been advancing for centuries, and should be followed out to its logical conclusion of complete non-interference on the part of both."[62] This ideal, once accepted and fully understood, seemed as if it would take Americans down the full length of its implications. As Abbot explained—when he asked his fellow Liberals to endorse the "TOTAL SEPARATION OF CHURCH AND STATE"—"It is a short phrase: but it has a long meaning."[63]

Antiecclesiastical Fears and Religious Yearnings

In seeking separation, many Liberals combined powerfully antiecclesiastical fears with intense desires of an almost religious character. Notwith-

---

[61] *Report of the Centennial Congress of Liberals,* 92.

[62] *Annual Report of the Board of Education of the City of Madison, for the Year 1879,* 18 (Madison: 1880). The superintendent, however, was reluctant to go so far.

[63] *Report of the Centennial Congress of Liberals,* 38. Separation seemed to have an inexorable logic, albeit a very different logic for Liberals and nativists. The old nativist, Daniel Ullmann, argued: "Three maxims are fundamental in America:—First,—The Sovereignty of the people; Second,—An absolute separation of church and state: and Third,—That republican institutions cannot permanently exist, unless the people are virtuous and intelligent." From these he concluded: "Now, if virtue and intelligence be the bulwark of American institutions, then free and universal education is a supreme necessity. If the maxim that there shall be no connection between church and state be fundamental then the schools

standing that the National Liberal League devoted itself to separation or the secularization of government, most individual Liberals also had higher ambitions for the abolition of all clergy, all Christianity, and all distinct religions. Yet even as they condemned all distinct religions and sought to keep them out of politics, they felt nearly religious passions on behalf of their secularized politics. Like some early nineteenth-century Republicans and mid-century nativists, these Liberals, as they sought to exclude religion from politics, devoted themselves to their cause with virtually religious zeal.

Most Liberals held highly unpopular, even unrespectable, anti-Christian opinions, and therefore Abbot and some other Liberal leaders attempted to distinguish between the positions of individual Liberals and the position of their League. Abbot had perceived that atheists, secular theists, and spiritualists could all find in separation a satisfying expression of their own, more varied, beliefs, and in this way he had unified Liberals in the National Liberal League. Yet when many Liberals sought to express their radical personal opinions in the public pronouncements of the League, Abbot feared that these Liberals risked alienating their fellow Americans, whose support the League needed if it was to obtain a constitutional amendment guaranteeing separation.[64] Most bluntly, the popular atheist speaker, Samuel P. Putnam, reminded the Congress of the political realities: "We propose to act on the question of the separation of Church and State, and where do we go to get that separation? We must go in the first instance to the Congress of the United States, and have it guaranteed in the Constitution: we must go to the State Legislature. How shall we go there? Shall we go as atheists? It may or may not be true that a majority of us are atheists; but that is not what we are driving at."[65] Hoping to reconcile his fellow Liberals to the limited

---

established by the state, and sustained by taxes levied upon the whole people, must remain unsectarian. These are logical sequences, from which there is no escape." *Amendments to the Constitution of the United States. Non-Sectarian and Universal Education. Veteran Association, Order of United Americans, Annual Dinner, New York, February 22d, 1876. Remarks of Daniel Ullmann, LL.D.*, 5 (New York: 1876).

[64] For example, when some Liberals proposed that their amendment should expressly mention that it aimed to protect the rights of atheists, Abbot attempted to put them off by arguing that "if you examine this article closely," one would see that "the atheist's right is as well protected as the theist's." *Report of the Centennial Congress of Liberals*, 47.

[65] Ibid., 49. The Report refers simply to "Mr. Putnam," who probably was the prominent freethinker.

public goal of the 1876 Congress, Abbot reminded them that he was "not only . . . not a Christian, but also . . . a determined anti-Christian, aye, to the very bone." Abbot and many other Liberals even believed that "Christianity and freedom are absolutely and totally irreconcilable." Yet precisely because Liberals held such views, they needed to make clear to their fellow Americans "that this National Liberal League, as such, is neither Christian nor anti-Christian."[66] Instead, as Abbot explained, it "is organized to carry out the principle of freedom and equal rights and secular government," and if any American "can reconcile these principles with his own idea of Christianity, however illogically,— why should he not do so?" Accordingly, Abbot urged: "Leave Christianity severely alone" and "Concentrate your entire energy on the one great object of the total separation of Church and State."[67]

Inescapably, however, many Liberals revealed a deep distrust of any religion that distinguished itself from others. In 1870 Judge Elisha P. Hurlbut proposed his constitutional amendment empowering Congress to prohibit the Catholic Church. He would soon become the elder statesman of the National Liberal League, but already in 1870 he revealed how his anti-Catholicism was but part of a broader antiecclesiasticism that would draw him to the Liberals. He had asked himself: "But is not the proposed amendment calculated to abridge religious liberty?" He answered in the negative, explaining: "There is a distinction to be taken between religious opinion and worship on the one hand, and organizations and practices in the name of religion on the other." Rather than oppose religious liberty, he merely rejected religious organizations. The "theocracy" of such groups was "a fungus of religion," which "may be

---

[66] Ibid., 72. Speaking of his own views and not those of the Liberal League, Abbot declared: "I believe, then, that Christianity and freedom are absolutely and totally irreconcilable. I believe that just in proportion as any nation is faithful to the creed of Christianity, it will put its heel on equal individual rights in religion, and is logically bound to do so. I believe that Christianity, being founded on the absolute 'Divine Authority' of Jesus Christ, is by its very nature hostile to individual and national liberty, and to equal individual rights. I am therefore logically bound to believe, and I do believe, that the National Liberal League, being founded on the great principle of EQUAL RIGHTS IN RELIGION, is necessarily hostile to the fundamental principle of Christianity; but I am extremely careful to tell you now that this is my individual view alone, and in no degree representative of the League as such." Indeed, the Liberals resolved "that the Christian or anti-Christian character of this movement is solely a question of private interpretation, to be answered by each member of the Liberal League, according to his own definition of Christianity." Ibid., 116.

[67] Ibid., 74.

eradicated without hurting religion itself. Restraint of theocracy, is the way to religious health and freedom."[68] More pleasantly, other Liberals sang about their fears, which similarly concerned not only government but also, perhaps more emphatically, the authoritative claims of church and clergy:

> We want no counsel from the priests,
>   No bishop's crook or gown,
> No sanctimonious righteousness,
>   No curse or godly frown.
>
> We want no Bibles in the schools,
>   No creeds nor doctrines there;
> We want no superstition's tools
>   The children's minds to scare.
>
> We want the rights of liberty,
>   With reason's lamp to try
> Each word and thought of other men
>   To solve our destiny.[69]

As Charles D. B. Mills declared at the Centennial Congress: "So long as the identification of religion with a certain determinate form of faith obtains (as with us Christianity, Bible, etc.), so long, the power of religious sentiment being what it is, there will be a strong tendency to the narrow, exclusive and intolerant spirit."[70] Another speaker at the Centennial Congress, Mrs. Pratt, believed of Christians: "The greater their faith, the more dangerous they are. If they believe that Jesus of Nazareth is the only God who can save men's souls, and if they want our souls saved, they will think it is their religious duty to burn our bodies." Seeing herself as a martyr to such intolerance, she added: "I have for fifteen years been burning for personal religious liberty; I am burning at the

---

[68] Hurlbut, *A Secular View of Religion in the State*, 22–23. He added: "I feel no difficulty therefore in asserting, that we can sever the connection between the Roman pontiff and the dignitaries of the Catholic Church in America, not only without violence to sound principles, but to the advantage of the state, and to the Church itself, which might then become truly Catholic, and command the respect of an age of light and liberty." Ibid., 23.

[69] "A Song for Liberals," in *The Truth Seeker Collection of Forms, Hymns, and Recitations. Original and Selected—For the Use of Liberals*, 377–378 (New York: D. M. Bennett, Liberal & Scientific Publishing House, 1877).

[70] *Report of the Centennial Congress of Liberals*, 145.

stake every day."[71] To these Liberals, any distinctive religion and especially Christianity seemed inimical to religious freedom.[72]

Nonetheless, Liberals possessed some of the very characteristics they condemned in distinct religions. Most prominently, while they declaimed against an intolerant Christianity, Liberals quickly acquired their own reputation for an intolerant censoriousness. Some worried about this. "Liberals are the last class of people that should be *bigoted*."[73] Yet more than many Christians, Liberals needed to remind themselves of this: "Above all things, let a spirit of liberality toward the opinions of others be duly exercised. Let a proper respect for the views of our fellows be generously maintained." It was "neither possible nor desirable that all should arrive at the same conclusions—that all should think alike as to all theological, scientific and philosophical subjects." Therefore, "[a]bove all things, let liberals not become bigots, and demand that others shall think precisely as they do."[74]

---

[71] Ibid., 61. At the request of T. B. Wakeman, the 1882 Congress of Liberals resolved to use a calendar measured from the martyrdom of Giordano Bruno in 1600, such that the year 1882 became 282 in the "Era of Man." As one Liberal generously observed, this "reform calendar did not survive its founder." George E. McDonald, *Fifty Years of Freethought Being the Story of* The Truth Seeker, *with the Natural History of Its Third Editor,* 317 (New York: The Truth Seeker Co., 1929). The tendency of nonbelievers to see themselves as martyrs and even in the image of Christ was not exclusively an American phenomenon. In England the radical printer, Richard Carlile, had declared, "I am the Jesus Christ of this Island, and this age" and even went so far as to clothe himself as if he were Jesus. Joseph Hamburger, Review of Joel H. Wiener, *Radicalism and Freethought in Nineteenth-Century Britain: The Life of Richard Carlile* (1983), in *Victorian Periodicals Review,* 17: 73, 75 (1984).

[72] In 1874, when proposing its constitutional amendment, the *Index* declared its hope of bequeathing to posterity "a supreme law freed from the last, lingering traces of a poisonous ecclesiasticism." "Wanted: A Religious Freedom Amendment . . . ," *Index* (Jan. 1, 1874), quoted in *Report of the Centennial Congress of Liberals,* 13. On the antiecclesiasticism of the *Index,* see Ahlstrom, "Francis Ellingwood Abbot," 2: 205.

[73] *The Truth Seeker Collection of Forms, Hymns, and Recitations,* 7. Of course, Liberals were not alone in noticing their intolerance. G. H. Andrews emphasized: "It is the Free-thinker who, under other skies, has felt the oppression of a State church, who is here intolerant of any religion." Andrews, "Should Church Property Be Taxed?" Letter No. 9, *New York Times,* 6 (Jan. 16, 1876).

[74] *The Truth Seeker Collection of Forms, Hymns, and Recitations,* 9–10. Some Liberals achieved a freedom from dogma—at least other people's dogma—in a town of their own, Liberal, Missouri. Founded in 1881 by G. H. Walser, "for the use and occupation of Freethought and Liberal-minded people," it had grown by 1885 "to an active business town of five hundred inhabitants, all of whom are honest, sober, and industrious; and, too, absolutely free from church dogmatisms and political serfdom of all kinds." Such, at least, was how they advertised themselves. Indeed, "The people of Liberal pride themselves in the fact that they have practically demonstrated to the world that Freethought and free expression

Although Liberals mocked religious ceremonies, creeds, and organizations, some of them craved similar forms and practices. At the end of life, for example, many Liberals hoped to avoid a Christian funeral service but anxiously adopted, instead, a Liberal ceremony, in which they were eulogized for being "untrammeled by the chains of priestly creeds and fables."[75] Similarly, at the beginning of life, Liberals who wanted to ensure their children's conformity to their beliefs adopted a mode of Liberal baptism: "In publicly naming the infant now before us we recognize the parents' desire to identify their offspring with the Liberal party."[76] Some Liberals even attempted to overcome their divisions and disorganization by admonishing each other to follow the example of the Catholics: "A single individual cannot accomplish great physical deeds, but a body of men joined together with one purpose can perform wonders. The Romish branch of the Christian Church is probably the strong-

---

do not tend to a lower grade of humanity; that the happiest and best community is that one which is the freest from the dogmas of religion; THAT MAN'S SAVIOR MUST BE MAN ALONE." "The Town of Liberal," Advertisement, in *The Truth Seeker Annual and Freethinkers' Almanac*, 96 (New York: Truth Seeker, 1885).

[75] *The Truth Seeker Collection of Forms, Hymns, and Recitations*, 66. For an extensive example of the religious imagery and feelings in some funeral services of Freethinkers, see the commemorations on the death of May L. Collins (who was discovered with Samuel Putnam, "asphyxiated by illuminating gas, their lifeless bodies having been found that morning lying upon the floor of Miss Collins's rooms in a Boston apartment house"). *Union and Federation, Arguments for Religious Equality, Compiled from Addresses Delivered at the Congress of the American Secular Union and Freethought Federation, Memorial Volume to Samuel P. Putnam and May L. Collins*, 59 (Chicago: 1896). According to one tribute, "[t]here seemed to be a voice divine calling to this girl," which said:

> Come up higher
> And burst your prison bars,
> And from out the mist and fire
> Of Christian myth and ire
> Arise and bathe the spirit
> In the sunlight and the stars.

Josephine K. Henry, "Personal Tribute," in ibid., 117–119.

Of course, Liberals were aware of allegations that their elevation of reason might be inadequate as a substitute for the emotional features of religion. Charles Watts wrote: "It is objected by some persons that reason is inadequate as a monitor, because it ignores too much the emotional part of our nature. This, however, is not so. Secularists do not neglect the emotions; they only endeavor to control and regulate them. Secularism teaches that the intellectual should predominate over the emotional, not the emotional over the intellectual. Where this rule is not observed religion frequently degenerates into wild fanaticism, and pleasure into licentiousness." Charles Watts, "Address," in ibid., 10.

[76] *The Truth Seeker Collection of Forms, Hymns, and Recitations*, 61.

est religion and political power on the earth today. It is the result of a thorough and effective organization. Whether for good or for ill, the result is the same. In Union There is Strength."[77] Liberals could hardly adopt religious forms, creeds, and organizations of the sort they condemned among Christians, but Liberals sorely desired the continuity and cohesion such practices could bring.

Indeed, while hostile to Christianity and any other distinct religion, the Liberals glowed with religious intensity. For many Liberals, their advocacy of separation was a manifestation of their otherworldly impulses. Abbot believed that "[t]he religion of every free State is free religion; and free religion, on its political side, is absolute secularism."[78] More generally, at the 1876 Congress in which the Liberals demanded their separation amendment, a suffragist and aspiring lawyer, Carrie Burham Kilgore, explained: "'Religion, as a soul-emotion, is universal,' and is the grand motive power of humanity. Every people (as also every individual legislator, if true to himself) will unwittingly incorporate its conceptions of the relation of humanity to the unknown, and the consequent relation of individuals each to the other, into its laws."[79] Charles D. B. Mills believed that if individuals and society were "penetrated and inspired perpetually and wholly by . . . high ideals," then "society itself shall be a church and all life worship."[80] Liberals could "build upon the foundations of the everlasting, build for the eternal verities and the welfare of humanity universal."[81]

In America in particular, according to Abbot, "the republic has its own purely secular religion"—a religion "declared luminously in its Constitution and exemplified (with sad deviations) in its history." Such was "the religion of political and personal freedom, of widely diffused education, of equal and universal human rights, of justice between man

---

[77] Ibid., 7.
[78] *Report of the Centennial Congress of Liberals,* 15.
[79] Ibid., 80. Her husband was the Spiritualist, Damon Kilgore. See Ahlstrom, "Francis Ellingwood Abbot," 2: 203.
[80] *Report of the Centennial Congress of Liberals,* 150.
[81] Ibid. Obviously many Liberals drew upon ideas that Comte had popularized in the middle of the century as the Religion of Humanity. Most notably, Octavius Brooks Frothingham— president of the Free Religious Association from 1867 to 1878 and a vice president of the National Liberal League—had published in 1873 his own volume advocating faith in "essential human nature," *The Religion of Humanity: An Essay.* Among the organizations represented by accredited delegates at the 1876 Congress of Liberals was the First Congregation of the Religion of Humanity of New York City. Ibid., 184.

and man and the brotherhood of universal benevolence which inevitably grows out of justice between man and man." Thus far, few were prepared to admit that "these glorious yet simple things are enough to constitute a religion; yet what do they lack? They have proved their vitalizing power as a religion by creating a political organism of majestic proportions." They "have proved their power to kindle fires of self-devotion, self-sacrifice, and moral enthusiasm," inspiring in the nation "an inextinguishable faith in its own future." Abbot declared: "Freedom, justice, knowledge, equal rights,—these are the religion that builds no churches and hires no priests, but makes every honest citizen's heart an altar and the republic itself a temple."[82] As one Liberal asked, "May not their *religion* be defined as liberty?"[83]

The religiosity of many of those who sought to separate church and state became most directly evident in Liberal religious services, in which Liberals rejected Christianity but not, apparently, religious emotions. A glimpse of one of the more elaborate of such services appears in a report of an 1888 reception or "festival" given by the Chicago Secular Society for the president of the American Secular Union, Samuel P. Putnam. The Union was one of the successors to the National Liberal League, and its president traveled so frequently across the country to lecture on free thought—"preaching the Gospel of Humanity"—that he came to be known as "the Secular Pilgrim."[84] The Chicago Secular Society held their reception for him at their regular meeting place, a former church, now called The Forum. This "temple of humanity" was "ablaze with glory; flowers and flags decorated the rostrum and the stars and stripes waved triumphantly above a prostrate cross." When Putnam arrived, "[t]he splendid Secular Union choir opened the services with a 'Greeting Glee.'" Then followed a series of recitations and songs. At the "intermission" came welcome refreshments, including ice cream. In the evening, by request, Putnam delivered his lecture on "The Glory of Infidelity."[85]

---

[82] Ibid., 15–16. Adopting a Christian image, Abbot similarly declared: "I confess I am waiting, with such patience as I can command, for a new Pentecost—never mind the metaphor—a new Pentecost to arouse the American people to a larger and higher affirmation of their fundamental rights." Ibid., 60.

[83] E. C. Alphonse, Letter to Abbot (1875), in ibid., 17–18.

[84] George E. Light, "Personal Tribute," in *Union and Federation, Arguments for Religious Equality,* 95; McDonald, *Fifty Years of Freethought,* 516.

[85] *Freethought: A Liberal Journal,* 1 (no. 40): 484 (Oct. 6, 1888); McDonald, *Fifty Years of Freethought,* 459. In transforming a church into The Forum, these Liberals acted out a Lib-

In Oregon in the mid-1890s such religious activity would lead the American Secular Union to name it "the Banner state for Secularism." Formed in 1889 and incorporated in 1893, the Oregon Secular Union had for its objects "the realization of the Nine Demands of Liberalism and the organization of local churches and Sunday-schools." Foreseeing "the wreck of the Union if some effectual and permanent work were not done at once," Katie Kehm Smith organized the First Secular Church of Portland and, shortly thereafter, the Portland Secular Sunday School, other Sunday schools, and various churches—"all proving very successful." In Silverton the Oregon secularists established "Liberal University" and published a weekly secular paper, *The Torch of Reason*. By these means Liberals hoped to make secularism "an aggressive and effective enemy against that devilish trinity, superstition, ignorance, and hypocrisy, all under the one great godhead of Christianity."[86]

Even the atheists who associated with the Liberals recognized the religious yearnings of their adherents and therefore published in 1877 *The Truth Seeker Collection of Forms, Hymns, and Recitations*. It collected numerous hymns set to church music and prayers or invocations that each ended in an "Amen." The prayers included a "secular prayer" by Austin Holyoake and "A Prayer under Pressure," which began, "Oh, Lord, you know that I do not believe in you, as you are described in the Bible and believed in by the church." Most such prayers sought in different ways to "[d]isperse the clouds that darken our way and illumine the altar of our being with the flame of truth," although one—a "Prayer to the Devil" written in response to the Christian prayer of an opponent of free

---

eral ideal, as expressed in a Liberal toast of the 1870s: "May churches and chapels be converted into Temples of Reason and Secular institutions for the people." "Sentiments & Toasts," in *The Truth Seeker Collection of Forms, Hymns, and Recitations*, 116. Of course, many other Liberal meetings did not adopt a religious tenor. For example, when in 1890 the Washington Secular Union held its first convention, the speakers' end of the hall was hung with a mammoth oil painting that reproduced a *Truth Seeker* cartoon of "Uncle Sam and His Parasites," over which a red, white, and blue banner proclaimed "Keep Church and State Forever Separate." To the right was a banner: "Infidelity is Liberty—All Religion is Slavery." To the left, above a portrait of Paine: "To Do Good is My Religion." "Washington Secular Union," *Freethought: A Liberal Journal*, 3 (no. 8): 121 (Feb. 22, 1890).

[86] Pearl W. Geer, "Address," in *Union and Federation, Arguments for Religious Equality*, 19–22. The Congress of the American Secular Union and Freethought Federation resolved: "That we unreservedly commend the Secular churches and the Secular Sunday-schools of the state of Oregon, and urge all Liberals to establish such organizations everywhere." Ibid., 32.

thought—daringly invoked Lucifer himself: "O, Lucifer, bearer of light! O, Beelzebub, Lord of Scorpions! O, Beliel, Lord of the Opposite! . . . O, Devil, Prince of Demons in the Christian Hell!"[87] Recognizing the incongruity of a Liberal prayer book, the volume insisted that its recitations could be efficacious only in satisfying emotional needs:

> It is not to be supposed that invocations or prayers can possibly effect a change upon any mysterious, unknown being, above or outside of the Universe. Nor upon the Universe itself. But they may have a salutary influence upon the person who utters them sincerely and upon the audience who listens to them. They are calculated to produce a harmonious, reverential feeling and to induce a united, emotional spirit upon those in attendance. Many persons are in favor of them. For this reason a few forms are given.[88]

Even in separating themselves from religion, these Americans poignantly acknowledged the strength of their religious desires.

Political Failure

Liberals imagined that they would achieve their separation amendment by means of a Liberal political party. Yet while Liberals dreamed of entering politics on behalf of their secular, anti-Christian version of separation, the Republicans attracted vast numbers of Americans to their party by advocating the very different, Protestant, anti-Catholic version of separation. Nothing better reveals the futility of the Liberals' hopes than the political success of those whose conventional, Protestant conception of separation left the Liberals so disappointed.

In 1876, at the height of their prominence, the Liberals optimistically hoped to influence the two main political parties and then run their own presidential campaign. They recognized that they were not "strong enough yet" to "nominate our candidate for the Presidency" and therefore resolved to have their directors "ascertain, if possible, by direct inquiry, whether the Presidential candidates of the Republican and Democratic parties are in favor of strictly secular government and of the special

---

[87] *The Truth Seeker Collection of Forms, Hymns, and Recitations,* 28, 41, 24, 45. This hymnal was published for all classes of "liberalists," including both Materialists and Spiritualists, and it therefore included different types of hymns and recitations in the hope that it might thereby satisfy the various types of Liberals. Ibid., 7.
[88] Ibid., 23.

measures we advocate."[89] Unfortunately for the Liberals, however, these parties took more interest in separation as a nativist slogan than as a systematic policy.

Shortly after the Liberals began to organize their national movement for a separation amendment, President Ulysses S. Grant made separation part of the Republicans' agenda. Prior to the Civil War, Grant had briefly been a member of the Know Nothings. Two decades later, on September 30, 1875, he astutely relied on some of his old nativist ideas when speaking in Des Moines to a reunion of the Army of the Tennessee. Aiming to rally his troops for the coming election, he warned them of the danger of a second civil war:

> If we are to have another contest in the near future of our national existence, I predict that the dividing line will not be Mason and Dixon's, but it will be between patriotism and intelligence on one side, and superstition, ambition and ignorance on the other. In this centennial year, the work of strengthening the foundation of the structure laid by our forefathers one hundred years ago, should be begun. Let us all labor for the security of free thought, free speech, free press, and pure morals, unfettered religious sentiments, and equal rights and privileges for all men, irrespective of nationality, color or religion. Encourage free schools, and resolve that not one dollar appropriated to them shall be applied to the support of any sectarian school. Resolve that neither the State or nation, nor both combined, shall support institutions of learning other than those sufficient to afford every child in the land the opportunity of a good common school education, unmixed with atheistic, pagan, or sectarian tenets. Leave the matter of religion to the family altar, the church, and the private school, supported entirely by private contribution. Keep the Church and State forever separate.[90]

Newspaper editorials across the nation thrilled to this patriotic theme, and Grant therefore returned to it on December 7, 1875, in his annual message to Congress. Blending Republican ideas about federal protection and nativist concepts of "American" liberty, Grant urged the House and the Senate to adopt a constitutional amendment separating church from state—particularly, the Catholic Church from the American states. The

---

[89] *Report of the Centennial Congress of Liberals,* 73, 118.
[90] *American State Papers Bearing on Sunday Legislation,* 203–204 (New York: National Religious Liberty Association, 1891) (editorial italics deleted). For a dispute as to Grant's phrasing, see ibid., 204, note 1.

amendment, he said, should require states to provide public schools, and it should prevent states from giving public funds to any schools that taught "sectarian tenets," lest Americans "sink into acquiescence to the will of intelligence, whether directed by the demagogue or by priest-craft." Grant proposed that the amendment should make education compulsory so far as to "deprive all persons who cannot read and write from becoming voters," and he hoped it would tax "all property equally, whether church or corporation, exempting only the last resting-places of the dead, and possibly, with proper restrictions, church edifices." Most broadly, Grant thought the amendment should "[d]eclare Church and State forever separate and distinct, but each free within its proper sphere."[91]

The proposed amendment's intrusion into traditional state powers provoked astonishment among such Americans as were not utterly blinded by anti-Catholicism. For example, the Presbyterian Samuel Spear wrote that Grant's church property amendment "would be very appropriate in a Governor's message, addressed to a State Legislature; but we do not see that Congress has any thing to do with the question."[92] Similarly, G. H. Andrews—an official of the New York City tax office— observed that the exemption of churches from state property taxes had previously been "a matter for State or municipal control," adding with dry humor: "It is something quite new for the General Government to express solicitude because property of any kind is not subjected to mu-nicipal or State taxation." Indeed, most church property (other than houses of public worship and school houses) was already taxed in New York, if not in most states, which left Andrews to ask, with his usual understatement, why Grant bothered to propose a federal amendment on the subject.[93] In various ways, Grant's amendment was both intrusive and unnecessary, and it never became a reality.

Nonetheless, the amendment served a purpose. Grant himself re-vealed that it was designed to rouse the prejudices of a majority, for,

[91] *Congressional Record*, 4(1): 175, 181 (Sen., Dec. 7, 1875).
[92] Spear, *Religion and the State*, 20.
[93] G. H. Andrews, "Should Church Property Be Taxed?" Letter No. 1, *New York Times*, 4 (Dec. 30, 1875); ibid., Letter No. 10, in ibid., 4 (Jan. 17, 1876). Incidentally, Andrews's twelve essays (which appeared in the *New York Times* between December 30, 1875 and January 24, 1876) constitute one of the more sophisticated and discerning early accounts of the exemption of churches from taxation. For related essays, see "A Protestant" (Jan. 8, 1876), in ibid., 6 (Jan. 9, 1876); "Churches and Taxes" in ibid., 4 (Jan. 28, 1876).

when suggesting the taxation of church property, he recited an exaggerated list of such property in the United States and then hinted to Catholics that they should submit quietly, unless they desired a worse fate: "The contemplation of so vast a property as here alluded to, without taxation, may lead to sequestration without constitutional authority and through blood." Grant used this standard anti-Catholic threat, couched in the usual solicitude, to stir the basest passions of his fellow Americans. Not surprisingly, the part of the president's message that "excited the most attention" was "that which relates to education and the church property."[94]

A week after Grant proposed the various components of his separation amendment, Congressman James G. Blaine pursued the most popular of them by introducing his constitutional amendment against public school funds coming "under the control of any religious sect." Since the 1840s some states had adopted various constitutional prohibitions on the distribution of benefits to sectarian-controlled schools, and in 1871 the U.S. Senate had considered constitutional amendments on the subject.[95] During the fall of 1875, as Blaine contemplated his chances for the presidency, he waited for an opportune time to introduce a school amendment, and in December 1875, after Grant had popularized the idea, Blaine supplied a concrete proposal.[96] His nomination in the Republican National Convention of June 1876 was delivered by the most famous of the Liberals, the eloquent atheist, Robert G. Ingersoll, who departed from the purified secularism of the National Liberal League to support Blaine and his amendment. Ingersoll told his fellow Republicans that "[t]hey demand a man who believes in the eternal separation and divorcement of church and school," and "[t]hat man is James G. Blaine."[97] Although the Republicans selected Rutherford B. Hayes as their candidate, they adopted a platform that supported Blaine's amendment.[98] Of course, commentators understood that "this issue will unite

[94] "Education and Church Property," *Boston Investigator*, 5 (Jan. 5, 1876) (quoting *Harper's Weekly*).

[95] See note 28 above.

[96] Marie Carolyn Kinkhamer, "The Blaine Amendment of 1875: Private Motives for Political Action," *Catholic Historical Review*, 42: 24 (1956–1957).

[97] *Proceedings of the Republican National Convention, Held at Cincinnati, Ohio*, 74 (Concord: 1876).

[98] Republican Platform (1876), in Thomas Hudson McKee, *The National Conventions and Platforms of All Political Parties . . . 1789 to 1900*, 171 (Baltimore: 1900).

the whole Liberal element in this country with the anti-Catholic element, and these two elements form a vast majority all over the land."[99] Less charitably, it may be suspected that the Republicans hoped to transcend sectional divisions by embracing sectarian strife—a strategy that would unite not only liberal and nativist sentiment but also North and South in a campaign against Catholicism.[100] As the election approached, Blaine's proposal passed in the House by 180 to 7, but in the Senate it fell two votes short of the two-thirds required for a constitutional amendment.[101] The Republicans failed to obtain a constitutional amend-

[99] "Church Politics" (from *The Israelite*), in *Boston Investigator*, 5 (Dec. 29, 1875). The *Index* explained: "For 'sectarian' (quoting from the platform), read 'Catholic,' and you have the full meaning of that ambiguous seventh plank, which is worded as to catch, if possible, the Evangelical and the Liberal votes at the same time." *Index*, 426 (Sept. 7, 1878), as quoted by Green, "The National Reform Association," 94.

[100] One senator said of the Blaine amendment, "the object was to remove the fear which had been raised as a bugaboo throughout the country for political purposes." Senator Eli Saulsbury, in *Congressional Record*, 4(6): 5246 (Sen., Aug. 7, 1876). In this, the Republicans followed the example of some earlier nativists. See, e.g., *Principles and Objects of the American Party*, 9 (New York: 1855). Unlike many of his supporters, Blaine apparently had no desire that his amendment should be adopted in the Constitution. He had Catholic family ties and may have acted in part to allay suspicions that he harbored Catholicising sympathies. Kinkhamer, "The Blaine Amendment of 1875." As months passed while Blaine allowed his proposal to languish in committee, the *Nation* observed that Blaine meant "not to pass" his amendment "but to use it in the campaign to catch anti-Catholic votes." Green, "The National Reform Association," 94. Indeed, when the amendment finally came to a vote, he did not even attend.

[101] For the process by which the proposal was weighed down with amendments, see Green, "The National Reform Association," 113–128. Echoing the National Liberal League's amendment and especially Blaine's, nativist Protestants made their own proposals. For example, in February 1876, at the annual dinner of the Veteran Association of the United Order of Americans in New York, Daniel Ullmann—the former nativist politician—suggested two amendments to the U.S. Constitution:

> 1. No State shall make any law respecting an establishment of religion, or prohibiting the free exercise thereof; and no money raised, or property acquired by taxation in any State for the support of public schools, or derived from any public fund therefor, shall ever be under the control of any religious sect; nor shall any money so raised, or property so acquired, ever be given or loaned to any religious sect or denomination.
> 2. "The United States shall guarantee to every State in this Union, a republican form of government," AND AN ADEQUATE SYSTEM OF FREE AND UNIVERSAL UNSECTARIAN EDUCATION.

Amendments to the Constitution of the United States. Non-Sectarian and Universal Education, 11–12. For a similar, later proposal by the Junior Order of United American Mechanics, see M. D. Lichliter, *History of the Junior Order United American Mechanics of the United States of North America*, 241 (Philadelphia: J. B. Lippincott Co., 1908). See also, for example, the

ment, but they elicited support by raising "American" issues, such as separation, church property, and school funding.[102]

Other parties soon competed for the separation vote. The Democrats declared their "faith in the total separation of church and state, for the sake alike of civil and religious freedom," although, at the same time, they protested that Republicans had created "a false issue with which they would enkindle sectarian strife in respect to the public schools."[103] Even the Prohibition Party attempted to sound as if it supported separation, declaring itself for "[t]he separation of the government in all its departments and institutions, including the public schools and all funds for their maintenance, from the control of every religious sect or other association, and the protection alike of all sects by equal laws, with entire freedom of religious faith and worship." This separation of government and sect, which carefully accommodated the Prohibition Party's theological objections to a separation of church and state, reveals how even a party opposed to separation felt obliged to seem as if it supported this principle.[104]

---

proposal of the Minute Men, "The Amendment to Prohibit Sectarian Appropriations," *Guardian of Liberty*, 1 (no. 3): 24 (March–April 1913), and the "Sisson Constitutional Amendment," in ibid., 3 (no. 28): 524 (July 1916). The National Reform Association also continued to urge an expressly Christian version of the Blaine amendment. For example, see S.R. 86, 50th Congress, 1st Session, and the discussion of it in *The National Sunday Law. Argument of Alonzo T. Jones before the United States Committee on Education and Labor Dec. 13, 1888*, 96–97 (Sentinel Library, No. 18, Sept. 15, 1889).

[102] Separation remained a part of Republican campaigns. See, e.g., *Letters of Acceptance of Hon. J. A. Garfield and Gen. C. A. Arthur, and the Platform Adopted by the Republican National Convention* (ca. 1880). Revealingly, in 1892 the Republican platform explained that it supported religious liberty "but" opposed a union of church and state: "The ultimate reliance of free popular government is the intelligence of the people and the maintenance of freedom among all men. We therefore declare anew our devotion to liberty of thought and conscience, of speech and press, and approve all agencies and instrumentalities which contribute to the education of the children of the land; but while insisting upon the fullest measure of religious liberty, we are opposed to any union of church and state." Republican Platform (1892), in McKee, *National Conventions and Platforms*, 272.

[103] Democratic Platform (June 28, 1876), in ibid., 163, 166. See also Green, "The National Reform Association," 109. State conventions also voiced their opinions. For some details, see Samuel W. Barnum, *Romanism As It Is*, 784 (Hartford: 1882).

[104] Prohibition Platform (1876), in McKee, *National Conventions and Platforms*, 176–177. This platform also supported "[t]he national observance of the Christian Sabbath, established by laws prohibiting ordinary labor and business" and "[t]he free use of the Bible . . . in our public schools." Ibid. For a less artful effort by a temperance organization to adopt and simultaneously qualify the principle of separation, see *Centennial Temperance Volume. A Memorial of the International Temperance Conference, Held in Philadelphia, June, 1876*, 320–321 (New York: National Temperance Society & Publication House, 1877).

Against the Utah Territory's toleration of polygamous relations, many Americans in-

Some Liberals understood that the Democrats and Republicans did not take their secular separation seriously—that "both political parties are coquetting with us." As Dr. Mary Pratt bluntly observed, they supported only a complacent Protestant version of separation: "Both the Republican and Democratic parties profess to be in favor of the separation of Church and State. If the question is put to these candidates individually as to what is meant by the separation of Church and State, I think you will find them declaring that the matter is all right as it stands now. Some of them are undoubtedly too stupid to understand that Church and State are not separated now."[105] Separation was becoming a focus of presidential politics, but the American people and their parties neither desired nor even comprehended the full extent of what separation implied. Accordingly, in 1877 the National Liberal League declared its formation of a presidential ticket for the 1880 election with the much beloved atheist, Robert G. Ingersoll, for president and Abbot for vice president.[106] Their platform declared: "TOTAL SEPARATION OF CHURCH AND STATE, to be guaranteed by amendment of the United States Constitution: including the equitable taxation of church property, secularization of the public schools, abrogation of Sabbatarian laws, abolition of chaplaincies, prohibition of public appropriations for religious purposes and all other measures necessary to the same general end."[107] In 1879 in

---

sisted upon a separation of church and state, and, in this way, the Mormons gave extra respectability to the parties' advocacy of separation. Mormons insisted that they conformed to this American ideal, but other Americans were skeptical. "While professing a complete divorce of church and state, their political character and administration is made subservient to the theocratical or religious element." J. W. Gunnison, *The Mormons, or Latter-Day Saints, In the Valley of the Great Salt Lake; A History of Their Rise and Progress, Peculiar Doctrines, Present Condition, and Prospects Derived from Personal Observation; During a Residence among Them,* 23 (Philadelphia: Lippincott, 1860). In 1878, as already noted, Chief Justice Waite, in *Reynolds v. United States,* employed Jefferson's phrase about separation in dicta in his opinion upholding a Mormon's conviction for polygamy. 98 U.S. 145, 164 (1878). Similarly, the Republicans adopted a platform in 1888 that pledged support for "appropriate legislation asserting the sovereignty of the nation in all territories where the same is questioned, and in furtherance of that end to place upon the statute-books legislation stringent enough to divorce the political from the ecclesiastical power, and thus stamp out the attendant wickedness of polygamy." Republican Platform (1888), in McKee, *National Conventions and Platforms,* 242. In 1895 the Utah Constitution declared "there shall be no union of church and state." Utah Const. of 1895, Art. I, §4.

[105] *Report of the Centennial Congress of Liberals,* 123.

[106] The ticket collapsed almost immediately, as Ingersoll was absent and Abbot backed out. Ahlstrom, "Francis Ellingwood Abbot," 2: 216.

[107] National Liberal League, "Platform for the Presidential Election of 1880 Adopted at Rochester, N.Y., Oct. 26 1877," *Index* 9: 1 (Sept. 19, 1878).

Cincinnati Liberals organized a National Liberal Party. Yet by that date they lacked even such political strength as they once had, and their party did "[l]ittle or nothing" during the 1880 election.[108] Although the Republicans could gain votes by seeking a Protestant, anti-Catholic separation, the Liberals, who demanded a secular anti-Christian separation, had little hope of prevailing in national party politics.

Obscenity and Collapse

Nothing did more to finish off the political ambitions and even the existence of the National Liberal League than its internal quarrels over obscenity. These disputes completed the destruction of the movement for a separation amendment.[109]

For Liberals the "hardest obstacle to overcome" was "the popular belief that the Church party alone stands for *morality*."[110] Worried about Protestants who vilified the Liberals as the "party of license," Abbot sought "to make it known that, at least in our own estimation, we are proposing to do nothing which shall not conduce to the genuine morality of all human life." It was especially important that "those in the churches who believe in the fundamental principles of this movement, and are yet not inclined to go with the radicals to the extent of their radical opinions, should be left in no uncertainty as to our moral purposes."[111] Abbot emphasized the morality of his secular movement because the connection between religion and morality was at the heart of the matter. One of Abbot's staunchest allies, B. F. Underwood, explained:

> Here we have the real difference reduced to its last terms between many of those who would Christianize and those who would secularize the government. Both parties hold to the importance of good morals. But one believes there can be no true morality except in connection with Christianity; while the other maintains that morality is natural and secu-

---

[108] McDonald, *Fifty Years of Freethought,* 281. See also the comments of Thomas Curtis at ibid., 317.

[109] Underlying the failure of the Liberals was also their distance from popular religious behavior, culture, and sentiments. Unlike the English secularist movement, which was thoroughly working class, the Liberal movement included numerous men and women from America's educated and wealthy elites.

[110] *Report of the Centennial Congress of Liberals,* 74.

[111] Ibid., 45–46.

lar, and does not depend for its existence, or for the practice of its precepts, upon any religion whatever.

As in the election of 1800, separation was part of a dispute about the necessity of religion, particularly Christianity, as the foundation of morality and government. "Thus is involved in this contest the true nature and the real basis of morality, without an understanding of which there can hardly be an intelligent appreciation of the merits of the controversy."[112]

The moral issue on which Liberals felt most vulnerable was obscenity. Rejecting religious orthodoxy of any sort, but animated by strong feelings that often seemed religious, Liberals had refocused these passions into free religious inquiry. Abbot turned to a scientific theism; Robert Ingersoll to freethought; Damon Kilgore to spiritualism. Steven Pearl Andrews concocted his own faith of Universology.[113] De Robique Mortimer Bennett moved restlessly from one mode of religious expression to another, including Shakerism, Spiritualism, and freethought, but re-

[112] Ibid., 104. In describing his individualistic moral and sociological views, Abbot found a kindred spirit in Herbert Spencer. Ibid., 58. Indeed, at a later date, in discussing conflicting claims of conscience, he explained that "there is no possible solution save through the laws of 'natural selection' and 'survival of the fittest.' Let that conscience triumph which shall prove itself to be most thoroughly conscientious—most enlightened, most just, and most powerful." "The Catholic Conscience and the Natural Conscience" (from the *Index,* Dec. 25, 1879), in W. Creighton Peden and Everett J. Tarbox, Jr., eds., *The Collected Essays of Francis Ellingwood Abbot,* 1: 146 (Lewiston: Edwin Mellen Press, 1996).

[113] Andrews sought "by positive discovery, *an absolute science of universal things,* or, in a word, Universology." Not entirely without reason, many of Andrews's fellow "Positivistic" Liberals feared that he had reduced scientific religion to gibberish. For example, he held that his life was "devoted to the exposition, promulgation, and practical institution of Universology, Alwato, and the Pantarchy." According to Andrews, "Universology is the intellectual recognition, in their profundities, exactitudes, and entirety, of Individuality, Unity, and Univariety, in their widest application to the Universe at large; and, thence, specifically, within the social sphere. Alwato is the correspondingly accurate discovery and use of the true technique or lingual expression of all universological ideas; the future vernacular of the planet. Pantarchy is the correspondingly accurate adjustment of Humanity and its conditions at large." He gave this explanation in the hope that he could "clear the way for the better understanding of Universology by those gentlemen of the Positivistic school who have always scrutinizingly scrutinized me, from the suspicion that I was engaged in 'scrutinizing the inscrutable.'" Interestingly, he adopted the Catholic Church as a metaphor for his ambitions: "New Catholic Church means simply the Universal Church of the Future, which, recognizing *the essential rightfulness* and *indispensable need* of *infinite Individuality,* or Variety as well as of Unity, shall devote itself to the rallying, sympathetically, or heartwise, of all the energies of mankind *to the practical sustentation of the University-State.*" Stephen Pearl Andrews, "The New Civilization," in *The Truth Seeker Annual and Freethinkers' Almanac,* 93, 96 (New York: Truth Seeker, 1885).

mained consistent, as did many of his fellow Liberals, in a sense of unsatisfied desires.[114] Such yearnings for a better world and a communion with something larger than the self had once found expression in the conventions of local Christian worship. Increasingly, however, many Americans, including many Liberals, pursued such feelings in various other ways—scientific and supernatural, abstemious and indulgent—and one such avenue for these feelings seems to have been sex or, at least, the free discussion of it.

The question of obscenity had already arisen at the 1876 Congress of Liberal Leagues, where many atheistical Liberals demanded that the National Liberal League take a stand against the laws prohibiting obscenity, particularly the notorious Comstock Laws, which forbade the distribution of obscene materials through the U.S. mails. These atheists and the more traditional theists in the National Liberal League avoided a conflict over the Comstock Laws by agreeing that, although obscenity should be prosecuted, it should be punishable only under such laws as clearly defined the offence:

> That this League, while it recognizes the great importance and the absolute necessity of guarding by proper legislation against obscene and indecent publications, . . . disapproves and protests against all laws which, by reason of indefiniteness or ambiguity, shall permit the prosecution and punishment of honest and conscientious men for presenting to the public what they deem essential to the public welfare, when the views thus presented do not violate in thought or language the acknowledged rules of decency; and that we demand that all laws against obscenity and indecency shall be so clear and explicit that none but actual offenders against the recognized principles of purity shall be liable to suffer therefrom.

Long before the Supreme Court addressed such matters, the Liberals condemned the laws that, by their "indefiniteness or ambiguity," threatened with prosecution persons who were not "actual offenders."[115]

Yet, as Liberals and their friends increasingly faced arrest and prison

---

[114] As a fellow freethinker observed: "All idealisms not included in the Christian scheme might hope for Bennett's allegiance." McDonald, *Fifty Years of Freethought*, 173.

[115] *Report of the Centennial Congress of Liberals*, 170. For the further development of such ideas, see Theodore Schroeder, *"Due Process of Law" in Relation to Statutory Uncertainty and Constructive Offenses* (New York: Free Speech League, 1908); David M. Rabban, *Free Speech in Its Forgotten Years*, 38, 139–141 (Cambridge: Cambridge University Press, 1997).

for medical, moral, and other high-minded sexual publications, Abbot and those who preeminently desired a separation of church and state feared that this common objective would be sacrificed to the "side-issue" of obscenity. For Abbot and his theist allies, obscenity was both morally repugnant and a distraction from separation. In contrast, for many atheists among the Liberals, sexual freedom seemed of almost religious importance, and increasingly, therefore, these atheists sought freedom of sexual discussion. They were outraged by the arrest of Ezra Heywood in 1877 for his free-love pamphlet, *Cupid's Yokes,* and especially by the arrest in the following year of a Liberal leader, D. M. Bennett, who mailed copies precisely in order to challenge the Comstock Laws.[116] As the atheists organized to oppose the obscenity laws, Abbot worried about the League's reputation for morality—a reputation that he and other theists had so assiduously cultivated, both from personal conviction and from a lucid understanding of the political realities. As one of the atheists later observed, Abbot and his fellow theists were "frightened," and they "hunted cover when their Liberal associate, Bennett, was accused."[117] Of course, Abbot continued to defend Heywood and the serious discussion of any topic, but he opposed the use of the National Liberal League to defend those accused of obscenity, lest this disreputable association jeopardize the movement for the separation of church and state.

Accordingly, the National Liberal League fell apart. At its Second Annual Congress, held in Syracuse in October 1878, the atheists seized control of the League to ensure that it would seek the repeal of Comstock's obscenity laws. Therefore, in the same town where, a dozen years earlier, Abbot had left the Unitarians, he once again walked away in protest.[118] Together with Judge Hurlbut, Abbot and the other theists left

[116] For further details, see ibid., 32–38; G. W. Morehouse, "What Is Liberalism?" (December 1879), in *Truth Seeker,* 178 (March 20, 1880). According to Ahlstrom, Bennett also was arrested in 1877 for writing an "Open Letter to Jesus Christ" and an essay on the reproductive habits of marsupials. Ahlstrom, "Francis Ellingwood Abbot," 2: 225–227.

[117] McDonald, *Fifty Years of Freethought,* 284. McDonald complained of Abbot that the ground he had taken for his Nine Demands and separation "was his limit. The state might be separated from the church but not from Comstockery." Ibid., 231. See also Persons, *Free Religion,* 123; Ahlstrom, "Francis Ellingwood Abbot," 2: 226.

[118] Abbot was well aware of the parallel, writing in his diary entry for Oct. 26, 1878, "The second 'Battle of Syracuse.'" Harvard University Archives, HUG 1101.3 (Box 1), Diaries of F. E. Abbot. Upon arriving at Syracuse, Abbot took precautions: "I strictly forbade the janitor to permit any sale of books, pamphlets, papers &c., on the premises, for I suspected Bennett & allies would sell *Cupid's Yokes* if permitted to, and disgrace the N.L.L. by getting

the Congress of the National Liberal League and reassembled nearby, in the Syracuse House Parlors, where they reorganized as the National Liberal League *of America,* retaining much of the original constitution and officers.[119] Not only did this new version of the National Liberal League quickly fall into desuetude, but the old League suffered yet further "centrifugalism."[120] At the 1880 Congress of the original National Liberal League, held in Chicago, another group of dissenters, led by Ingersoll, departed over the obscenity issue. As Ingersoll told the 1880 Congress:

> This obscene law business is a stumbling-block. Had it not been for this, instead of a few people voting here—less than one hundred—we should have had a congress numbered by thousands. Had it not been for this business, the Liberal League of the United States would tonight hold in its hand the political destiny of the United States. Instead of that we have thrown away our power upon a question in which we are not interested.[121]

The Liberals had destroyed their cause of separation over the issue of obscenity.

Four years later, the National Liberal League split further between Spiritualists and Freethinkers, leading the Freethinkers in 1885 to rename the organization the American Secular Union.[122] In their pursuit

---

arrested. Lucky I did this, as it turned out." Harvard University Archives, HUG 1101.3 (Box 1), Diaries of F. E. Abbot (Oct. 25, 1878). Abbot's precautions, however, were not enough to prevent the division of the League. Rabban, *Free Speech in Its Forgotten Years,* 38.

[119] "The Syracuse Congress," *Index,* 9: 534 (Nov. 7, 1878).

[120] *Report of the Centennial Congress of Liberals,* 17. In 1879 Abbot and the others who had departed attempted to distance even the name of their new League from the old by calling it the "American Liberal Union." Its existence, however, soon became a mere formality. Ahlstrom, "Francis Ellingwood Abbot," 2: 242.

[121] McDonald, *Fifty Years of Freethought,* 282. As late as August 1879, Ingersoll had been confident in the Liberals, writing that they should not worry about those who still wanted their organization to agitate on obscenity: "I am delighted to hear that the Free Lovers are against us. I want nothing to do with them. Let them spend their time examining each other's sexual organs and letting ours alone." Letter of Robert G. Ingersoll to Thaddeus Burr Wakefield (Aug. 15, 1879), in Frank Smith, *Robert G. Ingersoll: A Life,* 166 (Buffalo: Prometheus Books, 1990).

[122] The renaming process was completed at the next year's Congress in Cleveland. McDonald, *Fifty Years of Freethought,* 362, 386, 390. See also *The American Secular Union,* 4 (Philadelphia: n.p., n.d.). Another splinter group was the Freethinkers' Association, which was formed in 1878 but which still supported the National Liberal League's pursuit of separation. The objects of the Freethinkers' Association were "*First.* To stimulate free thought and investigation among the people in relation to their civil, religious, and political rights, and encourage the investigation of questions relating to religion, science, and reform, and to that end sustain Freethought speakers, hold Liberal meetings, and circulate Liberal,

of what Sidney Ahlstrom has called "a form of extra-ecclesiastical mysticism," the Spiritualists had actively supported separation and the National Liberal League. Eventually, however, the Spiritualists and the Freethinkers quarreled, and the Freethinkers formed the American Secular Union to pursue the secularist goal of separation without the distraction of other issues.[123] The Union continued to emphasize a version of Abbot's "Demands of Liberalism"—now the "Nine Demands of Secularism"—and it still sought "to secure the total separation of church and state."[124] Indeed, the Union boasted that it "alone, among Liberal societies, welcomes to its ranks all who work for total separation of Church and State, whatever additional principles they may uphold."[125]

Yet the various types of Liberals who remained in the American Secular Union increasingly went their own ways. The dispute over obscenity had shattered not only the National Liberal League but also the moral reputation and national political strength of the Liberal cause.[126] Even after shedding the rubric of "Liberal" in favor of "secular," the group had been unable to restore its political strength.[127] No longer with

---

scientific, and reform papers and periodicals." Also: "*Second.* To act as an auxiliary of the National Liberal League in its efforts to accomplish the total separation of Church and State, and to organize Local Liberal Leagues in the State in accordance with the provisions of the Constitution of the National Liberal League." *The Proceedings and Addresses at the Freethinkers' Convention Held at Watkins, N.Y., August 22d, 23d, 24th, and 25th, '78*, 5–6 (New York: D. M. Bennett, Liberal Publisher, 1878).

[123] The words are Ahlstrom's. "Francis Ellingwood Abbot," 2: 157A, 199–200.

[124] *Freethought: A Liberal Journal*, 2 (no. 46): 632 (Nov. 16, 1889). This was article two, which did not change in the 1889 amendments. Ibid., 2 (no. 48): 761 (Nov. 30, 1889).

[125] *The American Secular Union*, 5. Robert Ingersoll explained: "Each issue must have its own organization. Differentiation is the law of civilization, and the law of reform. Reform may be essentially one, but it has many instrumentalities. The American Secular Union is one of these. It is not a general association, a congress for all subjects. . . . The individual, of course, is interested in a thousand other things, for life is far broader and deeper than politics, but an organization is not a combination of individuals for the expression of all their individual desires, but a combination for a particular purpose." R. G. Ingersoll, "The Congress," *Freethought: A Liberal Journal*, 2 (no. 42): 510 (San Francisco: Oct. 20, 1888).

[126] The reputation that Abbot feared was not easily escaped. A decade later Comstock wrote that "the only sect or class that, as a sect or class, have attempted to repeal the law against the transmission of obscene matter by mail is the 'Infidel' and so called 'Liberal,' as represented by the former 'National Liberal League.'" Anthony Comstock, "Lawlessness of the Liberal Leagues," *Our Day*, 1 (no. 5): 393–394 (1888).

[127] Seeking to establish their position with a simple metaphor, the Union toyed for a while with a most unlikely symbol, a flower—an approach that suggests the degree to which they had lost touch with popular American politics: "There is, however, need of a badge which shall express at first glance, without complexity of detail, that basic principle of *freedom of thought* for which Liberals of all isms are contending. This need seems to have

much hope of immediate political power, Freethinkers sought comfort in their beliefs. "Let us place ourselves in a niche of the temple of Free-thought, guarding it against the invasion of the armies of theological bigotry; and, if we perish in the work, we shall die in the noble act of duty. Even if the laurels of victory never adorn our age, we despair not, believing as we do that the day of triumph will surely come."[128] Of course, their retreat to "a niche in the temple of Freethought" only made more certain that they would not win the "the laurels of victory." With-out expectations of worldly political success, many Freethinkers felt free to insist on a purity of membership and sought to exclude Spiritualists, Unitarians, and Jews because of their distinctive religious affiliations. Thus, like the National Liberal League, the American Secular Union col-lapsed. Although during the mid-1880s Liberal newspapers and organi-zations continued to demand a constitutional amendment ensuring sep-aration of church and state, the heady days of 1876, when an amendment seemed a real possibility, were long past.

---

been met by the Freethinkers of France, Belgium, Spain and Sweden, who have adopted the *pansy* as their badge (French *pensée,* meaning *thought*). We join with them in recom-mending this flower as a simple and inexpensive badge of Freethought. . . . Let every patriot who is a Freethinker in this sense, adopt the pansy as his badge, to be worn at all times, as a silent and unobtrusive testimony of his principles. In this way we shall recognize our brethren in the cause, and the enthusiasm will spread; until, before long, the uplifted standard of the pansy, beneath the sheltering folds of the United States flag, shall every-where thrill men's hearts as the symbol of religious liberty and freedom of conscience." *American Secular Union,* 7.

[128] Charles Watts, *The American Secular Union: Its Necessity and the Justice of Its Demands,* 31–32 (New York: n.p., n.d.).

12

Interpretation

AFTER the failure of the Liberal and Protestant proposals for a constitutional amendment, advocates of separation focused on constitutional interpretation. They quickly forgot about arguments that an amendment was necessary and claimed instead that American constitutions had already, since their inception, fully guaranteed a separation of church and state. In taking this new perspective, some Americans acted quite deliberately. Most, however, seem to have responded much less self-consciously, perceiving their constitution in accord with their hopes and wishful expectations.

Abandoning Aspirations for an Amendment to the U.S. Constitution

Both Liberals and nativist Protestants abandoned their hopes for a federal constitutional amendment on separation. With different conceptions of their shared ideal, they had to temper their ambitions in different ways, but both groups had to adjust their goals, typically seeking only some of the implications of separation and attempting to do so by means less sweeping than an amendment to the U.S. Constitution. The Liberals responded to the failure of their political campaigns and their unpopularity by shifting their tactics in the 1880s to seek a gradual, piecemeal influence on American culture and legislation. Nativist Protestants also failed to obtain a federal constitutional amendment but, because of the strength of anti-Catholic feeling, managed to secure local versions of the Blaine amendment in a vast majority of the states. Obliged to reduce their ambitions for federal amendments to these incomplete local measures, both Liberals and nativist Protestants had reason to give greater emphasis to constitutional interpretation.

In the mid-1880s Liberals redefined their mission in broadly legislative and cultural terms. Already in the 1870s, when organizing on behalf of a constitutional amendment, Liberals had sought to influence opinion and legislation—although this was not yet their main goal. For example, between 1873 and 1875 the *Index* and the Boston Liberal League petitioned against the Massachusetts tax exemption for churches and private educational institutions.[1] In the middle of the next decade, however, Liberals began to devote their energies to local agitation. Most dramatically, the American Secular Union successfully joined with the *Truth Seeker* to demand that New York City keep its museums in Central Park open on Sundays. No less significantly, the Union and the Freethought Federation agitated in numerous communities across the nation, using meetings and circular letters against Sunday laws and against the use of the Bible in public schools.[2] By focusing on these and other

---

[1] Sydney E. Ahlstrom, "Francis Ellingwood Abbot: His Education and Active Career," 2: 200–203 (Ph.D. diss., Harvard University, 1951). According to Steven Pearl Andrews— the Liberal adherent of "Universology"—he and a group of other Liberals met with President Grant in 1875 to present him with a statement against the exemption of churches from taxation, an idea Grant included in his proposals for a constitutional amendment. George E. McDonald, *Fifty Years of Freethought Being the Story of* The Truth Seeker, 181– 182 (New York: The Truth Seeker Co., 1929). Of course, Liberals were not alone in seeking such a measure. In 1874, for example, James Garfield declared: "The divorce between the church and the state ought to be absolute. It ought to be so absolute that no church property anywhere in any State or in the nation should be exempted from equal taxation; for if you exempt the property of any church organization, to that extent you impose a tax upon the whole community." *Congressional Record,* 2(6): 5384 (H.R., June 22, 1874).

Like many nativists, Liberals tended to believe that without taxation of church property, churches would become so powerful as to threaten civil government. Indeed, a Boston Liberal League pamphlet quoted a twenty-year-old letter from Mortimer De Motte to Erastus Brooks—the New York senator who helped to lead the nativist assault on Catholic church property. "The rapid and constant accumulation of property by the prelates of the Romish Church, to descend and be added to by them in perpetual succession, would, in the first place, carry into operation the principle of entailment, wisely forbidden by our national Constitution, and, in the next place, would in time concentrate in them an amount of property and power which would render them formidable adversaries to cope with." *No. 1: An Appeal for Equal Taxation and No Exemption,* 3 (Boston: Boston Liberal League, n.d.) (copy in Harvard University Archives, HUG 1101.74). Incidentally, the same pamphlet also argued that taxation was necessary because wealthy churches would "block up the pathway of all religious progress." Ibid., 3.

[2] McDonald, *Fifty Years of Freethought,* 394. For a richly detailed account, see *Union and Federation, Arguments for Religious Equality, Compiled from Addresses Delivered at the Congress of the American Secular Union and Freethought Federation, Memorial Volume to Samuel P. Putnam and May L. Collins,* 19, 28, 73–74 (Chicago: 1896).

very practical goals that they derived from separation, and by seeking local, legislative, and administrative remedies, these successors to the National Liberal League achieved at least some successes.

At the very beginning of the 1880s, one of Francis E. Abbot's fellow theists, William Potter, adumbrated the change in approach. In particular, he urged Liberals to abandon their battle for a Liberal political party devoted to obtaining an amendment, and he proposed that, instead, they seek gradually to attain cultural influence over legislation. Since 1877 many Liberals had anticipated "the organization of the League as a distinct political party." Potter, however, was "decidedly opposed to turning the Leagues into a political organization." The time for "political action" had not yet come in 1877, and now in 1880 "it is even further off than three years ago." As things stood, the League "does not deal with questions that can be most effectively advanced by a separate political organization." Indeed, Potter felt "it would seem better for the liberal cause if all the national organizations for Liberal League work should, at least temporarily disappear, and the local Leagues, under changed names, should reorganize for active enterprises of local benefit." The Liberals could best achieve "the complete secularization of the State" by attempting to persuade all parties to support separation and by avoiding identification with any particular political organization or rubric, especially their own. "For the present, and for a good while to come, wise and wide discussion of its questions is needed in order to form the public opinion which in any event will be necessary worthily to sustain a political party and which may, when strong enough to do that worthily, accomplish the desired reforms without a distinctive political organization."[3]

Potter's hopes for the "gradual enlightenment and liberalization of legislators of all parties"—for a cultural campaign that would transcend political differences—soon became the express object of Liberal organizations. In the 1876 constitution of the National Liberal League, the Liberals had declared separation their "general object" and a constitutional amendment guaranteeing separation their primary "specific object." Yet in 1879 the annual Congress of Liberals resolved that separation was "to be secured under present law and proper legislation, and finally to be guaranteed by amendment of the United States Constitution"—a locution that conveniently deferred the amendment.[4] In 1885, when Robert

---

[3] "Liberal League Objects," *Index*, 12 (new ser., vol. 1) (Oct. 7, 1880).
[4] W. S. Bush, *The Liberal League and National Elections*, 2 (Washington, D.C.: 1880).

G. Ingersoll, Samuel P. Putnam, and others formed the American Secular Union out of the old National Liberal League, these Liberals completely dropped the amendment from the organization's constitution. Instead, they stated that the Union's "specific work shall be to advocate" the "Nine Demands."[5] Putnam explained that "in order to give increased vitality to our movement . . . political action on the basis of the Nine Demands must be begun." This was to be "legislative action"—by which Putnam meant "not party politics, . . . but fundamental politics, which touches what is deepest and dearest to human life."[6]

At about the same time that Liberals shifted focus, nativist Protestants also put aside their hopes for a federal amendment, but these Protestants enjoyed options far more attractive than those within the reach of the Liberals. The Liberals had made themselves unpopular with their secular vision of separation, their anti-Christian beliefs, and their defense of sexually candid publications, and therefore they had little choice but piecemeal lobbying and cultural agitation. In contrast, although nativist Protestants failed to amend the U.S. Constitution, they enjoyed sufficient popularity to prevail in other, relatively dramatic ways. Not only did they renew their efforts to obtain state constitutional prohibitions on the distribution of benefits to sectarian-controlled schools, but they also demanded that Congress require such clauses in the constitutions of territories seeking admission to the Union.[7] Thus, even if only

---

[5] *Constitution of the American Secular Union Adopted at a Congress Held in Philadelphia, Oct. 26, 1889,* 2 (Philadelphia: 1889). See also "The Objects of the Washington Secular Union in 1890," *Freethought: A Liberal Journal,* 3 (no. 8): 8 (San Francisco: Feb. 22, 1890). Already in 1881, one Liberal leader declared rather unambitiously that the "aim" of the National Liberal League was "to secure a complete separation of the church from the state. . . . The means used to carry these ideas into effect are the establishment of auxiliaries, which are generally societies of men and women who meet once a week to hear a lecture on the some topic suggested by our platform." A. L. Rawson, "The Conditions of Freethought in the United States" (June 25, 1881), in *Truth Seeker,* 410 (September 1881).

[6] *The Truth Seeker Annual and Freethinkers Almanac,* 42 (New York: The Truth Seeker Co., 1886). In 1895, when the American Secular Union and Freethought Federation was organized "to . . . secure . . . a practical compliance with the principles involved in the Demands of Liberalism," and thereby "to effect a total separation of church and state," it specified that the "means to be employed . . . shall be lectures, conventions, and agitations through the rostrum and press." *Union and Federation, Arguments for Religious Equality,* 5.

[7] For Congress's requirement for new states, see McCollum v. Board of Education, 333 U.S. 203, 220 (1948) (Frankfurter concurring). More generally, see Elwyn A. Smith, *Religious Liberty in the United States: The Development of Church-State Thought since the Revolutionary Era,* 118–119, note 63 (Philadelphia: Fortress Press, 1972), and works cited there. Of course, nativists, like the Liberals, also hoped for cultural influence. For example, the Guardians of Liberty "called for a *campaign of education* for the purpose of bringing to the

through state constitutions, Protestants achieved what they considered the most important practical effect of the separation between church and state.

Events in New York illustrate the nativist shift to local amendments. To combat Catholic influence in New York State, Protestants formed the Central Committee for Protecting and Perpetuating the Separation of Church and State, which, beginning in 1885, protested against Catholic-supported legislation that led to the religious classification of orphans, prisoners, and others in custody of the state. (On the basis of this legislation, state prisons and orphanages allowed their residents to avoid generic Protestant services and attend services of their own faith, and judges similarly committed wards to institutions of their own denomination.) The Central Committee objected on grounds of separation and requested "every voter in the State to support, as candidates for the Senate and Assembly, only those who place principle above party, and patriotism above politics; and who will steadfastly sustain the American principle of The Separation of the functions of Church and State."[8] Giving focus to such requests, the Central Committee joined the agitation for a state constitutional convention and demanded an amendment requiring that *"The Legislature shall make no law respecting an establishment of religion, or enforcing the dogmas of any creed, or the rites or ceremonies of any sect."*[9]

---

clear understanding of all American citizens the gratitude which they owe to the wise and honored founders of our glorious republic in assuring to all citizens religious liberty (the complete separation of church and state), freedom of speech, and freedom of the press; of clearly showing what these rights imply." "The Practical Issues," *Guardian of Liberty*, 1 (no. 4): 40 (May 1913).

Some nativist groups continued to hope for a federal constitutional amendment. For example, Boston's Committee of One Hundred argued "for Congress to adopt such an amendment to the National Constitution as shall cover the appropriations of the public funds by Federal, State, county, or municipal authorities for any sectarian purposes whatever." See J. B. Dunn, *Constitutional Safeguards against the Appropriation of Public Funds for Sectarian Purposes*, 8 (Boston: Congregational House, Committee of One Hundred Series No. 10, July and August 1889). Incidentally, although largely a clerical operation run out of Congregational House, the Committee was not adverse to quoting Francis E. Abbot against its Catholic opponents. Committee of One Hundred, *An Open Letter to the Friends of Free Schools and American Liberties*, 12 (Committee of One Hundred Series No. 1, October 1888) (Boston: 1889). Nonetheless, it seems to have avoided formally taking a position on separation, probably for theological reasons.

[8] Central Committee for Protecting and Perpetuating the Separation of Church and State, *To the People of the State of New York: Appeal No. 3*, 4 (New York: September 1885).

[9] Central Committee for Protecting and Perpetuating the Separation of Church and State, *To the People of the State of New York: Appeal No. 1–No. 5* (New York: 1885–1886) (italics in original); *Report of the Secretary, Mr. Charles Plumb, to the Central Committee for Protecting and Perpetuating the Separation of Church and State* (New York: Dec. 2, 1886). Since 1875 Catho-

Eventually such requests made an impression. When New York finally held a constitutional convention in 1894, the convention's committee on education reported out a state version of the Blaine amendment with the observation that "there is no demand from the people of the state upon this Convention, so unmistakable, widespread, and urgent," and "none moreover, so well-grounded in right and reason." Reflecting the agitation of the prior decade, the committee's draft amendment, like the provisions in some other states, applied not only to schools but also to some other institutions, such as orphanages. In particular, it prohibited state financial aid for "any school or institution of learning wholly or in part under the control or direction of any religious denomination, or in which any denominational tenet or doctrine is taught." This language, the committee explained, drew a distinction between sectarian and nonsectarian schools in accord with "the sound principle of separation of church and state." Lest there be any mistake about the sort of separation the committee intended, it explained that "the words proposed by us cannot with any reasonable interpretation or construction be taken to prohibit the reading of the Bible in the public schools."[10]

In the ensuing debate in the constitutional convention, many Prot-

---

lics in New York had attempted to secure the passage of a "Freedom of Worship Bill" that would require penal, reformatory, and other custodial, state-funded institutions to provide "religious instruction and ministration by the clergymen of such denomination as the individual inmates may respectively prefer or to which they belonged prior to confinement." Central Committee for Protecting and Perpetuating the Separation of Church and State, *Appeal No. 1*, 2 (1885). Few disputed that children and prisoners should be required to attend chapel. It was, however, the policy of at least some institutions, such as the New York House of Refuge, that all clergy were welcome "to address the children in the chapel on general topics," but that "[n]o sectarian preaching or instruction shall be allowed." Needless to say, this was "acquiesced in" by Protestants, who viewed generalized Protestant instruction as nonsectarian and therefore perhaps especially helpful for Catholics. In contrast, Catholics found this to be a state imposition of nonsectarian Protestantism, and they therefore sought their Freedom of Worship Bill and other remedies. According to the Committee, this legislation would violate separation of church and state, as it would involve the "paraphernalia and appurtenances" of worship and "the recognition and enforcement of sectarian teaching," which was in sharp contrast to the "due provision" already provided by state institutions for "the proper moral and religious instruction of the inmates, conformable to . . . humane and reformatory influences." Ibid.; see also *Appeal No. 4*, 4 (1886). According to the Committee, the Catholic bill was *"un-American," "seditious,"* and *"subversive of good government." Appeal No. 2*, 3 (1885). After reading *Appeal No. 1*, one reader scribbled: "There are more malicious lies in this book than there are liars in Hades." See copy in Detroit Public Library (Bar Code no. 3 5674 01512915 9).

[10] Charles Z. Lincoln, *The Constitutional History of New York*, 3: 560–562 (Rochester: Lawyers Co-operative Publishing Co., 1906).

estants welcomed this amendment as a means of enforcing their American principle of separation of church and state—but not without protest. When the amendment came before a committee of the whole, a Baptist delegate, Owen Cassidy, successfully substituted language precluding the use of state money "in aid or maintenance . . . of any school or institution of learning not wholly owned or controlled by the state or a subdivision thereof"—a standard that would have prevented the distribution of state funds to all private schools, including nonsectarian Protestant schools. In the convention, however, the Republican politician, Elihu Root, moved to restore the education committee's proposal and eventually, after lengthy debates, he prevailed.

During these proceedings there was fierce opposition to Root's amendment—mostly from a minority of Protestants who rejected discrimination against Catholics. For example, Cassidy repeatedly denounced the amendment's "bigotry" and asked why the state should cooperate with members of the American Protective Association to allow these "blood-thirsty dogs . . . to hunt down their religious prey."[11] Henry Alanson Powell—a Reformed minister and lawyer who hoped to distinguish himself as an "honest Protestant"—bluntly charged that the amendment "is intended to discriminate," explaining that it "cuts off Catholic schools and cuts off Hebrew schools, but . . . allows Protestant schools to draw public funds for their support."[12] The Catholic and other opponents of Root's motion complained that its backers "violate the very principle they claim to uphold" and that "the hidden purpose of the amendment . . . was to separate the State from one church, and one church only."[13] In the end, however, Root and his allies succeeded. They were deeply imbued with a sense of their "Americanism" and believed that separation required a prohibition on aid to sectarian schools. Therefore, with reiterated demands for the "separation of church and state," they added a Blaine amendment to New York's constitution. This state amendment fell short of President Grant's ambition for a federal amendment declaring church and state to be separate. Yet precisely because nativist Protestants had lost hope of a national provision on separation, they argued all the more forcefully that separation was a principle genu-

[11] *State of New York. In Convention,* 1695 (Record no. 95) (Aug. 31, 1894).
[12] Ibid., 1822, 1829 (Record no. 101) (Sept. 4, 1894).
[13] Ibid., 1696 (Record no. 95) (Aug. 31, 1894); ibid., 1819 (Record no. 101) (Edward Lauterbach, Sept. 4, 1894).

ine Americans already shared. As Root declared: "I believe that every true American, of whatever religion, will be for this section as it stands now. It is not a question of religion, or of creed, or of party; it is a question of declaring and maintaining the great American principle of eternal separation of church and State."[14]

Rewriting the History of Religious Liberty and the First Amendment

Separation increasingly became a matter of constitutional history and interpretation. As already seen, nineteenth-century advocates of separation, whether nativist or Liberal, had viewed separation as an American ideal, evident in early American constitutions, even if not specifically or entirely guaranteed there. Ever more frequently, however, Americans spoke of separation in a manner that suggested this ideal had been secured in the U.S. Constitution and even the First Amendment.

The Liberals shifted their account of separation's constitutional history by the end of the nineteenth century. Following the example of mid-century nativists, the Liberals and their liberal Christian allies had once described separation as a principle evident throughout American constitutions and other founding documents—not as a right guaranteed in the First Amendment or any other specific clause of the U.S. Constitution. For example, in 1871 the Rev. Henry W. Bellows—a Unitarian— preached on the historical foundations of separation: "Happily our founders were compelled, and by a blessed necessity, to introduce at the very beginning a truly scientific principle into the foundations of the national law and life. They declared a complete and perpetual divorce between the Church and the State."[15] Similarly, the National Liberal

---

[14] Ibid., 1818 (Record no. 101) (Jesse Johnson, Sept. 4, 1894); ibid., 1728 (Record no. 96) (Elihu Root, Sept. 1, 1894).

[15] Henry W. Bellows, *Church and State in America*, 6 (1871). Similarly, the Rev. J. C. Adams—a Universalist who identified himself with "Liberal Christianity"—wrote that separation was new and coeval with the nation itself: "there grew up in the newly formed nation, a theory of the State, as new in the history of politics as in the history of religion." Rev. J. C. Adams, "The Church and the State," *Universalist Quarterly and General Review*, 14: 310– 311 (new ser., 1877). Nativist Protestants similarly insisted simply that separation had always been the goal of Americans, that it was a principle evident in American constitutions, and that it was the basis of American liberty. In his 1876 Republican election tract, *The Papacy and the Civil Power*, Richard W. Thompson went further than most when he claimed that separation was among the "principles of government distinctly and emphatically set forth" in the Constitution. Thompson, *The Papacy and the Civil Power*, 572–573 (New York: 1876).

League held that "[t]he Constitution of the United States, from beginning to end, in spirit and in letter, is framed in accordance with the principle of the total separation of Church and State."[16] Separation was a general principle of the Constitution, apparent throughout the document, and thus it was not specifically or fully secured, which is precisely what necessitated the Liberals' constitutional amendment.

Yet as Liberals switched strategies from seeking an amendment to seeking influence, they quietly, but quite self-consciously, suppressed their position that the Constitution had failed completely to guarantee separation. In 1885, when the newly formed American Secular Union dropped the National Liberal League's goal of an amendment, it also dropped almost all discussion of the constitutional status of separation. The Union's publications demanded the "repeal" of laws violating separation, without mentioning an amendment or even the U.S. Constitution.[17] Having recently insisted that the Constitution did not fully guarantee separation, these Liberals, who now sought merely legislative change, apparently recognized the advantages of silence.

Such fastidiousness did not last long. In 1889, writing in the *Truth Seeker*, G. H. Dawes began an article on the "Principles of American Liberty" by asserting that "[w]hen the fathers of the republic drafted the Constitution of the United States, it was their intention to effect a complete separation of church and state." Indeed, this was the source of the recent discontent among Christians. "Our Constitution has severed church and state, and as a consequence the church has been losing power and influence. She is, therefore, making desperate efforts to engraft her dogmas into the fundamental law of the land." Against such dogmas, Dawes insisted upon the "Nine Demands" of the American Secular Union, which "are in perfect harmony with the spirit of our American institutions and the strict letter of our Constitution."[18] Similarly, in 1902 the *Free Thought Magazine* editorialized that "the United States Constitution requires THE COMPLETE SEPARATION OF CHURCH AND STATE."[19]

---

[16] Constitution of the National Liberal League (July 1, 1876), in *Report of the Centennial Congress of Liberals*, 175 (Boston: National Liberal League, 1876).

[17] See, e.g., Charles Watts, *The American Secular Union* (New York: Truthseeker, n.d.); *The American Secular Union* (Philadelphia: n.d.).

[18] G. H. Dawes, "Principles of American Liberty," *Truth Seeker*, 338 (June 1, 1889); ibid., 354 (June 8, 1889).

[19] "Separation of Church and Creed," *Free Thought Magazine*, 20 (no. 11): 641 (November 1902).

In contrast to Liberals and their allies, who had particular reason to understand that they were switching from amendment to interpretation, most Americans adopted the new approach more unwittingly, as may be illustrated by the various religious denominations that competed for the honor of having first introduced religious liberty to America. In the late eighteenth and early nineteenth centuries, they had contended for this distinction without reference to separation. Congregationalists pointed to their Congregational principles and their escape from English persecution as evidence of their having first brought religious liberty to America. To this, Baptists responded that they had precedence and that they had led the long struggle against the state establishments, including those of the Congregationalists. Other sects, ranging from Quakers to Presbyterians, had their own claims to having originated American religious liberty. Of course, in this somewhat unseemly competition, each group sought to assimilate its history to what it expected other Americans would consider tolerant and patriotic. Congregationalists de-emphasized their harshness toward Quakers and Baptists; Quakers minimized the range of their departures from law and the ambiguities of their role during the Revolution; Presbyterians drew attention to their behavior in the struggle against the Anglican establishment in Virginia rather than to their earlier intolerance in Scotland; Catholics quoted Lord Baltimore's Charter, which seemed more appealing than papal encyclicals. Notwithstanding these arguments, it was a contest in which Baptists possessed a considerable advantage, for they had opposed establishments with greater consistency than any other denomination.[20]

In the nineteenth century Protestants began to compete for the history of religious liberty in terms of separation, and they thus contributed to the belief that it had been guaranteed in 1791. In particular, as Protestants came to conceive of religious liberty as a separation, they gave this

---

[20] In Leonard Bacon's reverential history of the early American Congregationalists, in which he attributed to them the principle of "elective affinity" or "separation" from other churches, this New Haven minister felt obliged to add, by way of introduction, that he should "not be understood as calling in question" the "right" of the Baptists to the "honor" of being "always foremost and always consistent in maintaining the doctrine of religious liberty." Bacon, *The Genesis of the New England Churches*, 477, vii (New York: 1874). A Baptist, George C. Lorimer, wrote: "The progress of religious liberty, both as a conception and a realization, is doubtless due to manifold agencies; but I am persuaded that to none other is it more indebted than to the Baptists of Europe and America." Lorimer, *The Great Conflict: A Discourse, Concerning Baptists, and Religious Liberty*, 12 (Boston: 1877).

principle different sectarian histories, which stretched from the origins of each denomination to the adoption of the U.S. Bill of Rights. In 1855 William H. Seward gratified Congregationalists who gathered at Plymouth by claiming that "[t]he Puritan principle draws closely after it the consequence of an absolute separation of Church and State." He argued that "[t]he separation of Church and State may therefore be regarded as a contribution made by the Puritans towards perfecting the art of government."[21] Ten years later, G. W. Warren similarly pointed to his Congregationalist forebears: "They brought here the two grand principles which have molded us into a great and flourishing country; the principle of the separation of Church and State, and the principle of Congregationalism,—of the independence of each individual church and society. These were the principles which they maintained and these principles were the foundation of our republic."[22] Apparently, the men who had banished Roger Williams were now to be honored for bringing to America the idea of separation between church and state.

Even Presbyterians made such claims. For example, in 1843, in a discourse delivered to the alumni of the Princeton Theological Seminary, the Rev. Thomas Smyth claimed that Calvin taught "the spiritual independence of the Church, its entire separation from civil government" and that this was among his "grand truths" that "drew the lovers of freedom to Geneva," that "revolutionized England, Presbyterianized Scotland, colonized New England, and founded this great and growing republic."[23] J. Harris Patton published the most elaborate of the Presbyterian claims for the honor of introducing separation. Like so many of his denomination, Patton regretted the reputation of Presbyterians for intolerance—a reputation earned by them in the seventeenth century and cultivated by their opponents for centuries afterward. In contrast, in his 1883 essay on the "The Separation of Church and State in Vir-

[21] William H. Seward, *Oration . . . at Plymouth. December 21, 1855,* 10–11 (Washington, D.C.: 1856).

[22] *Debates and Proceedings of the National Council of Congregational Churches Held at Boston, Mass., June 14–24, 1865,* 194 (Boston: 1866).

[23] Thomas Smyth, *Calvin and His Enemies: A Memoir of the Life, Character, and Principles of John Calvin,* 79 (1856; Philadelphia: 1881). Evidently, Smyth pleased his fellow Presbyterians. The substance of the discourse was also delivered "in Philadelphia, in the Second Presbyterian Church, during the sessions of the General Assembly"; it was republished in some religious papers; and it was published in 1856 as a book by the Board of Publication of the Presbyterian Church. For a less enthusiastic reception of Smyth's account of the relation between Calvinism and American liberty, see *Southern Quarterly Review,* 6: 259 (July 1844).

ginia," Patton sought to show that the Presbyterian Church "has ever been on the side of religious freedom and against intolerance." Although he graciously and prudently said he "would not detract one iota from the merit of the Baptists and the Quakers in this struggle," he argued that "their efforts were not as influential as the Presbyterians."[24] According to Patton, the late eighteenth-century antiestablishment memorials of the Presbyterians to the General Assembly of Virginia were demands for the "separation of church and state"—an interpretation he did not and could not support by pointing to the sect's actual use of this phrase or any equivalent. Nonetheless, on the basis of these memorials he believed: "The Presbyterians were thus the first in taking measures to secure the separation of Church and State." He concluded: "Justice and the truth of history demand that the services of those who accomplished this important result—the separation of Church and State in Virginia—should be recognized."[25] He thus gave separation a constitutional past.

Similarly, some Baptists began to claim that they had given the principle of separation to America. Baptists had not ordinarily advocated separation prior to the anti-Catholic disputes of the mid-nineteenth century. From 1840 onward, however, growing numbers of Baptists began to support separation, and, equating it with their traditional antiestablishment position, they described it as a distinctively Baptist idea. For example, in 1855 Thomas F. Curtis wrote that, at the start of the Revolution, the Baptists of Rhode Island, New York, and Philadelphia had coordinated "to awaken a spirit in favor of perfect liberty of conscience and the separation of Church and State" and had appointed Isaac Backus

---

[24] J. Harris Patton, "The Separation of Church and State in Virginia," *Presbyterian Review*, 4: 40, 38 (1883).

[25] Ibid., 30, 40. Like so many histories of separation, Patton's avoided extensive quotations and relied, instead, upon conveniently unrevealing summaries: "[A]t the first meeting of the Presbytery of Hanover after July 4, 1776, that body memorialized the Legislature or House of Assembly to dissolve the union of Church and State, and thus leave the support of the Gospel to its own friends. This memorial discussed the principles on which they demanded the separation." Ibid. In addition, Patton claimed that "[t]he influences that in process of time brought about the separation of Church and State in this country may be traced to the preaching of Jonathan Edwards and to the principles developed in his controversy in respect to what was termed the 'half-way Covenant.'" Ibid., 20–21. Wisely, Patton did not linger on this argument. After being lauded by his fellow Presbyterians, Patton republished his essay as a book. Jacob Harris Patton, *The Triumph of the Presbytery of Hanover, or, Separation of Church and State in Virginia* (New York: ca. 1887).

"the general agent of the Baptists for this purpose."[26] Later, in 1892 Professor John C. Long argued that "Baptists may claim as theirs the doctrine of a separation of Church and State," for, although individuals who were not Baptists had supported the idea, Baptists had adhered to it "as individuals and as a denomination." Thus Baptists had the "honor" of contributing the idea of separation, which Madison and others eventually adopted in the Virginia Bill of Rights. In this sense, "It *was* the Baptist idea; it *is* the American idea."[27]

By the early twentieth century, the many Baptists who made this historical claim about separation frequently associated it with popular nineteenth-century ideas about individualism. Such ideas seemed, at least in retrospect, to give a pleasingly simple and modern explanation of the complex, traditional Baptist ideas on religious liberty.[28] For example, in 1920 Austin Crouch argued that the "individualism" of Baptists "caused them, through all the ages, to stand for freedom of conscience, for religious liberty, and for the separation of church and state." Accordingly, "[t]he world owed the Baptists an everlasting debt of gratitude for their stand on and their work for these ideals."[29] In the same year, in a prominent speech on the steps of the U.S. Capitol, the well-known Baptist preacher and less well known Mason, George W. Truett, elaborated such claims. He contrasted Baptist *"Individualism"* to Catholic *"Absolutism"* and insisted that the Baptist message was the *"Exact Opposite of Ca-*

---

[26] Thomas F. Curtis, *The Progress of Baptist Principles in the Last Hundred Years*, 53 (Boston: 1855).

[27] John C. Long, *Separation of Church and State*, 10–11, 23, 27 (Philadelphia: American Baptist Publication Society, 1892). See also Charles F. James, *Documentary History of the Struggle for Religious Liberty in Virginia*, 206 (Lynchburg: 1900).

[28] Baptists had long combined individualistic ideas of religious liberty with strongly congregational assumptions about authority and church government, and the interpretation of these traditions through individualistic ideas drawn from John Stuart Mill and other nineteenth-century writers altered the character of much Baptist thought in a manner quite compatible with the increasing departure of Baptists from what they had considered their Calvinism. For the earlier emphasis on congregational authority and the consequent limits on Baptist individualism, see Gregory A. Wills, *Democratic Religion—Freedom, Authority, and Church Discipline in the Baptist South, 1785–1900*, 33 (New York: Oxford University Press, 1997).

[29] Austin Crouch, "Some Reasons Why Baptists Should Furnish Baptist Education to the World," *Baptist Education Bulletin*, 2 (no. 6): 7 (Birmingham, Ala.: November 1920). See also J. E. Dillard, "The Logical Dignity of Christian Education," in ibid., 1 (nos. 4 and 5): 14 (Birmingham, Ala.: November 1919).

tholicism." Describing how "our Baptist fathers" struggled for religious liberty, Truett declared: "They pleaded and suffered, they offered their protests and remonstrances and memorials, and, thank God, mighty statesmen were won to their contention. Washington and Jefferson, and Madison and Patrick Henry, and many others, until at last it was written into our country's Constitution that church and state must in this land be forever separate and free, that neither must ever trespass upon the distinctive functions of the other. It was a distinctively Baptist achievement."[30]

The Baptists who associated separation with their antiestablishment legacy grafted the concept onto their vision of church history. According to many Baptists, Constantine had ushered in the state establishment of religion and thus the era of the Anti-Christ, during which only some small congregations and sects remained untainted by Catholicizing pollutions. Nonetheless, Baptists argued that, in one way or another, they had some type of succession from Christ, even if only through the continued attachment of various unestablished groups to Baptist principles. As early as the mid-nineteenth century, Baptists were blending separation into this vision of their history. For example, Thomas F. Curtis held that "from the time of Constantine, when he united the spiritual and temporal power, there is every reason to feel assured that there has been a body of men who have opposed the whole of this, and have vigorously maintained freedom of conscience and the entire separation of Church and State."[31]

Similarly, in carrying forward this succession of Baptist principles through the Reformation, Baptists suggested that their advocacy of separation grew out of the heritage of the Anabaptists. In eighteenth-century controversies about disestablishment and conformity to law, American Baptists had disclaimed any connection to Anabaptists. In the nineteenth century, however, when arguing that they had brought religious liberty

---

[30] George W. Truett, "Baptists and Religious Liberty" (1920), in George W. Truett, *The Inspiration of Ideals,* 97, 90, 100–101 (Grand Rapids: Eerdmans, 1950). This speech has been described as "one of the most significant and momentous hours in the history of Southern Baptists." William Wright Barnes, *The Southern Baptist Convention,* 284 (Nashville: Broadman Press, 1954).

[31] Thomas F. Curtis, *The Progress of Baptist Principles in the Last Hundred Years,* 29–30. For the different Baptist views of succession, see Barnes, *The Southern Baptist Convention,* 100–103; W. Morgan Patterson, "The Development of the Baptist Successionist Formula," *Foundations,* 5: 331–345 (October 1962).

to America, Baptists increasingly asserted that some of these early "Baptists" (the emphasis being on those from Switzerland rather than Münster) had made noble efforts on behalf of "separation." In fact, Anabaptists hoped to withdraw not merely any institutional church but also individual Christians from the political world. For example, they refused to serve in civil office or to employ the legal processes of the state. Accordingly, this Anabaptist retreat from the world might seem a strange precedent for the standard of religious liberty Baptists claimed to have given to all Americans. Yet for many Baptist writers any opposition to an establishment sufficed as a precedent for the "Baptist principle and peculiarity" that they increasingly conceived of as a separation of church and state.[32] They lumped together, under the name of "Baptists," the sixteenth-century Anabaptists and innumerable, mostly hypothetical sects and congregations that were said to have existed in the prior thousand years; then, under the rubric of "separation of church and state," they obliterated any distinctions such sects may have drawn among their various conceptions of religious liberty. However inaccurate, this Baptist genealogy gave a splendid, timeless legitimacy to Baptists, to separation, and to the Baptists' claim that this was their distinctive contribution to America. Inadvertently, Baptists thereby also supplied an historical foundation for the arguments that separation had been guaranteed in American constitutions from the time of their drafting.

In the course of their struggle for pride of place in introducing separation, Baptists relied upon Roger Williams. Williams had left the tiny

---

[32] For the Baptist view of Anabaptists, see, e.g., the Rev. Henry M. King's attempt to trace the Baptists back through the Anabaptists of Switzerland and Germany. *An Address Delivered February 14, 1901, by Dr. Henry M. King before the R.I. Veteran Citizens' Historical Association,* 2 (Providence: ca. 1901). With greater caution than some Baptists, he did not specify separation until he reached the seventeenth century: "The Baptists in London in 1611 published a confession of faith in which the absolute separation of church and state was declared to be the law of Christ." Ibid. In 1936 J. L. Presser wrote: "If we cannot trace New Testament churches in every century up to the Reformation, then there was a period in which there was not a known New Testament church on the earth. This we know can not be true; for Jesus declared that his church should never cease." On such reasoning he concluded that "in accordance with Jesus' prediction, there has been a people in every century from the days of the apostles, whose churches . . . were like true Missionary Baptist churches of the present day." Among these were the Anabaptists, who believed in "separation of church and state" and other principles current among modern Baptists, leading Presser to infer: "Surely this is sufficient to identify the Anabaptists with Baptists of today." J. L. Presser, *The True Church and Her Enemies,* 126, 129, 137 (Kansas City, Mo.: Western Baptist Publishing Co., 1936).

Baptist congregation in Rhode Island almost as soon as he had joined it. Nonetheless, beginning in the eighteenth century, Baptists claimed Roger Williams as one of their own. In the nineteenth century, when Baptists associated themselves with Williams to show that they had first introduced the principle of separation, they did not attribute this idea to Williams on the basis of anything in particular he had written. Rather, they simply assumed that, as an advocate of religious liberty, Williams carried out such a separation of church and state.[33] For example, in 1875, at the fiftieth anniversary of the formation of the Rhode Island Baptist State Convention, A. H. Granger—pastor of the Fourth Baptist Church in Providence—broadly said of Williams and his fellow settlers at Providence: "The separation of church from state was the distinctive feature of their government. . . . In effecting this divorcement between these two realms—the civil and the ecclesiastical—our fathers were certainly making an experiment, were for the first time bringing long-cherished principles to the test."[34] Vaguely citing Williams and then claiming that Baptists had separated church and state in Rhode Island, Granger and other Baptists contributed to the impression that separation was an early American and, eventually, a founding idea.

Americans often took Jefferson to be the author of American religious liberty, and therefore different denominations claimed that he had borrowed the idea of separation from them. For example, Patton argued that, contrary to the suggestions of "certain authors," Jefferson intro-

---

[33] In the eighteenth century, for example, although John Callender celebrated Williams's advocacy of religious liberty, this historian of Rhode Island did not mention Williams's passage about separation of the church and the world. Callender, *An Historical Discourse on . . . Rhode-Island*, ed. Romeo Elton (Collections of the Rhode Island Historical Society, vol. 4) (Providence: 1838). This pattern was followed in the late eighteenth century by Isaac Backus, *History of New England*, 133–145 (New York: Arno, 1969), and in the nineteenth century by various Baptist biographers of Williams and historians of Rhode Island.

[34] A. H. Granger, *History of the Rhode Island Baptist State Convention, 1825–1875. A Semi-Centennial Discourse Delivered May 12, 1875*, in *Hymns, Odes and Discourses, Delivered at the Fiftieth Anniversary of the Formation of the Rhode Island Baptists State Convention, May 12, 1875*, 38 (Providence: 1875). See also, for example, King, *An Address*, 3; Henry C. Vedder, *A Short History of the Baptists*, 191, 321 (Philadelphia: American Baptist Publication Society, 1897). Incidentally, mid-nineteenth-century nativists had already joined the Baptists in celebrating Williams. For example, Thomas Whitney said, "When Roger Williams announced the doctrine of man's accountability to God alone, for his religious belief, he revealed a new light—a new light, which, like an electric flash, illuminated the souls and judgments of the Christian world." "Ecclesiastical Tenures. Speech of Hon. T. R. Whitney, in Senate of New York February 5, 1855," *Daily American Organ*, 2 (Feb. 19, 1855).

duced his Bill for Establishing Religious Freedom in response to a memorial of the Presbytery of Hanover—the document that was "the first to intimate the necessity for the separation of Church and State." Thus the Presbyterians led the dissenters, and "Jefferson joined them, not they him."[35] Of course, other denominations had a different view of the matter.

Protestants sometimes played a trump card in this battle of attribution by arguing that the authority for separation came from a source higher than themselves or Jefferson. In 1875 in Washington, D.C.—a favorite battleground for these denominational disputants—an orotund Methodist, John P. Newman, suggested that Jesus had authorized separation: "Let us to-day thank God that while the Divine Author of Christianity has declared the mutual and reciprocal relations of Church and State for the well-being of our race, yet he has authorized their separation and announced their independence."[36] By this means, Newman, who was popularly known as "Grant's pastor," sanctified Republican aspirations for separation and claimed this principle on behalf of all Protestants. Methodists did not have much hope of associating the history of their own denomination with the separation of church and state, and therefore Newman and other Methodists emphasized that the idea came from Jesus and was the equal inheritance of every Protestant. Almost a half century later, the Southern Baptist leader, George W. Truett, stood on the steps of the U.S. Capitol and spoke of Jesus but did so on the rather different assumption that Baptists in particular had perpetuated his ideals. "The utterance of Jesus, 'Render unto Caesar the things which are Caesar's, and unto God the things that are God's,' is one of the most revolutionary and history-making utterances that ever fell from those

[35] Patton, "The Separation of Church and State in Virginia," 40.

[36] John P. Newman, *Religious Liberty. A Sermon in the Metropolitan Memorial Methodist Episcopal Church, in Washington D.C., on November 25, 1875*, 7 (Washington, D.C.: 1875). See also Thomas Taylor, *Essay on Slavery* (1851), quoted in Chapter 9, at note 21. Another nineteenth-century author wrote: "But time will prove that Paul and the framers of the federal constitution, and those who achieved the separation of church and state, were right." *Internal Relations of the Cities, Towns, Villages, Counties and States of the Union; or, the Municipalist*, 8–9 (2d. ed., New York: 1859). Rabbi J. Bloch of Portland presented a Jewish version of these approaches in his address before the Secular Union Convention in 1889: "And speaking of the prophets of old . . . all of these from Moses to Samuel, and from Samuel to Malachi, all were the strongest advocates of the separation of church and state." "Separation of Church and State," *Freethought: A Liberal Journal*, 2 (no. 44): 697 (San Francisco: Nov. 2, 1889).

lips divine. That utterance, once for all, marked the divorcement of church and state."[37] Clearly, in competing over the history of religious liberty, Protestants disagreed about the origins and genealogy of the principle of separation, but, whether citing Jefferson or Jesus, they created consensus about the idea's legitimacy. Although they developed different theological histories of freedom, they all dated separation back at least to the American founding and thus seemed to confirm that separation had been guaranteed in American constitutions.

Historians increasingly gave credibility to some of these claims for separation. For example, an historian of Virginia's Baptists during the last quarter of the eighteenth century concluded: "During all those years the Baptists followed with passionate eagerness the ideal of religious freedom to its logical consequence of absolute separation of Church and State. In the process they had a large share, and for the result they deserve immense credit."[38] In his *History of American Christianity*, Leonard Woolsey Bacon acknowledged that "[s]o far as this work [of religious liberty] was a work of intelligent conviction and religious faith, the chief honor of it must be given to the Baptists. . . . [T]he active labor in this cause was mainly done by the Baptists. It is to their consistency and constancy . . . that we are chiefly indebted for the final triumph, in this country, of that principle of the separation of church from state which is one of the largest contributions of the New World to civilization and

---

[37] Truett, "Baptists and Religious Liberty," in Truett, *The Inspiration of Ideals*, 95. Of course, he also had much to say about Catholicism: "The Baptist message and the Roman Catholic message are the very antipodes of each other. The Roman Catholic message is sacerdotal, sacramentarian, and ecclesiastical. In its scheme of salvation it magnifies the church, the priest, and the sacraments. The Baptist message is non-sacradotal, non-sacramentarian, and non-ecclesiastical. . . . [T]he Catholic conception of the church, thrusting all its complex and cumbrous machinery between the soul and God, prescribing beliefs, claiming to exercise the power of the keys, and to control the channels of grace—all such lording it over the consciences of men is to the Baptist mind a ghastly tyranny in the realm of the soul and tends to frustrate the grace of God, to destroy freedom of conscience, and to hinder terribly the coming of the Kingdom of God." Ibid., 90. According to Truett, "When we turn to the New Testament, . . . we find that superemphasis is everywhere put upon the individual. The individual is segregated from family, from church, from state, and from society, from dearest earthly friends or institutions, and brought into direct, personal dealings with God. . . . Let the state and the church, let the institution, however dear, and the person, however near, stand aside." Ibid., 91–92.
[38] William Taylor Thom, *The Struggle for Religious Freedom in Virginia*, 91 (Johns Hopkins University Studies, series 18, nos. 10, 11, 12) (Baltimore: Johns Hopkins Press, 1900).

to the church universal."[39] Similarly, some historians sanctified Roger Williams. For example, Edward Eggleston—a writer of fiction who would soon become president of the American Historical Association—wrote: "Here at the very outset of his American life we find that Williams had already embraced the broad principle that involved the separation of Church and State and the most complete religious freedom, and had characteristically pushed this principle to its logical result some centuries in advance of the practice of his age. . . . In the seventeenth century there was no place but the wilderness for such a John the Baptist of the distant future as Roger Williams. He did not belong among the diplomatic builders of churches like Cotton, or the politic founders of States, like Winthrop. He was but a babbler to his own time, but the prophetic voice rings clear and far, and ever clearer as the ages go on."[40]

Throughout the twentieth century even professional historians have in various ways perpetuated such misperceptions about separation. For example, in 1910 the learned archivist of the Virginia State Library, H. J. Eckenrode, wrote his *Separation of Church and State in Virginia*. Although he focused on the language of the religious dissenters, his title and his occasional generalizations about the struggle for "the separation of church and state" legitimized popular historical assumptions about the idea.[41] In 1948 Professor William Warren Sweet (once called the "dean of

[39] Leonard Woolsey Bacon, *A History of American Christianity*, 221–222 (American Christian History Series, vol. 13) (New York: Christian Literature Society, 1897). Whereas for Leonard Woolsey Bacon this observation was an integral part of his history of American Christianity, for his father it had been an awkward appendage to his history of Congregationalism. By recognizing this and other ecumenical themes from the start, the son wrote a more balanced history.

[40] Edward Eggleston, *The Beginners of a Nation: A History of the Source and Rise of the Earliest English Settlements in America with Special Reference to the Life and Character of the People*, 272, 306 (New York: Appleton & Co., 1896). According to Eggleston, Williams opposed the "ceaseless dogmatism of his age" and "was the herald of a time yet more modern than this laggard age of ours." Ibid., 304–305. See also William Addison Blakely, ed., *American State Papers Bearing on Sunday Legislation*, 63, 629 (1890; Washington, D.C.: Religious Liberty Association, 1911). In this tradition, Mark DeWolfe Howe treats Williams as expounding ideas characteristic of the late eighteenth century. See Introduction at note 18.

[41] H. J. Eckenrode, *Separation of Church and State in Virginia—A Study in the Development of the Revolution*, 91 (Richmond: 1910). Among others, Justice Rutledge relied upon Eckenrode in preparing for the *Everson v. Board of Education* case, describing it as one of "the two most valuable things I ran into." Christine L. Compston, "The Serpentine Wall: Judicial Decision Making in Supreme Court Cases Involving Aid to Sectarian Schools," 99–100 (Ph.D. diss., University of New Hampshire, 1986), quoting Letter of Wiley B. Rutledge to Irving Dilliard (Feb. 19, 1947).

the historians of Christianity in America") argued that "[i]t was the triumph of left-wing Protestantism in eighteenth-century colonial America which underlay the final achievement of the separation of church and state"—a pronouncement that, notwithstanding its brevity, managed to be misleading in several ways.[42] In later decades innumerable other academics continued to interpret eighteenth-century dissenters and their allies as demanding the "separation of church and state." Like other Americans, these professional historians were not immune to the culture in which they lived. They had been told that separation was their American heritage, and they were attracted to what they understood to be American ideals. Accordingly, even the most learned and tolerant scholars, who were quite devoid of anti-Catholic sentiment, readily perceived and wrote about early American religious freedom as a separation of church and state. In this way, they gave historical credence to separation's constitutional authority.[43]

---

[42] Sidney E. Mead, *The Lively Experiment: The Shaping of Christianity in America*, 33 (New York: Harper & Row, 1963); William Warren Sweet, *The American Churches, An Interpretation*, 30–31 (New York: Abingdon Cokesbury Press, 1948). Although not unsympathetic to Catholics, Sweet nonetheless wrote of their "swarming" to the United States and the role of the Church in restraining and controlling "these teeming millions of foreign-speaking people." Ibid., 94, 100, 107.

[43] Edmund S. Morgan, *Roger Williams: The Church and the State*, 62–63 (New York: Harcourt, Brace & World, Inc., 1967); Bernard Bailyn, *The Ideological Origins of the American Revolution*, 249–250 (Cambridge, Mass.: Belknap Press, 1967); Gordon S. Wood, *The Creation of the American Republic*, 428 (Chapel Hill: University of North Carolina Press, 1969); William G. McLoughlin, *New England Dissent*, 1: 591, 600 (Cambridge: Harvard University Press, 1971); Douglas Adair, "James Madison," in Trevor Colbourn, ed., *Fame and the Founding Fathers*, 188 (1974; Indianapolis: Liberty Fund, 1998); Leonard W. Levy, *The Establishment Clause: Religion and the First Amendment* (Chapel Hill: University of North Carolina Press, 1994). McLoughlin backs away from such language later in his opus. In contrast, Bailyn and Morgan are emphatic. Bailyn goes so far as to claim that "some [eighteenth-century New England dissenters] ended by advocating explicitly the complete separation of church and state." *The Ideological Origins of the American Revolution*, 249–250. Morgan writes: "In the government of the United States, from the adoption of the Constitution to the present day, one of the outstanding characteristics of American freedom has been the strict separation of church and state." Morgan also uses the language of "separation" rather broadly to characterize seventeenth-century Massachusetts: "Massachusetts, so far from presenting an identification of church and state, had made a long step toward that separation which was to become the American way. The step was not long enough to suit Williams, but it was long enough to differentiate Massachusetts sharply from most of the rest of the world at the time." Edmund S. Morgan, *Puritan Political Ideas*, xxv, xxvi, xxix, xxxii (Indianapolis: Bobbs-Merrill, 1965). See also Morgan, *Roger Williams: The Church and the State*, 62–63. Morgan makes an important point, but he hardly increases its clarity by using the label of "separation." See Chapter 3, note 2.

At the same time that sectarian disputants and professional historians made historical arguments that had the effect of legitimizing separation, some religious groups directly advocated separation as an historical constitutional right. No group did so more vigorously than the Seventh-Day Adventists. In the late nineteenth and early twentieth centuries, as the Seventh-Day Adventists increasingly litigated and lobbied for a freedom from Sunday laws, they began to seek their liberty in terms of the secular, Liberal version of separation, and they attributed this separation to the founders and the U.S. Constitution. One of their most prominent advocates, Alonzo T. Jones, joined many other Protestants in finding historical support for separation in Christianity, the Reformation, and the founding:

> [T]he Reformers clearly saw the distinction *and* the separation that should be made between the ecclesiastical and the civil power, and between religion and the State. They clearly made and proclaimed this distinction and separation, and steadily maintained it as one of the essential principles of The Reformation.
>
> And this is how it is that "the people of the United States," making this the fundamental principle of their government, were truest of all people to The Reformation and to Christianity, *and so* "changed the face of the world."

As revealed by Jones's careful pairing of "this distinction and separation," he understood that the distinction between church and state advocated during the Reformation did not quite amount to the separation of these institutions, but he would hardly let this knowledge stand in the way of his belief that the Reformation had established separation. Of course, this belief about the Reformation seemed significant for the Constitution: "The separation of *Church* and State was a question already settled, and was in the past, before there was even begun the contest that ended only in the establishment of the Religious Liberty of the Constitution."[44] Although other Adventist writers did not feel obliged to go back quite so far in history, they all tended to begin with at least the Revolution or the founding. For example, in 1914 Charles Snow ex-

---

[44] Alonzo Jones, *Lessons from the Reformation*, 232, 68 (Boston: Forum Publishing Co., n.d.). Similarly, the magazine *Liberty* argued that "the principles of the Reformation . . . demanded the entire separation of church and state." *Liberty*, 1 (no. 1): 3 (April 1906). For a biography of Jones, see *The American Sentinel of Religious Liberty*, no. 101 (July 1923).

plained that "in colonial days . . . the founders of the new nation determined to separate the two," and that therefore "[t]he American government was established upon the principle of the complete separation of church and state." On this basis, according to Snow, the "mind that is free" could drive "a shaft of light . . . up to the mount of God"—a light that "has been shining in the New World from the day the American nation was founded."[45]

Eventually, some Adventists even depicted Roger Williams as one of the founders of the United States. For example, borrowing from Augusta W. Hinshaw, Charles Smull Longacre argued that, "much more than we have realized," Williams was "the practical founder of the new republic," for "Democracy and human liberty cannot be maintained on any other basis than the complete separation of church and state as advocated by Roger Williams." Through Longacre's historical sleight of hand, the Separatist who had departed from Boston in 1636 had become, in effect, the essential framer of the Bill of Rights one hundred fifty years later: "We must look to Roger Williams, more than to Jefferson or Madison, as the true builder of our American Bill of Rights, because all the provisions of civil and religious liberty as set forth in the matchless Constitution of the United States, were incorporated in principle in the charter of Rhode Island as conceived and framed by Roger Williams."[46]

[45] Charles M. Snow, *Religious Liberty in America*, 10, 236, 11 (Washington, D.C.: Review and Herald Publishing Association, 1914). Snow argued that "the interests of religion are best conserved when they are least entangled with the affairs of the state." Ibid., 10. Beginning in 1906, the Seventh-Day Adventists published *Liberty*, which declared itself "[a] Magazine of Religious Freedom Devoted to the American Idea of Religious Liberty Exemplified in the Complete Separation of Church and State." Moreover, in their 1908 "Memorial to the Honorable Senate and House of Representatives," the Adventists demanded "the complete separation of church and state" in opposition to various Sunday closing laws and, after quoting the religion clauses of the First Amendment, concluded of the founders: "Thus they founded a nation—the first in all history—upon the Christian idea of civil government—the separation of church and state." *Liberty*, 3 (no. 1): 16, 20 (First Quarter 1908).

[46] Charles Smull Longacre, *Roger Williams: His Life, Work, and Ideals*, 13, 14, 33, 82 (Takoma Park, Washington, D.C.: 1939). In support of his position that Williams was the "builder" of the Bill of Rights, Longacre made the astonishing argument that Williams's late eighteenth-century "followers" in Rhode Island refused to ratify the U.S. Constitution until it had a Bill of Rights guaranteeing separation: "When the Constitutional Convention in Philadelphia, in 1787, left the question of the establishment of a state church and of religious liberty untouched and undecided in the Constitution which it submitted to the people for ratification, the people of Rhode Island deliberately refused to ratify the Constitution, and

Among all of the publications of the Seventh-Day Adventists, the most scholarly was the compendium of sources known as *American State Papers Bearing on Sunday Legislation.* Edited by a lawyer, William Addison Blakely, and published by the Adventists' Religious Liberty Association, the volume first appeared in 1890, shortly after the failure of the Liberals to obtain a separation amendment. As suggested by its title, it was designed to appear as an authoritative collection of historical sources—an impression reinforced by Thomas Cooley's brief foreword to the 1911 and later editions.[47] The Adventists had not, in the mid-nineteenth century, emphasized separation as an argument against Sunday laws, but *American State Papers* was prepared by a man of somewhat Liberal sympathies, who unobtrusively but persistently interpreted his early American documents in terms of separation—a separation he went out of his way to distinguish from the merely anti-Catholic, Protestant conception of separation by presenting it occasionally as a separation of religion and government. As Blakely explained in his preface: "It is to set forth the true American idea—absolute separation of religion from the state—absolute freedom for all in religious opinions and worship—that these papers are collected and republished."[48]

Blakely's method was to print various documents, which he glossed in his notes as evincing authority for his position. In the margin of a letter written by Madison against "the alliance between church and state," Blakely assisted readers by explaining: "Theory of entire separation of religion and law." Blakely reproduced Madison's recommendation of "a perfect separation between ecclesiastical and civil matters."

---

served notice to the Federal Government that they would never ratify it unless and until a Bill of Rights was added that guaranteed absolute separation of church and state, the noninterference of the Federal Government in religious matters, and the unmolested and free exercise of the conscience of the individual in religious concerns." Ibid., 183. "Thus the great principle of religious liberty and the separation of church and state as well as the principle that civil government should function 'in civil things only,' which Roger Williams established in the founding of Rhode Island in 1636, became an established principle in the founding of the Federal Government under the Constitution of the United States, as the result of the persistent refusal of the followers of Roger Williams to ratify the Constitution, until assured of religious freedom under the Constitution. Indirectly, Roger Williams became the builder, through the adoption of his ideals, of the greatest republic in the world." Ibid., 186–187.

[47] Blakely, ed., *American State Papers Bearing on Sunday Legislation* (1890; Washington, D.C.: National Religious Liberty Association, 1911).

[48] William Addison Blakely, ed., *American State Papers Bearing on Sunday Legislation,* 10 (New York: National Religious Liberty Association, 1891).

However, not content with these words, Blakely praised Madison's "progressive" and "liberal spirit" and concluded by quoting General Grant's stern warning: "Keep church and state forever separate." Similarly, Blakely reproduced an 1808 letter in which Jefferson had written that he considered himself "interdicted by the Constitution" from proclaiming days of fasting or prayer or otherwise "from intermeddling with religious institutions, their doctrines or exercises." To this, Blakely appended a note asserting that Jefferson and Madison "were mainly instrumental in securing the first ten amendments which now stand as a part of that instrument. And, now, after having secured the first amendment, among the others, he [Jefferson] was desirous of having it strictly carried out—not to have it stand as a dead letter; he was desirous that it might fulfil the ends for which it was adopted—to separate entirely and forever every connection between religion and the state in the United States of America."[49] Thus Blakely exaggerated Jefferson's role in securing the Bill of Rights and relied upon a later letter in which Jefferson did not even mention separation. Such was the skill with which Blakely showed that the First Amendment had been adopted to achieve a complete separation.

This purportedly dispassionate volume conformed to a pattern already becoming commonplace in the writings of historians, lawyers, and lobbyists. Viewing all American arguments for religious liberty as varying formulations of a more or less consistent principle of separation between church and state, Blakely blended diverse eighteenth- and nineteenth-century arguments for religious liberty—the distinct positions of different sects and writers—into a single, uniform idea. Concomitantly, he did not hesitate to attribute to opponents of separation the ignominy of advocating establishments. Hardly eager to explore the improbability that many eighteenth-century Christians, including dissenters, would have desired a separation of church and state, he conveniently focused upon the opinions of Jefferson and other, carefully selected notables, especially after 1800. To the extent Blakely discussed eighteenth-century dissenters, he tended to describe them in Jeffersonian and separationist terms.[50] In this way he depicted the First Amendment's guarantees of

[49] Ibid., 77, 57.
[50] See, e.g., ibid., 95.

religious liberty as the culmination of a patriotic struggle for separation of church and state.

Thus, for quite diverse reasons, a wide range of Americans came to portray separation as a freedom that had been guaranteed in American constitutions since the eighteenth century. Some of these Americans were expansively anti-Christian; others were narrowly anti-Catholic. Some, without any animus, simply wanted to adopt what they had been told was the American principle of religious liberty. These variously motivated Americans included Liberals, denominational writers, professional historians, and, increasingly, advocates for religious organizations. As will be seen below, the Americans who interpreted their constitutions to guarantee separation also included nativists.

13

≡⇒·◇·⇐≡

Differences

As AMERICANS increasingly understood the U.S. Constitution to guarantee a separation of church and state, they had all the more reason to worry about what separation meant and whether they really wanted it. Separation clearly limited Catholicism, but Americans disagreed about the Liberal, secular version of separation, which, more broadly, limited Christianity. Further differences arose within denominations—for example, within the Southern Baptist Convention, in which Baptists struggled to reconcile the separation of church and state with their theological vision of their moral obligations in a modern world. These two types of disagreements—as to the logical extent of separation and as to how this principle could be reconciled with the moral responsibilities of both church and state—had been evident among advocates of separation already in the nineteenth century. In the twentieth century, however, an ever wider range of Americans both agitated for separation and self-consciously attempted to live in accord with this principle. As a result, growing numbers of Americans became aware of the tensions raised by separation and thought about them in detailed, concrete ways.

Practical Implications—Liberal and Protestant

The practical implications of separation continued to divide the advocates of a Liberal, secular separation and the adherents of a more nativist, Protestant separation. Liberals and their twentieth-century heirs understood separation to purify civil government of any distinct religion. Vast numbers of Protestants, however, still assumed that separation had severe consequences for the Catholic Church but not for the Protestant religion.

The organizations that continued the National Liberal League's fight for separation enumerated the practical implications of separation in lists that imitated Abbot's "Demands of Liberalism" and that thereby emphasized a radical disconnection of church and state. In 1885 the American Secular Union made its "Nine Demands." Similarly, in 1901, when the founders of the new American Secular Union and Freethought Federation hoped to revive Liberal cooperation on behalf of separation, they expressly harked back to Abbot's declaration thirty years earlier, specifying "that religion and religious worshiper must pay its and his own bills, and also refrain from encroaching upon the rights of others in religious matters, as is now done by our Sunday laws, the reading of the Bible and religious books in the public schools, the exemption of churches from taxation, and in various other ways indicated in the Nine Demands of Liberalism."[1]

In the first half of the twentieth century, this Liberal vision of separation was most self-consciously perpetuated by the Freethinkers of America. In 1929 Joseph Lewis and others affiliated with the Freethinker Society of New York expanded their local efforts for separation to a national scale by founding the Freethinkers of America. Although their most concentrated lobbying and litigation continued to focus on New York, they sought a broader visibility. For example, they made honorary vice presidents of various notables, including the British academics Harold Laski and Bertrand Russell, and Americans such as Clarence Darrow and Theodore Schroeder. In the tradition of the National Liberal League, the Freethinkers of America forthrightly proclaimed themselves "[a] Militant Organization Which Is Working To Accomplish and Maintain the Separation of Church and State."[2] It was a struggle for enlightenment

---

[1] "Call for the Annual Congress of the American Secular Union and Free Thought Federation," *Free Thought Magazine*, 20 (no. 11): 661 (November 1902).

[2] Freethinkers of America, *Bulletin*, 2 (April 1937). According to a 1938 judicial opinion, "The Freethinkers of America, Inc., is a New York corporation, which was incorporated in 1929, and its charter declares that the purposes or objects for which it was organized were as follows, viz.: 'To enlighten all people upon the philosophy of free thought and by all legal means to uphold the fundamental American principle of the complete separation of church and state." Old Colony Trust v. Welch, 25 F. Supp. 45 (D. Mass. 1938).

they manifested even by wearing blue "Freethinker emblem pins" with "a miniature gold relief of the Statue of Liberty."[3] Occasionally, they indulged in open anti-Catholicism, as when they published articles under the headlines "Catholics Urge Totalitarian State" and "The Menace of Catholic Action."[4] More typically, however, like earlier Liberals, they took the high ground and recited generalities about separation of church and state. They assumed that "[o]ur form of government is fundamentally based upon the constitutional principles providing for the strict separation of Church and State"—a constitutional standard they propounded in a version of Abbot's nine "Demands of Liberalism":

1. That no religious instruction be given or religious observance be held in public schools.

2. That churches and other ecclesiastical property shall be no longer exempt from taxation.

3. That all public appropriations for educational and charitable institutions of a sectarian character shall cease.

4. That all religious services now sustained by the government shall be abolished.

5. That all laws directly or indirectly enforcing the observance of Sunday as the Sabbath shall be repealed.

6. That the judicial oath in the courts and in all other departments of the government shall be abolished.

7. That the appointment by the President or by governors of the various states of all religious festivals shall wholly cease.

8. That no special privileges or advantages shall be conceded to any established or special religion whatsoever.

9. That the employment of Chaplains by federal and state institutions shall be abolished.[5]

These were "What Freethought Demands." Certainly, they were what the Freethinkers demanded in their litigation and lobbying.[6]

---

[3] Freethinkers of America, *Bulletin*, 3 (August, September, October 1937). "The words 'Freethinkers of America' is engraved in gold against a blue background," which encircled the relief. "For ladies the pins are made with a safety catch to guard against loss, and for the men a screwed-on button hole attachment." They cost $1.25. Ibid.

[4] Ibid., 1 (December 1938); ibid., 3 (May 1939).

[5] Ibid., 2 (April 1937).

[6] For a summary of the legal battles of the Freethinkers between 1930 and 1937, see Old Colony Trust v. Welch, 25 F. Supp. 45 (D. Mass. 1938). In these struggles the Freethinkers of America followed in the path pursued earlier by the Freethinker Society of New York, which, under the presidency of Joseph Lewis, also litigated to obtain a separation of church

The Freethinkers clarified what these demands meant in their *Bulletin*. In some *Bulletin* articles the Freethinkers condemned legislation influenced by religious organizations. For example, in a leading statement, Joseph Wheless—one of the organization's most active lawyers—denounced what he called "Catholic legislation." From this perspective, he opposed secular laws supported by Catholics on religious grounds and complained that "the amendment to the divorce law in Albany was defeated by Catholics" on the basis of their "religious beliefs," that "Catholic opposition fought birth control at Washington, and in Englewood, N.J.," and that "Catholicism led the fight against the Child Labor Amendment."[7]

According to the Freethinkers, not only the influence of religious organizations but also the benefits they received violated separation, even if such organizations met purely secular qualifications. For example, in 1937 and 1938 in *Judd v. Board of Education*, Wheless assisted the plaintiffs in suing to enjoin a board of education in Hempstead, New York, from using public funds for the transport of children to and from parochial and other private schools—his argument being that the New York Constitution's 1894 version of the Blaine amendment forbade the use of public money in aid of "any school . . . wholly or in part under the control or direction of any religious denomination, or in which any denominational tenet or doctrine is taught."[8] Wheless not only obtained an opinion from the Court of Appeals against busing for students at parochial schools but also persuaded the court to suggest in dicta that any public contributions to any private school violated the New York Constitution's concept of "complete Separation of Church and State," in spite of the fact that this constitution said nothing about "separation."[9]

Catholics responded by seeking two amendments to the state constitution. One allowed the legislature to "provide the transportation of children to and from any school or institution of learning." According to the Freethinkers' *Bulletin*, this "insolent and dangerous" proposal would

---

and state—for example, against released time for religious instruction in Mount Vernon. "School Time for Religion Barred," *New York Times*, 12 (June 23, 1925).
[7] Joseph Wheless, "The Catholic Church and Politics," in Freethinkers of America, *Bulletin*, 2 (May 1937).
[8] N.Y. Const., Art. XI, §3 (1894).
[9] Judd v. Board of Education, 278 N.Y. 200, 210–211, 15 N.E.2d 576, 581–582 (Ct. of App. 1938).

undermine "our hallowed Constitution of the State of New York," which had been "for more than a century a safeguard and bulwark for the separation of church and state." Freethinkers asked: "Must a victory on the field of battle be denied by politicians who sell their birthright for a mess of pottage?" Yet the "real joker" was another proposed amendment. In response to the broad judicial dicta prohibiting public contributions to private schools, Catholics sought an amendment requiring "[t]hat health and welfare services be provided for school children in both public *and denominational schools"*—a proposal that, according to the Freethinkers, would "grant to children of parochial schools, among other things, textbooks, supervision, teachers, free dental service, health inspection, shoes, clothing and lunches!" Freethinkers feared these amendments would lead to "the breakdown of the constitutional provisions providing for the separation of church and state."[10]

Although Freethinking and Protestant advocates of separation tended to agree about the application of this principle to Catholicism, they disagreed whether separation applied to Protestants who acted as part of a nondenominational majority. Many Protestants assumed that they, unlike Catholics, brought their religion into politics as free individuals who were not subservient to a single denomination or church, and therefore they criticized Catholics on grounds of separation, without questioning their own political participation. Similarly, many Protestants attacked aid to private schools if it found its way to Catholics, without questioning their own receipt of government benefits in either the public schools or nondenominational private schools.

Liberals shared this anti-Catholic Protestant view of separation as far as it went, but they were disappointed that it was not generally anti-Christian and completely secular. As the Liberals had earlier pointed out about the late nineteenth-century Central Committee for Protecting and Perpetuating the Separation of Church and State: "It falls short . . . of aiming at thorough state secularization, in that while demanding the exclusion of Catholic teachings from public institutions, it does not oppose the maintenance or introduction of unsectarian Protestant religious services. It still tacitly recognizes Christianity as the religion of the country. Therefore, while wishing the Committee for Protecting and Perpetuating the Separation of Church and State every success as far as its de-

---

[10] "A Grave Warning!" in Freethinkers of America, *Bulletin*, 1 (August 1938).

mands go, Liberals must still depend upon their own exertions for full and complete secularization."[11] Gradually, the Liberal understanding of separation would appeal to larger numbers of Americans. In the late nineteenth century, however, and throughout the first half of the twentieth, the Protestant conception remained popular and even flourished.

The most dramatic and least anti-Catholic of those who built upon the Liberal tradition—who insisted that separation applied to Protestants as well as Catholics—was the vehement W. C. Brann of Waco, Texas. Waco provided a home not only for many Baptists but also for a thriving community of freethinking Liberals, and it was there that Brann—a self-educated man of Liberal leanings—began in the 1890s to publish and edit his periodical, the *Iconoclast*.[12] Possessed of conspicuously acerbic literary talents, "Brann the Iconoclast" regularly wrote editorials that blasted any sort of humbug. Yet he enjoyed only a brief career. In 1898 he made accusations about sexual irregularities at Baylor University, and he thereby provoked a critique that left even Brann unable to respond. The man who had taunted the most feared nativist organization, the American Protective Association, by saying that he could "ridicule it out of existence" and "drive it off the earth with goosequills—despite its 'magazine guns' "—and who had assaulted Baylor University with innuendos and accusations of hypocrisy, was silenced, assassinated.[13] Shot in the back, "right where the suspenders crossed," Brann swiveled round to empty six bullets from his revolver—all hit his assailant—but even from the ground, his attacker propped himself up for a final volley. Brann collapsed with three bullet wounds and bled to death later that night.[14]

Although his life was short, and although his career as "the Iconoclast" lasted only four years, Brann made a profound impression on Texas Baptists. One such Baptist, who regretted Brann's atheism and his accusations against Baylor, but who also recognized his astonishing talent, was the young Joseph Martin Dawson, who would soon become a leader in his church, and to whom this book will have occasion to return. After learning of Brann's funeral, Dawson's father had opined that the

---

[11] *The Truth Seeker Annual and Freethinkers Almanac,* 18 (New York: Truth Seeker Co., 1886).
[12] For an illustration of Freethought Hall in Waco, see ibid., 24.
[13] W. C. Brann, "The A.P.A. Idiocy," in *The Iconoclast,* 1: 206 (Waco: Herz Bros., 1911).
[14] Joseph Martin Dawson, "Image-Breaker Brann Six Decades After," *Southwest Review,* 43: 148 (Spring 1958); Charles Carver, *Brann and the Iconoclast,* 178 (Austin: University of Texas Press, 1957).

journalist, rather than be cremated, should have been "burned alive."[15] The younger Dawson, however, understood some of the passions that burned in Brann while he lived. Dawson arrived in Waco to attend Baylor University in 1899, less than a year after Brann's death, and, while there, was moved to write:

> . . . Thy life, like a full-orbed
> Meteor in its trail across a star-lit sky,
> Lighted all the world for one brief moment,
> Leaving in its wake a path of fire
> That withered all and ended with a crash
> Unutterable. Thy glowing mind extinguished
> Forever, round thee, lying wounded, weltering
> In their blood, the helpless and the dead. Sorrow
> Broods amid the ruin wrought by thee,
> Who was in utterance like a very god,
> Yet owned a devil's passion.[16]

Whether or not he lighted "all the world," Brann certainly scorched through the pieties of Texas Baptists.

Brann excoriated Protestants, especially those of the American Protective Association (APA), for their proscription of Catholics and their hypocritical violation of their own principle of separation of church and state. In the late 1880s and early 1890s the APA advocated the "Perpetual separation of Church and State" and, to this end, condemned Catholics for participating in American politics, whether on school boards or in Congress.[17] In addition, the APA persuaded Protestants to fire Catholic employees and boycott Catholic businesses. In some cities they even purchased substantial quantities of arms in preparation against the massacre of heretics they expected at the hands of Catholics. To Brann, who sought a Liberal, secular separation in opposition to both Catholics and Protestants, the APA's one-sided application of this principle seemed utterly hypocritical.

---

[15] Joseph Martin Dawson, *A Thousand Months to Remember, An Autobiography,* 47 (Waco: Baylor University Press, 1964).

[16] Ibid., 59; Dawson, "Image-Breaker Brann Six Decades After," 148; *Oral Memoirs of Joseph Martin Dawson,* 124 (1972), The Texas Collection, Baylor University, Waco, Texas.

[17] Arthur Preuss, *A Dictionary of Secret and Other Societies,* 27 (St. Louis: B. Herder, 1924), quoting W. J. H. Traynor, president of the APA, in St. Louis *Globe Democrat* (Dec. 16, 1894).

Brann let loose with particular vigor against Joseph Slattery. This former priest had become a Baptist minister and a popular APA speaker. Like other nativist lecturers, he revealed the "truth" about Catholicism and roused particularly strong passions in voyeuristic speeches enticingly offered "FOR MEN ONLY."[18] In his lectures at the Opera House in Waco, Slattery denounced Catholic attempts to win school board elections, even as he also boasted of Protestant political successes. After listening to Slattery, Brann expostulated in his *Iconoclast:*

> The Pope, it appears, is a veritable Guy Faux, who is tunneling beneath our national capitol with a keg of giant powder in one hand and a box of lucifer matches in the other. What's the evidence? Why, out in San Francisco, so Slattery says . . . a Catholic school-board was elected and employed only Catholic teachers. The same awful thing happened in Detroit. . . . Then what? With a pride worthy a more American act, this illogical idiot informs us that "when the Protestants captured the school-boards of those cities they discharged every one of the Catholic teachers and put only good Protestants on guard."

Slattery's denunciation of Catholics for removing Protestants and his delight in the exclusion of Catholics resonated with his Baptist audience. Brann caustically reported:

> And at that Baptist brethren—with water on the brain—who boast of Roger Williams, cheered so loudly as to be in danger of lockjaw. In the exuberant imagination of Slattery and his dupes there appears to be a wonderful difference between tweedledum and tweedledee. It doesn't seem to have occurred to them that what is sauce for the Protestant goose should be sauce for the Catholic gander. They damn the Catholics for

---

[18] Carver, *Brann and the Iconoclast*, 8, 13. For some of Slattery's APA speaking adventures in the 1890s and the Catholic riots that ensued, see Gustavus Myers, *History of Bigotry in the United States*, 230, 241–242 (New York: Random House, 1943). Slattery continued to lecture and provoke mayhem well into the twentieth century, as when, on March 1, 1916, he appeared "under the auspices of the Guardians of Liberty at Boulevard Masonic hall, Chicago"—an event that was broken up by a Catholic mob. William Lloyd Clark, *The Knights of Columbus Unmasked*, 21 (Milan, Ill.: Railsplitter Press, ca. mid-1920s), copy in Knights of Columbus, Supreme Council Archives, SC-11-1-145, New Haven, Connecticut. Whether either side was very tolerant may be doubted. Incidentally, joining Slattery in his patriotic publishing endeavors was "Sister Mary Elizabeth (Otherwise Mrs. Joseph Slattery)," whose expertise in anti-Catholic propaganda was displayed in her *Convent Life Exposed* (Cliftondale, Mass.: 1892).

doing the very thing for which they commend the Protestant. That's the
logic of the A.P.A.—the Aggregation of Pusillanimous Asses.[19]

This APA, this "un-Christian and un-American movement"—"the bas-
tard spawn of Ignorance and Intolerance"—was attempting "to debar
an American citizen from the honors and emoluments of a public office
on account of his religious faith."[20]

In contrast to Slattery and other nativists, Brann insisted that "we've
got to keep religion of *all* kinds out of our politics, just as the framers
of the federal constitution intended that we should do. Mixing religion
and politics is like mixing whiskey and water—it spoils both."[21] He himself could "care never a copper whether a man takes his theology from
the Pope or Dalai-Lama, John Calvin or Joseph Smith, so long as he
doesn't persist in mixing it with American politics."[22] Disgusted by what

---

[19] W. C. Brann, "Brann vs. Slattery," in *The Iconoclast,* 1: 126–127.

[20] Ibid., 125. Similarly, Brann mocked those who attacked Catholics for exercising their
constitutional freedom of speech. One such, a Mr. George Knoll (who declared himself
neither Protestant nor Catholic) protested that "the Catholic church in this country openly
violates the constitution by demanding a portion of the free school fund for the support
of their parochial schools." He added that "Catholics persistently attempt to have nuns
placed in our public schools as teachers." Moreover, they "requested" that these nuns "be
permitted to wear their convent garb." Brann retorted with characteristic vigor—condemning what Catholics sought but defending their right to seek it:

> Now will Mr. Knoll kindly turn to his copy of the Federal Constitution and inform us
> what article and section these dangerous Romanists "openly violate by demanding a
> portion of the free school fund for the support of their parochial schools?" I am
> unalterably opposed to such diversion of the free school fund—even in a commu-
> nity where the Catholics pay nine-tenths of the taxes; but before shelling the Vati-
> can and assassinating the papal legate, I want to know wherein such "demand" is
> subversive of the fundamental law of the land. Because I disapprove a thing it does
> not follow, as a matter of course, that it's either *malum in se* or unconstitutional.
> What in the name of Lindley Murray has the Federal Government to do with the
> school system of a sovereign state? It doesn't even prohibit Texas setting up a reli-
> gious establishment and supporting it by general taxation. The public school fund
> of Texas is the property of the people, to do with as seemeth unto them best. The
> Catholics, as a portion of the people, have a right to be heard in the matter, but
> must bow to the will of the majority. So long as they do the latter they are patriotic
> Americans, true to the principles of democracy. They have as much right to ask
> that nuns be employed as teachers and that they be permitted to wear their convent
> garb as I have to ask the appointment of Baylor graduates and that they be com-
> pelled to wear bloomers.

"A Wail from the A.P.A.," in ibid., 2: 59, 61–62.

[21] "Brann vs. Slattery," in ibid., 1: 127.

[22] The A.P.A. Idiocy," in ibid., 1: 204.

he saw as Protestant hypocrisy toward Catholics and atheists, Brann asked, "Could 'Pagan Bob' Ingersoll be elected president? He could not. Why? Protestant prejudice—the admixture of religion and politics by those clamoring for 'complete separation of church and state.'"[23] Although Brann differed from most nineteenth-century Liberals in sympathizing with Catholics and defending their freedom, he joined other Liberals as a thorn in the side of the Protestants who advocated separation and denied that it applied to themselves.

Gradually, some Protestants, especially some nativists, adopted elements of the Liberal conception of separation, but they made little headway against those who continued to adhere to a distinctively Protestant separation. Such, for example, was the experience of some of the leaders of the Guardians of Liberty—one of the most prominent and respectable of American anti-Catholic organizations. Founded in 1911 in New York by former military officers apparently associated with the Masons, the Guardians of Liberty were devoted to various nativist ideals, especially the separation of church and state. Their declaration of principles stated: "As the fathers established, so are we resolved to maintain the complete separation of Church and State," and their periodical, the *Guardian of Liberty*, hammered away at this message.[24] Yet some of the leaders of this group, including the editors of the *Guardian*, had a different vision of separation than much of the membership. Although almost all Guardians shared a virulently anti-Catholic understanding of separation, they disagreed as to whether this was a secular principle that also constrained Protestants. Their different perspectives on separation first became apparent in 1913 in Long Island, when a school board election focused on Bible reading in public schools. The supreme courts of several states had recently questioned this practice, leaving many Americans concerned about the role of religion in public education. Like many other Protestants, the Guardians of Liberty in Long Island "declared themselves in favor of the Bible in the public schools." The editors of the *Guardian*, however, reproved the local members for failing to understand the secu-

---

[23] "A Wail from the A.P.A.," in ibid., 2: 66. Incidentally, although Brann had the breadth of mind to reject Protestant prejudice against Catholics, it should not be assumed that his understanding extended to all minorities, as he made clear in essays such as "The Buck Negro," in ibid., 1: 24; "Slandering the South. Southern Colonels Who Love the Coon," in *The Complete Works of Brann the Iconoclast*, 7: 5 (New York: Brann Publishers, 1919).
[24] "Declaration of Principles," *Guardian of Liberty*, 1 (no. 1): 5 (January 1913).

lar character of separation, arguing that, "[a]ccording to this principle, the Bible ought not to be read in schools established and supported by the government." Teaching religion was *the church's business.*"[25] More broadly, although the *Guardian* focused its animosity on Catholics and their violations of separation, the paper also complained of Protestant infractions, which were due to "the failure of many Protestants rightly to understand what a consistent application of the basic principles, upon which our liberties rest, demand. As a result we have chaplains in the army and navy, supported by the government; chaplains opening the meetings of congress and legislatures and political meetings; religious exercises in state schools; Sunday legislation demanded on religious grounds, and the like."[26]

Yet most Guardians continued to reject the secular separation. They made their preference for a Protestant separation most forcefully clear to their leadership in 1922. That year at a meeting of the Guardians' National "Court," some officers sought to amend the Guardians' constitution in a way that would have required new members to declare their support for an utterly secular separation. Most prominently, one officer—the so-called "Chief Vigilant," B. H. Coatney—moved to alter the portion of the constitution that governed the order's ritual. Arguing that "[m]any members of the order fail to comprehend the full meaning of the principle of the complete separation of Church and State, and what is necessary to obtain it," he proposed that each court of the Guardians

---

[25] "The Public School and the Bible," in ibid., 1 (no. 4): 40–41 (May 1913). When one reader protested, "Are your readers to understand that 'The Guardian of Liberty' thinks it would be best to have public schools without the Bible?" the paper responded that it was the duty of parents and the church to teach "such knowledge," although it attempted to find common ground by pointing but that the Bible could be appropriately taught in the schools "as literature." "Question-Box: Shall Roman Catholics Be Barred from Teaching in Our Public Schools," *Guardian of Liberty*, 1 (no. 5): 68 (June 1913). More generally, the *Guardian* attempted to reassure subscribers by adding articles emphasizing the value of the Bible. It also disagreed with Seventh-Day Adventists about Sunday laws, arguing that they did not violate separation if they did not require that Sunday be observed as a day of worship. "Sunday-Observance Law," *Guardian of Liberty*, 1 (no. 5): 77 (June 1913). Later, however, the magazine questioned released time. Percy S. Brown, "Religious Instruction as Part of the Public School Curriculum," *Guardian of Liberty*, 3 (no. 25): 451 (October 1915).

[26] "Violations of Fundamental Principles," *Guardian of Liberty*, 1 (no. 5): 56–57 (June 1913). Of course, the Catholic "violation of the principle of separation of church and state" seemed far more threatening, as it arose from "the religious-political activity of the Roman Catholic Church." This was "in diametrical opposition to the First Amendment of the Constitution and the Bills of Rights of the several states." Ibid.

be required to hold its meetings assembled around a table or altar supporting various symbols: "the American Flag, the Declaration of Independence, or the Constitution of the United States." He further proposed
that, when initiated into a court, each new member should be questioned about his understanding of separation. The "Ceremonial" of the
Guardians already stipulated that the Master Vigilant of each court had
to ask: "Do you believe in the complete separation of Church and State?"
Now, however, it was proposed that he also ask: "Do you believe . . . that
this principle should apply equally to ALL Churches, and except NONE?" If
the candidate answered affirmatively, the Master Vigilant was to instruct
him:

> . . . This Order demands the ABSOLUTE, COMPLETE, UNEQUIVOCAL AND ETERNAL
> separation of CHURCH and STATE, and we define this to mean that churches
> and other church property shall no longer be exempt from taxation; that
> the employment of chaplains in any department of the Government, or
> in any institution supported in whole or in part by public money, shall
> be discontinued; that no public money shall be appropriated to any insti-
> tution of a sectarian character; that all religious services now sustained
> by the Government, or any State or Municipality, and especially the use
> of the Bible in the public schools, whether as a text-book, or as a book
> of religious worship, shall be prohibited, and that not only in the Consti-
> tution of the United States, but also in the practical administration of the
> same, no privilege or advantage shall be conceded to any religion, and
> that our entire political system shall be founded and administered on a
> purely secular basis.

If, after further inquiry, the candidate agreed that he was "in harmony
with these principles," he was to be admitted.

This ritual was designed to instill an explicitly secular understanding
of separation. The majority of Guardians, however, like most other Protestants, tended to prefer the older, Protestant version of this principle.
Accordingly, they voted to table the secularizing proposals, explaining
"that our constitution and ritual on these points is liberal and clear and
could not be benefitted or strengthened any by the adoption of the
same."[27]

[27] "Proceedings of the 16th Annual Convention of the National Court, Guardians of Liberty,
Held June 12th, 1922, Cincinnati, O[hio]," *Guardian of Liberty*, 8 (no. 6): 70–71 (June
1922). Similarly, a member of the Columbia Court, No. 16, William J. Faulkner, failed to
get approval for his motion to amend the Declaration of Principles: "Inasmuch as ours is
a wholly *secular* as well as a non-partisan organization, that we are solemnly pledged to

Notwithstanding the efforts of Brann, some leading Guardians, and various others who adopted elements of the Liberal tradition, most Protestants during the first half of the twentieth century understood the U.S. Constitution to guarantee their distinctively Protestant concept of separation. Even when influencing politics as Protestants, or when benefiting from government as Protestants, they did not believe they violated this constitutional principle. From their perspective, whereas Catholics acted in subservience to a church—indeed, the Church—Protestants acted freely as individuals who did not constitute a single sect or church. Of course, this was largely a theological distinction. As Brann recognized in a slightly different context, "it is the spiritual rather than the supposed temporal power of the Pope that is troubling the A.P.A."[28] Yet, having reached the conclusion that they should view Catholics as adherents of the Church and themselves as nonsectarian individuals, Protestants could quite logically insist upon the separation of church and state while welcoming the Bible in public schools and other connections between their religion and the state. In the words of one Protestant, *"Constitutional Barriers are Against the Church, Not the Bible,"* and "[t]he State . . . in divorcing herself from the Church did not divorce herself from religion."[29]

---

do our utmost to keep Church and State forever separate, not only separate, but as far apart as possible, I deem it wise and conducive to that end to eliminate from this third section the word God, to be consistent, and thus remove all suggestions of any ecclesiastical connection." Ibid., 72.

[28] W. C. Brann, "The A.P.A. Idiocy," in *The Iconoclast*, 1: 202, 203.

[29] S. M. Ellis, *The Bible Indispensable in Education*, 84, 86 (Pittsburgh: National Reform Association, 1926). To non-Protestant immigrants—not only Catholics—this Protestant version of separation could seem quite threatening. The intimidating character of the Protestant separation (and the consequent appeal of the secular version) was poignantly chronicled by Bagdasar Krekor Baghdigian—an Armenian who, upon fleeing Turkey, eventually came to America and settled in St. Louis. Having lost most of his family in the Armenian massacres of the early twentieth century, and having found safety in the United States, he felt a profound "faith in America." Yet he worried about the fate of his fellow immigrants in the United States—particularly the "stupidly honest and inexperienced immigrants" whose lives were burned up in "industrial flames." The native-born took advantage of them, while despising them as "'criminals' and 'scums.'" Baghdigian's initial horror of industrial life in America led him to doubt whether it was the promised land, but he eventually "discovered that which I had been looking for—the America with its tremendous spiritual significance, the America with its prophetic future." Having the "wounds of religious intolerance" all too "fresh in my memory," he particularly welcomed "the separation of the church from the state" as "one of the cardinal points of the first ten amendments to the Constitution of the United States." Adopting this higher conception of America, he questioned the nativist attempts to "force" and "intimidate our new neighbors into being

Occasionally, Protestants worried that their advocacy of separation might be misunderstood as support for the Liberal, secular version of this principle, but they usually had little difficulty clarifying the sort of separation they desired—as may be illustrated by some preachers from Washington, D.C. In 1912, on account of "that essential principle of our National life—the separation of church and state"—the federal Office of Indian Affairs had ordered the Catholic nuns employed as teachers in Indian schools to "leave off" the "distinctive garb" of their "denomination."[30] This order would have, in effect, displaced many of the women

Americanized" and argued that immigrants would more completely "assimilate our ideals" if allowed to do so voluntarily. Above all, he resented the "religious organizations who are in 'Americanization' work because it affords an undetected avenue to further a program of proselyt[iz]ing"—organizations that attempted to convert Jews and various non-Protestant Christians "under the guise of Americanization" and thereby undermined the confidence of immigrants in their new nation. The "so-called Americanization activities of these religious organizations . . . tend to bring religion and the state closer together and thus violate the first amendments to the Constitution of the United States, which once and for all time, separated the church from the state." With this sort of training in Americanism, Armenians and "the other nationalities to whom the church is an inseparable part of the state" were apt to misunderstand American ideals, especially separation. Bagdasar Krekor Baghdigian, *Americanism in Americanization*, 13, 19, 138, 36, 50, 88, 99, 102–103, 109, 111 (Kansas City, Mo.: Burton Publishing Co., 1921).

Baghdigian's devotion to American principles and his sorrow that they were abused reached almost religious heights. This became particularly clear in his *Psalms of a Naturalized American Citizen*. For example, in his Psalm 37 he declared:

1. Democracy is my standard and redeemer of man; what other form of government shall I uphold? Americanism gives strength of my convictions; why should I be misled by erring Americans?
2. Though many should misuse Americanism, my heart shall not waver; though misjudgment shall rise against me, even in this will I not fret.
3. One thing have I desired of America, that will I seek after; that I may continue to grow spiritually and help lead my fellow men to paths of justice and mercy . . .

Bagdasar Krekor Baghdigian, *The Psalms of a Naturalized American Citizen*, 60 (Psalm 37) (Kansas City, Mo.: Burton Publishing Co., 1921). See also Psalms 36, 43, 56, and 59.

[30] On January 27, 1912, Robert G. Valentine—Commissioner of Indian Affairs—issued an order to superintendents in charge of Indian schools prohibiting the wearing of religious garb. This order, in Circular 601, declared: "In accordance with that essential principle of our National life—the separation of church and state—as applied by me to the Indian Service, . . . I find it necessary to issue this order . . . to cover the use . . . of insignia and garb as used by various denominations. . . . In Government schools all insignia of any denomination must be removed from all public rooms, and members of any denomination wearing distinctive garb should leave such garb off while engaged at lay duties as Government employees." Teachers who could not comply were to be given time, not exceeding the end of the school year, to find other employment. "Bar Catholic Garb at Indian Schools," *New York Times*, 2 (Feb. 4, 1912). President Taft recalled the order, explaining: "I fully believe in the principle of the separation of Church and State on which our govern-

who had founded the Indian schools. When President Taft hesitated to enforce the order, Protestant clergymen met in groups across the nation to pass resolutions demanding that the order be carried out. Like so many of these clergymen, the group of over one hundred who met in the capital declared that the wearing of Roman garb in publicly supported schools violated the separation of church and state. Yet these Washington preachers, being aware of the secular, Liberal understanding of separation, worried that their resolution to exclude religious garb on grounds of separation might be misconstrued to imply that Bible and prayers should also be prohibited. Accordingly, they went out of their way to clarify their Protestant perspective: "We mean the separation of *Church* and State: *not* the separation of *Christianity* and the State." This resolution was "endorsed by the whole body with applause."[31]

So pervasive was the Protestant interpretation of "separation of

---

ment is based, but the questions presented by this order are of great importance and delicacy." In particular: "They arise out of the fact that the Government has for a considerable period taken over for the use of the Indians certain schools heretofore belonging and conducted by distinctive religious societies or churches. As a part of the arrangements then made the school employees who were in certain cases members of religious orders, wearing the distinctive garb of these orders, were continued as teachers by the Government." On this basis, Taft pointed out, "The Commissioner's order almost necessarily amounts to a discharge from the Federal service of those who have thus entered it. This should not be done without careful consideration of the matter, nor without giving the persons directly affected an opportunity to be heard." "Taft Recalls Order Aimed at Catholics," in ibid., 5 (Feb. 5, 1912). Protestant clergymen protested vociferously, as did the Guardians of Liberty and other even less savory groups. See, e.g., ibid., 5 (March 13, 1912); ibid., 10 (April 9, 1912); ibid., 5 (May 17, 1912). The "Catholic authorities were willing that no more members of Catholic orders should be appointed as teachers" but sought to protect the relatively small number of existing teachers who were members of such orders. "Taft Lets Nuns Keep Their Garb," in ibid., 5 (Sept. 23, 1912). In the end, the Secretary of the Interior concluded that the prohibition on distinctive garb should not be revived. His report observed, among other things, that "[a]n Episcopalian or Quaker has been at liberty to wear any garb distinctive of religious calling or a particular sect, just as Catholic Sisters have been permitted to wear their distinctive garb." Ibid.

[31] Alonzo Jones, *Lessons from the Reformation*, 68–70 (n.p., n.d.). In 1921 the Supreme Court of Georgia relied upon the idea of separation to justify an ordinance of the city of Rome, according to which, on each school day, the principal of every school had to offer prayers and read portions of the King James Bible in the hearing of the pupils. In defending this ordinance and a mandamus enforcing it, the court observed that, "under the leadership of Roger Williams of Rhode Island, the movement for the separation of Church and State proceeded with ever-increasing volume and strength"—adding, by way of explanation, "It should be distinctly understood that this is not a movement of separation of the state from Christianity, but specifically a separation of Church and State." Wilkerson v. City of Rome, 152 Ga. 762, 769 (1921).

church and state" that in 1912 Alonzo Jones felt it necessary to reformulate this expression. As already seen, this prominent advocate of religious liberty on behalf of the Seventh-Day Adventists had seized upon the Liberal, secular version of separation in his arguments against Sunday laws.[32] Yet, in attacking such laws as violations of the constitutional right of separation, Jones felt stymied by the Protestant assumption that the diverse Protestant majority, which desired Sunday laws, did not constitute a church. Accordingly, unlike the Washington, D.C., preachers, he believed it was "important especially to emphasize . . . that the American and Constitutional principle of Religious Liberty is . . . the separation of *Christianity* and the State, and *not* merely the separation of *Church* and State." In other words, the generic "separation of *Church* and State . . . is* specifically the separation of *Christianity* and the State." Jones claimed that this separation of Christianity was simultaneously the "American and Constitutional principle" and the "Protestant and Christian principle." Nonetheless, he admitted that his Liberal vision of separation of church and state—his attempt to apply separation to all Christianity—appealed to only a minority of Protestants. Indeed, "hardly one in a thousand of the professed Protestant preachers in the United States recognizes it or will allow it."

The Southern Baptists and the Social Gospel

Although Protestants increasingly understood separation to be a constitutional right, some still worried that separation might limit their own denominational or more broadly Christian role in society—a role that seemed, to many Baptists, all the more important in the modern world. This tension was especially significant for Baptists, because they, more than any other denomination, had come to conceive of separation as their own distinctive contribution to American life. The awkwardness of this tension can be illustrated by the Southern Baptist Convention in particular, which had difficulty reconciling its principle of separation

---

[32] Incidentally, Jones's magazine, *The American Sentinel,* continued after his death to argue that "[s]ome Protestants do not as yet comprehend the true meaning of a total separation of church and state. They are still insistent that certain religious obligations shall be legalized and enforced by the civil magistrate under civil penalties, like compulsory Sunday observance." Claremount Lovington, "Roman Catholic Designs," *The American Sentinel of Religious Liberty,* No. 126 (December 1925).

with its commitment to the social gospel.[33] At stake was not only the principle of separation but also the role of Christians in encouraging government to alleviate the ills of twentieth-century American society.

It will be recalled that numerous Baptists found separation an expressive image of their religion and religious liberty. Whether in denouncing Catholic priests or, more positively, in expounding religious liberty, Baptists tended to find the principle of separation attractively antihierarchical. Moreover, this ideal seemed to carry few if any risks for their individualistic vision of religious experience or their congregational conception of authority. Numerous Baptists, including those who still thought of themselves as "Calvinist," emphatically rejected the religious authority of incorporated ecclesiastical bodies and even of their own associations.[34] Many doubted whether Baptists constituted a "church," and some went so far as to question whether there was a universal church.[35] Thus, from the perspective of many Baptist congregations, their church in any larger sense had, theologically, a very attenuated role or even existence. Accordingly, separation did not, in constraining the church,

---

[33] These tensions are also explored by Edward Earl Joiner, "Southern Baptists and Church-State Relations 1845–1954" (Doctor of Theology thesis, Southern Baptist Theological Seminary, 1959); Thomas G. Sanders, *Protestant Concepts of Church and State: Historical Backgrounds and Approaches for the Future* (New York: Holt, Rinehart & Winston, 1964); Elwyn A. Smith, *Religious Liberty in the United States: The Development of Church-State Thought since the Revolutionary Era,* 131–133 (Philadelphia: Fortress Press, 1972).

[34] In 1803, when arguing against their state establishment, Connecticut's Baptists had formulated an early and unusually clear statement of this position: "The calling of ministers is an act of divine power, and the employing and supporting them, are religious duties, enjoined by the word of God on all peoples *as individuals,* and not as legally incorporated bodies. Such corporate body is incapable of performing religious duties, it is not a moral agent, and no moral precept nor command can be addressed to it, in its corporate capacity." *To the Honorable General Assembly of the State of Connecticut, to Be Holden at Hartford, on the Second Thursday of May, 1803, the Remonstrance and Petition of a Convention of Elders and Brethren of the Baptist Denomination, Assembled at Bristol, on the First Wednesday of February, 1803* (broadside) (Feb. 2, 1803).

[35] Many Baptists often considered themselves members of particular Baptist congregations but not of any larger Baptist Church. For example, in the mid-1850s a Southern Baptist journal declared: "We can excuse a Pedobaptist for saying 'The Baptist Church,' but how to excuse a Baptist we scarcely know." Review of D. C. Haynes, *The Baptist Denomination,* in *Southern Baptist Review and Eclectic,* 2: 492 (1856). For a much later example, see Philip L. Jones, *A Restatement of Baptist Principles,* 47–48 (Philadelphia: American Baptist Publication Society, 1909). Fewer Baptists rejected the notion of a universal church, but in 1912 the president of the Baptist Theological Seminary, Edgar Young Mullins, had to argue: "The universal church is as real as the Kingdom of God. . . . We are not warranted . . . in refusing to employ the word church in this general sense." E. Y. Mullins, *Baptist Beliefs,* 64 (Louisville: Baptist World Publishing, 1912).

seem to limit the religious potential of Christians. Indeed, by hindering the worldly ambitions of the papal hierarchy, separation seemed to give all Americans, especially Catholics, the opportunity to enjoy freedom and an unadulterated Christianity. Accordingly, numerous Baptists felt drawn toward the principle of separation.

Coexisting with tendencies favoring separation, however, were others less clearly compatible with the principle, and these came to the surface when the Baptists adopted the social gospel. In accord with the remnants of their Calvinist heritage, some Baptists still believed that the state was divinely ordained and that the church should encourage the state to attend to its Christian obligations. Simultaneously, being ever more Arminian on the question of grace, Baptists increasingly saw in each individual a capacity for salvation, and they began to perceive human effort in this world as a means of redeeming the unregenerate. With this mixture of theological foundations—a Calvinist understanding of the state and an Arminian conception of grace—Baptists joined the social gospel movement in large numbers and thus came to ponder the implications of separation for themselves even as they increasingly employed this idea in opposition to Catholics.

In adopting the social gospel, many Southern Baptists refocused their desires for redemption toward this world and its worldly government. As the Southern Baptist Convention resolved in 1908:

> Civic righteousness and the Kingdom of God are bound up in each other. We are learning anew that Christ's commission to his followers is not primarily to increase the census of heaven, but to make down here a righteous society in which Christ's will shall be done, his kingdom come. Therefore, be it
>
> Resolved, that this Convention holds that to redeem society and to purify and perfect government, are results to be directly expected from the preaching of the gospel and the Christian education of young people of this rising generation, and that, therefore, every wrong, public and private, political and social, retards the consummation of the commission of our King.[36]

These Baptists took a new, more active view of Christianity's relation to the state. They had long demanded temperance laws, but, now, in

---

[36] *Proceedings of the Southern Baptist Convention,* 35 (1908); also quoted by Joiner, "Southern Baptists and Church-State Relations 1845–1954," 341, App. III.

welcoming ever broader worldly activities, many of them envisioned government at the center of their theology. The Convention's Temperance Committee put it bluntly in 1910: "On the far off horizon of time we see the fulfillment of the glowing pictures of the prophets in the coming Christian State. Salvation pertains to the State as well as to the individual."[37]

Of course, anti-Catholicism contributed to the attractions of both separation and the social gospel. On the one hand, separation would prevent the Catholic Church from influencing government or receiving benefits from it. On the other, the social gospel (not least, prohibition) would ameliorate the problems associated with Catholic immigrants and progressively lead these deluded individuals away from vice and Catholicism toward virtue and Protestantism. Thus, against Catholicism, Baptists tended to endorse separation; however, in developing a social policy against the worldly ills that seemed to impede conversion, many Baptists welcomed cooperation with government.

Incidentally, Northern as well as Southern Baptists felt these conflicting tendencies, as can be illustrated by two "standard works" published by the American Baptist Publication Society in 1909 and even advertised on the same page of their Annual Report.[38] In *A Restatement of Baptist Principles*, Philip L. Jones, who was theologically liberal, emphasized "Individual Freedom" and "independence of thought" and condemned the opposition to Darwin, Herbert Spencer, and other "prophets" of "individual progress." In a chapter on "The Absolute Severence of Church and State," he vigorously advocated the idea, although even he quietly equivocated by avoiding any discussion of an "absolute" separation and by stating that "[t]he Church and State must . . . be distinct and separate. They are interrelated but independent."[39] His overall emphasis, however, was on individualism, progress, and separation.

In contrast, in *The Christian State*, Samuel Zane Batten—a Northern advocate of the social gospel—discussed "the relations of Christianity to

---

[37] *Proceedings of the Southern Baptist Convention,* 56 (1910); also quoted by Joiner, "Southern Baptists and Church-State Relations 1845–1954," 147.

[38] Report of American Baptist Publication Society, in *Proceedings of the Northern Baptist Convention,* 16 (1909).

[39] Jones, *A Restatement of Baptist Principles,* 88, 87, 86, 67. Similarly, Edgar Young Mullins focused on individual freedom, progress, and separation. See Mullins, *Freedom and Authority in Religion,* 11, 13 (Philadelphia: Griffeth & Rowland Press, 1913).

the State" and "how important it is that its principles and its influence should be incorporated into the structure and dealings of the State." Batten complained that frequently "it has been assumed that the Church has to do with sacred things and the State with secular interests, and inasmuch as these realms are separate and isolated, Church and State must be separate." Yet this "modern argument in favor of the separation of Church and State has too often been based on wrong premises."[40] In particular, Batten denied that "the State is a non-religious realm," and argued: "They who say that the church is the one sole institution of religion, and that religion has nothing to do with social and political affairs, utterly misconceive the work of the church and the nature of religion." Contrary to their assumptions, "[r]eligion is a universal principle and has to do with all life." With these views, Batten dissented from the social Darwinism of Herbert Spencer and others who opposed government assistance to the poor and the weak: "Modern society, . . . being more and more motivated by the spirit of Christ, will never again allow the defective and unfit to live uncared for and to die unpitied." Society "must declare that there shall be no unfit and defective members in the state," and must ensure that "the weakest and least promising member" is "lifted up into strength and fitness."[41] More generally, Batten rejected self-interest and utility and opposed the "isolation" and "separation" of church, state, and individuals. Instead, unlike Jones, he emphasized the "mutual aid, social co-operation, and self-sacrifice" of a more "organic" society.[42]

Southern Baptists similarly encountered a conflict between separation and the social gospel and typically resolved the incompatibility simply by applying separation to Catholics but not to Baptists. When criticizing others, especially Catholics, the Southern Baptists insisted upon an unqualified separation. For example, in 1912, when Catholic "garb" in Indian schools was of widespread concern, the Convention condemned public institutions that permitted Catholics to teach while wearing habits and other symbols of their faith. Like other Protestants, Southern Baptists ignored the possible distinction between Catholic images affixed to the wall of a schoolroom and the cross and clothing of an individual

[40] Samuel Zane Batten, *The Christian State: The State, Democracy and Christianity*, 300–301 (Philadelphia: Griffeth & Rowland Press, 1909).
[41] Ibid., 351.
[42] Ibid., 301, 315, 325.

Catholic teacher. All of these expressions of Catholicism seemed to violate the principle of separation:

> And because the Baptists, by reason of the testimony which their fathers have borne in this and other countries, and the consistency with which they have followed and are following this principle, are peculiarly gratified to be guides of thought in this great matter; therefore be it
> *Resolved,* That this Convention at this time proclaim its unfaltering and uncompromising adherence to the principle of the separation of church and state, and protest against the use in schools and other institutions supported by public funds, of any device, symbol, picture, garb or aught else which would tend to serve the peculiar interests or promote the distinctive purposes of any religious sect, body or denomination whatsoever;
> *Resolved,* That this Convention reaffirm the principle of separation of church and state in the appropriation of public funds for the support of sectarian institutions . . .[43]

This must have been a profoundly satisfying didactic exercise.

In contrast, when the Southern Baptist Convention proclaimed the social gospel and therefore had to discuss its own role in the world, it almost expressly rejected separation. For example, in 1915 the Convention adopted a report on "Temperance and Social Service" that urged a muscular Christian involvement in this world:

> Some think of the kingdom of God as narrow, effeminate and sentimental. The exact opposite is true. It is broad, masculine and practical. It goes to the heart of every human issue and condition. "The kingdoms of this world are to become the kingdom of our Lord and his Christ." We interpret that to mean the kingdom of Asia, Europe and America. May it not mean the kingdom social, the kingdom industrial and the kingdom political? May it not mean these even more than those? So long as there is social inequality, industrial injustice or political crime, the kingdom of God is not fully come, and you and I have a message and mission. The kingdom of God is not a Sunday affair. It must pervade the factory that runs six days in the week as well as the Sunday morning service.

Accordingly, Christians had to do more than worship:

---

[43] *Proceedings of the Southern Baptist Convention,* 85 (1912), quoted by Joiner, "Southern Baptists and Church-State Relations 1845–1954," 343, App. IV. See also *Proceedings of the Southern Baptist Convention,* 58 (1912); ibid., 78 (1913).

So long as the housing conditions are bad and the crowded tenement sections of our great cities, so long as the tenantry problem is unsolved in the country, there is a cry for help that ought to stir the hearts of Christian men. So long as there is heartless greed in corporate wealth and graft in politics, so long as there is bribery in any legislative hall or temple of justice, the Christian citizen and the messenger of the kingdom of heaven must cry aloud and spare not. So long as the slimy leech of the liquor traffic sucks the life blood from the withering veins of our people and then pumps into those veins its poison of death, and all this under the sanction of government, the prophets of God are under inescapable obligation to breathe their message in words that burn.

Calling upon "the prophets of God" to speak out, these Baptists brought Calvinist obligations concerning government to bear upon Arminian hopes for the redemption of all. These Baptists therefore denied that government could be considered secular:

Many a thoughtless Christian has set politics and government off to themselves and labeled them secular, thus assigning to government qualities which it doesn't possess and thus excusing themselves from assuming fair and rightful share of the burden and responsibilities of the state. Government of itself is not secular. It is neither immoral, unmoral nor irreligious. In some high sense which we may not now fully understand, all governments, even the worst, are of God.[44]

Government and its moral responsibilities could not be segregated from religion.

Southern Baptists negotiated some of the tensions between their Protestant political engagement and their mostly anti-Catholic separation by assuming the usual distinction between the Catholic Church and the Protestant religion. For example, in 1916, when America's entry into the war with Germany became an ominous probability, a committee

---

[44] *Proceedings of the Southern Baptist Convention*, 82 (1915). Of course, many churches were troubled that government accepted their support during wartime but not afterward. For example, at the Methodist Episcopal Church (60th Street and Madison Avenue, New York), the Rev. Ralph W. Sockman preached: "Separation of church and state is a cardinal principle of American politics in time of peace. But in time of war the Church that would keep separate is called treasonable. This inconsistency cannot continue. Governments which expect the Church to support their programs which involve moral issues should heed the Church in the formation of their programs." "Bids State Heed Church," *New York Times*, 24 (Dec. 7, 1925).

of the Southern Baptist Convention examined the practice of appointing army and navy chaplains:

> And, since this custom of the government [of appointing chaplains] may, in our opinion, tend in the direction of a violation of the sacred and dearly-bought principle of separation of church and state, we would earnestly urge that no ecclesiastical system be allowed to fasten itself upon any branch of the public service.
>
> We, therefore, recommend that a copy of this report be sent to the Secretary of the Religious Welfare League for the Army and Navy, as briefly representative of the attitude of the Southern Baptist Convention, and that our pastors be encouraged to use all proper and available means to secure for our soldiers and sailors the pure gospel of Jesus Christ.[45]

To permit Catholic chaplains would be to allow an "ecclesiastical system" to "fasten itself" upon the government in violation of the "sacred" principle of separation between church and state. Yet, apparently because Baptist pastors were not part of such a system, the principle did not prevent them from securing "for our soldiers and sailors the pure gospel of Jesus Christ."[46]

---

[45] *Proceedings of the Southern Baptist Convention,* 59 (1916). Even to take a position on this subject, the committee first had to reassure itself and the Convention that Baptists were not thereby violating the principle of separation: "That they conceive it to be well within our province, and not inimical to the historic and fundamental Baptist doctrine of the separation of church and state, for this Convention to express earnest sympathy with all proper measures looking to the moral and religious welfare of the army and navy." Ibid.

[46] Some other resolutions were far more vehement. Provoked by "the presence of a papal legate" in America as representative of the Vatican, by "the presence of . . . national representatives in their official capacity at e[cc]lesiastical functions, and the manifest disposition . . . of some of our politicians to show deference to so-called church dignitaries," and by "the sentencing of any person" by judges to serve in a "religious institution," the Southern Baptist Convention resolved:

> WHEREAS, The combination of church and state has resulted in relentless religious persecution and crimsoned the pages of the past with the blood of the saints; therefore be it
>
> *Resolved,* That we, the representatives of two and a half millions of Baptists in Convention assembled, while reaffirming our age-long contention of the right of every man to worship God according to the dictates of his own conscience, we deny the right of any man or organization to force the conclusions of conscience upon any man, woman or child.

Proceedings of the Southern Baptist Convention, 93 (1914). The next year, on the motion of W. A. Jarrell of Texas, the Convention "repasse[d]" this resolution. *Proceedings of the Southern Baptist Convention,* 71 (1915). His motion also added statements against Catholic attempts to obtain federal legislation against transportation by U.S. mail of "publications which are, or are represented to be, a reflection on any form of religious worship practiced

The Southern Baptists and Education

The potential conflict between separation and other Baptist ideals came home to Southern Baptists when the principle of separation began to limit their capacity to educate their children in their faith. Many Southern Baptists were poor, and therefore the denomination welcomed the development of public schools in the South. In the aftermath of World War I, however, many Baptists became uneasy about the effect of separation on education. Before and during the war, as numerous parents became worried about the failure of public schools to provide adequate or even any religious instruction, some school districts allowed released time for religious training. In many districts, however, parents had to resign themselves to exclusively secular education and the difficult task of transmitting their religion to their children without reinforcement in school. Reflecting on the recent tendency "toward the complete secularizing of education," the Birmingham minister, J. E. Dillard, thought it had "grown out of an overemphasis of our doctrine of religious freedom." He acknowledged separation as a Baptist principle but felt that Baptists "have been so insistent on the separation of church and state that we have almost completely separated education and religion to the serious detriment of both."[47] It was a fear that he and many other Baptists explored in the pages of the Southern Baptist Convention's *Baptist Education Bulletin*, published in Birmingham beginning in 1919. Far from completely rejecting separation or entirely advocating it, they struggled to reconcile this conception of religious liberty with their hopes for an education that would perpetuate their faith.

---

or held by any citizen of the United States." Ibid., 72. Incidentally, nativists interpreted the 1914 resolutions as favoring their cause, even as late as the 1920s. See "Baptists Are on Record as Foes of Catholicism," *Searchlight*, vol. 3 (no. 2) (Jan. 16, 1922).

[47] J. E. Dillard, "The Logical Dignity of Christian Education," *Baptist Education Bulletin*, 1 (nos. 4 and 5): 7 (Birmingham, Ala.: November 1919). Somewhat similarly, another Baptist worried that the suspicion of creeds had united Liberals and Christians in a common, secularizing endeavor: "Two forces, from opposite sides, have cooperated toward this general secularizing of our education. . . . First, the Christian forces insisted on the absolute separation of Church and State, and thought of all religion in terms of church creeds and forms. Hence they set themselves against the teaching of Christianity in schools supported by public funds and controlled by public boards of education. At the same time non-Christian influences were exerted by men who, like the churchmen, identified religion with the creeds of organized churches and felt that the churches would produce friction and confusion in the schools, would lay a hindering hand on freedom of thought and investigation. Thus the two operated together to eliminate religion from our education."

In explaining their desire for the religious education that seemed to be jeopardized by separation, some Baptists spoke of the wholeness and interconnectedness of knowledge. For example, Dillard explained that "complete knowledge" was "forever out of our reach" but "we do not even have an adequate knowledge of any truth until we see it in its relation to ultimate truth—God." Quoting Josiah Strong, Dillard argued that "[w]hat we call separate truths are only partial manifestations of the God whose nature is truth." To those who said that "Christ taught only religion," Dillard responded that the objection implied an "arbitrary" distinction "conceived by men, that there are the two spheres of secular and religious life. Really, there is no such division or distinction. Christ's intention was to make the whole of life sacred. To infuse his principles into the entire life, transmuting the most menial of pursuits into the sacred, and this is his aim still."[48] Similarly, when Charles B. Williams—president of Howard College in Birmingham—pleaded for contributions to allow Baptist colleges to eliminate tuition, he declared, poetically, his hopes for a place where not only education but also the mind was free:

> Where the world has not been
> broken up into fragments by
> narrow domestic walls.[49]

In Baptist schools an undivided education remained possible.

As Baptists came to recognize the potential implications of separation for public schools—implications that increasingly were being shaped by the Liberal understanding of the concept—they realized that they needed somehow to provide religious education on a scale they had not previously anticipated. Public education was becoming more secular in conformity with the principle of separation, and therefore

---

W. O. Carver, "Some Aspects of Education in the Light of the War's Revelations," in ibid., 1 (nos. 7 and 8): 15 (March 1920).

[48] J. E. Dillard, "The Logical Dignity of Christian Education," 9, 28–29. See also James F. Sulzby, *Annals of the Southside Baptist Church Birmingham Alabama 1886–1936*, 178 (Birmingham: Birmingham Printing Co., 1947). Incidentally, Dillard later sat on the board of a church school that conducted Birmingham's first released-time program, which was organized in 1924 at the South Highlands Grammar School. Ibid., 185.

[49] Charles B. Williams, "Christian Colleges and the Re-Creation of the World," *Baptist Education Bulletin*, 1 (no. 6): 16 (January 1920). The verse was quoted from *Geetanjali* by the Bengali poet, Rabindranath Tagore, who had won the Nobel prize for literature in 1913.

Baptists were "now face to face with the demand for Christianizing our education with a thoroughness of extent and content which we have not heretofore realized."[50] The "fathers of our Republic separated the church from the state," Dillard explained, and "a majority must not impose its religious convictions upon a minority." This was "good sense and good Baptist doctrine. But it carries with it tremendous obligations."[51]

One solution was to establish denominational schools. After condemning the parochial education of Catholics for more than half a century, many Baptists were hardly ready to establish a substantial program of denominational schools. Therefore, the proponents of these institutions had to defend "the Baptist Right to Function in Distinctive Baptist Education."[52] According to these advocates, Baptists had "a perfect right" in their own schools to hire Baptist teachers.[53] More broadly, George W. Truett reminded his fellow Baptists that the "only complete education" was "Christian education" and that therefore, "[b]y the very genius of our government, education by the State cannot be complete." Accordingly, "[w]e must build here institutions of learning that will be shot through and through with the principles and motives of Christ, one Master over all mankind. . . . Wisdom has fled from us if we fail to magnify, and magnify now, our Christian schools."[54]

Yet among a people as impoverished as the Baptists, denominational

---

[50] Carver, "Some Aspects of Education in the Light of the War's Revelations," 15.

[51] J. E. Dillard, "Education and the 75 Million Campaign," *Baptist Education Bulletin*, 1 (no. 3): 9 (September 1919).

[52] Austin Crouch, "Some Reasons Why Baptists Should Furnish Baptist Education to the World," in ibid., 2 (no. 6): 7 (November 1920).

[53] W. E. Denham, "Why Denominational Schools?" in ibid., 2 (no. 1): 5 (June 1920).

[54] George W. Truett, "Our Christian Schools," in ibid., 2 (no. 4): 8–9 (September 1920). Of course, such disputes about denominational education also affected other denominations, as may be illustrated by a brief report of differences among some Lutherans. At the 1922 Augustana Synod, the Rev. Carl Solomonson of Rockford, Illinois, "led the movement in favor of a parochial school system. Charging that the public schools failed to provide adequate moral and religious instruction for the youth of the land," he "advocated that the church establish its own schools, where children might be given at least one year of religious training in addition to the regular public school education." He faced vigorous opposition, however, from other Lutherans, including the presidents of the California Conference and Iowa Conference, on the ground that "the parochial school system is un-American." Accordingly, instead of denominational schools, the Synod endorsed Saturday religious schools and "the week-day religious instruction plan in connection with the public schools as adopted by various states, and also the religious summer school." *St. Paul Pioneer Press* (June 17, 1922), as quoted in "Lutherans Are All Right," *New Age Magazine*, 30: 503 (August 1922).

schools seemed burdensome, and therefore some Baptists urged religious contact with students in public institutions. In Alabama, for example, where public schools had become available in all counties by 1918, parents soon abandoned their Baptist schools.[55] Accordingly, it became clear that "[o]ur churches must not lose touch with their young people whether they be in denominational schools or in State schools." In particular, "It may be that it will be necessary for us to have high school and college visitors who will visit these institutions and look after the interest of our Baptist boys and girls" and "it may be that we should have in all our State universities student pastors working in conjunction with the local pastors."[56] Accepting that "the state must not function in the sphere of religion," various denominations, especially in the North, had appointed "student pastors or secretaries" and had established buildings that could be used as "social and religious centers under denominational control."[57] Attracted to this solution, Walter N. Johnson—the Secretary of Southern Baptist State Missions in North Carolina—wrote to the *Bulletin* that "we should *make vital contact with State Education*." In particular, he urged putting "well equipped church buildings in every educational center of the State." He also argued that the "work of the Bible school in each church should be enlarged and co-ordinated with the work of the day-school of each community throughout the State." Understanding that his approach needed to be reconciled with separation, Johnson explained, "The Church and State are separate, yet they must be given legitimate contact, or else death ensues. There is no danger in Church and State working together so long as the Church is doing something for the State; mischief begins when the State tries to do something for the Church." Yet, even with this wishful thinking, he understood some of the difficulties, observing that "it is not clear where Missions and Education meet in Christian work in State education centers."[58]

---

[55] Avery Hamilton Reid, *Baptists in Alabama: Their Origin and Witness,* 239 (Montgomery, Ala.: Alabama Baptist State Convention, 1967). According to Reid, most Baptist academies had closed by 1924, and all Baptist secondary schools had shut by 1932. Ibid.

[56] "A New Day for New Schools," *Baptist Education Bulletin,* 1 (no. 6): 5 (January 1920).

[57] "Second Annual Report of the Education Board," in ibid., 2 (no. 12): 13 (May 1921).

[58] Walter N. Johnson, "Enlarging Education," in ibid., 2 (no. 4): 5–6 (September 1920). He also wrote: "We are . . . under the most solemn obligation to make the teaching of the Bible accessible to every student in a State school in such a way as not to force a State interpretation of the Bible upon the student"—a remarkably Protestant conception of the problem. Ibid., 6.

Joseph Martin Dawson

Eventually, some Baptists embraced ideas of separation that included elements drawn from the Liberal, secular version of this ideal. One of these Baptists was Joseph Martin Dawson. Although this Texas pastor had only a minor role in the developments studied here, his career can illustrate how some Baptists moved away from a narrowly Protestant concept of separation.

The growing division following World War I between fundamentalists and theological liberals seems to have encouraged some Baptists to move in the direction of a relatively secular version of separation. This split over separation divided Southern Baptists along very different lines than had the social gospel. In effect, it realigned disagreements over separation in a way that reflected disputes over Darwinism. Baptist fundamentalists rejected evolutionary teachings and other challenges to a literal reading of Scripture, and they distrusted the modernism of their liberal Baptist opponents. In Texas few Baptists felt the ire of the fundamentalists more than Joseph Dawson, who preached the social gospel, liberal theology, racial tolerance, and ecumenical relations with other denominations and religions. Although careful not to endorse Darwinism, Dawson vigorously defended the Baptist colleges that refused to fire their Darwinist teachers. On this account he had to put up with fierce attacks in which fundamentalists equated "Darwinism and Dawsonism" and condemned both as "Rank Infidelity."[59]

These educational divisions over fundamentalism and broader disputes over public schools seem to have affected Dawson's conceptions of separation between church and state. As a student at Baylor, Dawson had argued for the necessity of denominational colleges by suggesting that only in such institutions could Baptists enjoy a Baptist education without violating the separation of church and state.[60] At one point or another, perhaps in the 'teens and twenties, Dawson apparently became familiar with nativist and especially progressive, liberal ideas and thereby came to value public schools and a somewhat secular separation. In particular, after fundamentalists attacked the teaching of Darwinism in public schools, and after persons educated in Liberal ideals (most promi-

[59] *Oral Memoirs of Joseph Martin Dawson,* 114–116, 119. For Dawson's liberal attitudes, see ibid., 132.
[60] Dawson, *A Thousand Months to Remember,* 69.

nently, Clarence Darrow) defended such teaching, Dawson and other Baptist opponents of fundamentalism seem to have moved further toward the Liberal, secular concept of separation.[61]

Dawson eventually found a means to pursue his ideals in the Joint Conference Committee on Public Relations. In 1936 the Southern Baptist Convention reconstituted its Committee on Army and Navy Chaplains as a Committee on Public Relations, which was designed to act for the Convention more broadly in church-state relations.[62] Initially, the new Committee had five members, one of them being the lawyer, E. Hilton Jackson. In 1937 another Southern Baptist lawyer, Senator Hugo Black, joined the Committee, although he had to depart when nominated to the Supreme Court later that year. Similar public relations committees were formed by the Northern Baptist Convention and the black National Baptist Convention, U.S.A. These three committees eventually were authorized to cooperate in a Joint Conference Committee on Public Relations, which established a permanent Washington office in 1946, choosing Dawson to serve as the Committee's first Executive Secretary.[63]

The constitution of the Joint Conference Committee incorporated the ambiguities of the Baptist position on separation of church and state. On the one hand, it gave the Committee power "to enunciate, defend, and extend the historic, traditional Baptist principle of religious freedom with particular application to the separation of church and state as embodied in the Constitution of the United States." On the other hand, it authorized the Committee "to inform the Baptist constituencies of governmental movements and measures affecting principles held essential to true relations between church and state and the right application of Christianity to the life of the Nation."[64] For some Baptists the right application of Christianity to the life of the nation was at odds with separation, especially the secular version of this ideal. Dawson, however, had no such worries, and, from his position as Executive Secretary, he would

---

[61] Ibid. A reference by Dawson to the "little red school house" suggests the partly nativist context in which he came to value public education. Ibid.

[62] Stanley LeRoy Hastey, "A History of the Baptist Joint Committee on Public Affairs, 1946–1971," 18 (Doctor of Theology diss., Southern Baptist Theological Seminary, 1973).

[63] Pam Parry, *On Guard for Religious Liberty: Six Decades of the Baptist Joint Committee,* 7–8 (Macon, Ga.: Smyth & Helwys, 1996); Hastey, "A History of the Baptist Joint Committee on Public Affairs, 1946–1971," 17–26, 46–47.

[64] William Wright Barnes, *The Southern Baptist Convention 1845–1953,* 299 (Nashville: Broadman Press, 1954).

work devotedly for his conception of the Baptist and American principle of separation between church and state. Of course, as Dawson would soon learn, although most Baptists shared his understanding of separation in its application to Catholicism, they had no such consensus about his relatively secular version of this principle and its application to Protestants.

This account of conflicting attitudes among Baptists—whether in response to the social gospel or public education—should serve as a reminder of the substantial doubts and divisions over separation within the many denominations and other groups that sometimes supported the idea. These doubts lingered, notwithstanding the confidence of men such as Dawson, and usually focused (as in the nineteenth century) on the risk that the nation and its government might be freed from moral and social accountability. For example, like the Southern Baptists, a publication such as the *New Republic* could support separation but also sometimes question it. In 1926—when discussing church-state tensions in Mexico—the *New Republic* began by acknowledging that separation was the "modern" approach:

> To anyone who comes to the controversy between the Mexican government and the Catholic Church from the traditional assumptions of modern civilization, the issue seems clear and to take sides is easy. The church may be a necessary and harmless institution so long as it renounces temporal power and attends merely to the spiritual needs of its charges. If, however, it has a large economic stake in the community, if it presumes to take part in politics and even to controvert the dicta of the state, it is a public enemy and must be restricted to its proper function. For the state and the church should be separate and independent. . . . The church can teach what it likes about the salvation of the soul and the next world, but it must keep its fingers off the government of this. These are the liberal assumptions which have become established since the sixteenth century.

Yet, after reciting these "traditional assumptions of modern civilization," the *New Republic* paused to consider the potential of religion to supply moral restraints on capitalism:

> Anyone who has studied history, however, especially if he has recently read Mr. R. H. Tawney's stimulating book on Religion and the Rise of Capitalism, may well hesitate to rest his partisanship precisely on these grounds. Are we really content to admit the supreme sovereignty of the

state even when it strives to nullify our own scruples? Are we prepared
to say that there is really, or should be, a complete separation between
economic or political conduct and morals? Can we conceive the world
as composed of two separate and independent realms, the one "temporal" and the other "spiritual"? This sounds altogether too much like the
super-patriot who makes a religion of war, like the mill owner who objects that the churches are leaving their proper sphere when they investi-
gate strikes or promulgate social creeds, like the economist who perceives
beneficent automatism in the operation of "economic law" unchecked
by humanitarian controls. It is, in fact, a strictly modern conception, un-
dreamed of before the rise of capitalism.[65]

The *New Republic* wrote from a very different perspective than Southern
Baptists, but it could share both the Baptist desire for separation and the
Baptist hope for a society in which each person and institution, including
the government, was morally accountable. Whether in pursuit of a traditional or a progressive social order, and whether for religious or secular
reasons, Americans of various persuasions felt some of the attractions
and some of the unease illustrated here by the Southern Baptists.

[65] "The Church or the State?" *New Republic*, 323–324 (Aug. 11, 1926).

14

⇒·◇·⇐

An American Constitutional Right

NOTWITHSTANDING that some Americans had doubts concerning separation, growing numbers celebrated it as a constitutional right. They were not all anti-Catholic, and they had varying understandings about what separation entailed. Yet vast numbers of Americans from remarkably diverse backgrounds perceived separation to be an "American" constitutional right, which protected Americans from Catholic or, more broadly, ecclesiastical subjugation. In this manner, separation became established in popular opinion and eventually even in judicial opinions as a fundamental First Amendment freedom.

The Diverse Advocates of Separation: The Example of Jews and Masons

In the early decades of the twentieth century, many different Americans—seemingly incompatible in their aims—advocated separation. Diverse groups, including not only atheists and Baptists but also, for example, Jews and Masons, feared claims of religious authority and envisioned themselves as independent individuals. Accordingly, notwithstanding their differences, including somewhat divergent views of separation, they could share a belief in this principle. Indeed, through their variety, they gave separation an almost pervasive cultural strength as part of an American faith that transcended their otherwise fragmented religious, political, and other affiliations.

Jews had long suffered persecution under the Catholic Church, and they therefore eagerly welcomed separation. Some so strongly suspected

Catholics and so eagerly desired to become fully American that they allied themselves with nativists. In 1845, for example, the virulent Lewis C. Levin entered Congress on the ticket of the American Party.[1] Most Jews, however, recognized the dangers of popular anti-Catholic prejudice and attempted to adopt the nativist ideal of separation without the violent antipathies that often came with it.[2] For example, like many Jews of later generations, Rabbi Isaac M. Wise of Cincinnati identified with Jefferson as one who "combated long enough with the clergy of this country, to disconnect the State from the Church." Yet this founder of Reform Judaism in America rejected discrimination against Catholics, asking: "If the idea of Romanism is dangerous to the republic, are the Catholics not a small minority? have we not a free press, liberty of speech? are these powerful instruments not strong enough to guard our republican institutions?" Looking back over history, it was difficult to believe that "Protestant fanaticism is any better than Catholic fanaticism."[3]

For a while, many Jews contentedly supported the Protestant version of separation and even cooperated with Protestants in organizing religious education in public institutions. Some New York rabbis, for example, formulated the religious principles for a manual of morals to be used in the public schools:

1. The existence of God.
2. The responsibility of man to his Maker.
3. The immortality of the soul.[4]

---

[1] Morton Bordon, *Jews, Turks, and Infidels,* 54–58 (Chapel Hill: University of North Carolina Press, 1984).

[2] Ibid., 54.

[3] Isaac Wise, "Politics," *The Israelite,* 2 (no. 2): 12 (July 20, 1855). Wise also asserted: "We are citizens of this country, not by the tolerance of any sect, but by right and justice, hence we must always stand on the side of justice." Ibid. Although Jews often joined Protestants against public funding of Catholic schools, they also helped Catholics to exclude the Bible from public schools, and, later in the century, Wise would make such an alliance in Cincinnati. For the mixed partnerships of Jews in the nineteenth century, see Arthur Gilbert, "Jewish Commitments in Relations of Church and State," in Elwyn A. Smith, *Church-State Relations in Ecumenical Perspective,* 58 (Pittsburgh: Duquesne University Press, 1966).

[4] *American Hebrew* (May 14, 1886, and March 2, 1888), as quoted by Jonathan D. Sarna and David G. Dalin, *Religion and the State in the American Jewish Experience,* 19 (Notre Dame: University of Notre Dame Press, 1997); Naomi W. Cohen, *Jews in Christian America: The Pursuit of Religious Equality,* 85 (New York: Oxford University Press, 1992). Protestants

In this generic religiosity and in their distrust of Catholicism, Jews could become allies with Protestants. As put by the nativist Central Committee for Protecting and Perpetuating the Separation of Church and State: "Intelligent Hebrews always have been found ready, not only to accept such common basis for religious instruction as the State saw fit to permit in its institutions, but also to oppose any attempt to introduce Sectarian teaching."[5]

Eventually, when the Liberals advocated separation against both Catholics and Protestants, many Jews, especially members of the Reform movement, adopted a clearly secular, Liberal conception of separation. For example, in 1876 the editor of the *Jewish Times*, Moritz Ellinger, and Rabbi Isaac Wise, who edited the Cincinnati *Israelite*, agreed to become vice presidents of the National Liberal League.[6] Jews understood that the Liberals could become allies against the full range of Christianizing tendencies that suffused American public life. More profoundly, they perceived in the Liberal version of separation of church and state, which unambiguously separated Christianity from government, a satisfying expression of their fears of religious persecution and their hopes for equal citizenship. Most radically, they saw in the Liberal concept of separation an opportunity to escape the burdensome legislation that, even when secular, still accommodated the practices of the Christian majority, such as Sunday laws and laws that took for granted the Christian calendar. In this sense, for Jews separation defined a vision of America in which they enjoyed not only equal rights but also equalized strength—a vision

---

quickly modified these principles to read: "First.—The existence of a God. Second.—The responsibility of every human being to God. Third.—The deathlessness of the human soul. Fourth.—The reality of a spiritual state beyond the grave, in which condition must be determined by character." *Report of the Secretary, Mr. Charles M. Plumb, to the Central Committee for Protecting and Perpetuating the Separation of Church and State, New York, December 2d, 1886,* 8 (New York: 1886). Plumb explained: "To the Hebrew rabbis of New York belong the credit of formulating a basis for a manual of morals for the State schools, which seems to be entirely inoffensive to any body of religionists. It adopts the three intuitive religious beliefs which are universal, and if the fourth can not be accepted by all as a cherished belief, all will admit that it is unobjectionable, and conducive to morality." Ibid.

[5] The Central Committee for Protecting and Perpetuating the Separation of Church and State, *To the People of New York: Appeal No. 4, Roman Catholic Demands in Civil Affairs Inconsistent with American Principles,* 13 (New York: 1886).

[6] Sydney E. Ahlstrom, "Francis Ellingwood Abbot: His Education and Active Career," 2: 195–196 (Ph.D. diss., Harvard University, 1951); Cohen, *Jews in Christian America,* 71; Sarna and Dalin, *Religion and the State in the American Jewish Experience,* 173.

of America in which the Christian majority could not exercise its majority power even through secular laws, and in which Jews could avoid any sense of being different.

Reform Jews often perceived their "unbiased separation" as an extension of the liberal theology they borrowed from Protestant contemporaries. For example, Max Lilienthal—the Reform rabbi of the Bene Israel Congregation in Cincinnati—condemned the theology of dogmatism, of churches, and of the Orthodox Judaism he had abandoned, and he contrasted such theology with the religion of love he now embraced. In his 1869 sermon at the dedication of his congregation's new temple, Lilienthal declared:

> Theology is dogmatism; religion is love. . . . Theology dreams of a superiority and supremacy of the clergy; religion teaches you shall all be a kingdom of priests and a holy nation. Theology, claiming the superiority of the church over the state and human society attempts to make the highest interests of the human race subservient to obsolete medieval dogmas and imaginary claims; religion, rejoicing in the sacred principles of civil and religious liberty and equality, leaves the mode of worshiping our Heavenly Father to the private conviction and responsibility of the individual.

On the basis of this "radical difference between theology and religion," Lilienthal adopted not only liberal Judaism but also a liberal Americanism, in which he exalted the separation of church and state: "And hence the immortal fathers of this, our glorious country, when laying down the fundamental principles of our free institutions, at once decreed the final and thorough separation of church and state. Blessed be their sacred memory!"[7]

---

[7] David Philipson, *Max Lilienthal, American Rabbi: Life and Writings*, 68–69 (New York: Bloch Publishing Co., 1915). In the mid-1880s, looking back on his twenty-five years at Temple Bene Israel, Lilienthal hinted at the secular benefits of his theologically liberal emphasis on love. This shared essential allowed Jews to find common ground with Christians and thereby escape the bigotry of religious difference:

> Open the Bibles of the various nations and religions; they all teach and preach the same doctrine; it is the true revelation of the divine spirit enthroned in the human heart and mind. Let this doctrine of universal unsectarian love once be acknowledged, then the Kingdom of God will be near at hand; fanaticism, bigotry and prejudice will die out, and under the most various forms and ceremonies we will worship but one Father. We will hold divine services becoming our age, as love will be the officiating high priest, love the only sacrifice demanded by divine justice and mercy.

In 1868, at the laying of the cornerstone of the Mound Street Temple in Cincinnati, Lilienthal described two principles as "the spiritual cornerstone on which our new temple shall rest." One was "the supreme authority of the American Constitution," which "Jews consider and revere . . . almost like a new revelation." The second was that Jews "shall always join the ranks of those who advocate the separation of state and church." On these foundations Jews could "become 'Americanized' in every way and respect" and thus could find deliverance in their new promised land:

> For we Israelites of the present age do not dream any longer about the restoration of Palestine and the Messiah crowned with a diadem of earthly power and glory. America is our Palestine; here is our Zion and Jerusalem; Washington and the signers of the glorious Declaration of Independence—of universal human right, liberty and happiness—are our deliverers, and the time when their doctrines will be recognized and carried into effect is the time so hopefully fore[tol]d by our great prophets.[8]

In such ways, as he later explained, he worked "for Israel's redemption in this land of virgin liberty."[9]

Lilienthal indulged in extravagant language about separation and secular salvation, but his underlying sentiments were not unusual. Many Jews understood separation to be synonymous with their freedom in America. Therefore, as Lilienthal expected, they increasingly devoted themselves to the "time honored American tradition" of separation more consistently than to any tradition of their own.[10]

Although different types of Jews took different approaches to separation, the various branches of Judaism tended until the middle of the

---

In departing from the violence of theology, this religion of love led to "the American doctrine of separating church and state," which Lilienthal preached as the application of "the principles and essential doctrines of our Jewish religion." Ibid., 73–74.

[8] Ibid., 455–456, 457.

[9] Ibid., 74.

[10] "Inquiry on Religion in Nation's Schools," *New York Times,* 11 (April 15, 1925). Later, the leaders of the American Jewish Committee would reject Zionism in language very similar to Lilienthal's. Naomi W. Cohen, *Not Free to Desist: The American Jewish Committee,* 104 (Philadelphia: Jewish Publication Society of America, 1972). For the departure of the Orthodox from separationist views in the early 1960s, and for the tendency of American Jews to discuss separation of church and state on the basis of American rather than Jewish law, see Arthur Gilbert, "Jewish Commitments in Relations of Church and State," in Smith, *Church-State Relations,* 59–64, 68.

twentieth century to follow the leadership of Reform Jews in supporting a mostly secular version of this ideal. The approach to separation that developed under Reform leadership was least secular in matters of public education, for many Reform rabbis, like their Conservative and "Orthodox" counterparts, hoped that the generic religious foundations of morality would be inculcated in public schools.[11] On other issues, however, especially in opposition to Christianity, Reform leaders led other Jews in supporting a more thoroughly secular vision of separation. Much later, after the middle of the twentieth century, Reform Jews would take an increasingly secular stance on public schools. At the same time, Orthodox Jews would break with the Reformers and would directly challenge the concept of separation. Until then, however, the Orthodox did not adopt a distinctive stance. Instead, they went along with their liberalized brethren, who usually took the lead in making public declarations on religious liberty. In this manner, during the first half of the twentieth century, the largely secular separation advocated by the Reform movement dominated the positions on religious liberty taken by all branches of Judaism.[12]

In addition to Jews, Masons joined the demands for separation—albeit the more traditionally Protestant or nativist type of separation. Sympathetic to free inquiry and free institutions, Masons had long sought a fellowship that transcended religious divisions. Accordingly, they had welcomed diverse types of Protestants and sometimes also Jews and Catholics. Yet what Masons viewed as their tolerance, the Catholic Church feared was indifference—if not outright hostility—to the claims of the Church. Certainly, the vision of Masonic fellowship that required Masons to put aside their religious differences was at odds with the

---

[11] Cohen, *Jews in Christian America*, 83, 85; Sarna and Dalin, *Religion and the State in the American Jewish Experience*, 19–20; Eugene Lipman, "The Conference Considers Relations between Religion and the State," in Betram Wallace Korn, ed., *Retrospect and Prospect: Essays in Commemoration of the Seventy-Fifth Anniversary of the Founding of the Central Conference of American Rabbis 1880–1964*, 114–120 (New York: C.C.A.R., 1965). One of the traditionalists who worried that a separation of church and state would stand in the way of spirituality in public education was Bernard Drachman. Yet he revealed no such hesitation when applying this "American" ideal against the "participation of the clergy in politics." Drachman, *Looking at America*, 196–199, 121–123 (1934; Freeport, N.Y.: Books for Libraries, 1970).

[12] Cohen, *Jews in Christian America*, 75, 87. Cohen writes, "Reformers shaped the response of the community on all significant church-state issues for fifty years after the Civil War." Ibid. 75. Their ideas of separation, even if sometimes qualified, remained dominant even longer.

Church's conception of religious conformity and its expectation that it should have a pervasive role in society. Therefore, a series of popes criticized the Masons, and eventually in his 1884 encyclical, *Humanum Genus*, Pope Leo XIII accused them of seeking a separation between church and state: "They work . . . obstinately to the end that neither the teaching nor the authority of the Church may have any influence; and therefore they preach and maintain the full separation of the Church from the State." To this, the Sovereign Grand Commander of the Scottish Rite, Southern Jurisdiction, and the preeminent author of its rituals, Albert Pike, responded with the hyperbole typical of late nineteenth-century anti-Catholicism. He argued that the encyclical, "under the guise of a condemnation of Free-Masonry," was, in fact, "a declaration of war, and the signal for a crusade, against the rights of man individually and of communities of men as organisms; against the separation of Church and State, and the confinement of the Church within the limits of its legitimate functions; against education free from sectarian religious influences."[13] In response to this papal threat, Pike and many other Masons joined the Protestant chorus demanding the separation of church and state.

Yet the Masons' challenge to the Catholic Church and their advocacy of separation went deeper than a simple difference over religious liberty, for in their lodges and temples, Masons provided an alternative to sectarian identities. Most dramatically, they did so by adopting eclectic rituals drawn from religions across the globe and throughout human history. Paradoxically, while echoing ceremonies of diverse religions, Masons homogenized religious experience and, in effect, denied the distinctiveness of any particular religion. Most notably, Albert Pike created exotic, putatively ancient rituals, with which he gave symbolic expression to his understanding of the underlying unity or fundamental equivalence of different religions.[14] Scarcely less elaborate than the ceremonies of the Catholic Church, and often alluding to them, nineteenth-century Masonic rituals had profound appeal in an organiza-

---

[13] *The Letter "Humanum Genus" of the Pope, Leo XIII, against Free-Masonry and the Spirit of the Age, April 20, 1884, and the Reply for the Ancient and Accepted Scottish Rite of Free-Masonry*, 26 (Letter) and 3 (Reply) (Charleston, S.C.: Gr. Orient of Charleston, 1884). See William L. Fox, *Lodge of the Double-Headed Eagle: Two Centuries of Scottish Rite Freemasonry in America's Southern Jurisdiction*, 106–107 (Fayetteville, Ark.: University of Arkansas Press, 1997).

[14] Fox, *Lodge of the Double-Headed Eagle*, 75.

tion that "was often a convenient focal point of an otherwise formless and ubiquitous American Protestant culture."[15] Although these evolving Masonic rituals were liberal in their eclecticism and their intimations of equivalence among religions, they increasingly mimicked the severity of orthodox theology—allowing Masons to enjoy in their lodges a staged version of the emphasis upon sin and punishment they had rejected in their churches. Once suggestive of the goodness of man, Masonic rituals now dramatized his sinfulness; once acknowledging the kindness of the Almighty, they now drew attention to his wrath.[16] These increasingly severe ceremonies typically were written and led by liberal Protestant ministers, who often served as Masonic High Priests, Prophets, and Chaplains, and the new sort of ritual attracted members "largely from the urban middle class, where religious liberalism found its greatest support."[17] Such Masons typically viewed lodge and church as completely compatible and vehemently denied that their lodges challenged American denominations. Not surprisingly, however, many traditional clergymen—not only Catholics but also some Protestants—had nagging doubts.[18] Certainly, they had reason to fear that the eclectic religiosity of Masonic ritual was not specifically Protestant or even Christian. Many Masons insisted that theirs was the most ancient of ritual orders, from which other fraternal orders and even religions had drawn their ceremonies. According to the Masonic periodical, *The New Age,* Masonry could not be reduced to any one religion because it underlay them all. "Masonry *is religion.*" Indeed, "all . . . Ists and Isms of religion are embraced in, and spring from, Masonry. Masonry is the mother church, existing before there were either popes or prelates, Romanists or Protestants."[19]

[15] Ibid., 106. Incidentally, as their critics noted, the Masons and other secret groups were "usually organized like an army into a central host under general officers"—not unlike the structure of authority Protestants feared in the Catholic Church. I. J. Lansing, "Secrecy and Citizenship," in *New England Christian Association, Prize Essays,* 13 (Boston: 1897).

[16] Mark C. Carnes, *Secret Ritual and Manhood in Victorian America,* 52 (New Haven: Yale University Press, 1989). Carnes further interprets the Masons and other, largely male, orders as a response to the dominance of feminine domestic mores.

[17] Ibid., 61. In the early 1920s one commentator observed: "Our lodges are crowded while our churches are empty. The language of symbolism, . . . having been chased from the temple, has installed itself around the corner—but the name is changed." R. Dana Skinner, "Is the Ku Klux Klan Katholik?" *The Independent,* 111: 243 (Nov. 24, 1923).

[18] See, e.g., Charles A. Blanchard, *Modern Secret Societies* (Chicago: National Christian Association, 1903). Blanchard was president of Wheaton College.

[19] Carl F. Schader, "The Trinity of Masonry," *The New Age Magazine,* 26 (no. 2): 53 (February 1918).

There were even Masons who hoped in their fraternalism to found a "new religious movement outside of an[d] independent of any established church system"—a "Church of the Future" that would, in the opinion of one advocate, take its place after the successive failures of Judaism, the early Christian Church, and Protestantism.[20] In these conceptions of their fellowship, Masons pursued new-age eclecticism toward a vague, individual religiosity. They created an identity that transcended distinct institutional religions, and with this understanding of themselves as independent of churches, especially the Catholic Church, many came to believe—quite devoutly—in the separation between church and state.[21]

Of course, most Masons tended to understand separation differently than Jews, and therefore these groups cannot be lumped together any more than atheists and Baptists. Yet precisely because such groups, each for its own reasons, opposed ecclesiastical authority and welcomed separation, they seemed to confirm what nativists had long claimed—that separation had the support of all true Americans. Through their diversity they gave the impression that separation was a pervasive "American" ideal.

Nativist Organizations, Including the Ku Klux Klan

In addition to atheists, Baptists, Jews, and Masons, various nativist organizations demanded separation, and it is the support for separation among these groups that particularly needs documentation. Leaping from Jefferson's 1802 letter to Hugo Black's *Everson* opinion in 1947, the modern myth of separation omits any discussion of nativist sentiment in America and, above all, omits any mention of the Ku Klux Klan. Yet nativists had popularized separation in America in the nineteenth century, and, during the first half of the twentieth, they continued to distinguish themselves as the leading proponents of this ideal. Although

[20] Rev. Edgar Franklin Blanchard, *The Lodge and the Church of the Future*, 43–44 (Chicago: Vital Problem Publishing Co., n.d.).

[21] See, e.g., Justin A. Peterson, *Secret Societies, A Sermon* (Minneapolis: Augsburg Publishing House, 1924). More generally on these issues, see Lynn Dumenil, *Freemasonry and American Culture 1880–1930*, 42–71 (Princeton: Princeton University Press, 1984). On the individual religiosity that has flourished in America, see Sidney E. Mead, *The Lively Experiment: The Shaping of Christianity in America*, 134 (New York: Harper & Row, 1963).

conveniently forgotten, the advocacy of separation by myriad twentieth-century nativist organizations—of which the Klan was simply the most prominent—illustrates some continuities in the history of American religious liberty and reveals how broad a range of Americans perceived separation as a fundamental constitutional right.

Separation flourished in a nation that resounded with nativist sentiments, even in the most educated and genteel quarters. For example, in 1911, at the Cathedral of St. John the Divine in New York City, the members of the New England Society met on "Forefather's Sunday" to hear their annual sermon, in which the Rev. William M. Grosvenor bluntly stated their fears: "If the Pilgrim Fathers were a righteous remnant, we their sons are certainly a minority. We are scattered throughout the land. We have lost control of New England. Faneuil Hall is in an Irish city. Many beautiful colonial dwellings under the elms are crowded with Slavs and Poles and Italians and French Canadians. The Roman Catholic spire overshadows the Meeting House. More than that, the *Anglo-Saxon* is now a minority." Accordingly, these descendants of the Pilgrims had to struggle for their ideals:

> We must fight for the Constitution with its checks and balances, the bulwark of our freedom. We must fight to keep Church and State forever separated. We must fight for our public schools against the machinations of an Italian hierarchy that is today endeavoring to undermine and destroy them. . . .
>
> Before it is too late and the hordes of Europe and Asia have engulfed us, let us arise and fight, not with dreadnoughts, but for Puritan ideals and Puritan morals, for Anglo-Saxon freedom and Anglo-Saxon discipline, for Almighty God who is still for us, King of Kings and Lord of Lords, for Christ.

These men of New England would in this way fight for "the Messiah . . . whose law is love and whose service is perfect freedom."[22]

A far greater number of men pursued a more populist nativism in a widely circulated newspaper, the *Menace*. Published beginning in 1911 in Aurora, Missouri, by Wilbur Franklin Phelps, this paper reached over

---

[22] William M. Grosvenor, *The Puritan Remnant: The Twelfth Annual Sermon of the New England Society in the City of New York, Preached at the Cathedral of Saint John the Divine on Forefathers' Sunday, December 17th, 1911*, 2–3, 10, 11 (n.p., n.d.).

a million readers across the nation. Like many of his subscribers, Phelps seems to have channeled various fears and desires, including frustrated progressive hopes, into a fiercely nativist anti-Catholicism.[23] The head-lines of the *Menace* appealed to the most lurid anti-Catholic anxieties: "The Mother of Harlots and Her Children," "The Rape of Civic Honor—Americanism Betrayed," "Rome the Rum Dealer," and "Alice—The Cincinnati Convent Slave!"[24] Its masthead, however, departed from this sexually allusive, anti-Catholic hysteria and proclaimed a principled concern for liberty: "Published for the preservation of liberty, the promotion of progress and the advancement of civilization. As a means to this end we advocate the absolute separation of church and state, the taxation

---

[23] John Higham calls this anti-Catholicism "a displacement or distortion of antimonopolistic sentiment" and "an outlet for expectations which Progressivism raised and then failed to fulfill." John Higham, *Strangers in the Land: Patterns of American Nativism 1880–1925,* 180–181 (New York: Atheneum, 1963). See also Walter Kaufmann, *Faith and Fraternalism: The History of the Knights of Columbus,* 181 (New York: Simon & Schuster, 1992).

[24] Such topics held an inexhaustible fascination for nativists. For example, the *Rail Splitter* advertised a platform that included not only "Separation of church and state" but also "Convent inspection." "The Rail Splitter" (advertisement), in *Searchlight,* 3 (no. 9): 7 (March 4, 1922). At its most lurid, the *Rail Splitter* attracted readers with a combination of race, religion, and sex. After condemning "papalized politicians" who served "a bloated hierarchy," it promised to unmask "the Roman church from the harlotry of the Vatican to the vice dens of Chicago. . . . Read about protected vice and immunity rings. Little girls living lives of shame to enrich corrupt politicians. White girls forced to serve niggers and chinks. . . . The Rail Splitter in the name of God, and home, and school, and church, and country . . . hurls its defi[ance] in the faces of priest, bishop and arch-bishop." "Chicago Patriots—Attention" (Milan, Ill.: Rail Splitter, n.d.), an advertising leaflet in Knights of Columbus Archive, SC-11-1-145, New Haven, Connecticut. Similarly, during the 1928 election, *The True American* informed its readers about the "girls that are subjects of the priests" and had to "submit, surrender and yield to the often times half drunken, licentious, lustful priests be he black (negro) or white." R. C. Garner, "What Goes On in the Nunneries or the Difference between a Convent and a Nunnery," *The True American,* 1 (no. 2): 19 (Mattoon, Ill.: October 1928), copy in Knights of Columbus Archive, SC-11-1-056. Evangelist Garner was well known from the lecture circuit. For example, in Durham, North Carolina, he advertised a series of presentations at the Banner Warehouse, one of which—for "Men only"—was on that apparently ever-interesting topic, "Why Priests don't marry." Of course, the twenty-five cents paid by each listener was not an entrance fee but, rather, part of the "Collection." It barely requires mentioning that the "Protestant Committee" that purportedly organized the series ecumenically invited "All White Sects Creeds and Denominations." Advertising leaflet, in Knights of Columbus Archive, SC-11-1-55. In contrast to the *Menace,* the *Rail Splitter,* and many other nativist publications, *The Guardian of Liberty* emphasized in its advertisements not only that the *Guardian* was "AUTHORITATIVE" AND "CONVINCING" but also that "IT IS CLEAN." *Guardian of Liberty,* 1 (no. 6): 84 (July–August 1913).

of all church property and the compulsory education of all children up to the age of fourteen years in the public schools."[25] With these ideals the *Menace* opposed the "system . . . which crushes and stultifies the individual, demanding cringing obedience and lickspittle subserviency to a dishonest and grafting hierarchy."[26]

The *Menace* actively supported separation of church and state in political campaigns. For example, it regularly provided extensive publicity for the Guardians of Liberty. The Guardians assisted local anti-Catholic politicians across the nation, and, in advertising the Guardians' "organized resistance to popish aggressions," the *Menace* viewed itself as "an agitator—an educator—a light shining in the dark—a voice speaking to the people."[27] The *Menace* carried out this vision even in presidential poli-

---

[25] This declaration appeared in the top right corner of the front page from at least No. 52 (April 13, 1912) through No. 118 (July 19, 1913). On one side of its masthead appeared a skull and bones, crowned with a papal tiara, labeled "TEMPORAL POWER A PUBLIC MENACE"; on the other side, a public school building entitled "THE ANTIDOTE FOR PAPAL POISON." Earlier, in the top right corner, the *Menace* printed not the declaration reproduced in the text here, but the paper's "platform," which proposed "1. Relig[ious?] toleration. 2. Equality of all before the law. 3. Consent of the governed. 4. Civil marriage. 5. Free thought, free speech, and free press. 6. Submission to and recognition of rightly constituted authority." Soon after it began publication, however, at least by issue No. 18 (Aug. 19, 1911), the *Menace* altered the platform in order to defend itself against accusations of intolerance: "This publication does not condemn the Catholic religion, nor does it censure the honest, well meaning Roman Catholic communicant; but, it takes issue with the Roman Catholic organization in its political intrigues, its interference with established American institutions and government." Eventually, in early 1912 the paper replaced this "platform" with the quotation reproduced above in the text, giving more positive expression to its ideals. Yet, by July 1913 Catholic legal actions against the *Menace* left the editors feeling embattled, and they adopted an increasingly aggressive stance, changing their declaration in the top right corner of the masthead to read: "This is a nation of religious liberty and a man has a right to worship according to the dictates of his own conscience, but he DOES NOT have the right to impose his religion upon others. The menace to this nation from Catholicism lies in the fact that the avowed purpose of the hierarchy from the pope down is to make America Catholic, set the church above the state and dictate the religion of this republic." *Menace*, No. 119 (July 26, 1913). The last issue with this paragraph was No. 176 (Sept. 5, 1914). Thereafter, in response to a financial reorganization of the paper, the masthead included a commercial reminder concerning subscriptions.

[26] "Its Not the Laity," *Menace*, No. 68 (Aug. 3, 1912).

[27] "The Guardians of Liberty," *Menace*, No. 49 (March 23, 1912). When the publishers visited the national headquarters of the Guardians (apparently at the Masonic Grand Lodge at 50 West 24th Street, New York City), they were "given an insight into its aims and objects," and they thereby became "convinced that it is the greatest movement in the memory of the present generation." Ibid., No. 52 (April 13, 1912). Soon, the *Menace* was publishing a special "Guardians of Liberty Edition." Ibid., No. 65 (July 16, 1912), advertising No. 66. The Guardians were not the only organization to recognize the role of the

tics. During the 1912 election, it urged: "If you are in favor of the separation of church and state, the preservation of the flag and the American public school system, and opposed to the appropriation of public money for sectarian purposes, get busy now and spot the candidates who stand for the same things."[28] Americans understood what such exhortations meant, as revealed by a contemporary rhyme:

> Read the Menace
> Get the Dope
> Go to the Polls
> And defeat the Pope.[29]

Such were the means by which Protestants would achieve separation.

Another organization that joined the nativist campaign for separation was the Prohibition Party. In the nineteenth century the party could not agree about separation. Suspicious of Catholicism, some members favored the separation of church and state. Yet most hesitated to go so far, probably for theological reasons, including "Calvinist" or Reformed expectations about the role of the church. Accordingly, in 1876, it will be recalled, the Prohibition Party evasively supported the "separation of the government . . . from the control of every religious sect or other association."[30] When some in the party insisted upon a less equivocal separation, others vigorously objected. For example, in 1888 at the California state convention of the Prohibition Party, held in San Francisco, a majority "hissed down the principle of the separation of church and state, and adopted a platform recognizing the Lord as supreme ruler, 'to

---

Menace in providing communication among nativists. For example, one of the leaders of the revived American Protective Association (APA) had "plans to get the support of various anti-Catholic publications, such as 'The Menace.'" "Reorganizing the A.P.A. with Old Aims," *Catholic Standard and Times* (Nov. 29, 1913), clipping in Knights of Columbus Supreme Council Archive, SC-11-1-010, New Haven, Connecticut.

Incidentally, the relationship among nativist publications was complex. For example, in the early 1920s the *Rail Splitter* advertised in local Klan papers to provide its syndication services to individuals who wanted to start up their own papers. See, e.g., "Publish Your Own Patriotic Paper," *Oklahoma Fiery Cross*, 1 (no. 27): 3 (May 22, 1924), copy in Knights of Columbus Supreme Council Archive, SC-11-1-250. In this way, not only could the *Rail Splitter* increase its revenues, but local ventures could also enjoy independence while participating in the larger Klan and more broadly nativist movement.

[28] *Menace*, No. 68 (Aug. 3, 1912).

[29] *Amerika* (Nov. 2, 1914), clipping in Knights of Columbus Archive, SC-11-1-010.

[30] Prohibition Platform (1876), in Thomas Hudson McKee, *The National Conventions and Platforms of All Political Parties . . . 1789 to 1900*, 176–177 (Baltimore: 1900).

whose laws all human laws should conform.'"[31] Eventually, however, especially in the South, nativist support for separation reshaped the party's agenda. In the months before the 1912 election, the platform committee of the Prohibition Party considered planks supporting "Separation of church and state" and "No government appropriations for sectarian purposes." Although in the end the committee rejected these positions, it did so only after warm debate. The *Menace* complained: "Knowing the South as we do, and being in touch as we are with American sentiment throughout the country, we do not hesitate to say that the insertion of these planks in our party platform would have added a quarter of a million of the very best and most desirable of our citizens to our party vote."[32] In the years following, those who shared the views of the *Menace* continued to demand support for separation, and in 1916 they prevailed. In that year in response to nativist sentiments, the Prohibition Party at last acknowledged in its platform: "We stand for the preservation and development of our free institutions and for absolute separation of church and state, with the guarantee of full religious and civil liberty."[33]

Some local nativist endeavors emphasized separation even more dramatically, as can be illustrated by events in Birmingham, Alabama. In that city, prior to the spectacular growth of the Revised Klan in the 1920s, the Guardians of Liberty—known locally as "True Americans"—vigorously advocated separation, and they made this a central issue in the municipal election of 1917.[34] Led by the virulently anti-Catholic pastor of the First Baptist Church, A. J. Dickinson, the True Americans backed a Baptist candidate, Nathaniel A. Barrett, who had earlier been a local suburban mayor and who had led a campaign to ban Sunday movies.[35] Eventually, Barrett declared that he was a True American and

---

[31] Charles M. Snow, *Religious Liberty in America,* 282 (Washington, D.C.: 1914).

[32] "A Criticism Criticized," *Menace,* No. 73 (Sept. 7, 1912).

[33] *Platform of the Prohibition Party,* 5 (Chicago: Prohibition National Campaign Committee, 1916).

[34] The Guardians had already prevailed in other local political contests, one of the earliest being the 1913 election in St. Louis, where they supported the Republican against a Catholic Democrat. Afterwards, the Guardians explained that "[t]hey did not bring religion into politics, as they were accused of having done, but on the contrary made it their business to keep religion out. St. Louis is safe for another four years." "The Campaign at St. Louis," *Guardian of Liberty,* 1 (no. 4): 48 (May 1913). By 1914 they were moving their organization into the South. "A State Court Has Just Been Organized in Virginia—Now Watch the South," *Guardian of Liberty,* 2 (no. 14): 216 (May 1914).

[35] Carl V. Harris, *Political Power in Birmingham, 1871–1921,* 86 (Knoxville: University of Tennessee Press, 1977).

an ardent supporter of the "T.A." platform—a typical nativist document that began by declaring "complete separation of church and state" and then specified the implications of this principle. The platform's significance was clear enough, but to force its meaning into the open, a labor newspaper, which opposed the True American candidate, reprinted the platform together with a commentary explaining "the real platform as practiced by the T.A. society":

> 1. "The complete separation of church and state," *to the extent that no Catholic or friend of a Catholic shall hold any elective or appointive position under any city, county, state or national government.*
>
> 2. "The Public Schools"—*No Catholic or friend of a Catholic, or one who has not taken the oath of the T.A. Society, shall hold any position under the public school system of the city, county, state or national school system. . . .*[36]

[36] Michael A. Breedlove, "Progressivism and Nativism: The Race for the Presidency of the City Commission of Birmingham, Alabama in 1917," *Journal of the Birmingham Historical Society,* 6: 6, 7 (July 1980). The platform in full was:

> 1) complete separation of church and state, 2) the public school, no appropriations of public funds or land for any sectarian purposes whatsoever, 3) inspection of all public and private institutions, 4) civic righteousness, 5) the Bible in every school, 6) restriction of immigration, 7) the election to office of patriots only—men imbued with true American ideals, 8) free speech and free press, 9) appointment of those men and women only as public school teachers or principals whose Americanism is unquestioned, and 10) respect for Old Glory as the highest emblem of authority in the land.

Ibid., 6. This platform was backed up with action, such as "dismissals and boycotts against merchants who refused to dismiss Catholics." Ibid.

Other such platforms followed more or less the same formula. For example, the American Federation of Patriotic Voters had as the first plank of its platform that "[w]e demand absolute separation of church and state, as guaranteed by the constitution"—the second being that public schools "should be free from ecclesiastical influence or control" and that "persons disloyal to the government or to the public schools should be rigorously excluded from teaching therein." Typescript copy (May 9, 1938) of Patrick Henry Winston, "American Catholics and the A.P.A.," quoting the *Western Catholic* (Oct. 31, 1913), in Knights of Columbus Supreme Council Archive, SC-11-1-010. Similarly, the new APA declared: "(1) We unite to protect the institutions and Government of our country from the operations of the Roman Catholic hierarchy political machine, which is working under the guise of the Knights of Columbus and similar papal societies; (2) we are resolved to maintain a complete separation of Church and State by securing legislation to tax all church property and prevent any public money being given to Roman Catholic orphan asylums, parochial schools or other sectarian institutions; (3) it is our aim to fill every office of the nation, State and municipality with men of ability, integrity and pure patriotism. Roman Catholics, members of the Knights of Columbus, swear allegiance to the Pope, above any other authority, and therefore it is impossible for such men to be American patriots; (4) all patriotic citizens who believe that the Roman Catholic political machine is the deadliest menace to American liberties and civilization are invited to join this association." "Reorganizing the A.P.A. with Old Aims," *Catholic Standard and Times.*

Clause by clause, the whole platform was translated in this vein. None-theless, the True American candidate won—after which he promptly fired Birmingham's sole Catholic official, the police chief, and replaced him with a member of the Ku Klux Klan.[37] Like the *Menace* and the Prohibition Party platform, the True American campaign in Birmingham suggests the sort of nativism that made separation so popular.

Many nativists, including those who agitated for separation, recog-nized that they might seem unduly harsh toward Catholicism, and there-fore they often emphasized their cordial relations with Catholics and their deep concern for them as individuals. For example, in 1910, in his *Jeffersonian Magazine*, Thomas E. Watson wrote that "[f]or the individual Roman Catholic who finds happiness in his faith, I have no word of unkindness. Some of my best friends are devout believers in their 'Holy Father.' . . . The Roman Catholic Organization is the object of my pro-foundest detestation—Not the belief of The Individual."[38] In 1912 the *Menace* reminded its readers "that we have no ill will whatever for a man simply because he is a Roman Catholic." On the contrary, "[t]he writer of this article himself has Catholic relatives and Catholic friends." These and other members of "the laity" deserved "sympathy," for they were being crushed by "the Roman Catholic political machine," and it was "this machine" rather than the laity "that we are fighting."[39] Similarly, in the 1920s T. W. Callaway—pastor of the Baptist Tabernacle in Chatta-nooga and "a 100 per cent American"—denounced the Catholic Church as "simply a religio-politico organization" rather than a "spiritual body" and as a "relentless enemy" of "American" values (being "against separa-tion of Church and State, a fundamental in the Constitution of the United States"). Yet he went out of his way to "disclaim any ill-will to-ward a Catholic individual, or his religion." Callaway even praised the Catholics whom, because of their faith in Jesus, he respected "as Chris-tians, friends, and neighbors." Thus Callaway opposed "the Roman 'sys-tem,' and not the Catholic individual."[40] With these predictable lines,

---

[37] Harris, *Political Power in Birmingham*, 86. The nativist candidate won with strong subur-ban support, notwithstanding opposition from the downtown business community. Ibid.
[38] William W. Brewton, *The Life of Thomas E. Watson*, 325 (Atlanta: published by the author, 1926), quoting August 1910 issue of Watson's *Jeffersonian Magazine*.
[39] "It's Not the Laity," *Menace*.
[40] T. W. Callaway, *Romanism vs. Americanism*, 6–7 (Atlanta: Index Printing, 1923). For a much earlier Baptist example, see George C. Lorimer, *The Great Conflict: A Discourse, Concern-ing Baptists, and Religious Liberty*, 112–113 (Boston: 1877).

nativist Protestants could reconcile their prejudices with their individualistic ideals and neighborly relationships.

No nativist or Protestant organization more prominently supported the ideal of separation than the Revised Klan. Founded in 1915, this second Ku Klux Klan enjoyed particular success between 1921 and 1926, when it had about five million members and innumerable sympathizers. It exerted profound political power in states across the country and, probably more than any other national group in the first half of the century, drew Americans to the principle of separation.

The Klan, like so many earlier nativist orders, advocated separation as part of its vision of Americanism. The new leader of the Klan, Hiram Wesley Evans, exhorted Americans to adhere to the fundamental instincts of "race pride and loyalty," "patriotism," and "spiritual independence"—the last being "a revival of the individualism which sprang up just as the Nordic races began to assert themselves in their great blossoming of the last four centuries, and which found its chief expression in Protestantism." In contrast, the Catholic Church had a "habit of grouping aliens together and thus creating insoluble alien masses," which "strongly impede Americanization." Explaining how the Church was "actually and actively alien, un-American and usually anti-American," Evans argued that "its claim to full authority in temporal as well as spiritual matters" made "it impossible for it as a church, or for its members if they obey it, to cooperate in a free democracy in which Church and State have been separated." In particular, Catholics engaged in politics: "[T]here is the undeniable fact that the Roman Church takes an active part in American politics. It has not been content to accept in good faith the separation of Church and State, and constantly tries through political means to win advantages for itself and its people—in other words, to be a political power in America, as well as a spiritual power. Denials of Catholic activity in politics are too absurd to need discussion. The 'Catholic vote' is as well recognized a factor as the 'dry vote.' All politicians take it for granted." Unlike the dry vote, which was Protestant and the product of individual choice, the Catholic vote was that of a church exercising authority over "insoluble alien masses," and this violated "the separation of Church and State."[41]

---

[41] Hiram Wesley Evans, "The Klan's Fight for Americanism," *North American Review,* 223: 36, 45, 47 (1926). See also "Sheaves of Thought Gleaned from the Mind of Hiram Wesley

Separation became a crucial tenet of the Klan. When recruiting members, the Klan sometimes distributed cards listing "[t]he separation of church and state" as one of the organization's principles.[42] Bearing this out, Klan pamphlets declared that "[t]he fathers" and "the founders of our republic" had "wisely provided for the absolute divorce of Church and State."[43] Both in the South and the North, members even recited in their "Klansman's Creed": "I believe in the eternal Separation of Church and State."[44] Commenting on such vows, an "authoritative" writer— identified only as "931KNOIOK"—explained: "The Klan is pledged to maintain inviolate and perpetuate forever the principle of complete separation of Church and State, and the Roman Catholics fight this, because no sincere and devout Roman Catholic does or is permitted to believe in the separation of Church and State. The Roman Catholic Church is first, last and forever opposed to the separation of Church and State and

---

Evans," *The Kourier Magazine,* 2: 8 (September 1926); *Papers Read at the Meeting of Grand Dragons Knights of the Ku Klux Klan at Their First Annual Meeting Held at Asheville, North Carolina, July 1923,* 113–117 (n.p., n.d.).

[42] See example quoted in a broadside, *Does Bonham Need a Ku Klux Klan: A Sermon Delivered at the First Methodist Church, of Bonham, Texas, by the Pastor, Geo. C. French, Sunday Night, January 15, and Repeated by Request Friday Night, January 24th, at the South Bonham Church* (Texas: probably 1922 but possibly 1919), copy in Knights of Columbus Supreme Council Archive, SC-11-1-263.

[43] C. Lewis Fowler, *The Ku Klux Klan: Its Origin, Meaning and Scope of Operation,* 27, 33–34 (Atlanta: ca. 1922). Similarly, in a speech before assembled Klansmen in Dallas, the Rev. R. H. Tharp quoted Jesus on what should be rendered unto Caesar and added: "Following this principle as enunciated by Christ, our fathers established this nation on the basis of the separation of church and State. We must maintain that principle against all aggressors." *Searchlight,* 3 (no. 11): 10 (March 18, 1922). Such language about "our fathers" echoed earlier nativist rhetoric but attributed constitutional significance to what once had been a claim about the native paternity of the principle of separation. For example, in 1888 Justin D. Fulton had simply claimed: "Our fathers clamored for a separation of Church and State. Let their children go on with the work." Fulton, *Washington in the Lap of Rome,* 254 (Boston: Tremont Temple, 1888).

[44] The Creed began: "I believe in God and in the tenets of the Christian religion and that a godless nation can not long prosper." It also included: "I hold no allegiance to any foreign government, emperor, king, pope or any other foreign, political or religious power" and "I believe that our Free Public School is the cornerstone of good government and that those who are seeking to destroy it are enemies of our Republic and are unworthy of citizenship." *To the Citizens of Michigan* (n.p., ca. 1920s). The Creed was employed in Klan church services, such as in Birmingham, where, on a Sunday evening in January 1925, men, women, and children of the Klan met at the United Brethren Church for the usual mixture of Christ and Klan, ending with a recitation by the preacher, the Rev. G. A. Weaver, of the Klansman's Creed. *TWK Monthly* (Birmingham), 2 (no. 8): 28 (February 1925), copy available in Ku Klux Klan Scrapbook, vol. 1, Microfilm 257, at 79–95, Birmingham Public Library, Archives, Birmingham, Alabama.

in favor of the absolute control and domination of the State by the Roman Catholic Church."[45] At least in his account of the Klan's position, "931KNOIOK" was accurate. When new Klan members took their oath of allegiance in a formal and often dramatic ceremony, ablaze with light, they concluded with the climactic paragraph:

> I swear that I will most zealously—and valiantly—shield and preserve—by any and all—justifiable means and methods—the sacred constitutional rights—and privileges of—free public schools—free speech—free press—separation of church and state—liberty—white supremacy—just laws—and the pursuit of happiness—against any encroachment—of any nature—by any person or persons—political party or parties—religious sect or people—native, naturalized or foreign—of any race—color—creed—lineage or tongue whatsoever.
>
> All to which I have sworn by THIS oath—I will seal with my blood—be Thou my witness—Almighty God—
> AMEN!

Other than "white supremacy," there was nothing in this that Klansmen would take more seriously than "separation of church and state" and the related concern for "free public schools."[46]

---

[45] As quoted by "A Defense of the Ku Klux Klan," *The Literary Digest*, 76 (no. 3): 18–19 (Jan. 20, 1923). The anonymous "931KNOIOK" had written in *Brann's Iconoclast*, a Chicago publication issued after Brann's death.

[46] "Oath of Allegiance," 3 (Klan form printed for use in ceremony), inserted in Charles A. Fell, *Memoirs*, 2: 123, in Birmingham Public Library, Archives, 978.2.1.1.2. On behalf of the Klan, Evangelist C. P. Roney wrote: "The Knights of the Ku Klux Klan stand unequivocally for separation of church and state." *Is the Knights of the Ku Klux Klan Scriptural?* 7–8 (Shreveport, La.: ca. 1920–1925). For letters from Klansmen describing the "complete separation of church and state" as a Klan belief, see "Separation of Church and State Subject of Interest to All Americans Everywhere Now," *Searchlight*, 3 (no. 9): 7 (March 4, 1922). In Lincoln, Nebraska, in 1926 the participants in the annual Klan parade carried signs such as "'Long Live the Little Red School House,' 'We Believe in Separation of Church and State,' and 'Do you Believe in Upholding Our Constitution?'" Michael W. Schuyler, "The Ku Klux Klan in Nebraska, 1920–1930," *Nebraska History*, 66 (no. 3): 236 (Fall 1985). As if to ensure that these principles were not reduced to mere slogans, the women of the Nebraska Klan met to discuss such topics, including separation. Ibid., 238. See also ibid., 240; *Principles and Purposes of the Knights of the Ku Klux Klan Outlined by an Exalted Cyclops of the Order*, 4 (n.p., ca. 1920s); John Stephen Fleming, *What Is Klu Kluxism?: Let Americans Answer—Aliens Only Muddy the Waters*, 35 (Birmingham, Ala.: 1923); W. C. Wright, *The Ku Klux Klan Unmasked*, 4 (Dallas: Dallas Press, Inc., ca. 1924).

As Klansmen began to notice that there was a competing secular version of separation, they occasionally felt obliged to explain their conception of the principle. For example, in their Creed, Klanswomen declared: "WE BELIEVE that church and state should continue separate in administration and organization, although united in their mission and purpose to serve mankind unselfishly." "Creed of the Klanswomen," in *America for Americans as*

Many members of the Klan dedicated themselves to the separation of church and state with religious intensity, as became most strikingly evident in the ceremony conducted by the order's popular female branch, known as the Women of the Ku Klux Klan. In their second degree, "The Degree of the Kriterion Konservator," these women began their meetings by arranging themselves in a "quadrate" together with various symbols, including "the Bible and Torch at the Kludd's station; Sword at the Klokard's station; flag on the stand at the right of Excellent Commander; Fiery Cross at left of E.C.—and, in addition to these, there is on the Klaliff's station a copper penny (one of the large, old-fashioned ones), and an hourglass." The symbols in place, the Excellent Commander opened her Konklave of the Kriterion Konservators. What followed was a mixture of patriotic and Protestant music, the pledge of allegiance, and the placing of the symbols on "the Sacred Altar of the Klan." With a pitcher of water, the women celebrated "purity"; with the sword, "law enforcement"; with the Bible, the "Divine light upon the pathway of all Christian men and women"; with the hourglass, the "sands of time" during which the women would dedicate themselves to "Patriotism." The penny, however, had another meaning.

> (As the Kouriers place the penny and the hour-glass upon the altar, the music stops. The Kouriers step back two paces to their original positions.)
>
> *E.C.:* "Second Kourier, what is the symbol you deposited upon the altar?"
>
> *Kourier No. 2:* "A copper penny."
>
> *E.C.:* "Klaliff, its meaning?"
>
> *Klaliff:* "'They asked Him, "Tell us, therefore, what thinkest thou? Is it lawful to give tribute unto Caesar, or not?" But Jesus per-

---

Interpreted by the Women of the Ku Klux Klan, 6 (n.p., ca. 1920s). The *Kourier* explained: "While standing for complete separation of church and state, the Klan, recognizing the necessity for moral teaching, stands for the reading of the Bible in the public schools." "The Klan and the Public School," *Kourier Magazine*, 25 (May 1925). Similarly, Klansmen argued that they were not intolerant in their support for separation, as when Professor J. Q. Nolan—a spokesman for Imperial Wizard Joseph Simmons—insisted that "the Klan stands unalterably for separation of church and state, but it stands just as firmly for religious freedom." "Two Thousand Klansmen Hear Lecturer Tell Aims of Order," *Searchlight*, 3 (no. 11): 10 (March 18, 1922). Of course, in taking such positions, Klansmen assumed that it was the Catholic Church that was intolerant, and that "a real American . . . is tolerant of anything except intolerance." "The Real American," *Kourier Magazine*, 29 (July 1925).

ceived their wickedness and said, "Why tempt ye me, ye hypocrites? Show me the tribute money." And they brought unto Him a penny. And He saith unto them, "Whose is this image and superscription?" And they say unto Him, "Caesar's." Then saith He unto them, "Render therefore unto Caesar the things which are Caesar's, and to God the things that are God's."''

E.C.: "And in this Degree of Kriterion Konservator we are especially reminded of this lesson—that Church and State ought forever to be kept separate. . . ."

It was a devotion echoed in the Closing Ceremony, when the Excellent Commander spoke of "[t]he Copper Penny, like the tribute money of old," that stands for "our determination that Church and State shall forever be kept separate." Less than a minute later, she would order the Night Hawk to "extinguish the Fiery Cross," and the women would sing "The Old Rugged Cross." As the Night Hawk put out the flames, she would say: "I will extinguish the material fire . . . but will ever keep burning in my heart the ideal"—a sentiment she emphasized (in imitation of Catholic ritual) by giving the sign of the "O.F.C." or Old Fiery Cross.[47]

The men and women of the Klan devoted themselves to separation not only in their ceremonies but also in their towns and schools, where the Klan cooperated with other nativist organizations to create the appearance of unanimity. Such was the case in the New Jersey town of

---

[47] *Ritual in the Second Degree of the Women of the Ku Klux Klan,* 3, 9–10, 15 (Little Rock: Imperial Headquarters, Women of the Ku Klux Klan, ca. 1923). For female Klan ritual, see Kathleen M. Blee, "Gender Ideology and the Role of Women in the 1920s Klan Movement," *Sociological Spectrum,* 7: 87 (1987). The Klan was not alone in incorporating separation into its rituals. See, e.g., the Guardians of Liberty in Chapter 13, at note 27. From a decidedly more ecumenical perspective, E. Stacy Matheny—a former chaplain to the Ohio state senate—published a prayer entitled "Separation of Church and State":

> SHELTER us and keep us unafraid in Thy secret place, O God.
> We thank Thee for the Church and the State, and for our American idea of their separation forever. Thou knowest, O God, that we differ widely in questions of theology, and disagree on political problems and issues. . . .
> O God, we earnestly pray that all of the creeds may be swallowed up in pure and undefiled religion. May the wicked spirit of sectarianism lose itself in the Kingly Truth of the Infinite.

Matheny, *American Patriotic Devotions,* 284 (New York: Association Press, 1932). This prayer was followed by one for "Our American Schools." Ibid., 285.

Belleville, where in 1923 the local council of the Catholic Daughters of America impudently donated a copy of the *Catholic Encyclopedia* to the town's high school. Catholics had systematically sought to have the *Encyclopedia* placed in school libraries across the country, and nativist publications had urged Protestants to defend against this threat to American freedom.[48] In Belleville the Board of Education soon received protests from fifteen residents, including representatives of the Junior Order of United American Mechanics, the Patriotic Order of Sons of America, and the Ladies of the Grand Army of the Republic—all nativist orders founded in the nineteenth century. As if this were not enough, two anonymous letters arrived, one from "The Keeper of the Sacred Seal of Martha Washington, Council No. 9, Ladies of the Invisible Empire" (a female Klan auxiliary), and the other from "Belleville Chapter, No. 6, Royal Riders of the Red Robe" (a Klan-supported order that flourished mostly on the West Coast). Both letters had Belleville postmarks but bore return addresses in Oregon. Their spirit is suggested by the letter from the Royal Riders, which protested "against the acceptance of the nineteen volumes of the Catholic Encyclopedia . . . inasmuch as this would be an intermingling of Church and State, something to which we are absolutely opposed." With the benefit of such advice, the board— that is, the four out of five members who were not Catholic—voted to remove the offending tomes to the public library (although when the school superintendent tried to obey this instruction, he found that a volume had been stolen).[49]

In pursuit of separation, individual independence, and other "American" ideals, the Klan advocated compulsory public education—

[48] For example, *The Protestant* warned "Patriots everywhere" that "Roman literature," particularly the *Catholic Encyclopedia*, was "being intruded into the public schools to warp and poison the plastic minds of young children." "Catholic Encyclopedia in Schools," *The Protestant*, 2 (no. 12): 185 (February 1923). Incidentally, two months later, this journal reported the Belleville incident, and it was still complaining about the *Encyclopedia* almost a year later. "Papal Encyclopedia in Schools," in ibid., 2 (no. 2): 26 (April 1923); "Not Catholic, but Roman, Encyclopedia," in ibid., 3 (no. 11): 165 (January 1924).

[49] "Bar Catholic Books from High School," *New York Times*, 6 (March 21, 1923). Incidentally, the representations of the Junior Order were made by a trolley conductor, Henry Snyder. The logic of the Royal Riders was not uncommon among nativists. For example, the revived APA argued that "[a] cardinal is a member of the Papal court and cannot, therefore, have any other connection with another government or state, nevertheless cardinals hold citizenship in America." C. I. J. Arthur Petersen, *The Impending Collapse of Protestantism* (San Francisco: The American Protective Association, Form No. 23, 1-7-23), copy in Knights of Columbus Archive, SC-11-1-11.

most successfully in Oregon. Oregon had been a "Banner state" for Liberals because of the success they had enjoyed there when establishing numerous secular churches, and it was no less a place of high hopes for nativists. Although relatively few Catholics or recent immigrants resided in Oregon, nativists led a strongly anti-Catholic campaign there in the summer and autumn of 1922. Eventually, in November they captured the legislature and passed a law, by referendum, requiring all children between eight and sixteen to attend public schools.[50]

The Klan followed a well-trodden path when it sought mandatory state education. Nativists and Liberals had not typically argued that separation required compulsory public schooling, but they had long perceived public education as an essential means of preserving American principles—especially, perhaps, separation.[51] Only the government could ensure appropriate instruction in America's "glorious heritage of civil and religious liberty," and, on this account, already in the mid-nineteenth century nativist legislatures had contemplated requiring attendance at public schools or, at least, the certification of private school teachers.[52] Later in the century, Liberals joined nativists in seeking com-

[50] This account is based largely on Edwin V. O'Hara, "The School Question in Oregon," 2–4 (a typed memorandum) (n.p., ca. 1923), in Knights of Columbus Archive, SC-11-1-32; "History and Record of the Oregon School Case," 4 (n.p., ca. 1925), in Knights of Columbus Archive, SC-11-1-22; William G. Ross, *Forging New Freedoms: Nativism, Education, and the Constitution, 1917–1927*, 148–173 (Lincoln: University of Nebraska, 1994). See also David B. Tyack, "The Perils of Pluralism: The Background of the Pierce Case," *American Historical Review*, 74 (no. 1): 74 (October 1968). For the records of an Oregon klavern during this period, see David A. Horowitz, *Inside the Klavern: The Secret History of a Ku Klux Klan of the 1920s* (Carbondale: Southern Illinois Press, 1999). For Klan organizing in Oregon, see "Klan Activities in Oregon," *Searchlight*, 3 (no. 10): 7 (March 11, 1922).

[51] For example, in 1886 the Central Committee for Protecting and Perpetuating the Separation of Church and State argued that, "in founding parochial schools, and in withdrawing their children from the public schools where they would be under *American influences*," Catholics and their Church sought "civil encroachments" and the Church of Rome "thus places itself in antagonism to American thought." The Central Committee for Protecting and Perpetuating the Separation of Church and State, *To the People of New York: Appeal No. 4*, 13. According to John Jay, "The duties of the American citizen for which the public school is intended to fit him are those of a sovereign ruler. He is to be independent of the world, and especially of every foreign prince or potentate; he is to be governed by allegiance to the Republic, and to obey its constitution and laws expressed in the constituted will of the American people; and to maintain the fundamental principles of civil and religious freedom, and the separation of church and state." John Jay, "Public and Parochial Schools," in *The Two Sides of the School Question*, 59 (Boston: Arnold Publishing Co., 1890).

[52] For example, *Report of Massachusetts House Committee on Education*, as quoted by Orestes Brownson, "A Know-Nothing Legislature," *Brownson's Quarterly Review*, 398 (July 1855).

pulsory public education. For example, in 1876, when pursuing separation, the National Liberal League resolved: "That universal education is the only safeguard of universal liberty; that no child in the republic should be permitted to grow up without at least a good common school education."[53] Drawing upon the liberal theological ideals that had become a pronounced feature of Americanism, the Klan argued that intellectual independence and therefore also the foundations of American liberty depended upon public education. According to the Klan, in public schools, unlike in Catholic institutions, the young would "be taught *how to think, not* what to think."[54] On such assumptions, which sometimes came remarkably close to those of liberal intellectuals, the Klan and allied organizations, including many Masonic lodges, joined movements for obligatory public schooling in various states, including Alabama, Arkansas, California, Michigan, Nebraska, Ohio, Oklahoma, Oregon, Texas, Washington, and Wyoming.[55]

See also Ross, *Forging New Freedoms,* 24. Nativist Protestants continued to hold such views. Thus in 1888 Justin D. Fulton insisted that politicians "will insist upon a separation of Church and State; upon maintaining a public school system, in which all the children of the State *shall* be educated. The Bible shall be unbound." Fulton, *Washington in the Lap of Rome,* 255.

[53] Not surprisingly, the League added "that the public school system cannot be sustained in equal justice to all except by confining it strictly to a secular instruction; that all religious exercises should be prohibited in the public schools." National Liberal League, *Patriotic Address to the People of the United States,* 11 (Boston: National Liberal League, 1876). See also, for example, *The Third Annual Congress of the National Liberal League Held at Cincinnati, Ohio, September 13 and 14, 1879,* 97 (New York: D. M. Bennett, Liberal and Scientific Publishing House, n.d.).

[54] *The Ku Klux Klan Presents Its View of the Public Free School,* 2 (n.p., ca. early 1920s). Such ideas were commonplace among nativists. For example, Allen Hill Autrey observed: "to be a good Roman Catholic you must give up liberty of conscience, all civil and political rights, and even the privilege of THINKING for yourself." Autrey, *Warning Signals or Romanism an American Peril,* 126 (Little Rock: Doctrinal Interpreter, 1911). He elaborated: "Shall we send our sons to teachers who have not been trained in schools of independent thought, by the clash of mind with mind." Ibid., 128. A leading Mason from Mississippi held that "[o]ur schools inspire youth with the ideals of personal freedom and self-government and teach them to read and think for themselves." M. R. Grant, *Americanism v. Roman Catholicism,* 165 (Meridian, Miss.: Truth Publishing Co., 1920). For related ideas at a later date, see John T. McGreevy, "Thinking on One's Own: Catholicism in the American Intellectual Imagination, 1928–1960," *Journal of American History,* 84: 97 (June 1997).

[55] Ross, *Forging New Freedoms,* 142. For the Alabama measure, see "Compulsory School Law for Alabama," *The Protestant,* 3 (no. 7): 104 (September 1923). In Michigan a campaign song for the public school amendment began:

> Our boys and girls must go to school,
>   In Michigan, my Michigan;
> And learn to live the golden rule,
>   In Michigan, my Michigan;

In 1922 in Oregon a committee of Scottish Rite Masons, led by the Masons' state Inspector-General, P. S. Malcolm, circulated petitions to obtain a referendum on compulsory public schooling. Arguing that support for the referendum was a Masonic obligation, Malcolm and his Masonic allies took for their authority a 1920 resolution by the Supreme Council, 33°, of the Scottish Rite of Freemasonry, Southern Jurisdiction of the United States (which included much of the country, including both the South and the West). According to the Supreme Council's resolution, "we recognize and proclaim our belief in the free and compulsory education of the children of our nation in public primary schools" in which "all children shall attend and be instructed in the English language only . . . as the only sure agency for the perpetuation and preservation of the free institutions guaranteed in the Constitution of the United States."[56] The Supreme Council also endorsed "[t]he entire separation of church and state and opposition to every attempt to appropriate public moneys, directly or indirectly, for the support of sectarian institutions."[57] At about

---

Each boy to be a gallant knight,
    Each girl to help make laws that's right,
And save us from the papast [sic] blight,
    In Michigan, my Michigan.

An Amendment comes before our folks,
    In Michigan, my Michigan;
To rid our state of all paroks,
    In Michigan, my Michigan;
So awake ye freemen, sleep no more,
    Until our Public Schools are sure,
Let's keep them free forevermore,
    In Michigan, my Michigan.

Rev. F. F. DeLong, *The K.C. Oath Confirmed* (Ortonville, Mich.: n.d.), copy in Knights of Columbus Supreme Council Archive, SC-11-1-223. DeLong also published *Making America Catholic* and the more lurid *Convent Cruelties* by "ex-nun Helen Jackson." Ibid.

[56] Supreme Council, 33°, *Transactions*, 11 (1920); "History and Record of the Oregon School Case," 2. William G. Ross observes: "Virtually every issue of the *New Age*, for example, contained at least one article or editorial that advocated mandatory public schooling." Ross, *Forging New Freedoms*, 70.

[57] The Supreme Council created a news bulletin, *The Scottish Rite Clip Service*, devoted to reporting on the pursuit of some basic Masonic principles, which were published on the back page of each issue:

The Supreme Council Favors:

1. A Federal department of education with a secretary in the President's Cabinet, and federal aid for public school purposes, under the absolute control of the states.
2. A national university at Washington, supported by the Government.

the same time, the Supreme Council, together with the Klan, began to lead the struggle for a federal "Department of Education with a Cabinet Secretary at its head."[58] In this context, the Oregon Masons demanded in 1922 that the state adopt their principle of compulsory public education. Although many Oregon Masons, particularly in the business community, opposed the Oregon school referendum as a threat to freedom, the Masonic advocates of the measure apparently had greater strength.[59]

Not far behind the scenes lurked the Ku Klux Klan. With suburban and rural support, the Klan seems to have been responsible for the success of the referendum. Indeed, the Klan dominated the election. To win the Klan vote and the governorship, the Democratic nominee, Walter Marcus Pierce, backed the school measure, and, largely on this "progressive and enlightened" issue, both Pierce and what was described as a Klan legislature were swept into office.[60] Ensuring this victory for the

----

3. The compulsory use of English as the language of instruction in the grammar grades.

4. Adequate provision for the education of the alien populations, not only in cultural and vocational subjects, but especially in the principles of American institutions and popular sovereignty.

5. The entire separation of church and state and opposition to every attempt to appropriate public moneys, directly or indirectly, for the support of sectarian institutions.

6. The American public school, non-partisan, non-sectarian, efficient, democratic; for all the children of all the people; equal educational opportunities for all.

7. The inculcation of patriotism, love of the flag, respect for the law and order and undying loyalty to constitutional government.

For example, see *Scottish Rite Clip Service*, No. 7 (Sept. 17, 1923). This statement continued to appear for decades in succeeding publications, including The Supreme Council, 33°, *Bulletin*, and the *Masonic Bulletin*.

[58] *The Ku Klux Klan Presents Its View of the Public Free School*, 2; Fox, *Lodge of the Double-Headed Eagle*, 193. The National Education Association joined the demands for a Department of Education on July 6, 1922. In advocating compulsory education, separation of church and state, and a Department of Education, the Masons abandoned their proclaimed reticence about politics and thereby "signaled a major shift in the public life and profile of the Scottish Rite from the temple to the secular world." Ibid., 192.

Incidentally, the U.S. Bureau of Education worked closely with the Scottish Rite, Southern Jurisdiction, and other fraternal organizations. Beginning in 1915, *New Age* contained "Educational Notes" that were "furnished by the U.S. Bureau of Education." Ibid., 179. Moreover, within a few years, the Masons, as well as other "fraternal and patriotic organizations," were cooperating with the Bureau of Education in the Americanization of immigrants. Supreme Council, 33°, *Transactions*, 44 (1917).

[59] "History and Record of the Oregon School Case," 4.

[60] "School Bill Sweeps Oregon," *The Protestant*, 2 (no. 10): 158 (December 1922); Ross, *Forging New Freedoms*, 151. For Pierce's relationship to the Klan, his appearance at Klan meetings, and his apparent Klan membership, see David A. Horowitz, "The Klansman as Outsider," *Pacific Northwest Quarterly*, 80 (no. 1): 18 (January 1989).

Klan and its referendum were not only Klansmen but also numerous like-minded women, who exercised their recently acquired freedom by voting for compulsory education.[61]

The supporters of the Oregon movement for compulsory public education often argued that nothing less was at stake than the free and independent character of Americans. Asking themselves, "How is the spirit of a free people to be formed, animated and cheered," they an-

---

[61] For the role of women, see David A. Horowitz, "Social Morality and Personal Revitalization: Oregon's Ku Klux Klan in the 1920s," *Oregon Historical Quarterly*, 90 (no. 4): 371 (Winter 1989); Blee, "Gender Ideology and the Role of Women," 82. Many emancipated women supported compulsory public education and other nativist ideals. For example, in July 1922 the League of Protestant Women was formed with national headquarters in Houston for various nativist (and anti-Communist) purposes, including, as stated in its constitution, "to maintain and perpetuate the absolute separation of Church and State; to maintain forever the supremacy of the white race; to support, defend, and further advance and improve our public schools," and so on. These goals were the foundation of a more practical agenda that included "A PROTESTANT BIBLE TO BE PLACED AND READ IN EVERY PUBLIC SCHOOL; EVERY CHILD TO ATTEND PUBLIC SCHOOL THROUGH ALL ELEMENTARY GRADES; EVERY SCHOOL IN THESE UNITED STATES TO BE AN AMERICAN INSTITUTION; THE COMPLETE RESTRICTION OF ALL IMMIGRATION FOR A PERIOD OF TEN YEARS; THE PURIFICATION OF CAUCASIAN BLOOD." Advertisement cut out of *Colonel Mayfield's Weekly* (ca. November 1922), in Knights of Columbus Supreme Council Archive, SC-11-1-263. Incidentally, the byline of the *Weekly* was "BIGGER AND BETTER PUBLIC SCHOOLS AND MORE OF 'EM."

Widely associated with the compulsory public schooling campaigns was the image of the little red school house. This symbol had been popularized by the Order of the Little Red School House and by numerous images, such as little stickers depicting a red school house flying an American flag, which were advertised as "the little firebrands of the PROTESTANT movement." *Little Red School House Stickers* (Earlville, N.Y.: American Press, n.d.). In Philadelphia, in a parade organized by the Philadelphia County Federation of Protestant Patriotic Fraternities, Protestants even created a series of little red school house floats. "National Court Officers Review Great Patriotic Parade," *Guardian of Liberty*, 3 (no. 25): 465 (October 1915). The role of this image in the compulsory schooling campaign may be illustrated by a lead article in a local Masonic journal that introduced an argument for compulsory public education with an epigraph evincing almost poetic pretensions:

> Elections are
> Near.
> Primaries
> Are nearer.
> See that your vote
> And influence
> Are given to a friend
> Of the
> Little Red Schoolhouse
> And of the American
> Public School System.

Frank G. Burroughs, "Eternal Vigilance," *The Idaho Freemason*, 1 (no. 2): 1 (July 1922).

swered "only by free public schools."[62] One voter explained: "By supporting the public school, we support the foundation of true Americanism" and "teach children . . . to become Americans in reality and to
support America's ideals and traditions."[63] In contrast, "any sectarian
school is a menace to our nation's progress in that it has a tendency to
shape the plastic mind of the child into a molded path from which there
is small chance to escape at maturity."[64] According to another Oregon
nativist, this dangerous tendency of sectarian schools violated the U.S.
Constitution: "The fathers of the framers of that immortal document had
come out from under the yoke held over them by Rome and her daughters. They sought freedom to worship . . . and they found it under that
great constitution, yet today . . . Rome and her daughters would . . .
violate that very document, and desire to take the young under their
wing, under the guise of 'private school,' and for years . . . instill in that
unmatured mind, their peculiar church doctrines. Thus in a very strong
way moulding the conscience of the child."[65]

[62] John L. Schmudla, "Naught to Do with Religion. School Bill Is Purely Educational
Matter . . ." (Letter to editor, Portland, Oct. 31), in *Morning Oregonian*, 12 (Nov. 2, 1922).
[63] W. H. Gordon, "School Bill Held Just. American Ideals Declared First Need of All Children" (Letter to editor, Portland, Nov. 3), in ibid., 9 (sec. 4) (Nov. 5, 1922). This voter
wanted "all schools, public or private, inspected by the proper authorities" and hoped to
"[b]ar out all so-called religions which are sectarian and let each and every soul have full
freedom to worship God as he thinks will fit his case." In arguing that "[r]eligious creeds
have no place in our public schools," he explained: "Religion is one thing; creed and dogma
are another, hence are personal and cannot have any place in the school room under the
federal constitution. . . . Religion as taught by Christ is divine law. Religion as taught by
the different sects is not divine, but the creeds and dogmas of man." Ibid.
[64] A. G. Fries, "Sectarian Schools Rapped. Menace to Nation's Progress . . ." (Letter to editor,
Portland, Nov. 3), in ibid., 9 (Nov. 5, 1922). Accordingly, religion was not to be taught in
school, "except when a child has reached maturity and takes up the study of its own free
will, after it has enjoyed the blessed privilege of mingling . . . [and] exchanging ideas with
children of every other sect and religion." Ibid.
[65] W. A. Goodwin, "Why the School Bill Fought. Private Schools Declared Trying to Teach
Own Doctrine" (Letter to editor, Boardman, Nov. 3), in ibid. Revealing his sense of outrage,
this writer also asked, "Is it not true that the reason they want private schools is that they
may teach the young mind the beliefs of their peculiar churches." Ibid.
   Catholics had to struggle largely on their own in the courts to get the referendum overturned. During the months prior to the vote, Catholics had found allies in nonsectarian
schools and among the ministers and schools of some Protestant denominations (including
Episcopalians, Presbyterians, Lutherans, and Seventh-Day Adventists). Edwin V. O'Hara,
"The School Question in Oregon," 2–4. After the referendum passed, however, secular
and Protestant private schools received quiet assurances that they would be accommodated, leaving Catholics almost alone to challenge the law. Catholics apparently waited
until the decision in *Meyer v. Nebraska* (1923) before commencing their suit. They chose

In this dimly lit landscape, in which the foreign hierarchy imposed a stultifying mental subjugation, the Klan struggled to keep alight the torch of Protestantism, Americanism, and individual enlightenment. The Klan advocated compulsory public schooling and the separation of church and state as part of this fiery vision of individual independence— a vision radically Protestant in its conception and symbolized by burning crosses. Accordingly, the Klansmen who demanded separation, public schooling, and conformity to ideals of independence assumed that they, rather than their opponents, were fighting ignorance and submission to authority. Thus, in Rhode Island when Protestants were drawn to the anti-Catholic flames of the Klan, they formed the Roger Williams Klanton.[66] Similarly, in both the South and the North, it was not only to terrorize former slaves and their children but also to illuminate the ignorant with a religious and patriotic vision of freedom that Klansmen lit their fires—burning crosses in Catholic neighborhoods and occasionally even torching Catholic churches.[67]

Worshiping under their flaming crosses, Klansmen merged Klan and Christianity. In both Klan meetings and church services, Klansmen strangely combined Klan and Christian ritual. In the South and West they marched into churches on Sundays in full regalia to demonstrate their support for local congregations.[68] In Alabama the Klan so strongly

---

as their plaintiff the Society of the Sisters of the Holy Names of Jesus and Mary, which was backed by the newly formed Catholic Civic Rights Association and financed mostly by the Knights of Columbus. A single secular school, the Hill Military Academy, aligned itself with the Catholics, although its costs were such that Catholics eventually had to provide it with financial support. In 1925 the Supreme Court overturned the Oregon compulsory school law. Pierce v. Society of Sisters, 268 U.S. 510 (1925). After the Supreme Court's decision, it was observed that "Oregon's idea of separation of Church and State would mean . . . not Church but only State." "Oregon School Law Declared Invalid by Supreme Court," *New York Times*, 2 (June 2, 1925). For a much earlier treatment of the danger that compulsory public education would infringe upon religious and educational freedom, see a particularly interesting pamphlet on religion in the public schools: Zim Tod, *America's Great Peril*, 40–44 (St. Louis: 1879).

[66] For the Roger Williams Klanton, see Norman W. Smith, "The Ku Klux Klan in Rhode Island," *Rhode Island History*, 37 (no. 2): 41 (1978).

[67] For a church burning in 1916 in Birmingham, see Glenn Feldman, *Politics, Society, and the Klan in Alabama 1915–1949*, 58 (Tuscaloosa: University of Alabama Press, 1999). For an example of such arson in 1921 in Illinois, see Higham, *Strangers in the Land*, 293.

[68] In May 1924 in Cyril, Oklahoma, for example, when Klansmen attended a revival meeting in a local church, the minister, upon the request of the congregation, delivered an enlightening lecture on "The Ku Klux Klan and American Institutions." Apparently the minister "did a thorough 'job.'" "Klan Wears Evergreen on Cyril Church Visit," *Oklahoma*

identified with Protestantism that some Klansmen once paraded into a meeting of black Baptists, rendering them utterly astonished.[69] Although many ministers conducted Klan services and participated in other acts of solidarity, some ministers went so far as to institutionalize the Klan's connection to Protestantism. For example, in 1924 in Garber, Oklahoma, the Rev. O. R. Miller began holding regular services in what purportedly was "the first church to be dedicated under the fiery cross of the Ku Klux Klan." Locally famous as "the parson who don't mince words," Miller opened his interdenominational Community Church of Christ to members of all Protestant creeds. Perhaps on this account, and perhaps because of his blunt lectures on a favorite anti-Catholic topic, the "history of the church," he quickly attracted a flock of 1,000 and therefore needed a new building. After raising $50,000 with ease, Miller initiated construction by having Masons and Klansmen lay the cornerstone. Lest the affiliation be unclear, he placed "two huge fiery crosses" on top of the church for the dedication ceremonies and had another more permanently installed in the baptistry.[70] Like so many original thinkers, Miller was not altogether alone. In Webster, Maryland, during the same year, the Rev. Milton W. Sutcliffe proudly established what he believed to be "the first Klan church . . . in the United States." While Sutcliffe was preparing for the consecration—"just before the time set for a Ku Klux ceremony"—the entire church was ignited, apparently by a critic with a sense of irony. Undeterred, Sutcliffe quickly rebuilt the structure

---

Fiery Cross, 1 (no. 27): 3 (May 22, 1924), copy in Knights of Columbus Supreme Council Archive, SC-11-1-250. In the South this sort of Klan visit was utterly mundane. What earned this press coverage was the "new style of regalia" sported by the Klansmen. In contrast, on the East Coast such visits were most unusual. For photographs of what was billed as the first of these visits in the East, see *State Gazette* (Trenton, N.J.), 10 (March 15, 1923).

[69] Feldman, *Politics, Society, and the Klan in Alabama,* 40.

[70] "Dedicate Church at Garber as Cross Burns," *Oklahoma Fiery Cross,* 1 (no. 27): 3 (May 22, 1924), copy in Knights of Columbus Supreme Council Archive, SC-11-1-250. More temporary arrangements were commonplace. For example, at a Klan service in the United Brethren Church in Birmingham, the Rev. G. A. Weaver draped his pulpit with "a large American flag upon which rested an illuminated cross." The service began with the singing of "America" and "The Old Rugged Cross," and a rendition by three ladies of "Let the Fiery Cross Be Burning." *TWK Monthly* (Birmingham), 2 (no. 8): 28 (February 1925), copy available in Ku Klux Klan Scrapbook, vol. 1, Microfilm 257, at 79–95, Birmingham Public Library, Archives, Birmingham, Alabama.

and, in a more successful Klan ceremony, consecrated the church, the steeple of which—at least in this second version—was "surrounded by an electric fiery cross."[71]

In the light of the cross, Protestant, American, and Klan conceptions of freedom could seem indistinguishable. Klan leaders in Alabama explained that they used the cross "to constantly remind us that Christ is our criterion of character and His teaching our rule of life." The flames signified that "Christ is the light of the world"—an illumination that could "dispel ignorance, superstition and intolerance and enable one to walk mentally and spiritually without falling in to the pitfalls of sin."[72] Of course, the ignorance, superstition, and intolerance such light would dispel hardly needed explanation. Similarly, Walter Reasoner wrote from Foley, Alabama, of the "the fiery cross blazing in glory with it's [sic] radiance like the statute [sic] of Liberty, enlightening the world with liberty, both civil and religious." He worried about the crosses "associated with the power of Rome" and declared that the fiery cross—"the emblem of pure Americanism"—should not be "put to an open compromise with papists," lest it lose "its worth and ideals."[73] In a nation illuminated

---

[71] "Fire Engine Guards Church as the Klan Dedicates It," *New York Times,* 1 (Aug. 25, 1924). The most technically advanced of such Klan churches was one in St. Louis, which advertised its brand of Protestantism with a "revolving fiery cross." "Fiery Cross Brings Back Man's Memory," *Oklahoma Fiery Cross,* 1 (no. 27): 3 (May 22, 1924), copy in Knights of Columbus Archive, SC-11-1-250.

[72] As quoted by Feldman, *Politics, Society, and the Klan in Alabama,* 178, quoting Alabama KKK Newsletter, 7 (January 1929).

[73] Walter Reasoner, "Interested in Klan," *Onlooker* (July 3, 1924), clipping in Knights of Columbus Archive, SC-11-1-159. Responding to demands that the Klan disrobe, Reasoner challenged Catholics to shed their religious garb first: "They want the Klans to unmask. Very well. But let them disrobe first. They have clothed themselves in Christ-like garments." Ibid. In a more positive tone, a 1924 Klan publication on "Klanishness" instructed Klansmen to look beyond the external, "alien" world toward the internal and thus to see the importance of "the border Realm of Karacter." Klansmen were to judge one another "not by the texture of the garment worn nor by the position held in the social, educational, political, financial or ecclesiastical spheres of the world's society." On the contrary, "we look well to the inner qualities of the heart, the mind and the soul; on these we base our estimate and the eye of scrutiny beholds him bathed in the penetrating light of the Fiery Cross and he stands before us our equal in that he possesses a klansman's heart and a klansman's soul." *First Lesson in the Science and Art of Klancraft. The Practice of Klannishness,* 1–2 (Atlanta: 1924) (Imperial Instructions Document No. 1, Series AD. 1924, AK. LVIII). In one Klan song, "Behind the Convent Walls," a woman trapped in a convent awaited her liberation by a host of Klansmen carrying flaming crosses and an American flag:

by these burning crosses and by the independence they were understood to represent, separation of church and state often seemed the most elevated of American and Protestant ideals.

Cooperation: The Role of Hugo L. Black

The diverse Americans who supported a separation of church and state sometimes cooperated against Catholics. Numerous groups converged in distrusting Catholics and desiring separation, and in so doing they occasionally joined forces. Yet even when focused on political campaigns, most anti-Catholic alliances remained as much cultural as political, and they developed more through personal cooperation than official agreement, allowing groups that could not formally affiliate to enjoy ambiguous relationships on the basis of the shared ideals of their members. Such cooperation, between the Klan and many Masons, has already been observed in Oregon.[74] It may also be observed in the career of Hugo L. Black with the Ku Klux Klan.

> A white-robed army brave and true
> For liberty shall stand
> And from the hand of tyranny
> Will break our every band.
> The Fiery Cross has lighted up
> The nation far and wide;
> They bear with them the Stars and Stripes
> 'Neath which our heroes ride.
>
> Be patient, O my soul, and wait!
> Their coming draweth near;
> Soon shall the rosy-tinted morn
> O'ver these dark walls appear. . . .

Bishop Alma White, *Klansmen: Guardians of Liberty,* 137 (New Jersey(?): Pillar of Fire, 1926).
    The Statue of Liberty took on much significance for many Klansmen. Among the frequent depictions of the Statue of Liberty by Klan and other nativist propagandists was a postcard, published by William Lloyd Clark of *Rail Splitter* fame, showing a pair of images, one of the Statute of Liberty in the daylight, and another of a similar statue of the pope at night, the base of his statue being labeled, "DUNGEON FOR HERETICS." Under the daylight picture was the caption: "THE PRICE OF LIBERTY IS ETERNAL VIGILANCE." Under the other: "THE PRICE OF POPERY IS ETERNAL SLAVERY" (Milan, Ill.: William Lloyd Clark, n.d.), copy in Knights of Columbus Archive, SC-11-1-145. Revealing the degree of overlap between Liberal and nativist anti-Catholicism, this and many of the other cards published by Clark were copied from Watson Heston's *The Freethinker's Pictoral Text Book* (New York: Truth Seeker Office, 1890 and 1898).
    [74] More generally, numerous Masons, especially in the Scottish Rite, Southern Jurisdiction, found much that was attractive in the Klan vision of Americanism. The Scottish Rite, Southern Jurisdiction, did not officially endorse the Klan. Yet many of its members joined

In the 1920s in Alabama this aspiring Birmingham politician skill-fully drew upon a confluence of Protestant, nativist, and progressive anti-Catholic forces. A Baptist, Black opposed the consumption of alco-hol and harbored deep suspicions of Catholicism.[75] A progressive, he adopted a populist stance on behalf of the poor. On these principles he ran for the Senate in 1925 and 1926 by appealing to the "DRY-PROTESTANT-PROGRESSIVE VOTERS of the State of Alabama."[76] Yet Hugo Black was more than simply a Baptist and a progressive. He was also a Klansman. In later years he would discount his association with the Invisible Empire of the

---

the invisible empire, and the Klan, when organizing in a town, would usually begin at the local Masonic lodge. Higham, *Strangers in the Land,* 289. Although some Scottish Rite Masons of the Southern Jurisdiction objected to this nebulous, unofficial cooperation, oth-ers, including some of the most prominent, equivocated when pressed to state their posi-tion about Klan membership. Fox, *Lodge of the Double-Headed Eagle,* 208.

In contrast, Masons in the Northeast felt the political liabilities of this association with the Klan and eventually repudiated it. In late 1922 leading Masons in New York publicly denounced Klan proselytizing among Masons there. "Ku Klux Denounced by Masonic Leader . . . ," *New York Times,* 1 (Nov. 25, 1922). Shortly afterward, in January 1923 Mayor Curley of Boston demanded that the "decent membership of the masonic order should be called upon to repudiate the so-called Scottish rite now openly in alliance with the Klan in the west." "Letter on Ku Klux Klan," article from *City Record* (Boston), 15: 93 (Jan. 27, 1923), in Julia E. Johnsen, ed., *Ku Klux Klan,* in *The Reference Shelf,* 1 (no. 10): 101 (revised ed., New York: 1923). Indeed, Frederick W. Hamilton—a 33rd-degree Mason who was Supreme Council Deputy for Massachusetts—warned that Klansmen were not entitled to membership and that "no Scottish Rite Freemason can consistently be a Klansman." He recognized that Scottish Rite Masons were "being solicited to join the Ku Klux Klan, on the ground that its announced purposes should commend themselves to Masons," but, although some of these purposes would commend themselves, "others should not." "De-nounces Klan in Warning to Masons," *New York Times* (Jan. 23, 1923), in ibid., 99.

[75] Indeed, as "Solicitor" or prosecutor for Jefferson County, Alabama, between 1914 and 1917, Black enforced the Liquor Advertising Law with vigor, threatening newspapers and newsdealers with arrest and with injunctions to close them down if they carried the pro-hibited advertisements. Library of Congress, Hugo Black Papers, File 514 (Scrapbook), pages 1, 13, 15, and passim. He was not the only Supreme Court justice to have made himself popular among dry, anti-Catholic nativists by such means. For example, when Justice Stone was nominated, the *Fellowship Forum* said he had a "Fine Record," observing that this attorney general had recently been "very active in the enforcement of the prohibi-tion laws." "Stone Named to Vacancy in Highest Court," *Fellowship Forum,* 4 (no. 30): 1 (Jan. 10, 1925).

[76] As quoted by Howard Ball, *Hugo L. Black: Cold Steel Warrior,* 63 (New York: Oxford Uni-versity Press, 1996). By May 1926 he was "becoming known as the 'candidate of the masses.'" "Black Making Progress in District Tour," *Tri-Cities Daily* (May 22, 1926), clipping in Library of Congress, Hugo Black Papers, File 515 (Scrapbook). One reporter wrote that Black "has been making some pitiful pleas over the State that he is the poor son of a poor farmer. . . . Mr. Black has ridden the 'poverty nag' to its death." "Black, the 'Poor Man' Makes a Confession," *Jasper Advertiser* (June 16, 1926), clipping in Library of Congress, Hugo Black Papers, File 515 (Scrapbook).

Ku Klux Klan. It was, he said, as innocent as his membership in various other fraternal organizations, including the Masons, the Odd Fellows, the Knights of Pythias, and the Knights of Khorassan. Yet Black's account of his participation in the Klan was, at best, understated.[77]

Black made his public debut with the Klan in 1921 by defending a Klansman against a charge of murder. The Klansman was the Rev. Edwin R. Stephenson—a Methodist and the sort of disreputable preacher who hung around the courthouse offering to marry youngsters in order to earn the fee. One day in August 1921 his daughter Ruth married a Catholic Puerto Rican, Pedro Gussman, at the nearby Catholic church, St. Paul's. Earlier that year Ruth had converted to Catholicism. To escape her brutal father, moreover, she had repeatedly run away from home. At such times as Ruth disappeared, Stephenson feared that Catholics were trying to kidnap her, and he roamed the town looking for persons to help him search St. Paul's and a local convent, where he feared "the Catholics had spirited her away" and had her "locked up."[78] In this state of mind, on the afternoon that his daughter eloped, the Rev. Stephenson pocketed his revolver and went looking for her. Eventually, in the early evening he walked to St. Paul's, where he found Father James E. Coyle sitting on the rectory porch, as he often did after dinner. Father Coyle explained that Ruth was not at the church. Coyle also mentioned that he had married Ruth and Pedro earlier that day. The Rev. Stephenson was already agitated. Upon learning of his daughter's misalliance, he

---

[77] Roger K. Newman, *Hugo Black: A Biography*, 89–121 (New York: Pantheon, 1994). My analysis of Black draws substantially from the work of Howard Ball and especially Roger K. Newman, although not specifically on the issue of separation of church and state. Ball, *Hugo L. Black*; Newman, *Black*. For the Klan in Birmingham, see William R. Snell, "Fiery Crosses in the Roaring Twenties: Activities of the Revised Klan in Alabama, 1915–1930," *Alabama Review*, 256 (October 1970); William R. Snell, "Masked Men in the Magic City: Activities of the Revised Klan in Birmingham, 1916–1940," *Alabama Historical Quarterly*, 206 (Fall-Winter 1972); and, especially, Glenn Alan Feldman, "The Ku Klux Klan in Alabama," 73 (Ph.D. diss. Auburn University, Alabama, 1996), and Feldman, *Politics, Society, and the Klan in Alabama*.

[78] Feldman, *Politics, Society, and the Klan in Alabama*, 234. Stephenson's domestic discipline had not reconciled his daughter to him—least of all when in May 1921, after she came home late, he tied her to a bed for three days, nailed the windows shut, and whipped her. "State of Alabama v. Edwin R. Stephenson, Murder, Circuit Court of the Tenth Judicial Circuit of Alabama, Birmingham, Alabama . . . Commencing on the 17th Day of October, 1921" (copy of trial transcript), in John Carroll Catholic High School Library, Birmingham, Alabama. More generally, on the Stephenson trial, see Paul M. Pruitt, Jr., "Private Tragedy, Public Shame," *Alabama Heritage*, 24 (Fall 1993).

became enraged. He denounced Father Coyle as "a dirty dog" and, after a brief tussle, shot him—thus presenting Birmingham with the edifying spectacle of a Methodist preacher killing a Catholic priest.[79]

In an era in which nativist publications denounced both Catholics and blacks, Stephenson could claim that he had been provoked in two ways, for the priest had married his daughter to a dark-skinned Catholic. Certainly, Stephenson's lawyer, Hugo Black, made the most of such arguments. Although not yet a Klansman, Black had been hired to defend the preacher by Grand Dragon Jim Esdale—the head of the Alabama Klan—and understood exactly what was expected.[80] Emphasizing that Gussman might have some "negro ancestry," Black arranged for Gussman to enter the courtroom only after the blinds and the lights had been adjusted to make the Puerto Rican's skin look dark. Black then called Gussman before the jurors but asked him no questions. Instead, Black asked the jury to look at Gussman's skin, hair, and eyes, explaining afterward that "I just wanted the jury to see that man."[81] The State had desperately emphasized that Gussman's parents came from Spain, to which Black retorted that, although Gussman may have been "of proud Castillian descent," he had "descended a long way."[82] Black took every opportunity, moreover, to draw attention to Gussman's foreignness and Catholicism, asking "whether he was a Greek, or Porta Rican, or Dago."[83] Particularly, in his summation, Black dwelt upon the full range of anti-Catholic fears: "Because a man becomes a priest does not mean that he is divine. He has no more right to protection than a Protestant minister. Who believes Ruth Stephenson has not been proselytized? A child of a Methodist does not suddenly depart from her religion unless someone has planted in her mind the seeds of influence. They say she was locked up. . . . I do not care how she was locked. . . . There is no such thing as imprisonment of the human will by influence, vice and persuasion.

---

[79] Newman, *Black,* 73.

[80] Apparently, Black was contacted by his law partner, Crampton Harris, on behalf of Esdale, who later described how he "set up the trial." Newman, *Black,* 86.

[81] Feldman, "The Ku Klux Klan in Alabama," 73; Newman, *Black,* 81–82. On cross-examination, Black questioned Gussman to suggest that the state had arranged to have "the curls worked out" and repeatedly asked "What else did they do to your hair? . . . Didn't smoothe it down? . . . Has anything been done to your hair?" Alabama v. Stephenson (copy of trial transcript), 484–485.

[82] Newman, *Black,* 83.

[83] Alabama v. Stephenson (copy of trial transcript), 289.

When you find a girl who has been reared well persuaded from her parents by some cause or person, that cause or person is wrong." Nothing could have been better calculated to inflame the prejudices of the jury. To ensure that the Klan majority on the jury understood what was at stake, Black even used a Klan hand signal.[84] Of course, Black obtained an acquittal—a result that led a former governor, Emmett O'Neal, to denounce Birmingham's "odious religious bigotry."[85]

The Klan provided Black with his path to the Senate. In September 1923 Black joined the powerful Richard E. Lee Klan No. 1 and promptly became Kladd of his Klavern—the officer who initiated new members by administering the oath about "white supremacy" and "separation of church and state."[86] In this, Black took a very different path than another Alabama Democrat, Senator Oscar W. Underwood, who vigorously condemned the hooded order. A strong presidential candidate, Underwood recognized that his criticisms would provoke many of his fellow Democrats. Indeed, at the 1924 Democratic convention, he lost the nomination after he and his allies failed to get the convention to adopt a motion denouncing the Klan. Yet Underwood stood by his principles. As one of his friends observed, "Oscar won't demagogue, not even a little." This was not true of Black. In the summer of 1925, when Underwood's failure to gain the Democratic nomination seemed to leave his Senate seat up for grabs, Black eagerly took advantage of the opportunity created by Underwood's unpopular views.[87] After Black decided to run, Grand Dragon Jim Esdale told him, "Give me a letter of resignation and I'll keep it in my safe against the day when you'll need to say you're not a Klan member."[88] Recognizing the wisdom of this suggestion, Black gave Esdale a brief letter of resignation, signing it, "Yours, I.T.S.U.B. [In The Sacred, Unfailing Bond], Hugo L. Black."[89]

---

[84] Newman, *Black*, 83, 86.

[85] Feldman, *Politics, Society, and the Klan in Alabama*, 67.

[86] Newman, *Black*, 94, 95. Black's position was high enough that his name, along with the names of two other officers, appeared on his klavern's stationery. Ibid., 655, note 6. Later, a Birmingham paper reported: "He was no inoffensive dupe of the clever leaders—he was one of the leaders." Ibid. His klavern, moreover, the Robert E. Lee Klan No. 1, was "[p]erhaps the most powerful klavern in the Southeast." Kenneth T. Jackson, *The Ku Klux Klan in the City 1915–1930*, 82 (New York: Oxford University Press, 1967).

[87] Gerald T. Dunne, *Hugo Black and the Judicial Revolution*, 114–116 (New York: Simon & Schuster, 1977).

[88] Ibid., 116; Newman, *Black*, 103.

[89] Ball, *Hugo L. Black*, 62; Newman, *Black*, 103.

Just how unfailing was their bond of shared fears and aspirations, and just what it meant to appeal to the dry, Protestant, progressive voters of Alabama became apparent in Black's campaign. It was a time and place in which many affiliations seemed to overlap: the Baptists supported the Anti-Saloon League, the League and the Klan often seemed to blur together, and the Klan included "nearly all the preachers."[90] According to Esdale, "Hugo didn't ask for Klan support. It was just understood." Black was, as the *Montgomery Advertiser* noted, "the darling of the Ku Klux Klan." Esdale served as Black's unofficial campaign manager. The candidate's finance chairman was his old law partner, Crampton Harris, who had since become Exalted Cyclops of the Lee Klan, and who now "went around and got money" from various klaverns.[91] In these ways the Klan provided an invisible campaign organization, allowing Black to declare that he had "no paid workers, no campaign managers, no 'organizations,'" and that "the people" ran his campaign.[92]

Black appealed directly to Klan and other anti-Catholic voters. According to Esdale, "I arranged for Hugo to go to Klaverns all over the state, making talks on Catholicism. What kinds of talks? Well, just the history of the church and what we know about it. Not to talk on politics. Hugo could make the best anti-Catholic speech you ever heard."[93] Such was his message, which he and Esdale took to "nearly all 148 Klaverns" in the State.[94] Unlike other political candidates in Alabama, Black spoke in churches, and he later recalled that he addressed a Baptist convention on the religious liberty guaranteed by the First Amendment.[95] Of course,

---

[90] Newman, *Black*, 91. Support for the Anti-Saloon League appears regularly in the pages of the *Proceedings of the Southern Baptist Convention* in the beginning of the century, although with hints of disquiet about the League's tactics. Ball records a Birmingham newspaper editor as saying that "it is hard to tell where the League ends and the Klan begins." Ball, *Hugo L. Black*, 61. Not far behind these male alliances were various women's groups, such as the Women's Christian Temperance Union, which supported Black as the dry candidate.

[91] Newman, *Black*, 103, 115.

[92] "Black's Keen Thrust at Opponents Monday Drew Sharp Applause," *Talledega Daily Home* (June 14, 1926), clipping in Library of Congress, Hugo Black Papers, File 515 (Scrapbook).

[93] Newman, *Black*, 104; see also Dunne, *Hugo Black and the Judicial Revolution*, 117.

[94] Newman, *Black*, 104.

[95] Newman, *Black*, 112 (citing letter of 1962). Wherever he gave this speech, it was not at the Alabama Baptist State Convention, for he apparently gave there "an excellent speech on 'Respect for and Enforcement of Law,'" which, of course, meant prohibition laws. *Alabama Baptist*, 57 (no. 31): 5 (Nov. 26, 1925); Annual of the Alabama State Convention, 121–122 (Alabama: 1925). During the election, Black's opponent, John Bankhead, accused Black of taking advantage of his religious and fraternal affiliations. In response, Black

Black did not make his anti-Catholicism explicit in his public platform but, instead, relied upon almost innocuous code words. For example, under the heading "ALABAMA FOR AMERICANS," he opposed further immigration until there had been time to "Americanize" the foreigners who had already arrived. At one point he even put in print: "The shuffling feet of myriads of immigrants fill my heart with dread. They murmur the doom of the America of our fathers. That murmur should be hushed."[96] More typically, however, he indulged in less sinister public pronouncements and wisely left topics such as "the history of the church" for his tour of the state's churches and klaverns.

After the primary the Robert E. Lee Klan No. 1 held a "Klorero" to celebrate the Klan's political successes in Alabama. Black listened to Klan leaders denounce both "Catholic and Negro." Then Imperial Wizard Hiram Evans awarded Black the very rare honor of a golden "grand passport." Upon receiving this, Black spoke of his gratitude for the Klan's support.

> I know that without the support of the members of this organization I would not have been called, even by my enemies, the "Junior Senator from Alabama." (Applause.)
>   I realize that I was elected by men who believe in the principles that I have sought to advocate and which are the principles of this organization.

Exactly which principles Black had in mind were not exactly clear, but at one point he alluded to Mexico, "where for 350 years the boys and girls have lived in blindness and darkness." After speaking about the need to "remain true to the American precepts and American princi-

---

"asserted that Bankhead himself had been guilty of 'playing politics in the church.'" "Black Answers John Bankhead," *Birmingham News* (July 8, 1926), clipping in Library of Congress, Hugo Black Papers, File 515 (Scrapbook).

[96] *Principles Advocated by Hugo Black Candidate for United States Senate* (broadside), copies in Library of Congress, Hugo Black Papers, File 515 (Scrapbook). In this publication Black wrote that the greater proportion of immigrants were "ignorant, illiterate and wholly incapable of appreciating, during a lifetime, the ideals and duties of American citizenship" and that the "melting pot idea" was "dangerous to our national inheritance." He added: "I oppose further immigration, and always believe our nation would be greatly benefitted by closing the gates until such time as we can Americanize and educate those already here. This nation has cost too much in sacrifice, toil, and blood to jeopardize its safety in order to swell the profits of Millionaire Coal Operators, Millionaire Mill-Owners and the Millionaire Steel-Makers." Ibid., also quoted by Ball, *Hugo L. Black,* 65.

ples," Black concluded by thanking his fellow members of "this great fraternity" that was "founded on the principles of that man who taught us to love our enemies."

> I thank you friends from the bottom of my heart. With my love, with my faith, with my trust, with my undying prayer that this great organization will carry on sacredly, true to the real principles of American manhood and womanhood, . . . loving the pride of Anglo-Saxon spirit—and I love it—true to the heaven-born principles of liberty which were written in the Constitution of this country, and in the great historical documents, straight from the heart of Anglo-Saxon patriots, with my love, and my faith, and hope and my trust, I thank you from the bottom of a heart that is yours. (Great applause.)[97]

In this tribute to "the heaven-born principles of liberty which were written in the Constitution of this country," Black gave his last known speech to a Klan gathering.[98]

Hugo Black's association with the Klan became public little more than a decade later, in 1937, when President Franklin Delano Roosevelt appointed Black as Associate Justice of the Supreme Court. The news of Black's Klan membership broke shortly after the Senate confirmed his

---

[97] "Black's Loyalty to Klan Shows in Fervid Pledge," *Pittsburgh Post-Gazette,* 2 (Sept. 15, 1937); "Black Quoted as Crediting Klan for His Victory in Senate Fight," *New York Times,* 3 (Sept. 15, 1937); Dunne, *Hugo Black and the Judicial Revolution,* 122; Newman, *Black,* 116. More generally on the Klorero, see William R. Snell, "Masked Men in the Magic City," 206, 220. Shortly after Black spoke, the Imperial Legal Advisor declared to the crowd: "To come down here now and find that you have given us a man named 'Black' who wears 'white',—do you get that boys—to occupy a seat in the Senate of the United States is like getting an inspiration just before baptism." *Pittsburgh Post-Gazette,* 2 (Sept. 17, 1937). Black revealed in his equivocations some understanding of the sort of organization he was working with: "The great thing I like about this organization is not the burning of crosses, it is not attempting to regulate anybody—I don't know, some may do that—but my friends, I see a bigger vision, I see a vision honored by the nations of the world." "Black's Loyalty to Klan Shows in Fervid Pledge," *Pittsburgh Post-Gazette,* 2 (Sept. 15, 1937); Newman, *Black,* 116. Whatever his vision was, it was attractive enough to him that he was willing to remain mute about the cross burnings and more serious attempts to "regulate" fellow citizens. No doubt, the Klan's principles or at least its politics loomed larger for Black than its violence. According to a recent student of the Klan in Alabama: "Men such as Hugo Black . . . would have to have been literally blind, deaf, and dumb not to have known about the epidemic of Klan violence in their midst as early as 1921." Feldman, "The Ku Klux Klan in Alabama," 21.

[98] Nonetheless, informal relationships persisted, for Imperial Wizard Hiram Evans later mentioned that, until about 1930, he "used to see him [Black] in Washington when he was a Senator." "Evans Denies Klan Had Life Members," *New York Times,* 3 (Sept. 15, 1937).

nomination. Horrified, many Americans—not least, Catholics—bitterly denounced the new justice. Black, however, gave a radio address, in which he successfully put the matter to rest. He began with what appeared to be a repudiation of the Klan: "The constitutional safeguard to complete liberty of religious belief is a declaration of the greatest importance to the future of America as a nation of free people. Any movement or action by any group that threatens to bring about a result inconsistent with this unrestricted individual right is a menace to freedom." Yet, as Black proceeded, his message seemed to concern not so much the Klan as another "menace" to "this unrestricted individual right":

> Let me repeat:
>   Any program, even if directed by good intention, which tends to breed or revive religious discord or antagonism can and may spread with such rapidity as to imperil this vital constitutional protection of one of the most sacred of human rights. . . .
>   During my recent absence on a short vacation abroad, a planned and concerted campaign was begun which fans the flames of prejudice and is calculated to create racial and religious hatred. If continued, the inevitable result will be the projection of religious beliefs into a position of prime importance in political campaigns and to reinfect our social and business life with the poison of religious bigotry.

With the old allegation of a Catholic plot—the "planned and concerted campaign"—Black suggested to Protestants that the accusations against him were part of a Catholic conspiracy and simultaneously hinted to Catholics that their complaints would prompt the bigotry of Protestants. Black left Catholics with no doubt about the consequences: "It will bring the political religionist back into undeserved and perilous influence in affairs of government. . . . It will resurrect practices and arguments from which this country suffered sorely in the Nineteen Twenties. It will revive the spirit which in 1928 caused a national campaign to be waged largely upon issues unworthy of a free people."[99] The consequences would include not only the unworthy politics of anti-Catholicism but also more immediate repercussions for Catholics. Following the example of earlier nativists, the Klan and other groups in Birmingham and else-

---

[99] "Justice Black's Speech," *New York Times,* 1, 3 (Oct. 2, 1937). He could afford to mention the 1928 campaign because, although profoundly suspicious of Al Smith's Catholicism, Black had not abandoned the Democratic ticket.

where had organized boycotts against businesses that were owned by Catholics or that were reluctant to dismiss their Catholic employees.[100] Now Black declared that opposition to him would provoke a repetition of such practices:

> It will bankrupt many business men whose sole offense is that they have religious beliefs which do not accord with the prevailing religion in their communities. It will punish the professional man whose patients and clients boycott him not because of lack of professional ability but because there are in his locality few members of his faith or his race. It will again set neighbor against neighbor.[101]

This was as much a threat as an apology.

Catholics, Republicans, and some others sharply denounced Black's performance. For example, in New York the *Herald Tribune* announced: "The effort of Senator Black to suggest that he is the real protagonist of tolerance and that his enemies are intolerant is perhaps the greatest item

---

[100] Indeed, the initials that formed the title of the Alabama Klan newsletter, *T.W.K.*, stood for Trade With the Klan, and many Protestants went out of their way to patronize Protestant and especially Klan businesses. Even more aggressively, nativist Protestants across the country revived the earlier movement to exclude Catholics from teaching in public schools. For example, in 1920 the Scottish Rite Masons of Alabama Consistory No. 1, of Birmingham, resolved, whereas "loyalty to the fundamental principles of democracy and the safety of the fabric of our government depend upon the intelligent citizenship of the masses. . . . That we urge upon school authorities throughout the state the importance of electing for our public schools only such teachers as are of unquestioned moral character, of approved academic and professional training, and of demonstrated loyalty to the American flag and devotion to the public schools of our country." "The Masonic Fraternity and the Public Schools," *Guardian of Liberty*, 6 (nos. 5–8): 93–94 (February 1920). Notwithstanding the efforts of some nativist Masonic leaders, the Supreme Council of the Scottish Rite, Southern Jurisdiction, did not go so far. For example, the Grand Commander of the Southern Jurisdiction was not successful when he asked the Supreme Council to request every state to "enact legislation that would give preference to public school graduates in appointments to public office." Fox, *Lodge of the Double-Headed Eagle*, 178. Probably without paying full attention to the implications of this passage, Fox writes that it was "certainly a well-intentioned, though perhaps unrealistic proposal." Ibid.

[101] "Justice Black's Speech," *New York Times*, 3. The speech left some to "wonder if Justice Black predicted a resurrection of the Ku Klux Klan if religious antagonisms were again created through what, he said, was a concerted attack upon him." "Radio Talk Is Brief," in ibid., 1, 3 (Oct. 2, 1937). Black's initial response in September to the accusation of Klan membership had also been less than reassuring. On vacation in London, Black had left a theater only to be confronted by a reporter who asked whether he had at any time belonged to the Ku Klux Klan. Black shot back "Who are you?" and, learning that his questioner was an American reporter, Black responded tensely, "I don't see you! I don't know you! And I don't answer you!" "Black Evades Klan Query," *Washington Herald* (Sept. 18, 1937).

of effrontery in a uniquely brazen utterance."[102] The *Chicago Tribune* observed that Black had once "thanked the Klan for its aid," and "even now in his careful public statement he did not condemn the Klan or Klansmen."[103] Kenneth F. Simpson—chairman of the New York County Republican Committee—more bluntly declared: "Mr Justice Black pulled the pillow case even farther over his head."[104] A "Negro" paper, the *Amsterdam News*, added a still more graphic commentary. In his speech Black had insisted that some of his "best and most intimate friends" were "Catholics and Jews," and that he was not "prejudiced against people of the Jewish or Catholic faiths." To demonstrate this, he secured a black Catholic messenger, he replaced his long-standing Protestant secretary with a Catholic, and he attempted to get a Catholic clerk—although, failing in this, he hired a Jew. Appalled, the *Amsterdam News* published a cartoon showing the justice in his white robes behind the bench of the Supreme Court, where he displayed diminutive employees—one Catholic, one Jewish, and one black—cradled in the white folds of one arm. Justice Black gesticulated with the other arm, explaining: "See, I ain't prejudiced!"[105] Yet much of the criticism came from Republicans, who saw Black's Klan affiliation as an opportunity to embarrass the president. Fearing this, Democrats and others, further to the left, tended to make ambiguous and defensive comments. Typically, they regretted Black's "opportunism" in joining the Klan but emphasized that the justice was "one of the country's most convinced and effective liberals"—an "enemy of reaction."[106] It was a response that led

[102] "Comment of Press Is Critical of Justice Black," *New York Times*. 2 (Oct. 2, 1937), quoting *Herald Tribune*. Similarly, the *Los Angles Examiner* asked, "who could have anticipated such amazing effrontery?" It added: "He brazenly denounces those who have patriotically exposed his Klan connection for the very faults—the very crimes against the peace and order of the state—for the commission of which he himself is guilty." "Quite as Black as He Is Painted," *Los Angeles Examiner*, 1 (Oct. 4, 1937).

[103] "Nation's Press Almost United in Denouncing Black Speech," *New York Times,* 2 (Oct. 3, 1937), quoting *Chicago Tribune.*

[104] "Black's Explanation Elicits Both Praise and Scorn in Comment," in ibid., 2 (Oct. 2, 1937).

[105] "Justice Black's Speech," in ibid., 3; *Amsterdam News* (New York: Oct. 9, 1937). Black's effort to hire Catholics and the announcement of their religious affiliation in the newspapers "just smelled too much" for Bernard Monaghan, the Catholic graduate of Harvard Law School whom Black first asked to be his clerk. In Monaghan's place, Black selected a clerk whose father Black knew from an Alabama Masonic lodge. As the Court took pains to declare in a public statement, "He is of the Jewish faith." Newman, *Black*, 267.

[106] "Rabbi Plotkin Defends Black, Flays Critics," cutting from unidentified newspaper, in Library of Congress, Hugo Black Papers, File 235, Supreme Court Nomination Clippings (Favorable Comments after Radio Speech). Some papers, such as the *Minnesota Leader,*

the *New York Times* to complain of "the new morality by which Liberals may defend a Klansman on the Supreme Court because he is sound on the Administration's economic program."[107]

Among the various responses to Black's speech, few revealed a better understanding of the justice's vision of religious liberty than those that lit up the sky. Only a "few minutes" before Black began his radio speech, residents almost all the way across the borough of Mountain Lakes, New Jersey, saw flames arise from the top of the Mountain Lakes Dam, where suddenly "a fiery cross loomed in the darkness." The next evening, in Worcester, Massachusetts, on a hill in the "exclusive residential district" near Bancroft Tower—an area where in the mid-1920s crosses had burned nightly—an eighteen-foot cross attracted attention shortly after midnight. A few minutes later, another "burst into flame in Marlboro, sixteen miles away."[108] With equal visibility, former Imperial Wizard Hiram Evans told the *New York Times* that Black gave "a very sincere speech" and that "[h]is concept of religious and political freedom is sound Americanism."[109] Less widely noticed was a meeting of the Baptist Ministers Conference of Newport News a month later. The ministers of this local Baptist organization conducted part of their meeting in the form of a Klan service, singing "The Old Rugged Cross" and listening to a reading of Romans 12—a favorite Klan text. Then the Rev. H. P. East of the First Baptist Church gave an "exposition of the tenets of the Ku Klux Klan, with reference to the religious life of Associate Justice Hugo

---

even attempted to argue that Black's speech "repudiate[d]" the Klan. In any case, Black had "championed every liberal cause." "The Black Speech," *Minnesota Leader,* 4 (Oct. 3, 1937).

The White House reacted more cautiously. The president had "no comment." *Washington Herald Extra* (Oct. 2, 1937). Roosevelt claimed not to have known about his nominee's Klan membership. Yet Roosevelt had ignored the rumors that circulated during the confirmation hearings, and, after the confirmation, the White House arranged for Black to take his oath of office with remarkable dispatch and secrecy. There were several possible reasons for this. Dunne, *Hugo Black and the Judicial Revolution,* 62. Later, some journalists wondered how much the White House had known. "Roosevelt Named Black Unaware of Link to Klan," *New York Times* (Sept. 15, 1937); "Black Took Both Oaths Required for Justices, Court Clerk Reveals," *Washington Daily News* (Sept. 15, 1937); "F.D.R. on Defensive," *Washington Daily News* (Sept. 16, 1937); "Choice of Black Roosevelt Secret," *New York Times,* 3 (Oct. 2, 1937).

[107] *New York Times* (Oct. 23, 1937), as quoted by Paul A. Fisher, *Behind the Lodge Door,* 120 (Bowie, Md.: Shield Publishing, 1989).

[108] "Cross Burned in Jersey As Black Makes Speech" and "Fiery Crosses Blaze Up in Massachusetts Towns," *New York Times,* 2 (Oct. 2, 1937).

[109] "Reaction to Black's Speech Is Diverse among Ex-Colleagues and Civic Leaders," *New York Times,* 2 (Oct. 2, 1937).

Black." The Rev. East complained about the prominent part played by Jews and Catholics in the opposition to Black's appointment, and he defended the Klan and Black's membership in it. The Reverend closed by recalling the heady days of the previous decade, particularly the 1925 Klan parade in Washington, in which so many Americans had demonstrated "for the Christian church, our free institutions, the separation of church and state and freedom of conscience, and our great free public schools."[110]

Black's association with the Klan has been much discussed in connection with his liberal views on race, but, in fact, his membership suggests more about the ideals of Americanism and, especially, American religious liberty that he shared with so many of his countrymen. The combination of progressive, Protestant, and Klan sentiment that brought Black to the Senate illustrates how anti-Catholicism and, more broadly, fears of ecclesiastical authority transcended the differences among vast numbers of Americans, creating loose alliances that Black, the Klan, and many others cultivated on behalf of themselves and their ideals. In this context the separation of church and state flourished as a constitutional ideal, bringing together disparate groups by appealing to their aspirations for America and their loathing for Rome.

An "American" Liberty in a Federal System

At the same time that nativist Protestants advocated separation of church and state as an American liberty, they also, far from coincidentally, contributed to another, broader constitutional development: the Supreme Court's application to the states of the liberties enumerated in the U.S. Bill of Rights. In the 1920s, 1930s, and 1940s, when the justices of the Supreme Court extended to the states the freedoms listed in the federal Bill of Rights, they relied upon their interpretation of the Fourteenth Amendment's due process clause. Yet the justices had the benefit of pop-

---

[110] "Ku Klux Klan Is Subject of Baptist Talk—The Rev. H. P. East Says Many Klansmen Are Finest Specimens of American Manhood," *Time-Herald* (Newport News: Nov. 2, 1937). For an example of the standard Klan use of Romans 12, see W. C. Wright, *The Twelfth Chapter of Romans as a Klansman's Law of Life* (n.p., n.d.)—an official Klan republication of a sermon "on the principles of klancraft." For the tradition of singing the "Old Rugged Cross" in Klan services, see, e.g., *TWK Monthly* (Birmingham), 2 (no. 8): 28 (February 1925), copy available in Ku Klux Klan Scrapbook, vol. 1, Microfilm 257, at 79–95, Birmingham Public Library, Archives, Birmingham, Alabama.

ular conceptions of the liberty inhering in individuals—conceptions of freedom that were not tied to any particular level of government and that therefore lent much plausibility to the idea that individuals enjoyed the same liberty under the states as under the federal government. These popular ideas included notions of human rights. Most prominently and popularly, however, they included nativist ideals of "American" freedom. Although initially developed by anti-Catholic nativists, these ideals eventually became widely popular, even among the opponents of nativism. Most nativists understood themselves to be in a struggle to preserve the separation of church and state from the threat of Catholicism, but they also hoped, more generally, to secure all of their "American" liberties. They thereby did much to recast the U.S. Bill of Rights as an enumeration of not federal, but American rights, which seemed to belong to individuals as Americans, regardless of the distinctions between the federal government and the states. Identifying with the nation and its American freedoms rather than merely with the states or even the federal government, these nativists not only advocated separation but also elevated concepts of American liberty in a way that eclipsed much of the layered, federal character of their constitutional freedoms.

Traditionally, Americans distinguished between the rights they held under state constitutions and those they held under the U.S. Constitution. Not least, they usually took for granted that the U.S. Bill of Rights did not constrain the states—each state having its own limitations in its own constitution's bill of rights. Although in 1789 James Madison persuaded his fellow congressmen to make part of the U.S. Bill of Rights apply to the states, the Senate rejected this proposal, and, ever since then, the opening words of the First Amendment—"Congress shall make no law"—reminded Americans of the exclusively federal role of the U.S. Bill of Rights, a narrow role that persisted with only unsuccessful court challenges through much of the nineteenth century.[111] These days, it is sometimes assumed that the Fourteenth Amendment already in 1868, when it was ratified, applied the U.S. Bill of Rights to the states. Certainly, the Fourteenth Amendment preserved the essential freedom of Americans—notably, black Americans—by imposing restrictions on the states. Yet whatever may have been accomplished in 1868

[111] Charles Warren, "The New 'Liberty' under the Fourteenth Amendment," *Harvard Law Review*, 39: 435–449 (1926).

by the resonant words of the Fourteenth Amendment, myriad late nineteenth-century Americans continued to assume that the liberties of the U.S. Bill of Rights had not been extended beyond the federal government.

The persistence of traditional assumptions about the reach of the Bill of Rights, even after the adoption of the Fourteenth Amendment, may be illustrated by the attitudes of Americans about the religious liberty guaranteed in the First Amendment.[112] Even the activists who desired First Amendment limitations upon the states assumed the necessity

[112] In discussing popular perceptions, there is no need to review the extensive controversy as to whether the Fourteenth Amendment was designed to apply or "incorporate" the U.S. Bill of Rights against the states.

More significantly, Akhil Amar and Kurt Lash suggest that the Fourteenth Amendment not only applied the Bill of Rights to the states but also expanded and thus "reconstructed" the freedoms guaranteed in the 1791 document—in particular, that the Fourteenth Amendment expanded upon the religious liberty protected by the First Amendment to ensure individuals at least some freedom from the state laws to which they had religious objections. Akhil Reed Amar, *The Bill of Rights: Creation and Reconstruction*, 256–257 (New Haven: Yale University Press, 1998), citing Kurt T. Lash, "The Second Adoption of the Free Exercise Clause: Religious Exemptions under the Fourteenth Amendment," *Northwestern Law Review*, 88: 1106 (1994). In support of their argument, they cite the mid-nineteenth-century abolitionists who adopted ideas of conscientious disobedience and the politicians who echoed such ideas in post–Civil War congressional debates.

Yet these abolitionists and politicians were commenting on race rather than religious liberty in general. To the extent Americans generally changed their views about religious liberty, they responded to their fears of ecclesiastical and particularly Catholic authority, and they thereby became increasingly suspicious of any religious challenge to American laws. For example, Protestants often perceived Catholics as loyal to a foreign prince and took offense at papal pronouncements that civil laws were subordinate to those of the Church. Indeed, in rejecting the supremacy of the Catholic Church, many Americans insisted upon the absolute supremacy of the state and its laws. Such attitudes were evident already in the mid-nineteenth century and were only hardened during the Civil War, when secular threats to loyalty and renewed papal claims left ever more Americans—not only members of nativist orders but also many others—profoundly worried about the threat posed by the Catholic Church. Thus it is true Americans redefined their religious liberty during the nineteenth century, but they typically did so in a manner that cast doubt on claims of religious exemptions. Moreover, when Americans attempted to constitutionalize elements of their new approach to religious liberty, they did so not in the Fourteenth Amendment but in their various amendment proposals against public support for "sectarian" schools, against foreign loyalties, and against other challenges to separation.

Incidentally, although separation was only part of the new, anti-Catholic and antiecclesiastical, vision of American religious liberty, its growing prominence led to its use in arguments against religious defiance of civil law. See, e.g., Reynolds v. United States, 98 U.S. 145, 164 (1878); Stephen F. Blackwell, *Garfield or the Pope. No Foreign Catholic Can Be an American Citizen While Owing Allegiance to the Pope of Rome*, 16 (St. Louis: 1880); Isaac J. Lansing, *Romanism and the Republic, a Discussion of the Purposes, Assumptions, Principles and Methods of the Roman Catholic Hierarchy*, 99 (Boston: Arnold Publishing Co., 1890).

of a further constitutional amendment. In 1870, for example, Elisha P. Hurlbut—the former New York judge—proposed an amendment to the U.S. Constitution that would have extended the First Amendment to the states and would have given Congress power to ban the Catholic hierarchy. Hurlbut explained: "The proposed amendment prohibits a *state* from establishing any religion, or preventing its free exercise. The writer has assumed, that there is nothing in the Constitution as it stands, which prevents a state from doing either." He understood that judges could strain to reach another conclusion, but he doubted the propriety of such an approach: "There are . . . clauses in the Constitution of the United States which might be tortured into a construction prohibitory of state establishment of religion, by a court which should lean against it; or might be held, as I think more properly by an impartial legal tribunal, not applicable to the case: such as the clauses which provide the privileges and immunities of the citizens of the several states shall be equal, and the United States shall guaranty to every state, a republican form of government." Apparently, Hurlbut did not consider any provisions of the recently adopted Fourteenth Amendment to be among the possible vehicles for an interpretation prohibiting state establishments. In any case, he rejected "tortured" interpretations, believing that "[i]t is better that a Constitution should speak plainly than hint its meaning." On such grounds he reiterated his assumption "that there is nothing in the Constitution as it stands, which forbids a *state* from establishing a religion."[113]

Hurlbut's contemporaries seem largely to have agreed, for they also demanded amendments. In January 1874, and again in 1876, the Liberals proposed their amendments that applied the First Amendment to the states and expanded the amendment's meaning. They explained the necessity of their 1874 proposal by reciting the Tenth Amendment and pointing out that "the Constitution . . . contains no provision prohibiting

---

[113] E. P. Hurlbut, *A Secular View of Religion in the State and the Bible in the Public Schools,* 14, 5 (Albany: 1870). The amendment, which had been drafted by a friend of Hurlbut's, altered Article I of the U.S. Bill of Rights: "ART. I. *Neither* congress *nor any state* shall make *any* law respecting an establishment of religion, or prohibiting the free exercise thereof; or abridging the freedom of speech, or of the press; or the right of the people peaceably to assemble and to petition the government for a redress of grievances. *But congress may enact such laws as it shall deem necessary to control or prevent the establishment or continuance of any foreign hierarchical power in this country, founded on principles or dogmas antagonistic to republican institutions."* Ibid., 5.

the *several States* from establishing a State religion, or requiring a religious test for office, or disqualifying witnesses in the courts on account of their religious opinions, or otherwise restricting their religious liberty."[114] In 1875 and 1876 not only the Liberals but also various nativists (such as Daniel Ullmann) and solicitous politicians (such as James Blaine) proposed amendments subjecting the states to the First Amendment. Although most of these Americans and their supporters sought to alter the standard set by the First Amendment, they all clearly assumed that the Fourteenth Amendment had not already applied the First Amendment's freedoms to the states.[115]

Gradually, however, assumptions about the application of the U.S. Bill of Rights would change, partly—but only partly—in response to slavery and the nationalization of the economy. In the mid-nineteenth century many antislavery advocates emphasized the federal character of basic personal rights, and some opponents of state economic regulations desired federal protection of property and other economic liberty. After the ratification of the Fourteenth Amendment in 1868, some Americans continued to complain about oppressive state laws, but they now could argue on the basis of the Fourteenth Amendment. For example, they often claimed that state legislation regulating property or economic conduct violated the amendment by denying liberty without providing due process. Although, in 1873, in the *Slaughter House Cases*, the Supreme Court resisted this sort of Fourteenth Amendment argument, it eventually, toward the end of the nineteenth century, adopted such reasoning to invalidate state regulation that seemed to infringe on property and contract rights.[116] At the same time, some lawyers and other Americans speculated that this due process reasoning might also be relevant in cases

---

[114] *Report of the Centennial Congress of Liberals, and Organization of the National Liberal League,* 12 (Boston: National Liberal League, 1876).

[115] This sort of inference from the Blaine amendment has been contested on the basis of the Slaughter House Cases, 83 U.S. 36 (1873). In particular, it is argued that this decision dampened hopes that the Fourteenth Amendment might be interpreted to protect a wide range of substantive freedoms from state infringement and that therefore the Blaine amendment was considered necessary to overcome the Court's interpretation of the Fourteenth Amendment in the *Slaughter House Cases.* Yet Blaine's amendment was not the only proposal that attempted to apply the First Amendment to the states, and one was Hurlbut's in 1870, three years prior to *Slaughter House.* Moreover, in the debates about the later proposals, including Blaine's, there is no indication that they were drafted in response to the Supreme Court's decision.

[116] Slaughter House Cases, 83 U.S. 36 (1873).

involving "personal" liberties, but only considerably later, beginning in the mid-1920s, did the Court go so far.[117]

The Court now argued that the Fourteenth Amendment's due process clause protected fundamental personal liberties from the states— liberties that most of the justices defined by looking to the federal Bill of Rights. In the 1930s and 1940s, when the justices abandoned the due process protection of economic rights, they elaborated the personal freedoms protected in this way and developed slightly different theories about the application of the Fourteenth Amendment. The justices disagreed, among other things, as to whether the Fourteenth Amendment directly "incorporated" the Bill of Rights against the states or, more vaguely, secured "fundamental" freedoms against the states. For example, Justice Black thought the Fourteenth Amendment incorporated the Bill of Rights, and he even insisted upon a "complete" incorporation of all of the first eight amendments. In contrast, Justice Frankfurter understood the Fourteenth Amendment to protect fundamental freedoms— freedoms that might not be exactly the same as those secured by the U.S. Bill of Rights.[118] Nonetheless, the justices increasingly agreed that, in one way or another, the Fourteenth Amendment applied to the states at least some of the liberties secured in the U.S. Bill of Rights, and they particularly agreed that it applied First Amendment freedoms to the states. As Justice Roberts said about the Fourteenth Amendment in 1940, on behalf of a unanimous court in *Cantwell v. Connecticut:* "The fundamental concept of liberty embodied in that Amendment embraces the liberties guaranteed by the First Amendment."[119]

Yet, in assuming that the personal freedoms in the Bill of Rights limited the states as well as the federal government, the justices drew upon a context that had little connection to the Fourteenth Amendment, that was as much cultural as it was legal, and that concerned religion more than race. Beginning in the mid-nineteenth century, when the nation was much engaged in lawyerly debates about slavery, nativists

---

[117] David M. Rabban, *Free Speech in Its Forgotten Years*, 147–149 (Cambridge: Cambridge University Press, 1997).

[118] Felix Frankfurter, "Memorandum on 'Incorporation' of the Bill of Rights into the Due Process Clause of the Fourteenth Amendment," *Harvard Law Review*, 78: 746 (1965). For these developments, see Richard C. Cortner, *The Supreme Court and the Second Bill of Rights*, 108–123 (Madison: University of Wisconsin Press, 1981); Ross, *Forging New Freedoms*.

[119] Cantwell v. Connecticut, 310 U.S. 296, 303 (1940).

entered into a less sophisticated controversy with foreign-born Catholics about American principles and freedoms. In this struggle, even more than in the antislavery campaign, Americans came to view their constitutional rights as generally American principles of liberty, which belonged to individuals as Americans, and which individuals could therefore enjoy in their relations with all levels of government. The nativists and, increasingly, others who, in the nineteenth and twentieth centuries, adopted versions of this perspective identified themselves not so much with either the federal government or the states as with America, and they perceived uniform American rights or, at least, American principles of freedom in all American constitutions—most emphatically, with respect to First Amendment issues. Accordingly, they could avoid objections that the U.S. Bill of Rights did not apply to the states. Whereas federal claims challenging state law had always been controversial, especially if on behalf of blacks, assertions of American liberty often transcended the distinction between the federal government and the states, especially if on behalf of religious liberty and the freedom of the press.[120] Thus the doctrine that the Fourteenth Amendment applied the U.S. Bill of Rights to the states would have been widely condemned as an infringement upon states' rights if it had been understood simply as an application of federal law against racist local policies. Yet, when perceived as a protection of "American" freedoms, particularly those associated with the First Amendment, this Fourteenth Amendment doctrine seemed largely unobjectionable and even popular.

---

[120] For an early example of the First Amendment issues, see, e.g., the views of the Public School Society in 1840, in Chapter 8 at note 80. In 1856 a variant of such arguments came from Rabbi Max Lilienthal, who employed a non-Protestant version of American principles to argue against state discrimination against Jews. After observing that the state of North Carolina had a statute disqualifying Jews from public office, he asked, "Why do our brethren living in that state not take immediate and prompt steps to have this clause abolished? It is against the constitution of the United States, and therefore illegal. We deem that the attention of the legislature has but to be called to such an illegality and that it will be removed promptly." Philipson, *Max Lilienthal, American Rabbi: Life and Writings,* 109, quoting Lilienthal, "Religious Instruction," *The Israelite,* 2: 404 (Cincinnati: June 21, 1856). By 1892, with considerable overstatement, Alonzo Jones—the advocate of religious liberty for the Seventh-Day Adventists—could observe: "It is generally supposed that the First Amendment to the national Constitution guarantees the free exercise of religion in the States." Incidentally, although Jones had every reason to desire such an interpretation, he acknowledged that the amendment "is of no force at all upon any State." Alonzo Jones, *"Due Process of Law" and the Divine Right of Dissent,* 17, note 1 (Battle Creek: National Religious Liberty Association, 1892) (The Religious Liberty Library No. 1, November 1892).

Revealingly, southerners took great satisfaction in the nativist conception of American liberty. Prior to the Civil War, many southerners had resisted nativist anti-Catholicism. In the century following the war, however, numerous southerners strongly identified with the nativist vision of Americanism. Having themselves recently posed a threat to the nation, they now eagerly joined the ranks of those who denounced the Catholic menace and found a new, intensely loyal identity for themselves in the nativist vision of American liberty.

Catholics and some political liberals, who objected to the Protestant version of American freedom, often defensively asserted their own understandings of their rights as the "Real Americanism." Although, in attempting to coopt the notion of Americanism, they sometimes liberalized nativist conceptions of American liberty by redefining this freedom to include all human rights, they thereby seemed to confirm the existence of American liberties. On their different Americanist assumptions more than any theory of federalism, nineteenth-century Liberals, Protestant nativists, and attentive politicians had proposed their constitutional amendments that would have stipulated a single standard of religious liberty for all Americans under all American governments—the states as well as the federal union. Similarly, in the nineteenth century and the first half of the twentieth, various nativists, Catholics, and political liberals developed their own versions of "American" constitutional liberty, but even as they developed different "American" perspectives, they helped to create a legal culture in which the distinction between state and federal rights became blurred, and in which the U.S. Bill of Rights seemed to be the guarantor not merely of certain rights held against the federal government, but of pervasive ideals of American freedom.[121]

---

[121] Catholics and others adopted ideals of Americanism in many disputes—for example, in response to the nativist arguments in Oregon for compulsory public education. The National Catholic Welfare Council "described the confrontation as 'a battle of religious liberty against religious intolerance; true freedom against false freedom; real Americanism against bogus Americanism.'" Lynn Dumenil, "The Tribal Twenties: 'Assimilated' Catholics' Response to Anti-Catholicism in the 1920s," *Journal of American Ethnic History*, 11 (no. 1): 30 (Fall 1991). Similarly, the Non-Sectarian and Protestant Schools Committee quoted the First Amendment and demanded the preservation of "Real Americanism." "In Justice to American Principles" (advertisement), in *Oregon Sunday Journal* (Portland), 15 (Nov. 5, 1922). See also Dumenil, "The Tribal Twenties," 24, 30–32, 35, 36, 43; Schuyler, "The Ku Klux Klan in Nebraska, 1920–1930," *Nebraska History*, 240, 247, 253.

The version of Americanism that was Catholic or sympathetic to Catholics coopted the

By the 1920s the Americans who assumed that they enjoyed a single body of American liberties often went so far as to minimize the distinctions among different bills of rights and even among different constitutions. Some reduced the U.S. Bill of Rights to "principles" of American liberty, summarizing these in a way that conveniently obscured or altogether omitted the Tenth Amendment (which had reserved to the states or the people such powers as had not been delegated to the United States).[122] Some combined Americanism with philosophizing generalities about government, as when in 1935 Alexander Meiklejohn asked, "What Does America Mean?" and "What Is the American Ideal?" He concluded that America had six ideals, mostly drawn from the First Amendment but also including "Universal Suffrage" and "Universal Education."[123] Other Americans acknowledged the distinction between the federal and state bills of rights but depicted these documents as guaranteeing the same American liberties.[124] Most astonishingly, some com-

---

nativist assumption that American liberties, notably those in the U.S. Bill of Rights, applied to the states. For example, Frances A. Kellor argued that "Nativism is no substitute for Americanism." Kellor opposed racial, class, and ethnic prejudices and rejected the "anti-American" character of nativism. Accordingly, Kellor sought to "restore Americanism to America" and hoped to return to "our real traditions of liberty"—traditions that seemed to include much of the Bill of Rights but not, of course, the Tenth Amendment. Kellor, *Straight America: A Call to Service,* 26–27, 31, 90 (New York: Macmillan, 1916). More cautiously, three academics wrote in their textbook, *The American Citizen:* "The governments of the United States and of the states are supposed to guarantee the citizen a wide range of human rights. These guarantees are included in the first ten amendments to the Constitution and are often referred to as the Bill of Rights." The authors then quoted the First Amendment and emphasized its special significance "for the liberty-loving citizens" and pointedly mentioned that "our citizens have discriminated against Catholics, Jews, and persons of different religious connections in many public places," particularly in schools and elections. John A. Kinneman, Richard G. Browne, and Robert S. Ellwood, *The American Citizen: A Textbook in Government and Current Problems,* 171–172 (New York: Harper & Bros., 1936). Significantly, neither of these publications, which rejected the anti-Catholic versions of Americanism, interpreted the First Amendment in terms of "separation."

[122] For example, in a discussion of whether Catholics should be allowed to teach in public schools, the Guardians of Liberty argued that the "complete separation of Church and State" was one of "[t]he fundamental principles of our American government and life." "Shall Roman Catholics Be Barred from Teaching in Our Public Schools?" *Guardian of Liberty,* 1 (no. 5): 60 (June 1913). (Not surprisingly, the answer was yes.) The Tenth Amendment guaranteed: "The powers not delegated to the United States by the Constitution, nor prohibited by it to the States, are reserved to the States respectively, or to the people."

[123] Alexander Meiklejohn, *What Does America Mean?* 89 (New York: W. W. Norton, 1935).

[124] For example, the Guardians of Liberty often assumed the relevance of the U.S. Constitution to the rights of individuals against the states, as when the headquarters of the Guard-

mentators expressed their conception of American liberty by compressing the diversity of American constitutions into a single, undifferentiated American constitution. For example, Klanswomen pledged: "WE BELIEVE in the supremacy of the Constitution of the United States and the several states, and consecrate ourselves to its preservation against all enemies at home and abroad."[125] Similarly, albeit with very different political views, Bagdasar Krekor Baghdigian—an Armenian immigrant who ardently advocated an unprejudiced, secular Americanism—wrote collectively of "the first amendments to the Constitution of the United States, which once and for all time, separated the church from the state."[126]

The Americans who, in these various ways, perceived American principles or freedoms in their bills of rights found it all the more easy to escape the text of any one of these bills of rights. Not least, as already suggested by the example of Baghdigian, they could easily assume that their constitutional rights included the separation of church and state. For example, William E. Scott—a former high school principal from St. Paul, Minnesota—introduced immigrants and their children to the "American Bill of Rights," in which there was a First Amendment but not a Tenth. On this foundation he had no difficulty emphasizing, in his account of the First Amendment, that *"Church and State are wholly sepa-*

---

ians advised its "Local Courts" to "keep in touch with the political situation not only in the country at large, but in their territories in particular, giving especial attention to any issues which may be in conflict with the liberties granted us by the Constitution of the United States and the Bills of Rights of the several states." "Our Question Box," *Guardian of Liberty,* 1 (no. 4): 52 (May 1913). In his text on *Loyal Citizenship,* Professor Thomas Harrison Reed wrote about "American liberty" in a way that treated different constitutions as largely the same: "By provisions of the Constitution of the United States, and by similar provisions in the constitution of the states, it [our country] *protects the individual against possible tyranny by government itself.* This is what makes American freedom so secure and useful." He then proceeded to discuss the "first ten amendments" to the U.S. Constitution, "known as *our* Bill of Rights," but he listed only some of these rights (not including the Tenth Amendment), and he illustrated them with pictures suggestive of rights against the states—most clearly, with a picture of an Illinois writ of habeas corpus. Reed, *Loyal Citizenship,* 63–67 (Yonkers-on-Hudson: World Book Co., 1922).

[125] "Creed of the Klanswomen," in *America for Americans as Interpreted by the Women of the Ku Klux Klan,* 6.

[126] Bagdasar Krekor Baghdigian, *Americanism in Americanization,* 109 (Kansas City, Mo.: Burton Publishing, 1921). For further details, see Chapter 13, note 29. A former chaplain to the Ohio state senate observed: "In different states the rights of citizens are protected by what is called the Bill of Rights. These documents are calculated to guard the rights of the citizens." Matheny, *American Patriotic Devotions,* 297.

rated in the United States."[127] Augustus Lynch Mason—a prominent Indianapolis lawyer—took a version of this approach in his text on "Americanism." Although he briefly distinguished "the Federal Constitution" from state constitutions, he wrote about the Constitution in a vague manner that hardly emphasized this difference and that reduced constitutional freedoms to an unspecified set of American principles: "Certain principles of Government, certain safeguards for the liberty and rights of our citizens, certain supports for the authority of Government itself, were placed in the Constitution. These provisions are the very essence of Americanism. Whoever violates them is un-American and disloyal." Although he did not immediately identify these provisions, he later explained, in his discussion of "AMERICANISM IN THE PUBLIC SCHOOLS," that "[u]nder our Government, Church and State are separate."[128] With one such vision of American liberty or another, numerous commentators perceived the U.S. Bill of Rights as applicable to the states and, in particular, perceived the First Amendment as a guarantee against state violations of the separation between church and state.[129]

---

[127] William E. Scott, *Citizenship for New Americans*, 92 (St. Paul: Scott-Mitchell Publishing Co., 1923). When Scott resumed his account of the amendments to the U.S. Constitution, he conveniently began with the Eleventh Amendment. Ibid., 146.

[128] Augustus Lynch Mason, *Guiding Principles for American Voters: An Introduction to the Study of Elementary Americanism*, 37, 75 (Indianapolis: Bobbs-Merrill, 1920). From the ideal of separation, Mason drew what he apparently thought an ecumenical conclusion: "Instruction in any form of religious faith can not be permitted in our schools. But it is proper and necessary that children should be taught respect and reverence for every form of the Christian religion, including also the religion of the Jews." He added: "Those parts of the Bible that have no relation to the disputes between different forms of religious belief, may be read and taught in our schools, and should by no means be neglected. The Ten Commandments, the Psalms, the Book of Proverbs, . . . the sayings of Jesus, should be persistently presented to youthful minds, as a basis for wise and patriotic citizenship." Ibid., 75–76. Of course, he wanted "school authorities" to be chosen only if they were "one hundred per cent. American." Ibid., 68.

[129] When writing about state schools, George S. Rainey observed that the First Amendment "says, in substance: 'That no person shall be compelled to worship God against the dictates of his own conscience, and no person shall be compelled to support or maintain, by law, any religion against his will, by taxation or otherwise, and that the church and state shall be forever separate.'" Rainey, *Bibles in the Public Schools, or A Plea for Religious Liberty*, 18 (Lafayette, Ind.: 1924). In *Pierce v. Society of Sisters*, Oregon's Assistant Attorney General argued: "The American people as a whole have unalterably determined that there shall be an absolute and unequivocal separation of church and state, and that the public schools shall be maintained and conducted free from influences in favor of any religious organization, sect, creed or belief." Pierce v. Society of Sisters, 268 U.S. 510, 513 (1925). According to a Seventh-Day Adventist who understood the religious liberty of the First Amendment as a separation of church and state, "Many of the States in the Union still have religious

The conception of the U.S. Bill of Rights as an enumeration of American liberties, including separation, could become quite literal, as may be illustrated by the efforts of an anti-Catholic writer, M. R. Grant. A 33rd-degree Mason and the Sovereign Grand Inspector General for Mississippi, Grant had already distinguished himself in Masonic circles by warning against the "everpresent menace" and by "preaching the gospel of Masonic responsibility"—a creed that included: "We believe in the absolute and perpetual separation of church and state, as taught by Jesus Christ."[130] In 1920 Grant displayed his talents in constitutional law by writing a Masonic "indictment of the Roman Catholic Hierarchy." In this pamphlet, *Americanism v. Roman Catholicism*, Grant brought the Catholic Church to trial before the "Bar of Public Opinion." To assist the public in its civic duty, he printed a summary of what he called the "Ten Rights Guaranteed to American Citizens by the Constitution of the United States." Reproducing the Bill of Rights in abbreviated form, he began:

1. The right of free speech, free press and free religious worship.
2. The right to arm, and to bear arms . . .

This summary continued unremarkably, until Grant reached the Tenth Amendment. Not content with the usual assumption that separation of church and state was an American freedom evident in the religious liberty clauses of American constitutions and especially the U.S. Constitution, Grant wrote separation into the U.S. Bill of Rights in a way that

---

statutes upon their books, which have been retained from colonial times when America had a union of church and state, and these religious laws are permitted to override the Federal Constitution and its guaranties of religious liberty to the individual." Charles Smull Longacre, *Roger Williams: His Life, Work, and Ideals*, 82–83 (Takoma Park, Washington, D.C.: 1939). In 1944 Conrad Henry Moehlman—a Baptist professor of church history, who had long advocated separation as an American principle—argued, in his account of the "American Way" in education, that "the First Amendment . . . profoundly affected and finally abolished the religious restrictions originally permitted in the several states." Lest this was unclear, he explained: "Although Amendment X let education be a state matter, education forthwith became a federal objective because interpreted as a pledge to national unity and an essential to popular government. Without education, the nation could not hope to survive or realize its ideals." Moehlman, *School and Church: The American Way*, 84, 85 (New York: Harper & Brothers, 1944).

[130] M. R. Grant, *Americanism v. Roman Catholicism*, advertisement on back cover and "Declaration of Principles" on inside of back cover (Meridian, Miss.: Truth Publishing Co., 1920). It should not be a surprise that he favored the inspection of Catholic institutions or that he quoted Thomas Watson and the *Menace*.

displaced the Tenth Amendment: "10. *The absolute separation and divorce of Church and State is also declared, and all union of the same is forever enjoined.*"[131] Grant's strange enumeration hardly became popular, but it reveals how the words of the U.S. Constitution typically posed no obstacle to anyone who saw separation as an "American" liberty in the Bill of Rights.

Even state courts were not immune to the culture of Americanism and its conception of separation as an American liberty. Already in 1881, in a prosecution for selling liquor on Sunday, the Supreme Court of Louisiana spoke of "the salutary doctrine of the complete separation of church and state; a doctrine which has dictated the brightest page of American history, and has always been the distinguishing feature of American freedom."[132] Similarly, in 1918, when the Supreme Court of Iowa held that a school board could not use public funds to support a parochial school, the court found separation in American principles more than in the religious liberty clause of the Iowa Constitution. "If there is any one thing which is well settled in the policies and purposes of the American people as a whole, it is the fixed and unalterable determination that there shall be an absolute and unequivocal separation of church and state."[133] This right, which was not in fact guaranteed in any

---

[131] Ibid., 7–8. Ironically, Grant, like some earlier anti-Catholic advocates of separation, also argued that "the Roman Catholic Hierarchy . . . is NOT a Church in the true sense of the word nor a religious institution." M. R. Grant, *Americanism v. Roman Catholicism,* Preface to Second Edition (Meridian, Miss.: Truth Publishing Co., 1921).

[132] Louisiana v. Baum, 33 La. Ann. 981 (1881).

[133] Knowlton v. Baumhover, 182 Iowa 691, 166 N.W. 202, 206, 5 A.L.R. 841 (1918). In 1938 the New York Court of Appeals enjoined busing to private schools on the ground that the federal government and the states had always adhered to separation: "[T]he Federal government and each State government from their respective beginnings have followed the new concept whereby the State deprived itself of all control over religion and has refused sectaries any participation in or jurisdiction or control over the civil prerogatives of the State. And so in all civil affairs there has been a complete separation of Church and State jealously guarded and unflinchingly maintained." Judd v. Board of Education, 278 N.Y. 200, 210–211, 15 N.E.2d 576, 581–582 (Ct. of App. 1938). With a similar sense of separation as a principle that transcended the boundaries between the federal and state governments, the Supreme Court of New York condemned a release-time program that "violates the provisions of the Constitution of the State and the nation, respecting religious liberty, and the separation of Church and State." Stein v. Brown and Others, Constituting the Board of Education of the City of Mount Vernon, 125 Misc. 692, 693 (1925). See also Ex rel. Ira Latimer v. The Board of Education of Chicago, 394 Ill. 233 (Ill. Supr. Ct. 1946); Murrow Indian Orphans Home v. Childers, State Auditor, et al., 197 Okla. 249, 252 (Okla. Supr. Ct. 1946).

one constitution, seemed, nonetheless, to be an American freedom or at least an American policy and purpose.

In the context of such assumptions about "American" freedoms—assumptions shared not only by nativists but also, increasingly, by their opponents—the U.S. Supreme Court began to move toward the position that the Fourteenth Amendment guaranteed, against the states, some fundamental personal freedoms in the U.S. Bill of Rights.[134] Well into the twentieth century, the Court hesitated to step clearly beyond its doctrine that the Fourteenth Amendment's due process clause protected economic rights from state regulation.[135] In 1925, however, in *Gitlow v. New York*, the Court spoke clearly about the Fourteenth Amendment's application to the states of the fundamental "personal" freedoms in the Bill of Rights, holding that "[f]or present purposes we may and do assume that freedom of speech and of the press—which are protected by the First Amendment from abridgment by Congress—are among the fundamental personal rights and 'liberties' protected by the due process clause of the Fourteenth Amendment from impairment by the States."[136]

[134] For the history of this doctrine in the late nineteenth and early twentieth centuries, see Rabban, *Free Speech in Its Forgotten Years*, 125, 130, 147–149, 367–369.

[135] The Court may have confined itself to its due process analysis of economic liberties largely because of the cases that came before it, some of which raised not quite traditional issues of free speech and free exercise. For example, in 1923, in *Meyer v. Nebraska*, the Court overturned a Nebraska law prohibiting most teaching in foreign languages, and in 1925, in *Pierce v. Society of Sisters*, the Court rejected Oregon's compulsory education law. Meyer v. Nebraska, 262 U.S. 390 (1923); Pierce v. Society of Sisters, 268 U.S. 510 (1925). In both cases, although the Court understood that personal freedom was at stake, it seems to have found advantages in relying upon its due process reasoning about economic freedom. For a richly detailed account of these and other nativist cases of this period, see Ross, *Forging New Freedoms*.

[136] Gitlow v. New York, 268 U.S. 652, 666 (1925). Warren and Ross point out the curious timing. Warren, "The New 'Liberty' under the Fourteenth Amendment," 455; Ross, *Forging New Freedoms*, 189. G. Edward White observes the difficulty of explaining the *Gitlow* decision: "The offhand fashion in which the justices who decided *Gitlow* endorsed the incorporation of the First Amendment's freedom of speech clause in the Fourteenth Amendment's Due Process Clause requires some explanation, given the state of orthodox constitutional jurisprudence at the time." White argues that the decision was a continuation of a doctrinal trend, in which the definition of the word "liberty" in the Fourteenth Amendment's due process clause was already being expanded. White, *The Constitution and the New Deal*, 141 (Cambridge: Harvard University Press, 2000). More generally, however, *Gitlow* drew upon decades of positions taken by litigants and by political organizations—positions that became ever more plausible in the context of conceptions of "American" liberty. For the litigants, see Warren, "The New 'Liberty' under the Fourteenth Amendment," 436. An illustration of how a political organization could enunciate its views may be found in a suffragette publication by Mary Sumner Boyd—"Chairman" of the Research Department

Just as the fundamental law of the Constitution trumped other law, so, through the Fourteenth Amendment, fundamental rights in the U.S. Bill of Rights transcended the distinctions among the rights enjoyed under different fundamental laws or constitutions.[137] In subsequent years the Court gradually expanded this protection of fundamental freedoms to other portions of the U.S. Bill of Rights, until, in the *Cantwell* case of 1940, it held that the fundamental liberties protected by the Fourteenth Amendment included the free exercise of religion. More generally, as already seen, it declared in this case that the Fourteenth Amendment "embraces the liberties guaranteed by the First Amendment," which was a hint that such liberties would include a protection against a religious establishment.[138]

Although the justices did not typically adopt an explicitly "American" approach, they developed their Fourteenth Amendment doctrine about the Bill of Rights in the cultural circumstances created by nativism, in which numerous individuals (including many who were far from nativist) assumed that separation and other personal freedoms were American rather than merely federal rights. On this assumption many individuals who otherwise might have been disposed to protest federal intrusions upon state power made no objection based on federalism to the Supreme Court's application of fundamental personal rights to the states—at least in cases involving First Amendment rights.[139] The justices probably had little sympathy for cruder nativist prejudices.[140] In 1925 in

---

of the Leslie Bureau of Suffrage Education. She wrote of the U.S. Constitution: "Its fourteenth amendment and its Bill of Rights are among the broadest powers given the Federal Government by its Constitution. The Bill of Rights—Amendments I–VIII—and the general summing up in Amendment XIV, Section 1, second half, 'No state shall deprive any person of life, liberty or property without due process of law, nor deny to any person within its jurisdiction the equal protection of the laws,' . . . have to-day superseded and made unnecessary the bills of rights which were regarded as the foundation stones of the early state constitutions." Mary Sumner Boyd, *The Woman Citizen: A General Handbook of Civics, with Special Consideration of Women's Citizenship,* 128 (New York: Frederick A. Stokes Co., 1918).

[137] For the tradition of "fundamental" rights in the late nineteenth-century decisions of the Court, see Rabban, *Free Speech in Its Forgotten Years,* 148, discussing Spies v. Illinois, 123 U.S. 131 (1887).

[138] Cantwell v. Connecticut, 310 U.S. at 303 (1940).

[139] In matters of race, the Court ventured only so far as to employ the due process clause to provide more mundane procedural protections. Dennis Hutchinson, "A Century of Social Reform: The Judicial Role," *Green Bag,* 4: 156 (2001).

[140] Justice McReynolds viewed the nativists in the *Meyer* case with contempt. Ross, *Forging New Freedoms,* 128.

Gitlow, and in subsequent cases applying the personal freedoms in the U.S. Bill of Rights to the states, they were interpreting the Fourteenth Amendment, and they hardly equated their doctrinal reasoning with either the nativist or a less prejudiced version of Americanism. Yet the justices and their contemporaries had grown up amid reiterated claims on behalf of human and, above all, American freedoms in the U.S. Bill of Rights—freedoms that transcended the jurisdictions of the states and the United States. In such circumstances the justices, like other Americans, may have become accustomed to thinking about the U.S. Bill of Rights as a repository of human and, especially, American freedoms that applied to the states as well as the federal government. At the very least, the justices extended personal liberties in the U.S. Bill of Rights to the states in a manner congruent with popular "American" ideals of freedom, and, in this cultural context, mostly in cases involving various First Amendment freedoms, their judicial doctrine met with little opposition and even flourished.

Expectations of Conformity

In the late 1940s—when the U.S. Supreme Court would eventually establish separation as a First Amendment freedom—many Protestants were participating in yet another surge of anti-Catholicism. They had a heightened sense of the respectable and liberal character of their principles, and they therefore confidently renewed their demands that Catholics conform to "American" ideals, especially in education.

The previous period of intense anti-Catholicism had been the decade following World War I, culminating in the 1928 presidential election. On account of the Catholicism of the Democratic nominee, Governor Al Smith of New York, many Protestants, even within Smith's own party, feared that he would place the presidency within the control of Rome. Therefore, in accord with venerable Old World practices, these Protestants demanded that Smith renounce his allegiance to the pope. In the manner of the New World, they also required Smith to avow his faith in the tenets of Americanism, especially separation. Delicately avoiding a renunciation of the pope, Smith otherwise complied:

> I summarize my creed as an American Catholic. I believe in the worship of God according to the faith and practice of the Roman Catholic Church.

> I recognize no power in the institutions of my Church to interfere with
> the operations of the Constitution of the United States or the enforce-
> ment of the law of the land. I believe in absolute freedom of conscience
> for all men and in equality of all churches, all sects, and all beliefs. . . .
> I believe in the absolute separation of Church and State and in the strict
> enforcement of the provisions of the Constitution that Congress shall
> make no law respecting an establishment of religion or prohibiting the
> free exercise thereof. . . . I believe in the support of the public school as
> one of the corner stones of American liberty.[141]

Yet even after Smith declared his devotion to this creed, Americans rejected him. As a correspondent to the *New York Times* anticipated in 1926:
"The American people have made up their minds for separation of
church and state and they interpret such separation as meaning that no
member of the Roman Catholic communion is eligible to the Presidency."[142] Not until 1960, when John F. Kennedy, more vigorously than
Smith, declared his freedom from the pope and his belief in an absolute
separation, would a Catholic be elected president.[143]

After the Depression and the Second World War, America emerged
triumphant, but (as after earlier conflicts) many Protestants worried that
they now faced "a head-on collision" with the Catholic Church. Substantial numbers feared that the pope planned to assert Catholic supremacy
in an open struggle with secular democracies. Even Protestants who did
not go to such extremes regretted the illiberal social policies of the Vati-

---

[141] *Atlantic Monthly*, 728 (May 1927). Incidentally, in 1928, although Black loyally supported the Democratic ticket, he privately complained that Al Smith was a "menace to
the country." Feldman, "The Ku Klux Klan in Alabama," 299, 101. To an old friend, Black
wrote: "Smith signed a bill passed by the Legislature of New York while he was Governor,
permitting in that state by legal enactment, the sale of beers and wines," which "was in
the teeth of the Prohibition Amendment and in effect placed New York in the position of
defying the Federal Government." Smith would appoint "a large number of Catholics . . .
to office" and, not least, it was "well known that most of the Catholics favor foreign immigration." Black concluded: "[D]ue to the immense power which a president is frequently
able to wield in bringing about the passage of laws, a man's religious faith . . . might be
important." For Black, at least, a man's religious faith was very important. Ball, *Hugo L.
Black*, 72.
[142] Elwyn A. Smith, *Religious Liberty in the United States*, 134 (Philadelphia: Fortress Press,
1972).
[143] In 1960 Kennedy declared before the Greater Houston Ministerial Association: "I believe
in an America where the separation of church and state is absolute—where no Catholic
prelate would tell the President (should he be a Catholic) how to act and no Protestant
minister would tell his parishioners for whom to vote." "Transcript of Kennedy Talk to
Ministers," *New York Times*, 22 (Sept. 13, 1960).

can and believed that the "maintenance of a kind of Protestant tone to government and society was more likely to preserve democracy than relinquishing that leadership to their Catholic rivals."[144]

The Southern Jurisdiction of Scottish Rite Masons remained a bastion of this hostility to Catholicism. At its most principled, the Southern Jurisdiction demanded "non-sectarian" public schools and the "entire separation of Church and State"—ideals that Masons such as Hugo Black saw emblazoned across the back page of each issue of the organization's *Bulletin*.[145] During the postwar years the Southern Jurisdiction and other Masonic groups could still claim among their brethren large numbers of liberal Protestants, including many who had become quite prominent. For example, in the late 1940s at least seven justices of the Supreme Court belonged to one Masonic organization or another, three being attached to the Southern Jurisdiction of the Scottish Rite.[146] Such statistics prove little about specifically Masonic influence. Yet they clearly suggest the persistent cultural significance of fraternal organizations and their theologically liberal vision of Americanism. In such circumstances suspicions of the Catholic Church continued to thrive.

Liberal anti-Catholic sentiments would find their most prominent exponent in Paul Blanshard, who brought liberal, Ivy League respectability to nativist anti-Catholicism. Blanshard presented his high-toned, theologically and politically liberal perspective in 1948 in the pages of the *Nation,* and a year later in his best-selling *American Freedom and Catholic Power,* published by the Unitarians' Beacon Press. With all the apparatus of academic learning and the dispassionate, even-handed tone of a scholar, Blanshard gave old fears a thoroughly modern cast by exploring the growing worries of political liberals that Catholicism impeded mod-

---

[144] Glenn L. Archer and Albert J. Menendez, *The Dream Lives On: The Story of Glenn L. Archer and Americans United,* 79 (Washington, D.C.: Luce, 1982); Philip Gleason, *Speaking of Diversity: Language and Ethnicity in Twentieth-Century America,* 211–212 (Baltimore: Johns Hopkins University Press, 1992).

[145] For Black's attention to the principles on the back page and for his concern that the editors were not sufficiently adhering to them, see his letter to Senator Lister Hill quoted by Fisher, *Behind the Lodge Door,* 146–148.

[146] Fisher, *Behind the Lodge Door,* App. A, citing Ronald E. Heaton, *Justices of the Supreme Court Identified as Masons* (Washington, D.C.: Masonic Service Association, 1969). Fisher suggests that the Masons on the Court participated in a Masonic conspiracy to adopt the idea of separation in *Everson v. Board of Education.* Obviously, the evidence does not support this conclusion. Incidentally, Fisher states that Frankfurter was a Mason but cites no evidence, and therefore this justice is not included in the numbers given here.

ern social policy. He concluded that it was necessary "to build a resistance movement designed to prevent the hierarchy from imposing its social policies upon our schools, hospitals, government and family organization." This movement would struggle against the "un-American" features of the Church's social agenda, including not only its "intolerant" legislative goals but also its "separatist" institutions. Naturally, as part of this resistance, Blanshard also wanted "a wall of separation between church and state," and he emphasized that Americans had to "make it real with no compromise."[147] His book became a sensation because it justified a liberal, genteel, educated anti-Catholicism. As John Dewey put it, "Mr. Blanshard has done a difficult and necessary piece of work with exemplary scholarship, good judgment and tact."[148]

In critiquing Catholicism, some political liberals took umbrage at the Church's rejection of Communism. After the United States worked with the Soviet Union to defeat the fascists, many left-leaning liberals openly sympathized with the Soviets and feared that "[t]he Vatican seemed ready to embark on a crusade . . . to ally the Protestant democracies of the West in a kind of holy war or crusade against Communism."[149] It was a time when Americans on the left, ranging from Communists to moderate liberals, increasingly were accused of un-American loyalty to a foreign power, and therefore they became all the more willing to lash out at Catholics for their un-American, foreign allegiance. Of course,

[147] Paul Blanshard, *American Freedom and Catholic Power*, 303–305 (Boston: Beacon Press, 1949). In a manner reminiscent of earlier nativist and Klan demands, Blanshard proposed "continuous and scientific inspection of all parochial schools"—partly for respectable purposes but also to ensure that "classes are taught in the English language and that textbooks do not distort history, science and sociology in an un-American manner for the benefit of the hierarchy." Ibid.

[148] Quotation from dustjacket of fifth printing, 1949; also discussed by McGreevy, "Thinking on One's Own," 97, who, more generally, discusses the anti-Catholicism among intellectuals during this period. The president emeritus of the Union Theological Seminary, Henry Sloane Coffin, gushed about Blanshard that "the gratitude of all freedom-cherishing Americans goes to him" and that his volume "should be in the hands of every thoughtful American." Blanshard, *American Freedom and Catholic Power* (dustjacket).

[149] Archer and Menendez, *The Dream Lives On*, 78, 77. Others viewed Catholics and Communists as twin evils. For example, many Masons wanted "to watch them both. . . . They shall not crucify our nation upon the cross of religion or upon the hammer and sickle." C. I. McReynolds, "Enemies of America," in *Scottish Rite News Bulletin*, No. 117: 1 (Aug. 5, 1947). See also "Un-American Activities Group Asked to View R.C. Practices," in ibid., 3. Dawson was among those who condemned both "political totalitarianism" and "ecclesiastical totalitarianism." J. M. Dawson, "Baptists of United States," in ibid., No. 125: 1 (Dec. 5, 1947).

Catholics, who for centuries had been accused of subversion, had always been quick to return the favor, and they now redoubled their accusations against Communists. Many liberals were outraged by this opposition to progress and blasted Catholics for their un-American obscurantism. In such ways numerous Catholics and liberals identified themselves with Americanism by damning each other's alien loyalties.

More broadly, increasing numbers of theologically and politically liberal Protestants complained that Catholics were "divisive." These Protestants, together with their allies among Reform Jews, sought ecumenical harmony by breaking down the differences among churches. They therefore viewed the desire of Catholics to preserve their distinct beliefs and institutions as a threat to unity and peace. In particular, the "segregation" of Catholic children into parochial schools seemed divisive and likely to inculcate intolerance, leading a few observers, including Felix Frankfurter, to question the decision in *Pierce v. Society of Sisters,* in which the Supreme Court had held Oregon's compulsory education law unconstitutional. Indeed, at a time when some Americans were beginning to perceive the injustices of racial segregation in public schools, substantial numbers of Protestants felt greater anxiety about religious segregation in Catholic private schools. Many Protestants perceived the Church's reluctance to abandon its parochial schools or otherwise to homogenize its religious differences, as a sign of its oppressive intentions. More generally, they worried that "increasing signs of militancy and aggressiveness in the Vatican" had begun "to jar the basic easy-going friendliness of most of the American Protestant churches."[150] Whether either side was entirely easygoing or friendly may be doubted.

These continuing suspicions of Catholicism and demands for confor-

---

[150] Archer and Menendez, *The Dream Lives On,* 77. For the doubts about *Pierce,* see Will Herberg, "Religion and Education in America," in James Ward Smith and A. Leland Jamison, eds., *Religious Perspectives in American Culture,* 38 (Princeton: Princeton University Press, 1961); Dunne, *Hugo Black and the Judicial Revolution,* 266; McGreevy, "Thinking on One's Own," 120. Already in the 1920s in the *Pierce* case, it had been argued on behalf of compulsory education that private schools were divisive. Pierce v. Society of Sisters, 268 U.S. 510, 525 (1925). Looking back on the late forties, a leader of Protestants and Other Americans United (POAU) recalled: "The official Catholic emphasis on a separate parochial school system was felt to be divisive by many Protestants." Archer and Menendez, *The Dream Lives On,* 80. See also the controversy over the alleged use of the word "divisive" by the president of Harvard, James Bryant Conant. Edmond G. Drouin, "The School Question; A Bibliography on Church-State Relationships in American Education: 1940–1957," 151–154, App. D (master's thesis, Catholic University of America, 1958).

mity grew all the more insistent as many Protestants increasingly viewed their public schools with almost religious reverence. "Protestant educators became some of the most enthusiastic proponents of the new spirituality"—a religious approach to public education in which "'separation' itself became a quasi-religious dogma, impervious to the criticism of fact or experience." "In some versions, the new 'Americanist' creed was regarded as superceding, at least for public purposes, an outworn Christianity; in other versions, however, it proved more generous and hospitable."[151] For example, in 1944 a theologically liberal Baptist professor, Conrad Henry Moehlman, argued that public schools served a religious function in a nation in which "[t]he religion of the . . . majority is democracy." According to Moehlman, "Direct religious education is generally recognized to be the burden of the churches. *But functionally viewed, American public education emancipated from sectarianism is indirectly the only universal teacher of religious values in the United States.*" Imbued with this "religion of public education," Moehlman ardently advocated separation. He regretted that Catholicism had remained "resistant to the demands of the American environment," but he took hope in observing that "[t]he parochial school is definitely on the defensive."[152] Such was the atmosphere in which the Supreme Court endorsed separation as a national ideal.

Everson v. Board of Education

The Supreme Court finally interpreted the First and Fourteenth Amendments to require separation of church and state in 1947, in the New

---

[151] Herberg, "Religion and Education in America," in Smith and Jamison, eds., *Religious Perspectives in American Culture*, 25, 30, 32.

[152] Moehlman, *School and Church*, x, 85, 100, 102, quoted by Herberg, "Religion and Education in America," 31. Moehlman had long before quite literally dedicated his scholarship to separation: "TO THE MEMORY OF MY PARENTS WHO FIRST TAUGHT ME THE AMERICAN DOCTRINE OF THE SEPARATION OF CHURCH AND STATE." Conrad Henry Moehlman, *The Catholic-Protestant Mind: Some Aspects of Religious Liberty in the United States* (dedication page) (New York: Harper, 1929). For his liberalism, see Grace Moehlman Forbes, *Conrad Henry Moehlman—The Man and the Message*, 215–217 (Geneva, N.Y.: G. M. Forbes, 1978). For his attitudes in 1948, after *McCollum v. Board of Education*, see Conrad Henry Moehlman, "Exclusiveness of Roman Catholicism," *Scottish Rite News Bulletin*, No. 8 (April 20, 1948). Incidentally, V. T. Thayer rejected any role for even a secularized religion in the public schools and complained about the "liberals in theology" who sought "a reinterpretation of the term and the concept of religion." Thayer, *Religion in Public Education*, 100 (New York: Viking Press, 1947).

Jersey case of *Everson v. Board of Education of the Township of Ewing.* Already in 1878, after nativists, Liberals, and Republicans had demanded separation, the Supreme Court had quoted Jefferson's letter to the Baptists to justify its rejection of a Mormon's claim that his religious obligations excused him from federal antipolygamy laws. More recently, in 1943, in a dissent, Justice Frankfurter referred in passing to "the doctrine of separation of church and state, so cardinal in the history of this nation and for the liberty of our people."[153] Only in 1947, however, did the Court clearly make separation the basis for a decision—opining that the First Amendment required separation, that the Fourteenth Amendment applied it to the states, and that New Jersey's subsidized school busing for both public schools and private schools did not violate the First and Fourteenth Amendments. In this way, the Court recognized separation as part of American constitutional law.

An old nativist order initiated the *Everson* case. The plaintiff, Arch R. Everson, had distinguished himself as executive director of the New Jersey Taxpayers Association. More significantly, he was also a member of the New Jersey chapter of the Junior Order of United American Mechanics. The original Order of United American Mechanics had been founded in 1845 in Philadelphia by Protestant workingmen resentful of Catholic and other immigrants. Later, in 1853, some members established the Junior Order as a feeder organization, which eventually became a highly successful independent order. Like so many other "patriotic" orders, the Junior Order restricted membership to white, native-born Americans who were "in favor of free education, and opposed to any union of Church and State." It had among its objects: to prevent "foreign competition" from immigrants and "[t]o maintain the Public School System . . . and to prevent sectarian interference therewith, and to uphold the reading of the Holy Bible therein."[154] In the late nineteenth century members of the Junior Order took a prominent role in the notorious American Protective Association, and in the early 1920s, at least in some states, the Junior Order cooperated with the Klan against Catholicism. Most openly, in Georgia the "Juniors" endorsed the viru-

[153] West Virginia State Board of Education v. Barnette, 319 U.S. 624, 655 (1943).
[154] "Junior Order United American Mechanics . . . Eligibility for Membership," *The American,* 2 (no. 16): 8 (May 18, 1889). For variants of the Junior Order's evolving objectives and requirements, see M. D. Lichliter, *History of the Junior Order United American Mechanics of the United State of North America,* 47–57 (Philadelphia: J. B. Lippincott, 1908).

lent Klan newspaper, *The Searchlight*, as an "OFFICIAL ORGAN" of their order and published in each issue a "Junior Order Department," which articulated the anti-Catholic sentiments so many Klansmen and "Juniors" shared.[155] In the 1930s, after the decline of the Klan, the Junior Order continued to stand "at the portals of our American public school system to guard it from sectarian and foreign influence." It proudly declared itself "Patriotic" and "Progressive" and preached the "glorious trinity" of "[t]he Bible, the Flag, and the School," in part by presenting flags and Bibles to public schools. The Bible, it argued, was valuable "not to teach sectarianism," but "because it contains the purest code of morals the world has ever known." The Junior Order exaggerated less than might be supposed when it boasted: "EVERY LAW for the promulgation of American principles, Compulsory Education, Free Text Books, Reading of the Holy Bible in the Schools, Placing the Flag upon the Schools . . . have in a large measure been prepared and fostered by the Jr. O.U.A.M."[156]

In the late 1930s and early 1940s, the New Jersey chapter of the Junior Order lobbied against school busing. In particular, it attempted to block New Jersey legislation under which the state would bus children to and from their schools, including private institutions, many of which were Catholic. In this endeavor the Junior Order joined forces with other groups, including the League of Women Voters, the Seventh-Day Adventists, the New Jersey State Board of Education, the New Jersey Taxpayers Association, and the Patriotic Order of Sons of America. The Patriotic Order was an old nativist ally of the Junior Order, and the two relied upon the same lawyer, Albert McCay, to represent them in the legislative hearings. Notwithstanding their formidable efforts, the Junior Order and

---

[155] For example, in one issue this "Department" denounced the pope; it claimed that Georgia's election of "Brother Thomas E. Watson" to the Senate was among the Order's "1921 JUNIOR ACCOMPLISHMENTS"; and it reported on a local meeting of "Juniors" at which Walter A. Sims denounced the Knights of Columbus as "a military organization" and argued that "the Roman Catholics have no right to teach in the public schools of this country, as they do not believe in public schools, and follow the dictates of the pope of Rome." "Junior Order Department—Ingleside Council Pledges Support to *Searchlight*," *Searchlight*, 3 (no. 2) (Jan. 16, 1922). The Junior Order's endorsement of *The Searchlight* apparently came with financial support and was emblazoned across the paper's masthead.

[156] National Council, Junior Order United American Mechanics, *Addresses*, 20, 24 (1935); *A Short Sketch of America's Greatest Patriotic Fraternity: Facts Every American Should Know*, 1, 3, 5, 7 (Tiffin, Ohio: National Orphans Home Printing Dept., n.d.). The Order's legislative activities first became substantial in the early 1890s, as documented by Lichliter, *History of the Junior Order*, 206–279.

its allies lost this legislative battle in 1941, when the busing bill finally became law. In response, in 1943 the New Jersey chapter turned to litigation, relying upon Arch R. Everson as the plaintiff and Albert McCay as his attorney. Everson was a resident of Ewing Township, and his suit seems to have been a test case prearranged by the Junior Order in consultation with the defendant, the Ewing Board of Education.[157]

Everson's counsel eventually argued on grounds of separation. McCay at first had not expected to win on such grounds, but, after losing in the New Jersey Court of Errors and Appeals, he arranged for other lawyers to take an appeal to the U.S. Supreme Court. In their brief for the Supreme Court, they repeatedly described the constitutional standard as separation.[158] They insisted that the busing amounted to school aid, which was "contrary to our conception of the absolute separation of church and state and to the principles enunciated in the Fourteenth Amendment as well as those in the First Amendment." The busing violated "the mandate of the separation of church and state, inherent in the First Amendment providing that there shall be no law respecting an establishment of religion."[159]

In support of Everson, the New Jersey Council of the Junior Order of United American Mechanics submitted an amicus brief, in which it explained that it had long "taken a keen interest in all matters pertaining to public schools" and was "dedicated to the principle of separation of church and state."[160] In accord with the standard history of separation, the Order argued: "The desirability of keeping the church separated from the state was apparent to the framers of the Federal Constitution," who were convinced "that complete religious freedom and separation of the

---

[157] Daryl R. Fair, "The Everson Case in the Context of New Jersey Politics," in *Everson Revisited: Religion, Education, and Law at the Crossroads*, 4–8, 10, ed. Jo Renée Formicola and Hubert Morken (Lanham, Md.: Rowman & Littlefield, 1997); Cortner, *The Supreme Court and the Second Bill of Rights*, 108–123; Gregg Ivers, *To Build a Wall: American Jews and the Separation of Church and State*, 17–19 (Charlottesville: University Press of Virginia, 1995). This is not to say, however, that the case was litigated without vigor, for the Catholic Church apparently assisted the Board of Education in its defense. Christine L. Compston, "The Serpentine Wall: Judicial Decision Making in Supreme Court Cases Involving Aid to Sectarian Schools," 113 (Ph.D. diss., University of New Hampshire, 1986).

[158] Fair, "The Everson Case," in *Everson Revisited*, 8, 14.

[159] Brief for Appellant, in Everson v. Board of Education of the Township of Ewing, 19, 26 (October Term, 1946, No. 52, U.S. Supr. Ct.).

[160] Brief of State Council of the Junior Order of United American Mechanics of the State of New Jersey, in Everson v. Board of Education of the Township of Ewing, 1 (October Term, 1946, No. 52, U.S. Supr. Ct.).

church and the state should be one of the basic principles in the new Government." Being a "basic principle," separation was apparent in all American constitutions: "Every state constitution guarantees religious liberty and in more or less detail defines the intention of the people to keep the church and state separated." With such arguments, this "American" order, which had opposed Catholics for more than 100 years, asked the Court to condemn "an aid to sectarian schools" that thus "violates the basic American principle of the separation of church and state."[161]

The other amici briefs on behalf of Everson similarly demanded separation.[162] Like Everson and the Junior Order, albeit with less emphasis, the Seventh-Day Adventists and the Baptists' Joint Conference Committee on Public Relations took for granted "the time-honored doctrine of the separation of Church and State safeguarded by the Constitution."[163] Taking a slightly different tack, the ACLU treated separation as the First Amendment's purpose and as a pervasive American ideal. In such ways, like some nativists, the ACLU avoided the awkward reality that no American constitution mentioned separation and that the First Amendment expressly constrained Congress rather than the states. "The purpose of the First Amendment, seen in the perspective of history, is clear enough. It was designed to bring about the complete separation of church and state. This separation was to be achieved by guaranteeing to every person freedom from state interference in his religion or religious establishment."[164] This was a freedom against the states because "[t]he ideals of religious freedom and separation of church from state . . . permeate our constitution and institutions." Thus "[t]he constitutional policy of our country has decreed the absolute separation of church and state."[165]

---

[161] Ibid., 2, 11, 12.

[162] For the solicitation of briefs by Everson's lawyer, see Cortner, *The Supreme Court and the Second Bill of Rights,* 117; Ivers, *To Build a Wall,* 19.

[163] Amicus Brief of General Conference of Seventh-Day Adventists and the Joint Conference Committee, in Everson v. Board of Education of the Township of Ewing, 2 (October Term, 1946, No. 52, U.S. Supr. Ct.).

[164] Amicus Brief of ACLU, in Everson v. Board of Education for the Township of Ewing, 7–8 (October Term, 1946, No. 52, U.S. Supr. Ct.).

[165] Ibid., 34–35. Incidentally, like some earlier advocates of separation, the ACLU blurred the distinction between, on the one hand, eighteenth-century laws that recognized, subsidized, and thereby established particular groups on the basis of their particular religion (or religions) and, on the other, the twentieth-century laws under which both secular or religious organizations could obtain benefits by meeting secular qualifications. The former were laws respecting religion or taking cognizance of it; they also were laws respecting the establishment of religion. In contrast, the latter made no mention of religion, but they

In defense, the Ewing Board of Education and its allies did not even contest the assumption that the Constitution required separation. The board apparently worried that it might be perceived as disloyal to this American principle. The board therefore emphasized its support for separation and disputed only this idea's implications:

> To the proposition . . . that the separation of Church and State is a fundamental principle of our government, we whole-heartedly agree. No one would wish it otherwise. But it does not follow from this, as appellant implies, either that the two are irretrievably committed to perpetual hostility, or that when the interests of both happen to coincide, the Constitution requires that the interests of both should be either ignored or frustrated.[166]

Similarly, in its amicus brief in support of the Ewing Board of Education, the State of New York accepted separation as the standard and questioned only whether total separation was possible. Observing that many state laws regulated and facilitated education, including the safety, health, and instruction of children in private schools, the attorney general of New York argued: "If the divorce of the State from the denominational school must be total, the State could not extend the provisions of any of these statutes to it."[167] He conceded that "[t]he principle of separation of church and state must ever remain inviolate in these United States," but he emphasized that it was not a complete separation. The principle therefore remained undisturbed even though the states, "under the police power, have legislated in a variety of respects for the wel-

---

seemed offensive to proponents of separation because these laws did not exclude religious bodies from receiving benefits. Treating these two types of legislation as indistinguishable—indeed, carefully blurring them together—the ACLU rewrote history, arguing that, after the adoption of the First Amendment, "religious institutions" were "[n]o longer . . . to be supported out of the public treasury." The problems involved in *Everson* "were fully known and experienced in essentially similar manifestations in the eighteenth century and long before, and had led, after a century-and-a-half struggle for religious freedom and the separation of church and state to the framing and adoption of the First Amendment." Amicus Brief of ACLU, 7–8. In suggesting that twentieth-century secular laws that did not discriminate against religious organizations were "essentially similar" to the eighteenth-century laws establishing Christian churches, the ACLU revealed much about the character of its argument and much about what its lawyers understood.

[166] Brief of Appellees, in Everson v. Board of Education of the Township of Ewing, 29–30 (October Term, 1946, No. 52, U.S. Supr. Ct.).

[167] Brief of the State of New York, in Everson v. Board of Education of the Township of Ewing, 8 (October Term, 1946, No. 52, U.S. Supr. Ct.).

fare of children in the denominational as well as in the public school."
On the assumption that this argument about regulation extended to the
provision of benefits, the attorney general concluded that "[t]he transportation of pupils by buses to schools does not spell danger to that principle [of separation]."[168]

The National Council of Catholic Men and the National Council of
Catholic Women also hesitated to challenge separation directly. Cardinal
Spellman of New York and Cardinal Stritch of Chicago had become worried when the *Everson* case reached the Supreme Court and therefore had
asked the two Councils to prepare an amicus brief in consultation with
the theologian, John Courtney Murray—apparently on the assumption
that the Supreme Court was a forum in which to expound theological
as well as legal principles. Certainly, the brief's style of reasoning approached the scholastic. After indulging in the metaphor that "[t]he 'Wall
of Separation' between Church and State is not undermined, breached
or cracked by this Transportation Law," the brief tentatively suggested
"[a]bandoning metaphor." Yet it questioned only its opponents' interpretation of the wall rather than the metaphor itself. Acknowledging that
the "Jeffersonian metaphor of a 'wall of separation' between Church and
State has validity," it merely added that, "[l]ike any metaphor, however,
it must be closely analyzed in order that its true content may be revealed."[169] In particular, the Catholic National Councils argued that there
was a wall only "between the distinct areas of the life of an individual,
over which the authority of the State and the authority of conscience
respectively rule." Everson had been "misled by the metaphor" and had
"transformed the legitimate 'wall' into an illegitimate 'iron curtain' separating areas between which there should be free passage." As a result,
he had made the mistake of suggesting that "the exercise of parental
choice in the matter of education" by sending children to parochial
schools would "necessarily 'wall off' some citizens from participation in
ordinary educational benefits," such as busing, that they received as citizens. Far from escaping or repudiating the metaphor, the Catholic National Councils confined themselves almost entirely within its walls.[170]

---

[168] Ibid.

[169] Brief of National Council of Catholic Men and National Council of Catholic Women,
in Everson v. Board of Education of the Township of Ewing, 4, 32, 33 (October Term,
1946, No. 52, U.S. Supr. Ct.). For the preparation of the brief, see Jo Renée Formicola,
"Catholic Jurisprudence on Education," in *Everson Revisited*, 85.

[170] Brief of National Council of Catholic Men and National Council of Catholic Women, 33–36.

On these arguments, in which no one disputed that the Constitution required the separation of church and state, Justice Black, writing for the majority, declared that separation was the constitutional standard:

> The "establishment of religion" clause of the First Amendment means at least this: Neither a state nor the Federal Government can set up a church. Neither can pass laws which aid one religion, aid all religions, or prefer one religion over another. Neither can force nor influence a person to go to or to remain away from church against his will or force him to profess a belief or disbelief in any religion. No person can be punished for entertaining or professing religious beliefs or disbeliefs, for church attendance or non-attendance. No tax in any amount, large or small, can be levied to support any religious activities or institutions, whatever they may be called, or whatever form they may adopt to teach or practice religion. Neither a state nor the Federal Government can, openly or secretly, participate in the affairs of any religious organizations or groups and *vice versa*. In the words of Jefferson, the clause against establishment of religion by law was intended to erect "a wall of separation between church and State." *Reynolds v. United States.*[171]

It was a proclamation of principle with which none of Black's brethren disagreed.

Nonetheless, Justices Rutledge, Jackson, Burton, and Frankfurter vigorously dissented from Black's conclusion, for, after Black so eloquently enunciated his views on separation, he and his majority upheld New Jersey's subsidized busing.[172] This contradiction astonished the dissenters. As Jackson wrote of Black's opinion: "[M]uch of its reasoning confirms my conclusions that there are no good grounds upon which to support the present legislation. In fact, the undertones of the opinion, advocating complete and uncompromising separation of Church from State, seem utterly discordant with its conclusion yielding support to their commingling in educational matters."[173]

Black, however, understood what he was doing. Only ten years before, when Black was appointed to the Court, Catholics vociferously con-

---

[171] Everson v. Board of Education, 330 U.S. 15–16 (1947). Black drew upon Charles Beard's 1943 *The Republic*, which Black considered "a great book" and the title of which, he thought, "might almost have been 'The Origin and Aim of the American Constitution.'" Newman, *Black*, 363, quoting Letter of Hugo Black to Clarence Mullins (Nov. 11, 1943).
[172] For details about how the justices reached their conclusions, see Compston, "The Serpentine Wall," 1–119.
[173] *Everson*, 330 U.S. at 19. For the voting in *Everson*, see J. Woodford Howard, "On the Fluidity of Judicial Choice," *American Political Science Review*, 62 (no. 1): 54 (March 1968).

demned him for his Klan membership. Now Black had an opportunity to make separation the unanimous standard of the Court while reaching a judgment that would undercut Catholic criticism. Black expected that his disarming conclusion would lead Catholics to think that they had succeeded in staving off the practical consequences of separation.[174] The justice, however, knew better, and, in a conversation with a clerk, he alluded to it as a Pyrrhic victory.[175] Perhaps not insignificantly, Joseph Martin Dawson later echoed this sentiment. Although initially disappointed by the decision, Dawson soon came to recognize that "[w]e had lost a battle, but won the war!"[176]

Black had long before sworn, under the light of flaming crosses, to preserve "the sacred constitutional rights" of "free public schools" and "separation of church and state." Subsequently, he had administered this oath to thousands of others in similar ceremonies and had spoken in churches and klaverns across Alabama on what his fellow Klan leader, Jim Esdale, euphemistically called "the history of the church." Like so many earlier nativists, Black emphasized his concern for Catholic individuals, protesting that he was not "prejudiced against people of the Jewish or Catholic faiths" and that "[s]ome of my best and most intimate friends are Catholics and Jews."[177] Indeed, in the 1920s Black had occasionally sought to protect individual blacks, Jews, and Catholics from the violence of his fellow Klansmen, which he found distasteful, but he proudly declared his "principles" to be those of the Klan. With this combination of sentiments, he observed in 1921 at the time of the infamous Stephenson trial: "A man may not like the Catholic Church, but

---

[174] John Courtney Murray even praised the opinion: "The essence of the decision is (1) in its loyal affirmation of the American doctrine of religious freedom and consequent 'separation of Church and State' and (2) in its refusal to see this doctrine so interpreted as to 'wall off' any group of citizens on religious grounds, from an equal share in the benefits of public welfare legislature. By reason of this affirmation and this refusal the majority opinion is a new buttressing both of religious liberty and of civic equality." He added: "This is good legal realism which cuts through all the unrealistic legalism shown in the dissenting opinions." John Courtney Murray, S.J., "Transporting All Pupils Serves Public Purpose Decision States," *Catholic News* (New York) (Feb. 22, 1947). Many Catholics, however, came to view the opinion as a threat—a response that Black said he thought "strange." Newman, *Black,* 364, quoting 1949 letter to Max Lerner.

[175] He "quoted King Pyrrhus, 'One more victory and I am undone.'" Newman, *Black,* 364–365.

[176] Joseph Martin Dawson, *A Thousand Months to Remember, An Autobiography,* 194 (Waco: Baylor University Press, 1964).

[177] "Justice Black's Speech," *New York Times,* 3 (Oct. 2, 1937).

may like some of its members."[178] Black's distaste for Catholicism did not diminish. Although after his nomination to the Court, Black himself rarely talked about the Klan, he continued to complain about "Roman Catholic hostility to Masons" and about Catholics who got "riled" on the assumption that "Masons were always freethinkers."[179] His son recalled:

> The Ku Klux Klan and Daddy, so far as I could tell, only had one thing in common. He suspected the Catholic Church. He used to read all of Paul Blanshard's books exposing power abuse in the Catholic Church. He thought the Pope and bishops had too much power and property. He resented the fact that rental property owned by the Church was not taxed; he felt they got most of their revenue from the poor and did not return enough of it.[180]

Holding such views, which Esdale himself had called "anti-Catholic," Black in 1947 led the Court to declare itself in favor of the "separation of church and state."

The Aftermath of Everson

In the year following the *Everson* decision, the advocates of separation feared all the more intensely for their principle. They misunderstood the significance of Black's opinion in *Everson* and therefore severely criticized it for undermining the separation Black had thought he was establishing. As a result, Black felt eager and even anxious to clarify that his opinion laid the foundation for separation.

The advocates of separation focused on the particular result in *Everson* rather than the reasoning and therefore felt profound disappointment. Understanding separation to be their historical right, they could sense how close they were to getting the Supreme Court to enforce it and, accordingly, felt all the more frustrated. The tone of the advocates of separation was set, in the days immediately after the decision, by hostile newspaper editorials, such as that of the *Washington Post*, which observed that "the principle at issue is one of the most fundamental in the Ameri-

---

[178] Newman, *Black*, 77.
[179] Dunne, *Hugo Black and the Judicial Revolution*, 268, quoting March 22, 1956 interview. See also McGreevy, "Thinking on One's Own," 124.
[180] Hugo Black, Jr., *My Father*, 104 (New York: Random House, 1974), also quoted by Dunne, *Hugo Black and the Judicial Revolution*, 269.

can concept of government—the separation of church and state." According to the *Post,* Justice Black gave "much lip-service to the principles of religious freedom" but used a "superficial argument" to permit subsidized bus service and thereby undermined the separation of church and state. The Southern Jurisdiction of the Scottish Rite Masons, the National Education Association, and both the Southern and the Northern Baptists concurred.[181]

Amid these public denunciations of Black's opinion in *Everson,* the Baptists' Joint Conference Committee on Public Relations had special reason to be disappointed with the Court. The Committee had written a brief in the *Everson* case, and it had arranged for its chairman, E. Hilton Jackson, to join Everson's counsel in the oral argument. The Committee was particularly dismayed by Black, for he had grown up a Baptist and had briefly in 1937 served as a member of the Southern Baptist group that had evolved into the current Committee.[182] The day after the decision in *Everson,* the Joint Conference Committee adopted a resolution that "deplored" Black's decision for "turning back the hands of the clock as far as religious liberty and the separation of church and state are concerned"—a resolution it later published in a pamphlet together with

---

[181] "Church and State," *National Education Association Journal,* 36: 380 (May 1947), quoting *Washington Post* (Feb. 13, 1947); J. M. Dawson, "United States Supreme Court Decision Deplored," *The Christian Index,* 127 (no. 10): 5 (Atlanta, Ga.: March 6, 1947); "U.S. Supreme Court 'Giving the Clock's Hand a Backward Turn,'" *Scottish Rite News Bulletin,* No. 106: 1–2 (Jan. 6, 1947).

Almost immediately after the *Everson* decision, its Scottish Rite critics threatened Catholics with a revival of old demands for "inspection." Parochial and private schools "should see clearly that some controls will always follow the aid." Taxpayers would insist "upon inspecting them, criticizing them, and maybe changing them in a number of ways." E.K., "Parochial Schools Really Want Outside Regulation?" in ibid., 3. Protestants even had an obligation "to demand control over the teaching in such schools." "Sharp Scrutiny of Parochial Textbooks Believed Due," in ibid., No. 108: 1 (March 20, 1947). See also "Prewar Catholic Editorial Opposes Accepting Aid Funds," in ibid., No. 107: 1 (March 5, 1947); "Taxpayers Empowered to Ask Control of Parochial Schools," in ibid., 3. Incidentally, among those who condemned the *Everson* case in the pages of the *Scottish Rite News Bulletin* was not only Joseph M. Dawson but also Gilbert O. Nations—a 32nd-degree Scottish Rite Mason who had made a career of editing nativist periodicals, including *The Menace, The Protestant,* and *The Fellowship Forum.* See Nations, "Jesuit on School Bus Case," *Scottish Rite News Bulletin,* No. 120: 1 (Sept. 20, 1947).

[182] For the October 2, 1946 directive to Jackson, see Stanley LeRoy Hastey, "A History of the Baptist Joint Committee on Public Affairs, 1946–1971," 70 (Doctor of Theology diss., Southern Baptist Theological Seminary, 1973). Black "drifted away from organized religion" and eventually attended All Souls Unitarian Church in Washington. Newman, *Black,* 521.

other critiques of Black's reasoning.[183] In an issue of the Committee's newsletter—which was filled with denunciations of the case—Dawson complained: "We consider this another encroaching step toward changing the Constitution in a manner to give the Catholic Church a privileged position."[184]

Less publicly, Black received many letters criticizing his opinion in the *Everson* case, and, although some of these letters came from cranks, many came from Baptist ministers. These clergymen included northerners, but most were from the South, and notwithstanding that some were liberals, it may be doubted whether all of these Baptists welcomed the application of the U.S. Bill of Rights to the states in opposition to racism. Nonetheless, they regretted that Justice Black had not applied the U.S. Bill of Rights more vigorously against the Catholic menace in the states. For example, a Southern Baptist from Alabama, Charles R. Bell—who had become pastor of the First Baptist Church in Madison, Wisconsin—wrote to Justice Black: "Here in Wisconsin we are living with a Catholic hierarch which watches the law broken with impunity, which will crush our freedom when given a chance and which is working feverishly to blot out liberalism. The national Catholic leadership is working, in my opinion, for war with Russia." This theologically liberal Baptist had already, in 1946, led Wisconsin's Protestants in a campaign against public busing to private schools. He now told Black that if the Court "interprets our Constitution as allowing churches to get tax funds then I see no alternative to working for an amendment which will state specifically and finally the Protestant position which is complete separation of church and state!" Black responded with courtesy, writing that it was "always a pleasure to receive your views on any question," but explaining that he was "not free to say anything" as to his own views, other than what he had written in his opinion.[185] From Sebring, Florida,

---

[183] *Government Aid to Church Schools* (Nashville, Tenn.: Sunday School Board of the Southern Baptist Convention, 1947); Hastey, "A History of the Baptist Joint Committee," 73; *New York Times*, 26 (Feb. 11, 1947).

[184] Hastey, "A History of the Baptist Joint Committee," 74.

[185] Letter from Charles R. Bell, Jr., to Hugo L. Black (Madison, Wis., Feb. 13, 1947) and Letter of Hugo L. Black to Charles R. Bell, Jr. (Feb. 21, 1947), in Library of Congress, Hugo Black Papers, File 285, *Everson* Case File, Public Correspondence. For Bell's liberal theology, and for his background as pastor of his "home" church in Anniston, Alabama, see [Charles R. Bell, Jr.], *The First Baptist Church Madison 1847–1947*, 20, 33, 34 (Madison: 1947). Bell had led Protestants to defeat the "unAmerican" Wisconsin transport referendum by holding "mass" meetings across the state, by distributing "450,000 pieces of literature," and by

another Baptist sent a telegram: "BY YOUR ACTION YOU ARE TRYING TO DESTROY ONE OF THE CHIEF CORNERSTONES OF AMERICA, SEPARATION OF CHURCH AND STATE. WE BAPTIST PEOPLE WILL RESIST SUCH ROMISH PRACTICES TO THE END."[186] T. F. Callaway—pastor of the First Baptist Church in Thomasville, Georgia—thought Black's decision "all but unbelievable. . . . You were about the last one from whom we could have expected such a decision." Recalling the controversy over Black's membership in the Klan, Callaway wrote: "Now, you are in the position of going to the other extreme in your efforts to show that you are freed from any former Klan influence; but, i[n] so doing, you have utterly sacrificed the sacred principle of separation of church and state. . . . We, especially in the South, can never feel that your decision expressed your real sentiment as a citizen or a justice." In the circumstances "you should have disqualified yourself from participation in this case." Callaway added that, more than anyone in the past hundred years, Black would be seen to have "destroy[ed]" the principle of separation and to have "open[ed] the way for a renewal of intense and bitter religious controversy."[187] Similarly, the pastor of the First Baptist Church of Attalla, Alabama, Charles J. Granade, felt "greatly alarmed" by Black's opinion, which "ignores the Bill of Rights . . . and begins anew in our Country the war for the separation of Church and State." Black was to "rest assured that Baptists and others resent this decision."[188]

---

eliciting "excellent support from the individual pulpits." In working against this threat to "the separation between church and state," Bell believed that "[t]he Protestant church itself" was "the guardian" of "our liberties." Charles R. Bell, Jr., *Pattern for Protestant Action: How Wisconsin Defeated the Bus Bill* (Madison: February 1947).

[186] Telegram from Charles Milton McMan[u?]us to Hugo L. Black (Sebring, Fla., March 8, 1947), in Library of Congress, Hugo Black Papers, File 285, *Everson* Case File, Public Correspondence.

[187] Letter from T. F. Callaway to Hugo L. Black (Thomasville, Ga., Feb. 12, 1947), in Library of Congress, Hugo Black Papers, File 285, *Everson* Case File, Public Correspondence. The pastor of the First Baptist Church in Camilla, Georgia, Charles Duncan, explained that he was "not a Catholic hater" and that he would defend the rights of Catholics but that Black's decision would allow public money to support the "RELIGIOUS CULTURE" of "the Romanists," which he considered "the most bigoted and sectarian of all major Christian groups." Letter from Charles Duncan to Justice Black (Camilla, Ga., March 8, 1947), in Library of Congress, Hugo Black Papers, File 285, *Everson* Case File, Public Correspondence.

[188] Letter from Charles J. Granade to Hugo Black (Attalla, Ala., Feb. 23, 1947), in Library of Congress, Hugo Black Papers, File 285, *Everson* Case File, Public Correspondence. Although some of the Baptist ministers wrote on their own initiative, some seem to have been participating in organized protests. The Birmingham Protestant Pastors Union formally deplored the decision on the basis of a "conviction that the time-honored institution

Less hostile, but suffused with a profound sense of regret, were the letters from "old friends." A former citizen of Alabama, J. T. Mainor, worried that it was "somewhat out of line to address you direct." Yet, "having watched your career from the beginning of your public life," and having thought that the outrage over Black's nomination was a "tempest in a teapot," he now pointed out that it had been a storm "brought on by the very same organized forces that you write an opinion to uphold." He told Black that "it is grievously disappointing to myself and many of your old friends to see you reach such conclusions, when as everyone knows, this is just an entering wedge for more and more taxes to be diverted to the political Roman Catholic Hierarchy, and a blow against our public schools system, which has been the bulwark of our freedom since the adoption of our Constitution and Bill of Rights." Not surprisingly, this correspondent explained that his was "not a prejudiced viewpoint" but was "based on a study of world history . . . for the

---

of separation of church and state should be upheld as guaranteed by the first amendment to the Constitution of the United States." "Resolutions Passed by Birmingham Protestant Pastors Union," clipping in Library of Congress, Hugo Black Papers, File 285, *Everson* Case File, Public Correspondence.

Various other types of Protestants also complained. For example, a Methodist from Montgomery, W. A. Eidson, wrote of his admiration for Black's work for the state and the nation but feared that the decision "will result in more aggravated relations between Protestants and Catholics." He candidly admitted that "I am prejudiced against Catholics," but added that "I do try to be fair-minded toward them." He and his wife—a Baptist— had taught for decades in the public schools of Alabama. According to Eidson: "Protestants wrote into the Constitution that church and state should remain separate. And now for Catholics to come to our country and inch by inch, here a little, there a little, and to culminate in getting the control here in this country, so that their church is supported by the public expense . . . well, it makes my blood temperature rise pretty high! Especially so, when I think that one of our own Alabamians . . . is contributing to that inching along of this powerful nonconforming religious group." Letter from W. A. Eidson to Hugo L. Black (Montgomery, Ala., Feb. 27, 1947), in Library of Congress, Hugo Black Papers, File 285, *Everson* Case File, Public Correspondence.

Of course, there were an assortment of ugly nativist critiques. Addressed to "FRAID US SU-PREME COURT. CARE BLAKIE," a postcard from the District of Columbia simply quoted Jeremiah 7:18–19 and included a pasted clipping about Catholic attitudes concerning "the Queenship of Mary in Heaven." Postcard (March 10, 1947), in Library of Congress, Hugo Black Papers, File 285, *Everson* Case File, Public Correspondence. From Cincinnati one who signed himself "100% American" told Black, in the language of earlier nativism, "You must either be a Cross back, beckoning to the higher-ups, or a half-ass Protestant . . . The Roman hierarchy have no love for our public schools system. Nor for our Constitution. In George Washington's time, you would hang." "100% American," Postcard (March 13, 1947), in Library of Congress, Hugo Black Papers, File 285, *Everson* Case File, Public Correspondence.

past approximately 2000 years."[189] Another correspondent, who in 1917 had been one of Black's Sunday school pupils, worried about "what some groups are doing little by little that would destroy eventually, what our forefathers fought for." He "never believed that any Southern Gentleman would have made the mistake you made and certainly not a Baptist from Alabama." What, he asked, would Black's "old friend Rev. Charlie T. Culpepper" have said if he were still living?[190] H. Ross Arnold—the pastor of the First Baptist Church in Jacksonville, Alabama—recalled that in 1926 he had supported Black's candidacy for the Senate "with no little enthusiasm and rejoiced greatly when you were elected." When Black was appointed to the Court, Arnold "was again delighted, for I felt that the real honest-to-goodness Americans, the types who had actually made America free and great, had a man who was also devoted to the cause of freedom and could be depended on." But now, after reading how Black had "voted to require the states to furnish transportation for Catholic students to their schools, thus striking a de[at]h blow at the Bill of Rights, my disappointment was equaled only by my distress. You had let us down!"[191] Less pugnacious—almost poignant, were it not anonymous—was a note typed on a blank cash-register slip:

> We in Alabama are shocked and above all, we do not understand.
> We are disappointed in you.
>   From an "old time" Friend[192]

This shocked incomprehension was typical among Black's many old time "friends." Far from being of merely personal significance, it reveals much about the American culture—including "American" ideas of separation and of the Bill of Rights—within which Black and his fellow justices formed and delivered their opinions.

---

[189] Letter from J. T. Mainor to Hugo Black (Forsyth, Ga., Feb. 17, 1947), in Library of Congress, Hugo Black Papers, File 285, *Everson* Case File, Public Correspondence.

[190] Letter from S. S. Co[?]ll to Hugo Black (Notasulga, Ala., Feb. 27, 1947), in Library of Congress, Hugo Black Papers, File 285, *Everson* Case File, Public Correspondence.

[191] Letter from H. Ross Arnold to Hugo Black (Jacksonville, Ala., March 13, 1947), in Library of Congress, Hugo Black Papers, File 285, *Everson* Case File, Public Correspondence. The outcry against Black was such as to lead some citizens and former residents of Clay County, including a former classmate of two of his brothers, to defend Black with a resolution commending him for his "stand for religious liberty." "We, the undersigned . . ." (May 3, 1947), in Library of Congress, Hugo Black Papers, File 285, *Everson* Case File, Public Correspondence.

[192] Library of Congress, Hugo Black Papers, File 285, *Everson* Case File, Public Correspondence.

Black could not openly reassure his Baptist and other critics, but he went out of his way to talk in private with one of them. Black tended to laugh at the letters he received from importunate Americans and he certainly had reason to laugh at some of the missives that he received after the *Everson* decision. Yet this is not to say that he fully disagreed with all of his critics. To Baptists and other correspondents who sought from Black some explanation of his seemingly inexplicable decision, the justice addressed formal letters in which he reminded them that he could not express his views on the subject. Yet, to Joseph Dawson—the Executive Secretary of the Baptist Joint Conference Committee and a fellow Mason, who had criticized Black's opinion in *Everson*—Black responded differently. As Dawson recalled in the early 1970s, "I had a lengthy discussion with Mr. Justice Black as to all phases of the Everson decision in his office upon his invitation. He brought up the subject, not I." In this "private conversation," Black "explained what was meant" by his opinion, "insisting emphatically" on the passage in which he had said, as Dawson later recited, "that neither directly nor indirectly shall a cent of tax money be given by the government to religious sects, in keeping with the First Amendment forbidding any establishment of religion"—a passage Black had concluded with Jefferson's words about separation. The justice "was ardent upon insisting that this statement represented the basic concept of the American system." He "declared that the Everson decision in nowise approved or encouraged the granting of any tax funds to church aid. . . . He said that all the Court did was to grant reimbursement to Catholic children in a New Jersey town for fares paid to public school buses which passed their parochial schools. One might construe it as a judgment in a specific case of more or less local nature. It was not in favor of bus aid to parochial schools."[193]

Justice Black had revealed much. He had disclosed his thoughts,

---

[193] *Oral Memoirs of Joseph Martin Dawson*, 194–196 (1972), Texas Collection, Baylor University, Waco, Texas. A less detailed account of this conversation appears in Dawson's autobiography. Dawson begins this version: "Amid the tremendous furor stirred by this unpopular decision, by accident, Mr. Justice Black, who wrote the majority opinion, talked with me privately." Dawson, *A Thousand Months to Remember*, 194. In 1947 the Committee on Public Relations reported to the Southern Baptist Convention: "The Committee has established many legitimate contacts with various departments of the federal government, and through Dr. Dawson has been represented at various Congressional hearings the subject of whose discussions were of concern to Baptists." *Proceedings of the Southern Baptist Convention*, 154 (1947).

moreover, to the effective head of the organization that had filed a brief in *Everson,* that had arranged for its chairman to argue before the justices in this case, and that was likely to be a litigant in future cases on separation. His candor in person may be contrasted to his correspondence with Dawson shortly afterward, in 1948, when Dawson sent him a copy of his book, *Separate Church and State Now*—a volume that began with a quotation from Black's opinion in *Everson* and closed with, among other things, a long appendix detailing, in nativist style, various Catholic pronouncements against religious liberty. In response, Black simply wrote: "Thank you for sending [a] copy of your book . . . which I have read with interest. I regret that I cannot feel free to discuss the contents of the book since the subject is one which, as you know, frequently comes before the Court."[194]

More publicly, Dawson "took the lead in organizing a national instrument for litigation," Protestants and Other Americans United for the Separation of Church and State.[195] The group had first been conceived in 1946 by the founder of the Joint Conference Committee, Rufus Weaver. After Weaver's death in February 1947, Dawson took up his plans, becoming the Recording Secretary of the new organization.[196] Much later, Dawson laconically explained that the "function" of the Joint Conference Committee "was, first of all, to inform, to proclaim, to witness, and to protest" and that members of the Committee thought litiga-

---

[194] Letter from Hugo L. Black to J. M. Dawson (Sept. 10, 1948), in Library of Congress, Hugo Black Papers, File 296, *McCullum* Case File, Favorable Public Response.

[195] *Oral Memoirs of Joseph Martin Dawson,* 158–159. See also Dawson, *A Thousand Months to Remember,* 194.

[196] Dawson, *A Thousand Months to Remember,* 196. Dawson and his allies seem to have gone to some length to drum up support for the new organization. For example, on March 10, 1947, the Baptist Birmingham Pastors Conference resolved:

> That the Birmingham Pastors Conference requested J. M. Dawson and the Joint Conference Committee on Public Relations to approach the Federal Council of Churches in America and all Protestant denominations, the Jews, the Masons, and other groups, looking to the formation of a national organization to combat every attempt to invalidate the American Bill of Rights and its corollary, the separation of church and state.
>
> According to reports which are reaching this office from Washington and elsewhere the people are at last getting their eyes open as to what is happening in this country.
>
> Unless something is done to offset the efforts of the Catholic hierarchy the first article of the Bill of Rights will exist in law but will be wholly invalidated in practice. . . .

"Birmingham Pastors Conference," *Alabama Baptist,* 3 (March 20, 1947).

tion "would complicate its functioning."[197] Unlike the Joint Conference Committee, which could witness on behalf of Baptists, the new organization, Protestants and Other Americans United, could advocate separation in the courts on behalf of all Americans and thus could more clearly present separation as part of a broadly Protestant and American agenda. Perhaps an even more important reason for the establishment of Protestants and Other Americans United was that Dawson and his theologically liberal allies had a more secular vision of separation than many of their fellow Southern Baptists, and they increasingly had reason to fear that a future majority in the Southern Baptist Convention might try to prevent the Joint Conference Committee from litigating for some of the broader implications of separation. Only a nondenominational organization could litigate without such interference.

Accordingly, Dawson worked for the creation of Protestants and Other Americans United. At a preliminary meeting in October 1947 with various other advocates of separation, including evangelicals, Seventh-Day Adventists, and Jews, one of Dawson's confederates, the president of the Southern Baptist Convention, Louie D. Newton, moved to create an organization "devoted to the single issue of maintenance of separation of church and state as provided in the First Amendment."[198] In its founding manifesto of January 1948, the new organization complained of "[a] powerful church, unaccustomed in its own history and tradition to the American ideal of separation of church and state," and it invited all Americans, including Jews and "fraternal orders," to join in the campaign for separation.[199] Of course, Protestants and Other Americans

---

[197] Hastey, "A History of the Baptist Joint Committee," 62, 65, quoting personal interview conducted in 1973; *Oral Memoirs of Joseph Martin Dawson*, 199.

[198] Hastey, "A History of the Baptist Joint Committee," 63.

[199] "Manifesto of Protestants and Other Americans United for the Separation of Church and State," in Joseph Martin Dawson, *Separate Church and State Now*, 203, 208, App. B (New York: Richard R. Smith 1948). According to its Manifesto:

The immediate objectives of PROTESTANTS AND OTHER AMERICANS UNITED may . . . be summarized as follows:

1. To enlighten and mobilize public opinion in support of religious liberty as this monumental principle of democracy has been embodied and implemented in the Constitution by the separation of church and state.

2. To resist every attempt by law or the administration of law further to widen the breach in the wall of separation of church and state.

3. To demand the immediate discontinuance of the ambassadorship to the papal head of the Roman Catholic Church.

United sought more than merely moral support, and it secured funding for its first year of operations from John H. Cowles—the Sovereign Grand Commander of the Scottish Rite Masons, Southern Jurisdiction— who could take satisfaction that so patriotic an enterprise was led by fellow Masons such as Newton and Dawson.[200] In the decades to come, Protestants and Other Americans United would assiduously litigate and lobby for separation. Looking back, Dawson observed, not without pride, that it "had grown to be very powerful."[201]

In the autumn of 1947, while Dawson was still organizing Protestants and Other Americans United, separation again came before the Supreme Court in *McCollum v. Board of Education.* An atheist, Vashti McCollum, objected to her Illinois school district's released-time pro-

---

4. To work for the repeal of any law now on the statute books of any state which sanctions the granting of aid to church schools from the public school treasury.

5. To invoke the aid of the courts in maintaining the integrity of the Constitution with respect to the separation of church and state, wherever and in whatever form the issue arises, and, specifically, to strive by appropriate constitutional means to secure a reconsideration of the two decisions of the Supreme Court upholding the use of tax funds (a) for providing the pupils of parochial schools with free text books, and (b) for the transportation of pupils to parochial schools.

6. To call out and unite all patriotic citizens in a concerted effort to prevent the passage of any law by Congress which allots to church schools any portion of a Federal appropriation for education, or which explicitly or implicitly permits the states to make such allotment of federal funds. This purpose in no wise prejudices pro or con the propriety of a Federal grant in aid of public education.

7. To give all possible aid to the citizens of any community or state who are seeking to protect their public schools from sectarian domination, or resisting any other assault upon the principle of separation of church and state.

8. In seeking these objectives we are determined to pursue a course that cannot be justly characterized as anti-Catholic, or as motivated by anti-Catholic animus. As Protestants, we can be called anti-Catholic only in the sense in which every Roman Catholic is anti-Protestant. Profound differences separate us in the area of religious faith, but these differences have no relevancy in the pursuit of our objectives as clearly defined in this manifesto. The issue of separation of church and state has arisen in the political area and we propose to meet it there.

Ibid., 209–210. See also "New Body Demands Church Separation: Protestants and Others Plan Drive, Charging Catholic Violations of Doctrine," *New York Times,* 1 (Jan. 12, 1948).
[200] Dawson, *A Thousand Months to Remember,* 202. Later in an interview Dawson explained: "Speaking of Catholics, it is pertinent to tell of my experience in responding to the request of numerous VIP's in patriotic circles who worked to save the Constitution. I arranged for organization of the Americans United." *Oral Memoirs of Joseph Martin Dawson,* 156. For the character of Cowles's patriotic ideals, see John H. Cowles, "The Truth Shall Make You Free" (Washington, D.C.: Supreme Council, 33°, Southern Jurisdiction, October 1930), especially the version that was distributed with annotations in the 1940s.
[201] *Oral Memoirs of Joseph Martin Dawson,* 158–159.

gram, in which Protestant, Catholic, and Jewish teachers could come into the public schools to give religious instruction to students whose parents consented. McCollum's lawyer argued that, "unless this principle is applied, a constitutional clause acting as 'a wall of separation between Church and State,' will become a wall uniting Church and State." Yet probably because of the adverse result in *Everson*, he did not rely much upon the principle of separation or upon the authority of *Everson*.[202] Instead, *Everson* and its principle of separation were introduced in an emphatic manner by two amici briefs—one from a pair of Jewish groups (the Synagogue Council of America and NCRAC) and another from Dawson's Joint Conference Committee.[203] Although the Joint Conference Committee had earlier deplored Black's opinion in *Everson*, the Committee now relied upon it as a precedent for the principle of separation. About a month later, McCollum's lawyer filed a supplemental brief that devoted a whole section to "'Separation of Church and State' as defined in the Everson case."[204]

From the beginning of McCollum's litigation before the U.S. Supreme Court, the Illinois Board of Education recognized that the principle of separation would play a central role, and therefore, in response to McCollum's initial brief, the board attempted to distinguish the Constitution from Jefferson's assertion about separation. Unlike the New Jersey Board of Education in the *Everson* case, the Illinois board argued, "This case involves an interpretation of the First Amendment, not of Madison's Remonstrance, the Virginia bill for religious freedom, or even of Jefferson's 'wall of separation between Church and State.'"[205] This Board of Education litigated without much skill or even vigor, but it at

---

[202] Appellant's Brief, in Illinois ex rel. McCollum v. Board of Education of School District No. 71, at 19–20 (October Term, 1947, U.S. Supr. Ct.).

[203] NCRAC was the National Community Relations Advisory Council.

[204] Appellant's Supplemental Brief, in Illinois ex rel. McCollum, Appellant, v. Board of Education of School District No. 71, Champaign County, Illinois, 11 (October Term, 1947, U.S. Supr. Ct.). Having switched to an argument that gave greater emphasis to separation, McCollum's attorneys felt obliged to limit the potential breadth of her position, and for this purpose they adopted an ecumenical version of the old nativist, Protestant distinction between religious individuals and religious organizations: "When a state acting through its legislature invites or employs a minister of the Gospel to deliver an invocation at the opening of sessions of the legislature, it is dealing with individuals qualified in its judgment to perform the services asked for; it is not dealing with any church as an institution or establishment." Ibid., 14.

[205] Appellee's Brief, in Illinois ex rel. McCollum v. Board of Education of School District No. 71, at 20 (October Term, 1947, U.S. Supr. Ct.).

least contested the claim that separation was a requirement of the First Amendment.

The Court held that the released-time program violated the First and Fourteenth Amendments, and, in his opinion for the majority, Black had the satisfaction of relying upon his *Everson* opinion. Quoting the passage in which he had recited Jefferson's letter about the "wall of separation between church and state," Black now could point out that "[t]he majority in the *Everson* case, and the minority . . . agreed that the First Amendment's language, properly interpreted, had erected a wall of separation between Church and State."[206] This time, however, Black could apply the principle of separation with a dissent from only one justice, Stanley Reed, who vainly protested that "[a] rule of law should not be drawn from a figure of speech."[207]

Although only this one justice dissented, Black failed to persuade all of the justices who had dissented in *Everson* to join his opinion quoting that case.[208] His chief opponent, as so often, was Frankfurter, who had dissented in *Everson* on the ground that the state-supported busing in that case violated the principle of separation. A secularized Jew with an "insistent" attitude about a secular separation, Frankfurter had a distinct distaste for Catholicism.[209] He had led the dissenting justices in *Everson,* and now he eagerly encouraged the "anti-*Everson* lads" to rectify the Court's position.[210] In particular, Frankfurter sought to avoid any reference to *Everson.* Upon learning this, Black wrote to the Conference that "I will not agree to any opinion in the *McCollum* case which does not make reference to the *Everson* case," explaining that he was convinced the decision in *Everson* was right and that he attached "great importance to the constitutional question involved."[211] At stake was whether Black's opinion in *Everson* would become the foundation of constitutional jurisprudence on separation of church and state or whether it would go un-

---

[206] McCollum v. Board of Education, 333 U.S. 203, 211 (1948).

[207] Ibid. at 247. According to Joseph Martin Dawson, the case "serves as the greatest single safeguard to separation of church and state outside of the First Amendment itself." "Our Public Relations Committee Brief," *Report from the Capitol,* 2 (March 1948), quoted by Hastey, "A History of the Baptist Joint Committee," 78.

[208] Justices Rutledge and Burton, however, concurred. More significantly, Justices Frankfurter and Jackson did not. 333 U.S. at 212.

[209] Compston, "The Serpentine Wall," 104.

[210] Dunne, *Hugo Black and the Judicial Revolution,* 267.

[211] "H.L.B., Memorandum for the Conference In re No. 90—McCollum v. Bd. of Education" (Feb. 11, 1947), in Library of Congress, Hugo Black Papers, File 395, *McCollum* Case File.

mentioned in *McCollum* and thus seem as if it had been an obstacle on the way to separation. The next day, Black wrote to Justices Rutledge and Burton: "It seems evident to me that Justice Frankfurter is not willing to base [the] decision in this case on principles that were commonly declared in the *Everson* opinion and in Justice Rutledge's dissent." As for himself, he explained, "I am willing to agree to any opinion which decides this case on the basis of those principles. I am not willing, however, to repudiate them expressly or by failure to refer to them in a Court opinion." He closed by adding: "Rather than that, I think it would be better that any who desire to continue the school bus fight in this case should do so in filed opinions. I shall not be prodded into participation in such a contest here, because I believe it would be detrimental to the great principle of separation of Church and State—a principle which I think crucial to survival of a free government."[212] Unable to defeat Black, Frankfurter (with the support of the other "anti-*Everson* lads") filed an opinion in which he declared what he considered his consistent attachment to separation: "Separation means separation, not something less." Quoting Rutledge rather than Black, Frankfurter concluded "that we have staked the very existence of our country on the faith that the complete separation between the state and religion is best for the state and best for religion."[213]

On account of the dispute between Black and the *Everson* dissenters, Black assembled a majority only with difficulty. From the start of the Court's consideration of the case, Justice Reed planned to dissent, and, until quite late, Justice Murphy remained undecided. Therefore, without support from any of the four anti-*Everson* justices, Black had reason to fear that he would have to write an opinion for a minority. Allegedly, however, two of the anti-*Everson* justices, Burton and Rutledge, reached an understanding with Black, according to which he "took out of his opinion everything except the noble sentiments that Black uttered in the *Everson* opinion, so that Rutledge and Burton could concur in his opinion and thereby make it an opinion of the Court." Such, at least, was what Frankfurter wrote in his diary. Frankfurter considered the compromise "ignominious" and wrote a separate opinion, joined by all

---

[212] "H.L.B., Memorandum to Wiley and Harold, In re McCollum" (Feb. 12, 1947), in Library of Congress, Hugo Black Papers, File 395, *McCollum* Case File.
[213] *McCollum*, 333 U.S. at 231–232.

of his fellow *Everson* dissenters, including Burton and Rutledge.[214] Clearly, substantial differences, both personal and principled, kept Black and Frankfurter apart, but these justices clearly shared, together with almost all their brethren, a profound devotion to the "noble" principle of separation.

Incidentally, Frankfurter understood the Fourteenth Amendment to apply the fundamental freedoms within the Bill of Rights, rather than the Bill of Rights itself, to the states. Therefore, in requiring the states to conform to the separation of church and state, he felt obliged to show that this principle had long prevailed in the states and that it would not alter their traditional policies. Arguing that "[s]eparation in the field of education . . . was not imposed upon unwilling States by force of superior law," he claimed that "the Fourteenth Amendment merely reflected a principle then dominant in our national life"—a principle that, at least for purposes of public education, "by 1875 . . . was firmly established in the consciences of the nation."[215] In support of this conclusion, he described the nonsectarian character of nineteenth-century public schools and quoted President Grant and Elihu Root. Frankfurter concluded:

> The public school is at once the symbol of our democracy and the most pervasive means for promoting our common destiny. . . . "The great American principle of eternal separation"—Elihu Root's phrase bears repetition—is one of the vital reliances of our Constitutional system for assuring unities among our people stronger than our diversities. It is the Court's duty to enforce this principle in its full integrity.[216]

Although Frankfurter surely was not fully conscious of the prejudice so plainly evident in the history he celebrated, he revealed how much he and his brethren were a part of that history.

The *McCollum* case made clear, as the *Everson* case had not, that the justices would go far beyond the Protestant version of separation of church and state. Whereas in *Everson* Protestants had sought to prevent children in Catholic schools from receiving state aid for busing, in *McCollum* an atheist aimed to prevent mostly Protestant children from receiv-

---

[214] Joseph P. Lash, ed., *From the Diaries of Felix Frankfurter,* 343 (New York: W. W. Norton & Co., 1974).

[215] Ibid., 215, 217.

[216] Ibid., 231. See Joseph Brady, *Confusion Twice Confounded,* 142–146 (South Orange, N.J.: Seton Hall University Press, 1954).

ing released-time religious instruction in public schools. It was a pattern already evident in the nineteenth century, when Protestants initially popularized separation, and then anti-Christian secularists and other theological liberals insisted upon their expanded understanding of it. This time, however, because of greater popular support and because of the substitution of the judicial for the amendment process, a relatively secular version prevailed.

Many relatively traditional Protestants felt stunned, leading them slowly to reconsider separation. They had sought their familiar Protestant separation and now suddenly found themselves confronted with a secular version, which threatened the nonsectarian religiosity of America's public institutions. It was an experience they would feel even more profoundly in the wake of later Supreme Court cases and that would gradually bring many Protestants to recognize that they faced a greater threat from secularism and separation than from Catholicism.[217] At first, the Protestants who recoiled against the *McCollum* case merely argued that separation should not be interpreted to limit the freedom of churches. For example, in 1948 the Oberlin Conference did not question separation but urged that "[t]he separation of church and state was intended primarily to guarantee religious freedom, rather than to circumscribe the activities of any religious group."[218] In the aftermath of *McCollum*, even most writers for the *Christian Statesman*—a journal that had once argued for a Christian amendment to the Constitution—conceded the constitutional status of separation and argued only that the principle should not be taken too far. Gradually, however, some Protestants began to point out that there were other ways to think about religious liberty than in terms of the separation between church and state. Among these Protestants was the Rev. Frank Dyer of Santa Monica, who wrote for the *Christian Statesman*, and who still clung to hopes for a "Christian nation," albeit not by constitutional amendment. Even with his theological vision of politics, Dyer revealed a clarity of understanding that eluded many other commentators: "The dictum of 'separation' is a false premise

---

[217] Ivers, *To Build a Wall*, 82.

[218] The Conference also worried that "[c]oncern over Roman Catholic influence should not lead Protestants to embrace a narrow concept of church and state relations that would accelerate the secularization of our culture." "The Secularism of Society" and "Separation of Church and State," in "Washington Report," *Social Action*, 14 (no. 9): 33, 39 (Nov. 15, 1948).

which only breeds confusion and conflict. The very abuse of the metaphor of 'separation' is proof of its dangerous nature. If we follow the Constitution we shall use 'freedom' instead. It is Biblical, Christian, constitutional and philosophically sound." Dyer further recognized that the Protestant version of separation had been the means of introducing the more secular variety—that "[w]hat began with the slogan 'Separation of Church and State' has now been widened to declare that it means: 'Complete separation between the State and Religion.'" Dyer's understanding, however, had its limits. Fearing that this secular separation "means a godless state," he announced, "It is time to be alert and to become active."[219] Of course, it was much too late.

By the middle of the twentieth century, the idea of separation between church and state had become an almost irresistible American dogma. In the decades that followed, the justices of the U.S. Supreme Court and myriad other Americans would continue to develop this American freedom. They would explore its application to school prayer, to religious displays on public land, and to government subsidies for private schools and charities. Some Americans would recognize that they could not take separation literally and would question the breadth of its application, but they would rarely reject or altogether abandon the metaphor. Even as Americans wondered about separation's meaning, they treated its constitutional legitimacy as sacrosanct. Having enshrined the doctrine of separation in their Constitution, they deferred to it with reverence and viewed any dissent from it as profoundly un-American.

---

[219] Rev. Frank Dyer, D.D., "Crusade against Supreme Court's Decision on Religion," *Christian Statesman*, 93 (no. 1): 3, 1 (January 1949).

Conclusion

IN 1855, at the height of the mid-nineteenth-century assault upon Catholics, Congressman Philip Phillips of Alabama observed that the real danger lay ahead. "The change now aimed at for excluding Catholics from their share in the government of the country, like all radical and revolutionary movements, must be effected, if effected at all, by gradual stages of progress, which inure us to the journey, and accustom us to the road."[1] As it happens, Phillips did not understand that American anti-Catholicism was part of a much longer journey, in which many of his countrymen would eventually seek to escape the authority of all religious groups. Nor did he anticipate the exact path Americans would take. But he foresaw how it would be traveled. Ever more Americans would gradually, step by step, become conditioned to their prejudice. In a similar manner, while traveling along the same road, Americans would become accustomed to the separation of church and state. Even those who were not anti-Catholic would come to assume that separation was an American principle. Habituated to this belief, they would come to think of separation as their historic religious liberty, as a fundamental American freedom, and even as a constitutional right protected by the First Amendment.

Separation and the Constitutional Religious Liberty

Underlying the story recorded here is the distinction between the separation of church and state and the constitutional freedom from a religious

[1] Philip Phillips, *Letter . . . on the Religious Proscription of Catholics,* 5 (Washington, D.C.: 1855).

establishment. For many Americans, the difference between these ideals has become difficult to discern. The difference, however, was of profound importance to earlier Americans.

The dissenters who campaigned against establishments did not ordinarily demand a separation between church and state. They could not accept the establishment argument that there existed between religion and government the sort of connection that justified government financial benefits for established religions. Yet these protestors typically did not reject the utterly conventional assumption that there was a necessary and valuable moral connection between religion and government. Accordingly, they were hardly inclined to seek a separation of church and state. The pervasive assumption about a necessary connection tempted some establishment clergymen, following the example of Richard Hooker, to charge dissenters with seeking a separation of religion from government. This was, however, a canard. Although the dissenters rejected what they sometimes called a "union of church and state," they also avoided the other extreme. In particular, rather than demand a separation, dissenters opposed their state establishments by seeking various limits on the power of government.

To the extent that separation was a demand rather than an accusation, it was asserted by only a small number of eighteenth-century men—most prominently, a few political, anticlerical Europeans, who sought to limit not merely civil governments and their establishments of religion but also churches and their clergies. Already in the seventeenth century, Roger Williams employed the metaphor of a wall separating the church from the world on behalf of his vision of Separatist churches and their religious liberty. Hoping for churches purified beyond what even most of his Separatist colleagues thought possible, and desiring constraints on both government and the clergy, Williams had little reason to be troubled by the implications of his wall of separation. In the eighteenth century James Burgh and the Marquis de Condorcet came closer to advocating separation—each finding it unobjectionable from the perspective of his anticlerical agenda.

Separation became a substantial part of American conceptions of religious liberty only in the nineteenth and twentieth centuries, when Americans felt growing fears of churches, especially the Catholic Church. Separation first clearly entered public debates as a demand in the election of 1800, when some leading Republicans employed a version of the idea to elicit antiestablishment votes and to criticize and even intimidate the Federalist clergymen who spoke or wrote against Jefferson. Later, in the mid-nineteenth century, nativists adopted the idea against Catholics who were presumptuous enough to demand the same legal rights as Protestants. Nativists and, more broadly, Protestants assumed that the separation of church and state limited Catholics in their relations with government but not Protestants, because whereas Catholics seemed to defer to their church and act on its behalf, Protestants presumably followed the dictates of their individual consciences and, in any case, belonged to diverse denominations. Eventually, as adherents of liberal theology came to fear all ecclesiastical authority, these liberals developed a more secular version of separation. Most prominently, the anti-Christian theists and atheists known as "Liberals" adopted the idea of separation as an expansively antiecclesiastical principle that limited all distinct religions.

In one version or another—whether Protestant, secular, or some combination of these—separation became an increasingly pervasive cultural assumption. Although not all Americans who supported separation were anti-Catholic, Americans were ever more distrustful of ecclesiastical authority, and nativist anti-Catholicism gave respectability and popular strength to their suspicions. Accordingly, by the first half of the twentieth century a remarkably broad array of groups—including Baptists, Jews, atheists, Masons, Klansmen, and, indeed, almost all who emphasized their Americanism—viewed separation of church and state as an essential part of their liberty. In this manner separation came to be established as a matter of patriotic faith and a central tenet of the American constitutional creed.

Constitutional Authority

As should be clear from the contrast between separation and the religious liberty guaranteed by the First Amendment, the constitutional authority for separation is without historical foundation. True, Thomas Jefferson, in his letter to the Danbury Baptist Association, wrote that the First Amendment built a wall of separation between church and state. The Baptists, however, do not seem to have agreed. Later, when anti-Catholic nativists and the Liberals popularized separation, few of them argued that the U.S. Constitution had already guaranteed a separation of church and state. Instead, they suggested that separation was a political principle underlying the Constitution. While Liberals sought an amendment to remedy the Constitution's imperfect guarantees of separation, and while President Grant and others appealed to nativists with an amendment proposal declaring church and state separate, Americans had little reason to develop historical or interpretive claims for separation. Gradually, however, as it became clear that hopes for an amendment to the U.S. Constitution were unrealistic, advocates of separation easily persuaded themselves and others that separation was the religious liberty already guaranteed by the First Amendment.

To modern lawyers and judges anxious for legal authority and unfamiliar with the history examined here, Jefferson's role has often seemed profoundly important. In fact, in the history of separation, Jefferson is but a passing figure, less important for what he wrote than for the significance later attributed to it. Ironically, the pope did more than Jefferson to popularize the idea of separation of church and state in America, for by condemning separation among French Catholics, the pope made it all the more attractive to American Protestants. Nonetheless, Jefferson's participation is revealing. It is no coincidence that the separation he endorsed was contrary to what Baptists and other dissenters sought. Nor is it mere happenstance that Jefferson's principle has been incompatible with the lives of many Americans or that it has simplified and impoverished discussions of religious liberty in ways that have obscured the necessarily complex and textured relationships between civil and religious societies. Although Jefferson took justifiable pleasure in his contributions to religious liberty, he was indifferent to the religion of most of his countrymen and downright hostile to their religious institutions. Not until he came under scrutiny as president did he publicly suggest that he considered religion essential to the preservation of liberty. Even then, unlike many of his contemporaries, he certainly did not consider American religious groups and their clergy valuable for this purpose. On the contrary, traditional religious organizations and their clergy, even if purely voluntary, seemed to Jefferson a threat to religious and civil freedom. Indeed, Jefferson hoped to revolutionize Americans into a citizenry of republican individuals unbound by the customs, hierarchies, and superstitions that might divert them from their rational pursuit of equal freedom under government. Only since the mid-twentieth century, when large numbers of Americans were able to take this sort of society for granted, and when courts began to enforce it, has Jefferson's letter to the Danbury Baptist Association come to seem widely attractive as authority for the constitutional imposition of a separation of church and state.

In an era in which Americans often assume they have a living constitution—a constitution that evolves in response to their prevailing needs and ideals—the fig leaf of Jefferson's letter should not obscure the development of the First Amendment's religious liberty. Like so much legal change, this evolution occurred under the cover of an historical myth that conveniently allowed Americans to avoid perceiving the changing character of their constitutional law. Yet, once the fig leaf is stripped away, it becomes clear that the constitutional religious freedom of Americans developed in accord with popular expectations—that minority rights were redefined to satisfy majority perceptions of them. This supple response of the Constitution conformed (in all but its historical cover) to the increasingly popular conception of constitutional law as flexible. Yet whether it preserved religious freedom—for unpopular religious minorities or even most other religious groups—may be doubted.

Of course, the principle of separation between church and state may be valuable even though it lacks an historical foundation in the Constitution. If only as a matter of prudence, churches and their clergy often have good reason to separate themselves from partisan politics. Moreover, separation may offer a plausible legal solution to a wide range of issues, including clerical authority and hierarchy, church property and power, religious speech and influence, foreign claims of authority, and divided loyalties. Nonetheless, in discussions of these and other issues, separation ought not be assumed to have any special legitimacy as an early American and thus constitutional idea. On the contrary, precisely because of its history—both its lack of constitutional authority and its development in response to prejudice—the idea of separation should, at best, be viewed with suspicion.

Diminished Freedom

The separation of church and state not only departed from the religious liberty guaranteed by the U.S. Constitution but also undermined this freedom. In the election of 1800 Republicans used the idea of separation to limit the speech of clergymen in political matters. Beginning in the mid-nineteenth century, Protestants repeatedly relied upon the concept to deny Catholics equal rights in publicly funded schools and to discourage Catholic political activity. In the 1870s the National Liberal League attempted to use the idea of separation of church and state to limit the political participation of religious groups and to challenge otherwise secular laws that benefited these groups, that were influenced by them, or that coincided with their distinctive moral obligations.

Today, many Americans still sometimes draw such conclusions from separation. For example, on the basis of this principle, many Americans question the right of others to bring their distinct religious views to bear on politics, and some courts limit the rights of religious organizations to receive government benefits distributed on entirely secular grounds. Put more generally, separation has barred otherwise constitutional connections between church and state. It even has discriminated among religions, for it has placed especially severe limitations upon persons whose religion is that of a "church" or religious group rather than a mere individual religiosity. In all of these ways, the First Amendment, which was written to limit government, has been interpreted directly to constrain religion.

Separation protected not so much individual liberty as the liberty of individuals who were understood to be independent of a church. At first, therefore, few Americans advocated separation. In the seventeenth century the sole advocate of what might be considered a sort of separation, Roger Williams, had been a minority of one with so refined a fear of impurity as to be unwilling to remain even in his own tiny Baptist congregation for more than a few months. Eventually, however, politicians and even political majorities adopted visions of citizenship in which individuals were expected to put aside any group loyalty that might compete with that to the state. Accordingly, in the nineteenth and twentieth centuries the advocates of separation usually were self-proclaimed defenders of "American" liberty, who conceived of themselves as intellectually independent and who held profoundly coercive expectations that others should conform to their ideals. Thus separation became part of a majority's oddly conformist demands for individual independence and strangely dogmatic rejections of authority.

That American majorities used the separation of church and state to impose their vision of their religion and their Americanism upon religious minorities is a sober reminder that as religious liberty becomes more individualistic, it does not necessarily increase individual liberty. Particularly if, as was true of separation, a concept of religious liberty directly limits religious groups, it can impose substantial costs upon members of religious minorities who refuse to abandon their distinctive identity, affiliation, and sense of authority. It can even place burdens on members of the majority, who have not always been as independent of religious groups as they have sometimes perceived themselves to be.

Looming at the edges of the dispute over separation have been two conflicting visions of liberty and its relationship to religious groups. The traditional perspective of numerous eighteenth-century Americans—most vocally, establishment ministers but also many dissenters—remains familiar in the version presented by Alexis de Tocqueville when he observed the role of religion in the United States. By inculcating morals, by encouraging mutual love and forgiveness, and by directing ambitions toward another world, religion could diminish injurious behavior, dissension, and distrust. Accordingly, it could reduce the necessity of civil coercion—a necessity that might otherwise lead a people to desire harsh or even tyrannical government. Religion could also establish a lasting foundation in public opinion for the various rights that seemed particularly vulnerable to fluctuations in popular sentiments. It thereby could temper the selfish passions and oppression to which republics were all too prone. Thus religion—specifically, the Christianity inherited and shared by a community—seemed essential for the preservation of liberty.

Increasingly, however, this perspective coexisted with another, very different, point of view, drawn from European experiences and fears—a perspective that survives most prominently in the writings of Thomas Jefferson. Together with expanding numbers of other Americans, Jefferson feared that clergymen, creeds, and therefore most churches undermined the inclination and ability of individuals to think for themselves. He worried that individuals would defer to their church's clergy and creed in a way that would render them subservient to a hierarchy and would deprive them of intellectual independence. In such ways, the clerical and creedal religion of most churches appeared to threaten the individual equality and mental freedom that Jefferson increasingly understood to be essential for the citizens of a republic.

As such fears about the influence of religious groups became increasingly widespread, many Americans began to depart from the Jef-

fersonian precept that there was time enough for government to interfere "when principles break out into overt acts against peace and good
order."[2] Numerous Americans, including Jeffersonians, Jacksonians,
theological liberals, and nativists, feared assertions of clerical authority.
Increasingly, Americans worried in particular about the claims of the
Catholic Church and concluded that the adherents of Rome ought not
have all of the secular rights enjoyed by Americans who held more popular, individualistic conceptions of their faith. Undoubtedly, it was imprudent for any religious minority to enter the political fray with principles not shared by other Americans. Perhaps, moreover, the doctrines
believed by some Christian groups were more irrational and dangerous
than those espoused by others. Nonetheless, to deny secular rights on
the basis of religious beliefs was a violation of the liberty that, in the
eighteenth century, both Jefferson and most evangelical dissenters had
so carefully sought to protect.

A Simple Metaphor

Separation of church and state is an attractively simple metaphor. Like
so many beguiling metaphors, however, it is an oversimplification, and
on account of its appeal, it has gradually rendered Americans ever
less inclined to appreciate the more measured positions advanced by
eighteenth-century evangelical dissenters.

Separation has increasingly come to seem the only alternative to
another metaphor, the union of church and state. If Americans were to
avoid a union of church and state, had they any option except to maintain a separation between the two? Of course, union and separation
were not the only possible alternatives, as revealed by the Baptists and
other dissenters whose struggle for religious freedom led to the adoption
of the First Amendment. They no more wanted a separation of church
and state than they wanted an establishment. Yet, with each decade
since the Republican campaign for separation in 1800, growing numbers
of Americans have forgotten that there are myriad connections between
religion and government that do not amount to an establishment, let
alone a full union of church and state. Accordingly, they have mistak-

---

[2] "An Act for Establishing Religious Freedom," in William Waller Hening, *Statutes at Large
. . . of Virginia*, 12: 84 (Richmond: 1823).

enly assumed that such connections infringe upon their constitutional freedom. They have come to believe that even nonestablishment connections between religious organizations and government amount to a union of church and state and that anything less than a complete separation of church and state is, in effect, a union of these institutions. On this basis, they have often leapt to the conclusion that persons who question separation desire an establishment, as if the rejection of separation were a renunciation of freedom and disestablishment. Happily, some commentators have noticed that union and separation are overgeneralizations between which lies much middle ground. These principles are, in fact, extremes along a continuum very different than that between establishment and disestablishment. In a society, however, in which many are willing to view their surroundings in seductively simplistic terms, the distinction between union and separation has distracted most Americans from other conceptions of their religious liberty.

Unfortunately, opponents of separation have often lent credence to the belief that separation is the only alternative to a union of church and state. In the nineteenth century, many Protestant critics of separation speculated about a Christian nation without indicating whether they meant a voluntary or an established Christianity. Some proposed laws clearly unconstitutional under the First Amendment. Others naively sought a Christian amendment to the Constitution. Even more dramatically, many Catholic priests and intellectuals, following the pope, claimed for their church a power superior to secular authority. In so doing, these various Christians gave the impression that the alternative to separation was an establishment or "union of church and state." Presented with this alternative, most Americans preferred separation.

Contributing to the appeal of this simplistic vision and the abandonment of more sophisticated, traditional conceptions of religious liberty has been the association of separation with Americanism. Following a pattern set by mid-nineteenth-century nativists, those advocating separation, including theological and political liberals, have long presented this ideal as an American freedom. Even today they work through organizations with names such as "People for the American Way" or "Americans United for the Separation of Church and State." In defense of separation, its advocates, both religious and secular, have recited its development in tones suggestive of sacred history. Whether striving for the "purity" of church and state, defending the "altar" of American freedom, or staking the existence of the nation on their "faith" in separation, they have often depicted separation in the image of religion and have sometimes denounced dissent from their creed as an almost heretical deviation from Americanism and its principles of freedom. Even the nineteenth-century Liberals, who, at least until 1885, were so endearingly honest as to draw attention to the difference between their separationist principles and the realities of the U.S. Constitution, declared in that year that "[a]ny sect, church, or 'religion' that militates against these principles openly or covertly, directly or indirectly, is the enemy of American liberty and of the American people"—an aggressive demand for conformity little less strongly felt than in a theocracy.[3]

It should not be a surprise, therefore, that the simple metaphor of separation has largely eclipsed other points of view. Even within churches, the history of other perspectives on religious liberty has often been neglected or disparaged. For example, when an interviewer asked Joseph Dawson whether his views were really typical of his church, Dawson adamantly insisted that there had been "an amazing continuity and uniformity," adding: "Deviates have been exceptional and [have] usually been motivated by some real or imaginary need."[4] Sometimes more knowingly, and often with an eye on the Supreme Court, advocates of separation have contributed to a huge semihistorical literature that blurs together different types of early American religious liberty under the rubric of separation. Accordingly, looking back, it has been all too easy to see a single American religious liberty, the separation of church and state—at times disputed as to how far it should be taken, but, nonetheless, usually conceded to be the American freedom.

Etching this metaphor on the minds of Americans with particular vividness has been the mental image of a wall of separation. By reducing the complexity of religion and its place among nations to a bold visual construct—by allowing Americans to see in tangible terms the abstractions they might otherwise have to cogitate—the wall of separation has achieved much popularity. Yet this and other visual metaphors— whether the candle, the dark lantern, the prostrate cross draped with the American flag, the Mary who was mother of George, or the fiery

---

[3] *The Truth Seeker Annual and Freethinkers' Almanac,* 29 (New York: Truth Seeker, 1885).
[4] *Oral Memoirs of Joseph Martin Dawson,* 204 (1972), Texas Collection, Baylor University, Waco, Texas. When pressed, Dawson insisted: "I am typical of Southern Baptists on church and state relations, and most other matters." Ibid., 206.

cross—have encouraged Americans to see their world with more clarity than accuracy. While allowing a broad populace to perceive richly delicate questions with ease, such images have all too often encouraged learned and unlearned alike to envision these matters in sharp contrasts of light and dark—a chiaroscuro more dramatic than revealing. Indeed, the inaccuracy of such depictions makes them poor guides for conduct. The image of the candle—whether in the wilderness or the garden—is profoundly appealing. Yet no one sees a light or reads the Bible in an entirely individuated, independent way, without the knowledge, experience, and preconceptions acquired in society and its groups. It is difficult to conceive how any religion, as an institution, could exist among a people so individuated as never to acknowledge or defer to communal beliefs. Similarly, the image of a wall of separation between church and state is appealing. Yet no state or church can develop its laws and beliefs in a cultural vacuum, separate from the other institutions in society. Churches are distinct from states but are not entirely separate from states, and it is difficult to understand how they could be fully separated, unless either churches or states were to be completely abandoned. Thus the stark image of separation, especially that of a wall of separation, lends itself to demands for a purity not possible in this world. As a result, the metaphor bodes ill for actual churches and states, which must function as institutions and must coexist in a far from metaphorical realm. In particular, separation and all the barriers it creates portend ill for individuals who value their participation in religious as well as civil associations and who hope to flourish and even, perhaps, find some truth in each.

Separations in Society

Of course, the history of the separation of church and state cannot be confined to an account of religious liberty, for this separation developed amid broader separations in American society. At the very least, the idea of separation between church and state seems to have been part of a reconceptualization of religious liberty that had particular appeal for Americans who conceived of themselves as independent of clerical and ecclesiastical claims of authority. Whereas eighteenth-century demands for disestablishment were often made by dissenters who were unified in their desire to limit the power of government, the nineteenth- and twentieth-century demands for separation were made by those who sought to limit religious groups as much as government. Separation was especially attractive for Americans who feared churches that emphasized the authority of their creeds and clergies. In such churches, it seemed, individuals were unlikely to remain free or to become independent citizens, loyal to the United States and devoted to its civil and religious liberty. Most fundamentally, Catholics who "submitted" to the clergy or creed of their church seemed incapable of the intellectual independence needed in Americans. Viewed as a challenge to individual freedom, a claim of clerical or church authority was, by extension, also frequently perceived as a threat to the state and the majority that lay not far behind it—as the old *imperium in imperio,* albeit now, in the fashion of the New World, a danger to the independence of individuals in their dealings with the state. Gradually, in response to their fears of church authority, especially Catholic Church authority, Americans reconceptualized their religion, their citizenship, and their sense of themselves in highly individualistic ways, and, concomitantly, they redefined their religious liberty to protect themselves from the groups they feared, making separation of church and state part of their broader reconception of their individual, religious, and national identity.

More generally, as Jefferson himself suggested, the separation of church and state has been attractive in a modern world of specialization—in a world in which people divide their knowledge and their lives into specialized fields, such as medicine, law, politics, and religion. Engaged in very different activities and idealizing their sense of independence, Americans have expected to be free to attend to their specialized professions, interests, and activities without interference from persons focused upon other fields, and even without much obligation to reconcile their own conduct in different areas of endeavor. In this specialized world, Americans found that the sort of religion that once had harmonized them now seemed oppressive and divisive. Accordingly, Americans increasingly insisted upon pursuing their various secular activities, including politics, without complaint or instruction from churches and clergymen. Like the cigar-loving member of the American Secular Union who had difficulty finding a cigar on a Sunday and therefore gave generously to defeat Sunday laws, many Americans, even if not hostile to Christianity, did not want it to intrude upon areas of their lives in which they sought freedom. In this sense "[e]very open violator of the Sabbath is to be counted in their ranks. Every railroad corporation that runs its trains on the Sabbath is a part of their forces."[5] Americans resented demands that they should integrate religion with the rest of their already specialized lives, and therefore they eagerly reduced not only their professions but also politics and even religion to specialized activities. In this spirit, they increasingly supported a separation of religion from other worldly activities, especially a separation of church and state.

Ironically, even as religion has been separated from politics, politics has become, in a sense, religious. Although this peculiar development has had many causes, including a general secularization, it surely is no coincidence that many of the very groups that have sought to exclude churches from politics have pursued their political goals by appealing to religious passions and aspirations—to the intense feelings and improbable hopes, including aspirations for purity and transcendence, that have, traditionally, seemed unlikely to be satisfied in this world. Perhaps the powerful emotions and desires associated with religion are unavoidable and, if not channeled through conventional religious institutions, are likely to find other outlets. Certainly, advocates of separation participated in the transformation of politics into a venue for aspirations and feelings once more typically focused on another world. Indeed, some spoke of their hopes for an "absolute" or "total" separation or for a state "purified" of clerical influence in almost religious tones. The displacement of religious feelings from the organized communal channels of denominational fellowship, identity, and expression has affected not only politics but also other activities. In diverse areas of life, ranging from the most personal to the most public, many Americans candidly describe feelings of intensity and transcendence akin to the religious. Perhaps there is no earthly reason to regret that Americans have concentrated with almost religious zeal upon secular, worldly aspirations. Yet it remains unclear whether powerful yearnings for purity and transcendence are less dangerous when focused on this world than on another.

In the end, these various separations and the associated displacement of passions suggest that the history of the separation between church and state cannot be understood simply as the history of religious liberty and its protection by American institutions. On the contrary, sep-

---

[5] *Proceedings of the National Convention to Secure the Religious Amendment of the Constitution of the United States. Held in Pittsburg, February 4, 5, 1874,* 28 (Philadelphia: 1874).

aration needs to be recognized as part of much broader social and cultural developments. In particular, separation became a popular vision of religious liberty in response to deeply felt fears of ecclesiastical and especially Catholic authority. These anxieties intensified as Americans increasingly identified with their specialized roles and worried about the failure of minorities to conform to what were elevated as Protestant and American ideals of individual independence. In the transfiguring light of their fears, Americans saw their religious liberty anew, no longer merely as a limitation on government, but also as a means of separating themselves and their government from threatening claims of ecclesiastical authority. Americans thereby gradually forgot the character of their older, antiestablishment religious liberty and eventually came to understand their religious freedom as a separation of church and state.

Index